THE

BAPTIST HAND-BOOK

FOR

1896.

PUBLISHED UNDER THE DIRECTION OF

THE

COUNCIL OF THE

Baptist Union of Great Britain and Ireland.

London:
CLARKE & CO.,
13 AND 14, FLEET STREET, E.C.

1895.

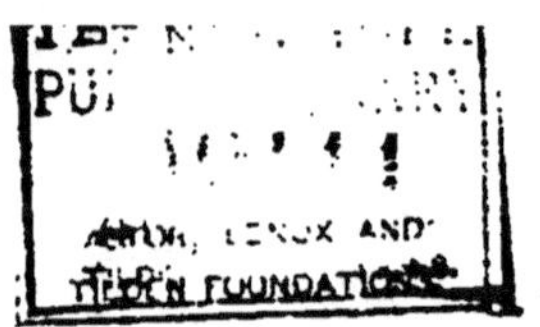

NOTICES.

The Spring Assembly for 1896 of the Baptist Union of Great Britain and Ireland will be held in London on Monday, Wednesday, and Thursday, April 27th, 29th, and 30th. Further details will be announced in the denominational papers.

The time for, and place of holding the Autumn Assembly will be announced in denominational periodicals, as soon as the arrangements are made.

The Editor again presents his sincere thanks to the Secretaries of Associations, to the "Correspondents" named on page 7, and to numerous other friends who have assisted him in the endeavour to secure accuracy in the information given, and he cordially invites such assistance for the future. He also thanks those who have enriched the HAND-BOOK with the Memoirs of Deceased Ministers.

All communications to be sent to the Secretary of the Baptist Union, 19 Furnival-street, E.C. Corrections for the next issue of the HAND-BOOK should be in the hands of the Secretary not later than September 14th. (See Notice on page 332.)

This scarce antiquarian book is included in our special *Legacy Reprint Series*. In the interest of creating a more extensive selection of rare historical book reprints, we have chosen to reproduce this title even though it may possibly have occasional imperfections such as missing and blurred pages, missing text, poor pictures, markings, dark backgrounds and other reproduction issues beyond our control. Because this work is culturally important, we have made it available as a part of our commitment to protecting, preserving and promoting the world's literature. Thank you for your understanding.

10 Baptist 7VP

CONTENTS.

PART VI.

PART VII.

PART VIII.

PART IX.

APPENDIX.

MAGIC LANTERNS.

THE MARVELLOUS

PAMPHENGOS.

The most Powerful Oil Light in the Market.

OVER 3,000 SOLD.

(HUGHES' PATENT.)

TESTED. TRIED. PROVED.

Further Improvements.
Greater Volume of Light.
Cannot be Surpassed.

It has Challenged Comparison for over 14 Years.

SIMPLE, RELIABLE & SAFE.

Suitable for Missionaries.

No Smell. No Smoke. No Broken Glasses

PRICES OF LAMP:

£2 2s., £1 10s., £1 1s.

WHY IS THE PAMPHENGOS SUPERIOR TO ALL OTHERS? Because it is carefully and scientifically constructed, and not made commercially and sold under a variety of *noms de plume*. **Because** it is a pure white light. **Because** the conoidal glasses resist heat and are proof against fracture. **Because,** being technical, it has no dampers or chimney lengtheners, which are evils to be eschewed. **Because** it gives a good 12 to 14 feet disc unparalleled, therefore will largely take the place of limelight and thus save the risk and danger of gas explosions.

Do not have any other lantern or lamp than the **MARVELLOUS PAMPHENGOS,** a really superb, substantial, and effective instrument. Waste not your money on inferior imitations.

HUNDREDS OF TESTIMONIALS. Supplied to Colleges, Institutions, Missionaries, Clergy, and the Gentry. Particulars free.

PRICES: Complete **PAMPHENGOS,** beautifully constructed, solid brass fronts, with high-class lenses, **£6 6s., £4 4s.,** and **£2 10s.**

THE DOCWRA TRIPLE Prize Medal, highest award. Supplied to Dr. H. Grattan Guinness, Capt. C. Selwyn, Madame Adelina Patti, and the Royal Polytechnic, &c., &c.

MINIATURE MALDEN TRIPLE. Supplied to B. J Malden, Esq.; unparalleled results; Capt. Chas. Reade, R.N.; Rev. Canon Scott, and principal exhibitors.

THE UNIVERSAL LANTERN, four wicks, four inch condensers, **£1 2s. 6d.**; three wicks, **19s. 6d.**; elegant mahogany biunials, brass front, **£6 10s.**; blow through jets, **8s. 6d**; mixed, **12s.**; life models, subjects coloured **1s. 3d** each; Scripture, hymns, temperance tales, &c., &c.

THE CHEAPEST AND BEST HOUSE FOR COMPLETE LANTERN OUTFITS.

50 Slides on loan for **3s.,** in special despatch boxes.

BEFORE PURCHASING be sure to get **Mr. HUGHES' MAGNIFICENTLY ILLUSTRATED CATALOGUE** of great Inventions in the art of **OPTICAL PROJECTION,** a volume to be prized, over 160 Original Illustrations—not commercial. Price 6d., postage 3d.; ditto, including detailed list of 60,000 slides, 10d., postage 5d. The slide list 6d., pamphlets free.

W. C. HUGHES (Specialist),

(Over 25 Years' Reputation for Highest Class Results in the Art of Optical Projection, &c.)

Brewster House, 82, Mortimer Road, Kingsland, London, N.

INDEX.

2 *

CALENDAR 1896.

JANUARY—31 Days.

MOON'S CHANGES.

Last Quar. 7th day, 3h. 29m. p.m.
New Moon 14th day, 10h. 29m. p.m.
First Quar. 23rd day, 2h. 40m. a.m.
Full Moon 30th day, 8h. 55m. a.m.

1	W	Slaves (U.S.A.) freed 1863
2	Th	[lished 1649
3	F	Commonwealth estab-
4	S	Robt. Morrison b 1782,
5	S	[d 1834
6	M	
7	Tu	Robert Robinson b 1735,
8	W	[d 1790
9	Th	Proclamation against Con-
10	F	[venticles 1661, Penny
11	S	[Post established 1840
12	S	G. Fox d 1690, b 1624
13	M	Dissentg. Dep. met 1736
14	Tu	Brit. Museum opd. 1759
15	W	[ed Antwerp 1526
16	Th	(cir.) Tyndale's Bible print-
17	F	(cir.) Cov'rdale's B.p. 1535
18	S	Baptist W. Noel d 1873
19	S	Bd. of Bap. Min. fd. 1723
20	M	
21	Tu	Lord Bacon b 1560, d 1626
22	W	
23	Th	[d 1806
24	F	C. J. Fox, b 1749 [d 1716
25	S	Dr. Williams [Libr.]
26	S	Abraham Booth d 1806,
27	M	[b 1734
28	Tu	Dr. J. Ryland b 1753,
29	W	[d 1825
30	Th	39 Articles sub. 1562
31	F	C. H. Spurgeon d 1892

FEBRUARY—29 Days.

MOON'S CHANGES.

Last Quar. 6th day, 0h. 36m. a.m.
New Moon 13th day, 4h. 13m. p.m.
First Quar. 21st day, 9h. 15m. p.m.
Full Moon 28th day, 7h. 51m. p.m.

1	S	
2	S	Span. Inqn. ablsd. 1813
3	M	J. Rogers burnt 1555
4	Tu	
5	W	D. L. Moody b 1837
6	Th	Andrew Fuller b 1754, d '15
7	F	Baptist Chapels, Jamaica,
8	S	[dest. 1832
9	S	Hooper burnt 1555
10	M	Queen Vict. married 1840
11	Tu	Lond. Univ. Chrtr. 1826
12	W	C. Darwin b 1809, d 1882
13	Th	Bill of Rights 1689
14	F	
15	S	Galileo b 1564, d 1642
16	S	Melancthon b 1497, d 1560
17	M	[Henry Martyn b 1781, d '12
18	Tu	Raikes' first S.-sch. 1781
19	W	
20	Th	Negro suffrage 1869
21	F	
22	S	Bapt. Missionaries reached
23	S	[Jamaica 1814
24	M	F. Bampfield, M.A., sent
25	Tu	[to Newgate 1683
26	W	[Longfellow b 1807, d 1882
27	Th	Corn Laws repealed 1846
28	F	(cir.) Sax. B. MS. 706-995
29	S	

MARCH—31 Days.

MOON'S CHANGES.

Last Quar. 6th day, 11h. 29m. a.m.
New Moon 14th day, 10h. 46m. a.m.
First Quar. 22nd day, 11h. 57m. a.m.
Full Moon 29th day, 5h. 22m. a.m.

1	S	Nat. Covenant Scot. 1638
2	M	J. Wesley d 1791, b 1703;
3	Tu	[Jo. Robinson d 1625
4	W	(c.) Wyclif 1st Eng. B. 1380
5	Th	B. & F. Bible Soc. fd. 1804
6	F	First Missny. Tahiti 1797
7	S	
8	S	
9	M	Meth. Stds. ex. fr. Ox. 1768
10	Tu	Bishops exp. fr. Parl. 1640
11	W	[werp, 1526; 1st E. B. print
12	Th	(cir.) Tyndale's Bib. Ant-
13	F	English Revolution 1688
14	S	Reform Bill, 1832 [1672
15	S	Decl. Ind'ul. Charles II.
16	M	(cir.) First Eng. Bible at
17	Tu	[Geneva, 1557-60
18	W	Eman. Russ. Serfs 1861
19	Th	(cir.) Bishop's Bible 1568
20	F	Sir Isaac Newton d 1727
21	S	Cranmer burnt 1556
22	S	Jonathan Edwards d 1758
23	M	
24	Tu	
25	W	LADY DAY.
26	Th	
	F	John Bright d 1889
	S	
	S	Test Act 1673
30	M	
31	Tu	Caxton's Book on Chess [fin. 1474

APRIL—30 Days.

MOON'S CHANGES.

Last Quar. 5th day, 0h. 22m. a.m.
New Moon 13th day, 4h. 29m. a.m.
First Quar. 20th day, 10h. 47m. p.m.
Full Moon 27th day, 1h. 47m. p.m.

1	W	John Howe d 1705, b 1630
2	Th	
3	F	GOOD FRIDAY.
4	S	Daniel Neal d 1743
5	S	EASTER SUNDAY
6	M	BANK HOLIDAY
7	Tu	Quakers' Oaths abol. 1839
8	W	Legh Richmond d 1827
9	Th	Lib. of Conscien. decl. 1687
10	F	Ed. Wightman mart. 1612
11	S	Civil War (U.S.A.) 1861
12	S	Catholic Eman. 1829
13	M	
14	Tu	
15	W	
16	Th	Conventicle Act pd. 1664.
17	F	John Fox d 1587, b 1517;
18	S	[Livingstone bur. 1874
19	S	Long Parliament dis. 1653
20	M	David Brainerd b 1718,
21	Tu	C. Bronte, [d 1747
22	W	[b 1816, d 1855
23	Th	Shakespeare d 1616, b 1564
24	F	Serampore Ch. fnd. 1800
25	S	
26	S	
27	M	Chaucer d 1400
28	Tu	Benjamin Keach b 1640
29	W	Anti State Ch. Conf. 1844
30	Th	

MAY—31 Days.

MOON'S CHANGES.

Last Quar. 4th day, 3h. 29m. p.m.
New Moon 12th day, 7h. 49m. p.m.
First Quar. 20th day, 6h. 21m. a.m.
Full Moon 26th day, 9h. 37m. p.m.

1	F	Slavery abolished 1807
2	S	Robt. Hall b 1764, d 1831
3	S	
4	M	David Livingstone d. 1873
5	Tu	
6	W	Humboldt d 1859, b 1769
7	Th	And. Fuller d 1815, b 1754
8	F	Cong. Union formed 1832
9	S	Rel. Tract Soc. fd. 1799
10	S	Test & Cor. Act rep. 1828
11	M	Puritans s. for Amer. 1620
12	Tu	D. G. Rossetti b 1828, d 1882
13	W	
14	Th	
15	F	Disr. Ch. of Scotland 1843
16	S	
17	S	New Test. R. V. pub. '81
18	M	Bishop Butler born 1692
19	Tu	Act of Unifor'ty pd. 1662
20	W	Coverdale d 1569, b 1487
21	Th	[J. S. Mill b 1806, d 1873
22	F	Sol. Leag. & Cov. bt. 1661
23	S	[Toleration
24	S	WHIT SUNDAY. Act of
25	M	BANK HOLIDAY
26	Tu	Bengalee N. T. pub. 1800
27	W	
28	Th	Wm. Pitt b 1759, d 1806
29	F	Charles II. restored 1660
30	S	Jerome of Prague bt. 1416
31	S	1st Newsp. Orient. lang. [Ind. Seramp. Press 1818

JUNE—30 Days.

MOON'S CHANGES.

Last Quar. 3rd day, 8h. 3m. a.m.
New Moon 11th day, 8h. 49m. a.m.
First Quar. 18th day, 11h. 41m. a.m.
Full Moon 25th day, 6h. 55m. a.m.

1	M	(cir.) Luther's Bib. 1522-
2	Tu	[1532
3	W	
4	Th	Partic. B. Fund fd. 1717
5	F	Adam Smith b 1723, d 1790
6	S	[Reform Bill psd. 1832
7	S	Gen. Bap. N. Con. fd. 1770;
8	M	Seven Bishops sent to
9	Tu	Dickens d 1870 [Tower 1688
10	W	
11	Th	
12	F	Dissents. Mtg. Plumbers
13	S	[Hall, Anchor-la. 1567
14	S	Battle of Naseby 1645
15	M	[Bisp. Butler d. 1752
16	Tu	Univer. Tests abol. 1871
17	W	
18	Th	B. of Waterloo 1815
19	F	Mag. Charta signed 1215
20	S	Accss. Q. Victoria 1837
21	S	Longest day
22	M	Baptist Union fd. 1813
23	Tu	Dissts. adm. to Oxf'd Un.
24	W	MIDSUMMER DAY [1854
25	Th	First Wesleyan Conf. 1744
26	F	[G.B. An. rsld. on Algm. '91
27	S	G. Bap. Miss. Soc. fd 1816
28	S	Q. Victoria crowned 1838
29	M	
30	Tu	

CALENDAR 1896.

JULY—31 Days.

MOON'S CHANGES.

Last Quar. 3rd day, 1h. 29m. a.m.
New Moon 10th day, 7h. 35m. p.m.
First Quar. 17th day, 4h. 4m. p.m.
Full Moon 24th day, 5h. 45m. p.m.

1	W	W'minster Assembly 1643
2	Th	Dl. Wilson b 1778, d 1858
3	F	[1776, ack. Nov. 30, 1782
4	S	American Indep. asserted.
5	S	Star Chamber and High-
6	M	[Com. abolished 1641
7	Tu	John Huss burnt 1415
8	W	
9	Th	
10	F	Jn. Calvin b 1509, d 1564
11	S	Board of Three Denomi-
12	S	[nations fnd. 1727
13	M	Sun. Sch. Un. est. 1803
14	Tu	Bastille stormed 1789
15	W	Peto's Trust Deed Act
16	Th	[passed 1850
17	F	Dr. Watts b 1674, d 1748
18	S	Ballot Act passed 1872
19	S	Dr. A. Gifford d 1784
20	M	Christmas Evans d 1838
21	Tu	Span. Arm. deftd 1588
22	W	Un. Eng. and Scot. 1706
23	Th	New Toleratn. Act 1812;
24	F	[Jews adm. Parlt. 1858
25	S	
26	S	Irish Ch. disestabd. 1869
27	M	Six Noncons. burnt at
28	Tu	[Brentford 1558
29	W	Wilberforce d 1833, b 1759
30	Th	Penn d 1718, b 1644
31	F	Comp. Ch. rates ab. 1868

AUGUST—31 Days.

MOON'S CHANGES.

Last Quar. 1st day, 6h. 34m. p.m.
New Moon 9th day, 5h. 2m. a.m.
First Quar. 15th day, 9h. 3m. p.m.
Full Moon 23rd day, 7h. 4m. a.m.
Last Quar. 31st day, 10h. 55m. a.m.

1	S	Slavy. in W. Ind. abl. 1834.
2	S	Endd. Schs. Act 1869
3	M	BANK HOLIDAY
4	Tu	
5	W	
6	Th	Tennyson b 1809, d 1892
7	F	[Goethe b 1749, d 1832
8	S	Meth. New Con. fd. 1797
9	S	Elementary Educ. Act, '70
10	M	Hugh S. Brown b 1823,
11	Tu	[d 1886
12	W	[1613
13	Th	Jeremy Taylor d 1667, b
14	F	Richard Jefferies d 1887
15	S	Sir Walter Scott d 1832
16	S	Whitfield b 1714, d 1770
17	M	Mar. & Reg. Act. pd. 1836;
18	Tu	[W. Carey b 1761, d 1834
19	W	Pascal d 1662, b 1623
20	Th	Dr. Wenger d 1880
21	F	[b 1781
22	S	G. Stephenson d 1848
23	S	Pompeii dest. A.D. 79
24	M	Noncons. ejected 1662
25	Tu	
26	W	Adam Clarke d 1832
27	Th	
28	F	
29	S	
30	S	
31	M	Jn. Bunyan d 1688, b 1628

SEPTEMBER—30 Days.

MOON'S CHANGES.

New Moon 7th day, 1h. 49m. p.m.
First Quar. 14th day, 4h. 10m. a.m.
Full Moon 21st day, 10h. 59m. p.m.
Last Quar. 30th day, 1h. 59m. a.m.

1	Tu	J. Howard b 1726, d 1790
2	W	Mg. Gn. Ass. Bp. Def. 1689
3	Th	Cromwell d 1658, b 1599
4	F	
5	S	Samuel Morley, d 1886
6	S	Pilgrim Fathers embkd.
7	M	[in Mayflower 1620
8	Tu	
9	W	
10	Th	Tea First Imported 1591
11	F	
12	S	Bapt. Church formed at
13	S	[Wapping 1633
14	M	
15	Tu	
16	W	
17	Th	Jno. Foster b 1770, d 1843
18	F	Dr. Johnson b 1709, d 1784,
19	S	Hansard Knollys d 1691
20	S	Ital. Troops ent. Rome '70
21	M	Lnd. Miss. Soc. fnd. 1795
22	Tu	Capture of Delhi 1857
23	W	
24	Th	
25	F	Cong. Board found. 1727
26	S	Thomas Clarkson d 1846
27	S	Jesuits formd. 1540; Wm.
28	M	[of Wykeham d 1404
29	Tu	MICHAELMAS DAY.
30	W	

OCTOBER—31 Days.

MOON'S CHANGES.

New Moon 6th day, 10h. 18m. p.m.
First Quar. 13th day, 2h. 47m. p.m.
Full Moon 21st day, 4h. 17m. p.m.
Last Quar. 29th day, 3h. 21m. p.m.

1	Th	Lon. Univ. open. 1828
2	F	Bap. Miss. Soc. fnd. 1792
3	S	[John Angell James d 1859
4	S	
5	M	J. Edwards b 1703, d 1758
6	Tu	Tyndale martyred 1536
7	W	B. U. Annuity Fund
8	Th	[estd. 1875
9	F	Arminius d 1609, b 1560
10	S	Samuel Pearce d 1799
11	S	America discovered 1492
12	M	Elizabeth Fry d 1845
13	Tu	B. Keach pilloried 1664
14	W	Dr. Gill d 1771, b 1697
15	Th	
16	F	Ridley & Latimer bnt. at
17	S	[Ox. 1555; H. Martyn
18	S	[d 1812, b 1781
19	M	Henry Kirke White d 1806
20	Tu	Wm. Ward b 1769, d 1823
21	W	Coleridge b 1772, d 1834
22	Th	
23	F	
24	S	Revoc. of Edict Nantes
25	S	[1685
26	M	Doddridge d 1751
27	Tu	Servetus burnt 1553
28	W	Vavasour Powell d in
29	Th	[Prison 1670
30	F	
31	S	Five Mile Act 1665

NOVEMBER—30 Days

MOON'S CHANGES.

New Moon 5th day, 7h. 27m. a.m.
First Quar. 12th day, 5h. 41m. a.m.
Full Moon 20th day, 10h. 25m. a.m.
Last Quar. 28th day, 2h. 4m. a.m.

		[1638
1	S	Episcopacy abol. in Scot.
2	M	[Torbay 1688
3	Tu	William III. landed at
4	W	Geo. Peabody d 1869
5	Th	Gunpowder Plot 1605
6	F	Dr. Joseph Stennett b
7	S	[1692, d 1758
8	S	John Milton d 1674
9	M	Prince of Wales b 1841
10	Tu	Mn. Luther b 1483, d 1546
11	W	Carey landed at Serampore
12	Th	[1793
13	F	B. U. incorporated, 1890
14	S	
15	S	Andrew Marvel d 1678
16	M	John Bright b. 1811
17	Tu	(cir.) Foxe, martyrologist,
18	W	[b 1517, d 1587
19	Th	
20	F	John Williams martyred
21	S	[Erromanga 1839, b 1796
22	S	
23	M	
24	Tu	John Knox d 1572, b 1505
25	W	
26	Th	Cowper b 1731, d 1800
27	F	Dan Taylor d 1816
28	S	
29	S	
30	M	

DECEMBER—31 Days.

MOON'S CHANGES.

New Moon 4th day, 5h. 51m. p.m.
First Quar. 12th day, 0h. 29m. a.m.
Full Moon 20th day, 4h. 5m. a.m
Last Quar 27th day, 0h. 9m. p.m.

1	Tu	Princess of Wales b 1844
2	W	
3	Th	
4	F	Suttee in India abold., 1829
5	S	[Carlyle b 1795, d 1881
6	S	
7	M	
8	Tu	Baxter d 1691, b 1615
9	W	John Milton b 1608
10	Th	Burning of Pope's Bull by
11	F	[Luther 1520
12	S	
13	S	Council of Trent 1545
14	M	Prince Albert d 1861;
15	Tu	[Washington d 1799
16	W	Oliver Cromwell made
17	Th	[Lord Protector, 1653
18	F	
19	S	Rev. of Prayer Book 1661
20	S	
21	M	Shortest day
22	Tu	
23	W	
24	Th	
25	F	CHRISTMAS DAY
26	S	BANK HOLIDAY
27	S	
28	M	
29	Tu	W. E. Gladstone b 1809
30	W	Royal Soc. Instd. 1660
31	Th	Wycliffe d 1384, b 1324

REIGNING SOVEREIGNS AND PRINCES, AND PRESIDENTS.

Austria-Hungary, Emperor-King, Francis Joseph I.; *aged* 65; *accession*, Dec. 1848.
Bavaria, King, Otto; *aged* 47; *accession*, June, 1886. (*Regency*.)
Belgium, King, Leopold II.; *aged* 60; *accession*, December, 1865.
Brazil, President, Dr. Prudente José de Moraes Barras; *appointed*, November, 1894.
Bulgaria, Prince, Ferdinand, *aged* 34; *elected*, July, 1887.
China, Emperor, Kuang Hsü; *aged* 24; *accession*, January, 1875.
Denmark, King, Christian IX.; *aged* 77; *accession*, November, 1863.
Egypt, Khedive, Abbas Pasha; *aged* 21; *accession*, January, 1892.
France, Republic, President, Felix Faure; *aged* 55; *elected*, January 17, 1895.
Germany, Emperor, William II.; *aged* 37; *accession*, June, 1888.
Great Britain, Queen, Victoria; *aged* 76; *accession*, June, 1837.
Greece, King, George; *aged* 50; *elected*, March, 1864.
Holland, Queen, Wilhelmina I.; *aged* 15; *accession*, November, 1890. (*Regency*.)
Italy, King, Humbert I.; *aged* 51; *accession*, January, 1878.
Japan, Mikado, Mutsuhito; *aged* 43; *accession*, February, 1867.
Madagascar, Queen, Ranavalona III.; *aged* 33; *accession*, July, 1882.
Persia, Shah, Nasir-ed-Din; *aged* 66; *accession*, September, 1848.
Portugal, King, Carlos I.; *aged* 32; *accession*, October, 1889.
Roumania, King, Charles I.; *aged* 56; *proclaimed*, March, 1881.
Russia, Emperor, Nicholas II.; *aged* 27; *accession*, November, 1894.
Saxony, King, Albert; *aged* 67; *accession*, October, 1873.
Servia, King, Alexander; *aged* 19; *accession*, March, 1889.
Spain, King, Alfonso XIII.; *aged* 10; *accession*, May, 1886. (*Regency*.)
Sweden and Norway, King, Oscar II.; *aged* 66; *accession*, September, 1872.
Switzerland, President, M. Zamp; *elected* December, 1894.
Turkey, Sultan, Abdul Hamid II.; *aged* 53; *proclaimed*, August, 1876.
United States, President, Grover Cleveland; *aged* 58; *elected*, November, 1892.
Wurtemberg, King, William II.; *aged* 47; *accession*, October, 1891.

THE ROYAL FAMILY OF GREAT BRITAIN.

Queen (Alexandrina) Victoria, born May 24, 1819; succeeded to the throne June 20, 1837; married February 10, 1840, to the late Francis Albert, Prince of Saxe Coburg and Gotha. *Issue*: 1. Princess Victoria Adelaide (Princess of Prussia, January 25, 1858, German Empress, March 9, 1888), born November 21, 1840.——2. Albert Edward, Prince of Wales, born November 9, 1841; married March 10, 1863, to the Princess Alexandra of Denmark, born December 1, 1844, and has issue George Frederick Ernest Albert (Duke of York), born June 3, 1865; married July 6th, 1893, to Princess Victoria Mary of Teck: Louise Victoria Alexandra Dagmar (Duchess of Fife), born February 20, 1867; Victoria Alexandra Olga Mary, born July 6, 1868; Maud Charlotte Mary Victoria, born November 26, 1869, betrothed, 1895, to Charles, second son of the Crown Prince Denmark.——3. *Princess Alice Maud Mary* (Grand Duchess of Hesse, July 1, 1862), born April 25, 1843; died December 14, 1878.——4. Prince Alfred Ernest Albert, Duke of Edinburgh and Duke of Saxe-Coburg-Gotha, born August 6th, 1844; married to the Grand Duchess Marie Alexandrovna of Russia, January 23, 1874.——5. Princess Helena Augusta Victoria, born May 25, 1846; married to Prince Christian of Schleswig-Holstein, July 5, 1866.——6. Princess Louise Carolina Alberta, born March 18, 1848; married to the Marquis of Lorne, March 21, 1871.——7. Prince Arthur William Patrick Albert, Duke of Connaught, born May 1, 1850; married to Princess Louise Margaret of Prussia, March 13, 1879.——8. *Prince Leopold George Duncan Albert*, Duke of Albany, born April 7, 1853; married to Princess Helen of Waldeck-Pyrmont, April 27, 1882; died March 28, 1884.——9. Princess Beatrice Mary Victoria Feodore, born April 14, 1857; married to Prince Henry of Battenberg, July 23, 1885.

(1) George William Frederick Charles, Duke of Cambridge, born March 26, 1819.

(2) Ernest, Duke of Cumberland (son of the Ex-King of Hanover), born September 20, 1845: married, December 21, 1878, to Princess Thyra of Denmark.

(3) Princess Augusta Caroline, sister of (1) (Duchess of Mecklen-burg-Strelitz), born July 19, 1822; married June 28, 1843, Frederick, Duke of Mecklenburg-Strelitz.

(4) Princess Mary Adelaide, sister of the Duke of Cambridge, born Novembe 27, 1833; married to H.H. the Duke of Teck June 12, 1866.

HER MAJESTY'S CHIEF OFFICERS OF STATE.

Prime Minister and Secretary of State for Foreign Affairs—Marquis of Salisbury, K.G.
Lord High Chancellor—Lord Halsbury.
Lord President of the Council—Duke of Devonshire.
Lord Privy Seal—Viscount Cross, G.C.B.
First Lord of the Treasury—Arthur James Balfour, M.P.
Chancellor of the Exchequer—Sir Michael Edward Hicks-Beach, Bart., M.P.
Home Secretary—Sir Matthew White Ridley, Bart., M.P.
Secretary for the Colonies—Right Hon. Joseph Chamberlain, M.P.
Secretary for War—Marquis of Lansdowne, K.G.
Secretary for India—Lord George Francis Hamilton, M.P.
First Lord of the Admiralty—George Joachim Goschen, M.P.
President of the Board of Trade—Charles Thomson Ritchie, M.P.
Chancellor of the Duchy of Lancaster—Lord James of Hereford.
President of the Local Government Board—Henry Chaplin, M.P.
Lord Lieutenant of Ireland—Earl Cadogan, K.G.
Secretary for Scotland—Lord Balfour of Burleigh
First Commissioner of Works—Aretas Akers-Douglas, M.P.
President of the Board of Agriculture—Walter Hume Long, M.P.

The above form the Cabinet.

Chief Secretary for Ireland—Gerald William Balfour, M.P.
Postmaster-General—Duke of Norfolk.
Vice-President of the Committee of Council on Education—Sir John Eldon Gorst, Q.C., M.P.
Junior Lords of the Treasury—Henry Torrens Anstruther, M.P., William Hayes Fisher, M.P., Lord Stanley, M.P.
Patronage Secretary to the Treasury—Sir William Hood Walrond, Bart., M.P.
Financial Secretary to the Treasury—Right Hon. Robert William Hanbury, M.P.
Civil Lord of the Admiralty—Joseph Austen Chamberlain, M.P.
Under Secretary for Foreign Affairs—Right Hon. George Nathaniel Curzon, M.P.
Under Secretary for India—Earl of Onslow, G.C.M.G.
Under Secretary for the Colonies—Earl of Selborne.
Under Secretary for Home Department—Jesse Collings, M.P.
Under Secretary for War—Hon. William St. John F. Brodrick, M.P.
Secretary to the Admiralty—William Grey Ellison-Macartney, M.P.
Secretary to the Board of Trade—Earl of Dudley.
Secretary to the Local Government Board—Thomas Wallace Russell, M.P.
Paymaster-General—Earl of Hopetoun, G.C.M.G.
Comptroller of the Household—Lord Arthur Hill, M.P.
Lord Chamberlain—Earl of Lathom.
Attorney-General—Sir Richard Everard Webster, Q.C., M.P.
Solicitor-General—Sir Robert Bannatyne Finlay, Q.C., M.P.

SCOTLAND.

Secretary—Lord Balfour of Burleigh (See Cabinet, above).
Lord Justice General—James P. B. Robertson (Lord Robertson).
Lord-Advocate—Sir Charles John Pearson, Q.C., M.P.
Keeper of the Privy Seal—Marquis of Lothian.
Lord Justice Clerk—Lord Kingsburgh (John Hay Athol Macdonald, C.B.)
Lord Clerk Register—Duke of Montrose.
Solicitor-General—Andrew Graham Murray, Q.C., M.P.

IRELAND.

Lord-Lieutenant—Earl Cadogan (See Cabinet, above).
Chief Secretary—Gerald William Balfour.
Lord Chancellor—Lord Ashbourne.
Attorney-General—John Atkinson, Q.C., M.P.
Solicitor-General—William Kenny, Q.C., M.P.

PUBLIC BUSINESS, 1896.

JAN. 1.—Dog licences renewable.—Licences for Armorial bearings to be renewed by 31st inst.—Quarter Sessions commence this week.

—— 9.—Insurances renewable at Christmas expire.

FEB. 1.—Within 21 days clerks of peace of counties and town clerks of boroughs to forward printed copy register of voters to Secretary of State.

APRIL 6.—Bank Holiday.—Quarter Sessions commence this week.

—— 8.—Clerks of peace and town clerks to send precepts to overseers as to registration of voters.

—— 9.—Insurances renewable at Lady-day expire.

MAY 25.—Bank Holiday.

JUNE 1.—Overseers to give notice by 20th that voters who have not paid poor rates, due 5th January, by 20th July, will not be entitled to be inserted in list of voters.

—— 20.—Overseers to publish list of persons entitled to vote as owners, and notices to persons qualified to vote for counties to send in claims.

—— 22.—Quarter Sessions commence this week.

JULY 9.—Insurances renewable at Midsummer expire.

—— 22.—*See* June 1.—Overseers to make out lists of persons who have not paid poor rates, due January 5.

—— 31.—Game and gun licences expire.—Overseers to make out list of ownership claimants, occupiers' list, and old lodgers' list.

Aug. 1.—Borough and county lists to be affixed to doors of churches and chapels for 14 days.

AUG. 3.—Bank Holiday.

—— 20.—Last day for leaving with overseers objections to county and borough electors; and for service of objections on electors in counties or their tenants.

—— 20.—Last day to claim as borough electors.—Last day for lodger claims.

—— 25.—Overseers to send list of claimants and objections, and copy of register of county voters, to clerk of peace.

—— 31.—All taxes and rates payable on March 1 must be paid on or before this day by persons claiming to be enrolled as burgesses under the Municipal Corporation Act.

SEPT. 2.—Town clerks in boroughs to affix in public places the list of claims and objections to freemen, from this day to the 16th.—Overseers to make out burgess lists.—Lists of objections to county electors and claims and objections for borough lists to be affixed to church doors till 16th.

—— 8.—Between this day and October 21, registration courts are to be held by the revising barrister. Claims of persons omitted in the burgess lists, and objections to persons inserted, to be given to the town clerk in writing on or before this day; notice of the objection also to be given to the person objected to.

OCT.—An open court to revise the burgess lists under Municipal Reform Act, to be held some time between the 1st and 15th of October—three clear days' notice being given.

—— 12.—Quarter Sessions commence this week.

—— 14.—Insurances renewable at Michaelmas expire.

NOV. 1.—Borough councillors to be elected. NOV. 9.—Election of Mayors and Aldermen of Boroughs.

DEC. 26.—Bank Holiday. DEC. 31.—Various Licences expire.

CHRONOLOGICAL NOTES FOR THE YEAR 1896.

Golden Number ..	16	Solar Cycle	1	Roman Indiction ..	6
Epact	15	Dominical Letters	E.D.	Julian Period ..	6,609

The year 5657 of the JEWISH ERA commences on September 8th; RAMADÂN (Month of Abstinence observed by the Turks) commences on February 15th; the year 1314 of the MOHAMMEDAN ERA commences on June 12th.

ECLIPSES IN 1896.

In the year 1896 there will be two Eclipses of the Sun and two of the Moon:—

(1) February 13.—An Annular Eclipse of the Sun, invisible at Greenwich.
(2) February 28.—A Partial Eclipse of the Moon, partly visible at Greenwich.
(3) August 8.—A Total Eclipse of the Sun, invisible at Greenwich.
(4) August 22.—A Partial Eclipse of the Moon, partly visible at Greenwich.

LAW SITTINGS AND UNIVERSITY TERMS, 1895.

	LAW SITTINGS.		UNIVERSITY TERMS.			
			OXFORD.		CAMBRIDGE.	
	Begins.	Ends.	Begins.	Ends.	Begins.	Ends.
Hilary	Jan. 11	April 1	..	..	..	..
Lent	..	..	Jan. 14	Mar. 28	Jan. 8	Mar. 27
Easter	April 14	May 22	April 8	May 22	April 18	June 24
Trinity	June 2	Aug. 12	May 23	July 11	..	..
Michaelmas ..	Oct. 24	Dec. 21	Oct. 10	Dec. 17	Oct. 1	Dec. 19

BANK HOLIDAYS.

The Bank Holidays in *England and Ireland* are Easter Monday, the Monday in Whitsun week, the first Monday in August, the 26th of December, if a week day, or, if a Sunday, the 27th.—In *Scotland*, New Year's Day, Christmas day (if either of these days falls on a Sunday, the next following Monday shall be a Bank Holiday), Good Friday, the first Monday of May, and the first Monday of August.

THE SEASONS.

Spring Quarter commences	March 20	Autumn Quarter commences	September 23
Summer Quarter commences	June 21	Winter Quarter commences	December 21

USEFUL LEGAL INFORMATION.

REGISTRATION OF BIRTHS.

An Infant should be registered within six weeks after birth. No fee is then payable, but after 42 days a fee of 7s. 6d. is chargeable.

REGISTRATION OF DEATHS.

Notice should be given of deaths to the district registrar. Let this be done early that the undertaker may have a certificate to give the minister who performs the funeral service.

APPOINTMENT OF NEW TRUSTEES.

This may now be made under the Titles of Religious Congregations (Sir Morton Peto's) Act, 1850, and the Acts of 1869 and 1890 extending same, now together called the Trustees Appointment Acts, 1850 to 1890, or by the Conveyancing and Law of Property Act, 1881. These Acts apply to land held in trust for the purposes of chapels, endowment of chapels, or ministers' residences, burial grounds, places for education and training of students, schools, residences for a minister, schoolmaster, or caretaker. When there is an existing power of appointment, the appointment may be effected in the manner, and by the person appointed by the instrument, creating the trust; if there is no existing power, or the appointment under the power be not made within twelve months, then recourse should be made to the above Acts, under which the appointment is made, in the case of Peto's Act, by resolution of the church as by the Act provided, or, in the case of the Conveyancing Act, by Deed executed by the persons therein mentioned, the trust property in the former case vesting in the new trustees by virtue of the appointment alone, and, in the latter case, by virtue of a declaration forming part of the Deed. The document should bear a stamp duty of 10s. in respect of the appointment, and 10s. in respect of the vesting of the property.

If none of these modes of appointment are feasible, resort should be had to the powers of the Charity Commissioners, and in the last instance to the Court of Chancery, though this latter course should not be adopted without a certificate of its necessity from the Commissioners.

No form of appointment is prescribed by the Conveyancing Act, 1881, but in Sir Morton Peto's Act a form is given for cases under that Act only, and is as follows:—

Memorandum of the choice and appointment of new trustees of the chapel, situate in the parish of in the county of at a meeting duly convened and held for that purpose at on the day of 18 . Chairman.

Names and description of all the trustees on the constitution [*or last appointment of trustees*] made the day of

Adam Bell, of	George Hurst, of	Matthew Norman, of
Charles Dixon, of	John Jackson, of	Octavius Parker, of
Edward Forster, of	Kenneth Lucas, of	

Names and descriptions of all the trustees in whom the said chapel and premises now become legally vested.

1st. Old continuing trustees.

John Jackson, now of	Matthew Norman, now of	Octavius Parker, now of

2nd. New trustees now chosen and appointed.

Benjamin Adams, of	Jonathan Edmonds, of	John Horne, of
Charles Bell, of	Richard Baxter, of	

Dated this day of 18 .

WILLIAM HICKS, (L.S.)
Chairman of the said meeting.

Signed, sealed, and delivered by the said William Hicks, as chairman of the said meeting, at and in the presence of the said meeting, on the day and year aforesaid, in the presence of
A. B.
C. D.

N.B.—The Baptist Union Corporation, Limited, is prepared to act as trustee for new chapel property, thus obviating with perpetual succession the recurring expense and trouble of re-appointment on the death or resignation of individual trustees. Application should be made to the Secretary of the Corporation, 19 Furnival Street, E.C. For Memorandum and Articles of Association see page 29.

Chapel Burial-Grounds.

32 & 33 Vic. c. 26.—By this Act the provisions of 13 & 14 Vic. c. 28, entitled "An Act to render more simple and effectual the titles by which congregations and societies for purposes of religious worship or education in England and Ireland hold property for such purposes," are extended to burial-grounds which have been or hereafter shall be acquired by any congregation or society, or body of persons associated for religious purposes, and whether such burial-grounds are now in use or closed. Proviso that nothing in Act contained shall interfere with Burial Acts. The Acts render unnecessary any transfer of the property or the appointment of new trusteess The property is to vest by virtue of the appointment alone.

Exemption from Rates.

It is enacted by 3 & 4 William IV., cap. 30, that "no person or persons shall be rated, or shall be liable to be rated to, or to pay any church or poor rates or cesses for, or in respect of, any churches, district churches, chapels, meeting-houses, or premises, or such part thereof, as shall be exclusively appropriated to public religious worship, and which (other than churches, district churches, or Episcopal churches of the Established church), shall be" registered under 18 & 19 Vic., cap. 81. as a place of meeting for religious worship. (See Sec. 3.) "Provided always that no person or persons shall be hereby exempted from any such rates or cesses, for or in respect of, any parts of such churches, district churches, chapels, meeting-houses, or other premises which are not so exclusively appropriated, and from which parts not so exclusively appropriated, such person or persons shall receive any rent or rents or shall derive profit or advantage." Section 2 proceeds, "Provided always that no person or persons shall be liable to any such rates or cesses because the said churches, district churches, chapels, meeting-houses, or other premises, or any vestry-rooms belonging thereto or any part thereof, may be used for Sunday or infant schools, or for the charitable education of the poor." It is difficult to say what user of part of a chapel or school premises would bring the case within the exception from the exemption. It is believed that no case on the point has as yet come before the courts. With regard to the certification of places of Worship, see *post* "Registration." It will be seen from the foregoing that churches of the Establishment and chapels are on the same footing.

Other Rates.

By the Public Health Act the incumbent or minister of any building exempted by law from the poor rate is also exempt from rates for sewering, paving, and lighting leviable by any authority administering the Act. It may be questioned whether such user (if any) of chapel or school premises as would subject the chapel or premises to the liability to pay poor rates, might not also involve liability to rates levied under the Public Health Act. This Act does not apply to the metropolis, which is governed by the Metropolis Management Act, 1855. From that Act the exemption clause was omitted (*qu: per incuriam?*) and it has been practically held that Dissenting places of worship are "houses," and are not exempt from the paving, sewering, and lighting rates leviable thereunder. In the great majority of cases the persons who are rateable under this Act are the Trustees of the property. The owners of an Established church are not liable under the Act. This inequality should be remedied by Parliament as soon as practicable.

Charitable Assurances.

The law relating to gifts and sales of lands and other property for charitable uses (amongst which are included the erection of chapels, schools, &c.), has been recently consolidated by the Mortmain and Charitable Uses Act, 1888 (51 & 52 Vic. cap. 42). No attempt should be made to give effect to sales of more than two acres of land, or to gifts for such purposes without competent legal advice. Land not exceeding two acres in extent may be conveyed to "trustees on behalf of any society or body of persons associated together for religious purposes," "for the erection thereon of a building for such purposes," "or whereon a building used or intended to be used for such purposes has been erected," without any special formalities, provided that such conveyance be made in good faith, for full and valuable consideration. It is no longer necessary to enrol either the conveyance or the deed declaring the trusts in such cases, though the trustees may enrol such deed if they think fit.

Further change has been made in the law relating to charitable assurances by an Act of the Session of 1891, namely, The Mortmain and Charitable Uses Act, 1891, by virtue of the provisions of which land may now be assured by will to or for the benefit of any charitable use, but such land, notwithstanding anything in the will contained to the contrary, must be sold within one year from the death of the testator.

Charitable Trustees Incorporation Act.

35 & 36 Vict. c. 24.—This Act, entitled "An Act to facilitate the Incorporation of Trustees of Charities for Religious, Educational, Literary, Scientific, and Public Charitable Purposes, and the Enrolment of certain Charitable Trust Deeds," was passed 27th June, 1872.

The object of this Act is to facilitate the incorporation of the charities indicated in the title, and to diminish the expense of enrolment under an Act passed in the thirtieth year of the reign of her present Majesty. Owing to the option of granting a certificate being by the Act vested in the Charity Commissioners for England and Wales, and to the latter having held that such certificate should be refused in cases where the property might be vested in the official trustee of the Commissioners under the Charity Commission Acts, the incorporation Act has become practically almost useless.

Charitable Trusts (Recovery) Act, 1891.

This Act, entitled "An Act to facilitate the recovery of rent-charges and other payments owing to charities," was passed on 11th May, 1891. It provides for the institution of proceedings by the Charity Commissioners for England and Wales for the recovery of any property the gross annual income of which does not exceed £20 per annum, and which appears to belong to a charity; and regulates the procedure to be adopted thereon.

Upon such proceedings it enacts that the printed report of the Charity Commissioners shall be admissible as *primâ facie* evidence of the documents and facts therein stated. Also that, where any yearly or other periodical payment has been made in respect of any land to or for the benefit of any charity or charitable purpose for twelve consecutive years, such payment shall be deemed subject to any evidence which may be given to the contrary *primâ facie* evidence of the perpetual liability of such land to such yearly or other periodical payment, and no proof of the origin of such payment shall be necessary.

Bequests to Charities.

(1) *Bequest of an ordinary pecuniary Legacy.*—In this case there is no need for the provision formerly inserted in wills directing the legacy to be paid exclusively out of such parts of the testator's estate as might lawfully be disposed of for charitable purposes. The bequest may be in the following form :—

" I give to the treasurer or treasurers for the time being of the Society the sum of pounds, free of duty, for the general purposes of the said society, and his or their receipt shall be a sufficient discharge for the same."

(2) *Bequest of a pecuniary legacy made payable out of the proceeds of sale and conversion of the testator's real and personal estate, or of a share of such proceeds.*—Very frequently a testator gives his real and personal estate, or his residuary estate, to trustees on trust to sell, and out of the proceeds of sale to pay the legacies previously bequeathed, which may include a legacy to a charitable society, and a testator may now bequeath a share of such proceeds to such society. In these cases, although perhaps not essential, it is considered prudent, at all events until the interpretation of the Mortmain and Charitable Uses Act, 1891, noted above, has been settled by Judicial decision, to add to the gift of the pecuniary legacy or share to the society the following direction :—

"And I direct that in case all the real and leasehold estate comprised in the devise and bequest in trust for sale herein contained shall not be sold within one year from my death, then the said legacy (or share) herein bequeathed to the said treasurer or treasurers for the time being of the society, and the duty thereon shall be paid out of the proceeds of sale and conversion of my personal estate and the proceeds of sale of such of my real and leasehold estate as shall be sold within one year after my death, in priority to all other legacies (or shares) payable thereout."

Dissenting Registers of Births, Baptisms, and Burials.

These registers and records, which were collected, examined and approved by a Royal Commission, are now deposited in the custody of the Registrar-General, at the Non-Parochial Register Office, Somerset House, London, which, for the purposes of the Act of 3 & 4 Vic., c. 92, is deemed a branch or part of the General Register Office. Searches and extracts from these registers and records will be granted on every day except Sundays, Christmas Day, and Good Friday, between the hours of ten and four, upon personal application only, and payment of legal fees. *Applications by letter for search or extract cannot be complied with.* Persons residing in the country, therefore, who may require searches of certificates, must, of necessity, apply to a friend in London, or employ an agent. All other communications by letter, on the subject of the above-mentioned registers and records, must be addressed to the "Registrar-General, General Registrar Office, London," and it is requested that the words "Non-Parochial Registers" may be written on the outside of all such letters, the postage of which may be left unpaid. The fee for each search is 1s., and for each certificate 2s. 6d.

The foregoing paragraph applies only to Dissenting records. In the case of other registers, application for copies of certificates can be made either personally or by letter to the Registrar-General.

Registration of Chapels.

Dissenting chapels, not already registered, may be certified, in writing, to the Registrar-General, through the superintendent-registrar of the district, who will furnish the legal form of certificate, and forward them (in duplicate) to the Registrar-General for record. Afterwards one of the forms will be returned, through the registrar, to the party certifying. At the office of the superintendent-registrar, a list of all chapels certified and not afterwards cancelled is open for inspection on the payment of 1s. The Registrar-General's certificate (which is legal evidence) of a chapel being registered may be obtained for a fee of 2s. 6d. Every place of worship *registered under the present law in the office of the Registrar-General* is exempt from poor rates (see above), and is exempted from the operation of the Charitable Trusts Act, by which the Charity Commission was instituted. In order that a chapel may be registered for the Solemnisation of Marriages it must be "certified," and must have been *used* as a place of religious worship by the congregation requiring it to be registered, during one year at the least preceding such registration. If the building be one erected and used *in lieu* of some other building which had been previously registered and subsequently *disused* as a place of religious worship, the registry of the disused building must be cancelled, whereupon the new building may be immediately registered in its stead. The fee for merely certifying a place of worship is 2s. 6d.; for registering the same for marriages, £3.

Law of Marriage.

England.

The law regulating Dissenting Marriages in England is contained in five Acts of Parliament—viz., the 6 & 7 Will. IV., c. 85; 1 Vict., c. 22; 3 & 4 Vict., c. 72; 19 & 20 Vict., c. 119; and 49 Vict., c. 14. Particulars or explanations may always be obtained from the district registrars or superintendent-registrars. Marriage may be solemnised in any registered building, or in district register office (otherwise than by banns in the church, as by law established), either by certificate (without licence) or by licence. If by *certificate* (without licence) notice (accompanied with fee of 1s. for entry in "Marriage Notice Book") must be given by *one* of the parties, if both live in one district, to superintendent-registrar, on form furnished for purpose, containing solemn declaration of absence of impediment to intended marriage, certifying that *one* of the parties has dwelt at least seven days in district, and must be signed in presence of registrar or deputy; but if parties live in different districts, notices must be sent to respective superintendent-registrars. *Twenty-one* clear days after entry of notice the certificate (for which 1s. must be paid) will be granted on application.

The same applies if one party lives in Ireland, only notice must be given on form used in Ireland. If one party lives in Scotland, Scotch certificate of proclamation of banns will be accepted as equal to certificate.

If by *licence*, though both parties do not dwell in same district, only *one* need give notice (on a form impressed with a 2s. 6d. stamp), certifying that he or she has resided at least *fifteen* days in district, though marriage may be had in district of either party. Both parties, however, must be in England at time of notice, though only *one* clear day is required (unless marriage take place in Ireland with someone there, when *seven* days are required) between notice and granting of licence. Cost of licence, £2 4s. 6d.

The law is substantially the same in the Channel Islands and the Isle of Man.

If there be no registered building in the district according to the rights or ceremonies desired by parties, by endorsing notice with such declaration, marriage may be held in another district.

If usual " place of worship " at which ceremony is desired be out of district of either's dwelling, by inserting words :—" Such building being usual place of worship of said——, and situate not more than two miles beyond limits of district of——," certificate will be granted accordingly.

The marriage must take place in the registered building specified in certificate, with open doors, between hours of eight in the morning and three in the afternoon, within three calendar months from day of entry of notice, in presence of registrar (or deputy), and two or more credible witnesses besides minister, if any. At some part of ceremony the words must be said :—" I do solemnly declare that I know not of any lawful impediment why I —— may not be joined in matrimony to ——" ; and each must say to other : " I call upon these persons here present to witness that I —— do take thee —— to be my lawful wedded wife (or husband) " ; without which it is not a marriage.

Registrar's fee for attending marriage by licence, 10s.; by certificate (without licence), 5s.

In marriages in district registry office, the same conditions (only *superintendent-registrar* must be present) and words as above must be observed. There must, however, be no religious service, though this does not prevent such service being subsequently held if desired.

Quakers and Jews are excepted so far from the ordinary operation of Marriage Acts as to be allowed their respective usages, provided due notice be given and certificate shall have issued.

SCOTLAND.

Ceremony can be performed by minister of any denomination, in any place, at any time, without any particular form. The law, however, recognizes as marriage a contract of mutual consent, though there be no minister nor ceremony of any kind, provided one of the parties has been twenty-one days in Scotland.

IRELAND.

Certificates and licences are granted Protestant Nonconformists on exactly the same conditions as in England, except that notice must be given on form used in Ireland, and immediately before *licence* is granted (which is on *eighth* day, instead of second as in England) an oath must be administered or solemn declaration taken.

Marriage may also be had by special licence granted by president of that religious body (except Jews) to which *both* parties belong.

A marriage can take place in Ireland when one party resides in England only by *licence* granted seven days after date of certificate of *licence* obtained by other party in England. It is the same if one party resides in Scotland, only certificate of proclamation of banns is accepted as equal to English certificate of licence.

The Burials Acts.

The following digest of the leading provisions of the Burial Laws Amendment Act, 1880 (43 & 44 Vict., c. 41), which became law on the 7th of September of that year, has been prepared by the "Liberation Society" for the guidance of those whose duty it may be to make arrangements for interments. Further information, and copies of the Act, and of the requisite forms, may be obtained by addressing "The Secretaries," 2, Serjeant's Inn, Fleet-street, London:—

I.—The Notice of Burial.

1. The notice of an intention to bury in accordance with the Act, in either churchyards or the consecrated parts of parochial cemeteries, should be given with as little delay as possible, and must not be later than *forty-eight hours* before the time proposed for the burial.

2. The notice may be given by any relative, friend, or legal representative having charge of, or being responsible for, the burial.

3. It must be in writing; must be endorsed on the outside "Notice of burial"; must be signed with the name and address of the person giving it, and be in the form, *or to the effect*, following:—

"I,   of   being the relative [*or* friend, *or* legal representative, *as the case may be, describing the relation, if a relative*] having the charge of, or being responsible for, the burial of A. B., of   , who died at   , in the parish of   , on the pay of   do hereby give you notice that it is intended by me that the body

of the said A. B. shall be buried within the [*here describe the churchyard or graveyard in which the body is to be buried*] on the   day of   , at the hour of   , without the performance in the manner prescribed by law of the service for the burial of the dead according to the rites of the Church of England; and I give this notice pursuant to the Burial Laws Amendment Act, 1880.

"To the rector [*or, as the case may be*] of   ."

[N.B.—While it is desirable to keep to this form, the person receiving it will not be at liberty to object to its sufficiency because the exact words are not used, the Act requiring that the notice shall be in the form, "*or to the effect,*" of the above.]

4. In the case of a *churchyard*, the notice is to be left at the house of the clergyman, or, in his absence, of the clergyman in charge of the parish, or of any person appointed to receive such notices.

5. In the case of a parochial *cemetery*, if there is a chaplain for the consecrated ground, the notice is to be addressed to him, but is to be left at the office of the Clerk of the Burial Board.

6. In the case of a pauper, notice may be given to the Incumbent, or the chaplain, and also to the Master of the Workhouse, or to the Clerk to the Guardians, by the husband, wife, or next-of-kin. The Guardians will be bound to allow the burial to be in accordance with the Act.

II.—Change of Time for Burial.

7. The person receiving the notice may object to the time proposed for the burial in the following cases:—

(*a*) As to burials in both *churchyards and parochial cemeteries*: if the burial be inconvenient on account of some other service having been *previously to the receipt of the notice* appointed to take place.

(*b*) As to burials in parochial cemeteries only: if the time proposedinfringes any regulations in force limiting the times at which burials may take place

Unless some other time be mutually arranged within *twenty-four hours* from the time of giving the notice, the person from whom the notice has been received must be informed in writing at what other hour *on the same day* the burial is to take place. But if no such intimation of change of hour is sent the burial is to take place at the time named in the notice. There is therefore *no necessity for receiving the consent of the clergyman;* as, in the event of his not objecting, within the time named, the funeral may take place in accordance with the notice, as a matter of *course.*

[N.B.—Unless it be otherwise mutually arranged, burials must be between 10 and 6 o'clock from April 1 to October 1, and between 10 and 3 from October 1 to April 1.]

8. In the case of a *churchyard*, if the Incumbent objects to a burial on Sunday, Good Friday, and Christmas Day, he must name a time on the following day. He must also state his reason for doing so, in writing, to the person from whom he has received the notice. This objection cannot be taken in the case of *cemeteries*, unless Sunday funerals are prohibited by the cemetery regulations.

III.—CHARACTER OF BURIAL SERVICES.

9. A burial may take place either without any "religious service," or "with such Christian and orderly religious service," at the grave, as the person responsible for the burial may think fit, and "any person or persons," whether ministers or laymen, who may be invited, or authorised, may conduct such service, or take part in any religious act thereat. The words "Christian service" include "every religious service used by any church, denomination, or person professing to be Christian."

10. All burials must be decent and orderly, and any one guilty of riotous, violent, or indecent behaviour, or of obstructing any service, will be guilty of a misdemeanour.

11. So also will any person who shall "deliver any address, not being part of, or incidental to, any religious service" permitted by the Act; or who wilfully endeavours "to bring into contempt, or obloquy, the Christian religion, or the belief, or worship, of any church, or denomination of Christians, or the members, or any minister of any such church or denomination, or any other person."

12. The clergyman, the cemetery authorities, and all other authorised persons, will have the same power to preserve order, and to prevent, or to punish, disorderly behaviour, or obstruction, as they now possess in the case of burials in accordance with the rites of the Church of England. All persons may have free access to the place of burial.

[N.B.—It is most desirable that those who are responsible for the conduct of funerals should carefully avoid, not only the commission of any legal offence, but any proceedings which may afford just ground for complaint.]

IV.—THE REGISTRY OF BURIALS.

13. The person having charge of a burial under the Act must, either on the same day or the day after, send to the Incumbent, or his representative—or, in the case of a cemetery, to the clerk—a certificate in the following form:—

"I, , of , the person having the charge of [or, being responsible for] the burial of the deceased, do hereby certify that on the day of , 189 , of aged was buried in the churchyard [*or* graveyard] of the parish [*or* district] of

"To the rector [*or, as the case may be*] of

Any person wilfully making a false statement in such certificate, or any person whose duty it is to make such entries, refusing or neglecting to enter the burial in the parish or cemetery register, will be guilty of a misdemeanour.

V.—SERVICES BY THE CLERGY OF THE CHURCH OF ENGLAND.

14. The clergy of the Church of England are at liberty to use the burial service of that Church in any unconsecrated burial ground, or in the chapel therein. The relatives may have such service performed in unconsecrated ground by *any* clergyman of the Church of England who may be willing to perform the same.

15. In cases where the Church of England service cannot legally be used, and in any other case, *at the request of the relatives*, the clergy may use some other than the ordinary burial service of the Church of England, provided that it has been approved by the Bishop, and is taken wholly from the Bible and Prayer Book.

VI.—MISCELLANEOUS.

16. The Act does not entitle anyone to be buried in any place in which there would be no right of burial if the Act had not passed. The Act relates only to burial *services.*

17. Neither does it affect previously existing regulations or authority in regard to the position of graves, inscriptions on gravestones, etc. The same fees will also have to be paid as though the burial were in accordance with the rites of the Church of England.

18. The Act applies only to England and Wales and the Channel Islands.

THE OATHS ACT, 1888.

The Act to amend the Law as to Oaths, passed on the 24th December, 1888, enacts that every person upon objecting to being sworn, and stating, as the ground of such objection, either that he has no religious belief, or that the taking of an oath is contrary to his religious belief, shall be permitted to make his solemn affirmation instead of taking an oath, in all places and for all purposes where an oath is or shall be required by law, which affirmation shall be of the same force and effect as if he had taken the oath. Every such affirmation shall be as follows:—"I, A. B., do solemnly, sincerely, and truly declare and affirm," and then proceed with the words of the oath prescribed by law, omitting any words of imprecation or calling to witness.

DISSENTERS IN ESTABLISHED CHURCH PULPITS.

The Act by which it is considered that the clergy are restrained from inviting Dissenters to occupy their pulpits is the Act of Uniformity of 1662 (13 & 14 Car. II., c. 14). By this Act no one may act or preach as a lecturer (in which capacity it is conceived a Dissenter or layman would appear, if so invited to preach) without a licence from the Bishop, and it has been decided that the discretion of the Bishop to grant or withhold his licence cannot be questioned. Any lecturer who acts in contravention of this enactment "shall suffer three months' imprisonment without bail or mainprize." No penalty, however, appears to be incurred by a parson inviting or permitting an unlicensed lecturer to use his pulpit; though a Bishop who grants a licence to anyone who has not first subscribed to the Three Articles concerning "the King's supremacy, the Book of Common Prayer, and the 39 Articles," will have to suffer the serious inconvenience of being suspended from giving licences to preach for the space of twelve months.

RECENT STATUTES.

The Acts of Parliament of 55 & 56 Vict. may be usefully consulted on the following subjects:—Chapter 11, Mortmain and Charitable Uses Act Amendment; Chapter 15 Charity Inquiries (Expenses); Chapter 23, Foreign Marriage; Chapter 32, Clergy Discipline Act, 1892.

THE CENSUS, 1891.

The Census taken on 5th April, 1891, gives the population of the British Isles as 37,880,764, viz.:—

	Persons	Males.	Females.	Increase since previous Census 1881.	Decennial Rate of Increase per cent.
England and Wales.. ..	29,002,525	14,052,901	14,949,624	3,028,086	11·65
Scotland	4,025,647	1,942,717	2,082,930	290,074	7·77
				Decrease.	Decrease.
Ireland	4,704,750	2,318,953	2,385,797	470,086	9·08
				Increase.	Increase.
Channel Islands	92,234	43,226	49,008	4,532	3·8
Isle of Man	55,608	26,329	29,279	2,050	5·16

STAMPS, DUTIES, &c.

Receipts.

For sums of £2 or upwards (persons receiving the money are to pay the duty) .. 1d.

Drafts, Bills, &c.

Draft or *Order* for the payment of any sum of money to the bearer, or to order, on demand, including bankers' cheques .. .. 1d.

Inland Bill, Draft, or *Order*, payable otherwise than on demand:—

		£	£	s.	d.
Not exceeding	.. ..	5	0	0	1
Exceeding £ 5,	and not exceeding	10	0	0	2
10,	"	25	0	0	3
25,	"	50	0	0	6
50,	"	75	0	0	9
75,	"	100	0	1	0

and 1s. for every additional £100 or fractional part thereof.

House Duty.

On premises of the annual value of £20 and under £40—Shops, 2d. in £.
" " " " Houses, 3d. in £.
" " " £40 and not exceeding £60—Shops, 4d. in £.
" " " " Houses, 6d. in £.
" " exceeding £60—Shops, 6d. in £.
" " " Houses, 9d. in £.

Apprentices' Indentures

Instrument of .. .. 2s. 6d.

Licence for Marriage.

Special, in England or Ireland, £5; not special, in England, 10s.

Income Tax.

Duty is not chargeable when the income does not exceed £160 a year. The rate of duty is 8d. per £. A deduction of £160 is allowed before charging duty in any case in which the total income does not exceed £400, and when the total income exceeds £400 but does not exceed £500, a deduction of £100 is allowed.

RATES OF POSTAGE, &c.

The rate of postage on letters passing between any two places in the United Kingdom, including the Orkney, Shetland, Scilly, and Channel Islands, and the Isle of Man, is as follows:—

If not exceeding 1 ounce .. .. 1d.
Exceeding 1 ounce, but not exceeding 2 ounces .. .. 1½d.
" 2 ounces " " 4 ounces .. .. 2d.
" 4 ounces " " 6 ounces .. .. 2½d.

And so on at the rate of a halfpenny for every additional two ounces, or fraction of two ounces.

Unpaid letters are charged double postage on delivery; those insufficiently prepaid, double the amount of such insufficiency.

All letters should be clearly addressed in a plain hand. The stamp should stand above the address, to the right hand of the writer.

No charge is made for the re-direction of letters, provided that the letters are re-posted not later than the day after delivery, and that they do not appear to have been opened.

If coin be enclosed in an ordinary letter, the letter will be charged a registration fee of 8d. on delivery.

No letter may be above 18 inches in length, 9 inches in width, or 6 inches in depth, unless it be sent to or from one of the Government Offices.

Registration.

Inland letters, book packets, parcels, and newspapers may be registered upon payment of a fee of 2d. over and above the postage. All letters containing coin should be enclosed in a registered letter envelope, which may be obtained at any Post Office on payment of 2½d. (which includes the registration fee), or in packets of twelve at 2s. 2½d. per packet (small sizes).

Compensation.

Compensation is given for loss or damage of Inland Registered Postal Packets of all kinds, subject to certain conditions, on payment of an Insurance Fee, which either consists of or includes in each case, the ordinary registration fee of 2d.; and the scale of fees, and the respective limits of compensation are:—

Two pence for	£5
Three pence for	£10
Four pence for	£15
Five pence for	£20
Six pence for	£25

and so on up to a maximum limit of £50.

The following rates of postage are also in operation —

Book Packets.

Inland, ½d. for every 2 ounces or part of 2 ounces. No book packet may exceed 5 pounds in weight, 18 inches in length, 9 in width, or 6 in depth, unless it be sent to or from a Government Office.

Letter Cards.

1¼d. each; 3½d. for three; 9d. for eight, &c.

Newspapers.

Newspapers (which have been registered as such at the General Post Office), whether posted singly or with others in a packet, ½d. each between any two places in the United Kingdom. If more than one paper be sent under the same cover the packet is not chargeable with a higher rate than would be chargeable on a book packet of the same weight.

Newspaper Wrappers.

Bearing ½d. stamp, 3½d. for six wrappers; bearing 1d. stamp, 8½d. for eight wrappers, &c.

Postcards (thin).

1¾d. for three cards, 3½d. for six cards, or in packets of ten at 5½d. per packet.

Postcards (stout).

3d. for five cards, 5d. for eight, or 6d. per packet of ten cards.

Reply Postcards (thin).

3¼d. for three, 6½d. for six, 11d. for ten, &c.

Reply Postcards (stout).

3¾d. for three, 7½d. for six, 1s. for ten, &c.

MONEY ORDERS (INLAND).

Money Orders are granted and paid at every Head Office, and also at several thousands of Branch and Sub-offices and Town Receiving Houses in the United Kingdom, the commission on which is as follows:—

For sums not exceeding £1	..	..	2d.
For sums above ..	£1 and not exceeding	£2 ..	3d.
" ..	£2 "	£4 ..	4d.
" ..	£4 "	£7 ..	5d.
" ..	£7 "	£10 ..	6d.

An order may be crossed like a cheque, at the time of issue, thus: & Co., and thus be payable only through a bank. Payment of an Order must be obtained within twelve months.

In case of the miscarriage or loss of a Money Order, a duplicate is granted without charge on a written application (with the necessary particulars) to the Controller of the Money Order Office of the Kingdom in which the original Order was issued, provided the loss is in the transmission to the payee, but if otherwise a charge of 1s. or 2s. (according to the amount of the Order) is made for the issue of the duplicate Order.

Money Orders are also issued on many foreign countries, the British Colonies, &c.—

For sums not exceeding £2 ..	..	£0	0	6
" " £5 ..	..	0	1	0
" £7 ..	..	0	1	6
" " £10 ..	..	0	2	0

TELEGRAPH MONEY ORDERS

May be sent by payment of double he commission on Money Orders, and a minimum charge of 9d. in addition for the Official Telegram authorizing payment, and the repetition thereof.

POSTAL ORDERS

Are issued for fixed sums as follows, and paid at all Money Order Offices in the United Kingdom, and at Malta, Gibraltar, India, Straits Settlements, Hong Kong, Newfoundland, and Constantinople, within three months of issue; and thereafter on payment of a second poundage.

Amount of Order	Poundage.
1s. and 1s. 6d. ..	½d.
2s., 2s. 6d., 3s., 3s. 6d., 4s., 4s. 6d., 5s., 7s. 6d., 10s., and 10s. 6d. ..	1d.
15s. and 20s. ..	1½d.

Broken amounts may be made up by the use of Postage Stamps, not exceeding 5d. in value, affixed to the face of any one Postal Order.

SAVINGS BANKS.

Deposits are received at every Postal Savings Bank Office during the hours appointed for the sale of stamps in amounts from 1s. upwards, and upon every complete pound yearly interest is given at the rate of £2 10s. per cent. Deposits not to exceed £50 in one year, ending 31st December, and £200 in all, inclusive of interest. See *Post Office Guide*.

GOVERNMENT ANNUITIES AND LIFE INSURANCES.

Immediate or deferred annuities from £1 up to £100, may be purchased through the Post Office on the life of any person over 5 years of age. These annuities are payable by equal half-yearly instalments on the 5th January and the 5th July, or on the 5th April and the 10th October, according to the date of purchase. Life insurances, from £5 to £100, can be granted to persons between 14 and 65 years of age. Children between 8 and 14 years of age can be insured for £5. See Post Office *Guide*.

EXPRESS DELIVERY OF LETTERS AND PARCELS.

Letters and parcels are now accepted at all Express Delivery Offices in the United Kingdom for immediate delivery by special messenger in any part of the same town or rural district. Letters and parcels may also be handed in at any Post Office which is not an Express Delivery Office for despatch in the ordinary course of post to the nearest available Express Office for delivery by special messenger. Letters and parcels forwarded by mail in the regular course of post to any Express Delivery Office in the Kingdom are also delivered by special messenger if desired by the sender.

INLAND PARCEL POST.

Parcels *not exceeding* 11 *lbs. in weight* are received at any Post Office for transmission between places in the United Kingdom.

In order that a packet may go by Parcel Post, it must be tendered for transmission as a parcel, and should bear the words "Parcel Post," which should be clearly written in the left-hand top corner.

Every Post Office is open to the public for Parcel Post business on week days during the same hours as for general postal business. No Parcel Post business is transacted in the United Kingdom on Sundays, nor in England and Ireland on Christmas Days and Good Fridays; nor in Scotland on Sacramental Fast Days.

The following are the principal conditions and regulations:—

The size allowed for an Inland Postal Parcel is—

Greatest length	3 ft. 6 in.
Greatest length and girth combined	6 ft. 0 in.

For example—

A parcel measuring 3 ft. 6 in. in its longest dimension may measure as much as 2 ft. 6 in. in girth, *i.e.*, round its thickest part; or

A shorter parcel may be thicker; thus, if it measure no more than 3 ft. in length, it may measure as much as 3 ft. in girth, *i.e.*, round its thickest part.

The rates of postage are, for a Parcel—

Not exceeding 1 lb. in weight			.. .. ..	3d
Exceeding 1 lb. and not exceeding 2 lbs.			..	4½d
,,	2 lbs. ,, ,,	3 lbs.	..	6d.
,,	3 lbs. ,, ,,	4 lbs.	..	7½d.
,,	4 lbs. ,, ,,	5 lbs.	..	9d.
,,	5 lbs. ,, ,,	6 lbs.	..	10½d.
,,	6 lbs. ,, ,,	7 lbs.	..	1s. 0d.
,,	7 lbs. ,, ,,	8 lbs.	..	1s. 1½d.
,,	8 lbs. ,, ,,	9 lbs.	..	1s. 3d.
,,	9 lbs. ,, ,,	10 lbs.	..	1s. 4½d.
,,	10 lbs. ,, ,,	11 lbs.	..	1s. 6d.

No parcel is accepted which weighs more than 11 pounds, or is not sufficiently paid. The postage must, in all cases, *be paid in advance*, and by ordinary postage stamps, which must be affixed by the sender before tendering a parcel for transmission by Parcel Post at a Post Office.

Care must be taken that every parcel bears a clear address, and has the words "Parcel Post" legibly written on the left-hand corner of the address.

Parcels must not be posted in a letter box, but must be taken into a Post Office and handed over the counter. If a packet, which either bears the words "Parcel *Post," or from its* appearance seems to be intended for transmission as a parcel, is not posted in accordance with this regulation, it is treated as a letter or book packet, if it is fully prepaid at the rate proper to either, and is otherwise in accordance with the letter or book post regulations. If such a packet is not fully prepaid at the letter or book post rate, it is treated as a parcel, and is charged on delivery a fine of 1d., together with the deficient postage, if any, at the Parcel Post rate.

By filling up a blank form—obtainable at Post Offices—a "Certificate of Posting" can be had under the Stamp of the Post Office.

INLAND PATTERN AND SAMPLE POST

"Is intended for the transmission of *bona fide trade patterns and samples of merchandise*. . . . No article sent for sale or in execution of an order, or otherwise than as a trade pattern or sample, will under any circumstances be admissible; and if any such packet be posted prepaid at the pattern rate only, it will be charged with double the deficient postage, *at the letter rate*, together with a fine of 6d."

Trade patterns and samples of merchandise may be sent between places in the United Kingdom, at the following rates of postage—

For a packet weighing not more than 4 ounces .. .. 1d.

For a packet weighing more than 4 ounces, but not more than 6 ounces 1½d.

For a packet weighing more than 6 ounces, but not more than 8 ounces 2d.

No packet may exceed 8 ounces in weight. The limits of dimensions are 12 in by 8 in. by 4 in. If either of these conditions be infringed, the packet will not be forwarded, but will be returned to the sender.

TELEGRAM RATES.

The charge for any message of twelve words throughout the United Kingdom (including the Channel Islands, Orkney, Shetland, the Isle of Man, and the Scilly Isles), is 6d., and ½d. for every additional word. Postage Stamps are used for payment; to be affixed as upon letters. Books of 20 forms, interleaved with a sheet of carbonic paper, and with embossed stamp, may be had at 10s. 2d. each.

FOREIGN POSTAL ARRANGEMENTS.

Full details as to days of despatch, rates of postage, &c., to Foreign Countries may be obtained from any Post Office, or from the *Post Office Guide*, which is published quarterly. These arrangements vary quarter by quarter, and reliable information cannot, therefore, be given for the whole year in this annual publication.

The prepaid postage of 2½d. per ½ ounce is now applicable to letters for all parts of the world outside the United Kingdom.

COLONIAL AND FOREIGN PARCEL POST.

Parcels can now be received at any Post Office in the United Kingdom for transmission to many foreign countries. The system undergoes frequent revision. For rates, &c., see *Post Office Guide*, or apply at any Post Office.

PASSPORTS.

An Englishman travelling on the Continent seldom needs a Passport, but it is nevertheless *advisable* to carry one, as it is at all times proof of identity, and frequently secures admission to museums and similar buildings when otherwise closed. A Passport is *necessary* for Russia, Turkey, Roumania, Bosnia and Herzegovina, and is desirable for Spain and Portugal. Passports are also required when persons are making any long stay in France, Germany, or Switzerland.

Passports are issued to British-born subjects by the Foreign Office or the various British Consuls on presentation of a recommendation from a Banker *under seal*, or upon the production of a Certificate of Identity, signed by a Magistrate, Clergyman, Physician, Solicitor, Notary, or M.P., and countersigned by the person on whose behalf the certificate is granted. Passports are issued to naturalised British subjects only on *personal* application at the Foreign Office. The charge for issue of a Passport is 2s., and for Visas—Austria-Hungary, 2s. ; Belgium, 2s. 6d.; France, 8s.; Germany, 1s. 6d. (visa renewable annually); Greece, 2s. 6d.; Holland, 4s. 2d.; Italy, 4s.; Portugal, 8s. 11d ; Roumania, 4s. 2d. (1s. to British *born* subjects): Russia, 4s. 10d. (must state religion); Servia, 2s. 6d. ; Spain, 8s. ; Switzerland, 2s.; Turkey, 4s.; Persia, 4s. Agency fee 1s. extra for Passport and each Visa.

PART I.

BAPTIST UNION OF GREAT BRITAIN AND IRELAND.

OFFICERS, COUNCIL, ETC., 1895–96.

Officers.

President—Rev. JOHN GERSHOM GREENHOUGH, M.A.

Vice-President—Rev. THOMAS VINCENT TYMMS.

Treasurer—Mr. WILLIAM WILBERFORCE BAYNES, J.P.

Secretary—Rev. SAMUEL HARRIS BOOTH, D.D., 19 Furnival Street, E.C.

Members of the Council.

(1) *REPRESENTATIVES OF ASSOCIATIONS*

(In Membership with the Baptist Union).

BEDFORDSHIRE UNION.—Mr. R. Goodman, Flitwick.

BERKSHIRE.—Rev. J. Cave, Wokingham.

BRISTOL.—Mr. S. Iles, Bristol.

BUCKINGHAMSHIRE.—Rev. H. J. Lester, Aylesbury.

CAMBRIDGESHIRE.—Rev. J. Carvath, Willingham.

DEVON.—Mr. W. Hawkes, J.P., Devonport; Mr. H. E. Lilley, Honiton.

EAST MIDLAND.—Rev. T. Barrass, Peterborough; Mr. W. B. Clark, Leicester; Rev. W. F. Harris, Derby; Rev. W. Woods, London.

ESSEX UNION.—Rev. E. Dyer, Southend.

GLOUCESTERSHIRE AND HEREFORDSHIRE.—Rev. E. Ashton, Gorsley.

HERTFORDSHIRE UNION.—Rev. C. M. Hardy, B.A., St. Albans.

KENT AND SUSSEX.—Mr. G. Osborn, J.P., St. Leonards; Rev. W. Townsend, Canterbury.

LANCASHIRE AND CHESHIRE.—Rev. C. Bonner, Southampton; Rev. R. Lewis, Liverpool; Mr. G. W. Macalpine, J.P., Accrington.

LONDON.—Rev. J. Fletcher, Rev. G. P. McKay, Mr. H. Marnham.

NORFOLK.—Rev. J. M. Hamilton, Lowestoft.

NORTHAMPTONSHIRE.—Mr. J. Campion, Courteenhall.

NORTHERN.—Rev. J. T. Forbes, M.A., Edinburgh.

OXFORDSHIRE.—Rev. T. Bentley, Chipping Norton.

SHROPSHIRE.—Rev. A. Lester, Dawley.

SOUTHERN.—Rev. C. Joseph, Portsmouth; Rev. J. P. Williams, Portsmouth.

SUFFOLK AND NORFOLK UNION.—Mr. R. Mattingly, J.P., Sudbury.

WESTERN.—Rev. H. Hardin, Montacute.

WEST MIDLAND.—Rev. E. W. Cantrell, Birmingham; Mr. H. P. Chapman, Birmingham.

WILTSHIRE AND EAST SOMERSET.—Mr. W. B. Wearing, Swindon.

WORCESTERSHIRE.—Mr. J. Smallwood, J.P., Stratford-on-Avon.

YORKSHIRE.—Mr. W. Best, Bradford; Mr. J. R. Birkinshaw, Bradford; Rev. A. P. Fayers, Rawdon.

ANGLESEY.—Rev. T. M. Rees, Holyhead.

CARMARTHENSHIRE AND CARDIGANSHIRE.—Rev. J. A. Morris, Aberystwyth; Mr. I. Phillips, Burry Port; Rev. E. U. Thomas, Carmarthen.

DENBIGH, FLINT AND MERIONETHSHIRE.—Rev. E. K. Jones, Brymbo; Rev. T. Shankland, Rhyl; Rev. D. Williams, Llangollen.

GLAMORGANSHIRE AND CARMARTHENSHIRE (E.)—Mr. J. Davies, Cardiff; Rev. W. G. Davies, Penarth.

MONMOUTHSHIRE (E.)—Rev. H. Abraham, Newport.

NORTH WALES ENGLISH UNION.—Rev. J. Raymond, Llandudno.

OLD WELSH.—Rev. T. E. Williams, Newtown.

(2) *EX-PRESIDENTS OF THE BAPTIST UNION.*

1865 Rev. J. Angus, M.A., D.D., London.
1866 Rev. J. Aldis, Beckington.
1873 Mr. E. B. Underhill, LL.D., London.
1875 Rev. A. McLaren, B.A., D.D , Manchester.
1876 Rev. W. Landels, D.D., Edinburgh.
1877 Rev. J. T Brown, Northampton.
1882 Rev. J. J. Brown, Birmingham.
1884 Rev. R. Glover, D.D., Bristol.
1885 Rev. S. G. Green, B.A. D.D. London.
1886 Rev. C. Williams, Accrington.
1887 Rev. J. Culross, M.A., D.D., Bristol.
1888 Rev. J. Clifford, M.A., LL.B., B.Sc., F.G.S., D.D., London.
1890 Rev. J. Owen, Swansea.
1892 Rev. R. H. Roberts, B.A., London.
1893 Rev. T. M. Morris, Ipswich.
1894 Rev. G. Short, B.A., Salisbury.

(3) *PRINCIPALS OF DENOMINATIONAL COLLEGES*

(*In Membership with the Baptist Union.*)

Rev. J. Culross, M.A.. D.D., Bristol (*see above*—Ex-President).
Rev. G. Davies, D.D., Bangor.
Rev. T. W. Davies, B.A., Nottingham.
Rev. W. J. Henderson, B.A., Bristol.
Rev. R. H. Roberts, B.A., London (*see above*—Ex-President).
Rev. T. V. Tymms, Rawdon (*see under* "*Officers*"—Vice-President).

(4) *HONORARY MEMBERS.*

Mr. A. H. Baynes, London.
Mr. J. Brooke, J.P., Huddersfield.
Mr. D. Clarke, C.A., High Wycombe.
Rev. J. H. Cooke, London.
Mr. E. Mounsey, J.P., Liverpool.
Rev. E. Parker, D.D., Manchester.
Mr. W. R. Rickett, London.
Rev. A. Tilly, Cardiff.
Rev. J. W. Todd, D.D., London.
Mr. W. Willis, Q.C., London.
Rev. W. Woods, London (*see* "*East Midland*" *Association*).

(5) ELECTED MEMBERS.

(Under Sections 5 & 6, Article VIII. of Constitution.)

Mr. F. Arnold, J.P., Great Yarmouth.
Rev. J. H. Atkinson, Liverpool.
Rev. J. Bailey, B.A., Sheffield.
Rev. J. Baillie, London.
Rev. B. Bird, Plymouth.
Mr. W. B. Bembridge, J.P., Ripley.
Rev. W. E. Blomfield, B.A., B.D., Coventry.
Mr. J. Bowden, Barnet.
Rev. S. W. Bowser, B.A., Birkenhead.
Rev. J. Bradford, Leytonstone.
Rev. J. T. Briscoe, Bristol.
Rev. C. Brown, London.
Mr. S. B. Burton, Newcastle-on-Tyne.
Mr. G. M. Carlile, Bristol.
Mr. J. Chown, London.
Mr. R. Cleaver, J.P., Northampton.
Rev. W. Cuff, London.
Rev. J. Dann, Oxford.
Rev. D. Davies, Brighton.
Mr. R. O. Davies, J.P., London.
Rev. N. Dobson, Deal.
Rev. W. Dyson, London.
Rev. W. Evans, Leicester.
Rev. J. W. Ewing, M.A., London.
Rev. E. G. Gange, London.
Rev. G. P. Gould, M.A., London.
Mr. H. P. Gould, Norwich.
Mr. R. F. Griffiths, London.
Mr. J. J. Gurney, J.P., Newcastle-on-Tyne.
Rev. R. F. Guyton, Huntingdon.
Rev. J. Haslam, Gildersome.
Rev. J. Hasler, Andover.
Rev. G. Hawker, London.
Rev. E. Henderson, London.
Rev. D. J. Hiley, Bristol.
Rev. G. Hill, M.A., Nottingham.
Mr. T. R. Hope, J.P., Redhill.
Mr. E. Jackson, Reading.
Rev. F. A. Jones, London.
Mr. J. Marnham, J.P., Boxmoor.
Rev. E. Medley, B.A., London.
Mr. T. Penny, Taunton.
Rev. J. Porteous, Burton-on-Trent.
Rev. A. F. Riley, London.
Mr. H. Rogers, J.P., Hereford.
Rev. J. H. Shakespeare, M.A., Norwich.
Mr. Alderman G. Shepherd, J.P., Bacup.
Rev. C. W. Skemp, Bradford.
Rev. W. R. Skerry. London.
Rev. E. Spurrier, Colchester.
Mr. P. H. Stevenson, Nottingham.
Rev. J. Stuart, Watford.
Rev. T. G. Tarn, Cambridge.
Rev. J. Turner, Blaby.
Rev. C. W. Vick, London.
Rev. S. Vincent, Plymouth.
Mr. W. R. Wherry, J.P., Bourne.
Mr. T. Whitley, Southsea.
Rev. W. E. Winks, Cardiff.
Rev. J. R. Wood, London.

The Committees, as also the Council, for the Year 1896-7 will be found in the Baptist Union Report, which will be issued immediately after the Spring Assembly

CONSTITUTION (1894).

I.—Name.

The Baptist Union of Great Britain and Ireland.

II.—Constituency.

The Union shall consist of the Churches, Associations of Churches, and persons whose names are given in the Baptist Handbook for each year as comprising the membership of the Baptist Union.

III.—Declaration of Principle.

In this Union it is fully recognised that every separate church has liberty to interpret and administer the laws of Christ, and that the immersion of believers is the only Christian baptism.

IV.—The Objects of this Union.

1. To cultivate among its own members respect and love for one another, and for all who love the Lord Jesus Christ.

2. To spread the Gospel of Christ by employing ministers and evangelists, by establishing Christian churches, by forming Sunday-schools, by distributing the Scriptures and religious tracts, and by adopting and using such other methods as the Council shall deem advisable.

3. To afford opportunities for conference, for the public declaration of opinion, and for joint action on questions affecting the welfare of the churches and the extension of the denomination, both at home and abroad.

4. To promote fraternal correspondence between Baptists in this and in other countries.

5. To obtain accurate information respecting the organizations, labours, and sufferings of Baptists throughout the world.

6. To confer and co-operate with other Christian communities as occasion may require.

7. To maintain the right of all men everywhere to freedom from disadvantage, restraint, and taxation in matters purely religious.

V.—Operations.

This Union shall act by its Assembly, and through its officers and Council.

VI.—Membership.

The application of any Church, College, Association, or person, for admission to this Union shall be laid before the Council, and no application shall be complied with unless a majority of those present are in its favour. The constituency and list of members may be revised by the Council, and their decision shall be duly notified to the persons concerned, who shall have the right of appeal to the Assembly.

VII.—The Assembly.

1. The Assembly shall consist of representative, personal, and honorary members.

(A) Representative members shall comprise:—
- (*a*) Ministers of Churches,
- (*b*) Principals and Tutors of Colleges, and
- (*c*) Delegates from Churches and Associations of Churches,

in membership with the Baptist Union.

Churches not exceeding 150 members may appoint one delegate; more than 150, two delegates; and more than 300, three delegates.

Associations may appoint two delegates each.

Delegates shall be appointed annually, or for each meeting of the Assembly, and their appointment be duly accredited and notified to the Secretary before *March 31st* and August 31st respectively.

(B) Personal Members shall be members of Churches, who, being Baptists, shall have been duly accredited in writing by at least three members of the Assembly, and accepted by the Council, and who are donors of £10, or yearly subscribers of not less than one pound, or, in the case of Ministers not in pastoral charge, of not less than five shillings, to the General Expenses Fund of the Union.

(C) Honorary Members shall be chosen by a resolution of the Assembly, on the nomination of the Council, and the Officers and Ex-Presidents of the Baptist Union shall be *ex-officio* Honorary Members.

2. The Assembly shall meet in London in the Spring, and in the provinces if possible, in the Autumn, at such place as the Council may arrange.

VIII.—The Council.

The operations of the Union shall be conducted by a Council, consisting of: (1) one representative from each affiliated Association for every fifty Churches in its membership, or part of fifty, the names of such representatives to be certified to the Secretary not later than 1st February; (2) the Officers and Ex-Presidents of the Union; (3) the Principals of denominational Colleges in membership with the Union; (4) such persons as the Assembly may think fit (having been nominated for that purpose by the Council) to be Honorary Members of the Council; (5) forty-five members of the Assembly, who shall be chosen in the Assembly by ballot, and who, together with the representatives from Associations and Colleges, the Officers and Ex-Presidents, and the Honorary Members of the Council, shall make it their first business to elect (6) fifteen other nominated members of the Assembly. In the event of any vacancy occurring, the number under (5) and (6) may be made up to sixty by the Council electing a member of the Assembly to serve until the ensuing Spring Assembly.

Eleven members shall form a quorum.

IX.—The Officers.

The Officers of the Union shall be the President, Vice-President, Treasurer or Treasurers of the Funds of the Union, and Secretary.

X.—Alteration of Constitution.

No proposal for change in this Constitution shall be entertained without notice having been given in writing at a previous meeting of the Assembly.

BYE-LAWS.

I.—Election of Officers.

The Officers shall be elected at the first Session of the Spring Assembly. The Vice-President (who shall be the President of the next year) shall be elected by ballot, without discussion, a majority of the total votes given being necessary to election. Should no person have such majority on the first ballot, the four names for which the largest number of votes has been given shall be read out with the number of votes given for each, and, if needful, successive ballots shall be taken. After every such ballot the name receiving the smallest number of votes shall be struck off the list until the requisite majority of votes has been given for one person. Should such person fail to enter upon the office, the Council shall appoint a Vice-President.

II.—Election of Council.

1. Any member of the retiring Council may be nominated for re-election.

2. Nominations for the sixty "elected members" of the Council must be forwarded in writing to the Secretary on or before March 31st, signed, if made by resolution of a Church or Association, by the Chairman; or otherwise by not less than three members of the Assembly.

3. Voting papers shall be printed, containing a list of the persons nominated, with the attendances of the Council, which shall be distributed to members on entering the first Session of the Spring Assembly, and no change shall be made in the list after its distribution.

III.—Appointment of Scrutineers.

Scrutineers shall be appointed by the President to receive and examine all voting papers, and to announce the result as early as possible.

IV.—Sessions of the Assembly.

1. The Sessions of the Assembly shall be advertised as the Council may direct—the advertisements to include, as nearly as may be, a statement of the proceedings in their proposed order.

2. Admission to the Sessions shall be by ticket only, to be issued by the Secretary, under direction of the Council.

3. To secure a place on the Agenda paper as arranged by the Council, notices of motions or of amendments, signed by the Proposer, should be in the hands of the Secretary seven days before the first Session of the Assembly. Other notices of motions received subsequently must also be in writing, and shall be considered in the order determined by the Officers.

V.—Finance.

1. To defray the General Expenses of the Union an annual subscription shall be required of not less than 5s. from each Church, and not less than £1 from each College and each Association in membership with the Union.

2. Subscriptions for each year shall fall due on the 1st January, and, until paid, no cards of admission to the Assembly shall be granted.

3. Auditors for the year shall be appointed by resolution at the first Session of the Spring Assembly.

4. The financial year shall terminate on the 31st of December.

VI.—Meetings of Council.

1. The Council shall meet not less than twice a year, at fixed dates.

2. Meetings of Council shall be summoned by the Secretary, and special meetings on the written request of five members of the Council, stating the objects.

3. The expected business shall be named in all summonses of the Council.

4. The attendance of members at meetings of the Council and Committees shall be registered in a book kept for the purpose.

VII.—Committees.

The Council shall appoint from its members separate Committees for the conduct of its business as necessity may arise, and each Committee shall elect its own Chairman at the first meeting after its appointment.

The report of each Committee shall be given to the Council in writing by the Secretary.

Separate accounts shall be kept of all funds contributed to the objects of the Union, and such funds shall be devoted exclusively to the objects for which they are given. No legacy or other fixed funds or investments bequeathed and belonging, or hereafter to be bequeathed and to belong, to any object or fund of the Union shall be applied in any other way than has been, or may be, specified by the donors or testators of such funds respectively.

VIII.—The Hand-Book.

The matters to be published in the Hand-Book shall be determined by the Council.

IX.—Change of Bye-Laws.

No proposal to alter any of these Bye-laws shall be entertained until after twenty-eight days' notice has been given in writing to the Secretary, signed by the proposer.

CORRESPONDENTS.

The Secretaries of the Associations and of the Baptist Unions of SCOTLAND, WALES and IRELAND.

FRANCE, Rev. Aimé Cadot, Chauny, Aisne.

ITALY, Rev. W. K. Landels, 51, Corso Siccardi, Torino Rev. E. Clarke, Casa Alberto, Spezia.

GERMAN BAPTIST UNION, Mr. J. G. Lehmann, Borgfelde, Mittelweg 98, Hamburg.

DENMARK, Rev. Marius Larsen, 20, Griffensfellgade, Copenhagen.

HOLLAND, Rev. B. Roeles, Zutphen.

SWEDEN, Rev. Prof. Drake, 18, Engelbrehtigatan, Stockholm.

NORWAY, Rev. P. Helbostad, Trondhjem.

RUSSIAN BAPTIST UNION, Rev. A. Liebig, 4, Johannisstr., Stettin, Germany.

FINLAND, Rev. E. Jansson, Potalax, Finland.

MADEIRA, Rev. F. A. Jefferd, 29, Rua do Consalheiro, Funchal.

CAPE VERDES, Rev. G. S. C. Eveleigh, St. Vincent.

ST. HELENA, Rev. J. R. Way, Jamestown.

SOUTH AFRICA, Rev. H. J. Batts, King William's Town.

CANADA, Mr. B. H. Eaton, Q.C., 35, Bedford Row, Halifax, N.S.; Rev. D. M. Mihell, M.A., B.Th., St. George, Ont.

UNITED STATES, Rev. Lansing Burrows, D.D., Augusta, Ga.; (and for Free Baptists) Rev. G. H. Ball, D.D., Keuka College, N.Y.

AMERICAN BAPTIST MISSIONARY UNION, Rev. H. C. Mabie, D.D., Boston, Mass.

SOUTHERN BAPTIST CONVENTION, FOREIGN MISSION BOARD, Rev. R. J. Willingham, D.D., Richmond, Va.

AMERICAN FREE BAPTIST MISSION, Rev. T. H. Stacy, Auburn, Mass.

WEST INDIES, Rev. P. Williams, Sec. Jamaica Baptist Union, Bethel Town, P.O. Jamaica.

ARGENTINE REPUBLIC, Rev. Paul Besson, Buenos Ayres.

NEW SOUTH WALES AND N.S.W. MISSIONARY SOCIETY., Rev. F. Hibberd, Holden Street, Ashfield.

VICTORIA, Mr. C. W. Walrond, Cotham Road, Kew.

Do. MISSIONARY SOCIETY., Rev. A. W. Webb, Aberdeen Street, Geelong.

QUEENSLAND, Rev. W. Higlett, Albion, Brisbane.

Do. MISSIONARY SOCIETY., Rev. W. Poole, South Brisbane.

SOUTH AUSTRALIA, Mr. R. W. M. Waddy, The Almonds, Magill.

Do. MISSIONARY SOCIETY., Rev. R. McCullough, Parkside.

NEW ZEALAND, Rev. A. H. Collins, Auckland.

Do. BAPTIST MISSIONARY SOCIETY, Rev. H. H. Driver, 3 George Street, Dunedin.

TASMANIA, Rev. E. Harris, Launceston.

EX-PRESIDENTS OF THE BAPTIST UNION.

1864. *MURSELL, REV. J. P., Leicester.
1865. ANGUS, REV. JOSEPH, M.A., D.D., London.
1866. ALDIS, REV. JOHN, Beckington.
1867. *NOEL, HON. and REV. BAPTIST WRIOTHESLEY, M.A., London.
1868. *GOTCH, REV. F. W., M.A., LL.D., Bristol.
1869. *BROCK, REV. WILLIAM, D.D., London.
1870. *ROBINSON, REV. WILLIAM, Cambridge.
1871. *BIRRELL, REV. CHARLES M., Liverpool.
1872. *THOMAS, REV. THOMAS, D.D., Pontypool College.
1873. UNDERHILL, MR. EDWARD BEAN, LL.D., Hon. Sec. Baptist Missionary Society.
1874. *STOVEL, REV. CHARLES, London.
1875. MCLAREN, REV. ALEXANDER, B.A., D.D., Manchester.
1876. LANDELS, REV. WILLIAM, D.D., Edinburgh.
1877. BROWN, REV. JOHN TURLAND, Northampton.
1878. *BROWN, REV. HUGH STOWELL, Liverpool.
1879. *GOULD, REV. GEORGE, Norwich.
1880. *TRESTRAIL, REV. FREDERICK, D.D., Bristol.
1881. *DOWSON, REV. HENRY, London.
1882. BROWN, REV. JOHN JENKYN, Birmingham.
1883. *CHOWN, REV. JOSEPH PARBERY, London.
1884. GLOVER, REV. RICHARD, D.D., Bristol.
1885. GREEN, REV. SAMUEL GOSNELL, B.A., D.D., London.
1886. WILLIAMS, REV. CHARLES, Accrington.
1887. CULROSS, REV. JAMES, M.A., D.D., Bristol College.
1888. CLIFFORD, REV. JOHN, M.A., LL.B., B.SC., D.D., London.
1889. WIGNER, REV. JOHN THOMAS, London.
1890. OWEN, REV. JAMES, Swansea.
1891. GRIFFIN, COL. JAMES THEODORE, London.
1892. ROBERTS, REV. ROBERT HENRY, B.A., Regent's Park College.
1893. MORRIS, REV. THOMAS MEW, Ipswich.
1894. SHORT, REV. GEORGE, B.A., Salisbury.

* Deceased.

ASSOCIATIONS IN MEMBERSHIP WITH THE BAPTIST UNION.

ENGLAND.

Bedfordshire Union of Christians.
Berkshire.
Bristol.
Buckinghamshire.
Cambridgeshire.
Cornwall.
Devon.
East Midland.
Essex Union.
Gloucestershire and Herefordshire.
Hertfordshire Union.
Kent and Sussex.
Lancashire and Cheshire.
London.
Norfolk.
Northamptonshire.
Northern.
Oxfordshire.
Shropshire.
Southern.
Suffolk and Norfolk Union.
Western.
West Midland.
Wilts. and East Somerset.
Worcestershire.
Yorkshire.

WALES AND MONMOUTHSHIRE.

Anglesey.
Carmarthenshire and Cardiganshire.
Denbigh, Flint and Merioneth.
Glamorganshire and Carmarthenshire (E.).
North Wales English Union.
Old Welsh.
Monmouthshire English.

COLLEGES IN MEMBERSHIP WITH THE BAPTIST UNION.

Aberystwyth.
Bangor.
Bristol.
Midland.
Rawdon.
Regent's Park.

CHURCHES IN MEMBERSHIP WITH THE BAPTIST UNION.

Churches (affiliated to the Baptist Union) of not exceeding 150 *Members, may appoint one delegate; more than* 150, *two delegates; and more than* 300, *three delegates, to the Spring and Autumn Assemblies of the Union.*

ENGLAND.

BEDFORDSHIRE.

Ampthill.
Bedford—
  Bunyan Meeting.
  Mill-street.
Biggleswade, Old Meeting.
Dunstable, West-street.
Houghton Regis.
Keysoe.
Leighton Buzzard, Lake-street.
Luton—
  Castle-street.
  Park-street.
Maulden (U.).
Ridgmount.
Sandy.
  Blunham, Old Meeting.
Shefford (U.).
Stotfold.
Thurleigh.

BERKSHIRE.

Abingdon, Ock-street.
Bourton (Shrivenham).
Brimpton.
Faringdon.
Maidenhead, Marlow-road.
Newbury, North Brook-street.
Reading—
  Carey.
  King's-road.
  Wycliffe.
Sunningdale.
Wallingford, Thames-street.
Windsor, New, Victoria-street.
Wokingham.

BUCKINGHAMSHIRE.

Amersham, Lower Meeting.
Chesham—
  Broadway.
  Lower Chapel.
Dinton.
Drayton Parslow Group.
Fenny Stratford.
Gold-hill (Chalfont).
Haddenham.
Kingshill, Little.
Long Crendon.
Missenden, Great.
Olney.
Princes Risborough.
Speen.
Stantonbury.
Stony Stratford and Loughton.
Wendover.
Weston Turville (U.).
Winslow, Tabernacle.
  Swanbourne.
Wycombe, Union Church.

CAMBRIDGESHIRE.

Burwell.
Cambridge—
  St. Andrew's-street.
  Zion.
Caxton.
Chatteris, West Park-street.
Cottenham, Old Meeting.
Gamlingay.
Harston.
Histon.
Isleham, High-street.
March, Centenary Church.
Melbourn.
Prickwillow.
Shelford, Great.
Soham.
Swavesey Bethel.
Waterbeach, High-street.
Willingham, Tabernacle.
Wisbech—
  Ely-place.
  Upper Hill-street.

CHESHIRE.

Altrincham.
Audlem.
Birkenhead, Grange-road.
  Jackson-street.
Chester, Grosvenor Park.
  Northgate-street (W.).
Crewe, Union-street.
  Victoria-street.
Egremont, Liscard-road.
Frodsham (U.).
Hill Cliff.
Hyde.
Latchford.
Little Leigh.

Macclesfield, St. George's-street.
Nantwich.
Onston.
Poynton.
Sale.
Stalybridge—
 Cross Leech-street.
 Wakefield-road.
Stockport, Greek-street.
Tarporley.
Wheelock Heath.

CORNWALL.

Calstock and Metherill.
Falmouth.
Helston.
Launceston.
Penzance.
Redruth.
Saltash.
St. Austell.
Truro.

CUMBERLAND.

Carlisle.
Maryport.
Millom.
Workington.

DERBYSHIRE.

Belper.
Chesterfield.
Clay Cross.
Derby—
 Green Hill, Trinity.
 Osmaston-road
 St. Mary's Gate.
Heanor
Ilkeston, Queen-street.
Long Eaton—
 Chapel-street.
 Station-street.
Measham and Netherseal.
Melbourne and Ticknall.
Riddings and Swanwick.
Ripley.
Sawley.
Smalley.
Swadincote.
Wirksworth.

DEVONSHIRE.

Appledore.
Barnstaple.
Bideford.
Bovey Tracey.
Bradninch.
Brayford.
Brixham.
Budleigh Salterton.
Combmartin.
Cullompton.
Devonport, Hope Church.
Dolton.
Exeter, Bartholomew-street.
 South-street.
Frithelstock Group.
Hatherleigh.
Hemyock and Saint Hill.
Honiton.
Ilfracombe.
Kilmington and Loughwood.
Kingsbridge.
Lifton.
Malborough and Salcombe.
Modbury.
Newton Abbot.
Okehampton.
Paignton.
Plymouth—
 George-street.
 Mutley.
Teignmouth.
Tiverton.
Torquay, Upton Vale.
Torrington, Great.
Totnes.
Uffculme and Prescott.
Upottery, Newhouse.

DORSETSHIRE.

Bridport.
Dorchester.
Gillingham.
Iwerne Minster.
Lyme Regis.
Poole.
Weymouth.

DURHAM.

Bishop Auckland.
 Witton Park.
Consett.
Crook.
Darlington, Grange-road.
Gateshead, Durham-road.
Hamsterley.
Hartlepool.
Hartlepool, West.
Middleton-in-Teesdale.
Rowley and Blackhill.
South Shields—
 Tabernacle.
 Westoe-road.
Spennymoor.
Stockton, Northcote-street.
Sunderland—
 Lindsay-road.
 Monkwearmouth, Barclay-street.

Waterhouses.
Wolsingham.

ESSEX.

Ashdon.
Barking, Linton-road.
Burnham-on-Crouch.
Colchester Eld-lane.
Earl's Colne.
Grays, Tabernacle.
Halstead, North-street.
Harlow.
  Potter-street.
Maldon, Crown-lane.
Romford.
Saffron Walden, High-street.
Sampford, Great.
Southend, Tabernacle.
Thorpe-le-Soken.

GLOUCESTERSHIRE.

Avening.
Blakeney.
Bourton-on-the-Water.
Bristol—
  Bedminster, East-street.
  Broadmead.
  City-road.
  Clifton, Buckingham.
  Cotham-grove.
  Counterslip.
  Horfield.
  Hotwells, Buckingham Hall.
  Old King-street.
  Redland, Tyndale.
  Stapleton-road.
  Totterdown.
Bristol Itinerant Society Station—
  Dundry.
Chalford, Tabernacle.
Cheltenham—
  Cambray.
  Salem.
Chipping Campden.
Chipping Sodbury.
Cinderford.
Cirencester.
Coleford.
Downend.
Eastcombe.
Fishponds.
Gloucester—
  Brunswick-road.
  Corn Exchange.
Hanham.
Kingstanley.
Longhope.
Lydbrook.
Lydney.
Minchinhampton.
Nailsworth, Shortwood.
Naunton and Guiting.
Nupend.
Old Sodbury.
Parkend.
Ruardean Hill.
Stow-on-the-Wold.
Stroud, John-street.
Tetbury.
Thornbury.
Uley.
Wotton-under-Edge.
Yorkley.

HAMPSHIRE.

Aldershot.
Andover.
Ashley.
Boscombe.
Bournemouth—
  Lansdowne.
  West Cliff Tabernacle.
Broughton
Fleet and Hope.
Isle of Wight—
  Cowes, West.
  Newport.
  Niton.
  Ryde, Park-road.
  Ventnor.
  Yarmouth.
Lymington.
Lyndhurst.
Milford.
Odiham.
Portsmouth—
  Lake-road.
  Landport, Commercial-road.
  Portsea, Kent-street.
  Southsea, Castle-road.
    Elm-grove.
Romsey, Bell-street.
Shirley (U.).
Southampton—
  Carlton.
  East-street.
  Portland.
Waterlooville.
Whitchurch.
Winchester.

HEREFORDSHIRE.

Ewias Harold.
Fownhope.
Garway and Orcop.
Gorsley.
Hereford, Commercial-road.
Leominster.
Ross, Broad-street.
Ryeford.

HERTFORDSHIRE.

Berkhamsted.
Bishop's Stortford.
Bovingdon.
Boxmoor.
Chipperfield.
Hemel Hempstead.
Hitchin—
Tilehouse-street.
Walsworth-road.
King's Langley.
Northchurch.
Rickmansworth.
St. Albans—
Dagnall-street.
Tabernacle.
Tring, High-street.
Watford—
Beechen-grove.
New Bushey.

HUNTINGDONSHIRE.

Bluntisham.
Huntingdon, Trinity (U.).
Ramsey, Great Whyte.

KENT.

Brabourne.
Brasted.
Canterbury, St. George's-place.
Chatham, Clover-street.
Deal.
Dover—
Biggin-street.
Eden Bridge.
Eynsford.
Eythorne.
Faversham.
Folkestone.
Gravesend, Windmill-street.
Hawkhurst.
Headcorn.
Herne Bay.
Loose.
Maidstone, Union-street.
Margate, New Cross-street.
New Brompton.
New Romney.
Orpington.
Plumstead, East, Station-road.
Ramsgate—
Cavendish.
Ellington (U.).
St. Peter's.
Sandhurst.
Sevenoaks.
Sheerness, Strode-crescent.
Sittingbourne.
Smarden, Zion.
Tenterden, High-street.
Tunbridge, High-street.
Tunbridge Wells, Calverley-road.
West Malling.
Woolwich, Queen-street.
Yalding.

LANCASHIRE.

Accrington, Cannon-street.
Ashton-under-Lyne.
Atherton.
Bacup—
Acre Mill.
Doals, Weir-terrace.
Ebenezer.
Irwell-terrace.
Zion.
Barrow-in-Furness.
Blackburn, Montague-street.
Blackpool.
Bolton—
Astley Bridge.
Claremont.
Zion.
Bootle—
Brasenose-road.
Derby-road.
Briercliffe, Hill-lane.
Burnley—
Colne-road.
Enon.
Mount Olivet.
Mount Pleasant.
Yorkshire-street.
Bury—
Chesham Chapel.
Knowsley-street.
Church.
Clayton-le-Moors.
Cloughfold.
Clowbridge.
Colne.
Dalton-in-Furness.
Darwen.
Edgeside.
Garston.
Goodshaw.
Haslingden—
Bury-road.
Trinity.
Heywood, Rochdale-road.
Inskip.
Lancaster.
Leigh.
Littleborough.
Liverpool—
Everton-road.
Kensington.
Myrtle-street.
Earlestown.
Pembroke.
Prince's-gate.
Richmond.

Liverpool (*continued*)—
Toxteth Tabernacle.
Walton, Carisbrooke.
Rice-lane.
Manchester—
Brighton-grove.
Broughton.
Coupland-street.
Eccles, Peel-street.
Gorton, Wellington-street.
Gorton, West, Birch-street.
Clowes-street (U.).
Grosvenor-street, Chorlton.
Moss-side.
Openshaw, Higher.
Oxford-road (U.).
Pendleton.
Salford, Great George-street.
Stretford, Edge-lane (U.).
Upper Brook-street.
Middleton.
Millgate.
Mills Hill.
Nelson, Carr-road.
Ogden.
Oldham—
King-street.
Manchester-street.
Pitt-street.
Oswaldtwistle.
Padiham, Burnley-road.
Preston—
Ashton-on-Ribble.
Fishergate.
Pole-street.
Ramsbottom.
Rawtenstall.
Rochdale—
Drake-street.
Newbold, Milnrow-road.
West-street.
Royton, Oldham-road.
Sabden.
St. Anne's-on-the-Sea.
St. Helen's—
Boundary-road.
Hall-street.
Park-road.
Southport, Hoghton-street.
Sunnyside.
Tyldesley (W.).
Ulverston.
Warrington, Golborne-street.
Waterbarn.
Waterfoot.
Wigan—
King-street
Scarisbrick-street.

LEICESTERSHIRE.

Arnsby.
Barton Fabis.
Blaby.
Castle Donington.
Coalville, London-road.
Countesthorpe.
Foxton.
Hinckley.
Hose, Chapel-street.
Hugglescote.
Husband's Bosworth.
Ibstock.
Leicester—
Archdeacon-lane
Belgrave (U.).
Belgrave-road Tabernacle.
Belvoir-street.
Harvey-lane.
Carley-street.
Charles-street
Dover-street.
Friar-lane.
Melbourne Hall.
New Park-street
Victoria-road.
Loughborough—
Baxter-gate.
Wood-gate.
Market Harborough.
Melton Mowbray.
Oadby.
Quorndon.
Shepshed, Charnwood-road.
Sutton-in-the-Elms.
Syston.
Whitwick.

LINCOLNSHIRE.

Boston, Salem.
Bourne.
Coningsby.
Crowle.
Epworth and Butterwick.
Fleet.
Grantham, Wharf-road.
Great Grimsby—
Victoria-street.
Holbeach.
Kirton-in-Lindsey.
Lincoln—
Mint-street.
Monk's-road.
Thomas Cooper Memorial.
Long Sutton.
Louth, East-gate.
Spalding.

METROPOLITAN.

(Includes Churches within the limits of the Metropolitan Postal District, and also Churches outside that District connected with the London Baptist Association).

Acton, Church-road.
Alperton.

Balham, Ramsden-road.
Barnes.
Barnet, New.
Battersea—
  Battersea Park Tabernacle.
  York-road.
Beckenham.
Belle Isle.
Belvedere.
Bermondsey, Drummond-road.
Bexley Heath.
Blackheath, Shooter's Hill-road.
Bloomsbury.
Bow, High-street.
Bow Common, Blackthorn-street.
Brixton, Wynne-road.
Brixton Hill, New Park-road.
Brockley-road.
Bromley (Kent), Park-road.
Brompton, Onslow.
Brondesbury.
Camberwell—
  Camberwell New-road, Clarendon.
  Cottage Green.
  Denmark-place.
Camberwell-gate, Arthur-street.
Camden-road.
Catford Hill.
Chelsea, Lower Sloane-street.
Child's Hill.
Clapham, Grafton-square.
Clapton, Downs Chapel.
Clerkenwell—
  Spencer-place, Goswell-road.
Commercial-road East.
Croydon, South—
  Croham Road (U.).
Croydon, West.
Dalston, Queen's-road.
Deptford, Octavius-street.
Ealing, Haven-green.
Edmonton, Lower.
Erith, Queen-street.
Finchley, East, High-road.
Finchley, North.
Forest Gate, Woodgrange.
Forest Hill, Sydenham Church.
Greenwich, Lewisham-road.
Gunnersbury.
Hackney—
  Lauriston-road.
  Mare-street.
Hampstead, Heath-street.
Harlesden.
Harlington.
Harrow-on-the-Hill.
Highbury Hill.
Highgate—
  Archway-road.
  Southwood-lane.
Holborn—
  John-street.
  Kingsgate-street.

Holloway, Upper.
Honor Oak, Mundania-road.
Hornsey, Ferme Park-road.

Ilford.
Islington—
  Cross-street.
  Salters' Hall.
Kentish Town, Bassett-street.
Kilburn, Canterbury-road.
King's Cross—
  Handel-street.
  Vernon-square.
Lambeth, Upton Chapel.
Lee, High-road.
Leytonstone, Fairlop-road.
Loughton.

Marylebone—
  Church-street.
Norwood, South, Holmesdale-road.
Norwood, Upper, Central Hill.
Norwood, West, Gipsy-road.
Notting Hill, Ladbroke-grove.
Nunhead, Edith-road.
Old Kent-road, Maze Pond.
Paddington—
  Praed-street, Westbourne Park and Bosworth-road.

Peckham—
  Peckham Park-road.
  Rye-lane.
Penge, Maple-road.
Plumstead—
  Conduit-road.
  Park-road.
Poplar, Cotton-street.
Putney, Werter-road.

Regent's Park.
Richmond, Duke-street.
Rotherhithe—
  Bush-road, Midway-place.
  Rotherhithe New-road.
Shepherd's Bush-road.
Shoreditch Tabernacle.
Sidcup.
Southgate, New.
Southwark, Borough-road.
Stockwell.
Stoke Newington, Devonshire-square.
Stratford—
  Carpenter's-road.
  The Grove.
Streatham, Lewin-road.
Surbiton Hill, Oaklands.
Sutton.

Tooting, Upper, Trinity-road (U.).
Tottenham, High-road.
Victoria Park, Grove-road.

Wallington.
Walthamstow, Boundary-road.
Walworth-road.

Wandsworth—
East Hill.
Northcote-road.
Wandsworth-road, Victoria.
Westbourne-grove.
Westminster, Romney-street.
Whitechapel, Commercial-street.
Woodberry Down.
Wood Green, Finsbury-road.
Woolwich, Parsons Hill.

MIDDLESEX.

Harefield.
Pinner.
Teddington.

NORFOLK.

Aylsham.
Buckenham, Old.
Downham Market.
Fakenham.
Lynn—
Stepney Chapel.
Union Chapel.
Norwich—
Gildencroft.
St. Mary's.
Unthank's-road.
Stalham.
Swaffham.
Upwell.
Yarmouth, The Park.

NORTHAMPTONSHIRE.

Blisworth.
Braunston.
Brington.
Buckby, Long.
Bugbrook.
Burton Latimer.
Clipstone.
Desborough.
Earl's Barton.
Guilsborough.
Hackleton.
Harpole.
Kettering, Fuller Chapel.
Kingsthorpe.
Middleton Cheney.
Moulton.
Northampton—
College-street.
Far Cotton.
Grafton-street.
Mount Pleasant.
Princes-street.
Peterborough, Queen-street.
Ringstead.
Roade.
Rushden, Old Chapel.
Spratton and Ravensthorpe.
Thrapston.
Towcester.
West Haddon.
Weston-by-Weedon.

NORTHUMBERLAND.

Alnwick.
Berwick.
Broomhaugh and Broomley.
Newcastle—
Jesmond.
Rye-hill.
Westgate-road.
North Shields.

NOTTINGHAMSHIRE.

Beeston.
Collingham.
Mansfield.
Newark, Albert-street.
Nottingham—
Arkwright-street.
Basford, New, Chelsea-street.
Palm-street.
Basford, Old.
Broad-street.
Bulwell.
Carrington.
Derby-road.
George-street.
Hyson-green.
Lenton, New, Church-street.
Mansfield-road.
Woodborough-road.
Retford and Gamston.
Southwell, Park-street.
Sutton-in-Ashfield, Wood-street.

OXFORDSHIRE.

Banbury, Bridge-street.
Caversham, Free Church.
Chadlington and Charlbury.
Chipping Norton.
Coate.
Hook Norton.
Little Tew and Cleveley.
Milton.
Oxford—
Commercial-road.
New-road.
Woodstock.

RUTLANDSHIRE.

Oakham, Melton-road.

SHROPSHIRE.

Bridgnorth.
Dawley.
Lord's Hill, Snailbeach.
Market Drayton.
Oswestry—
  Castle-street (W.).
  Salop-road.
Pontesbury.
Shrewsbury, Claremont.
Wellington.
Wem.
Whitchurch.

SOMERSETSHIRE.

Banwell.
Bath—
  Hay-hill.
  Manvers-street.
Beckington.
Boroughbridge.
Bridgwater.
Burnham.
Burton (Stogursey).
Chard.
Cheddar.
Crewkerne, North-street.
Fivehead and Isle Abbots.
Frome—
  Badcox-lane.
  Sheppard's Barton.
Hatch Beauchamp.
Highbridge.
Keynsham.
Minehead.
Montacute.
North Curry and Stoke St. Gregory.
Paulton.
Pill.
Radstock.
Stogumber.
Taunton, Silver-street.
Twerton-on-Avon.
Watchet and Williton.
Wedmore.
Wellington.
Wells.
Weston-super-Mare—
  Bristol-road.
  Wadham-street.
Wincanton.
Yeovil, South-street.

STAFFORDSHIRE.

Bilston, Wood-street.
Brierley Hill, South-street.
Burton-on-Trent—
  New-street.
  Station-street.
Coseley—
  Darkhouse.
  Providence.
Cradley Heath.
Hanley—
  Eastwood Vale and Fenton.
  New-street.
Longton.
Newcastle-under-Lyme.
Prince's End.
Stafford, Water-street
Stoke-on-Trent.
Walsall—
  Stafford-street.
  Vicarage-walk.
West Bromwich, High-street.
Willenhall, Lichfield-street.
Wolverhampton, Waterloo-road.

SUFFOLK.

Bardwell.
Brandon.
Bury St. Edmunds, Garland-street.
Eye.
Ipswich—
  Burlington.
  Stoke-green.
  Turret-green.
Lowestoft, London-road.
Stoke Ash.
Sudbury.
Walton.
West Row (Mildenhall).

SURREY.

Addlestone.
Dorking.
Esher.
Guildford, Commercial-road.
Horley, Brighton-road.
  Victoria-road.
Kingston.
Molesey, East.
Redhill and Reigate, London-road.
Woking, Goldsworth-road.
York Town.

SUSSEX.

Brighton—
  Florence-road.
  Queen-square.
  Sussex-street.
Crawley.
Crowborough, Forestfold.
Eastbourne, Ceylon-place.
Hastings, Wellington-square.

Portslade-by-Sea.
Shoreham.
St. Leonards.

WARWICKSHIRE.

Alcester.
Attleborough.
Birmingham—
Aston Park.
Bristol-road.
(Cannon-street), Graham-street.
Erdington.
Great King-street.
Hagley-road.
Handsworth, Hamstead-road.
Harborne.
Heneage-street.
Highgate Park.
King's Heath.
Moseley, Oxford-road.
Selly Park.
Small Heath, Coventry-road.
Smethwick.
Sparkbrook, Stratford-road.
Spring Hill.
Warwick-street.
Coventry—
Gosford-street.
Queen's-road.
St. Michael's.
Henley-in-Arden.
Leamington, Warwick-street.
Longford, Salem.
Monk's Kirby and Pailton.
Nuneaton.
Rugby.
Stratford-on-Avon.
Studley.
Warwick, Castle Hill.

WESTMORLAND.

Kirkby Stephen Group.

WILTSHIRE.

Bradford-on-Avon, Zion.
Bratton.
Calne, Castle-street.
Chippenham, Station-hill.
Corsham, Priory-street.
Damerham.
Devizes, Sheep-street.
Downton, South-lane.
Imber.
Melksham, Broughton-road.
Salisbury, Brown-street.
Shrewton.
Swindon, Tabernacle.
Trowbridge—
Back-street.
Bethesda.
Warminster.
Westbury, Penknap.
West End.
Westbury Leigh.

WORCESTERSHIRE.

Astwood Bank.
Atch Lench and Dunnington.
Bewdley.
Bromsgrove, New-road.
Cinderbank.
Cutsdean.
Droitwich.
Dudley, New-street.
Evesham, Cowl-street.
Kidderminster, Church-street.
Malvern, Great.
Pershore, Broad-street.
Redditch.
Shipston-on-Stour.
Stourbridge.
Stourport.
Upton-on-Severn.
Westmancote.
Worcester, Sansome Walk.

YORKSHIRE.

Armley.
Barnsley—
Parker-street.
Sheffield-road.
Batley, Park-road.
Beverley, Well-lane.
Birchcliffe.
Bishop Burton.
Blackley.
Bradford—
Allerton, Central Ch.
Girlington.
Hallfield.
Heaton.
Leeds-road.
Ripley-street.
Sion Jubilee Ch.
Tetley-street.
Trinity.
Westgate.
Bramley—
Salem.
Zion.
Brearley.
Bridlington.
Clayton.
Cowlinghill.
Dewsbury.
Doncaster, Chequer-road.
Driffield.

Earby-in-Craven.
Eccleshill.
Farsley.
Gildersome.
Golcar.
Halifax—
  Lee Mount.
  North Parade.
  Pellon-lane.
  Trinity-road.
Harrogate.
Haworth, West-lane.
Hebden Bridge.
Heptonstall Slack.
Horsforth, Cragg Hill.
Huddersfield—
  Lindley.
  Lockwood.
  New North-road.
  Primrose Hill.
Hull—
  Beverley-road.
  George-street.
  South-street.
Idle.
Keighley.
Leeds—
  Blenheim.
  Burley-road.
  North-street.
  South Parade.
Lineholme, near Todmorden.
Lydgate.
Malton, Castlegate.
Middlesbrough—
  Linthorpe-road.
  Marton-road.
  Newport-road.
Milnsbridge.
Mirfield.
Morley.
Nazebottom.
Ossett.
Polemoor.
Pudsey.
Queensbury.
Rawdon.
Rishworth.
Rotherham.
Salendine Nook.
Scapegoat Hill.
Scarborough—
  Albemarle.
  West Gate.
Sheffield—
  Attercliffe.
  Cemetery-road.
  Glossop-road.
  Port Mahon.
  Townhead-street.
Shipley—
  Bethel.
  Rosse-street.
Shore.
Skipton, Otley-street.
Slaithwaite, Zion.
South Bank, Normanby-road.
Staincliffe.
Steep-lane.
Sutton-in-Craven.
Thornaby-on-Tees.
Todmorden—
  Roomfield.
  Wellington-road.
Wainsgate.
Wakefield.
West Vale.

WALES
AND
MONMOUTHSHIRE.

ANGLESEY.

Holyhead, New Park-street.

BRECKNOCKSHIRE.

Brecon, Kensington.
Brynmawr, Calvary.
Builth, Ebenezer.
Garth, Pisgah.
Glasbury and Penyrheol.
Maesyberllan.
Nantyffin.
Talgarth, Tabernacle.

CARDIGANSHIRE.

Aberystwyth—
  Alfred-place.
  Baker-street.
Cardigan, Mount Zion.

CARMARTHENSHIRE.

Carmarthen, Lammas-street.
Cwmifor.
Ferryside, Salem.
Llanelly—
  Greenfield.
  Horeb, and Ponthenry.
  Moriah.
Whitland, Nazareth.

CARNARVONSHIRE.

Bangor (E.).
Gilfach.
Llandudno, Mostyn-street.
Llanfairfechan, Libanus.
Nevin, Sion.

DENBIGHSHIRE.

Abergele.
Brymbo (W.).
Cefnmawr, Ebenezer.
Colwyn, Old.
Colwyn Bay (E.).
Llangollen, Penybryn.
Ponkey, Zion.
Wrexham, Chester-street.

FLINTSHIRE.

Bagillt.
Buckley.
Holywell.
Nantmawr.
Rhyl, Sussex-street.

GLAMORGANSHIRE.

Aberavon, Water-street.
Aberdare—
  Calvaria.
  Carmel.
Barry District—
  Holton-road, Barry Dock.
  Mount Pleasant, Cadoxton.
Bridgend, Hope.
Briton Ferry, Jerusalem.
Caerphilly—
  Mount Carmel.
  Tonyfelin.
Cardiff—
  Bethany.
  Bute Docks, Bethel.
  Canton, Hope Chapel.
  Grange Town.
  Riverside.
  Roath, Salem.
  Splott-road.
  Tabernacle.
  Tredegarville.
  Walker's-road.
  Woodville-road.
Clydach, Calvaria.
Cowbridge.
Dowlais, Beulah.
  Caersalem.
Gelligaer, Horeb.
Hengoed.
Hirwain, Ramoth.
Knelstone.
Lisvane (Cardiff).
Llancarvan.
Llangyfelach—
  Craigcefnparc, Elim.
Loughor, Penuel.
Maesteg—
  Castle-street.
Melincrythan (Neath).
Merthyr Tydvil—
  Ainon.
  High-street.
  Morlais.
  Tabernacle.
Mountain Ash, Nazareth.
Neath—
  Christchurch.
  Orchard-place.
Penarth—
  Stanwell-road.
  Tabernacle.
Penclawdd, Trinity.
Penrhiwceiber, Bethesda.
Pontyclun.
Pontycwmmer—
  Noddfa.
  Zion.
Pontypridd, Carmel.
Porth, Salem.
  Tabernacle.
Swansea—
  Gorse Lane.
  Landore, Salem.
  Mount Pleasant.
  St. Helen's.
Tirphil, Tabernacle.
Tondu, Carey.
Treharris, Bethel.
Treherbert—
  Bethany.
Treorky, Noddfa.
Wauntrodau, Ararat.
Ynyshir (E.).
Ystalyfera, Zoar.

MERIONETHSHIRE.

Barmouth.
Corwen.

MONTGOMERYSHIRE.

Llanfair-Caereinion.
Machynlleth.
Newtown.

PEMBROKESHIRE.

Blaenconin Clynderwen.
Blaenffos.
Blaenywaen and St. Dogmell's.
Broadhaven.
Cresswell Quay.
Croesgoch.
Haverfordwest, Bethesda.
Letterston.
Llangwm.

Martletwy.
Middlemill.
Milford, North-road.
Moleston (Narberth).
Narberth.
Newport, Bethlehem.
Newtonpants, Bethlehem.
Pembroke.
Pembroke Dock—
Bush-street.
High-street.
Pennar.
Tenby.

RADNORSHIRE.

Bwlchysarnau and Cefnpole.
Dolau, Nantmel.
Llandrindod Wells.
Presteign.
Rock.

MONMOUTHSHIRE.

Abercarn (E.).
Abercarn (W.).
Abergavenny—
Bethany.
Frogmore-street.
Abersychan (E.).
Abertillery, Blaina Gwent (W. & E.).
Bassaleg—
Bethel (W. & E.).
Bethesda.
Bedwas (W.).
Blackwood, Mount Pleasant.
Blaenavon—
Horeb.
King-street.
Blaina, Salem (W. & E.).
Caerleon.
Caerwent.
Castletown (W. & E.).
Chepstow.
Cross Keys.
Cwmbran, Siloam (W. & E.).
Ebbw Vale, Briery Hill.
Nebo (W.).
Griffithstown.
Llanddewi Rhydderch.
Llanfihangel Crucorney, Zoar.
Llanfihangel Ystern Llewern.
Llanvaches, Bethany.
Llanwenarth (W. & E.).
Machen, Siloam (W. & E.).
Maesycwmmer.
Magor.
Michaelstone-y-Vedw, Tirzah.
Newbridge (E.).
Beulah (W.).
Newport—
Alma-street.
Commercial-road.
Commercial-street.
Duckpool-road.
Maindee.
St. Mary-street.
Stow-hill.
Norton (Skenfrith).
Ponthir.
Pontnewydd.
Pontnewynydd.
Pontrhydyryn.
Pontypool, Bridge-street.
Crane-street.
Raglan, Usk-road.
Risca, Bethany.
Moriah (W. & E.).
St. Mellon's (W. & E.).
Talywain, Pisgah (W. & E.).
Tredegar, Church-street.
Usk.
Whitebrook and Llandogo.

SCOTLAND.

Aberdeen, Union-grove.
Kirkcaldy, Whyte's Causeway.
Paisley, Victoria-place.

IRELAND.

Ballymena.
Banbridge.

CHANNEL ISLES.

Jersey, St. Helier.

HONORARY MEMBERS OF THE BAPTIST UNION.

	Date of Election.
Aldis, Rev. J., Beckington	1874
Angus, Rev. J., M.A., D.D., London	1878
Baynes, Mr. W. W., J.P., Bromley, Kent	1894
Booth, Rev. S. H., D.D., London	1894
Brown, Rev. J. J., Birmingham	1887
Brown, Rev. J. T., Northampton	1887
Clifford, Rev. J., M.A., D.D., London	1894
Culross, Rev. J., M.A., D.D., Bristol College	1888
Edwards, Rev. E., Torquay	1888
Glover, Rev. R., D.D., Bristol	1888
Green, Rev. S. G., B.A., D.D., London	1874
Greenhough, Rev. J. G., M.A., Leicester	1894
Griffin, Col. J. T., London	1894
Landels, Rev. W., D.D., Edinburgh	1884
McLaren, Rev. A., B.A., D.D., Manchester	1874
Morris, Rev. T. M., Ipswich	1894
Owen, Rev. J., Swansea	1894
Roberts, Rev. R. H., B.A., Regent's Park College	1894
Short, Rev. G., B.A., Salisbury	1894
Tymms, Rev. T. V., Rawdon College	1895
Underhill, Mr. E. B., LL.D., Hon. Secretary to Baptist Missionary Society	1874
Underwood, Rev. W., D.D., Derby	1877
Wheeler, Rev. T. A., Hoveton St. John, Norfolk	1888
Wigner, Rev. J. T., London	1894
Williams, Rev. C., Accrington	1888

PERSONAL MEMBERS OF THE BAPTIST UNION.

	Date of Enrolment.
Acomb, Rev. W. J., Birmingham	1890
Acworth, Mr. J., Bradford	1878
Aldis, Rev. J., Beckington (See *Honorary Members*)	1874
Anders, Mr. H., London	1892
Anderson, Rev. J. H., Loughton	1895
Anderson, Rev. W. M., Epworth	1895
Anderton, Mrs. A. Bury, Southport	1895
Angus, Rev. J., M.A., D.D., London (See *Honorary Members*)	1874
Angus, Mr. W., Newcastle-on-Tyne	1895
Anstie, Mr. T. B., J.P., Devizes	1889
Appleton, Mr. W., Sutton (*Surrey*)	1895
Apthorpe, Mr. G., Cambridge	1877
Archer, Rev. W. E., Leeds	1874
Arnold, Mr. F., J.P., Great Yarmouth	1887
Ashwell, Mr. H., J.P., Nottingham	1889
Avery, Mr. J., St. Albans	1888
Avery, Rev. W. J., London	1895
Bacon, Mr. A., Brentwood	1889
Bailey, Rev. G. T., Leyton	1891
Baines, Mr. J., London	1876
Baker, Rev. T., B.A., Lewes	1895
Balding, Mr. E., London	1895
Barker, Mr. A. H., Ditchling	1893
Barran, Mr. A., J.P., *Leeds*	1888

	Date of Enrolment.
Barran, Sir John, Ilkley	1878
Barrass, Rev. T., Peterborough	1877
Barry, Mr. W., Scarborough	1888
Bartlett, Mr. J. M., Newcastle-on-Tyne	1895
Bate, Mr. R., C.C., Tarporley	1889
Baynes, Mr. A. H., London	1874
Baynes, Mr. W. W., J.P., Bromley, Kent (See *Honorary Members*)	1874
Beach, Mr. W. C., New Barnet	1895
Beattie, Mr. W., Sunderland	1889
Beecliff, Rev. R. J., London	1895
Bell, Rev. J., Leeds	1895
Bembridge, Mr. W. B., J.P., Ripley, Derby	1889
Benham, Mr. J., London	1875
Benham, Mr. W. J., B.A., London	1886
Bentley, Rev. T., Chipping Norton..	1874
Bergin, Rev. J. M., York Town	1893
Best, Mr. W., Bradford	1888
Betts, Mrs., St. Albans	1895
Bexon, Mr. A., Nottingham	1889
Black, Mr. J., Ford, Cornhill-on-Tweed	1893
Bompas, Mr. H. M., Q.C., London	1878
Bond, Mr. J. T., Plymouth	1884
Booker, Mr. W. H., Nottingham	1889
Booth, Rev. S. H., D.D., London (See *Honorary Members*)	1874
Bourne, Mr. J. P., Bristol	1874
Bowden, Mr. J., New Barnet	1888
Bowman, Rev. W. R., B.A., London	1894
Bowser, Mr. H., Glasgow	1884
Bowser, Mr. W. A., London	1888
Bright, Mr. J., Nottingham	1896
Brooke, Mr. J., J.P., Huddersfield	1889
Brooks, Mr. R. H., London	1881
Brown, Rev. J. A., London	1888
Brown, Rev. J. J., Birmingham (See *Honorary Members*)	1888
Brown, Rev. J. J., Cromer	1895
Bruce, Rev. F. W. C., Liverpool	1895
Bryan Rev. W. C., Hunstanton	1893
Bult, Mr. A., London	1892
Burns, Rev. Dawson, D.D., London	1891
Burton, Mr. S. B., Newcastle-on-Tyne	1881
Butlin, Rev. J., M.A., Leamington	1882
Carlile, Mr. G. M., Bristol	1887
Cartwright, Mr. H. S., London	1894
Cartwright, Mrs. R., London	1895
Cayford, Mr. E., J.P., London	1884
Chandler, Mr. B. W., F.C.A., London	1880
Chapman, Mr. A. A., Taunton	1892
Chapman, Mr. H. P., Birmingham	1882
Chapman, Mr. I., Trowbridge	1895
Chapman, Mr. W. M., Banbury	1892
Chappell, Mr. J., Calne	1879
Charles, Mr. E., Bassaleg	1892
Charlesworth, Rev. V. J., London	1888
Chedburn, Rev. W. S., Aberdeen	1881
Chick, Mr. S., London..	1878
Cholerton, Mr. G., Derby	1889
Chown, Mr. J., London	1886
Clark, Mr. J., London	1878
Clark, Rev. C., Bristol	1888
Clark, Rev. T., Ashford	1881

	Date of Enrolment.
Clarke, Mr. D., C.A., Wycombe	1885
Clay, Mr. J., Halifax	1889
Cleaver, Mr. R., J.P., Northampton	1895
Clifford, Rev. J., M.A., D.D., London (See *Honorary Members*)	1888
Cole, Rev. T. J., London	1895
Collier, Mr. E. P., J.P., Reading	1888
Collier, Rev. J. T., Salisbury	1895
Colman, Mr. S. C., Peterborough	1889
Cook, Mr. M., J.P., Dunstable	1895
Cook, Rev. G. S., London	1888
Cooke, Rev. J. H., London	1882
Coombs, Rev. W., Aylesbury	1895
Cooper, Mr. J. O., Boscombe	1892
Cork, Rev. D., Budleigh Salterton	1895
Cornford, Mr. J. E., Stourbridge	1891
Cowdy, Rev. S., LL.D., London	1886
Cox, Mr. G., London	1876
Cox, Mr. T., Luton	1888
Cripps, Mr. J., J.P., Liverpool	1887
Crossley, Mr. D. J., J.P., Hebden Bridge	1874
Culross, Rev. J., M.A., D.D., Bristol College (See *Honorary Members*)	1888
Cumberlidge, Mr. G., J.P., Tunstall	1886
Curtis, Mr. E. C., Neath	1895
David, Mr. A. J., B.A., LL.M., London	1872
Davidson, Rev. G. W., Milton, Chipping Norton	1888
Davies, Rev. B., Pontypridd	1895
Davies, Rev. D., Brighton	1886
Davies, Rev. D. M., B.A., Colwyn Bay	1895
Davies, Rev. E., Monmouth	1895
Davies, Rev. G., D.D., Bangor College	1895
Davies, Mr. R. O., J.P., London	1889
Davies, Rev. T. Witton, B.A., Nottingham	1895
Davies, Mr. W., Swansea	1888
Davies, Mr. W. J., Newbury	1895
Davis, Rev. E. T., Sidcup	1894
Davis, Rev. J., Bristol	1888
Davis, Rev. J. U., B.A., London	1882
Dawbarn, Mr. R. Y., Derby	1895
Dawson, Mr. E., J.P., Middlesbrough	1895
Denny, Mr. C. W., London	1895
Derrington, Mr. J. P., Birmingham	1888
Dicks, Mr. J., Cheltenham	1895
Dixon, Mr. B., Sheffield	1889
Dodwell, Rev. J., Haddenham, Thame	1895
Douglas, Rev. J., Teignmouth	1885
Dowen, Rev. Z. T., M.D., London	1881
Drabble, Mr. R. C. H., L.D.S., Sheffield	1895
Drayton, Mr. E., Montacute	1893
Drew, Rev. J., St. Leonard's	1895
Dunckley, Rev. J., London	1895
Dyson, Rev. W., Harrow-on-the-Hill	1877
East, Rev. D. J., Watford	1894
Eaton, Mr. J., Sheffield	1895
Eccles, Rev. R. K., M.D., Salem, Ohio, U.S.A.	1887
Edwards, Rev. E., Torquay (See *Honorary Members*)	1885
Edwards, Rev. F., B.A., Harlow	1878
Edwards, Rev. H., Anstruther	1894
Ellis, Mr. E. C., Derby	1874
Ellis, Rev. W. C., *Sandy*	1895

	Date of Enrolment.
Engall, Mr. T. H., London	1895
Ennals, Rev. G. T., Upminster	1889
Erith, Mr. H. G., London	1886
Etheridge, Rev. B. C., London	1895
Evans, Mr. J., Brecon	1878
Faulkner, Mr. A., London	1891
Fisk, Mr. J., J.P., St. Albans	1895
Fisk, Miss E., St. Albans	1895
Fisk, Miss S., St. Albans	1895
Foster, Rev. J., London	1870
Foulkes, Mr. A., Abergele	1888
Francis, Mr. F. C., London	1888
Freeman, Mr. T. Kyffin, F.G.S., F.S.S., London	1893
Freer, Mr. F. A., Bristol	1895
Fuller, Rev. F., Bedford	1895
Fuller, Mr. W. M., Newport, Mon.	1875
Fuller, Rev. J. J., London	1895
Gamman, Mr. F., Bedford	1895
Garland, Mr. T., London	1877
Gibson, Mr. E. A., New Barnet	1888
Godfrey, Rev. W. S., Croydon	1894
Goodman, Mr. R., Flitwick	1889
Goodman, Mr. T., Royston	1888
Goodman, Rev. W., B.A., London	1895
Gordon, Mr. R., London	1883
Gould, Mr. A. P., M.S., London	1888
Gould, Mr. H. P., Norwich	1888
Gould, Rev. G. P., M.A., London	1889
Grace, Mr. R., London	1889
Gray, Rev. A. C., London	1895
Green, Mr. G., Norwich	1892
Green, Mr. J. A., London	1888
Green, Prof. J. R., D.Sc., London	1894
Griffiths, Rev. P., London	1895
Haddon, Mr. S., Weston-super-Mare	1891
Haines, Rev. W. W., London	1877
Hainsworth, Mr. A. W., Farsley	1889
Hall, Rev. S., Hindley Green	1895
Hammer, Mr. G. M., Eden Bridge	1894
Hammond, Mr. N., Seaford	1889
Hanson, Mr. J. S., Worcester	1888
Hanson, Rev. J., Henshaw, Yeadon	1876
Harcourt, Rev. J., Leicester	1895
Harper, Rev. J., Ledbury	1874
Harris, Mr. G., London	1895
Hart, Mr. S. J., Chatham	1890
Harvey, Mr. J., Sandwich	1874
Haslam, Rev. J., Gildersome	1874
Hawkes, Mr. W., J.P., Devonport	1884
Hayman, Rev. J. J., London	1895
Henderson, Rev. H., Plymouth	1888
Henderson, Rev. W. J., B.A., Bristol	1895
Henderson, Rev. W. T., London	1888
Hetherington, Rev. W., Walthamstow	1889
Hewson, Rev. J. M., London	1888
Hill, Mr. I., Derby	1892
Hill, Rev. W., London	1877
Hine, Mr. A., J.P., Maryport	1889

	Date of Enrolment.
Hodges, Mr. E. A., Redditch	1894
Holmes, Mr. J., Rawdon	1892
Holmes, Mr. R., Bradford	1888
Hope, Mr. T. R., J.P., Redhill	1877
Horsfall, Mr. J. C., J.P., C.C., Cross Hills, Keighley	1895
Hougham, Mr. W., Birmingham	1891
Howard, Mr. J. B., New Barnet	1881
Hughes, Mr. E. W., London	1878
Hurtley, Mr. R. J., J.P., Burnley	1878
Hutchison, Mr. G. A., Leytonstone	1875
Iles, Mr. S., Bristol	1891
Illingworth, Mr. W., Bradford	1878
Jefferson, Rev. J., Rawtenstall	1895
Jennings, Rev. D., Stratford-on-Avon	1895
Johnston, Rev. R., London	1874
Jones, Mr. S., J.P., C.C., Wrexham	1895
Jones, Rev. E., Maesteg	1895
Jones, Mr. W., Orpington	1895
Juniper, Rev. W. J., Rangoon, Burmah	1895
Kent, Mr. W., South Croydon	1882
Kerry, Rev. G., Calcutta	1882
King, Mr. G., Hereford	1888
Knee, Mr. H. F., Withington, Manchester	1886
Knight, Rev. B. G., Swavesey	1892
Knight, Mr. W. D., Broadbridge Heath	1878
Lees, Mr. E. A., Birmingham	1895
Leonard, Rev. H. C., M.A., Bristol	1884
Levinsohn, Rev. I., London	1883
Lewarn, Mr. G., Plymouth	1888
Lewarn, Mr. W., Plymouth	1888
Lewis, Mr. E. W., Wolverhampton	1895
Lewis, Mr. G., London	1885
Lewitt, Rev. J., Cheltenham	1890
Lloyd, Mr. G., Bridgnorth	1895
Lovatt, Mr. S. G., Stafford	1895
Lowden, Rev. G. R., Hanwell	1878
Lowe, Rev. R., Welford, Rugby	1896
Luntley, Mr. P. H., Bromley, Kent	1874
Lush, Mr. P. J. F., M.A., M.R.C.S., London	1895
Macalpine, Mr. G. W., J.P., Accrington	1889
Mace, Rev. D., Market Harborough	1895
Mack, Mr. J., London	1892
Mansfield, Mr. S., Trumpington	1895
March, Rev. W., Birmingham	1895
Marnham, Mr. H., London	1895
Marnham, Mr. J., J.P., Boxmoor	1886
Martin, Rev. T. H., Glasgow	1888
McKenzie, Rev. A. P., Potter Street, Harlow	1888
McMaster, Mr. J. S., London	1877
McPherson, Rev. D. P., B.D., Exeter	1894
Mead, Mr. J. B., London	1877
Meadows, Mr. W., jun., Kettering	1895
Medley, Rev. W., M.A., Rawdon	1895
Merrick, Mr. A. B., Exeter	1895
Meyer, Rev. F. B., B.A., London	1895

	Date of Enrolment.
Miller, Rev. W., Chesham	1895
Minns, Mr. G. C., London	1892
Mitton, Mr. E. M., Birmingham	1881
Moore, Rev. J. H., Oxford	1892
Mostyn, Rev. J., Ipswich	1889
Moulson, Mr. Ald. W., J.P., Bradford	1895
Mounsey, Mr. E., J.P., Liverpool	1878
Myers, Rev. J., Longwood	1884
Myers, Rev. J. B., London.	1885
Needham, Rev. G , Loughborough	1895
Neobard, Rev. J., Reading	1874
Newell, Rev. W., Downend	1895
Newman, Mr. W., Louth	1895
Newton, Rev. F. H., London	1876
O'Dell, Rev. J., Hull	1895
O'Neill, Rev. A. G., Birmingham	1889
Osborn, Mr. G., J.P., St. Leonards	1891
Osborne, Rev. A. T., King's Lynn	1895
Parker, Mr. H. R., London	1891
Parker Rev. E., D.D., Manchester	1875
Parker, Rev. J., M.A., Ilford	1891
Parkinson, Mr. W. C., London	1877
Parrett, Rev. C. H., Boscombe	1895
Payne, Mr. W., London	1874
Peak, Mr. H., Guildford	1877
Pearce, Rev. F., Trowbridge	1874
Pedley, Mr. G., Sutton (*Surrey*)	1888
Penny, Mr. T., Taunton	1888
Penny, Mr. T. S., Taunton	1888
Perrin, Mr. H. S., Stony Stratford	1891
Pewtress, Mr. E., London	1885
Pewtress, Mr. H. W., London	1895
Pewtress, Mr. J. W., London	1895
Phillips, Rev. G., Newtown	1895
Philp, Rev. C., Gosport	1895
Plumb, Rev. G., Norwich	1895
Porter, Mr. W. R., Southsea	1888
Potter, Mr. H., London	1893
Powell, Mr. C., Chadwell Heath	1889
Prestige, Mr. G., Exmouth	1895
Priestley, Mr. J. G., London	1895
Pullar, Mr. L., Lower Weston, Bath	1886
Purchase, Rev. W. H., Birmingham	1895
Radburn, Rev. W., Henley-in-Arden	1888
Rees, Rev. W., Blaenavon	1895
Rickett, Mr. W. R., London	1875
Rickett, Mrs. W. R., London	1895
Ridley, Mr. A. C., Ipswich	1895
Riley, Rev. A. F., London	1894
Roberts, Mr. R. G., Swansea	1895
Robertson, Rev. F., Bath	1891
Robinson, Mr. E., J.P., Bristol	1874
Robinson, Mr. K., Bristol	1888
Robinson, Mr. W. L., Coventry	1895
Rogers, Mr. H., J.P., Hereford	1888
Rose, Mr. J. S., Bristol	1874
Rouse, Rev. G. H., M.A., D.D., Calcutta	1892

	Date of Enrolment
Rowson, Rev. H., Birmingham	1895
Russell, Mr. J., Ardrossan	1877
Russell, Rev. J. R., Astwood Bank	1888
Ryan, Mr. J., London	1895
Salisbury, Rev. J., M.A., Derby	1895
Saul, Mr. T., J.P., Great Yarmouth	1888
Saunders, Rev. J., Dinton	1877
Saville, Rev. C., Middleton Cheney	1890
Scholefield, Mr. J. W., J.P., Bootle	1888
Scudamore, Rev. G., London	1893
Seager, Rev. J., Bristol	1895
Sharman, Mr. W. J., Bittleswell	1891
Sharman, Rev. W., Fleet (*Hants.*)	1895
Sharp, Mr. S., Morley	1889
Sharp, Rev. D., Bristol	1895
Shaw, Mr. W. D., Longwood	1888
Sheen, Mr. J., London	1893
Shepherd, Mr. Ald. G., J.P., Bacup	1895
Short, Rev. G., B.A., Salisbury (See *Honorary Members*)	1877
Simmons, Mr. W. R., Boscombe	1889
Small, Mr. W., Nottingham	1896
Small, Rev. G., M.A., Leytonstone	1879
Smalley, Rev. J., Blackburn	1895
Smallwood, Mr. J., J.P., Stratford-on-Avon	1888
Smith, Mr. A. Gurney, Bromley, Kent	1889
Smith, Mr. F. E., Sheffield	1895
Smith, Mr. J. F., London	1887
Smith, Mr. J. J., J.P., Watford	1874
Smith Mr. N., London	1888
Sowerby, Rev. R. C., Stirling	1895
Spice, Mr. W. H., Leeds	1888
Spurr, Rev. F. C., London	1893
Stanford, Mr. J., J.P., Eden Bridge	1874
Stevenson, Mr. G., J.P., Leicester	1889
Stiff, Mr. E., Worcester Park, Surrey	1888
Stocker, Mr. T., St. Austell	1895
Stocker, Miss, St. Austell	1895
Stowe, Mr. G. S., Penarth	1895
Sturge, Rev. A., Dartford	1885
Styles, Rev. W. J., London	1891
Tarbox, Rev. E. W., Guildford	1893
Tarver, Mr. G., Burton-on-Trent	1886
Tawell, Mr. J. A., Earl's Colne	1895
Taylor, Mr. B., Bristol	1889
Taylor, Mr. H., Birmingham	1895
Taylor, Rev. W. J., London	1895
Terry, Mr. P., London	1888
Terry, Mr. P., jun., London	1878
Thomas, Rev. J., Exmouth	1887
Thomas, Mrs., Llanelly	1895
Thompson, Miss A., Harrogate	1895
Thompson, Rev. J. C., Heathfield	1895
Thompson, Mr. S., Beckenham	1877
Thomsett, Rev. W. E., Reading	1877
Thorne, Mr. G. R., Wolverhampton	1891
Tilly, Rev. A., Cardiff	1894
Todd, Rev. J. W., D.D., London	1888
Toll, Rev. J., Great Ellingham	1877
Townsend, *Mr. C., J.P., Bristol*	1888

	Date of Enrolment.
Tresidder, Rev. H. J., London	1890
Trotter, Mr. M. H., Coleford	1876
Tuckett, Mr. C. H., Bristol	1895
Turner, Mr. J. E., J.P., Gloucester	1876
Turner, Rev. J., Blaby	1895
Turner, Rev. J., Eastbourne	1895
Turtle, Mr. S. T., London	1894
Tyrer, Mr. R. H., London	1889
Underhill, Mr. E. B., LL.D., London (See *Honorary Members*)	1874
Underwood, Rev. W., D.D., Derby (See *Honorary Members*)	1888
Upward, Mr. E. J., J.P., Sandown, I.W.	1874
Varley, Rev. J. W., St. Anne's-on-the-Sea	1894
Vasey, Rev. W. B., Sale	1895
Vaughan, Mr. J., Dowlais	1895
Walduck, Mr. T. H., Bexley Heath	1888
Wales, Mr. H. C., J.P., Cheshunt	1889
Warmington, Mr. F. W., London	1876
Warmington, Miss H. B., London	1895
Warren, Mr. G. A., London	1877
Wates, Mr. J., London	1888
Watkins, Mr. H., Swansea	1888
Watkins, Rev. S., Withington, Hereford	1895
Watson, Mr. A., Salisbury	1888
Watson, Mr. R., Rochdale	1889
Watson, Mr. S., London	1881
Watts, Rev. H., Grantham	1895
Wearing, Mr. W. B., Swindon	1889
Webb, Mr. P. C., London	1894
Webb, Mr. W., Chesham	1895
Weymouth, Dr. R. F., Brentwood	1875
Whale, Rev. W., Brisbane, Australia	1893
Wheatley, Rev. T., London	1895
White, Mr. Ald. G., J.P., Norwich	1895
Whiteman, Mr. W. H., Croydon	1888
Whitley, Mr. T., Southsea	1888
Whitley, Rev. W. T., M.A., LL.M., Melbourne, Australia	1888
Whittaker, Mr. C. D., M.A., B.Sc., Harlow	1895
Whittard, Mr. T., Cheltenham	1895
Wigner, Rev. J. T., London (See *Honorary Members*)	1878
Wiles, Mr. J., St. Albans	1895
Wilford, Mr. Ald. J., Leicester	1896
Wilkin, Mr. M. H., London	1874
Williams, Rev. C., Accrington (See *Honorary Members*)	1886
Willis, Mr. W., Q.C., London	1877
Wilshere, Rev. D., Nassau, Bahamas	1874
Wilshire, Mr. L. W., Derby	1892
Wilson, Mr. G. D., Darlington	1888
Wilson, Rev. J. L., Ulverston	1895
Winterton, Mr. J., London	1885
Wood, Mr. H., J.P., London	1895
Wood, Mr. H. E., London	1894
Woodroffe, Mr. C. G., London	1888
Woods, Rev. W., London	1894
Woollard, Mr. F. W., Stony Stratford	1889
Woolley, Mr. T. B., London	1876
Yeo, Mr. J., Plymouth	1888

DEPARTMENTS OF THE BAPTIST UNION.

I.—BAPTIST UNION CORPORATION, LIMITED.

The Memorandum and Articles of Association of "The Baptist Union Corporation, Limited," which are given below, were duly registered on 14th November, 1890. They allow the Baptist Union to hold securities and other property under a common seal in the name of the Corporation, thus obviating the trouble and expense involved in transferring such property upon the death of individual trustees.

The Corporation is prepared, under certain conditions, to act as the trustee for chapel property in accordance with the terms of the following Memorandum and Articles of Association:—

I.—MEMORANDUM OF ASSOCIATION OF THE BAPTIST UNION CORPORATION, LIMITED.

1. The name of the Company is "The Baptist Union Corporation, Limited."

2. The Registered Office of the Company will be in England.

3. The objects for which the Company is established are:—

(A) The promotion of the interests of the Baptist Denomination.

(B) The acquisition by purchase, hire, or otherwise, and the acceptance by way of gift, subscription, donation, devise, bequest, or otherwise, and the holding of buildings, lands, securities, stocks, shares, and debentures, money, and other property in the United Kingdom or elsewhere, whether for the purposes of the Corporation or to be held by the Corporation as trustee for or on behalf of or otherwise for the use or benefit of any person, church, society, association, committee, or cause connected with the Baptist Denomination in the United Kingdom.

(C) The selling, exchanging, mortgaging, letting, or demising of lands, buildings, or houses, or other property vested in or held by the Corporation.

(D) The acceptance, taking, and holding, whether as bare trustee or otherwise, of any property, whether real or personal, which may from time to time be conveyed, transferred, assigned, or otherwise vested in the Corporation, upon any trust or trusts, for the benefit of or in any manner calculated to advance the interests of any person, church, society, association, committee, or cause connected with the Baptist Denomination.

(E) The performance of any duty, function, or act, whether ministerial or otherwise, in compliance with and the carrying into effect any directions or instructions relating to any trust property vested in the Corporation, which may be given to the Corporation by any duly constituted body entitled to give such directions or instructions, whether the same relate to the corpus or to the income of such trust property.

(F) The administration, management, and conduct as trustees, factors, or agents, in accordance with any trusts, express or implied, affecting the same, of any trust property vested in the Corporation, otherwise than as bare trustees, and the exercise of any rights of ownership or any rights or powers, discretionary or otherwise, relating to the administration, management, and conduct of, or in any manner to, any such trust property.

(G) The giving of bonds or guarantees on account of any covenants, titles, trusts, or agencies that may be undertaken by the Corporation.

(H) The erection of any building, office, room, chapel, manse, or other building, or of any part of the same, and the repair and restoration of the same, for the purpose of the Corporation, or of any church direction, or chapel trus

(I) The support of agents, preachers, teachers, colporteurs, when such may be deemed necessary for the work of the Corporation or any church, society, association, committee, or cause for whom it may become trustee.

(J) The printing and publishing of annual reports, year books, papers, circulars, pamphlets, books, tracts, magazines, newspapers, and other documents, either for the advantage and profit of the Corporation, or for that of any church, society, association, committee, or cause for whom it may become trustee.

(K) The recovery of rents and of charges for burial or other matters connected with chapels or property vested in the Corporation or held by them.

(L) The raising or borrowing of such money as the Corporation may from time to time determine to raise or borrow, upon banking account or otherwise upon such security, whether by way of mortgage or otherwise, and on such terms as to interest, powers of sale, and otherwise, as the Corporation may from time to time deem expedient.

(M) The instituting, conducting, defending, or compromising of legal proceedings by and against the Corporation or its officers.

(N) The investing of all or any part of the funds held by the Corporation on such securities and terms as may be directed, or as the Corporation may deem fit, and the varying of such investments.

(O) The acquiring by purchase, amalgamation, or otherwise, the undertaking and business of any other society, association, or corporation having for its objects or some or one of them the promotion, in any form whatsoever, of the interests of the Baptist Denomination, or of any section or part thereof.

(P) The making of bye-laws for the government of the Corporation generally, and the alteration or rescission of such bye-laws or any of them.

(Q) The doing of all such other lawful things as are incidental or conducive to the attainment of the above objects.

4. Every Member of the Corporation undertakes to contribute to the assets of the Corporation in the event of the same being wound up during the time that he is a Member, or within one year afterwards, for the payment of the debts and liabilities of the Corporation contracted before the time at which he ceases to be a Member, and of the costs, charges, and expenses of winding up the same, and for the adjustment of the rights of the contributors among themselves, such amount as may be required not exceeding Five Shillings.

5. If, upon the winding up or dissolution of the Corporation there remains after the satisfaction of all its debts and liabilities any property whatsoever, the same shall not be paid to or distributed among the Members of the Corporation, but shall be given or transferred to the society known as the Baptist Union of Great Britain and Ireland, if that shall be in existence and willing to accept it, and if not to some other institution having objects similar to the objects of the Corporation, to be determined by the Members of the Corporation at or before the time of dissolution, or, in default thereof, by such Judge of the High Court of Justice in England as may have or acquire jurisdiction in the matter.

6. The Articles of Association of this Corporation shall be subject to the condition that no alteration in any clause which defines the conditions of membership (whether with the object of increasing or diminishing the number of those having a right to become Members), or in any clause relating to the qualification or election of Directors, shall be made without the previous assent of the Baptist Union. For the purpose of obtaining such assent, a notice shall be served upon the Secretary of the Baptist Union at least twenty-one days before the first day of the spring, or autumn, or other regular assembly of the Baptist Union, and such notice shall set forth a copy of the clause which it is proposed to alter, and a copy of the clause as it would stand after being altered as proposed. If the Baptist Union at such assembly shall pass a resolution prohibiting such alteration, or modifying the terms thereof, such prohibition shall take away from this Corporation the power of altering such clause, save in so far (if at all) as such alteration may be effected within the limits of the resolution of the Baptist Union; Provided that in case no prohibition or modification be made the Corporation shall be free to make the notified alteration if it so deem expedient; Provided also that the said Baptist Union may at a future assembly vary or annul any such resolution as aforesaid.

II.—ARTICLES OF ASSOCIATION OF THE BAPTIST UNION CORPORATION, LIMITED.

1. For the purposes of registration the number of the Members of the Corporation is declared not to exceed One hundred and fifty.

2. These Articles shall be construed with reference to the provisions of the Companies Acts, 1862 to 1890, and terms used in these Articles shall be taken as having the same respective meanings as they have when used in those Acts. The term "Baptist Union" means the society known as the Baptist Union of Great Britain and Ireland.

3. The Directors may, when they think fit, register an increase of Members.

Membership.

4. Every Member of the Council of the Baptist Union, and all the Officers of the Baptist Union who shall subscribe a copy of these Articles, shall be Members of the Corporation.

5. The rights and privileges of every Member shall be personal to himself; they shall not be transferable by his own act or by operation of law.

6. Any Member may withdraw from the Corporation by giving one calendar month's notice in writing to the Secretary of his intention so to do, and upon the expiration of the notice he shall cease to be a Member.

7. The Directors shall have power, by resolution duly passed and entered in their minute book, to determine the membership of any Member who shall by any means cease to be a Member of the Council of, or an Officer of the Baptist Union.

Directors and Officers.

8. The Directors of the Corporation shall be the persons who have signed the Memorandum of Association until the first General Meeting, and thereafter the Directors shall be the Members and Officers for the time being of the Council of the Baptist Union, who shall be the Board of Directors herein referred to as the Board.

9. The President of the Baptist Union for the time being subscribing a copy of these Articles, shall be President of the Corporation. The Secretary of the Baptist Union, for the time being, shall be the Secretary of the Corporation. There shall be two Auditors, who shall be elected annually in General Meeting, one of whom shall not be a Member of the Corporation.

Procedure of Board.

10. The Board shall meet in the spring and autumn of each year, and at such other times as the Directors may appoint. The Board may make such regulations as they think proper as to the summoning and holding of meetings, and for the transaction of business thereat, and they may adjourn any meeting.

11. The Directors may from time to time fix the quorum necessary for the transaction of business at any meeting to be held after such quorum shall have been fixed. Previous to the first General Meeting the quorum shall be three, and thereafter, until the Directors shall otherwise determine, the quorum shall be eleven.

12. The President alone or any five Directors may at any time summon a Meeting of the Corporation.

13. The President shall take the chair at all meetings of the Directors, and if at any Meeting he shall not be present within ten minutes after the time appointed for holding the same, the Directors present shall choose some one of their number to be Chairman of the Meeting.

14. Every question, matter, or thing which shall be brought up at any Meeting of the Directors shall be decided by a majority of votes, and in case of an equality of votes, the Chairman shall have a second or casting vote.

15. A Director may at any time resign his Directorship by giving one month's notice in writing to the Secretary.

16. Fifteen of the Directors of the Corporation for the time being may constitute themselves into a special Board for the transaction of any business of the Company which in their opinion demands instant attention, provided that before transacting such business such Directors enter a declaration, signed by each of them in the minute book, certifying that the business is urgent and that the best notice possible during the interval in which the knowledge of urgent business has existed has to the best of their knowledge been given to each of the Directors. The Directors so assembled shall be competent, by resolution passed unanimously, to exercise all the powers of the Directors in regard to such business. It shall be the duty of the Secretary to acquaint absent Directors as soon as practicable with the nature of the urgent business so transacted.

Powers of Directors.

17. The Directors for the time being shall have the management of all the affairs and business of the Corporation, and shall conduct the same in such manner as they in their discretion shall think fit; and may exercise all the powers of the Corporation.

18. Without prejudice to the generality of the last preceding Article, it shall be lawful for the Directors, immediately upon the incorporation of the Corporation, to do all or any of the following things in the name and on behalf of the Corporation:—

(A) They may undertake, administer, and carry into execution, any trust or other duty, ministerial or otherwise, and accept and hold any trust or other property.

(B) They may receive, act upon, and carry into effect any instructions or directions that may be given to the Corporation by any person or body in whom may be invested the management or administration of any trust property held by the Corporation.

(C) They may buy, sell, exchange, mortgage, demise, or let any real or personal property of the Corporation.

(D) They may exercise any power of borrowing or raising money and give bonds or guarantees.

(E) They may invest and vary investments of any moneys belonging to, or under the control, or in the custody of the Corporation.

(F) They may affix the Seal of the Corporation to, or otherwise make and execute, any documents, deeds, powers of attorney, authorities, or other instruments which may be necessary, useful, or advisable for the conduct of the affairs of the Corporation. The Seal to be affixed in the presence of two Directors and the Secretary.

(G) They may institute, prosecute, defend, compromise, or abandon any suit, action, or other proceeding at law.

(H) They may appoint at any time a temporary substitute for the Secretary, who shall have all the powers of the Secretary for the time being.

(I) They may enter into contracts and carry on all matters of business permitted by the Memorandum of Association.

(J) The Directors may delegate any of their powers to Committees, consisting of such Member or Members of their body as they think fit. Any Committee so formed shall have the same powers in relation to the matters delegated to them or placed under their supervision or control as the Directors originally had, except the power of sub-delegation. The Directors may withdraw such delegated power whenever they deem fit, provided that no prior act of the said Committee shall be invalidated by a subsequent regulation of the Directors if the same would have been valid except for such regulation.

Provided always that any cheque or other negotiable instrument shall be signed by a Director, and countersigned by the Secretary.

General Meetings.

19. The first General Meeting shall be held at such time, not being more than four months after the incorporation of the Corporation, and at such place as the President of the Corporation may determine.

20. Subsequent General Meetings shall be held at least once in every year, and on such days, at such time and place, as may be prescribed by the Corporation in General Meeting, and if no time or place is so prescribed, as shall be determined by the Secretary for the time being, or if there be no Secretary, by the President. Such meetings may be adjourned from time to time until the business is ended, and at and to such place as may be determined by the General Meeting.

21. The above-mentioned General Meetings shall be termed Ordinary Meetings, all others shall be Extraordinary Meetings.

22. The Directors may convene an Extraordinary Meeting, and when required by any twelve Members, by a notice in writing left at the Registered Office, shall convene an Extraordinary General Meeting.

Proceedings at General Meetings.

23. Notice specifying the place, the day, and the hour of meeting, and in case of special business, the nature of such business, shall be served upon every Member of the Corporation, in manner hereinafter provided, but the non-receipt of such notice by any Member shall not invalidate the proceedings at any General Meeting.

24. No business shall be transacted at any meeting unless a quorum of Members is present.

25. Twelve Members shall be a quorum at any General Meeting of the Corporation.

26. If within one hour from the time appointed for the Meeting a quorum of Members is not present, the meeting shall stand adjourned to such day, time, or

place as may be appointed in the agenda or bye-laws for the time being, and if at such adjourned Meeting a quorum of Members is not present, it shall be adjourned *sine die*.

27. The President of the Corporation shall preside as a Chairman at every General Meeting, or in his absence such person as shall there and then be elected by the General Meeting.

28. The Chairman may, with the consent of a majority of the General Meeting, adjourn any General Meeting from time to time and from place to place, but no business shall be transacted at any Adjourned Meeting other than the business left unfinished at the Meeting from which the adjournment took place.

29. At any General Meeting, unless a poll is demanded by at least ten Members, a declaration by the Chairman that a Resolution has been carried, and an entry made to that effect in the minute book, shall be sufficient evidence of the fact, without proof of the number or proportion of the votes recorded in favour of or against such resolution.

30. If a poll is demanded in manner aforesaid, the same shall be taken in such manner as the Chairman shall direct, and the result of such poll shall be deemed to be the Resolution of the Corporation in General Meeting.

Votes of Members.

31. Each Member shall have one vote only, and such vote must be given personally and not by proxy.

Bye-laws.

32. In addition to the powers vested in the Corporation by the Companies Acts, 1862 to 1890, the Corporation shall have power by Resolution passed in General Meeting, whether Ordinary or Extraordinary, from time to time to make such bye-laws for the government of the Corporation, as do not under the said Acts require to be passed by Special Resolution as being alterations of the regulations of the Corporation contained in the Articles of Association.

Accounts and Audit.

33. Accounts shall be kept of the moneys received and expended by the Corporation, and the matters in respect of which such receipt and expenditure takes place, and of the property and liabilities of the Corporation.

34. The accounts of the Corporation, and also the balance-sheet thereof, shall be audited every year by one or more Auditors, and such Auditor or Auditors shall have power to require the production of all books of account belonging to the Corporation, and of all vouchers which they may deem necessary to be produced.

Miscellaneous.

35. A notice may be served by the Corporation upon any member either personally or by sending it through the post in a prepaid letter addressed to such Member at his registered address in the United Kingdom.

36. Any notice served by post shall be deemed to have been served at the time when the letter containing the same was put into the post office, and in proving such service it shall be sufficient to prove that the letter containing the notice was properly addressed and put into the post office.

37. All notices required by the Companies Acts, 1862 and 1890, and by any Acts amending the same, to be given by advertisement shall be advertised in such newspapers as the Directors may select.

38. A certificate signed by the President and Secretary of the Baptist Union, or either of them, shall be sufficient proof that any person was or is a Member of the Council of, or an officer of, the Baptist Union, or that any minute or resolution has been passed by the Assembly of the Baptist Union.

II.—GENERAL EXPENSES FUND.

For Officers, Lists of Subscriptions, &c., see Baptist Union Annual Report.

This Fund bears the entire cost of working the general business of the Baptist Union. Towards this the subscriptions from associations, churches and personal members contribute. Grants in aid are made from the Annuity, Home Mission, and Augmentation Funds towards the working expenses. The Council have resolved, however, that it is desirable, if possible, to raise the income of the General Expenses Fund to such an amount as that the whole of the contributions to each of the Funds under the direction of the Council shall be devoted to the objects for which they are given, without any deduction for office expenses. In order to do this the income of the General Expenses Fund must be raised to at least £2,000 a year.

Subscriptions become due annually on 1st JANUARY. It is earnestly requested that they be paid on that date.

Subscribers of 10s. and upwards are entitled to a copy of the *Handbook*, post-free, and other Subscribers can obtain it from the Publishers for 1s. 8d. or for 2s. post-free. The price to non-subscribers is 2s., or post-free, 2s. 4d.

INCOME for 1894, including £650 voted from Annuity, Home Mission, Church Extension and Augmentation Funds ..	£1,779	5	9
EXPENDITURE for 1894	1,922	16	8

III.—LITERATURE FUND.

Chairman—REV. G. P. GOULD, M.A.

For Committee, &c., see Baptist Union Annual Report.

The Council of the Baptist Union publish *The Union Mission Hymnal* at (words only) one penny, and (Music and Words), 1s. 6d., 2s. 6d., 3s., and 5s., according to style. Under the direction of the Assembly, they are publishing a series of Manuals for the Instruction of Young People in Baptist Principles. The first volume, by Mr. Richard Heath, on "Anabaptism," and the second by Rev. J. Culross, D.D., on "Hanserd Knollys," are already issued.

INCOME for 1894 (including vote of £279 13s. 6d. from General Expenses Fund)..	£528	0	6
EXPENDITURE for 1894	677	7	8

IV.—HOME MISSION.

Chairman—MR. D. CLARKE, C.A.

For Committee, Lists of Subscriptions, &c., see Baptist Union Annual Report

The Mission was formed in 1797, under the title of the "Baptist Home Missionary Society," and in 1882 was incorporated in the amended constitution of the Baptist Union, together with the "Baptist Irish Society," under the title of the "British and Irish Home Mission." The Irish department of the joint Mission was transferred to the Irish Baptist Association on and from 1st January, 1890, and is now under the control of a Committee of that Association.

THE OBJECT is defined in the Constitution of the Baptist Union as follows:—"To spread the Gospel of Christ by employing Ministers and Evangelists; by establishing Christian churches; by forming Sunday-schools; by distributing the Scriptures and religious tracts; and by adopting and using such other methods as the Council shall deem advisable."

INCOME for 1894	£3,084	12	5
EXPENDITURE for 1894	£3,254	16	3

V.—CHURCH EXTENSION FUND.

Chairman—Rev. J. H. SHAKESPEARE, M.A.

For Committee, &c., see Baptist Union Annual Report.

This Fund was started in 1893, for Baptist Church Extension in large towns, under the following scheme adopted by the Assembly of the Baptist Union:—

1. That a fund be established, to be called the "Baptist Union Church Extension Fund," which shall be under the control of the Baptist Union Church Extension Committee, subject to the confirmation of the Council of the Baptist Union.

2. The objects of the Fund are to undertake the formation of Baptist Churches in towns where local effort is inadequate, and to provide means for:—

(*a*) The purchase of sites for prospective Baptist chapels;

(*b*) Grants and loans in aid of chapels built in connection with this scheme;

(*c*) A Pastor's Sustentation Fund.

3. The sphere of the operations of the Fund shall be limited to the large towns of the United Kingdom.

4. Local Church Extension Societies may be affiliated with the Fund on the recommendation of the Church Extension Committee, by the Council of the Baptist Union.

5. The Fund shall be formed from donations, subscriptions, and legacies, church collections and contributions from affiliated local Church Extension Societies.

6. The Committee may—

(*a*) Purchase sites for prospective chapel building, vesting them in the Baptist Union Corporation, Limited, with power of sale or transfer to local bodies, and may (*b*) make grants in aid of the purchase of sites and of chapel building, provided that no such grant shall exceed one-half of the amount contributed totally to the same object, but (*c*) not more than one-third of the income, apart from sums received as the repayment of loans (and such sums as may be given by the donors for special purposes), shall be applied to the purchase of sites and to grants in aid of chapel building.

7. The Committee may make loans in aid of the purchase of sites and chapel building, subject to such terms of repayment as may be agreed upon.

8. A Local Church Extension Society making any contribution to the National Fund shall have a prior right to a loan of a similar amount in aid of *bonâ fide* Church Extension which has received the sanction of the Local Committee.

9. An application for a grant must be signed by at least two-thirds of a Local Church Extension Society, who shall also, in case of a loan, furnish the names of four guarantors and certify their sufficiency.

10. The Committee shall have power to guarantee an adequate salary to the pastor of any new church formed under the auspices of this Fund, or of any local Baptist Church Extension Society, for a term not exceeding four years, such guarantee in every case to be a gradually diminishing amount with a view to the Church becoming self-supporting at the end of the period.

11. Donors may appropriate their gifts for particular cases, or to any department of the Fund.

12. That to be eligible for assistance, a church must be in membership with the Baptist Union, and that no grant be made in aid of purchasing a site or the cost of building unless the trust deed shall first have been submitted to the Committee and approved.

13. That all chapels erected under the auspices of the Baptist Union shall be suitable in size and architectural conditions to the neighbourhood in which they are placed.

14. That the first pastor of any church formed in connection with this movement, *if aided by the* Central Fund, shall be elected by the Local Church Extension *Committee and the Church* Extension Committee of the Baptist Union.

15. That the Baptist Union Church Extension Committee shall endeavour to promote the better distribution of Baptist churches in towns' areas, having regard to the existence of other Evangelical Nonconformist chapels.

16. That the Baptist churches in large towns and in their vicinity be invited to form local Church Extension Societies, having for their chief objects and methods—

(*a*) To secure prospective sights for churches in suitable and increasing neighbourhoods;

(*b*) To make grants to the Local Building Fund of new chapels;

(*c*) To make grants to a Pastor's Sustentation Fund for a certain term of years.

17. That Associations and Local Unions be invited to undertake Church Extension in towns on a larger scale than in the past, and especially in towns where the Baptist cause is weak or not represented.

18. That all contributions to affiliated societies for the purpose of this scheme, whether Associations or Local Unions, or Church Extension Societies, be included in the annual balance-sheet of the Baptist Union Church Extension Fund, such Societies being duly credited with them.

19. That in order to realise the brotherhood of the Baptist churches, and to promote the common cause of the strong and the weak, the local Church Extension Societies be urged to contribute 25 per cent. of their local funds to the National Fund, retaining the remaining 75 per cent. for use in their districts.

INCOME for 1894	£3,248 12 11
EXPENDITURE for 1894	2,062 10 9

VI.—ANNUITY FUND.

Chairman—REV. C. WILLIAMS.

For Committee, Lists of Subscriptions, &c., see Baptist Union Annual Report.

N.B.—Applicants for Beneficiary membership are requested to make themselves thoroughly acquainted with the Rules. All communications to be addressed to the Secretary, 19, *Furnival-street, E.C.*

RULES

TITLE.

The Baptist Union of Great Britain and Ireland undertakes to administer a fund to be formed partly by voluntary donations, and partly by subscriptions of Beneficiary members, and to be designated "THE BAPTIST UNION ANNUITY FUND FOR RETIRED MINISTERS, AND MINISTERS' WIDOWS AND ORPHANS."

DESIGN.

1. The object of the Fund is to provide Annuities for its Beneficiary members and Annuities for their widows and orphans.

MANAGEMENT.

2. The Fund shall be administered by a Committee of not less than fifteen members thereof, not being annuitants, and by a Treasurer, and Secretary or Secretaries, who shall be annually appointed by the Council of the Baptist Union. The Treasurer and Secretary or Secretaries of the Fund, and the Officers of the Baptist Union for the time being, shall be members of the Committee *ex officio*.

3. The Baptist Union Corporation, Limited, shall be the Trustee of the Fund.

4. Three Auditors shall be appointed by the Assembly of the Baptist Union.

5. The Committee shall meet to transact business as often as may be required. Seven Members shall form a quorum All questions shall be decided by a majority of votes, the Chairman having a second or casting vote when the numbers are equal.

6. An account shall be kept with a bank approved by the Committee in the joint names of the Treasurer and Secretary for the time being, into which all moneys shall be paid, and all payments shall be made by cheque, signed by both parties, after receiving the order of a Committee Meeting, which shall be their authority for payment.

7. Proper books shall be kept by the Committee, Treasurer, and Secretary, containing minutes or accounts of their respective transactions.

8. The Council of the Baptist Union shall once in each year submit to the Assembly a report of the proceedings for the year ending on the 31st December preceding and the Treasurer shall at the same time present a statement of accounts for the same period duly audited.

Membership.

9. Members of the Fund shall be either Honorary or Beneficiary: the former including all who contribute five shillings or upwards annually, or who shall have paid in one sum not less than five pounds; the latter all who subscribe for benefits to be received by themselves.

10. The persons eligible for Beneficiary membership shall be Pastors of Baptist Churches, Tutors of Baptist Colleges, Officers of Baptist Institutions, and Missionaries of Baptist Missionary Societies.

11. Every applicant for Beneficiary membership must be either a resident within the United Kingdom or a Missionary of one of the Baptist Missionary Societies of the United Kingdom.

12. Every applicant who shall satisfy the Committee with respect to his character, health, and age, may be received by the Committee as a Beneficiary member.

13. In the event of the Committee not being satisfied with regard to the health of any applicant, they shall have power to fix special terms for his reception as a Beneficiary member.

14. The Committee shall determine the amount of the payments, whether by way of subscription or of single payment, to be made by a Missionary becoming a Beneficiary member.

15. In the event of a Beneficiary member, subsequently to his reception, accepting the pastorate of a Baptist Church beyond the limits of the United Kingdom, or becoming a Missionary of one of the Baptist Missionary Societies aforesaid, he shall within one month of his acceptance of a pastorate, or of his having become a Missionary as aforesaid, give notice thereof in writing to the Secretary of the Fund.

16. A Beneficiary member so accepting a pastorate beyond the limits of the United Kingdom, or becoming a Missionary as aforesaid, shall duly make such additional payments (if any) as the Committee shall determine, whether by way of increased subscription or further single payment.

17. In the event of failure to give such notice and to make such additional payments as are prescribed by Rules 15 and 16, the interest of the Beneficiary member in the Fund shall entirely cease.

18. The Committee, with the consent of the Council, shall have full power to assume the Liabilities and Assets of other Societies having similar objects, on such terms and conditions as may be agreed upon.

Subscriptions of Beneficiary Members.

19. Every Beneficiary member shall pay an entrance fee and an annual subscription, according to Table I. in the subjoined schedule, or he may commute the same by a single payment, according to Table II. in the same schedule.

20. An annual subscription shall cease to be payable by a Beneficiary member upon his becoming an annuitant; but if an annuitant shall accept any post which would render him eligible for Beneficiary membership, his annuity shall cease as from his acceptance of such post, and he shall be entitled to resume his Beneficiary membership upon the terms of his paying as from his acceptance of such post the same annual subscription as that paid by him prior to his becoming entitled to his annuity.

21. In the event of a Beneficiary member who has commuted his annual subscriptions by a single payment and has become an annuitant, accepting any post which would render him eligible for Beneficiary membership, his annuity shall cease as from his acceptance of such post, but he shall resume his Beneficiary membership as from that date without making any further payment.

22. If any Beneficiary member shall desire to secure the benefits of the Fund for his Widow and Orphans, he shall pay an entrance fee and annual subscription for them according to Table III. in the subjoined schedule, or he may commute the same by a single payment according to Table IV. The subscription for a Widow and Orphans shall be according to a Beneficiary member's age at the time of his wife's admission, and shall cease at her death or upon his becoming entitled to an annuity. Any Beneficiary member proposing, after his own admission, to secure the benefits of the Fund for his then wife and their children, shall produce a satisfactory medical certificate of his health. A Beneficiary member who shall subsequently contract another marriage, and desire to secure the benefits of the Fund for his widow, shall pay an entrance fee and subscription according to his age at the time. If a Beneficiary member's wife shall be more than five years younger than himself, he shall pay such additional subscription as the Committee, with the advice of an Actuary, shall determine.

23. Beneficiary members, being Widowers, who may desire to secure the benefits of the Fund for their children, shall pay such subscription as the Committee, with the advice of an Actuary, shall determine.

24. A Beneficiary member may secure additional Annuities, not exceeding six (making seven in all), for himself and family respectively, upon payment of additional entrance fees and subscriptions; such additional subscriptions, however, shall give no claim to increased benefit from the free contributions to the Fund.

25. Any person, otherwise eligible under Rules 10 to 17 inclusive, may become a Beneficiary member on payment of half-rates, and, if he shall desire to secure the benefits of the Fund for his Widow and Orphans, he may do so on payment of half-rates, subject to the provision as to increase of benefits from the free contributions mentioned in Rule 32.

26. A Beneficiary member, or any Church on his behalf, may at any time commute the whole or any part of his annual subscriptions by one or more payments, upon such terms as the Committee shall determine.

27. Payments of entrance fees and single payments may, with the addition of five per cent. on the whole amount, be made in three equal yearly instalments.

28. Annual subscriptions of Beneficiary members shall become due in advance on the first of January or the first of July in each year, but such subscriptions may be paid half-yearly in advance with the addition of a charge at the rate of sixpence in the pound.

29. Any Beneficiary member whose subscription, whether annual or half-yearly, shall be in arrear, shall pay a fine at the rate of one shilling in the pound for the first completed period of three months, and a further fine at the rate of fourpence in the pound for every subsequent month or part of a month during which his subscription shall be in arrear.

30. (i.) Any Beneficiary member whose subscription, whether annual or half-yearly, shall have been in arrear for the period of twelve months shall cease to be a Beneficiary member as from the date when such subscription became due, provided there shall have been sent to him by the Secretary, at least one month prior to the expiration of such period of twelve months, notice that his subscription will, upon a date to be mentioned in such notice, be twelve months in arrear. (ii.) If any Beneficiary member shall, in the opinion of the Committee, be or become morally unfit to remain a member of the Fund, the Committee shall have power to determine his membership. But any Beneficiary member whose Beneficiary membership shall cease or be determined by either of the modes aforesaid, or by voluntary relinquishment, shall be entitled to be repaid two-thirds of the amount paid by him as subscriptions.

31. No Beneficiary member, while receiving benefit, shall be required to pay his subscription.

BENEFITS.

32. A Beneficiary member shall receive £15 per annum in respect of each single subscription; on his death his Widow, if subscribed for, shall receive £10 per annum for each single subscription; if there be no Widow, an Orphan shall receive £4 per

annum till 15 years of age, and, if there be more than one Orphan, the others shall receive £2 per annum each till the same age, but no Orphan family shall receive more than £10 per annum in all for any single subscription. The Annuities shall be increased from the funds obtained by free contributions, to such sums as the Committee, with the advice of an Actuary, may determine; but if a Beneficiary member shall have paid for himself or for his Widow and Orphans only half-rates, he or they, as the case may be, shall receive only half the increased benefit given to other Beneficiary members and their families from the free contributions to the Fund. All payments shall be made in quarterly instalments on the first days of January, April, July, and October.

33. An examination shall be made into the affairs of the Fund by an Actuary, to be appointed by the Committee, within six months after the 31st December, 1878, and so again within the same period after the expiration of every succeeding three years; and by the result of such examination the Committee shall be guided as to the benefit to be given to claimants, the proportionate scale as between Beneficiary members and their Widows and Orphans being maintained; provided that until the third triennial valuation the addition to Annuities from the free contributions shall not exceed £30 for Beneficiary members, and a proportionate sum for their Widows and Orphans.

34. The additions hitherto made to the Annuities shall henceforth cease to be payable. The Committee shall, after each Actuarial Examination, determine the amounts of the benefit to be given to claimants during the period ending with the next Actuarial Valuation, and such amounts shall be payable only until the Committee shall have made their next subsequent determination.

35. The wife and family of a Beneficiary member shall be entitled to the benefits of the Fund immediately upon his death, in accordance with Rule 32; but to be entitled to benefit for himself a subscriber must have been a Beneficiary member of the Fund for three years. If any applicant for membership over sixty years of age shall desire to secure an immediate Annuity for himself, he shall pay such additional subscription as the Committee, with the advice of an Actuary, may determine, and shall be entitled to share in the free contributions after the next valuation. And if any applicant for membership, whether a retired Pastor or the Widow of a Pastor of a Baptist Church, shall desire to secure an *Immediate Annuity*, he or she shall pay such additional subscription as the Committee, with the advice of an Actuary, may determine, but shall not be entitled to share in the free contributions.

36. Any Beneficiary member having subscribed for three years shall be entitled to claim the benefits of the Fund (i.) if he shall have relinquished office on or after attaining the age of sixty-five; or (ii.) if he shall have become permanently incapacitated for remunerative employment, and shall from time to time satisfy the Committee that he is so incapacitated.

37. Every annuitant shall make application in writing for each quarterly instalment of his annuity, and shall give satisfactory information respecting the ground of his claim. The claim, if admitted, shall take effect and be recognised only as from the receipt by the Secretary of such application.

38. If any Widow who is receiving benefit shall marry, her claims on the Fund shall thereupon cease, but the children of her former husband shall receive benefits as under Rule 32.

Relinquishment of Office.

39. If any Beneficiary member, at any time after his admission, but before he shall have become entitled to claim the benefits of the Fund, shall relinquish (whether permanently or otherwise) his qualifying office, he shall retain his Beneficiary membership; but his right and that of his Widow and Orphans (if subscribed for) to claim a share in the dividend from free contributions shall cease and determine as from the date of such relinquishment of office. Provided always that (i.) if such Beneficiary member shall, at the time of such relinquishment, have the intention of obtaining with all convenient speed some other qualifying office, and of such relinquishment and intention shall, within three months of such relinquishment, give written notice to the Committee, he and his Widow and Orphans (if

subscribed for) shall for the space of three years from the date of such relinquishment retain the right to claim a share in the dividend from free contributions; and at the expiration of such period the Committee shall determine whether he or his Widow and Orphans (if subscribed for) shall retain such right, and, if so, upon what conditions; such arrangements to be annually reviewed and altered or confirmed as the Committee may see fit, so long as he may remain out of office; ii.) if any Beneficiary member who has lost his right to share in the dividend from free contributions shall subsequently accept any qualifying office, the Committee may, if and upon such terms as they may think fit, restore the said right to him and to his Widow and Orphans (if subscribed for).

Funds.

40. The Funds not required to meet current liabilities shall be invested in the name of the Baptist Union Corporation, Limited, in Real or Government Securities, or in Debenture Stock of dividend-paying Railways in the United Kingdom, or in East India Government Stock, or in the Stock of Indian Railways guaranteed by the Indian Government, or in the Public Stocks of any of the British Colonies, until they shall amount, exclusive of interest, to the sum of £50,000. When the sum of £50,000 shall have been so accumulated, any further contributions to the Fund, above the capitalised sum aforesaid, shall be invested in the like description of securities, or in such other securities, including the security of mortgage of real or leasehold property belonging to or held in trust for any Baptist Church or Society now or hereafter to be established, and upon such terms as to time or mode of repayment, whether by instalments or otherwise, and with such collateral security, whether personal or otherwise, as the Committee may approve. The expressed wishes of Donors as to any particular Stocks in which their own contributions shall be invested, whether the same as or other than those before specified, shall at all times be regarded. The Committee may vary the securities from time to time, and make sale thereof respectively, within the limits above mentioned.

41. The capitalised sum aforesaid, together with such further free contributions as the Donors shall in writing so direct, shall form a Permanent Fund, the interest on which alone shall be available for the increase of Annuities. All other free contributions shall be applied by the Committee as the exigencies of the Fund shall from time to time seem to them to require.

Disputes.

42. The Council shall appoint an Arbitrator or Arbitrators, to whom shall be submitted any dispute arising between Beneficiaries and the Committee of Management, and the decision of the Arbitrator shall be conclusive and binding on all parties.

Alteration of Rules.

43. All Alterations in or Additions to the Rules shall be made by a vote of the Assembly at the Annual or Autumnal Session of the Union, and notice of any proposed Alteration must be given at the previous Session of the Union, such notice having been first sent in writing to the Secretary.

General.

44. If at any time the state of the Fund should not allow the payment in full of all the instalments payable in respect of Annuities, exclusive of any share in the voluntary contributions, all such instalments shall abate in the same proportion, and the deficiency on each instalment, together with interest on such deficiency, shall be a charge on the Fund, and shall rank next to the current claims in respect of Annuities in every subsequent quarter until paid.

45. The Treasurer and other Office-bearers, the Members of the Committee, and the Trustee, shall not be individually liable for the payment of Annuities, nor for any loss on investments, nor for any other loss which may happen to the Fund, unless the same shall happen through their own wilful fault or neglect; and each of them shall be accountable only for his own acts.

46. The foregoing Rules, as altered or amended from time to time in conformity with Rule 43, shall be binding on each Beneficiary member, and shall be printed on all schedules of application for admission as a Beneficiary member, and shall be signed by each applicant in token of his acceptance thereof.

SCHEDULE OF SUBSCRIPTIONS AND PAYMENTS.

The following Tables show the payments required to be made in respect of one Annuity only of each description according to a Beneficiary member's age next birthday at entry. Additional Annuities (not exceeding six, making seven in all) may be secured upon payment of proportionate Entrance Fees and Subscriptions; but such additional Annuities do not entitle to any additional benefit from the voluntary contributions. (*See Rule* 24.)

BENEFICIARY MEMBERS.

TABLE I.

Entrance Fee and Annual Subscription for one Annuity (£15).

Age under	Entrance Fee.	Annual Subscription.	Age under	Entrance Fee.	Annual Subscription.
	£ s. d.	£ s. d.		£ s. d.	£ s. d.
25	NONE	1 1 0	43	NONE	2 17 0
26	"	1 2 0	44	"	3 0 0
27	"	1 3 0	45	"	3 3 0
28	"	1 4 0			
29	"	1 5 0	46	3 0 0	3 3 0
30	"	1 6 0	47	6 12 6	3 3 0
			48	10 10 0	3 3 0
31	"	1 7 0	49	14 12 6	3 3 0
32	"	1 8 0	50	19 0 0	3 3 0
33	"	1 9 0			
34	"	1 11 0	51	23 12 6	3 3 0
35	"	1 13 0	52	28 10 0	3 3 0
			53	33 12 6	3 3 0
36	"	1 16 0	54	39 0 0	3 3 0
37	"	1 19 0	55	44 12 6	3 3 0
38	"	2 2 0			
39	"	2 5 0	56	51 0 0	3 3 0
40	"	2 8 0	57	57 17 6	3 3 0
			58	65 5 0	3 3 0
41	"	2 11 0	59	73 2 6	3 3 0
42	"	2 14 0	60	81 10 0	3 3 0

TABLE II.

Single Payment, in lieu of Entrance Fee and Annual Subscription, for one Annuity (£15).

Age under	Single Payment.	Age under	Single Payment.	Age under	Single Payment.
	£ s. d.		£ s. d.		£ s. d.
25	20 15 0	37	32 0 0	49	48 0 0
26	21 10 0	38	33 5 0	50	50 5 0
27	22 5 0	39	34 10 0		
28	23 0 0	40	35 15 0	51	53 0 0
29	24 0 0			52	56 0 0
30	25 0 0	41	37 0 0	53	59 5 0
		42	38 5 0	54	62 15 0
31	26 0 0	43	39 10 0	55	66 15 0
32	27 0 0	44	40 15 0		
33	28 0 0	45	42 0 0	56	71 0 0
34	29 0 0			57	75 10 0
35	30 0 0	46	43 5 0	58	80 10 0
		47	44 15 0	59	86 0 0
36	31 0 0	48	46 5 0	60	92 0 0

WIDOWS AND ORPHANS.

TABLE III.

Entrance Fee and Annual Subscription for one Annuity (£10).
(Subject to the exceptions mentioned in Rule 22.)

Age under	Entrance Fee.	Annual Subscription.	Age under	Entrance Fee.	Annual Subscription.
	£ s. d.	£ s. d.		£ s. d.	£ s. d.
25	NONE	2 7 0	43	1 0 0	3 3 0
26	"	2 8 0	44	1 17 6	3 3 0
27	"	2 9 0	45	2 15 0	3 3 0
28	"	2 10 0			
29	"	2 11 0	46	3 12 6	3 3 0
30	"	2 12 0	47	4 12 6	3 3 0
			48	5 15 0	3 3 0
31	"	2 13 0	49	7 0 0	3 3 0
32	"	2 14 0	50	8 15 0	3 3 0
33	"	2 15 0			
34	"	2 16 0	51	10 10 0	3 3 0
35	"	2 17 0	52	12 10 0	3 3 0
			53	14 10 0	3 3 0
36	"	2 18 0	54	16 12 6	3 3 0
37	"	2 19 0	55	18 17 6	3 3 0
38	"	3 0 0			
39	"	3 1 0	56	21 2 6	3 3 0
40	"	3 2 0	57	23 10 0	3 3 0
			58	26 0 0	3 3 0
41	"	3 3 0	59	28 10 0	3 3 0
42	0 10 0	3 3 0	60	31 2 6	3 3 0

TABLE IV.

Single Payment in lieu of Entrance Fee and Annual Subscription, for one Annuity (£10).

(Subject to the exceptions mentioned in Rule 22.)

Age under	Single Payment.	Age under	Single Payment.	Age under	Single Payment.
	£ s. d.		£ s. d.		£ s. d.
25	37 10 0	37	38 10 0	49	42 6 0
26	37 10 0	38	38 15 0	50	42 11 0
27	37 10 0	39	39 0 0		
28	37 10 0	40	39 5 0	51	42 15 0
29	37 10 0			52	42 18 0
30	37 10 0	41	39 10 0	53	43 0 0
		42	39 15 0	54	43 0 0
31	37 10 0	43	40 1 0	55	43 0 0
32	37 10 0	44	40 8 0		
33	37 10 0	45	40 16 0	56	43 0 0
34	37 15 0			57	43 0 0
35	38 0 0	46	41 5 0	58	43 0 0
		47	41 13 0	59	43 0 0
36	38 5 0	48	42 0 0	60	43 0 0

Enrolments are made on 1st January and 1st July in each year. Applications must be forwarded not later than a month previous to these dates, and the first payments made not later than two months after the date of enrolment.

The rates for ages over sixty and for "Immediate Annuities" may be ascertained on application to the Secretary.

SOCIETIES AMALGAMATED WITH THE BAPTIST UNION ANNUITY FUND.

THE NATIONAL SOCIETY FOR AGED AND INFIRM BAPTIST MINISTERS AND THEIR WIDOWS AND ORPHANS.

(*Established at Birmingham*, 1858.)

Resolutions passed by the Committee of the Baptist Union Annuity Fund on the 10th December, 1878:—

1. That this Committee do, as and from 1st January, 1879, assume and accept the liabilities and take over all the assets of the National Society for Aged and Infirm Baptist Ministers upon the terms and conditions following, being the terms and conditions agreed upon by the Committee of this Fund with the Committee of the said Society, and unanimously approved by a Special Meeting of Members of the said Society held at Walworth Road Chapel, London, on the 25th of April last, and assented to in writing by all the Beneficiary Members of the said Society; that is to say—

(1) That in January, 1879, the Members of the National Society become Members of the Baptist Union Annuity Fund, entitled to share and share alike with the other Members of the Fund in all its benefits.

(2) That the Members of the National Society be entitled to retire from the pastorate, and claim the benefit of the Fund, at the age of sixty, on the account of age only, and that the present Subscription of £3 3s. cover all the advantages of the Baptist Union Annuity Fund.

(3) That Messrs. Middlemore, C. T. Shaw, J. C. Woodhill, and T. Adams be added to the Trustees of the Annuity Fund.

2. That, in further pursuance of the said Agreement, Messrs. Middlemore, C. T. Shaw, J. C. Woodhill, and T. Adams be, and they are hereby, appointed Trustees of the Baptist Union Annuity Fund, subject to confirmation by the Union in accordance with Rule 3.

THE YORKSHIRE SOCIETY FOR THE RELIEF OF AGED AND INFIRM BAPTIST MINISTERS AND THEIR WIDOWS.

(*Established at Bradford*, 1845.)

Resolutions passed by the Committee of the Baptist Union Annuity Fund on the 10th December, 1878:—

1. That this Committee do, as and from 1st January, 1879, assume and accept the liabilities, and take over all the assets of the Yorkshire Society for the Relief of Aged and Infirm Baptist Ministers and their Widows, upon the terms and conditions following, being the terms and conditions agreed upon by the Committee of this Fund with the Committee of the said Society, and unanimously approved at the Annual Meeting of the said Society held at Bradford on the 2nd of October last, and assented to in writing by all the Beneficiary Members of the said Society; that is to say—

(1) That, in order to amalgamation of the Yorkshire Aged Ministers' Society with the Baptist Union Annuity Fund, the capital of the Yorkshire Society be made up to £8,000 by the Annuity Fund.

(2) That, in the event of amalgamation, the Trustees of the Yorkshire Society become Trustees of the Annuity Fund, and that two of the Trustees and two of the Committee of the Annuity Fund be chosen from Yorkshire, so that the county shall be represented in perpetuity on the Trust and on the Committee of the Annuity Fund.

(3) That the Members of the Yorkshire Society, when amalgamation shall take place, shall be subject to the Rules of the Annuity Fund, except—

(*a*) That they pay, as heretofore, three guineas each per annum as full payment for all benefits.

(*b*) That, on their retirement from the pastorate from any other cause than age or infirmity, they receive back one-third of the subscriptions paid by them from their admission into the Yorkshire Society.

(*c*) That they be entitled to retire from the pastorate on the ground of age only when sixty years of age.

(*d*) That in and from 1879 the payments to the claimants of the Yorkshire Society, on the ground of age or infirmity, shall be—

Ministers, per annum, £45.
Widows, per annum, £30.
Widows with 1 child under 16 years of age, £35 per annum.
Widows with more than 1 child under 16 years of age, £40 per annum.
Orphans under 16 years of age—1, £12 per annum; 2, £18 per annum; 3, £24 per annum; more than 3, £30 per annum.

(4) That the final agreement be printed in the Report of the Annuity Fund for 1879.

VII.—AUGMENTATION FUND.

Chairman—Rev. G. Short, B.A.

For Committee, Lists of Subscriptions, &c., see Baptist Union Annual Report.

The following are the Rules for Administering the Pastors' Income Augmentation Fund:—

1. The income of the Fund, after deducting working expenses, shall be distributed among those Pastors of contributing churches whose salaries are not less than £60 nor more than £150 a year. The items included in computing the stipend of a pastor are pew rents, weekly offerings, and other contributions within the church and congregation.

2. The pastor must have held office in the church on 1st October preceding the date of application, and have continued in the same pastorate until 30th June in the year of distribution.

3. The form of application, duly filled in, together with a Beneficiary subscription of £10, must be in the hands of the Secretary not later than 30th June, otherwise the case will be ineligible.

4.—A church or an individual contributing not less than £10 per annum shall be entitled to recommend an application, or two contributors of £5 each may join in a recommendation; but the recommendations shall not be in excess of the contributions—*i.e.*, they shall be at the rate of one recommendation for each £10 contributed.

5. The Beneficiary subscription from a church recommended in accordance with Rule 4 shall, if the case be approved by the Committee, be returned to the Pastor with an addition of not less than £10 from the voluntary funds.

6. The Secretary shall be authorised to receive applications not recommended according to Rule 4, to make inquiries respecting them, and to report thereon to the Committee; but no grant shall be made to such cases, except from a surplus left after meeting the claims of recommended cases, under Rule 4. Each application, whether recommended or otherwise, must be approved by the Committee before receiving a grant.

7. A church which has been constituted within two years of date of application shall be ineligible.

8. After receiving help for three years, a church shall be required to furnish a detailed report of its financial condition, and assistance from the Fund shall be discontinued unless the report be approved by the Committee.

9. A declaration by the Pastor as to his income shall be made at the foot of the schedule as follows:—"My annual income from all sources, whether mentioned in the foregoing items or not, does not exceed £150."

The amount distributed in December, 1894, to 181 pastors, was £3,442.

VIII.—EDUCATION FUND.

Chairman—Mr. R. Goodman.

For Committee, Lists of Subscriptions, &c., see Baptist Union Annual Report.

This Fund, under direction of the Baptist Union, aids Baptist pastors, by grants of money towards the cost of educating their sons and daughters. The schools are selected by the parents, subject to the approval of the Committee, and the grants are seldom renewed beyond three years.

The following are the Rules for Administering the Education Fund:—

1. That for the education of any child accepted by the Committee a sum not exceeding £15 per annum be granted by the Society in case of Boarding Schools, and in case of Day Schools a sum not exceeding £7 10s. per annum.*

2. That no child shall be admitted under eleven years of age, nor older than fourteen years, and the term of grant shall not exceed one year, unless specially determined by the Committee.

3. That subscribers of £10 per annum to the Fund may nominate one child for election in case of Boarding Schools, and subscribers of £5 per annum may nominate similarly in case of Day Schools.

	£	s.	d.
Income for 1894	£106	0	7
Grants Voted for 1894	85	0	0

IX.—BOARD OF INTRODUCTION AND CONSULTATION.

Chairman—Rev. J. Jenkyn Brown.

Constitution and Bye-Laws.

1. That a Board be elected by the Council of the Baptist Union for the purpose of introducing Pastors and Churches to each other, and for consultation in regard to ministerial settlements.

2. That the Board consist of twenty members of the Council, together with the Officers.

3. That the Board be appointed at the first meeting of the Council after its election.

4. That the action of the Board be limited for the present to the Churches in the following Associations, and that the members of the Board be resident in the

* For several years past the Committee have voted not more than £7 10s. per annum in any case.

districts into which the Associations are grouped, in the proportion of two members to each district:—

First District.
Northern. Yorkshire.

Second District.
Shropshire.
Lancashire and Cheshire.

Third District.
East Midland. West Midland.
Worcestershire.

Fourth District.
Oxfordshire. Berkshire.
Buckinghamshire. Northamptonshire.
Huntingdonshire.

Fifth District.
Cambridgeshire. Norfolk.
Suffolk and Norfolk Union.
Essex Union.

Sixth District.
London. Herts Union.
Beds Union. (Baptist Churches only.)

Seventh District.
Southern.
Wilts and East Somerset.

Eighth District.
Kent and Sussex.
Home Counties.

Ninth District.
Monmouthshire, English.
Gloucestershire and Herefordshire.
Bristol.

Tenth District.
Western. Devonshire.
Cornwall.

5. That the following be the bye-laws of the Board:—

(A) That the Board meet quarterly, and that in the interim the Secretary, along with a member of the Board residing in the district to which the vacant pastorate belongs, be empowered to act.

(B) That when desirable a communication be sent to churches without pastors giving particulars of the nature and objects of the Board.

(C) That ministers of churches desirous of introduction or advice with a view to settlement apply to the Secretary of the Board.

(D) That brethren who are accredited by the Board be placed on the register of ministers desiring settlement.

(E) That all the transactions of the Board be strictly confidential.

(F) That until the first name introduced to a Church by the Board has been dealt with, no second name be mentioned.

(G) That the Board undertake to furnish information as to character and general fitness for ministerial work.

(H) That the Board undertake to furnish to applying Churches information respecting the character and suitability of any Ministers who may be before them as candidates for the pastorate.

(I) That the Secretary of the Union be the Secretary of the Board.

REPRESENTATIVES FOR THE VARIOUS DISTRICTS, 1894-95.

First District.. .. Mr. J. J. Gurney, J.P., and Rev. A. P. Fayers.
Second „ .. .. Revs. C. Bonner and C. Williams.
Third „ .. .. „ J. J. Brown and W. Woods.
Fourth „ .. .. Mr. D. Clarke, C.A., and Mr. R. Cleaver, J.P.
Fifth „ .. .. Revs. T. G. Tarn and T. M. Morris.
Sixth „ .. .. „ F. A. Jones and J. Stuart.
Seventh „ .. .. „ J. Hasler and Mr. W. B. Wearing.
Eighth „ .. .. „ D. Davies and N. Dobson.
Ninth „ .. .. „ R. Glover, D.D., and Mr. H. Rogers, J.P.
Tenth „ .. .. Mr. T. Penny and Rev. S. Vincent.

X.—COMMITTEE OF ARBITRATORS.

Rev. J. ANGUS, D.D., London, *Chairman*.
Mr. W. B. BEMBRIDGE, J.P., Ripley, Derby.
Mr. D. Clarke, C.A., High Wycombe.
Rev. J. CLIFFORD, D.D., London.
Rev. E. PARKER, D.D., Manchester.

RULES ADOPTED BY THE ASSEMBLY AT MANCHESTER, OCTOBER 11TH, 1872.

(1) The Arbitration Committee shall have all the powers, and be governed by all the laws, belonging or applicable to Arbitrators legally appointed.

(2) The Arbitration Committee shall undertake the reference of any dispute cognisable by law, arising within or respecting any Church in the Baptist Union, which shall be duly submitted to it by the parties.

(3) The Arbitration Committee may delegate to any one or more of its members the duty of making investigations or taking evidence; but every award shall be made at a meeting of the Committee, and shall be deemed to be the act of the whole Committee, three members being a quorum, and every award shall be signed by at least three members on behalf of the whole Committee.

(4) The award of the Arbitration Committee shall be final.

(5) The Arbitration Committee may, from time to time, make Bye-laws for the management of its business, and particularly may require of Applicants a deposit for payment of necessary expenses, as a preliminary condition of reference.

(6) The Arbitration Committee shall take up any matter cognisable by law duly submitted to it; it may also, in its discretion, undertake any reference respecting ecclesiastical matters or discipline in our Churches, duly submitted to it, though such matter may not be cognisable by law.

In order to preserve intact the inalienable rights of Christian liberty, it is declared by this minute that reference to the Arbitration Committee shall be wholly voluntary.

BYE-LAWS ADOPTED BY THE COMMITTEE OF ARBITRATORS, APRIL 30TH, 1873.

(1) That the designation of the Committee in all documents shall be sufficient if named as "THE COMMITTEE OF ARBITRATORS OF THE BAPTIST UNION OF GREAT BRITAIN AND IRELAND."

(2) That, in order to satisfy the Committee that some difference between brethren exists which may properly be referred to its decision, the general nature of such difference shall be stated in writing, and be signed by the parties, who thereby shall express their consent to submit their differences to the award of the Committee, the statement consent in writing to be left, as a preliminary step, in the hands of the Secretary.

(3) That all written statements made to the Arbitrators or to the Secretary shall be regarded by them respectively as "private and confidential," until the final decision or award be made and announced in writing to both parties.

(4) Having regard to Rules 1 and 4, unanimously passed at the Autumn Meeting of the Baptist Union on the 11th October, 1872, it is agreed that no statement in writing or submission to the Arbitrators or any other paper shall be given up to either party to be used in a Court of Law or Equity, either before or subsequently to the publication of an award, without the written consent of each of the Committee of Arbitrators.

(5) That no fee or pecuniary reward shall be made or accepted by the Arbitrators for their services. Necessary expenses shall be provided for by *deposits*, to be made by each of the parties with the Secretary, equal in amount, before the case can be heard, which deposits shall be returned wholly or in part, and in such proportions as the Committee may direct.

(6) That for the purpose of remunerating the Secretary for his services, a small *payment* (the amount whereof to be determined by the Committee) shall be made to

him by each party on presentation of the submission or statement in writing, signed by the parties in difference.

(7) That, excepting cases of special business appointed for consideration by the Committee (and of which proposed appointment mention shall be particularly made in the notices of the meeting), the Committee shall meet in London.

(8) That of all meetings of the Committee a week's notice at least shall be given, which may be done by the Secretary, with consent of the Chairman, or by the Chairman as convener of the Committee.

(9) That suitable account books be provided in which shall be entered by the Secretary all deposits, receipts, and payments.

XI.—THE LIBRARY

In the Gallery of the Mission House, 19, Furnival-street, E.C., is designed mainly for the preservation of Literary Works written by Baptists or relating to the history of the Baptist Denomination.

Presented during the past year:—

By the Author—
Memorials of Bromsgrove Church. By Rev. J. Ford.

By the Author—
(1) Primitive Preaching;
(2) The Grand Old Book. By Rev. A. McCaig, B.A., LL.B.

By the Author—
Life and Labours of Rev. H. W. Holmes. By Rev. T. R. Lewis.

By the Author—
English Nonconformity. By Rev. E. C. Pike, B.A.

By the Author—
Armenian Crisis. By Rev. F. D. Greene, M.A.

By Rev. J. R. Godfrey—
The Barton Church Magazine, 1893-4.

By Mr. J. Hooper—
Baptist Manuals. 4 vols.

By the late Rev. F. Perkins—
The Baptist Reporter. 5 vols.
The Baptist Repository. 4 vols.
The Christian Witness. 7 vols.
The Church. 5 vols.
The Evangelical Register.
The Gospel Herald.
The Monthly Christian Spectator.

By Rev. J. Saunders—
Buckinghamshire Association Circular Letter, 1844.

THERE ARE THREE CATALOGUES—

I.—Alphabetical. II.—Arranged according to Subjects.

III.—Arranged according to Authors.

An order to use the Library must be obtained of the Secretary of the Baptist Union. Books are not allowed to be taken away.

Baptist Authors are requested to present to the Library a copy of each of their works during the year of publication.

Works on Ecclesiastical History and Modern Criticism are specially needed to add to the many valuable works already in the Library.

The Secretary will be greatly obliged if friends having copies of the *Baptist Manual* will communicate with him on the subject.

PART II.

BAPTIST UNION OF GREAT BRITAIN AND IRELAND.

PRESIDENTIAL ADDRESSES AND PAPERS READ BEFORE THE ASSEMBLY.

1863.—*London.*

Progress of the Baptists in the last Sixty Years ..	Rev. J. Angus, D.D.
State of the Baptist Denomination in Wales ..	Rev. T. Thomas, D.D.
State of the Baptist Denomination in Scotland ..	Rev. J. Patterson, D.D.
State of the Baptist Denomination in Ireland ..	Rev. C. J. Middleditch.

1864.—*London.*

President's Address	Rev. J. P. Mursell.
The Spiritual Aspects of the Churches	Hon. and Rev. B. W. Noel, [M.A.
Our Associations	Rev. C. Williams.
Chapel Building Finance	Mr. A. T. Bowser.
Ecclesiastical Relations	Rev. C. Stovel.

Birmingham.

President's Address	Rev. J. P. Mursell.
Romanism and Rationalism	Rev. G. Gould.
The General Baptist Denomination	Rev. W. Underwood, D.D.
The Influence of the Present Times on Personal Religion	Rev. C. M. Birrell.
Church Work in large Towns	Rev. J. P. Chown.
Individual Effort for the Conversion of Sinners ..	Hon. and Rev. B. W. Noel, [M.A.

1865.—*London.*

Baptists: Their Existence a Present Necessity ..	Rev. J. Angus, D.D.
Difficulties of the Village Ministry	Rev. J. T. Brown.

Bradford.

Christian Churches: their success proportionate to the presence and grace of the Holy Spirit..	Rev. J. Angus, D.D.
Our Colleges	Rev. N. Haycroft, M.A.
Our Associations	Rev. J. Mursell.

1866.—*London.*

The Nature and Claims of Dissent	Rev. J. Aldis.
Religious Beneficence among the Baptists ..	Rev. W. R. Stevenson, M.A.

Liverpool.

The Duty and Advantages of Domestic Worship ..	Rev. J. Aldis.
The Financial Duties of the Deacon's Office ..	Mr. James Benham.
Thoughts on Public Worship	Rev. S. G. Green, B.A.
The British and Irish Baptist Home Mission ..	Rev. C. Kirtland.
The Jamaica Insurrection	Mr. E. B. Underhill, LL.D.

1867.—*London.*

Sacerdotalism in the Church of England	Hon. and Rev. B. W. Noel, M.A.
The Ritualism of Churchmen and the Duties of Dissenters	Rev. C. Vince.

Cardiff.

A Brief View of the Churches associated in the Union	Hon. and Rev. B. W. Noel, M.A.
Baptist Principles and Religious Liberty	Rev. W. Walters.
Woman's Work in the Church	Rev. J. Jenkyn Brown.
Ministerial Education in Wales	Rev. T. Davies, D.D.
The Sacramental Theory of the Lord's Supper ..	Rev. G. Gould.

1868.—*London.*

The Special Duties of Baptists at the present time	Rev. F. W. Gotch, LL.D.
National Education	Rev. S. G. Green, B.A.

Bristol.

Christ the Centre	Rev. F. W. Gotch, LL D.
Ministerial Failures	Rev. W. Landels, D.D.
The Baptist College, Bristol; its History, Students, and Treasures	Rev. F. Bosworth, M.A.

1869.—*London.*

The Unstable and the Stable	Rev. W. Brock, D.D.
Church Membership, its Law and its Method ..	Rev. C. Bailhache.

Leicester.

Our Position to-day	Rev. W. Brock, D.D.
The Policy of Nonconformists in view of Ecclesiastical Disestablishment	Rev. C. Williams.
The Best Means of Overtaking the Religious Destitution of our large Towns	Rev. C. Short, M.A.
The Relation of the Sunday-school to the Congregation and the Church	Mr. S. R. Pattison.
Precision in Doctrine	Rev. D. Gracey.
The Essential Spirit of Puritanism in Relation to the Needs of To-day	Rev. W. T. Rosevear.

1870.—*London.*

The Foundation of our Faith	Rev. W. Robinson.
Improvement in the Mode of Public Worship ..	Rev. C. Stanford, D.D.

Cambridge.

A Few Lines of Baptist History and their Lessons	Rev. W. Robinson.
The Influence of Business on the Christian Life..	Rev. J. J. Goadby.
Missing Links in our Church Life	Rev. W. Brock, jun.

1871.—*London.*

The Character Demanded by the Times	Rev. C. M. Birrell.
The Best Means of Evangelizing the Masses ..	Mr. H. M. Bompas, M.A.

Northampton.

Northampton Memories	Rev. C. M. Birrell.
Arbitration	Mr. S. R. Pattison, F.G.S.
Education for the Ministry	Rev. S. G. Green, D.D.

1872.—*London.*

The Kingdom of Christ in Relation to the Aspects of the Present Time	Rev. T. Thomas, D.D.
The Divine Order of Christian Work	Rev. J. Culross, D.D.

Manchester.

The Baptists and Christian Union	Rev. T. Thomas, D.D.
Our Progress: Statistical and Spiritual	Rev. J. Angus, D.D.
The Religious Aspect of National Education ..	Rev. C. Stovel.

1873.—*London.*

Our Position as Baptists	Mr. E. B. Underhill, LL.D.

Nottingham.

The History of Baptist Missions	Mr. E. B. Underhill, LL.D.
The Changes Required in Sunday-school Education	Rev. R. Evans.
The Promotion of Spiritual Life among the Ministers of the Churches	Rev. G. Short, B.A.
The Increase of Spiritual Life in our Churches ..	Rev. T. Goadby, B.A.
An Appeal for our Foreign Missions	Rev. C. B. Lewis.
Ritualism	Rev. W. Landels, D.D.

1874.—*London.*

The Rule of our Fellowship	Rev. C. Stovel.
The Revival in the North cf England	Rev. J. Mursell.

Newcastle-on-Tyne.

The Privileges of our Fellowship	Rev. C. Stovel.
How may Members of Churches best help their Ministers?	Rev. J. Watson.
British and Irish Home Missions	Rev. J. Bigwood.
The Desirability of a Closer Connection between the Baptist Union and the leading Baptist Societies	Rev. R. Glover.

1875.—*London.*

The Gospel for the Day	Rev. A. McLaren, D.D.
Our Relation to Certain Religious Aspects of the Time	Rev. C. Bailhache.

Plymouth.

The Outward Business of the House of God .. Rev. A. McLaren, D.D.
Brethren Lately Deceased .. .. Rev. R. James.
The Early Baptists in Devon: their History, Sufferings, and Character .. .. .. Rev. F. Bosworth, M.A.
The Services to be Rendered by Young Men in the Work of the Churches .. .. .. Rev. T. Wilkinson.

1876.—*London.*

Our Denominational Position Internally and Externally Surveyed .. .. Rev. W. Landels, D.D.
Religious Education in Board Schools .. .. Rev. E. C. Pike, B.A.

Birmingham.

Our Duty as Baptists .. .. Rev. W. Landels, D.D.
Religious Life in the Rural Districts of England Rev. J. Clifford, M.A., LL.B.

1877.—*London.*

Christ and the Church.. .. .. Rev. J. T. Brown.

Newport, Monmouthshire.

The Ministry and Work of the Church in Relation to the People of Our Lord .. .. Rev. J. T. Brown.
The Evangelization of Cities and Villages.. .. Rev. J. H. Millard, B.A.
Welsh Churches and their Lessons .. .. Rev. J. Owen.

1878.—*London.*

Ministerial Apprenticeship .. .. Rev. H. S. Brown.
The Best Method of Calling Forth and Cultivating Local Evangelists in our Churches .. Rev. J. Aldis.
The Best Means of Using Unpaid Local Evangelists in our Churches in Town and Country .. .. Rev. J. R. Wood.

Leeds.

An Appeal to Well-Educated Young Men to Enter the Christian Ministry .. .. Rev. H. S. Brown.
Forms of Worldliness Prevalent in the Christian Church .. .. Rev. R. H. Marten, B.A.
Home Mission Work .. .. Rev. J. H. Millard, B.A.

1879.—*London.*

Our Present Outlook .. .. Rev. G. Gould.
The Evangelistic Work of the Baptist Union .. Rev. E. G. Gange.

Glasgow.

The Use and Disuse of Confessions of Faith .. Rev. G. Gould.
Our Attitude in Relation to the Prevalent Unsettlement of Religious Opinion and Belief.. Rev. W. Medley, M.A.

1880.—*London* (twice)

The Past and the Present .. .. Rev. F. Trestrail, D.D.
On the Moral Tendency and Influence of Infidelity Rev. F. Trestrail, D.D.
The Claims of Mission Work on the Support of the Churches .. .. Rev. J. B. Myers.

The Reality and Power of Evangelistic Work Dependent on the Spiritual Life of the Churches	Rev. J. W. Lance.
The Spirit and Method of Evangelistic Work ..	Rev. H. E. Stone.
Union Funds and Home Missions	Rev. W. Sampson.

1881.—*London.*

Our Union in Connection with the First Principles of Divine Truth	Rev. H. Dowson.
The Present Position and Prospects of the Annuity Fund	Rev. W. Landels, D.D.

Portsmouth and Southampton.

Spiritual Life in Connection with the Assemblies and Operations of the Union	Rev. H. Dowson.
The Condition and Needs of our Village Churches	Rev. G. W. Humphreys, B.A.
Christian Liberty in Relation to Modern Life ..	Rev. W. Brock.
Evangelistic Labour a Necessity of Christian Life	Rev. J. Stuart.

1882.—*London.*

The Spirit we need for our Time and Work ..	Rev. J. J. Brown.
The Church and the World	Mr. W. P. Lockhart.

Liverpool.

Practical Aspects of Church Life	Rev. J. J. Brown.
The Duties and Responsibilities of Church Membership	Rev. R. Lewis.
Evangelistic Church Work in Large Towns ..	Rev. T. V. Tymms.

1883.—*London.*

Christ in Christian	Rev. J. P. Chown.
The Union and the Associations	Rev. W. Woods.

Leicester.

Lessons from Leicester	Rev. J. P. Chown.
The Changes Passing over Religious Thought, and the Spirit in which we should meet them	Rev. B. Bird.
Christians not in Church Fellowship	Rev. W. C. Upton.
Church Life and Discipline	Rev. W. R. Skerry.
Church Finance	Mr. W. Payne.
Family Religion	Rev. C. Stanford D.D.

1884.—*London.*

The Gift of Prophecy	Rev. R. Glover, D.D.
Truths Essential to Church Prosperity	Rev. W. Anderson.
Glad Service	Rev. J. Aldis.

Bradford.

The Work of the Church To-day	Rev. R. Glover, D.D.
The Economy of Spiritual Power in our Churches	Rev. W. S. Davis.
The Pastor in the Sunday School	Rev. S. G. Green, D.D.
Juvenile Discipleship, and How to Deal with it ..	Rev. J. R. Wood.
The Progress of the Baptist Denomination during the last Twenty Years	Rev. J. Angus, D.D.
The Progress of the Church of Christ in this Country during the last Twenty Years ..	Rev. C. Williams.

1885.—*London.*

Signs of Revival	Rev. S. G. Green, D.D.
The Responsibilities of Church Members.. ..	Mr. J. Templeton, F.R.G.S.
The Quiet Heart	Rev. J. Culross, D.D.

Swansea.

The Kingdom of Christ	Rev. S. G. Green, D.D.
The Religious Condition of Wales	Rev. J. Jones (Felinfoel).
The Public and Private Use of the Revised Version of the Bible	Rev. H. C. Leonard, M.A.
The Answer of the Christian Church to the Bitter Cry of the Poor	Rev. W. Edwards, B.A.
Elder Classes: the Link Between the Sunday School and the Church	Mr. J. E. Tresidder.

1886.—*London.*

A Plea for Union among Baptists	Rev. C. Williams.
The Attitude of the Rural Populations to Christianity	Rev. T. M. Morris.
The Difficulties of our Village Churches	Rev. G. Jarman.
Our Duties as a Denomination to the Rural Districts	Rev. J. J. Brown.
The Strength and Beauty of the Sanctuary ..	Rev. F. Tucker, B.A.

Bristol.

A Plea for Puritanism..	Rev. C. Williams.
A Ministry of Power the Necessity of the Times	Rev. J. Clifford, M.A., D.D
Suggestions for the Formation of a Board of Reference	Mr. W. M. Fuller.
The Training of Sunday School Teachers ..	Mr. A. Sindall.
The Spiritual Harvest of the Sunday School ..	Mr. G. White.
The Best Means of Maintaining the Spirituality of our Church Membership	Rev. J. T. Briscoe.
The Best Methods of Using the Power of our Churches	Rev. J. R. Wood.

1887.—*London.*

The Testimony of Life	Rev. J. Culross, D.D.
Our Prayer Meetings	Rev. J. Aldis.

Sheffield.

Dost Thou Believe on the Son of God?	Rev. J. Culross, D.D.
The Churches and the Coming Ministry	Rev. G. P. Gould, M.A.
The Work of the Church amongst the Young ..	Rev. S. R. Aldridge, B.A., LL.B.
Fellowship Considered in some of its Ideal Aspects	Rev. E. Medley, B.A.
Church Fellowship	Rev. W. Landels, D.D.

1888.—*London.*

The Great Forty Years; or, the Primitive Christian Faith, its real Substance and best Defence	Rev. J. Clifford, M.A., D.D
The Supernatural the Essential Element in Church Life	Rev. T. G. Tarn.
Lay Preaching and Rural Nonconformity.. ..	Rev. W. Bishop.

Huddersfield.

The New City of God; or, the Primitive Christian Faith as a Social Gospel	Rev. J. Clifford, M.A., D.D.
The Perils of a Pleasure-loving Age; with Special Reference to the Young	Rev. T. V. Tymms.
The Cultivation of the Devout Life..	Rev. F. B. Meyer, B.A.
Family Religion	Rev. W. Cuff.

1889.—*London.*

Our Life in Christ, that Life for Him: or, Christ Living in us, we Living for Him	Rev. J. T. Wigner.
Young Women's Guilds	Mrs. Edward Medley.
Guilds for Young Men..	Mr. D. F. Gotch.
Higher Biblical Criticism	Rev. J. W. Todd, D.D.
The Relations of Employer and Employed in the Light of the Social Gospel	Mr. T. W. Bushill.

Birmingham.

Christian Citizenship	Rev. J. T. Wigner.
Woman's Work in the Church	Mrs. Dawson Burns.
Child Life in England: its Perils and our Duties	Rev. B. Waugh.
Some Phases of Ministerial Life and Work ..	Rev. J. Culross, M.A., D.D.
The Development and Perfecting of the Work of Local Preaching	Mr. Alderman W. R. Wherry.

1890.—*London.*

An Effective Ministry of the Word	Rev. J. Owen.
Sunday Morning Classes for Adults	Mr. Alderman W. White.
Centre and Suburb: a Plea for Christian Work in Large Towns	Rev. J. J. Brown.
The Growth of Clericalism	Rev. C. W. Vick.

Cardiff.

The Free Churches and the People	Rev. J. Owen.
The Culture of the Devout Life	Revs. J. P. Clark, M.A., and J. R. Russell.
The Organisation of Local Preachers	Mr. G. M. Carlile.
The Instruction of our Young People in Nonconformist Principles	Mr. C. A. Vince, M.A.
The Claim which our Churches have on the Best Services of their Best Men	Rev. W. Brock.
Charm in Church Life	Rev. G. Hawker.

1891.—*London.*

A Voice from the Pew	Col. J. T. Griffin.
Evangelistic and Philanthropic Work outside our own Churches	Rev. J. P. Tetley.
The Right Use of Wealth	Mr. A. Briggs, J.P.
The Sense of Responsibility for Personal Sin ..	Rev. G. Hill, M.A.
Individualism and Socialism..	Rev. J. G. Greenhough, M.A.

Manchester.

The Greater Forty Years; or, The Progress of Christ's Kingdom during the last Four Decades	Col. J. T. Griffin.
Our Colleges	Rev. J. Culross, D.D.
The Work of the Church for Elder Scholars ..	Mr. A. White.
Women's Work among the Sick Poor	Miss Farrer, M.B., B.S.
Women's Work in Connection with the Social Condition of the Poor	Miss Edith A. Angus.
The Christian Conception of Society	Rev. J. Clifford, M.A., D.D.

1892.—*London* (twice).

The Witness of the Bible to itself	Rev. R. H. Roberts, B.A.
Baptist Church Extension in Large Towns ..	Rev. J. H. Shakespeare, M.A.
The Witness of the Bible to the Kingdom of Heaven upon earth	Rev. R. H. Roberts, B.A.
Divine Power, the Need and the Heritage of Christian Workers	Rev. W. J. Henderson, B.A.

1893.—*London.*

Our Greatest Need	Rev. T. M. Morris.
Church Worship—	
Prayer	Rev. J. Bailey, B.A.
Praise	Rev. H. Bonner.
Labour Problems in the Light of the Gospel ..	Rev. J. C. Carlile, M.L.S.B.

Reading.

Our Proper Work	Rev. T. M. Morris.
The Better Equipment of Sunday School Teachers in View of the Demands of our Age	Rev. C. Brown.

1894.—*London.*

Baptists in Relation to other Christians and to some of the Special Questions of the Day ..	Rev. G. Short, B.A.
Ministerial Life and Work—	
The Aim and Results of an Evangelical Ministry	Rev. W. E. Winks.
The Distinctively Pastoral Relation of the Minister to his People	Rev. L. G. Carter.
The Spirit in which we should regard the Present Phases of Biblical Criticism	Rev. S. Vincent.

Newcastle-on-Tyne.

The Religious Instruction of the Young	Rev. G. Short, B.A.
Young People's Societies of Christian Endeavour	Rev. J. Stuart.
Indifference to Religion: its Roots and Remedies	Rev. J. R. Wood.
Broken Ideals	Rev. J. Thew.

1895.—*London.*

A Puritan Message to the Democracy	Rev. J. G. Greenhough, M.A.
The Betting Fever	Rev. J. Baillie.
Our Church Polity in relation to the Churches ..	Rev. R. Glover, D.D.
Our Church Polity in relation to the Pastors ..	Rev. J. Thew.
Consecration to Christ	Rev. B. Bird.

Portsmouth.

A Free Churchman's Thoughts about the Church	Rev. J. G. Greenhough, M.A.
Hymnody in our Churches	Rev. S. G. Green, D.D.
Hymnody in Mission Services	Rev. F. C. Spurr.
"Help Clement also"..	Rev. W. J. Styles.

PROCEEDINGS OF THE SPRING ASSEMBLY,

HELD IN

LONDON,

April 22nd, 23rd, 24th and 25th, 1895.

MONDAY, APRIL 23RD.

BLOOMSBURY CHAPEL.

HOME MISSION SERMON.

At noon, Rev. H. Arnold Thomas, M.A., of Bristol, preached the Annual Sermon on behalf of the Home Mission, from Romans x., 1.

FIRST SESSION.

DEVOTIONAL SERVICE.

At three o'clock a Devotional Service was held, conducted by the retiring President, Rev. G. Short, B.A. Prayer was offered by Rev. D. P. McPherson, B.D., of Exeter, and Mr. H. Dibben, of London.

NEW PRESIDENT.

At the close of this service, Mr. Short introduced, as his successor to the Chair, Rev. J. G. Greenhough, M.A., whose first business was to appoint the following gentlemen as

SCRUTINEERS

For the election of the Council and the Vice-President:—Rev. A. B. Middleditch (Convener), Mr. J. Carter, Mr. J. A. Curtis, Rev. R. A. Elvey, Rev. F. James, Mr. H. W. Pewtress, Mr. J. Ryan, Mr. J. Sheen, and Mr. H. W. Smith.

ANNUAL REPORT.

The Annual Report of the Council, copies of which had been circulated in the Assembly, was adopted on the motion of the Secretary, seconded by Mr. J. A. Compston, of Leeds.

HOME MISSION CENTENARY.

The following resolution was moved by Rev. C. Brown, of London, seconded by Mr. Alderman D. Clarke, of High Wycombe, Chairman of the Home Mission Committee, and carried unanimously:—

> "That this Assembly having heard the Report of the Council with regard to the urgent need for a larger income on behalf of the Home Mission, in order to continue the work already undertaken, and meet the pressing and increasing call for further help, and in view of the interesting fact that the Mission will attain its Centenary in 1897, hereby resolves that the Churches and Associations be requested to arrange for the making of collections and the gathering of subscriptions to further the work of the Mission, and worthily commemorate the Centenary by securing an adequate permanent increase of the Fund, and authorizes the Council to make an appeal accordingly."

ELECTION OF VICE-PRESIDENT.

Rev. A. B. Middleditch, on behalf of the Scrutineers, announced, in accordance with Bye-law I., as the result of a second ballot, the election of Rev. Thomas Vincent Tymms, of Rawdon College, as Vice-President of the Union for the ensuing year, and Mr. Tymms briefly responded, accepting the office.

ELECTION OF OFFICERS AND AUDITORS.

The election of the Officers of the Union and of Auditors for its Funds was moved from the Chair, seconded by Mr. R.

Cleaver, J.P., of Northampton, and unanimously carried as follows:—

(1) Officers:—(*a*) Treasurer—Mr. W. W. Baynes, J.P.
(*b*) Secretary—Rev. S. H Booth, D.D.

(2) Auditors:

(*a*) General Expenses Fund—Mr. W. E. Cove and Mr. B. W. Chandler, F.C.A.

(*b*) Home Mission Fund—Mr. H. R. Parker, Mr. H. Potter and Mr. B. W. Chandler, F.C.A.

(*c*) Church Extension Fund—Mr. A. T. Chew, Mr. R. Gordon and Mr. B. W. Chandler, F.C.A.

(*d*) Annuity Fund—Mr. A. Faulkner, Mr. A. Gurney Smith and Mr. B. W. Chandler, F.C.A.

(*e*) Augmentation Fund—Mr. J. Winterton and Mr. B. W. Chandler, F.C.A.

(*f*) Literature and Education Funds—Mr. Percy C. Webb and Mr. B. W. Chandler, F.C.A.

On the motion of the Secretary, the Session was adjourned at 5 p.m.

PUBLIC WORSHIP.

At seven o'clock, worship was conducted by the Vice-President, who read Psalm cxlv. and Acts iii., 24 to iv., 12.

PRESIDENT'S ADDRESS.

The President then delivered the following address:—

A PURITAN MESSAGE TO THE DEMOCRACY.

AMONG the various centenary celebrations of recent years there has been perhaps none more remarkable than the latest—the tercentenary of Archbishop Laud. It is not surprising that it awakened little interest—that most Churchmen ignored it, and not a few wished it had been let alone. The surprising thing is that it should have been thought of at all. To set up an image of Laud, and summon all men by sound of clerical sackbut and psaltery to come and bow down to it, is one of those anachronisms at which patience grows angry and charity smiles. The Bishop of Peterborough half apologized for the attempt by confessing *that the search* for heroes in those times was fruitless. We can understand his difficulty, though we do not share it. The exigencies of his position limited the field of his research; yet surely the annals of the Episcopal Church are not so barren of great names and memories worth reviving, that it must needs give this man a foremost place in its martyr roll, and invest him with the saint's aureola. The man who represented and embodied in his small person and unexpansive mind all those distorted views and stifling principles which our English nation has grown out of, and is almost ashamed to remember: the sworn foe of political and religious liberty, the champion of a close and cruel intolerance, the fussy inquisitor, the ubiquitous spy, the man who lost the patriot in the priest, the Christian in the ecclesiastic, the man in the machinery, the idolator of form and uniform, slave of etiquette and master of postures, who substituted gewgaws for grace, candles for conscience, rubrics for righteousness, and dead works for a living God. Surely it were better that this man should be allowed to slumber on in the oblivion to which kindly time has consigned him. There are some graves which it is well not to disturb. Even after the lapse of centuries the ashes do not smell sweet. Requiescat! we can easily forgive if we are only permitted to forget.

But this attempt to glorify Laud deserves our commendation in one respect. In these days it is refreshing to find people who are not ashamed of their forefathers—who believe that great men lived before the giants of the nineteenth century arose, and that the past is not a museum of forsaken idols and fossilised stupidities, but a pantheon of hallowed figures and a storehouse of inspiring memories. To mistake the objects of our reverence is an intellectual or moral blunder, but to have no reverence at all is the sin against the Holy Ghost. To glorify those who were unworthy of it is to follow marsh lights instead of heavenly stars, but to recognise no light save that which flashes from modern mirrors is to see our own faces in a glass and call them the faces of the Almighty. This age is too much disposed to fling scorn upon the dead: to fancy that their heroisms were crazes, their ideals delusions, and their thoughts childish gropings in the dark. We are afraid of not being up to date. The charge of being old-fashioned frightens a great many people out of their convictions, and some few out of their wits. We must have new altars, new prophets, and, alas, a "new woman." Our systems have issued from the Patent Office marked absolutely original. Our "isms" are of yesterday if they are not of to-day. Some of our theologies are like spring birds recently fledged—vain enough to think that their untried wings can carry them higher than St. Paul's soarings. We have even new Churches of which our fathers were ignorant—a Labour Church, a Church of Humanity, a

Church of Our Father, and a Church born in an Editor's room begotten by a Reviewer of Reviews, and happily stillborn. "Mons parturit et nascitur ridiculus mus." There is a popular idea that this modern age sprang fully formed like Athena from some Zeus's wise head: there was no groaning and travailing in pain to produce it. It was not the fruit of other men's labour. It was self-created. Its own wisdom laid the egg from which it was hatched.

But this self-conceit is the child of ignorance. If we despise our fathers it is because we do not understand them. We are so engrossed with the novel and the newspaper that we have not time to look back, and we think the clatter of modern tongues perfect music because they are the only voices we have heard.

And not to know the past is to misread the present. The problems of to-day are the outcome of many yesterdays. He who knows not what his fathers thought cannot think wisely himself. There is historical continuity in all things. We cannot build lasting fabrics with absolutely new material; there must be at least the old rock underneath if the bricks and mortar are modern. Our secularisms, socialisms, materialisms, agnosticisms, some of our very humanitarianisms have no solidity because they have no underground. We have seen them "spreading like a green bay tree," and we shall see the other thing which the Psalmist saw. They are the seed on stony ground which springs up forthwith, because it has no root and presently withers away. Men do not live on fashions but on faiths. We get our opinions, fads and fashions from floating things in the circumambient air; convictions are rooted in the deep soil of the past. Our thoughts are shaped, coloured and directed by the movements and exigencies of the time, but if they have any substance it is supplied by the best thoughts and doings of the great ones whom we have left behind.

"Those dead but sceptred sovereigns who still rule our spirits from their urns."

Forgive this somewhat stale philosophy, and bear with me as I try to point the application. I wish to speak about the men whom Laud vainly tried to squeeze into his ecclesiastical moulds, and shape into an unlovely and diminutive uniformity: the men with whom he carried on that battle of the dead letter against the living spirit, which always ends in one way, and which ended for him in a way that was not convenient. I wish to ask if those old Puritans have any message for the new age—for the democracy in particular, and if possible to look at certain questions of the day through Puritan eyes.

Perhaps to the general world whose fashion is to sneer at these men that it may be saved the trouble of understanding them, the proposal to learn anything from this quarter may seem as absurd as to animate fossils, or push back the wheels of time. But not to you: "Ye are the children of the prophets," not yet wholly ashamed of your ancestry, possessing, I trust, some of their spirit, and at least patient enough to bear with one who thinks that they were far above our scorning, and that some of the light which they had was not only clearer than Laud's candles, but more heavenly than the electric brilliance in which we walk.

I am not going to do them injustice by unmeasured and unqualified praise. Walking in their company one should at least learn to be honest and truthful, for they were nothing if they were not that; and either to extenuate their faults or laud extravagantly their virtues would be to offend their memories and prove that we are wanting in their best qualities. We understand many things better than they did. We take wider views because we stand upon their shoulders, and illumination from various sources has fallen upon human problems, and upon God's own revelation, which they were not privileged to see. The heavens have not been shut up through these centuries, nor has the praying heart found the vision always sealed and waited in vain for the fuller light to break through the clouds. To accept the Puritan theology as a complete and authoritative statement of God's thought is to credit men with omniscience, and to place a human limitation on the outflow of the Divine Spirit. To moor ourselves to that old anchorage is indeed to be safe from "every changeful wind of doctrine," but it is also to feel no more the mighty current of living spiritual force which bore them on to greatness.

The soul of Puritanism lives for ever, but some of the forms in which it appeared fall away. The body decays, it is even buried, the spirit survives. Every earnest age is animated by it afresh. Whenever Christ's power is unusually felt Puritanism comes from its grave again like Lazarus, but not to walk among living men in the grave clothes in which it was buried. It is arrayed in new garments of beauty and praise.

We have learned things which they knew not, or only saw "through a glass darkly," and which we would not willingly let go. We would not exchange the throbbing, tender, pitiful heart of this age for the sterner thoughts which gave them heroic strength, but often froze up the fountain of their tears. The sweet humanities of our times, the gentler sentiments, the broader charities, the larger hopes, we would not lose, even to get back their more virile faith, and rock-like righteousness.

They saw the majesty and sovereignty of God, His holiness and power, with eyes of awe and reverence to which we are strangers. They stooped lower at His feet in self-abasement than we do, and therefore were lifted up higher. But in veiling their faces from the splendour they lost sight of that rainbow which is around the throne, and of which the rain-drops are surely Divine tears. They believed that the throne of the universe was established in righteous and irresistible power, and the touch of Almightiness upon them made them mighty, but they sometimes forgot that in the midst of the throne there is a gentle and suffering Lamb, and that the central and deepest force of all is love, pity, and self-sacrifice. We know these things better than they did, not because we are wiser, more thoughtful, more logical, better theologians, we are not; but because we have done what the Master advised, we have carried into the study of these things more of the child's heart, and "the things which were hidden from the wise and prudent have been revealed unto babes."

I am more anxious, however, to emphasise the points in which they were, and still are, our masters. It is far easier to criticise their limitations than to take a just measure of their moral magnitude. The nineteenth century cannot get a proper perspective of the seventeenth. We are too luxurious to appreciate the Puritan's simplicities, too much the servants of forms and conventions to understand his rigorous sincerities, too pleasure-loving to give him credit for an honest disdain of the world's frivolities. Above all, we are not sufficiently imbued with religious thought to enter into the feelings of men who lived in the presence of God continually, who felt His hand upon them in their daily thoughts and work, who talked about Him as naturally as we talk about the weather or politics or business, and who carried a spirit of prayer into every resolve and act of their lives. Think how far we have left that religious atmosphere behind in which five hundred English gentlemen, members of Parliament, could kneel down together on the floor of the House of Commons, crying to God on behalf of their poor country, and shedding tears copiously as they prayed. Imagine the present House of Commons doing this, with Mr. Labouchere leading the supplications; think what a power of imagination is needed to reproduce that scene, and then judge how remote that world is from ours. It is so much the fashion now, indeed, to keep what religious convictions we have discreetly hidden in our own breasts, save on the stated occasions of worship, that we find it hard to believe in the absolute sincerity of men who spoke without reserve, in all *scenes* and companies, in letters and business transactions and political speeches, about their faith in God, and the solemnities of the world to come; and alas! there are comparatively few men now who could do it without some measure of affectation and unreality, because there are few who walk close enough to God to give the clear and honest ring to such language. We would gladly forego some of our modern accomplishments and crafts to get back the temper and spirit of men who did all their work under the great Taskmaster's eyes; who needed no press criticism to keep them up to their public duties; no paid overseers to watch them at their humbler labours, who believed that every word, action, and thought was weighed and scanned by Him, who walked always in the searching light of Divine omniscience, and in view of the judgment throne. It would save us from some fears and forebodings concerning the immediate future; it might even be better for our commercial interests, and it would certainly contribute greatly to the purifying of national morals if that searching light were felt a little more on the Stock Exchange, in the rooms where limited liability companies are floated and directed, and in the factories where the operative thinks that it is to the interest of his class to do as little work as possible. In these days when the law is so imposingly elaborate, and yet so impotent; the press so lynx-eyed, and yet so blind; and Trades' Unions so solicitous about increase of wages and shortening of hours, and often so indifferent about the conscientious discharge of duty, it would be an advantage, indeed, if we could add to the resources of civilization a little more of what those less polished fathers of ours called the fear of God.

And, truly, if the new democracy were not so intolerant of everything that is old, it might improve its temper and learn some lessons of moderation, and even of wisdom in the Puritan school. That school was the Bethlehem of the new age. The open Bible gave it birth, and it was cradled in Puritan homes. Then and there man discovered his own worth. He swept aside priestly veils and laid himself open to the direct light of God, and in that light he stood self-revealed. It showed him the infinite value of the individual soul, the preciousness of each single life in the eyes of the Redeemer, and the unconquerable energy of each single soul when allied by faith with the Almighty. There he found himself exalted to be a king and priest by divine right, ennobled by the imposition of a mightier hand than that of princes, raised immeasurably in the scale of being, and energized with a wonderful consciousness of human dignity. Puritanism was the upspringing of a new and larger manhood, in the presence of which titles and degrees, social distinctions, intellectual superiorities, and even royal pretensions became of slight and almost contemptible importance. From that fountain issued the ever broadening current of modern democracy which is carrying us all along to unknown and doubtful issues, issues however, which are only to be dreaded if the religious spirit which originated the movement is trampled out by gross material and secular forces. The Puritans believed that man was great not by virtue of his humanity, but by virtue of his kinship with God. He was nothing unless he was a temple of the Divine. It was the fatherhood of God that ennobled him. It was faith and spiritual receptivity that made him strong. It was moral qualities that gave him all his worth. They knew nothing of the modern rant which claims for all men a natural equality, which professes a sort of sublime indifference to moral distinctions, which demands for the indolent and thriftless the rewards of the sober and dutiful, and which in its insane endeavours to force a general levelling up would bring about a universal levelling down. The Puritans were not so blind to facts. The common talk about human equality is mere bubble blowing. Start from a religious foundation and there is some ground for it. Set it in the light of God and it may bear examination; acknowledge that we are the children of God, and alike dear to Him, and it may be thought of, but apart from that it is a theory which explodes in laughter. It is absurd to suppose that all inequalities are produced by social conditions. They are aggravated and intensified, undoubtedly, but with the most favourable social conditions most of them would remain. We are not born equal or gifted equally. We are born with an amazing and sometimes awful diversity of mental and bodily powers, clever and dull, feeble as cripples or abounding in energy, capable of only the lowest work, or fit for works of genius. And no contrivances can make men equal. Though you were to proclaim equality by a thousand Acts of Parliament you would not render it a fact or induce the world to believe it. And in every society, no matter how constituted, and though you employed all the machinery which collectivism could devise to chain men down to the same level, the inequality would assert itself, and there would be leaders and led, and the morally strong would get to the front, and the weak would be left in the rear, and in spite of all you could do to prevent it there would be diversity of rewards.

It is only in the sight of God and in our relationship to God that there can be anything approximating to human equality. Some puny crippled child says to his big strong brother, "I am in all things equal to you," and the brother good-humouredly laughs. "Yes," the feeble one says, "for my father thinks as much *of me* as he does of you. I am as dear in my mother's eyes as you are." Then the big brother takes the little one up in his arms and says, "Yes, that is true, we are equal, and for father's sake and for your sake because you are so weak, I will help to carry you until we reach the journey's end." I can understand that. That is Christian equality. Whatever we are, strong or feeble, brilliant or commonplace, capable of the highest work or only fit for drudgery, we have the same place at God's feet, the same share in His love. He does not think less of us because we can only limp along in the rear. "It is not His will that the least of His little ones should perish," and it is only as men feel that and recognise the obligation of brotherhood, and not by any forcing socialistic process, that we can attain to any real sense of human equality.

The doctrine of human brotherhood has no meaning save that which the Puritans gave to it. They found it in the Divine fatherhood. If they put limits upon the Divine fatherhood which to some of us are unwarranted, that is not the question. At least they were not guilty of the modern absurdity of thinking that there can be a family without a parentage. To-day some of the men who are most urgent in pressing the claims of human brotherhood are the men who want us to throw down our altars and put God out of our thoughts. We are to worship humanity, without knowing whence it came or whither it goes. They do not believe that we ever had a father, but they are clamorous in asserting that we are brothers. It is possible that we came not from Adam but from apes—nay, the latest scientific theory is that the origin of all things was a cell—the word is spelt with a "c"—and yet we are all brothers. What stuff is this? What is it but stealing the clothes of Christianity and rejecting the living body of it? It is playing with fine words that once had a meaning and have lost it. What makes brotherhood but fatherhood? How can there be a family if there has never been a parent? All this is juggling with names, and not even clever jugglery, for a child can see through the trick. Fraternity on a basis of materialism and agnosticism is an inverted pyramid, or like a spinning-top kept going by incessant lashing. There is no reason apart from God why the man of refinement and elevated thought should admit to brotherhood the man of soddened intellect and coarse nature; no reason why the strong should bear the burdens of the weak; no reason why the dismal science of political economy should not have free course, and self-interest be made supreme. It is only as we walk in the light Divine that we have fellowship one with another. We are united in family bonds by that same "golden chain of prayer" which binds us to the feet of the Father, and without that all the grand humanitarian sentiments which are so much boasted of would perish as lighted faggots go out when they are flung off from the parent fire.

The aim and ideal of modern democracy points to the equal elevation of all, and to that end it seeks the sweeping away of law-made distinctions, and of all fictitious and artificial superiorities. It is an ambition with which in all its nobler aspects we are in profound sympathy. Our ears are open to the bitter cries of city life, to the complaints of the unprivileged classes, and our hearts are with them in their aspirations after a better lot. If it were otherwise we should have no part with the Master. We want to see men everywhere rise to a proper conception of manhood, and endowed with power to become sons of God. "It shall come to pass in that day that the feeblest shall be as David and David as an angel of God." But the way to accomplish that is not to bring David down to the stature of the feeblest. The Puritan doctrine of election finds little favour now either among the proletariat or in Christian circles. It is often treated with a grimace, and to venture a word in its defence would be to place oneself among antiquarian curiosities. Yet the derision which it provokes is the derision of superficial minds—minds which have not discernment enough to distinguish between the husk and the grain. There is an imperishable body of truth beneath the changing form. "The outward man perisheth, but the inward man is renewed from day to day." There is always an election of grace. God carries the world forward by the instrumentality of leading spirits. He lifts the mass of men up through the few who are specially endowed with gifts and goodness; the sunlight shines upon the hilltop before it reaches the valleys below; the earth is saved by the salt of the earth. If we have no excellence in the front ranks we shall have less than mediocrity in the host behind. One may discern in the democracy a growing impatience of every kind of superiority. Its cry is "Make no more giants, God, but elevate the race"; and that cry recalls an older saying, "Whom the Gods wish to destroy they first make mad." If God makes no more giants we shall all be dwarfs. Let us beware lest in our crusade against individualism we crush individuality, and in our impatience of social differences abolish moral excellence. Pictures of a socialistic paradise, where all shall be equally strong and happy, are charming in the distance; seen close at hand they are made up of men and women as dull and uniform as waxwork, and all small. We look for the kingdom of God, and lo, we find a kingdom of Liliputians. If there be no free play for the individual forces there will be a speedy decay of manhood. We grieve over the evils wrought by excessive competition. They are manifest and deplorable, but the dead level and torpor that would ensue from the absence of competition would be hideous to contemplate. The schemes, organizations and trades' unions which would provide compulsorily for the indolent and improvident, secure a minimum wage for the worthy and the worthless, remove all incentives to superior industry, and chain the aspiring men down to the heels of the sluggish, would arrest all growth, clip the wings of energy and genius, and corrupt the very springs of honesty. In like manner, to propose that Government shall do everything for us is to propose that we abdicate and lose the power of doing anything for ourselves. To make the Government our nursing mother is not far removed from a return to babyhood. My Puritan blood revolts against Government drill. People who believe that religion needs no State support cannot consistently draw the line there. The State is no wiser than the average contents of the ballot-box, and its hands are bandaged in red tape. It is sufficiently clever to fashion imitative functionaries and automata; but manhood develops on surer lines when the State secures it room to work in, and then for the most part leaves it alone. If we have to submit to the rule of majority, there should be surely some limit to its power. The rights of man are more sacred than the whims of the greater number. The majority may be as unreasonably despotic as those Stuarts against whom our Puritan fathers fought, and collectivism may crush personal liberty as cruelly as Laud's forcing presses tried to do. We shall not raise the stature of the masses by cutting off all the tall men's heads; we shall not accelerate the forward movement of humanity by tying up the feet of the foremost. Give us more giants, God, for we want to see the race elevated. Give us more elect men. There never was a time when leaders were more needed; leaders who lead and are not content to follow; living and original voices, not mere echoes; men who believe in principles more than in policy, in conscience more than in votes, in the approval of God more than in the applause of the crowd; above all, men "predestinated to be conformed to the image of Christ," that the world in following them may come nearer to Him whose face they shew. Without them the march of the democracy will be but "the blind leading the blind until they both fall into the ditch."

The secular temper of the new age needs leavening with the spirit of the Puritans. Those men believed that righteousness exalted a nation, and that if we would have other things added we must seek *first* the kingdom of God. They verily thought that life was more than meat, and the body more than raiment, and that a man's well-being did not consist exclusively in "the abundance of the things" which he possessed. They kept moral and spiritual ideals ever before them. The Millennium for which they looked was not earth-born but heaven descended. It was not a paradise of material comforts but a sphere in which God's will would be supreme, and the blessings of obedience would fall upon a regenerate humanity. No lower ideal than that can ever be entertained by those who call themselves the children of the Puritans. We are confronted now by a very different spirit. There is a widespread conviction or sentiment that nothing more is needed for the redemption of society but a rearrangement of social conditions; salvation will be wrought by science and sanitation; the heart will be cleansed by an external application; lusts, envies, and hatreds will cease when the body's cravings are satisfied. Take care of the animal in man, and the spiritual will take care of itself. Brighten the material surroundings and you will bring in the golden age, and men will love as brothers, and peace will flow "as a river, and righteousness as the waves of the sea."

On the top of these vain dreams there comes the clamour for a social gospel, though what that phrase means it is not always easy to define. The preacher is to put into the back-ground the eternal truths that he may cater for temporal wants. He is "to forsake the word of God and serve tables;" he is to forget the soul's hunger in appealing for the necessities of the body. He is to resign the prophet's functions for the more popular arts of the demagogue. We are told even that if Christ were to come again He would come as a social reformer, as the champion of the labour party; to multiply loaves, and double wages, and satisfy the physical cravings of man. And our answer to all this is that if Christ were to come again He would come as He came before, to deliver men from the bondage of the devil and to save people from their sins, whether poor people or rich people. He would compassionate now as He did then, the sufferings, hunger, ignorance and wants of the toiling, groaning multitude. He would appeal to those who love Him to busy themselves in relieving every kind of human need. But His great work would still be to convince the world of sin, righteousness, and a judgment to come, to prove to men that the main cause of their misery is not in things external, but in their enmity to God, and the evil of their own hearts, and to lift them up by faith, repentance, and regeneration to a new and happier life.

And we cannot and dare not preach any other Gospel. Our work is moral and not political. Our weapons are spiritual, not carnal. It would be a happy thing indeed if we could raise all political and secular things to the high religious level as the Puritans did, but the tendency against which we have to guard is the reverse process, the letting down of religion to the secular plane, the surrender of the Divine ideal to the pressure of the lower nature. It is ours to declare with unwavering voice that "The Kingdom of God cometh not with observation," not from the outside, but grows up within. Each man must be made sober, pure, unselfish and loving by having a new nature given from above before the Millennium can come. Each member of society must have the heavenly mind before the whole of society can be coloured with heavenly hues, and the only way to happiness, whether for the individual or the race, leads through the straight gate which the Incarnation opened—the way of forgiveness, cleansing and renewal by the Holy Ghost.

I have said comparatively little about the Puritan theology, and about the Puritan anthropology nothing at all, nor will I speak of it save one word: We have all reacted more or less from their severe and uncompromising doctrine of total human depravity. Have not some in their revolt from that extreme position swung to a far more perilous extreme? The Puritans believed without qualification in what a greater Puritan called "The exceeding sinfulness of sin." Scoffers tell us that they exaggerated the disease in order to magnify the remedy. And it is true that the grace was very wonderful in their eyes, because the abyss from which it had saved them was so profound and dark. "Deep called unto deep"; redeeming love opened itself out to them in all its grandeur and pathos, because the guilt had been so great and the mercy so undeserved. Verily, sin was to them a terrible fact, the one grim reality compared with which physical pain, blood drops, tears, and even death, might be thought of as small evils. How much of this moral sensitiveness have we retained? The temper and spirit of the new age have very little of it. We are all shocked by the sight of bodily pain; we quiver like sensitive plants at the very thought of blood, and there is a weak sentimentality which would spare the most brutal offender the touch of the lash; but sin: what do we feel about that? The sense of sin in the democracy is conspicuously wanting. There is a keen sense of injustice and of wrong done by man to man, especially of wrong done to the unprivileged classes; but of sin, in the true meaning of that word, there is little or none. Nor is this defect confined to one class. We hear common talk about sin and moral responsibility, and we meet with it in a certain class of light literature, which threatens to remove and destroy all sense of wrong-doing, to strike at the very roots of conscience, and to obliterate the eternal distinction between right and wrong. Sin, nay even crime, have come to be regarded in some quarters not as things to be reprehended, but rather to be pitied. They are the result of inheritance, or a mental defect, or a disease, or a fault of training, or the inevitable effect of environment ; something to be deplored and sympathised with, and treated with lavender water and tears, and it is supposed that God will so regard them, and make things all smooth and well with the worst offender at the end. Ah, well ! I have something of the Puritans, and prefer as they did the old Bible ways, which have no respect for all this effeminate and hysterical sympathy, which waste no pity on confirmed wrong-doers, which uphold the sanctity of conscience, which are compassionate with the erring, and merciful to the penitent, but ever indignant and wrathful with those who harden themselves in their iniquity. If our theologies are defective, the defects generally have their origin here. They have no sufficient conception of the righteousness of God because they do not recognise the guilt of man, and they make even the Divine love a flaccid and almost immoral benevolence because they do not see anything to provoke its indignation. It is through the consciousness of sin that we reach up to the unsearchable riches of His grace, to the fact and mystery of Atonement, and to that very holiness without which no man can see God. And if we do not believe in the sin of the human heart, if we do not believe that sin is the one great evil of humanity, the one and only thing which God hates with an eternal hatred, we might as well tear up our creeds, burn our Bibles, and beg one another's pardon for wasting our lives in preaching a useless Gospel.

And now I come to the finish. I have not said these things to you because I think you need to be reminded of them, and because I fear you have become unfaithful to your best traditions. I have ventured to speak in this way because, though in some points you may differ from me, I am persuaded that on the main lines your thoughts run with mine. I would fain believe, and do believe, that whatever changes have affected our denominational faith and life, they have left unimpaired the richest and noblest elements of our Puritan inheritance. If we have lost a little we have surely gained more. Were one of these fathers to re-visit us I think he would bring less of the spirit of criticism than the spirit of congratulation. I can fancy him saying, "You are not so distinctly separate from the world as we were. You do not look upon its lighter diversions with our stern and scornful eyes. Perhaps we were somewhat too rigid, but may not you be getting a little too lax? We read nothing but grave and devout books, and our children's lives were a little too dull because we did not give them a touch of romance. Perhaps you are wiser in letting imagination have fuller play, but your popular literature is now so mixed, so sensuously realistic, some of it so defiled, that the young heart, and the old heart, too, can hardly escape contamination if it be allowed the free run of the field. You have made your public worship far less sombre than that which we knew. There is more beauty in your sanctuaries, and that is well if there be also as much strength. Your sermons have been cut shorter and shorter, chiefly in compliance with the dictates of the least religious. Take care that they do not dwindle to the vanishing point. You have pleasant Sunday afternoons, and sometimes pleasant Sunday evenings. I can forgive you, though that was not our way. I understand your difficulty; you belong to a pleasure-loving generation, which will hardly enter the Lord's house unless pleasure is written over the portals, and is reluctant to take its heavenly bread without a thick coating of earthly sugar—only remember that the religious life cannot be nourished wholly on sweets. You love music in your services better than we did, though we did not hate it so fiercely as is commonly reported. We swept the organs and choirs from the churches only because they had first driven out everything else, and it seems as if history were repeating itself, and you would by-and-bye have to borrow our broom again." These things the Puritan might say, but I think he would also say, "You have kept the Faith; you have jealously preserved the truths for which we fought and suffered; you have not cut away the Bible with German scissors. All that was deepest in us is as deep in you. You have the same sense of human unworthiness; the same trembling, yet mighty clinging to the Cross; the same impassioned love for Him who died thereon. He is to you as He was to us, Deity Incarnate, and the fairest of the sons of men. On His human side you understand Him better than we did, and have caught more of the spirit of His earthly ministry. Your sympathies are wider, if not stronger, than ours. You think less of the elect, but you have more solicitude for the world at large. The enthusiasm of humanity burns in you with a purer flame, and you have more hope than we had of bringing the whole guilty world to the Redeemer's feet."

In some such language would a truth-loving Puritan speak now if he could address us; and that at least is the voice in which I would speak. We cannot go back, and we would not if we could. My whole point has been not that the former days were better than these, but that there were some things in the former days which we should do well to recover if we have lost them, and to hold fast if we still retain. But if the Church of to-day could learn some things from the Puritans it could teach them more. It works in broader fields. It is more in touch with universal needs. It feels more the throbbings and heavings of the great human sea. Its heart is expanded with nobler charities, and its eyes shine with the light of a fuller promise. There has seldom been a time when the Church had a more forward look, when its veins and arteries were pulsing with more varied activities, when it had more assurance of the Master's living presence, and more confidence in His final and complete victory. And rarely has there been a time when its tendency and urgent and pathetic desire were more towards unity, towards the solid front which is needed by those who are fighting the Lord's battle.

Thank God, we as a denomination are *one* and in harmony, and yet not quite. There is a little rift in the lute; would to God it were healed. Would that those who went out from our Union could understand that their God-appointed place is with us. There passed away from us not long ago, it still seems but yesterday, one who was called, half in playfulness and half in reverence, " the last of the Puritans." He was not the last—there are many left, but none that could measure themselves against him, or wield with such power the sword of the Spirit. His memory will be forever sweet, and men can still conjure with his name. It were cruel to use the name for any office save that of love and healing. That grave which is still to all, a regret, which is to many a shrine of inspiration, should also be our place of re-union. If Jacob and Esau, who had so little in common, could join hands and mingle tears beside Isaac's grave, should not we who are one in all dear things let that grave bring us together again? There is nothing to forgive—there are only some things to forget, and, indeed, they are almost forgotten—let it be altogether. I know that if he could speak to us now from the clearer light in which he walks it would be to say, " Children, love one another." And if by these trembling words I could make all our brethren feel this as I feel it myself, I should be indeed thankful to God for this alone that you have called me to occupy this privileged position.

The Session closed at 8.48 p.m. with the Benediction.

TUESDAY, APRIL 23RD.

BLOOMSBURY CHAPEL.

SECOND SESSION.

The President took the Chair at three o'clock. Prayer was offered by Revs. E. Carrington, of Sheffield, and T. W. Medhurst, of Cardiff.

THE BETTING FEVER.

Rev. J. Baillie, of London, read a paper on "The Betting Fever." Revs. W. Evans, of Leicester, followed with some remarks upon the subject, and also seconded the following resolution, which had been moved by Mr. S. Watson, of London :—

> "That this representative meeting views with the greatest distress, the growth of gambling amongst all classes of the community, and would earnestly call upon the Legislature to turn their serious attention to this unspeakable evil, and, with a view to its abatement and ultimate suppression, to enforce the laws already existing, and enact such other measures as will bring about this desirable object."

ATROCITIES IN ARMENIA.

Mr. T. H. Bennett, of Derby, moved, and Rev. F. E. Robinson, B.A., B.D., of Leighton Buzzard, seconded, the following resolution, which was carried unanimously :—

> "This Assembly emphasizes the action of the Council of the Baptist Union in protesting against the atrocities which, on evidence which cannot be ignored, have been perpetrated on Armenian Christians, and implores Her Majesty's Government, in accordance with treaty obligations, to take immediate steps to prevent the continuance of such barbarous persecution."

It was also resolved, on the motion of Rev. J. Clifford, D.D., of London, that the Officers of the Baptist Union be deputed to attend the Conference of the Anglo-Armenian Association on 7th May. Rev. G. Short, B.A., of Salisbury, seconded, and at his suggestion, it was agreed that Dr. Clifford be also asked to represent the Union on that occasion.

BOARD OF CONCILIATION.

The following resolution was moved by Mr. Alderman G. White, J.P., of Norwich, seconded by Rev. W. J. Tomkins, of Rushden, and carried unanimously:—

"In view of the derangement to trade, of the widespread misery to families, and of many and often aggravated social evils consequent upon strikes and lock-outs, this Assembly of the Baptist Union appeals to Parliament, without distinction of party interests, on principles of fair dealing, to appoint a National Board of Conciliation to which disputes between employers and employed may be referred, with a view to settlement with promptitude and justice."

DISESTABLISHMENT IN WALES.

Rev. W. Thomas, of London, moved, and Rev. E. C. Pike, B.A., of Exeter, seconded, the following resolution, which was carried unanimously:—

"The Assembly of the Baptist Union records its satisfaction at the second reading by a substantial majority, of the Bill for the Disestablishment and Disendowment of the Episcopal Church in Wales, and hopes that with all proper dispatch such Bill in its main provisions will become law, believing—as this Assembly has always affirmed—that all State Establishment of Religion is opposed to the progress of Christ's Kingdom on earth, and consequently to the best interests of the nation."

TEMPERANCE REFORM.

The following was unanimously adopted, upon the motion of Rev. R. Richard, of Bristol, seconded by Rev. S. Vincent, of Plymouth:—

"This Assembly expresses its approval of the provisions of the Bill which has just been introduced to the House of Commons by the Chancellor of the Exchequer to establish local control over the traffic in intoxicating liquor, and urges that the Bill be pressed forward with the utmost energy, so that it may speedily become law."

The President pronounced the Benediction, and the Session closed at 5.10 p.m.

WEDNESDAY, APRIL 24TH.

MEMORIAL HALL, FARRINGDON STREET, E.C.

HOME MISSION AND CHURCH EXTENSION MEETING.

At half-past five o'clock refreshments were served, and at a quarter to seven o'clock the Chair was taken by Mr. Alderman *E. Wood, J.P.*, of Leicester.

Prayer was offered by Rev. G. Hider, Mission Pastor, Great Sampford, Essex.

After the Secretary had made a statement regarding the Home Mission and Church Extension Funds, addresses were given by (1) Rev. A. C. Batts, of Upwell, on "The Position and Prospects of Village Nonconformity; (2) Rev. C. Joseph, of Portsmouth, on "Christ and Civic Life;" and (3), Rev. W. J. Woods, B.A., Secretary of the Congregational Union of England and Wales, on "The Free Churches in English Cities."

The Vice-President pronounced the Benediction.

THURSDAY, APRIL 25TH.

BLOOMSBURY CHAPEL.

THIRD SESSION.

The President took the chair at ten o'clock.

Prayer was offered by Rev. G. E. Ausden, of Smarden, and Mr. T. Whittard, of Cheltenham.

DEPUTATION FROM SCOTLAND.

The President cordially introduced Rev. D. W. Jenkins, of Glasgow, President of the Baptist Union of Scotland, who was present to represent that body, and he conveyed its fraternal greeting to the Assembly in a short address.

THE MINISTRY AND THE CHURCHES.

Rev. R. Glover, D.D., of Bristol, gave an address on "Our Church Polity in relation to the Churches," and after prayer by Rev. W. Townsend, of Canterbury, Rev. J. Thew, of Leicester, read a paper on "Our Church Polity in relation to the Pastors." Mr. W. Payne, of London, then led in prayer, and discussion ensued, in which Rev. J. E. Bennett, B.A., of London; Mr. F. E. Smith, of Sheffield; Rev. G. Jarman, of Bristol, and Rev. E. C. Pike, B.A., of Exeter, took part. It was unanimously resolved, upon the motion of Rev. J. T. Brown, of Northampton, seconded by Rev. S. P. Carey, M.A., of Loughborough:—

> "That the Council be requested to take into their serious consideration, the question of how to secure a closer fellowship between our Churches, and to deal with those sources of weakness affecting our ministry which have been pointed out by Dr. Glover and Mr. Thew; and that a report be rendered to the Assembly at the earliest possible moment."

THE POPE'S LETTER.

The following resolution was moved by Rev. R. Glover, D.D., of Bristol, seconded by Rev. E. Medley, B.A., of London, and carried :—

" That the Officers of the Union be requested to prepare and submit to the Autumn Assembly a letter to the Pope in reply to his recent invitation to English Christians to return to the Church of Rome."

CLOSING ADDRESS.

Rev. B. Bird, of Plymouth, gave the closing Address to the Assembly on " Consecration to Christ."

CONCLUSION OF SESSIONS.

The Vice-President offered prayer, and this terminated the third and last Session of the Spring Assembly.

At the kind invitation of the London Baptist Association, the members of the Assembly partook of luncheon in the King's Hall, Holborn Restaurant, at two o'clock.

PROCEEDINGS OF THE AUTUMN ASSEMBLY,

HELD IN

PORTSMOUTH,

October 7th, 8th, 9th and 10th, 1895.

MONDAY, OCTOBER 7TH.

HOME MISSION AND CHURCH EXTENSION MEETING,

TOWN HALL.

At 5 p.m. refreshments were kindly provided by the Local Committee, and

At 7 p.m. the Chair was taken by Rev. C. Joseph, Chairman of the Local Committee, who gave a cordial welcome to the Union on behalf of the Churches in Portsmouth.

Prayer was offered by Rev. F. W. Reynolds, Mission Pastor, Redruth.

After the Secretary had made a statement regarding the Home Mission and Church Extension work of the Union, addresses were given by (1) Mrs. Bonwick, of London, on "The Evangelization of the Villages"; (2) Rev. J. H. Shakespeare, M.A., of Norwich, on "Some Conditions of Social Progress"; and (3) Rev. W. Cuff, of London, on "Men, Money and Movement."

TUESDAY, OCTOBER 8TH.

At 7.30 P.M. A

SPECIAL SERVICE

was held in Fareham (Wesleyan) Chapel by Rev. A. F. Riley, of London.

WEDNESDAY, OCTOBER 9TH.

At 7.30 a.m. Sermons were preached at (1) Kent-street Chapel, Portsea, by Rev. J. Wilson, M.L.S.B., of Woolwich, from Luke xv., 3 to 10; and (2) Elm-grove Chapel, Southsea, by Rev. J. W. Ewing, M.A., of London (to Christian workers), from Daniel xi., 32.

FIRST SESSION.

LAKE ROAD CHAPEL.

At 10.6 a.m. the President, Rev. John Gershom Greenhough, M.A., took the Chair. After prayer, offered by Rev. F. Pugh, of Swindon, and Mr. Councillor J. Baker, of Othery, the President delivered his address as follows:—

In the first address which I was privileged to give from the Presidential chair, I ventured to lead your thoughts on somewhat secular lines, and to examine, though I trust with Christian eyes, some of the problems and ideals which are agitating the popular mind. I had in view the mass of people whom, in religious phraseology, we roughly call the world, and though I did not overlook the welcome fact that in the great multitude which makes up the democracy there are not a few to whom Christ and Christian thoughts are dear, my glances were directed chiefly to those who would hardly regard themselves as belonging to the household of Faith, and whose main interests are not centred in what we call the Kingdom of God. And that has suggested the subject of my present address. For when we talk about the "World" we think of its co-relative the Church, and I have a notion that the imaginary Puritan whom I brought into your Assembly to discourse on the spirit and temper of the modern age, would hardly have been willing to retire until you had patiently endured his utterances on this dearer, if not greater, theme. I will not, however, introduce him to you again, but simply give you in my own poor words

"A FREE CHURCHMAN'S THOUGHTS ABOUT THE CHURCH."

And here the track on which I have to lead you has been well trodden. Your eyes must be content to rest on familiar objects, and your ears to suffer that which has become almost stale by repetition. The theme is one which hardly admits of novelty. My main purpose will be to re-state the things which are commonly believed among us, and "to stir up your pure minds by way of remembrance."

You will neither expect nor desire a discussion of the various questions of ecclesiastical polity which are suggested by the word Church, nor would it be profitable, even if it were within my capacity, to defend by force of argument those principles of Church life and government which we deem sacred and true. This Presidential chair is not the place for elaborate apologetics, nor would this Assembly, with all its intellectual keenness and long-suffering patience, be willing to follow any one less than a Doctor of Divinity through the dusty archæological chambers into which such a discussion would draw it. My task is both simpler and more practical. It is not to establish principles, but merely to emphasize and apply them.

Our idea of the Church needs no cumbrous and circumlocutory definition. When I address you first as representatives of Baptist churches, and then, lifting the survey over a wider ground, forget the sect in the community, and think of you as members of the one great family of faith, as living stones in that living temple which Christ doth fill, I have given you implicitly our conception of the Church, and expressed the only two meanings of that word which the Scriptures sanction by usage, and to which we attach any importance. We believe that wherever there is a company of men and women, be they few or many, united for the worship and obedience of Jesus, and seeking to do His will as the only will which they regard as authoritative and Divine, there is *a* Church. His own words carry us behind all ecclesiastical tradition and debate, and enable us to dispense with them: "Where two or three are gathered together in My Name there am I in the midst." All the essentials of a Church are briefly expressed in that. It is the charter of our ecclesiastical freedom. There is no question about the consecration of the building when He condescends to enter; no doubt about the validity of sacraments where the real presence is enjoyed; no need of bishops when the one Archbishop presides; no want of the Holy Ghost where He breathes upon the faces of His disciples; and no longing for communion unrealized, where souls are joined in mystical fellowship with Him. Where these conditions are satisfied *a* Church is found. And we have but to group together mentally these small communities in one great aggregate, to gather in one comprehensive and illumined vision all the assemblies in earth and heaven and all the individual hearts which are conscious of the same beloved Presence and inspired by the same sentiments, and there grows up before us that one vast eternal house which He has built, and is still building, for His praise, and which we call the Holy Catholic Church.

We do not *talk* about Catholicity in the confession of a creed and then empty the word of its meaning in practice. "God has brought us forth into a large place." We spurn with mingled charity and disdain the limitations which human pride or short-sighted zeal have put upon Christ's grand conception of His own household. We quietly ignore, if we do not despise, the narrowness of vision or vulgarity of sentiment which claims for a party what belongs to a commonwealth and regards as the monopoly of a sect that which is the universal privilege of believers. When we speak of *the* Church it is not with the insolent exclusiveness which violates brotherhood to exalt a class, but with the humbler glorying which loses self in the contemplation of a vast and innumerable fraternity.

To tell us that the Church is only found in conjunction with a certain rigid and unexpansive form of ecclesiastical discipline and polity, that there is no Church without a graduated hierarchy, a stereotyped creed, a certain confined channel of grace, and a real or fictitious line of apostolical successors, is to tell us that there can be no living body and throbbing heart without a particular fashion of dress: or that there can be no Divine force without one unvarying kind of machinery. It is to cramp the Holy Ghost within the confines of a system, and to reduce the manifold wisdom of God to the uniformity of a pattern.

The Church in all its essentials existed before ecclesiasticism was born, and it would remain in all essentials were every known form of ecclesiasticism dead and forgotten. If it does not date back to the twelve who formed the first company of disciples, it certainly dates back to that somewhat larger company on whom the affusion of Pentecost came. That Divine outpouring made the Church if it did not fall on one. There in substance and all fundamental things, there in its typical and prophetic beginnings, was the Church which was to fill the world with the witness of Christ's grace. A band of men and women, fired with the love of their crucified and risen Lord, and mighty through the power of the Holy Ghost, without organization, without machinery, without bishop, priest, liturgy, or ecclesiastical building, yet with all the equipment needed for their holy work and warfare; whatever came afterwards was but development, adaptation, organization, and expansion. And the Church of to-day, with all its manifold machinery, methods, and forms, is in all indispensable things just that little company indefinitely multiplied, with the same unseen Presence lending its forces, and the same unction from above conferring upon it superhuman gifts. It comprises, just as it did when the Apostle described it, all "the faithful in Christ Jesus called to be saints," all to whom the Name is inestimably dear, His Person their worship, His Word their unquestioned law, who love Him with a love that is more than human, who trust Him with a trust stronger than life, whose eager and fervent desire is to get His truth made known, His redeeming power proved, and His Name lifted above every name "until at the Name of Jesus every knee shall bow." In that Church we humbly and reverently trust that we have part, and if there be any other we know it not, nor should we aspire to a place in it, though it were the very highest.

There are certain words such as heresy and schism, which ecclesiastics have always employed as bogies to frighten children. We are too familiar with them to be scared. There has recently come from the pen of one whom we revere, that venerable statesman who has retired from the political arena to think and write thoughts dearer to him than any which he found there, a generous plea for modern heresy and schism. We do not lightly challenge the utterances of such a man, and we should be wanting in spiritual sensitiveness if we did not appreciate the pathetic tenderness of his tone, but when we find ourselves classed under one or both of those heads, and the Church defined as a visible organization whose corporate unity Christ designed and provided for by an unbroken line of apostolical succession, we feel that the hand which was intended to soothe has barely escaped inflicting a wound. We quietly repudiate those two words. They are offensive, however gently administered. If the writer had known how offensive I think he would not have used them. We know no heresy and schism except that which denies saving truth, or severs itself from the body of Christ, and we are more than innocent of both offences. It is strange how the most gifted minds may fail to see beyond the boundaries of the system in which they have been trained, may mistake the shibboleths of a regiment for the watchwords of the Christian army, and while burning with the desire to be both just and generous, may misunderstand the very alphabet of those who belong to another school. We have never dissented or separated ourselves in any degree from the company, visible and invisible, of the faithful, or from Him who is its living Head; we have only parted from a politico-ecclesiastical organization. We do not violate the unity of the Spirit, because we claim for the Spirit a diversity of operations, and if it seems to devout minds like that whose words I have quoted, that the witness of the Church for Christ is seriously weakened by its want of uniform order and centralized authority, our answer is that the real witness power of the Church is not in the imposing grandeur of an artificial solidarity, but in the measure of its service and moral elevation. Christ does not extend and perpetuate belief in Himself through hierarchies and sacramental machinery and cunningly carved channels of grace, but by reproducing Himself in the lives of disciples, by multiplying fair images of Himself in the faces and hearts of those who love Him. And any Christian community which can show this proof of His presence and inworking power may fairly answer every question about its catholicity in the proud words of an Apostle, "Henceforth let no man trouble me, I bear in my body the marks of the Lord Jesus."

Now these principles, clearly understood and firmly held, will determine our attitude towards some of those questions which are everywhere exciting, and perhaps suggesting larger hopes, to the Christian mind. One of the most important of these is the problem of Christian union, though that is not one question, but many, according to the more or less ambitious views which suggest it. With some it takes the form of a practical proposal to draw into closer bonds the Protestant Evangelical bodies; with others it is a scheme of vast dimensions but Utopian character that aims at nothing less than the re-union of Christendom; while a third party with more vague charity than vital conviction would construct a Universal Church on the creedless basis of good fellowship. Whatever form the question takes there is no doubt that it is arousing the widest possible interest. There is not a Christian conference or Church gathering held without some earnest utterance of a desire to discover what is practicable in this direction. A hundred gifted pens have expressed the longing of devout hearts for its attainment. The secular press, which does not readily lend its columns to religious topics, has devoted large space to its discussion. It has converted a Swiss mountain valley, erewhile the secluded haunt of tourists, into the happy meeting ground of world scattered divines, and perhaps made some sanguine dreamers think that "In this mountain the House of the Lord shall be established, and all nations flow unto it." It has elicited from the Archbishop of Canterbury a manifesto which follows an apostolic precedent in "becoming all things to all men," and "giving no offence in anything," which is for the most part sweetly vague, innocently unmeaning, and only strong at the point, if there be a point, where it claims for his own communion unrivalled authority and *unique* importance; and it has drawn from the amiable tenant of the Vatican a curious perversion of history, an emphatic re-assertion of errors which are revolting to every Protestant mind, and an exhortation to charity and meekness which contrasts strangely with the spirit that has usually ruled in that quarter.

Now I need not say that we follow these movements of thought not only with profound interest, but with prayerful sympathies. We rejoice in that deep undercurrent of unity which is beginning to be felt by the lovers of Jesus beneath the surface volume of denominational life, and we are anxious to take our full part in emphasizing essential oneness, and bringing into heartier co-operation those who are already closely akin in spirit, purpose and truth. But it is well that we should try to understand first, what is possible? and secondly, what is desirable? Many of the contributors to this discussion have but reminded us of the proverb that "In all labour there is profit, but the talk of the lips tendeth to penury," and some of them, instead of encouraging our hopes, have rather suggested despair. Between men who glory in the principles and doctrines of the Reformation and men whose eyes are towards Rome, who are avowedly much more wishful to fraternize with foreign herarchies than to join hands with their Christian fellow-countrymen, a closer approach is hardly within the range of present possibility. When men are willing to go with almost obsequious steps and cap in hand to beg for papal recognition of their orders, and their Primate can hardly conceal his disappointment that the Pope, like the deities on Carmel, "answers them not at all," they not only furnish what to a Protestant nation is an unedifying and humiliating spectacle, but they make us feel that there must be an entire change of spirit, and pehaps a new baptism of the Holy Ghost, before union between them and ourselves can be even thought of. And, further, when an assembly of bishops proposes as a basis of re-union the recognition of the historical Episcopate, we should regard it as an insult if we did not more charitably assign it to ignorance of our position. They seem incapable of understanding that we attach no value whatever to those orders which are with them of supreme importance, that we regard their solicitude in this matter, however conscientious it may be now, as the outgrowth of an anxiety to exalt the privileges of a priestly caste. We honour all the good and devout men who fill the Episcopal seats, and thank God for the gifts of mind and spirit which they have brought into the service of the Church. We are all richer when any of the real "Kings of the Earth do bring their glory and honour" into any part of the Holy City. All things are ours, whether Paul, or Apollos, or Cephas, or a golden-tongued Chrysostom, or modern bishops like those of

Worcester and Ripon, but our honour is given to the bishop who has proved his calling of God, and not to the bishop who has received his call from the first minister of the Crown. Our honour is given to the sanctified culture and energies, and not to any imaginary grace which the office confers, and to admit for the sake of union that our ministry needs their ordination would be to put in doubt our calling of God to submit to fallible human judgment the Divine gift of prophesying, and, in fact, to confess that our whole history has been a mistake, and some of our dearest convictions a folly and delusion.

Let it be clearly understood that union on any of these lines is not only unattainable, but to us well-nigh unthinkable.

Moreover, it is well that we should have a clear definition of aims. Do we all mean the same thing when we use the same language? Are some of us wrestling with substantial things and others only beating the air? Pope, Cardinal and Primate seem to be engaged in fondly nursing a dream, while we are praying for the realization of something both possible and substantial. When *we* talk about union, we mean a brotherhood of hearts amid a diversity of forms and administrations; when they talk about it they are thinking of a centralized human authority which shall either make different things one by giving them the same name, or secure the obedience of uniformity. The first would be valueless, even if it were not dishonest; the second is not within human power unless it should please God to re-create men all in one mould. It belongs to the region of fantastic imaginations. Some of us are too busy to pursue the rainbow, or start off again in search of the philosopher's stone, and we are all too old to cry for the moon, if we are not too wise. To have "the single eye" in the Saviour's sense is to be "full of light," but to have "the single eye" in the priest's sense is to dispense with the faculty of vision. We cannot, and we would not if we could, crush individuality, and force all minds through the same plaster of Paris cast. That is only man's narrowness and poverty challenging and defying God's rich diversity. It is not possible, and if it were possible we should oppose it with all our energy and prayer. It would produce sameness at the expense of force, originality, and life, and make peace through mental and spiritual torpor.

When the Archbishop of Canterbury writes, "We know that our divisions are a chief obstacle to the progress of the Gospel," we both assent to the proposition and we dissent from it. The obstacle is not in our divisions, but in the spirit that divides. In no other department would a proper division of labour be regarded as a hindrance to progress and production. The *hindrance lies not* in the multiplicity of operations, but in the want of sympathy and mutual recognition among the workers. It is not our divisions that retard the Gospel, but the envies, jealousies, prides, and uncharities which we bring into them, the poverty of love and imagination which claims for a small arc of the circle all the grace which God makes to flow through the whole circumference; the ungenerous competition which cares not how it weakens its neighbour's part of the wall if it may but strengthen its own; the personal vanities and disputes about the infinitely little, which needlessly multiply congregations; the haughtiness which monopolises a parish and insolently ignores all Christian fellow-labourers; the occasional malignity which puts the dissenting sanctuary and the beer-house into the same class, and the general waste of energy which compasses sea and land to make a proselyte when it might be moving heaven and earth to make a Christian. These are the things which grieve the hearts of all good men, and cause the enemies of the Lord to blaspheme, and these, alas! spring from unsanctified human nature to whatever system it belongs.

We ought not to allow ourselves to be befooled by any inconsiderate outcry against divisions, or be tempted to overlook the strength of denominationalism while lamenting and confessing its weaknesses and abuses. Let us not in our zeal for union give the world the impression that we are apologizing for our existence. I for one must decline to take part in that act of humiliation. The forces making for Religion in this land have been immeasurably augmented by the different channels and agencies through which they have operated. Let Collectivists argue if they will, that one centralized and unified Christian community would have done Christ's work better than separate organizations directed by the same free spirit; the facts of history are on the side of the Individualist in this as in other things. Even in the kingdom of God it is not monopolies that produce the grandest results. The witty Frenchman sneers at this little island of ours with its hundred religious sects, but these sects prove not less the intensity and earnestness of the religious element than its impatience of authority, and though we should be well content with a smaller number, we would rather have ten thousand sects than a land like the Frenchman's neighbour, Spain, where one sect dominates and cultivates the whole field and brings forth chiefly tares and corruption. The Pope, in that address which I have referred to, heaves a profound sigh of regret for the days when the Church was one. We cannot conjure up the ghost of a sigh. It never *was* quite one in the sense which he implies; there was always just enough independence of thought and just enough of dissent to prevent its sluggish waters from stagnating into death. But when it was nearest one, in the Romish sense, then was it most fit to be "spued out of" the mouth of Christ, and most a bye-word among the nations. Let us not forget the immense service which has been rendered to the Saviour's cause by the generous rivalry of the denominations, by their unconscious provoking one another to good works, and the saving agencies, countless in number and variety, which they have initiated. Especially let not that community which almost begrudges the denominations a place be unmindful of the immeasurable stimulus which it has received from their presence and labours. Let us remember, too, what is true now and always has been, that they are not the mere offspring of human caprice and error, but part of God's deliberate design for the ampler manifestation of His truth. His many-coloured wisdom shines forth more freely and beautifully through many windows. The full harmonies of His voice are better heard through many instruments. His saving grace reaches more hearts through many channels. The inspired seer tells us that he saw in the City of God twelve gates, and he probably knew the Divine mind better than those who would make one gate wide enough to admit all, and close the rest.

No, it is not by the effacement of denominational lines that we shall attain the end we all desire. A far nobler unity is within our reach, and, indeed, to all evangelical bodies is fast coming. It will have come when these various communities have equally grasped the central truth that "Christ is all and in all," Christ exalted above all, Christ loved better than all! That is the watchword of union; that is the grand Catholic note. If we love our creeds and forms and dignities and orders and ecclesiastical idols and sects and parties better than we love Him, unity is impossible, but if we truly lift His Name above all these names, unity is in our hands already. Details will slowly settle themselves if devotion to Him and adoration of His divine Person be the predominant sentiment. If there are thousands—as there undoubtedly are in every branch of Christ's Church—to whom He is the source of all spiritual life, aspiration and hope, the name loved best, the joy of all joys, the end of all desire, then the prayer for unity has been already answered for them, and in no other way but by the deepening in the whole Church of this spirit of concentrated love, can the prayer be answered for the rest.

There is one thing more to be kept in mind in our endeavours after a wider and richer fellowship. It is possible even in this to lose the substance in clutching at the shadow and to secure peace by the semi-denial of our deepest convictions. If faith profit nothing without charity, even charity is not worth winning by the sacrifice of faith. There must be great beliefs in common, or unity is a mere pretence. It is of no use joining hands around an empty shrine or marching together under a flag which means nothing in particular. It is easy to mistake pulpy sentiment for charity and to prostitute that angelic grace to the service of a loose indifferentism. In fact, the charity which believes that there is an equal amount of good in everything is not far removed from the cynical indifference which thinks there is no particular good in anything. The Church has been defined by one who ought to know, and who, moreover, sang an immortal song in praise of charity, as the "pillar and ground of the truth," and we at least are not likely to ignore that part of her function. A pillar and basement are intended to support something positive and substantial, and not a structure of airy negations and cloudy sentiments. We have never put our trust in creeds drawn up by human hands, nor are we likely to begin. We have no particular reverence for those ancient documents in which mysteries are set forth in bad metaphysics, more unintelligible than the mysteries themselves. We have no thirty-nine articles to stand as sentinels over the faith; nor do we believe that any number of such sentinels would keep dishonest men out of the fold. Elastic consciences will wriggle through any net, no matter how closely the meshes are drawn. But we cling—and always have clung—to those great and vital truths which have been substantially the heritage and jealously preserved treasure of the Universal Church, and only on the basis of these are we prepared to recognise communion. If men think they have part in the Church who have given up nearly every one of her distinctive doctrines, who call in question the incarnation, the divinity of our Lord, and it may be the supernatural and miraculous, it is not for us to deny their claim. We leave that to our Master's wiser judgment; but we should be guilty of disloyalty to Him if, for the sake of charity, we were to put the same light estimate upon these things which they do. And if we are told, as we shall be, that some of these men are great, tender, and reverent souls, we cheerfully admit it, we even confess that we are far behind them in graces of spirit; but we cannot on that account consent to forego our witness, nor can we understand how those to whom Christ is only human should wish to have fellowship in worship with those who pray to Him as Divine. One would rather have supposed they would say: "Ephraim is joined to idols, let him alone." No, there must be something like oneness in vital truths, or there will only be the semblance of unity and communion, and there is no attraction to us in a feast of brotherhood from which all the choicest viands are gone; the table covered with little more than empty dishes, and the guests only able to talk about surface things because, in their deepest beliefs, they are far apart. We are ready to work with all good men in furthering moral and righteous ends. In warring against iniquity we need not arrest the march to test the orthodoxy of the soldier by our side, and, indeed, men who have any sort of sincere Christian or religious convictions are incomparably nearer to us than those who have none. "I am a companion of all them that fear Thee, and of them that keep Thy precepts." But we must part company at those hallowed places where our Master meets with us, unless their lips and ours can say together, "My Lord and my God," foreven brotherhood must not be bought at the price of truth, and there is nothing in the world worth gaining by the sacrifice of honesty.

But while we will have no part in building up a comprehensive Church on the ruins of precious belief we should be careful to give a place in it to all the faithful, irrespective of condition and party. The Church is the Household of God. It is the place where a Father's welcome awaits all the children who seek His face, and where every one, no matter to what rank or section he belongs, should feel at home. It is the region of grand equalities, where the world's poor distinctions are forgotten in the profound needs felt by all, and in the condescending grace which stoops as much to save the greatest as the lowliest. The Church knows nothing about either the classes or the masses. These are terms which Society recognizes, but which have, or ought to have, no meaning in the fraternity of faith. The Church degrades itself when it takes sides. It is neither the paid retainer of the rich, nor the one-sided champion of the poor. It is the impartial servant of all alike. It cannot play the part of flatterer and cover with smooth words the weaknesses and vices of any class without forgetting its high calling, and losing its strength and purity; and if it is ever guilty of stirring up hatred and exasperating division when it should be healing breaches and kindling love it forfeits all right to its Master's name. Its part is to warn, rebuke, exhort and render equal justice fearlessly to every one, and to represent, as far as it can, that great Judge with whom there is no respect of persons. A Church which includes only one class is but a maimed and half-developed member of the body of Christ. It violates one of the primary conditions of its existence. A Church of millionaires would be a laughing stock. A Church of capitalists would die of its own surfeit if it survived the sneers of the world, and a labour Church is no less a travesty and a contradiction of the Divine idea. A Church must be Catholic in the social sense as well as the theological. If rich and poor cannot meet together *there we shall* look in vain for the Master's presence. If the labourer says, "I will have no dealings in worship with the employer," God will "cover Himself with a cloud which prayers cannot pass through," and if there is any sanctuary in which the labourer finds no welcome, God will remain outside with him, and the worshippers will be left to their respectabilities and idols. The Church is not a society, club, or a workman's federation, but the place of the Father's feet, where love makes all men equal.

And, further, if it would retain and fill its God-appointed place it will be the servant of the people and not of a party. The Church wears no political badge, and uses no political shibboleths. It has done this in times past, and always to its own loss and shame. It has too often, alas! made itself the obsequious servitor of parties that opposed human progress, and defrauded justice, and the penalty has been the sacrifice of its influence and the dwindling of its light. The Church has never gained anything but dishonour and enfeeblement from its political alliances, and never will. It can only be free to serve Christ, and become the minister of all by holding itself loose from these entanglements. The members of our Churches will be, individually, as they always have been, eager politicians, and their sympathies will always be given to that which makes for advance, righteousness, and equality of human opportunity, but, as Churches, we are unpledged and unattached. There is no section of Christ's one household which can afford to write over its doors, "We are all of one political colour here." If men are one with us in the great things of faith, we ask no questions about the other things. Our pulpits should give no voice to party cries—they should be lifted above the arena of political debate. They abuse their privilege when they become the mouthpieces of a section. They only use it nobly when they speak as God's messengers to all. Whether our ministers should take a leading part in politics outside is a matter which I am not presumptuous enough to discuss, and were I to express an opinion it would clash with the views of men far better and wiser than myself. If they can do it without imperilling their higher functions, without suffering a lowering of tone in their higher work, it is well. But some of us have lost all desire to take that part since we struck what seemed to us a deeper vein. It may be that we are nervously afraid of losing the fine spiritual touch which our weapons need if we engage too much in the rougher work. Perhaps we can never quite forget that the minister is hardly a free agent, that he cannot divest himself of his representative character, that he is supposed to be speaking for his people, and not simply for himself. Possibly we are ambitious to be true successors of those Apostles who gave themselves up wholly to the ministry, and certainly we need all the strength we have for the special work which the grace of God has made our own. On that point, however, I speak with modest hesitation, but with none whatever on the duty of keeping the sanctuary clear from the dust and contentions of the political world. There no word should be uttered which betrays political bias—there the words of mercy and judgment should be heard, words of warning and words of promise, great truths and great principles, burning utterances of indignation against manifest wrong, appeals steeped in love and hope to all the weary and the sinful. There the strife of tongues should be allayed, and the worshipper forget, in blessed moments of elevation, by what party name he is called. A Church is the peculiar possession of Christ, and can never lend itself to a party.

I do not think we can form too high an estimate of the work of a Church, nor can we demand from it a greater service than that which its Master asks, but we may easily mistake its functions, and by requiring from it that which is no part of its calling may cripple its true ministry, and even degrade it. The Church is to shed its influence everywhere, but it is not to meddle everywhere. It is to teach politicians righteousness, but not to be a politician; it is to help in making good and honest business men, but it is not to do their business for them; it is to furnish the principles by which all social problems must be solved, but it is not to undertake the solution of the problems; it is to give its sanction to pure recreation, and to utter its warning against all that defiles, but it is no part of its function to provide entertainment; it is to prescribe the diet, but not to be a purveyor of the food; it is to salt every department of human activities, if it can, but chiefly by attending to its own special calling. That calling is, above all things, to bear persistent witness for Christ, to keep His changeless image before the changeful minds and fashions of men, to teach them to do and observe all things which He commanded, to preach His Gospel and to exemplify it, to bring men under His saving power, and to raise their thoughts above the secular and material, to the spiritual, eternal and divine. A Church which is not doing that, whatever else it may be doing, is as salt that has lost its savour. Though it gain the whole world by ministering to men's lower desires it will but have lost its own soul and perhaps theirs.

Let our own Churches at least be on their guard against every temptation to substitute pleasurable devices for exercises of devotion, and sacred concerts for prayer and praise and the preaching of God's word. We thank God for the ministry of song. It will lift us up like angel's wings if we use it soberly, but nothing needs more to be kept in its own place and due *proportion—to have* too much of it can only gratify a religious self-indulgence. A Church may be inspired by heavenly melodies, and it may fall asleep and die to that sound if it hears no other. The modern tendency to disparage the teaching function will, if yielded to, be fatal to the Nonconformist Churches. They at least cannot live by music and æsthetics; they can only live by strong convictions, by intelligent apprehension of the truth, by prayerful study of God's word, and by that preaching which has always been God's instrument for soul-saving and the building up of holy lives. The Churches which still believe in the foolishness of preaching will need patience and grace enough to resist the attractive fashions of the day, but they will prove in the long run by their stability and growth that "the foolishness of God is still wiser than men."

And now I have but one word to add, and it may seem superfluous and even absurd. If we are to claim our part in the one great Church of Christ we must be *alive*, with ears open to His calls, with eyes that survey the wider fields before us, with hearts and minds that have understanding of the times. This is not a happy time for a slumberous and backward Church to live in, for the age, whatever its defects, is in grim earnest, and has nothing but scorn for the laggards. But this is a magnificent time for a Church which feels the Master's power within it and is burning to be in front of His battle. We are in the midst of a wide-spread religious revival which is not shewn by multitudes of conversions, but less ostentatiously in the deepening of the religious sentiment in nearly all classes of men. No observant eye can have failed to mark the reaction from materialism, agnosticism and negativism which is everywhere at work and constantly increasing. The witness of it comes from most unexpected quarters. Frederick Harrison, the Positivist, speaks almost the language of a Christian as he interprets the returning sigh of the human heart for something which Science and Nature cannot give. A statesman who was half regarded as an Agnostic, surprises the world by a positive treatise on the bases of belief. The scientific world has changed its tone from an almost aggressive hostility to Christianity to one of respectful and even reverent sympathy. The School of Huxley, with its coarse and well-nigh brutal antagonism to revealed truth, passed away with him who was its chief prophet. The stream of fictional literature, in which there is no God and no hope, is beginning to sicken those who have been long drinking of it, and in the great mass of the people there is a distinct turning towards the thoughts and ideals of Jesus if there is no direct movement towards the Churches. In the Church of Christ itself there is a growing impatience of mere negativism, of criticism which only whittles down and destroys, and an urgent demand for something that the feet can stand on and the heart hold fast. And truly the army of the Lord is feeling the impulse of this great spiritual movement. Its thoughts are all in the direction of advance, it is full of the energy of hope.

It is not the time for any denomination to stand still, "to let I dare not, wait upon I would," and to acknowledge before the world that its faith is too small to do more than hold its own. If a Church does not attempt larger things it loses what it has already gained. If it does not move forward with the moving host it not only loses the inspiration which comes to the host, but it severs itself from the Master who always marches in front, and it is slowly deserted by all the eager and ardent spirits. If our foreign missions are to sound the retreat for want of men and means—if our home missions are to languish crippled on the bed of annual deficits—if Church extension is to fail because the enthusiasm which God has kindled in a few souls provokes no answering fire in the rest—I shall then begin to believe that we *are*, what the oracles of the hierarchy tell us, schismatics, for these things can only be where a Church is no longer in living union with its Lord, and no longer feels the vitalizing, energizing current of His blood.

But I name the thing only to reject and spurn it. "I am persuaded better things of you though I thus speak." Our denomination has often had its moments of apathy or its moods of weariness, but it has soon recovered from them, and sprung up again to new and nobler enterprise. So it will be now. I will not finish with a despondent word or in accents of rebuke. I will rather beseech you by the mercies of God, by the passion of Jesus Christ, by the memories of all the grace you have received, and all the great things which the Lord has enabled you to do, by your illustrious traditions, and the names of your sainted dead, by all your martyrs and heroes, by all your past glories and all your hopes of future reward, to answer the calls which God makes upon you, and to command His blessing by expecting and attempting greater things.

THANKS TO PORTSMOUTH FRIENDS.

On the motion of Miss Hearn, of Northampton, seconded by Mr. W. Goode Davies, of Newcastle-on-Tyne, it was unanimously and cordially resolved:—

"That the Assembly hereby expresses its most cordial thanks to the friends of all denominations in Portsmouth and the district, and especially to the pastors, deacons, and members of the Baptist Churches, for their abounding hospitality to the members of the Baptist Union during its Sessions, and for the Christian courtesy they have shown to their guests; also to the Local Committee for the admirable arrangements they have made, and to the Mayor and Corporation for the generous way in which they have granted the use of the Town Hall for the public meetings of the Union."

Rev. J. P. Williams and Mr. T. Whitley responded on behalf of the Local Committee, as did also Rev. J. Oates (Congregational) on behalf of friends of other denominations.

LOCAL DELEGATIONS.

On behalf of a delegation of Ministers of the Portsmouth and Gosport Nonconformist Association, Rev. J. Kemp, Honorary Secretary, read the following address :—

To the Members of the Baptist Union of Great Britain and Ireland, met in Annual Assembly at Portsmouth, October 9th, 1895.

Honoured fathers and brethren,

The members and friends of the Portsmouth and Gosport Nonconformist Association, representing the Congregational, Wesleyan, Bible Christian, Presbyterian, Primitive Methodist, and Baptist Churches of this town and district, desire to offer you their most respectful and cordial greeting on this your second visit to our ancient borough.

We gratefully recognize that in the Providence of God the Baptists have been able for centuries to bear faithful testimony to the great central truths of our holy religion; and that, through good report and ill, you have upheld the banner of civil and religious freedom; and that for more than a hundred years you have been distinguished leaders in the noble enterprise of evangelizing the heathen world.

We rejoice also that amid the dangers which now threaten the principles of religious liberty, your Churches remain faithful to their noblest traditions. The rising tide of Sacerdotalism imposes upon all Protestant Christians a fresh responsibility in safe-guarding the ramparts of truth.

We believe that the vital doctrines of our Evangelical Nonconformity can alone counteract the subtle forces which are seeking to destroy the work accomplished by our Puritan fathers. The immediate access of the soul to God, the conscious sense of sins forgiven, the sanctifying presence of the Holy Spirit in the believer's life, the atoning virtue of the sacrifice of Christ availing to the uttermost of man's need—these and other vital truths of Christianity alone can repel the insidious advances of sacerdotal assumption.

In the defence and propagation of these, and all leading principles of of our common Evangelical faith, we are devoutly thankful to know that we stand in unbroken phalanx, with firm front to all the adversaries of the truth as it is in Christ.

We trust that this unity will be greatly strengthened by your visit to our town; and that your sojourn with us may be to you a season of refreshing from the presence of the Lord, as well as an occasion of spiritual quickening to all the Churches in this neighbourhood.

We pray that the benedictions of heaven, promised to those who dwell in brotherly unity, may rest like the dew of Hermon upon all the Churches —both yours and ours—and that the universal Church of Christ may be filled with the fruits of righteousness which are by Jesus Christ, unto the glory and praise of God.

Signed on behalf and by order of the Association,

A. E. SHARPLEY, B.A., *President.*
JOHN KEMP, *Honorary Secretary.*

Rev. Walter C. Talbot (Congregational), and Rev. C. H. Floyd (Chairman of the Portsmouth District of the Wesleyan Methodists), spoke in the name of the delegation, and the President replied.

On behalf of the Hampshire and Isle of Wight Band of Hope Union, Mr. W. Miller, Honorary Secretary, read the following address :—

To the Baptist Union of Great Britain and Ireland in Conference at Portsmouth.

9th October, 1895.

Amongst the many addresses which will be presented to you on the occasion of your visit to our ancient Borough, we on behalf of the Hampshire and Isle of Wight Band of Hope Union, embracing nearly 209 Bands of Hope and Juvenile Temperance Societies, with a membership of 23,000, including Portsmouth Union, with 66 Societies and 12,000 members, unite in giving you a hearty welcome, and in offering you our sincere congratulations, expressing an earnest desire that the deliberations of this Conference will tend to waken and deepen the interest of all those who are engaged in the extension of Christ's Kingdom.

The organization which we represent stands foremost in the ranks of social reform, having a twofold aim : that of inculcating in young people the principles of total abstinence from the use of intoxicating drinks, and that ot promoting habits of truth, self-control, and thrift, thereby conducing to good citizenship.

We rejoice to know that during the past ten years a more active interest has been taken in our movement throughout the United Kingdom, and in the spread of our principles. Physiological lectures have been given in Elementary Schools—in which Portsmouth and other parts of this county have taken a prominent position—Workhouse Bands of Hope have been established, visits paid to industrial homes, and last, but not least, a growing interest is being taken in our Christian Churches and Sunday Schools.

There is room in our ranks for all willing and earnest workers, for we are fighting no imaginary foe ; we, therefore, realizing the supreme importance of our work amongst the young, invite your hearty cooperation in the various districts represented here.

We wish you God-speed in the noble work in which you are engaged, and pray that the blessing of the Almighty may rest upon your labours.

Signed on behalf of the Union,

B. M. PORTSMOUTH, *President*,
R. OLDFIELD, *Treasurer*,
W. WILLIAMS, *Chairman*,
W. MILLER, *Hon. Sec.*,
W. CORNER, *President, Portsmouth Band of Hope Union*.

Miss Emily Weston spoke in the name of the delegation.

On behalf of the Portsmouth Temperance League (adult societies), Mr. W. Miller read the following address:—

To the Baptist Union of Great Britain and Ireland in Conference assembled at Portsmouth.

9th October, 1895.

The Adult Temperance Societies of the town, as represented in the "Portsmouth Temperance League," give a most cordial welcome to your Assembly on this your visit to our ancient Borough, and we most earnestly pray Almighty God that your deliberations may be crowned with success, and may be a means of blessing to many, not only in this town, but throughout the area covered by your Union. Our League has brought temperance workers of all classes more closely together, having affiliated societies from the B.W.T. Associations, C.E.T.S., Good Templars, Rechabites, Sons of Temperance, Sons of Phœnix, and Bands of Hope and Temperance Societies from various Nonconformist Churches; and, although the various branches have different modes of working, we recognise in the "drink traffic" one common enemy to all that is best and noblest in mankind, and all the societies are working in their own way for its removal from our midst. We are proud to know in the Baptist Union there are many stalwart workers for the Temperance cause, who fully understand our work and its difficulties. We are able to welcome you to a town represented by two Members of Parliament pledged to the hilt to support Temperance Legislation. We earnestly trust that among the many momentous questions that will be brought before your Conference during its sittings time will be found for the consideration and advancement of the Temperance movement. We thank you for affording us this opportunity of welcoming you among us, and pray that the blessing of Almighty God may crown your deliberations.

Signed on behalf of the League,

WILLIAM WARD, *President*.
JOHN CULL, *Hon. Secretary*.

Rev. E. C. Chorley (Wesleyan) spoke in the name of the delegation.

On behalf of the Portsmouth Sunday School Union, Mr. W. C. Ransom read the following address:—

To the Baptist Union of Great Britain and Ireland assembled at Portsmouth,

October, 1895.

Gentlemen,

We, the undersigned, as representing the Portsmouth Sunday School Union, comprising 45 schools, 1,240 teachers, and 13,757 scholars, beg to extend to you our most hearty welcome and greeting.

It is our desire and prayer that you may experience, from the Sessions and meetings at which you gather for deliberation in the interests of Christ's Kingdom, great blessing and stimulus, both in your own spiritual life and, on your return, in the various churches of which you are the honoured representatives.

Looking upon Sunday School work as "the Church's mission to the young," we feel that the interests of both are inseparably bound together, and, therefore, that the benefits and privileges which accrue to yourselves must in turn tell for the good of this branch of Christian work.

Trusting that much good may be the outcome of these great meetings,

We are,

On behalf of the Portsmouth Sunday School Union,

HENRY MARTIN, *President*,
W. LONGYEAR, *Chairman of Committee*,
W. C. RANSOM, *General Secretary*.

In a few appreciative words the President responded to the messages of the Temperance and Sunday School delegations, and the Session was closed with the Benediction at 1 p.m.

SECOND SESSION.

LAKE ROAD CHAPEL.

The President took the Chair at 3.5 p.m., and prayer was offered by Rev. E. W. Tarbox, of Guildford.

THE POPE'S LETTER.

In place of a letter to the Pope as directed by the Assembly on 25th April, 1895, the Vice-President submitted an "Address to the English People;" respecting "The Pope's Letter" on Christian Reunion, the adoption of which was seconded from the Chair. After discussion in which Rev. J. Lewitt, of Cheltenham; Rev. S. J. Jones, of Liverpool; Mr. R. Cleaver, J.P., of Northampton; Rev. T. M. Morris, of Ipswich; Rev. S. Vincent, of Plymouth; Rev. E. B. Woods, B.A., of Manchester; Mr. F. A. Freer, of Bristol; Rev. J. E. Jasper, of London; Rev. G. Short, B.A., of Salisbury; Rev. E. C. Pike, B.A., of Exeter; Rev. J. Collins, of Lymington; Rev. H. Hardin, of Montacute, and A. H. Lee, of Walsall, took part, it was eventually resolved upon the motion of Rev. G. P. McKay, of London, seconded by Rev. T. W. Medhurst, of Cardiff:—

"That the Address be referred back to the Officers, in order that it may be turned into an 'Open Letter' to the Pope, and forwarded to him accordingly."

The following is therefore the final form of the document:—

An Open Letter to Pope Leo XIII., respecting his Letter to the English People, dated April 14th, 1895.

In common with all "Englishmen who glory in the Christian name," we have carefully read the Letter addressed to us on Easter Sunday, 1895, and cordially reciprocate the good wishes therein expressed. We earnestly join in prayer to the Great Head of the Church that all who are united to Him by Faith, and are thus united to each other as members of His twice-born family, may speedily be united in visible bonds of mutual love, common service, harmonious worship, and undivided testimony to the world. We share the conviction that our Lord's prayer for His disciples reveals the eternal and invincible purpose of the Father's grace, and, therefore, undismayed by the disorders and strife which have weakened the Church and now hinder the triumphs of the Gospel, we believe that disciples are being "perfected into one" through the discipline of ages, and that all things—even those which now distress us—are working together for the ultimate consummation of our Lord's desire.

But inasmuch as the Unity which Christ prayed for can only come to pass by our ceasing to be "children tossed to and fro and carried about with every wind of doctrine, by the sleight of men, in craftiness after the wiles of error" (Ep. iv., 14), and by our universal attainment to "the unity of the faith, and of the knowledge of the Son of God: unto a full grown man, unto the measure of the stature of the fulness of Christ" (Ep. iv. 4), we deem it our duty to contribute towards this end by speaking in love what we believe to be the truth concerning those historical causes of ecclesiastical division, which compel us to maintain the Protest of our fathers against certain doctrines and practices of the Roman Church.

It would be untimely for us to traverse in detail the account given in the Letter, of Augustine's mission to the Anglo-Saxons, but we cannot admit its accuracy in many important particulars. We honour the desire of Pope Gregory to evangelize the pagan races which had driven out the already Christianized British people from the Eastern portions of this island, but we deplore the claim made by Augustine, as Gregory's representative, to be received as the ecclesiastical superior of the British Bishops. In that claim, with its disastrous consequences, we see a prominent illustration of the divisive influence which the assertion of supremacy by Roman Pontiffs has incessantly wrought in this fatherland, and we applaud the repudiation of it by the ancient British Church.

Descending to the Sixteenth Century, we observe that the Letter before us speaks of the efforts made by former Popes to oppose the Reformation and to minimize its results. The nature of these efforts is not referred to, but they are written in characters of blood upon our annals; and we lament that no confession of sin has ever been made on account of them by the official heirs of persecuting Popes and Bishops. We rejoice to hear, not threatenings, but kindly invitations to-day; yet, while hailing this new tone, we find no indication of changed principles or abated demands for absolute submission. We look back with devout thankfulness to God for those events of the Sixteenth Century which the Pope regrets. We mourn over the violence of the struggle, and the civil and military complications which obscured the religious issue and injured the spiritual life of that age; but the religious freedom then partially obtained, and since increased, is a heritage in which we exult, and it is impossible for us to regard with seriousness any proposals for unity which involve a surrender of that privilege for which so many of our forefathers suffered bonds, impoverishment, and death.

We cannot adopt the position that complete unity of opinion is an indispensable condition of Christian fellowship or inter-communion, but reunion with the Roman Church is rendered impossible by the maintenance of beliefs and practices which we deem subversive of the first principles of Christ; *e.g.*, at the present hour we, in common with a vast majority of English Christians, lie under the solemnly pronounced "Anathema" of the Roman Church, because we deny the following propositions:—

1. "That it is a dogma divinely revealed that the Roman Pontiff when he speaks *ex cathedra*, . . . is possessed of . . . infallibility . . . and

that therefore such definitions of the Roman Pontiff are *irreformable*."—*Decrees of the Vatican Council*.

2. That the Apostle Peter was "appointed the Prince of all the Apostles and the visible Head of the whole Church Militant," and "that the Roman Pontiff is the successor of blessed Peter in this primacy."—*Ibid.*

3. That the Virgin Mary and other saints are our intercessors in heaven, and that "it is good and useful suppliantly to invoke them."—*Decrees of the Council of Trent*.

4. That "honour and veneration" are to be given to "images of Christ, of the Virgin . . . and of the other saints," also to "the relics of saints."—*Ibid.*

5. That "there is a Purgatory, and that the souls there detained are helped by the suffrages of the faithful."—*Ibid.*

6. That Christ instituted an order of sacrificing Priests to "offer His own body and blood."—*Ibid.*

7. That the Lord's Supper is a propitiatory sacrifice in which bread and wine become the very body of Christ, and as such are offered to God.—*Ibid.*

8. That sacramental confession and penance were instituted by Christ.—*Ibid.*

9. That in "absolution" sentence is pronounced by the priest as a judge.—*Ibid.*

10. That "the power of granting Indulgences was granted to the Church."—*Ibid.*

11. That Baptism is necessary to salvation, and that by it we are made entirely a new creature.—*Ibid.*

Without discussing these doctrines, we reaffirm our conviction that they are anti-Christian; and that the Papal assertion of authority to define the doctrine of the Universal Church, and to anathematize all who think otherwise is an attempted usurpation, which only fails to excite indignation because so manifestly futile and absurd that it rather commands our compassion. Until such pretensions have been abandoned, overtures from Rome can only betray a pitiable failure to understand the minds of most Englishmen to-day.

While thus refusing to subject ourselves to spiritual and intellectual bondage for the sake of unity, we invite Pope Leo XIII. to seek unity with us in "the Liberty wherewith Christ hath made us free;" and we beseech all who now acknowledge his Primacy, to re-examine their position in the light which shines from the mind of Christ through those Scriptures which they and we revere.

We gladly note the Catholic sentiments expressed by the Archbishop of Canterbury in his Pastoral Letter of August 30th, 1895. With him we deplore "the recent appearance within the Established Church of certain foreign usages and forms of devotion;" and earnestly hope that his wise counsel will help to preserve the blessings of the Reformation, in so far as they are possessed by the Church over which he presides. We join with him in deprecating the narrow and schismatic spirit of the Pope's Letter, which ignores the existence of any Church outside the Roman communion, and hail with satisfaction his opinion that an intelligent aspiration after unity "must take account of Eastern churches, of non-Episcopal churches and bodies on the continent, at home, and among the multiplying populations of the new world."

We respectfully call the attention of Pope Leo XIII. to the large measure of brotherly love and fellowship already subsisting between ourselves and many Reformed Churches in English-speaking lands. Differing as we do, on various points of Church Polity, Biblical Interpretation, and the Administration of Ordinances, we are becoming increasingly conscious of our essential oneness in loyalty to Christ as the sole Head of the Church. We respect each other's fidelity to conviction, and are more truly one in this, even when it keeps *us somewhat* apart, than we should be if loyalty to the Master were sacrificed for the sake of a premature abolition of denominational distinctions. In this spirit we can work and worship side by side; and shall continue to pray without ceasing for the visible fulfilment of the Saviour's desire. Such prayer may be answered in part by judgments which will make the House of God to tremble, and consume whatever is perishable in ecclesiastical systems: but the trials and changes of the coming age can have no terror for those who love truth more than their own opinions, and are more solicitous for the Kingdom of God than for their own institutions.

We grieve to know that there are many Englishmen who do not glory in the Christian name; and we fear that they are encouraged in their unbelief by the faults and divisions of the Church. We are not surprised that the spectacle of what is called Christendom should seem to throw doubt on the Divine origin of the Church and on her future glory and triumph. We submit, however, that the troubled history of Churches confirms our faith that the Ideal Church after which all are striving is no vain dream, but a Divine thought given to the world by our Founder, and so imperishable that after eighteen centuries of comparative failure it is sought more ardently and with more definite conceptions of its worth and world-wide significance than at any former time. We invite men to judge and condemn our defects; but we entreat them not to spurn the Ideal because too sublime for present attainment, or because it has been travestied by unworthy institutions in the past. In many of the greatest matters of belief all Christians are agreed. We differ in things supplementary, and in our modes of presenting God's message to man, and man's worship to God; but we all believe that every good thing comes down from the Father, and that all human aspirations, prayer, praise, and service ascend to the Father through the Son of Man. Finally, we desire to unite with all our fellow Christians in praying earnestly for that Visible Unity which will be the crowning evidence of Christianity; and will usher in the ultimate desire of Christ for mankind:—"that the world may know that Thou didst send Me and lovedst them, even as Thou lovedst Me."

(Signed) On behalf of the Baptist Union, assembled in Portsmouth, October 9th, 1895.

J. G. GREENHOUGH, *President.*
T. VINCENT TYMMS, *Vice-President.*
SAMUEL HARRIS BOOTH, *Secretary.*

"THE CHILDREN IN THE SANCTUARY."

With the concurrence of Mr. G. A. Hutchison, of Leytonstone, and Rev. F. A. Jones, of London, who had been announced to open a Conference on this subject, it was agreed, in consideration of the lateness of the hour, to defer the discussion until the Spring Assembly.

The Benediction was pronounced by Rev. G. Short, B.A., of Salisbury, and the Session closed at 4.25 p.m.

SERMONS TO CHILDREN.

At 6 p.m. Sermons to children were preached at (1) Victoria-road Chapel, Forton, by Rev. G. Hay Morgan, B.Sc., of London, from Cant. ii., 15; (2) Lake-road Chapel, by Rev. C. Bonner, of Southampton, on "Christ, the Magnet of Souls"; and (3) Elm-grove Chapel, Southsea, by Rev. E. Medley, B.A., of London, from 2 Kings, v. 1-3.

PUBLIC MEETING,

TOWN HALL.

At 7 p.m. the Chair was taken by Sir John Baker, M.P. Prayer was offered by Rev. B. Brigg, of Margate. Addresses were given as follows:—(1) Rev. W. E. Blomfield, B.A., B.D., of Coventry, on "The Present Crisis in the Education Question"; (2) Rev. E. G. Gange, of London, on "Spiritual Power"; and (3) Mr. Alderman G. White, J.P., of Norwich, on "The Relation of Total Abstinence Associations to Social Reform."

SPECIAL SERVICES

were held as follows:—7.30 p.m.: (1) Emsworth, Rev. F. Thompson, of Luton; (2) Avenue-road, Gosport, Rev. R. G. Fairbairn, B.A., of Cheltenham; (3) Newport, I.W., Rev. T. Phillips, B.A., of Kettering; (4) Bell-street, Romsey, Rev. A. B. Middleditch, of London; (5) George-street, Ryde, I.W., Rev. F. C. Spurr, of London; (6) Sandown, I.W., Rev. T. Hancocks, of Ramsgate; (7) Shirley, Rev. W. H. M'Mechan, of London; (8) Waterlooville, Rev. F. C. Player, B.A., of Wolverhampton; (9) West Cowes, I.W., Rev. C. Williams, of Accrington; and (10) City-road, Winchester, Rev. P. H. Smith, of Northampton (at 8 p.m.).

THURSDAY, OCTOBER 10TH.

At 7.30 a.m. a Sermon was preached in Elm-grove Chapel, Southsea, by Rev. F. B. Meyer, B.A., of London, from Acts. xi., 15.

THIRD SESSION.

LAKE ROAD CHAPEL.

The President took the Chair at 10.5 a.m. Prayer was offered by Rev. W. Evans, of Downton, and Rev. C. E. P. Antram, of Stocksfield.

ELEMENTARY EDUCATION.

The following resolution was moved by Rev. C. Williams, of Accrington, seconded by the Secretary, and after remarks by Rev. I. A. Ward, of Sheffield, Mr. T. H. Engall, of London,

Rev. W. Woods, of London, and the Vice-President, was carried unanimously:—

"That this Assembly rejoices in the spread of education in our land, especially in the good work accomplished by School Boards since 1870, and demands that the School Board system shall be extended to every part of the country, and a Board School be placed within easy and reasonable distance of every family. That the Assembly renews its protest against the support from public funds of sectarian schools, and claims that no denominational formulary shall be taught in any State-aided school, that all scholars and teachers, whatever their religious opinions, shall be equally treated in all public elementary schools, and that all such schools shall be under the management of boards elected by the public. The Assembly also instructs the Council to co-operate with other representative Unions and Conferences in the formation of a National Vigilance Committee for the maintenance of the rights of Nonconformists."

DISESTABLISHMENT.

It was resolved, on the motion of Mr. J. R. Smith, J.P., of Southampton, seconded by the Secretary:—

"That this Assembly emphatically renews its solemn protest against all Establishments of religion by the State as unjust in principle, mischievous in operation, and totally at variance with the spirit of the religion of Jesus Christ. That the Assembly recognises and deplores the long catalogue of persecutions, wrongs, and sufferings which have been inflicted upon the noblest men by Established Churches, in the name of our Lord and Master; that the same spirit is inherent in all established churches, however the form may be modified; and that such establishments of religion have in every age injured the spirituality, the purity, and the usefulness of the Church of Christ. That the Assembly, therefore, calls upon the Free Churches of the United Kingdom, by the memory of the sufferings and sacrifices of their fathers, by their love of a pure and free Gospel, and by their loyalty to the Lord Jesus Christ, the Founder and sole Ruler of the Church, to realize their responsibility and bounden duty to promote, by all lawful means, the disestablishment and disendowment of the Churches 'by law established' in England, Scotland, and Wales."

TEMPERANCE REFORM.

The following resolution was moved by Mr. T. Kyffin Freeman, F.G.S., F.S.S., of London, seconded from the Chair, and carried unanimously:—

"That this Assembly regards with shame and sorrow the vice and misery which spring from the liquor traffic; and in view of the universal testimony of philanthropists, magistrates, and Her Majesty's judges, that drink is the fruitful source of the poverty and crime which crowd our workhouses and prisons, the Assembly expresses its conviction that experience has shown that irresponsible magistrates are unfit to be a licensing body, and hereby calls upon the Government to prepare some scheme by which the people may control the issue of licenses to houses intended for their use. That the Assembly is also of opinion that all clubs in which intoxicating liquors are sold should be licensed, and be subject to police supervision, as in the case of houses now licensed."

"HYMNODY IN OUR CHURCHES."

A paper on this subject was read by Rev. S. G. Green, D.D., of London, which was further discussed in relation to Mission Services by Rev. F. C. Spurr, of London.

Then followed a

DEVOTIONAL ADDRESS

by Rev. W. J. Styles, of London, on Phil. iv., 3, "Help... Clement also."

Rev. T. M. Morris pronounced the Benediction, and so terminated at 1.4 p.m. the third and last Session of the Autumn Assembly.

PUBLIC WORSHIP.

TOWN HALL.

At 3 p.m. a Sermon was preached by Rev. Charles New, of Hastings, from Mark ix., 29.

CLOSING PUBLIC MEETING.

TOWN HALL.

At 7 p.m. the Chair was taken by Mr. E. Robinson, J.P., of Bristol.

Prayer was offered by Rev. D. Davies, of Brighton.

Addresses were given as follows:—(1) Rev. J. Owen, of Swansea, on "An Evangelical Revival"; (2) Rev. J. Thomas, M.A., of Liverpool, on "The Sacerdotal Revival"; and (3) Rev. W. L. Watkinson, of London, on "The Influence of Sacerdotalism on National Prosperity."

At the meetings in the Town Hall on Monday, Wednesday and Thursday evenings organ recitals and choral selections were given under the direction of Mr. W. E. Green, and at the last meeting his efficient services, together with those of the organist and the choir, were suitably acknowledged on behalf of the Council of the Baptist Union, by the Secretary.

PART III.

BAPTIST SOCIETIES, COLLEGES, PUBLICATIONS, &c.

I.—SOCIETIES.

THE BAPTIST BOARD.

Originated Jan. 20, 1723. President, Rev. A. B. Middleditch ; Vice-President, Rev. W. Hamilton; Secretaries, Rev. J. H. Cooke, Ramleh, Coolhurst-road, Crouch End, N., and Rev. E. T. Davis, Sidcup R.S.O.; Committee, Revs. J. W. Boud, G. T. Ennals, W. H. King, R. E. Sears, G. Simmons, and W. J. Styles.

(For List of Members, see last page.)

RULES.

1. That the design of this Society is to afford an opportunity of mutual consultation and advice on subjects of a religious nature, particularly as connected with the interests of the Baptist Denomination.

2. That this Society do consist of approved Ministers of the Baptist Denomination, being, or having been, Pastors, residing in or about the Cities of London and Westminster.

3. That any Candidate for admission into this Society shall express his desire to the Secretary in writing, or through some Member of the Board ; and that his application having been laid before one meeting shall be decided at another, a majority of at least two-thirds of the Members present being necessary for his admission.

4. That this Society transact its ordinary business at meetings to be holden on the last Tuesday in each month, beginning with October, and ending with the following May, and that the meeting in March be the annual meeting of the Board.

5. That at the Annual Meeting of the Board, the Rules shall be read, the proceedings of the year reported, the expenses defrayed, a report for the general body of the three Denominations prepared, a Secretary chosen for the year ensuing, and any other business transacted that may be deemed necessary.

6. That Special meetings of the Board be summoned whenever necessary in the judgment of the Secretary, or upon a requisition signed by six Members.

7. That the expenses of the Board be met by a levy on the Members, to be agreed upon at the Annual Meeting; and that any individual not having paid, for a period of two years, his proportion of the sum called for, and not paying on a final application within three months after the expiration of this period, be no longer considered a Member.

8. That the Rules of the Board shall not be altered except at an annual meeting, or at a meeting specially called for the purpose.

9. That when any of the brethren are removed by death the Secretary be requested to ascertain the time and arrangements of the funeral, and communicate the same to the Members of the Board, in order that each of the brethren may have the opportunity of testifying his respect by attending.

THE WIDOWS' FUND OF MEMBERS OF THE BAPTIST BOARD.

Instituted 1872.

Treasurer—MR. H. WOOD, J.P.

Honorary Secretary—Rev. W. J. STYLES, 1, College-street, Islington, N.

OBJECT.—To provide a sum (at present about £25) available for the widow ; or if there be no widow, for the young children, if any, *immediately* on the death of a Beneficiary Member.

All accredited Baptist Ministers within the Metropolitan area (whether belonging to the Baptist Board or not) can be *Beneficiary* Members. The subscriptions of *Honorary* Members are gratefully received.

BENEFICIARY SUBSCRIPTIONS.—10s. 6d. if not more than 45 years of age; 15s. 9d. if above 45; £1 1s. if above 50, on joining, and similar amounts on the death of a member. A donation of five pounds or an annual subscription of One Guinea entitles to Honorary Membership.

PARTICULAR BAPTIST FUND.

Formed 1717. OBJECTS.—For the relief of ministers and churches of the Particular Baptist denomination in England and Wales; the education of young persons of the same persuasion for the ministry; donations of books to young ministers; and for any other charitable purpose (consistent with the general design) which the managers shall approve.

INCOME, year ending Feb., 1895	£3,086	5	11
EXPENDITURE, ditto	2,984	5	3

Treasurers—Mr. J. J. SMITH, J.P., REV. S. H. BOOTH, D.D., and Mr. C. PRICE.

Secretary—Mr. R. GRACE, 160, The Grove, Camberwell, S.E.

*** This Fund is managed by the Pastors and Messengers annually appointed by those churches which have subscribed towards the capital and make annual collections. Applications to be made in writing, addressed to the Secretary, the last week in August.

BAPTIST BUILDING FUND.

Formed 1824. 1. The object of this Fund is to assist, by loan without interest, in the building, enlargement, or repair of, or in the removal of building debts on, places of worship, including therein buildings for Sunday schools, class rooms, lecture rooms, and Home Mission halls in connection therewith, belonging to the Evangelical Churches of the Baptist Denomination throughout the United Kingdom; and also to undertake the custody of title deeds and other documents relating to any place of worship, school, college, or other property held in trust for any purpose of the Denomination. 2. Forms for the preparation of trust deeds for chapel property, and directions for the appointment of new trustees from time to time, are supplied gratis on application to the Honorary Secretary.

N.B.—In 1891 the funds of the General Baptist Building Fund, amounting to £6,400, were joined to the previous capital, which amounted to £43,000, in pursuance of a request intimated in a Resolution unanimously passed at a Session of the Baptist Union in 1889, and in accordance with Resolutions passed by the General Baptist Association, at Burnley, in June, 1891, and by Subscribers to the Baptist Building Fund at a Special General Meeting in October, 1891—the Amalgamated Fund continuing under the title of "The Baptist Building Fund."

1894-5—

	£	s.	d.	£	s.	d.
INCOME— Balance brought forward	£294	2	9			
Subscriptions and Donations	210	13	2			
Congregational Collections	51	4	8			
Liverpool Auxiliary	53	9	9			
Rent of Peniel Chapel	58	1	8			
Donation subject to Interest	60	0	0			
Loans repaid	10,637	0	0			
				11,364	12	0
EXPENDITURE—						
Loans to 41 Churches	£10,915	0	0			
Annuities in respect of Donations	64	18	4			
Working Expenses	251	7	1			
Balance at Bankers'	133	6	7			
				11,364	12	0

The Capital of the Fund is £51,442 17s. 1d.

Trustees—W. B. BEMBRIDGE, J.P., E. MOUNSEY, J.P., E. RAWLINGS, and W. R. RICKETT.

Committee.

Avery, Rev. W. J.
Benham, Mr. W. J., B.A.
Benson, Mr. J.
Bentley, Rev. W.
Bowser, Mr. W. A.
Chapman, Mr. J. W.
Cowdy, Mr. J.
Fletcher, Rev. J.
Gordon, Mr. R.
Griffiths, Mr. R. F.
Hill, Mr. H.
Mote, Mr. J.
Olney, Mr. T. H.
Payne, Mr. W.
Pewtress, Mr. S.
Stoneman, Mr. J.
Underhill, Mr. E. B., LL.D.
Wilkin, Mr. M. H.
Wood, Mr. H., J.P.
Woollacott, Mr. J. C.

Treasurer—Mr. J. B. MEAD, Endsleigh, Wickham-road, Brockley, S.E.

Auditors— Mr. J. WATES and Mr. G. ROBERTSON.

Honorary Secretary—Mr. J. HOWARD, 42, Old Broad-street, E.C.

Solicitor—Mr. S. WATSON, 12, Bouverie-street, Fleet-street, E.C.

Secretary for Deeds—Rev. W. BENTLEY, 227A, Brooke-road, Upper Clapton, N.E.

Travelling Secretary and Collector—Rev. F. H. NEWTON, 18, Ribblesdale-road, Hornsey, N.

Bankers—LONDON AND COUNTY BANK, Lombard-street, E.C.

DEPOSITORY FOR TITLE AND TRUST DEEDS.

A Strong Room, fire-proof, has been provided in the basement of the Baptist Mission House, Furnival Street, where the Deeds of Chapel and other property connected with the Baptist denomination will be securely kept, under the guardianship of the Baptist Building Fund. Officers of Churches are strongly advised to avail themselves of the security for their Chapel Deeds thus offered to them. For Forms of Application apply to Rev. W. Bentley, 227A, Brooke-road, Upper Clapton, N.E.

BAPTIST TOTAL ABSTINENCE ASSOCIATION.

President—Mr. Alderman G. WHITE, J.P., Norwich.

Treasurer—Mr. J. B. MEREDITH, Hawthorndene, Sydenham-road, Croydon.

Committee.

Rev. D. Burns, D.D.
,, J. H. Cooke.
,, R. A. Elvey.
,, A. C. Gray.
,, F. C. Hughes.
,, W. J. Mills.
Rev. G. H. Morgan, B.Sc.
,, J. Parker, M.A.
,, J. E. Shephard.
,, W. Stott.
Mr. S. B. Burton.
,, J. T. Dunn.
Mr. T. K. Freeman.
,, R. F. Griffiths.
,, G. Pedley.
,, J. Wates.
,, H. Wood, J.P.

Hon. Secretary—Mr. J. T. SEARS, J.P., 11, Crane-court, Fleet-st., E.C.

General Secretary—Rev. H. TROTMAN, 133, Spring Vale-road, Sheffield.

Travelling Secretary—Rev. J. M. HEWSON, 4, The Avenue, Acre-lane, Brixton, S.W.

This Association was formed to utilize to the greatest advantage the Total Abstinence power existing in the churches of the Baptist denomination. The Travelling Secretary devotes the whole of his time to visiting the churches and assisting in the formation of Temperance Societies and Bands of Hope. Its monthly organ is *The Bond of Union.*

All abstaining Baptist ministers, deacons, elders, professors and students of Baptist colleges, and abstaining delegates to the Baptist Union, and other Baptists who abstain, and contribute to the funds of the Association a donation of £5, or a subscription of at least 2s. 6d. per annum, are eligible for membership. The *Bond of Union* is sent, post free, to all subscribers of 5s. and upwards. The present ministerial membership is 1,424, and 206 students.

PLEDGE.—I hereby agree, by Divine assistance, to abstain from all intoxicating drinks as a beverage, and to promote the practice of abstinence throughout the community.

METROPOLITAN TABERNACLE COLPORTAGE ASSOCIATION.

Founded 1866 *by the late* Rev. C. H. SPURGEON.

President—Rev. T. SPURGEON.

Vice-President—Rev. J. A. SPURGEON, D.D., LL.D.

Honorary Secretary—Mr. C. P. CARPENTER.

Secretary—Mr. A. E. ALDER.

OBJECT.—The increased circulation of religious and healthy literature, blended with personal evangelistic effort by means of Christian Colporteurs, who devote all their time and visit every accessible house with Bibles and good books and periodicals for sale, and perform other missionary services, such as visitation of the sick and dying, and conducting meetings and open-air services as opportunities occur. The Association is unsectarian in its operations, "doing work for the friends of a full and free Gospel anywhere and everywhere," and a strict supervision is exercised over the books and periodicals issued for sale.

Last year seventy-three Colporteurs were employed in twenty-four counties. Expenditure, £5,663 0s. 7d. Sales, £8,125 8s. 10d.

The average cost of a Colporteur is £80, but the Committee will appoint a man to any district for which £45 a year is subscribed. For further information, application should be made to the "Secretary," Metropolitan Tabernacle Colportage Association, Pastor's College, Temple-street, Southwark, S.E.

SOCIETY FOR AGED OR INFIRM BAPTIST MINISTERS.

Formed 1816. OBJECT.—"The relief of Baptist ministers, being Beneficiary members, when they appear to be permanently incapacitated for pastoral duties by reason of age or infirmity."

CAPITAL invested	£13,204	0	0
INCOME, year ending June, 1895	621	12	11
RECEIPTS on account of Capital..	471	11	11
19 Shares to Claimants at £32 10s. each.	617	10	0

Number of Beneficiary Members, 115.

Treasurer—Rev. J. CULROSS, M.A., D.D., Bristol.

Secretary—Mr. W. SHERRING, Bristol.

Trustees—Mr. W. SHERRING, Mr. G. H. LEONARD, J.P., Mr. C. TOWNSEND, J.P.

Committee.

Brown, Rev. C., London.
Brown, Rev. J. J., Birmingham.
Burton, Rev. W., Minehead.
Evans, Rev. G. D., Totnes.
Glover, Rev. R., D.D., Bristol.
Gower, Rev. H. F., Bath.
Hawkes, Mr. W., J.P., Devonport.
Henderson, Rev. W. J., B.A., Bristol.
Hepburn, Mr. T. H., Hele.
Humphreys, Rev. G. W., B.A., Wellington.
Jarman, Rev. G., Bristol.
Knee, Rev. H., Bristol.
Medway, Mr. H. A., Bristol.
Moore, Rev. H., Bristol.
Penny, Mr. T., Taunton.
Skerry, Rev. W. R., London.
Tratman, Mr. A. R., Bristol.
Vincent, Rev. S., Plymouth.
Wood, Rev. J. R., London.

BAPTIST WESTERN SOCIETY

FOR WIDOWS AND ORPHANS.

Formed 1807. OBJECT.—The relief of necessitous Widows and Orphans of ministers of the Baptist denomination, in the counties of Cornwall, Devon, Dorset, Hants, Wilts, Gloucester, and Somerset, including the city of Bristol.

	£	s.	d.
CAPITAL INVESTED	£8,227	13	0
INCOME, year ending June, 1895	407	0	5
RECEIPTS on account of Capital	330	8	8
7 Widow Claimants, £34 18s. 6d. each	244	9	6
4 Widows and Children	159	15	6

Number of Beneficiary Members, 62.

Treasurer—Rev. J. CULROSS, M.A., D.D.

Secretary—Mr. W. SHERRING, Bristol.

Trustees—Mr. G. H. LEONARD, J.P., Mr. W. SHERRING, Mr. C. TOWNSEND, J.P., Mr. T. H. HEPBURN.

BAPTIST TRACT AND BOOK SOCIETY.

Formed 1841. OBJECT.—"To disseminate by means of tracts, books and other publications, the truths of the Gospel of the Lord Jesus Christ, and the teaching of the New Testament Scriptures respecting Christian Baptism."

	£	s.	d.
INCOME, year ending December 31, 1894	£1,035	6	2
EXPENDITURE	1,039	13	2

OFFICERS AND COMMITTEE FOR 1895.

Treasurer—Mr. M. H. WILKIN, Hampstead, N.W.

Editor—Rev. E. PARKER, D.D., Baptist College, Brighton-grove, Manchester.

Committee.

LIFE MEMBERS.

Bell, Mr. J. A., London.
Bland, Rev. S. K., Ipswich.
Box, Rev. J., London.
Cattell, Rev. J., Bessels Green.
Davies, Rev. Prof. G., D.D., Bangor.
Lynn, Rev. J. H., London.
Morris, Rev. J. A., Aberystwyth.
Parker, Rev. E., D.D., Manchester.
Reynolds, Rev. P., London.
Shaw, Mr. W. D., J.P., Longwood, Huddersfield.

ORDINARY MEMBERS.

Archer, Rev. G., Huddersfield.
Baillie, Rev. J., London.
Briggs, Rev. H., Todmorden.
Brown, Rev. H. D., M.A., Dublin.
Cuff, Rev. W., London.
Davies, Rev. D., Brighton.
Davies, Rev. Prof. T. W., B.A., Nottingham.
Hughes, Rev. J. S., Warrington.
Jenkins, Rev. D. W., Salendine Nook.
Marshall, Rev. J. T., M.A., Manchester.
Moore, Rev. S. H., New Malden.
Parry, Rev. A. J., Cefn Mawr, Ruabon.
Tarn, Rev. T. G., Cambridge.
Thomas, Mr. A., M.P., Cardiff.
Thomas, Rev. J., M.A., Liverpool.
Towler, Rev. R. E., Manchester.
Williams, Rev. C., Accrington.
Williams, Rev. R. E., London.
Wood, Mr. H., J.P., London.

Hon. Secretary—Mr. J. C. WOOLLACOTT, Tintern Cottage, New Malden.

Trade Manager—Mr. LUKE W. BICKEL.

Collectors—Mr. A. WHITEHEAD, Wood-villa, New Hey, near Rochdale. and Mr. W. K. BLOOM, 331, West Green Road, Tottenham, N.

Depository and Book Room—16, Gray's Inn Road, W.C.

THE BAPTIST UNION OF WALES.

See "Associations," Part VI.

THE PROVIDENT SOCIETY FOR AGED AND INFIRM BAPTIST MINISTERS IN WALES AND MONMOUTHSHIRE.

Established 1872. OBJECTS.—"To enable Ministers of the Baptist denomination in Wales and Monmouthshire to meet the exigencies of old age, sickness and death."

INCOME for 1894	£350	5	3
CAPITAL invested	2,739	17	3

Number of aged ministers relieved during the year, by £11 11s. 7d. each, 16.

Number of Members, 149. Annual Subscription, £1.

Chairman—Rev. W. HARRIS, Aberdare.

Secretary—Rev. W. MORRIS, Treorky, Pontypridd.

Treasurer—Mr. D. DAVIES, Merthyr.

Trustees—Rev. C. GRIFFITHS, Bristol; Rev. J. G. LEWIS, D.D., Swansea; Mr. D. DAVIES, Merthyr; Rev. W. EDWARDS, B.A., D.D., Cardiff; and Rev. H. C. WILLIAMS, Corwen.

BAPTIST BUILDING FUND FOR WALES.

Formed 1862. OBJECT.—"To assist, by loan without interest, in the building, enlargement, or repair of places of worship belonging to the Particular or Calvinistic Baptist denomination in Wales and Monmouthshire."

CAPITAL ACCOUNT.

To Loans in hands of the Churches	£7,748	15	0
Swansea Harbour Trust	500	0	0
Balances	27	0	6
	£8,275	15	6

Chairman for 1895-96—Rev. D. DAVIES, Llandudno.

Hon. Treasurer—Mr. D. DAVIES, 3, Glebeland, Merthyr Tydvil.

Hon. Solicitor—Mr. J. JONES PUGHE, Pontypridd.

Hon. Secretary—Mr. I. PHILLIPS, Burry Port R.S.O., Carmarthenshire.

WELSH BAPTIST ASSURANCE TRUST, LIMITED.

Chairman—Mr. O. LEWIS, St. Briavel's, Coleford, Glos.

Treasurers—Mr. W. R. EDWARDS, J.P., Carmarthen; Mr. R. D. EVANS, M.D., Festiniog.

Solicitor—Mr. J. JONES PUGHE, Pontypridd.

Secretary—Mr. I. PHILLIPS, Brynteg, Burry Port R.S.O., Carm.

CAPITAL, £10,000 in 2,000 Shares of £5 each.

OBJECT.—"To carry on the business of insurance of chapels, schools, class-rooms, vestries, &c., with their fittings; houses, colleges, libraries, and other property belonging to the Baptist denomination in Wales and Monmouthshire, or its Associations in the same."

WELSH BAPTIST TOTAL ABSTINENCE SOCIETY.

Established 1879.

President—Rev. J. W. MAURICE, Dinas Cross.

Vice-President—Mr. R. WILLIAMS, Garn, Dolbenmaen.

Secretary—Rev. J. GRIFFITHS, Llanfairfechan, N. Wales.

Treasurer—Mr. S. ELLIS, Llanfair, Welshpool.

Auditor—Mr. H. ABRAHAM, Porth.

The Society was formed for the purpose of combining the temperance power of the churches to check the great evil of intemperance. By its means the Colleges are visited annually by members of the Committee, who address the students; the conferences of the Associations are addressed; a paper is read at a meeting held in connection with the annual meetings of the Welsh Baptist Union; and various other agencies are employed. Almost all the students, and a majority of the ministers, enrol themselves as members of the Society.

BAPTIST UNION OF SCOTLAND.

See "Associations," Part VI.

BAPTIST HOME MISSIONARY SOCIETY FOR SCOTLAND.

CHIEFLY FOR THE HIGHLANDS AND ISLANDS.

Formed 1816. OBJECT.—"The dissemination of the Gospel of Christ in Scotland."

	£	s.	d.
INCOME for 1894-5, from Subscriptions, Donations, and Legacies	£2,250	17	10
EXPENDITURE for 1894-5—Salaries and Missionaries' Travelling Expenses, &c.	2,402	9	11
Legacy Fund	715	17	11
Oban Fund	44	13	3

Hon. Treasurer—Mr. W. O. GIBB, 21, Royal Terrace, Edinburgh.

Secretary—Mr. P. WAUGH, 69, Morningside Drive, Edinburgh.

The Committee consists of members of Baptist Churches in Scotland.

Twenty-three missionaries are supported, in whole or in part, by this Society. They are distributed as follows:—In the Shetland Isles, 3; in the Orkney Islands, 2; Caithness, 2; Forfarshire, 1; Perthshire, 1; Hebrides, 6; Argyllshire, 2; Ayrshire 2; Lanarkshire, 1; Roxburghshire, 1; Fifeshire, 2.

BAPTIST UNION OF SCOTLAND LOAN AND BUILDING FUND.

Established 1878.

OBJECT.—"To assist in the liquidation of Chapel debts by loans of money, without interest, and in the building, enlargement, or repair of places of worship connected with the Baptist denomination in Scotland."

Capital	£3,943	3	1
Subscriptions, 1894-95	2	12	0
Balance in Bank	120	4	1
Advanced to Churches during the year	800	0	0

Trustees—Mr. J. WILSON, Falkirk; Mr. H. BOWSER, and Mr. J. NIMMO, Glasgow; Mr. T. G. COATS, Paisley; and Mr. J. WALCOT, Edinburgh.

Convener—Mr. J. WALCOT, Edinburgh.

Law Agent—Mr. T. WHITE, S.S.C., Edinburgh.

BAPTIST UNION OF SCOTLAND MINISTERS' PROVIDENT FUND.

Established 1874.

INCOME, 1894-95	£277	4	4
EXPENDITURE	195	5	0
CAPITAL	6,100	12	10

BAPTIST UNION OF SCOTLAND BENEFICIARY FUND.

Established 1869.

OBJECT.—"The relief of aged and infirm ministers in Scotland."

INCOME, 1894-95	£36	11	0
EXPENDITURE	70	5	0
BALANCE AT CREDIT OF FUND	252	9	5

SCOTTISH BAPTIST TOTAL ABSTINENCE SOCIETY.

OBJECT:—"To promote the practice of Total Abstinence among the ministers, students, members, and adherents of the Baptist Churches in Scotland, and to further the interests of the Temperance cause in General.

President—Mr. R. LOCKHART Edinburgh.

Vice-Presidents.

Rev. W. GRANT, Edinburgh.
Rev. R. MACNAIR, M.A., M.D., Edinburgh.
Rev. W. TULLOCH, Edinburgh.
Rev. A. WYLIE, M.A., Edinburgh.
Rev. F. H. ROBARTS, Glasgow.
Mr. A. COATS, Paisley.
Rev. JOHN CROUCH ,,

Hon. Treasurer—Mr. J. S. BONE, 1, Park-terrace, Langside, Glasgow.

Hon. Secretary—Mr. F. SPITE, 6, The Crescent, Dalmuir, Dumbartonshire.

Committee.

Black, Mr. W., Edinburgh.
Johnston, Mr. J. W. ,,
McKenzie, Mr. ,,
Macdonald, Rev. G. ,,
Tait, Rev. D. ,,
Thomson, Mr. A. B., M.A., Edinburgh.
Urquhart, Mr. A., S.S.C. ,,
Watson, Mr. J. ,,
Way, Rev. T. W. ,,
Brown, Mr. A. K., Glasgow.
Elder, Rev. J. ,,
Graham, Mr. J. C. ,,
Last, Rev. E. ,,
Lockhart, Mr. D. ,,
Millar, Rev. W. J. ,,
Parker, Mr. A. ,,
Sharp, Mr. G. ,,
Young, Mr. A. ,,
Bisset, Rev. A., M.A., Aberdeen.
Dingwall, Mr. A. ,,
Gibb, Mr. A. ,,
Scott, Mr. F. J. ,,
Seivwright, Mr. J. ,,
Watt, Mr. W. ,,
Macintosh, Rev. W., Airdrie.
Edwards, Rev. H., Anstruther.
Fortune, Mr. R. ,,
Thomson, Mr. P. ,,
Carter, Mr. J., Dundee.
Clark, Rev. D. ,,
Ireland, Mr. D. ,,
Lawson, Mr. J. ,,
Lister, Rev. T. W. ,,
Hagen, Rev. J. T., Dunfermline.
Johnston, Rev. J. B., M.A., Galashiels.
Thomson, Rev. A., Galashiels.
Chrystal, Rev. J. R. B.D., Hamilton.
Seaman, Rev. W., Hawick.
Farquhar, Rev. J., M.A., Paisley.
M'Alpine, Mr. A., Paisley.
McCallum, Mr. J. M. ,,
Robinson, Rev. J. A. G., M.A., Perth.
McKinlay, Mr. A., Rothesay.
Swan, Mr. A., Stirling.
Yuille, Rev. G. ,,
Brown, Mr. G., Greenock.
Corbet, Rev. A. ,,
Glendening, Rev. R. E., Elgin.
Richards, Rev. W., Leith.
Brown, Rev. H. D., Ayr.
Hourston, Mr. D. ,,
Nicolson, Rev. W.B., M.A., Kirkintilloch.
Payne, Rev. A. J., Peterhead.
Hirst, Rev. S., St. Andrews.
Connor, Rev. J., Motherwell.

BAPTIST UNION OF IRELAND.

See "Associations," Part VI.

IRISH BAPTIST HOME MISSION.

Founded 1814 as the Baptist Irish Society.

Chairman—Rev. H. D. BROWN, M.A., Glengyle, Rathgar, Dublin.

Treasurer—Mr. H. A. GRIBBON, Holme Lea, Coleraine.

Secretary—Mr. T. R. WARNER, Rockefeller House, Harcourt Street, Dublin.

General Committee.

Atkinson, Mr. E. D., Tandragee.
Banks, Rev. S. J., Banbridge.
*Bennett, Mr. B., Waterford.
*Brown, Rev. H. D., M.A., Dublin.
Bury, Mr. A. U. G., M.A., Dublin.
Carson, Rev. R. H., Tubbermore.
*Clark, Rev. R., Belfast.
*Crosthwaite, Dr. Davenport, Dublin.
Dixon, Mr. J. L., Dublin.
Donald, Rev. C. S., Belfast.
*Drummond, Mr. W. H., Dublin.
Froste, Mr. R. P., B.A., Dublin.
*Glendinning, Mr. R. G., Belfast.
*Graham, Mr. H. H., Belfast.
*Gribbon, Mr. H. A., Coleraine.
Haughton, Mr. R. S., Dublin.
*Irwin, Mr. W., Donaghmore.
Kirker, Mr. H., Banbridge.
La Touche, Mr. J., J.P., D. L., Brannoxtown.
*M'Kelvey, Mr. D., Belfast..
McIntosh, Mr. H., Belfast.
Nixon, Surgeon F. A., Dublin.
*Pearson, Mr. J. D., Dublin.
Prendreigh, Mr. A., Cork.
Wallace, Mr. J. R., Limerick.
*Warner, Mr. T. R., Dublin.
Warner, Mr. W. C., sen., Dublin.
*Waters, Surgeon-Major, C.B., J.P. Tubbermore.
Weatherup, Mr. J., Carrickfergus.

* These constitute the Executive Committee.

INCOME for the year 1894	£2,154	15	5
EXPENDITURE	2,410	15	3

Eighteen agents employed.

BAPTIST MISSIONARY SOCIETY.

(Mission House, 19, Furnival-street, E.C.)

Formed 1792.

GROSS RECEIPTS, year ending March 31st, 1895	*£62,999	18	3
GROSS EXPENDITURE do.	*71,700	3	6
CASH RECEIPTS, during same period, for Centenary Fund	4,825	13	11
EXPENDITURE, during same period, on account of Centenary Fund	22,821	13	8

* These totals do not include amounts raised and expended at mission stations.

COMMITTEE AND OFFICERS, 1895-96.

Treasurer—MR. W. R. RICKETT.

Hon. Secretary—MR. E. B. UNDERHILL, LL.D.

General Secretary.—MR. A. H. BAYNES.

Association Secretary—REV. J. B. MYERS.

Secretary of Bible Translation Society Auxiliary—REV. W. HILL.

Committee.

Atkinson, Rev. J. H., Liverpool.
Bailey, Rev. J., B.A., Sheffield.
Baillie, Rev. J., London.
Barran, Mr. A., Leeds.
Bird, Rev. B., Plymouth.
Briscoe, Rev. J. T., Bristol.
Brown, Rev. C., London.
Chown, Mr. J., London.
Clarke, Mr. D., C. A., High Wycombe.
Collier, Mr. E. P., J.P., Reading.
Davies, Rev. D., Brighton.
Dobson, Rev. N. Deal.
Evans, Rev. B., Aberdare.
Forbes, Rev. J. T., M.A., Edinburgh.
Gange, Rev. E. G., London.
Glover, Rev. R., D.D., Bristol.
Gould, Rev. G. P., M.A., London.
Gray, Rev. R., Birmingham.
Greenhough, Rev. J. G., M.A., Leicester
Griffiths, Mr. R. F., London.
Hawker, Rev. G., London.
Henderson, Rev. E., London.
Hill, Rev. G., M.A., Nottingham.
Lush, Mr. Percy J. F., M.R.C.S., London.

Marnham, Mr. F. J., Addlestone.
Marnham, Mr. J., J.P., Boxmoor.
Martin, Rev. T. H., Glasgow.
Mead, Mr. J. B., London.
Medhurst, Rev. T. W., Cardiff.
Medley, Rev. E., B.A., London.
Morris, Rev. J. A., Aberystwyth.
Morris, Rev. T. M., Ipswich.
Morris, Rev. W., Treorky.
Olney, Mr. T. H., London.
Owen, Rev. J., Swansea.
Parkinson, Mr. W. C, L.C.C., London.
Payne, Mr. W., London.
Penny, Mr. T. S., Taunton.
Phillips, Rev. T., B.A., Kettering.
Price, Mr. C., Hampstead.
Roberts, Rev. J. E., M.A., Manchester.
Shakespeare, Rev. J. H., M.A., Norwich.
Short, Rev. G., B.A., Salisbury.
Skemp, Rev. C. W., Bradford.
Skerry, Rev. W. R., London.
Smith, Mr. J. J., J.P., Watford.
Spurrier, Rev. E., Colchester.
Tarn, Rev. T. G., Cambridge.
Thew, Rev. J., Leicester.
Vincent, Rev. S., Plymouth.
Wherry, Mr. Alderman W. R., J.P., Bourne.
Whitley, Mr. T., Southsea.
Williams, Rev. H. C., Corwen.
Wood, Rev. J. R., London.

And the Officers of the Zenana Mission.

Auditors—Messrs. J. Jennings, H. Keen, and W. W. Parkinson.

Bankers—Messrs. Barclay, Bevan, Tritton & Co., 54 Lombard Street, E.C.

Honorary Members of Committee.

Having rendered important Services to the Society.

Aldis, Rev. J., Beckington.
Allsop, Rev. S. S., Ripley, Derby.
Angus, Rev. J., D.D., London.
Barrass, Rev. T., Peterborough.
Baynes, Mr. W. W., J.P., D.L., Bromley.
Bembridge, Mr. W. B., J.P., Ripley, Derby.
Bompas, Mr. H. M., Q.C., London.
Booth, Rev. S. H., D.D., London.
Bowser, Mr. H., Glasgow.
Brown, Rev. J. J., Birmingham.
Brown, Rev. J. T., Northampton.
Burton, Mr. S. B., Newcastle-on-Tyne.
Clifford, Rev. J., M.A., D.D., London.
Culross, Rev. J., D.D., Bristol.
Edwards, Rev. E., Torquay.
Green, Rev. S. G., D.D., London.
Gurney, Mr. J. J., J.P., Newcastle.
Landels, Rev. W., D.D., Edinburgh.
McLaren, Rev. A., D.D., Manchester.
McMaster, Mr. J. S., Toronto.
Muller, Professor, Amsterdam.
Orton, Rev. W., Leicester.
Rawlings, Mr. E., London.
Robinson, Mr. E., J.P., Bristol.
Spurgeon, Rev. J. A., D.D., London.
Underwood, Rev. W., D.D., Derby.
Wheeler, Rev. T. A., Norwich.
Williams, Rev. C., Accrington.

Honorary Members of Committee (ex-officio), being Presidents or Principals of Denominational Colleges, in accordance with Regulation, p. 116.

Davies, Rev. Gethin, D.D., Bangor.
Davies, Rev. T. W., B.A., Nottingham.
Edwards, Rev. W., D.D., Cardiff.
Henderson, Rev. W. J., B.A., Bristol.
Parker, Rev. E., D.D., Manchester.
Roberts, Rev. R. H., B.A., London.
Tymms, Rev. T. V., Rawdon.

Plan and Regulations of the Society.

Name.—The name by which the Society has been, and is, designated, is "The Baptist Missionary Society," including "The Particular Baptist Missionary Society for Propagating the Gospel among the Heathen," which was formed in 1792, and "The General Baptist Missionary Society," which was formed in 1816.

Object.—The great object of this Society is the diffusion of the knowledge of the religion of Jesus Christ throughout the whole world, beyond the British Isles, by the preaching of the Gospel, the translation and publication of the Holy Scriptures, and the establishment of schools.

Members.—The following persons shall be considered members—viz., pastors of churches making an annual contribution; ministers who collect annually; and all Christian persons concurring in the objects of the Society, who are donors of ten pounds or upwards, or subscribers of ten shillings and sixpence annually to its funds.

General Meeting of Members.—A General Meeting of Members only shall be held annually, at which the Committee and Officers shall be chosen for the year ensuing, the Auditors of accounts appointed, and any other business pertaining to the Society transacted.

In choosing the Committee and Officers, the Chairman of the Meeting shall receive all names which it may be intended to propose. Out of the list so obtained, forty members of the Committee shall be chosen by ballot, those who have the greater number of votes being the parties elected, and the members so elected shall be empowered to fill up the number to fifty-four members, as required by the following rule, from the list of nominations presented at the Annual Meeting.

Committee.—That the affairs of the Society shall be conducted by a Committee of fifty-four persons, two-thirds of whom shall be residents beyond twelve miles of St. Paul's; the Committee to meet monthly, or oftener, in London, on a fixed day, for the despatch of business; seven members to be deemed a quorum; the Committee to be empowered to fill up vacancies

Public Meetings.—A Public Meeting of the Society shall be held annually, when the list of the Committee shall be read, the accounts presented, and the proceedings of the previous year reported. The Committee shall also be empowered to summon Public Meetings in London or elsewhere, whenever the interests of the Society may seem to require.

Corresponding Members.—All Treasurers and Secretaries of Missionary Auxiliaries shall be CORRESPONDING MEMBERS of the Committee, together with such persons as it may be found necessary to add to their number.

Honorary Members.—The General Meeting of Members shall also be empowered to appoint as HONORARY MEMBERS of the Committee any who have rendered important services to the Society; provided the nomination of such Honorary Members of Committee shall proceed only from a resolution of the General Committee of the Society, or from six members of the Society who are combined therein.

Honorary Members (ex-officio).—Presidents or Principals of Denominational Colleges shall be *ex officio* Members of the Committee of the Society.

Members of the Society entitled to Vote at Committee Meetings.—All Honorary and Corresponding Members of the Committee, and all Ministers, who are Members of the Society, who may occasionally be in London; and also Ministers residing in London, similarly qualified, together with the Treasurers and Secretaries of London Auxiliaries, shall be entitled to attend and vote at the Meetings of the Committee.

Funds.—All moneys received on behalf of the Society shall be lodged in the hands of the Treasurer, or of Trustees to be chosen by the Society. When the amount received shall exceed the sum needed for the current expenses of the month, it shall be invested in the Public Funds, until required for the use of the Mission.

Alteration of Constitution.—No alteration in the constitution of the Society shall be made without twelve months' notice having been given at a previous Annual General Meeting.

For further Particulars see Report published by the Baptist Missionary Society.

THE LADIES' ASSOCIATION FOR THE SUPPORT OF ZENANA WORK IN INDIA AND CHINA.

(IN CONNECTION WITH THE BAPTIST MISSIONARY SOCIETY.)

President—MRS. RICKETT.

Treasurer—MRS. UNDERHILL.

Hon. Secretaries
- Miss A. G. ANGUS, Miss E. A. ANGUS, 5, Ellerdale-road, Hampstead, N.W.
- Miss H. C. BOWSER, Sunnyside, Richmond Road, Ealing, W.

The object of this Society is to send the Gospel to the women of India and China, and it is carried on by lady missionaries and native Bible-women and school teachers. Zenanas are visited, schools established, and evangelistic, medical and village work maintained in 26 different stations, with a staff of 58 lady visitors and 200 native agents. Boarding, normal, and day schools contain 3,300 pupils, and 2,000 pupils are in Zenanas under regular instruction.

Committee.

Baillie, Mrs.
Barnard, Mrs.
Barran, Miss.
Baynes, Mrs. A. H.
Byerley, Miss.
Caine, Mrs.
Campagnac, Mrs.
Cowdy, Miss.
Fletcher, Mrs.
George, Mrs.
Gould, Mrs. A. P.
Gould, Mrs. H. P.
Green, Mrs.
Hawker, Mrs.
Henderson, Mrs. E.
Hill, Mrs. W.
Japp, Miss
Johnson, Mrs. G. L.
Kemp, Miss E. G.
Lewis, Mrs. P.
Medley, Mrs. E.
Murrell, Mrs.
Olney, Miss A.
Parkinson, Mrs.
Roberts, Mrs. R. H.
Robinson, Mrs. E.
Williamson, Mrs. R.
Rooke, Mrs. A. B.
Rose, Mrs. H.
Salter, Miss
Skerry, Mrs.
Smith, Mrs. J. J.
Southwell, Miss.
Spurgeon, Mrs. J. A.
Sturt, Mrs.
Trafford, Mrs.
Tritton, Miss.
Warmington, Miss.
Watson, Mrs. S.
Whitley, Mrs.

And the Treasurer and Secretaries of the Baptist Missionary Society.

Honorary Members: Mrs. J. F. Smith and Mrs. Sale.

INCOME, year ending March 31st, 1895 .. .. £9,005
EXPENDITURE 9,255

YOUNG MEN'S ASSOCIATION IN AID OF THE BAPTIST MISSIONARY SOCIETY.

Founded 1848. OBJECTS:—"To diffuse a missionary spirit, especially among the young, by the dissemination of missionary information, the establishment of missionary libraries, and the delivery of lectures; to form and encourage Sunday School and other juvenile missionary auxiliaries; and to promote systematic efforts on behalf of missions."

All moneys received by the Association for the Baptist Missionary Society are paid over direct, the working expenses being met by separate subscriptions.

President—Mr. H. M. BOMPAS, M.A., Q.C.

Vice-Presidents.

Rev. J. ANGUS, D.D.
Mr. A. H. BAYNES.
Mr. W. J. BENHAM, B.A.
Mr. T. H. OLNEY.
Mr. W. R. RICKETT.
Mr. E. B. UNDERHILL, LL.D.

Treasurer—Mr. F. J. MARNHAM.

Acting Hon. Secretaries—Messrs. J. EVERETT, F. W. FORD, and H. E. WOOD, 19, Furnival-street, E.C.

Committee.

Bell, Mr. D. S.
Bond, Mr. A.
Dyer, Mr. W. G.
Evans, Mr. H. W.
Field, Mr. F. E.
Ford, Mr. F. W.
Judd, Mr. G. H.
Lovejoy, Mr. T.
Maynard, Mr. J.
Myers, Rev. J. B.
Page, Mr. J. B.
Parkinson, Mr. W. W., L.C.C.
Wood, Mr. H. E.
Shepherd, Mr. A. J.
Taylor, Mr. W.
Thomson, Mr. H. O.
Tucker, Mr. F. E.
Tyrer, Mr. R. H.
Westwood, Mr. W. J.

One representative from Regent's Park College; one from Metropolitan Tabernacle College; and two representatives from each School.

School Visitor—Mr. J. EVERETT.

Auditors—Mr. C. E. SMITH and Mr. W. W. PARKINSON, L.C.C.

BIBLE TRANSLATION SOCIETY.

Formed 1840. OBJECT.—"It shall be the object of this Society to aid in printing and circulating those translations of the Holy Scriptures from which the British and Foreign Bible Society has withdrawn its assistance, on the ground that the words relating to the ordinance of Baptism have been translated by terms signifying immersion; and further to aid in producing and circulating other versions of the Word of God similarly faithful and complete."

INCOME, year ending March 31st, 1895	£1,276 2 8
EXPENDITURE	1,239 9 3

Treasurer—Mr. E. B. UNDERHILL, LL.D., Derwent Lodge, Thurlow-road, Hampstead, N.W.

Secretary—Rev. W. HILL, 9, St. Julian's-road, Kilburn, N.W.

Committee.

Angus, Rev. J., D.D. London.
Baynes, Mr. A. H. ,,
Booth, Rev. S. H., D.D. ,,
Clifford, Rev. J., M.A., D.D. ,,
Gould, Rev. G. P., M.A. ,,
Green, Rev. S. G., D.D. ,,
Griffiths, Mr. R. F. ,,
Myers, Rev. J. B. ,,
Rickett, Mr. W. R. ,,
Roberts, Rev. R. H., B.A. ,,
Scorey, Rev. P. G. ,,
Willis, Mr. W., Q.C. ,,
Wood, Rev. J. R. ,,
Barrass, Rev. T., Peterborough.
Brown, Rev. J. J., Birmingham.
Brown, Rev. J. T., Northampton.
Culross, Rev. J., D.D., Bristol.
Davies, Rev. G., D.D., Bangor.
Davies, Rev. T. W., B.A., Nottingham.
Edwards, Rev. W., D.D., Cardiff.
Henderson, Rev. W. J., B.A., Bristol.
Landels, Rev. W., D.D., Edinburgh.
Marnham, Mr. J., J.P., Boxmoor.
Morris, Rev. J. A., Aberystwyth.
Morris, Rev. T. M., Ipswich.
Owen, Rev. J., Swansea.
Parker, Rev. E., D.D., Manchester.
Shaw, Mr. T., Huddersfield.
Short, Rev. G., B.A., Salisbury.
Tilly, Rev. A., Cardiff.
Tymms, Rev. T. V., Rawdon.
Wheeler, Rev. T. A., Norwich.
Williams, Rev. C., Accrington.
Williams, Rev. H. C., Corwen.
Wherry, Mr. Ald. W. R., J.P., Bourne.

GERMAN BAPTIST MISSION.

COMMITTEE FOR DISTRIBUTION OF FUNDS SENT OUT FROM GREAT BRITAIN.

Treasurer—Rev. P. W. BICKEL, D.D., Hamburg.

Secretary—Pastor K. MASCHER, Dresden.

Pastor WIEHLER, Bremen.
,, E. MILLARD, Wiesbaden.
,, L. HORN, Elbing.
Pastor R. KROMM, Breslau.
,, WEERTS, Frankfurt-on-Main.
Herr PIELSTICK, Hamburg.
Rev. F. B. MEYER, B.A., London.

Treasurer for Great Britain—Mr. M. H. WILKIN, Hampstead, N.W.

Hon. Secretary for Great Britain—Mr. W. S. ONCKEN, Sunny Bank, Lincoln.

Amount received during 1894-95 in Great Britain, £499 6s. 3d.

SUMMARY FOR JANUARY 1ST, 1895, comprising the Churches in Germany, Switzerland, Austria-Hungary, Holland, Roumania, Bulgaria and South Africa.

Number of Churches	163	Number of Sunday Schools ..	513
,, Members	31,399	,, Sunday Scholars ..	21,460

Amount contributed by the German Churches to the work of this Mission, about £25,540.

N.B.—Five German Churches in South Africa, with 928 members, are included in the above summary. The Russian Churches, of which there are 48, have formed a separate Union, with a membership of over 15,000. The proceedings are in the Lettish, Esthonian and German languages. The 25 Danish Churches have also formed a separate Union, numbering 3,000 members.

STRICT BAPTIST MISSION.

Formed 1860. OBJECT.—"The diffusion of the Gospel in heathen lands, and the formation of churches in accordance with the principles of Strict Communion Baptists."

INCOME, 1894, including balance from 1893 of £455 16s. 8d. ..	£1,949	6	10
EXPENDITURE	1,362	12	8
BALANCE in hand	586	14	2

President—Mr. J Box.

Vice-President—Mr. R. E. SEARS.

Treasurer—Mr. W. ABBOTT.

Hon. Secretaries—Mr. J. BRISCOE, 58, Grosvenor-road, Highbury New Park, N.; Mr. I. R. WAKELIN, 33, Robert-street, Hampstead-road, N.W.; and Mr. F. J. CATCHPOLE, 11, Jerningham-road, New Cross, S.E.

This Mission has two centres of evangelical work—in India and Ceylon. In India there are eighteen stations and fifty-three sub-stations, with sixty-eight workers; in Ceylon there are four stations, and five workers.

BAPTIST DEACONESSES' HOME AND MISSION.

59, DOUGHTY STREET, LONDON, W.C.

Superintendent—Rev. W. BROCK, 16, Ellerdale-road, Hampstead, N.W.

Acting Treasurer—Mr. S. THOMPSON, 11, Wood-street, E.C.

Secretary—Rev. E. HENDERSON, 21, Victoria-road, Clapham, S.W.

Committee.

Baillie, Rev. J.
Chown, Mrs.
David, Mr. A. J., LL.M.
Denny, Mrs.
Gordon, Mrs.
Gould, Mr. A. P., M.S.
Grigg, Mr. F. R.
Hudson, Mrs.
Lush, Mr. Percy J. F., M.R.C.S.
McKay, Rev. G. P.
Micklem, Mr. N., LL.B.
Page, Rev. W., B.A.
Skerry, Rev. W. R.
Stiff, Mr. E.
Thompson, Mrs. S.
Vick, Rev. C. W.

The Central Mission is in Dorrington-street, Leather-lane, E.C., and the neighbourhood around. Seven sisters are engaged there, in visiting, nursing, and conducting meetings. A medical dispensary is open every Friday afternoon for the poor, and is conducted by Dr. Lush. There are also five sisters at work in various parts of London, in connection with Baptist Churches, and under the superintendence of their ministers.

INCOME, 1894	£906	19	4

HOME OF REST FOR BAPTIST MINISTERS AND MISSIONARIES.

CEFN-Y-COED, LLANFAIRFECHAN, NORTH WALES.

President—Rev. A. MCLAREN, D.D., Manchester.

Vice-Presidents.

Baynes, Mr. A. H., London.
Booth, Rev. S. H., D.D., London.
Brown, Rev. J. T., Northampton.
Clifford, Rev. J., D.D., London.
Culross, Rev. J., D.D., Bristol.
Glover, Rev. R., D.D., Bristol.
Greenhough, Rev. J. G., M.A., Leicester.
Medley, Rev. W., M.A., Rawdon.
Parker, Rev. E., D.D., Manchester.
Rickett, Mr. W. R., London.
Roberts, Rev. R. H., B.A., London.
Shakespeare, Rev. J. H., M.A., Norwich.
Short, Rev. G., B.A., Salisbury.
Tymms, Rev. T. V., Rawdon.
Williams, Rev. Chas., Accrington.

Committee of Management.

Atkinson, Rev. J. H.
Bonner, Rev. C.
Bowser, Rev. S. W., B.A.
Lewis, Rev. R.
McLaren, Rev. A., D.D.
Macalpine, Mr. G. W., J.P.
Roberts, Rev. J. E., M.A.
Streuli, Rev. A. W. H.

House Committee.

Rev. J. E. ROBERTS, M.A., Rev. A. W. H. STREULI, and the WARDEN.

Warden and Treasurer (pro. tem.)—Rev. C. BONNER, Southampton.

The Home of Rest is open throughout the year, and is under the care of a Lady Superintendent. Baptist Ministers or Missionaries, alone or with their wives, can, when in need of change, find a home there. All provision is made for comfort and recreation, at a much smaller cost than that incurred in the usual way of taking a holiday. Particulars may be had of the Warden.

II.—COLLEGES.

BRISTOL.

Instituted 1770.

INCOME, year ending June, 1895	£1,900 16 10
EXPENDITURE	1,878 19 5

Present number of Students, 22.

Trustees—Mr. T. H. HEPBURN, Mr. E. ROBINSON, J.P., Mr. W. SHERRING, Mr. C. TOWNSEND, J.P.

Joint Presidents { Rev. J. CULROSS, M.A., D.D.
Rev. W. J. HENDERSON, B.A.

The Study of Classical and General Subjects is pursued in the classes of Bristol University College.

During 1895, in the University of London, Mr. H. G. Hore passed the Intermediate Arts Examination, and Mr. A. Moore and Mr. J. Thomas matriculated, the former in the First Division and the latter in the Honours Division.

Treasurer—Mr. E. ROBINSON, J.P., Bristol.

Secretary—Rev. R. GLOVER, D.D., 15, Westfield Park, Bristol.

Financial Secretary—Rev. H. KNEE, Wellington House, Ashley-road, Bristol.

MIDLAND.

NOTTINGHAM.

Instituted 1797 *in London. Removed to Wisbech* 1814, *to Loughborough in* 1825, *to London in* 1841, *to Leicester in* 1843, *to Nottingham in* 1857, *to Chilwell in* 1861, *and to Nottingham in* 1883.

INCOME, year ending June, 1895	£961 0 0
EXPENDITURE	960 0 0

Present number of Students, 14.

Principal and Tutor in Biblical Languages and Biblical Theology—Rev. T. W. DAVIES, B.A.

Warden—Rev. W. EVANS.

Warden Elect—Rev. T. BARRASS.

Hon. Medical Officer—Mr. J. WATSON, M.B., C.M., M.R.C.S.

The Study of Classical, Mathematical, and Literary Subjects is pursued in he classes of Nottingham University College.

During 1895, in the University of London, Mr. J. H. Rushbrooke matriculated in *the First* Division and Mr. P. G. R. Monk in the Second Division.

Treasurer—Mr. J. S. SMITH, Mountsorrel, Loughborough.
Hon. Secretaries—Rev. W. EVANS, Leicester, Rev. R. SILBY, Nottingham, and (Finance) Mr. W. HUNT, Nottingham.

Life Governors.

Mr. W. B. Bembridge, J.P.
†Mr. A. Bradley.
Mr. R. F. Griffiths.
Mr. J. S. Smith.
Mr. Alderman W. R. Wherry, J.P.

Elected Members of Council.

*Aked, Rev. C. F.
Atkinson, Rev. J. H.
*Barrass, Rev. T.
Bennett, Rev. J. E., B.A.
*Bishop, Rev. W.
*Carey, Rev. S. P., M.A.
Carrington, Rev. E.
Clark, Rev. J.
*Clifford, Rev. J., M.A., D.D.
*Coleman, Rev. E. E.
*Douglas, Rev. J., B.A.
Ford, Rev. R. C., M.A.
Godfrey, Rev. J. R.
Handford, Rev. R. F.
Harris, Rev. W. F.
Jenkins, Rev. R.
Jones, Rev. W. R.
*McElwee, Rev. G. M., M.A., B.Sc.
Payne, Rev. C.
*Vick, Rev. C. W.
Ashby, Mr. W.
†Barwick, Mr. E.
Bennett, Mr. T. H.
†Bexon, Mr. A.
‡Bishop, Mr. C. T.
†Booker, Mr. F. W.
‡Bright, Mr. J.
†Bright, Mr. L.
‡Brownsword, Mr. A.
‡Cholerton, Mr. G.
‡Clark, Mr. W. B.
†‡Cullen, Mr. A. H.
*‡Forth, Mr. C.
*Granger, Prof. F. S., D. Lit., M.A.
†Hall, Mr. S.
‡Harrison, Mr. Alderman T. H., J.P.
Hoffman, Mr. G.
†Mallet, Mr. J. T.
Pochin, Mr. J.
*Stevenson, Mr. P. H.

Representatives of Baptist Union.

Booth, Rev. S. H., D.D.
Williams, Rev. C.

Representatives of East Midland Association.

*Ashwell, Mr. H., J.P.
Woods, Rev. W.

Representatives of West Midland Association.

Brown, Rev. J. J.
Lee, Rev. A. H.

* Academic Committee. † House Committee.
‡ Finance and Reference Committee.

RAWDON, NEAR LEEDS.

The "Northern Baptist Education Society," formed at Horton, Bradford, 1804.

College removed to Rawdon, 1859.

Present number of Students, 25.

INCOME, for year ending June 30, 1895	£1,431	15	11
EXPENDITURE	2,057	14	2
SPECIAL CONTRIBUTIONS TO ARREARS FUND, 1895 ..	625	0	0

COMMITTEE FOR 1895-96.

President and Tutor in Theology—Rev. T. V. TYMMS.

Tutor in Greek and Philosophy—Rev. W. MEDLEY, M.A.

Tutor in Hebrew, Greek Testament, and English—Rev. D. GLASS, M.A.

During 1895, at Edinburgh, Mr. W. H. Holdsworth took the degree of M.A.; and in the University of London, Mr. C. A. Charter took the degree of B.A.

Treasurers—Sir JOHN BARRAN, Bart., Leeds; Mr. W. TOWN, Keighley.

Secretary—Rev. C. W. SKEMP, Bradford.

Finance Secretary—Mr. W. R. BILBROUGH, Leeds.

Members of the Committee.

Arthur, Rev. D., Haworth.
Bailey, Rev. J., B.A., Sheffield.
Barran, Mr. A., Leeds.
Benskin, Rev. F. J., Huddersfield.
Best, Mr. W., Bradford.
Bilbrough, Mr. A., Leeds.
Birkinshaw, Mr. J. R., Bradford.
Bonner, Rev. C., Southampton.
Bonner, Rev. H., Birmingham.
Bowser, Rev. S. W., B.A., Birkenhead.
Bright, Mr. J., Nottingham.
Brooke, Mr. Ald. J., J.P., Huddersfield.
Chown, Mr. J., London.
Davies, Mr. W. G., Newcastle-on-Tyne.
Fayers, Rev. A. P., Rawdon.
Fearnside, Mr. E., Leeds.
Forbes, Rev. J. T., M.A., Edinburgh.
Fyfe, Mr. J. R., Shipley.
Gray, Rev. R., Birmingham.
Green, Rev. S. W., M.A., London.
Greenhough, Rev. J. G., M.A., Leicester.
Greenwood, Mr. J. F., Oxenhope.
Haslam, Rev. J., Gildersome.
Hill, Rev. G., M.A., Nottingham.
Horsfall, Mr. J. C., Sutton-in-Craven.
Hunter, Rev. W. J., Kirkcaldy.
Illingworth, Mr. W. K., Leeds.
Jones, Rev. W., Hebden Bridge.
Lewis, Rev. R., Liverpool.
Macalpine, Mr. G. W., J.P., Accrington.
Martin, Rev. T. H., Glasgow.
Medley, Rev. E., B.A., London.
Mursell, Rev. J., Derby.
Paget, Mr. S., Keighley.
Porteous, Rev. J., Burton-on-Trent.
Pratt, Mr. J. H., Rawdon.
Riley, Rev. A. F., London.
Roberts, Rev J. E., M.A., Manchester.
Scholefield, Mr. J. W., J.P., Bootle.
Skerry, Rev. W. R., London.
Smith, Mr. F. E., Sheffield.
Spencer, Mr. T., Manchester.
Stuart, Rev. J., Watford.
Taylor, Mr. R., Southport.
Thew, Rev. J., Leicester.
Town, Mr. J., Leeds.
Walker, Mr. A., Lindley.
Watson, Mr. R., Rochdale.
Watts, Mr. H., Liverpool.
Whitewood, Mr. J. E., Ben Rhydding.

Honorary Members of the Committee.

Acworth, Mr. J., Bradford.
Aldis, Rev. J., Beckington.
Crossley, Mr. D., J.P., Hebden Bridge.
Eaton, Mr. J., Sheffield.
Green, Rev. S. G., D.D., London.
Henderson, Rev. W. J., B.A., Bristol.
McLaren, Rev. A., D.D., Manchester.
Morris, Rev. T. M., Ipswich.
Mounsey, Mr. E., J.P., Liverpool.
Williams, Rev. C., Accrington.

REGENT'S PARK.

Instituted at Stepney, 1810. *Removed to Regent's Park*, 1857.

INCOME, 1894-95 .. .. £4,382

Present number of Ministerial Students, 29; Ministers educated from commencement, 400.

Emeritus Principal—REV. J. ANGUS, M.A., D.D.

Principal and Theological Tutor—Rev. R. H. ROBERTS, B.A.

Tutor in Philosophy and in New Testament Exegesis—Rev. S. W. GREEN, M.A.

Tutor in Church History and in Hebrew—Rev. G. P. GOULD, M.A.

Tutor in Classics, &c.—Mr. C. McEVOY, B.A., and Browne Medallist.

Treasurer—Mr. E. B. UNDERHILL, LL.D.

Secretary—Rev. W. W. SIDEY, 54, Lansdowne-road, Tottenham.

Committee.

Angus, Mr. C. J.
Baillie, Rev. J.
Balding, Mr. E.
Baynes, Mr. A. H.
Benham, Mr. W. J., B.A.
Bergin, Rev. J. M.
Booth, Rev. S. H., D.D.
Chown, Mr. J.
Cooke, Rev. J. H.
East, Rev. D. J.
Freeman, Mr. T.
Gange, Rev. E. G.
Green, Rev. S. G., D.D.
Lush, Mr. P. J. F., M.R.C.S.
Marnham, Mr. H.
Medley, Rev. E., B.A.
Wood, Rev. J. R.
Page, Rev. W., B.A.
Price, Mr. C.
Rawlings, Mr. E.
Rickett, Mr. W. R.
Skerry, Rev. W. R.
Thomas, Rev. E.
Todd, Rev. J. W., D.D.
Weymouth, Dr.

The following Managers of the Baptist Fund have been elected by the Fundees to serve on the Committee during the ensuing year, viz.:—

Mr. J. Eastty	Mr. P. Cadby	Rev. W. T. Henderson
Mr. R. Grace	Mr. J. J. Smith, J.P.	

The Session begins early in September. All applications to be sent in by the 15th of the preceding May.

During 1895, in the University of London, Mr. F. J. Shipway and Mr. W. A. Benton matriculated in the First Division, and Mr. D. J. Evans passed the Intermediate Arts Examination in the Second Division. At St. Andrews, Mr. J. E. Ennals, B.A., passed the second and final examination for the degree of B.D.

PASTORS'.

Instituted at Camberwell, 1856. *Removed to Metropolitan Tabernacle*, 1861.

INCOME, year ending December 31st, 1894	£4,068	2	9
EXPENDITURE	5,188	19	2

Present number of Students, 55.

President—Rev. J. A. SPURGEON, D.D., LL.D.

Tutors—Rev. F. G. MARCHANT, Rev. A. M'CAIG, B.A., LL.D., and Rev. W. USHER, M.D.

Tutors of Evening Classes—Messrs. S. JOHNSON, and T. F. BOWERS, B.A.

Secretary—Mr. E. H. BARTLETT.

During 1895, in the University of London, Mr. S. S. Sarson, Mr. E. P. Wright and E. M. Yeomans matriculated in the Second Division.

MANCHESTER.

BRIGHTON GROVE, MANCHESTER.

Established as the "Baptist Theological Institution," at Bury, October, 1866.

Present number of Students, 19.

President and Theological Tutor—Rev. E. PARKER, D.D.

Tutor in Classics, Hebrew, and Philosophy—Rev. J. T. MARSHALL, M.A., Lond.

Treasurer—Mr. W. D. SHAW, J.P., Huddersfield.

Secretary—Rev. H. ELLIS, M.A., Farsley, near Leeds.

Collector—Rev. R. E. TOWLER, Eltham Terrace, Levenshulme, Manchester.

Committee.

Bayley, Mr. C. H., Oswestry.
Crabtree, Mr. S., Bradford.
Delday, Mr. J. H., Scarborough.
Elias, Mr. J., Liverpool.
Fairbank, Mr. C., Ogden.
Fisher, Mr. H., Marsden.
Hanson, Mr. G. H., Huddersfield.
Harvey, Mr. W., Nantwich.
Hirst, Mr. W., Golcar.
Hurst, Mr. John, Rochdale.
Illingworth, Mr. W., Bradford.
Lewis, Mr. B., Cardiff.
Maden, Mr. J. H., Ramsbottom.
McMaster, Mr. J. S., Toronto.
Marshall, Mr. J. D., Farsley.
Mellor, Mr. D., Bradford.
Mitchell, Mr. J., Bradford.
Moulson, Mr. W., J.P., Bradford.
Pearce, Mr. Joseph, Leeds.
Shaw, Mr. Geo., Huddersfield.
Smith, Mr. J., Lindley, Huddersfield.
Sykes, Mr. T. E., Huddersfield.
Taylor, Mr. E., Milnsbridge.
Watson, Mr. P., Bradford.
White, Mr. J., Bradford.
Whitehead, Mr. W. A., Bradford.
Whiteley, Mr. J. W., Rishworth.
Wilkin, Mr. M. H., London.
Wilson, Mr. George, Bramley.

Together with (*a*) Ministers educated in the College, (*b*) Pastors of churches giving to the College an annual collection, and (*c*) Ministers accepted as Associates of the College.

CARDIFF.

Originally the Welsh and English Baptist Education Society. Instituted at Abergavenny, 1807. Removed to Pontypool, 1836, and to Cardiff, 1893.

INCOME, year ending June, 1895..	£1,319 2 9
EXPENDITURE	1,482 7 8

Present number of Students, 24.

President—Rev. W. EDWARDS, B.A., D.D.

Tutor—Rev. J. M. DAVIES, M.A.

During 1895, in the University of London, two students matriculated in the First Division, and in the University of Wales, one student matriculated in the First Division.

Chairman—Mr. H. PHILLIPS, J.P., Newport.

Treasurers—Mr. Councillor W. EDWARDS, J.P., Maindee, Newport, and Mr. Alderman R. CORY, J.P., Cardiff.

Secretaries—Revs. D. B. JONES, Caerleon, Mon., and W. MORRIS, F.R.G.S., Treorky, Pontypridd.

Auditors—Mr. D. JONES, Pontnewynydd, and Mr. T. JAMES, Blaenavon.

ABERYSTWYTH.

Instituted at Haverfordwest, 1839. *Removed to Aberystwyth,* 1894.

INCOME, year ending August 1st, 1895	£622 12 6
EXPENDITURE	920 7 6

Present number of Students, 16. Educated from commencement, 295.

Tutors—Revs. J. A. MORRIS, and T. WILLIAMS, B.A.

Treasurers—Mr. J. ROWLANDS, Haverfordwest, and Mr. J. MORGAN, J.P.; Aberystwyth.

Secretaries—Revs. J. JENKINS, Newport, Pembrokeshire; B. THOMAS, Letterston, Pembrokeshire, and D. F. ELLIS, Aberystwyth.

The College Term begins the Fourth Wednesday in October and ends the Second Wednesday in August.

BANGOR.

Instituted at Llangollen, 1862. *Removed to Bangor,* 1892.

INCOME, year ending Dec. 31st, 1894	£1,290 19 11
EXPENDITURE	1,248 9 6

Present number of Students 24. Ministers educated from commencement, 168.

Principal and Tutor in Theology, Apologetics and Hebrew—
Rev. G. DAVIES, D.D.

Tutor in Greek Testament, Philosophy and Church History—
Rev. S. MORRIS, M.A., (Lond.).

(Arts Students attend the classes and lectures at the University College.)

During 1895, in the University of Wales, Mr. E. C. Jones and Mr. D. O. Griffiths matriculated.

Treasurer—Mr. R. BECK, Bangor.

Secretaries—(*Minutes*) Rev. J. GRIFFITHS, Llanfairfechan; and (*Honorary*) Rev. O. DAVIES, D.D., Carnarvon.

The Session begins in October and ends the last week in June.

DR. WARD'S TRUST.

Trustees—Rev. J. ANGUS, D.D., Rev. S. G. GREEN, D.D., Mr. E. RAWLINGS.

Treasurer—Mr. J. J. SMITH, J.P.

Hon. Secretary—Rev. S. H. BOOTH, D.D., 19, Furnival-street, E.C.

John Ward, LL.D., a Professor in Gresham College, who died in 1758, had, in 1754, put in trust £1,200 Bank Stock, to be applied after his decease to the education for the Ministry of two young men or more, whose parents shall be Protestant Dissenters, living in England, or who shall have resided in England at the time of their decease (preference being given to those of Baptist parentage), and who when applying shall declare their intention to give themselves to the work of the ministry in South Britain. Such young men shall have made a good proficiency in the Latin and Greek languages, and the Exhibition shall be for their improvement in these languages, and for the acquisition of Hebrew. A Scheme by the Charity Commissioners (July, 1863) comprises these particulars, and also directs that an Exhibitioner shall not be more than twenty-one years at the time of his appointment, and shall not retain his appointment after the age of twenty-five years. The Scheme also directs that each Exhibitioner shall, during the tenure of his appointment, attend some established University or other Educational Institution in the United Kingdom, where provision is made for their preparing for a Degree, as determined by the Trustees. The number of Students at present aided by the Trust is five.

SCOTLAND.

THEOLOGICAL COLLEGE, GLASGOW.

Instituted 1894, in place of the Theological Hall of the Baptist Union of Scotland, which was instituted in 1869. The new College is in no way connected with the Baptist Union of Scotland. It is intended to provide for a complete course of ministerial education, which will comprise:—(1) A course in Arts in a Scottish University, qualifying for the M.A. Degree; and (2) a course in Theology, embracing (*a*) Biblical and Systematic Theology; (*b*) Biblical Criticism and Exegesis; (*c*) Church History and Apologetics, including the Historical position and Principles of the Baptists; (*d*) Homiletics and General Pastoral Work.

President—Prof. J. COATS, M.D.

Vice-Presidents.

BOWSER, Mr. H.	WALCOT, Mr. J.
NIMMO, Mr. J.	WILSON, Mr. J.

Treasurer—Mr. G. W. ELMSLIE.

Joint Secretaries—Mr. A. NIMMO, M.A., and Mr. C. H. BOWSER.

Trustees.

Bowser, Mr. H.	White, Mr. T., S.S.C.
Nimmo, Mr. J.	Wilson, Mr. J.
Somerville, Mr. R., M.D.	

Tutors—

Biblical and Systematic Theology—Rev. A. WYLIE, M.A.
Biblical Criticism and Exegesis—Rev, J. COATS, M.A.
Church History and Apologetics—Rev. J. McLELLAN.
Homiletics and General Pastoral Work, including the Historical Position and Principles of the Baptists—Rev. T. H. MARTIN.

IRELAND.

ROCKEFELLER HOUSE, HARCOURT-STREET, DUBLIN—TRAINING INSTITUTE.

Instituted 1892.

Present Number of Students, 8.

President—Rev. H. D. BROWN, M.A.

Vice-Presidents.

Mr. D. CROSTHWAITE, LL.D. | Mr. J. LA TOUCHE, D.L., J.P.

Secretary—Mr. T. R. WARNER.

Treasurer—Mr. F. A. NIXON, F.R.C.S.I.

Committee.

Adam, Mr. J.
Beater, Mr. O. P., M.D., LL.B.
Beater, Mr. H. W.
Bennett, Mr. B.
Clark, Rev. R.
Drummond, Mr. W. H.
Froste, Mr. R. P., B.A.
Gibb, Rev. A. G., M.A.
Glendinning, Mr. R. G.
Gribbon, Mr. H. A.
Haughton, Mr. R. S.
Lloyd, Mr. T. E.
O'Hara, Mr. E.
Pearson, Mr. J. D.
Warner, Mr. W. C.
Waters, Brigade-Surgeon, C.B., J.P.

Principal—Mr. A. BURY, M.A., T.C.D.

Mathematical Tutor—Mr. S. WILLIS (Siz., First Honorman T.C.D.).

English—Mr. E. RONEY.

III.—PUBLICATIONS.

THE UNION MISSION HYMNAL.

(See under "Literature Fund" of the Baptist Union, page 35.)

---

(1) PSALMS AND HYMNS.

First published in 1855.

---

(2) PSALMS AND HYMNS, WITH SUPPLEMENT.

First published in 1881.

---

(3) "THE TREASURY" CONGREGATIONAL TUNE BOOK.

Published 1886.

(4) PSALMS AND HYMNS FOR SCHOOL AND HOME.

Published 1882.—Enlarged 1892.

(5) "THE TREASURY" SCHOOL AND HOME TUNE BOOK.

Published 1883.—Enlarged 1892.

(6) YOUNG MEN'S CHRISTIAN ASSOCIATION HYMNS.

Also Hymn Sheets—Special for Various Occasions. Seventeen different sorts.
Published 1887—1894.

The entire profits of these six publications and hymn sheets are yearly distributed amongst the widows and orphans of Baptist ministers and missionaries. The amount distributed in 1895 was £950; and the total amount thus distributed is £19,526.

The next distribution will take place in April, 1896.

to whom application for Grants to Widows should be made before 25th March.

Published by the Psalms and Hymns Trust, 22A, Furnival-street, E.C.

Remittances to be made payable to the Secretary, as above.

(1) THE BAPTIST HYMNAL.

First published in 1879. Profits devoted to Denominational objects, *e.g.*, the Annuity and the Home Mission Funds of the Baptist Union, the Midland College, and the Baptist Building Fund.

---

(2) THE UNION HYMNAL.

Same book as the Baptist Hymnal, with undenominational title for the use of Union Churches.

---

(3) THE SCHOOL HYMNAL.

Published in December, 1880. A Collection of 343 hymns for the young, for use in Sunday Schools and families.

---

(4) THE INFANT-CLASS HYMNAL.

A Selection of Hymns from the preceding, for use in Infant Classes and Religious Services for Young Children.

---

(5) THE SCHOOL HYMNAL TUNE BOOK.

Published in May, 1882. Containing tunes for all the hymns in the School and Infant Class Hymnals, as well as for the hymns of peculiar metre in the Baptist Hymnal.

Editor of Tune Book—Mr. J. ADCOCK, Nottingham.

The Baptist Hymnal and four following publications, which were formerly the property of the General Baptist Association, are now issued solely under the direction of the undermentioned Trustees:—

Treasurer—Mr. J. T. MALLET, Brighton.

Secretary—Mr. P. H. STEVENSON, 2, Vickers-street, Nottingham.

Publishers—E. MARLBOROUGH & CO., 51, Old Bailey, London.

SELECTION OF HYMNS.

First published in 1829, by Trustees, for the benefit of the widows of Baptist ministers and missionaries.

GRANTS from the commencement till 1892 .. .. .. £13,625 0 0

Trustees—Mr. A. H. BAYNES, London; Mr. F. W. CARTWRIGHT, London. Mr. J. EASTTY, London; and Mr. C. PRICE, London.

Treasurer and Secretary—Mr. A. H. BAYNES, 19, Furnival-street, E.C.

Applications should be addressed to the Secretary in the month of September.

Publishers—Messrs. PEWTRESS & Co., 51, Old Bailey.

*** An edition is now published, under the title of "THE SELECTION ENLARGED," containing a large proportion of the Psalms and Hymns by Dr. Watts which are generally used in Public Worship.

OUR OWN HYMN-BOOK.

Compiled by the late Rev. C. H. SPURGEON.

To be had of the Publishers, Messrs. PASSMORE & ALABASTER, 4, Paternoster-buildings, Paternoster-row, London, E.C.

IV.—PERIODICALS.

YEARLY.

BAPTIST HAND-BOOK. Two Shillings. Clarke & Co., 13, Fleet-street, E.C., and Veale, Chifferiel & Co., Limited, Cursitor-street, Furnival-street, E.C.

BAPTIST ALMANACK. Twopence. R. Banks, Racquet-court, Fleet-street, E.C.

SPURGEON'S ILLUSTRATED ALMANACK. One Penny. Passmore & Alabaster.

MONTHLY.

BAPTIST MAGAZINE. Sixpence. Alexander & Shepheard.

BAPTIST MESSENGER. One Penny. Elliot Stock.

BAPTIST VISITOR. One Halfpenny. Baptist Tract Society.

BOND OF UNION. One Penny. Sears & Sons, 11, Crane-court, Fleet-street.

CHURCH AND HOUSEHOLD. One Penny. Marlborough & Co.

EARTHEN VESSEL AND GOSPEL HERALD. Twopence. R. Banks, Racquet-court, Fleet-street, E.C.

MISSIONARY HERALD. One Penny. Alexander & Shepheard.

JUVENILE MISSIONARY HERALD. One Halfpenny. Alexander & Shepheard.

SWORD AND TROWEL. Threepence. Passmore & Alabaster.

WEEKLY.

THE FREEMAN. One Penny; per annum, post free, Six and Sixpence. Alexander & Shepheard.

THE BAPTIST. One Penny; per annum, post free, Six and Sixpence. Elliot Stock.

WELSH.

THE WELSH BAPTIST HAND-BOOK. One and Sixpence, One Shilling, and Sixpence. Yearly. Llewelyn Griffiths, Cwmavon, Glam.

YR ADRODDIAD. Yearly. Sixpence. Jenkin Howell, Aberdare.

SEREN CYMRU (*Star of Wales*). Weekly. One Penny. W. M. Evans, Carmarthen.

SEREN GOMER. Bi-monthly. Sixpence. Jenkin Howell, Aberdare.

Y GREAL (*The Magazine*). Monthly. Threepence. W. Williams, Llangollen.

YR ATHRAW (*The Teacher*). Monthly. One Penny. W. Williams, Llangollen.

YR HERALD CENADOL (*Welsh Missionary Herald*). Monthly. One Penny. Lewis Evans, Cadoxton, Barry, Cardiff.

YR HAUWR (*The Sower*). Monthly. One Penny. Baptist Union of Wales Sunday School Committee.

THE BAPTIST RECORD. Monthly. One Penny. Date & Buston, Cardiff.

SCOTCH.

THE SCOTTISH BAPTIST MAGAZINE. Monthly. One Penny. Morrison & Gibb, Edinburgh.

IRISH.

THE IRISH BAPTIST MAGAZINE. Monthly. One Penny. W. W. Cleland, Belfast.

PART IV.

INSTITUTIONS & GENERAL RELIGIOUS SOCIETIES

IN WHICH BAPTISTS ARE MORE OR LESS INTERESTED.

UNIVERSITY OF LONDON:

BURLINGTON GARDENS, LONDON, W.

VISITOR—THE QUEEN.

Chancellor—The Rt. Hon. Lord HERSCHELL, D.C.L., F.R.S.

Vice-Chancellor—Sir JULIAN GOLDSMID, Bart., M.A., M.P.

Registrar—Mr. A. MILMAN, M.A.

This important corporation was created by Royal Charter, in the seventh year of the reign of William IV., and the first year of the reign of Queen Victoria, 1837, "To hold forth to all classes and denominations of Our faithful subjects, without any distinction whatsoever, an encouragement for pursuing a regular and liberal course of education: and considering that many persons do prosecute and complete their studies both in the United Kingdom and elsewhere, to whom it is expedient that there should be offered such facilities, and on whom it is just that there should be conferred such distinctions and rewards, as may incline them to persevere in these their laudible pursuits; *We do*, by virtue of our prerogative royal, and of our special grace, certain knowledge, and mere motion, by these presents, for Us, our heirs and successors," constitute William, Duke of Devonshire, &c., &c., one body politic and corporate, by the name of "*The University of London*," "for the purpose of ascertaining, by means of examination, the persons who have acquired proficiency in literature, science, and art, by the pursuit of such course of education, and of rewarding them by academical Degrees and certificates of proficiency, as evidence of their respective attainments, and marks of honour proportioned thereunto."

The original charter provides, that not only University College, and King's College, London, shall issue certificates to candidates for degrees in arts or laws, but also all other institutions, "corporated or unincorporated, established for the purpose of education, whether in the metropolis or elsewhere, which the Sovereign, under her sign-manual, shall authorise to issue such certificates." But the present charter, obtained in 1863, allows Degrees in Arts, Science, and Law to be conferred on any candidate who may have evinced sufficient merit at the specified examinations, whether he has studied at any college or not.

By a Resolution of the Senate passed July 27th, 1881, the Titles of the Examinations until then known as the First B.A., First B. Sc., First LL.B., First M.B., and First B.Mus., were changed to those of Intermediate Examinations in Arts, Science, Laws, Medicine, and Music, respectively.

EXAMINATIONS FOR MATRICULATION.

One commences on the second Monday in January, and the other on the second Monday in June. The pass list contains three divisions—Honours, First and Second Division.

12

Examinations for Degree of Bachelor of Arts (B.A.).

The Intermediate Examination in Arts commences on the third Monday in July. *The Examinations for Honours* take place in the same week and the following week.

The Degree Examination commences on the fourth Monday in October. *The Examinations for Honours* take place in the fourth, fifth and sixth weeks after the Pass Examination.

Master of Arts (M.A.).

The Examinations for the Degree of Master of Arts commence—Branch I. (Classics), on the first Monday in June; Branch II. (Mathematics), the second Monday in June; Branch III. (Mental and Moral Science), the third Monday in June; Branch IV. (any two of the following subjects: English Language and Literature, including Anglo-Saxon Language and Literature; French Language and Literature; German Language and Literature; Italian Language and Literature; the Celtic Languages and Literature; Hebrew Language and Literature, including Syriac Language and Literature; Sanskrit Language and Literature; Arabic Language and Literature), on the fourth Monday in June.

Doctor of Literature (D.Lit.).

The Examination for the Degree of *Doctor of Literature* takes place on the first Tuesday in December.

Examinations in the Hebrew Text of the Old Testament, in the Greek Text of the New Testament, in the Evidences of the Christian Religion, and in Scripture History (a first and a further Examination, with an Interval of One Year at least between them),

Take place on Tuesday and Wednesday in the week following the conclusion of the B.A. Examinations for honours.

Bachelor of Science (B.Sc.).

The Intermediate Examination in Science commences on the third Monday in July. *The Examinations for Honours* take place in the same week, and the first week and the second week after the Pass Examination.

The Degree Examination commences on the third Monday in October. *The Examinations for Honours* take place in the third, fourth and fifth weeks after the Pass Examination.

Doctor of Science (D.Sc.).

The Examination for the Degree of *Doctor of Science* takes place within the first twenty-one days of June, and is mainly based on a Thesis upon some branch of Science written and published by the candidate. The Examiners are at liberty to test the candidate's knowledge to any extent they may deem desirable; or they may, when the Thesis is of a high order of merit, pass him without further examination.

Bachelor of Laws (LL.B.)

The Intermediate and Degree Examinations for the Degree of *Bachelor of Laws* take place within the first fourteen days of January. Examinations for *Honours* take place in the second week after the Pass Examinations.

Doctor of Laws (LL.D.).

The Examination for the Degree of *Doctor of Laws* takes place in January, in the week next but one following the LL.B. Examination.

Provincial Examinations

For Matriculation, for the Examination in Arts, for the Intermediate Examination in Science, and the Preliminary Examination in Medicine, are also held in various towns and colleges upon application being made to the Senate of the University.

For full particulars respecting fees, subjects, honours, exhibitions, see the Calendar of the University of London for the current year, or "The Regulations," which may be obtained on application to "The Registrar of the University of London, Burlington-gardens, London, W."

N.B.—*All the foregoing Examinations, and likewise those in* Medicine *and in* Music, *together with all the Scholarships, Prizes, &c., attached thereto, are now open to* WOMEN *upon precisely the same conditions as to men.*

SENATUS ACADEMICUS OF THE ASSOCIATED THEOLOGICAL COLLEGES, BRITISH AND COLONIAL.

CONSTITUTION.

The Senatus consists of the Professors of the Associated Colleges, together with a delegation of three other gentlemen from each college, and such ministers as hold the diploma of Fellow. It is empowered to institute examinations in Theological and Biblical subjects, including Ethical Philosophy and Church History; and to grant certificates to those candidates who pass such examinations.

EXAMINATION FOR THE DIPLOMA OF ASSOCIATE (A.T.S.).

Candidates are required to show a competent knowledge of Apologetical and Doctrinal Theology, Exegesis of the Old and New Testaments, Homiletics, Church History, and Philosophy. If in one of the associated colleges, they must produce certificates of character and standing from the tutors; if ministers, from the Secretary of the Baptist Union or of the County Association. Prizes are awarded to present students who distinguish themselves in the examination.

EXAMINATION FOR THE DIPLOMA OF FELLOW (F.T.S.).

Associates may gain this by satisfying the Examiners in two separate years as to two or more of these branches:—Hebrew and Chaldee, Greek Testament, Septuagint and Vulgate, Theology, History of Christianity, &c., Apologetics.

Sixteen colleges are now members, including Rawdon, Manchester, Bangor, Aberystwyth, Cardiff, Regent's Park, and Midland; and more than fifty Baptist ministers hold its diplomas.

It is under consideration to apply for power to grant degrees.

The Examinations are held in June; particulars can be obtained of Rev. W. Farrer, LL.B. (one of the Registrars), New College, South Hampstead, N.W.

The following Students passed in 1895:—

Honours Division.—(1) with £20 Prize, Arthur Herbert West, B.A., Regent's Park; (6) David Jerman, Manchester.

First Division.—(1) John Bell, Regent's Park; (4) Ralph Holme, Midland, and Wm. A. Livingstone, Manchester, *equal*; (16) Robert William Davies, Bangor; (20, with another) Arthur Spelman Culley, Regent's Park; (23) George William Bloomfield, Manchester.

Second Division.—(2) John Richard Phillips, Bangor.

Rev. William Ernest Blomfield, B.A., B.D., of Coventry, passed with credit the first half of the further (or Fellowship) Examination.

[*Mem.*—The Senatus *does not give honours in single subjects*, but only in the Examination *as a whole*. The marks obtained by a candidate are furnished to the authorities of his College *for their private information, not for publication*].

DISSENTING DEPUTIES.

This important Association has now existed for upwards of a century and a half. It originated in a general meeting of the Protestant Dissenters of London, held in November, 1732, to consider an application to Parliament for the repeal of the Corporation and Test Acts. The want of a permanent body to superintend the civi concerns of Dissenters being strongly felt, it was resolved at a subsequent meetin held in January, 1735-36, that deputies from the several congregations in London should be chosen for that purpose. The first meeting of the deputies was held at Salters' Hall Meeting, January 12th, 1736-37, Dr. Benjamin Avery in the chair. The succession of gentlemen who have occupied the chair is as follows:—

1737 Benj. Avery, LL.D., deceased.
1764 Jasper Manduit, deceased.
1771 Thomas Lucas, deceased.
1777 William Bowden, deceased.
1779 Nathaniel Polhill, deceased.
1782 George Brough, deceased.
1785 Edward Jefferies, deceased.
1802 Ebenezer Maitland, deceased.
1805 William Smith, M.P., deceased.
1831 Henry Waymouth, deceased.
1844 John Remington Mills, deceased.
1853 Sir Samuel Morton Peto, Bart., M.P., deceased.
1855 Apsley Pellatt, M.P., deceased.
1864 Sir Samuel Morton Peto, Bart, M.P., deceased.
1869 Sir Charles Reed, M.P., LL.D., F.S.A., deceased.
1875 Henry Richard, M.P., deceased.
1889 Mr. William Woodall, M.P.

COMMITTEE OF DEPUTIES OF THE THREE DENOMINATIONS, PRESBYTERIAN, INDEPENDENT, AND BAPTIST, IN AND WITHIN TWELVE MILES OF LONDON, APPOINTED TO PROTECT THEIR CIVIL RIGHTS FOR THE YEAR 1895.

Chairman—Mr. W. WOODALL, M.P., Queen Anne's Mansions, S.W.

Deputy-Chairman—Mr. Alderman EVAN SPICER, Belair, Dulwich, S.W.

Treasurer—Mr..W. HOLBORN, Fern Lodge, Campden-hill, Kensington, W.

Mr. A. H. Baynes, 19, Furnival Street, E.C.
,, W. W. Baynes, J.P., Pickhurst Wood, Bromley, Kent.
,, W. T. Bolton, 4, Cumberland-park, Acton, W.
,, W. S. Caine, M.P., 33, North Side, Clapham, S.W.
,, J. Clapham, Queen's Head-street Board School, Essex-road, N.
,, J. J. Corbin, 85, Gresham-street, E.C.
,, J. Eastty, 86, Grange-road, Bermondsey, S.E.
,, W. S. Gard, Trewithen, Roslyn-hill, Hampstead, N.W.
,, W. G. Snowden Gard, 20, Upper Park-road, N.W.
,, W. Hazell, M.P., 15, Russell-square, W.C.
,, J. Laughland, 17, Highbury New-park, N.
,, H. Lee, J.P., 25, Highbury Quadrant, N.
,, B. S. Olding, Lissant House, St. Mary's-road, Long Ditton, Surrey
,, S. Robjohns, Marchmont, Hatherley-road, Sidcup R.S.O.
,, E. Unwin, Woodcote, Burnt Ash Hill, S.E.
,, G. S. Warmington, Stonycroft, 146, Burnt Ash-hill, Lee, S.E.
,, S. Watson, 179, New Park-road, Brixton-hill, S.W.
,, J. Carvell Williams, M.P., 21, Hornsey Rise-gardens, N.
Sir W. H. Wills, Bart., M.P., 25, Hyde Park-gardens, W.

Secretary—Mr. A. J. SHEPHEARD, 31 and 32, Finsbury-circus, E.C.

LONDON NONCONFORMIST COUNCIL OF EVANGELICAL FREE CHURCHES.

President—Rev. J. CLIFFORD, D.D.

Treasurer—Mr. R. W. PERKS, M.P.

Honorary Secretaries—Revs. J. MATTHEWS, W. J. AVERY, A. JEFFREY, and J. JACKSON (Memorial Hall, E.C.).

OBJECTS:—To furnish opportunities to Evangelical Nonconformists for taking concerted action upon questions affecting their common interests, or bearing upon the social, educational, moral, and religious welfare of the people. The Council will, as occasion requires, endeavour to influence public opinion upon such subjects as the following:—1. The moral state of London, and the best methods of suppressing intemperance, gambling, sweating, overcrowding, and social vice. 2. The social condition of the people, and the causes that hinder the acceptance of the *Gospel of Christ*. 3. The rescue and restoration of the lapsed and lost, and the removal of the causes of their degradation. 4. The liquor traffic and public house licences, the opium monopoly, the prohibition of the liquor traffic in heathen countries, the importance of moral character in our legislators, the adoption of arbitration in industrial and international disputes, religious persecution in rural districts. 5. The religious visitation of hospitals, workhouses, lodging houses, prisons, &c.; and the question of hospital nursing. 6. The representation of Nonconformists on Boards of Guardians, School Boards, County Councils, &c.

MEMBERSHIP.—The Council shall consist of the Minister and two representative members of each congregation within the Metropolitan area.

COUNTY PROVIDENT SOCIETIES.

FOR THE BENEFIT OF CONGREGATIONAL AND BAPTIST MINISTERS AND THEIR FAMILIES.

1. Bedfordshire and Huntingdonshire Provident and Benevolent Society. Formed 1812. For Nonconformist ministers who, through age or infirmity, retire from the pastorate, their widows and orphans. Secretaries, Rev. J. Brown, B.A., D.D., Bedford; Rev. P. Griffiths, 2, Heyworth-road, Clapton, N.E. Treasurer, Mr. C. P. Tebbutt, Bluntisham, Hunts. *Funds*, £6,100 invested. Distributed at last annual meeting, £244.

2. Cambridgeshire Benevolent Society, for the relief of necessitous Dissenting Ministers' widows and orphans. Capital, £4,385 3s. 1d., 2¾ per cent. Consols. Established 1807. Secretary, Mr. G. E. Foster, Cambridge.

3. Essex and Herts Benevolent Society for the relief of necessitous widows, and the children of Protestant Dissenting Ministers; and also of such ministers as through age or infirmity may be incapacitated for public service. Established 1789. Trustees, Mr. Ernest Ridley, Chelmsford, Mr. J. G. Smith, Watford, Herts, Mr. F. A. Wells, Chelmsford. Treasurer, Mr. F. A. Wells, London Road, Chelmsford. Secretary, Rev. E. T. Egg, Woodford Green, Essex. Amount of Funded Property, £9,300. Terms of Membership—(1) All Protestant Dissenting Ministers who have accepted an invitation to the stated discharge of the pastoral office in any congregation, in either of the two counties, are eligible for admission to beneficiary membership, provided that they make application to the Society *within four years* from the date of such acceptance, and provided also that at the time of his application he is not more than 48 years of age. (2) Every minister who wishes to become a Beneficiary member must be nominated by two members to whom he is personally known, at one general meeting, and be proposed and seconded (by proxy) by two other members, to whom also he is personally known, at the next general meeting. The payment of personal and congregational subscriptions is due from the time of nomination. (3) Personal Subscription, £1 1s.; Congregational Subscription, not less than £2; Beneficiary Life Membership, £10 10s.; Gentleman's Life Membership, £10 10s.; Lady's Life Membership, £5 5s. (4) In removing to some other county of the United Kingdom, or to the Continent, or to the Colonies, a minister is at liberty to continue his membership, or he may have his personal contributions returned to him on application to the Treasurer. The Committee are very desirous that both ministers and churches of the two denominations in the counties of Essex and Herts should take a greater interest in this Society, and they urge that further particulars should be obtained from the Secretary. An effort is being made to raise the capital of the Society to £10,000.

4. Watkinson's Trust. Secretary, Mr. W. Theobald, Cressing, near Braintree. The interest of £1,518 2¾ per cent. Consols. The trust deed declares—"That the income of the charity property shall be from time to time applied for and towards the relief, support and maintenance of poor Protestant Dissenters, ministers of the Gospel, commonly called Baptists and Independents, within the county of Essex. Or for and towards the relief and support of poor widows of such poor ministers aforesaid, as such of the major part of the trustees see fit." The proceeds of the charity are appropriated yearly in the month of July.

5. Kent Union Society, for the benefit of aged and infirm ministers of the Gospel in the county of Kent and the widows and orphans of ministers. Instituted 1802. The ministers assisted are only such as, being members of the Society, are, through age and infirmities, incapable of exercising the pastoral office. This Society partakes both of an equitable and benevolent character. Application for membership to be made within three years after the commencement of ministerial work in the county. Secretary, Rev. G. W. Cowper-Smith, Tunbridge Wells.

6. Norfolk. The Norfolk Protestant Dissenters Benevolent Society. Instituted 1800. Income, 1894-5, £444 10s. 11d. Beneficiaries 1894-5, 18. The Beneficiary members of this Society are ministers who through age or infirmity are rendered incapable of public service; also the necessitous widows and orphans of such ministers. Secretary, S. Cozens Hardy, Norwich.

7. Northamptonshire Baptist Provident Society. Instituted at Kettering in 1813. Capital, £7,392 10s. 10d. Beneficiary members—widows and orphans of ministers. and disabled or retiring ministers. Treasurer, Mr. D. F. Gotch, Chesham House, Kettering.

8. The Suffolk Benevolent Society for the Relief of Necessitous Widows and Orphans of Protestant Dissenting Ministers, and also of such Ministers as, through age or infirmity, may be incapacitated for public service in the county of Suffolk. The annual meeting is held on the third Friday in June. Hon. Secretary, Mr. H. F. Harwood, Tuddendam Hall, Ipswich. Hon. Treasurer, Mr. J. V. Webb, Combs, Stowmarket.

Aged Pilgrims' Friend Society. Treasurers, Mr. F. A. Bevan, 54, Lombard-street, E.C., Mr. W. J. Parks, 32, The Chase, Clapham Common, S.W. Secretary, Mr. J. E. Hazelton; Office, 83, Finsbury Pavement, E.C. Instituted 1807. For giving life pensions of 5, 7, and 10 guineas per annum to the aged Christian poor of both sexes, and of every Protestant denomination, who are not under 60 years of age, and give Scriptural evidence that they are of "The Household of Faith." During the last 89 years it has been the Lord's almoner in relieving the temporal necessities of upwards of 6,000 of His aged disciples. At the present time there are 206 pensioners on the 10, 338 on the 7, and 792 on the 5 guinea list. Upwards of £8,700 per annum is distributed in pensions alone. In the *Asylum* at Camberwell, 42 of the pensioners are provided with a comfortable home, coals, medical attendance, etc. The Asylum at Hornsey Rise accommodates 120 pensioners, the Home at Brighton 7 pensioners, and the Stamford Hill Home 9 pensioners. All the inmates of the Asylums and Homes enjoy the same privileges.

Apprenticeship Society. President, Mr. J. Wates. Vice-President, Mr. M. Holmes. Treasurer *pro. tem.*, Mr. J. Snow. Secretary, Mr. J. R. V. Marchant, 1, Gray's Inn-square, W.C. Object—To assist by grants of money Congregational or Baptist ministers or their widows in apprenticing their children or otherwise preparing them for business.

Army Scripture Readers and Soldiers' Friend Society. President, General Right Hon. Viscount Wolseley, K.P. Secretary, Col. Philips, late 4th Hussars. Office, 112, *St. Martin's-lane, W.C.*

Bible Lands (or Turkish) Missions Aid Society, 7, Adam Street, Strand, W.C. Honorary Secretary, Rev. W. A. Essery. Bankers, Messrs. Barclay, Bevan, Ransom, Bouverie & Co., 1, Pall Mall East, S.W. President, Earl of Aberdeen. Treasurer, Lord Kinnaird.

Book Society, for Promoting Religious Knowledge among the Poor. 28, Paternoster-row, E.C. Instituted 1750. Treasurer, Mr. W. Payne. Secretary, Mr. W. S. Payne.

British and Foreign Anti-Slavery Society, 55, New Broad-street, E.C. Patron, H.R.H. The Prince of Wales. President, Mr. A. Pease. M.P. Treasurer, Mr. J. Allen Secretary, C. H. Allen, F.R.G.S. Assistant Secretary, J. E. Teall. Organ of the Society, *The Anti-Slavery Reporter*, bi-monthly. *Price 1d.* Free to subscribers of 10s. and upwards.

BRITISH AND FOREIGN BIBLE SOCIETY, 146, Queen Victoria-street, London, E.C. Formed 1804. Secretaries, Rev. J. Sharp, M.A., and Rev. W. M. Paull.

BRITISH AND FOREIGN SAILORS' SOCIETY, SAILORS' INSTITUTE, Mercers'-street. Shadwell, E. Established 1818. Treasurer, Sir J. C. Dimsdale. Secretary, Rev. E. W. Matthews. Association Secretary, Mr. G. Clarke, R.N. Sustains and assists 150 agents in 97 home and foreign ports. Income last year, £24,912 5s. 3d.

BRITISH AND FOREIGN SCHOOL SOCIETY, Temple Chambers, Temple Avenue, London, E.C. Formed 1808. President for 1895-96, Right Hon. A. J. Mundella, M.P. Treasurer, Mr. J. G. Barclay. Secretary, Mr. A. Bourne, B.A. Normal Colleges and Practising Schools—Male: Borough-road (Isleworth), and Bangor; Female: Stockwell, Darlington, Swansea, and Saffron Walden.

BRITISH SOCIETY FOR THE PROPAGATION OF THE GOSPEL AMONG THE JEWS. Formed 1842. Secretary, Rev. J. Dunlop. Accountant, Mr. H. J. Wesson. Offices, 96, *Great Russell-street, Bloomsbury, W.C.*

CENTRAL ASSOCIATION FOR STOPPING THE SALE OF INTOXICATING LIQUORS ON SUNDAY. President, Mr. A. Pease, M.P. Vice-Presidents, the Archbishop of Canterbury; Duke of Westminster, K.G.; Mr. W. S. Caine, M.P.; Rev. C. Garrett; Rev. A. McLaren, D.D., &c., &c. Treasurer, Mr. G. C. Haworth, J.P. Hon. Secs., Mr. R. Whitworth, Rev. Canon Stowell, M.A., Rev. W. Young, B.A. Travelling Secs., Mr. E. Thomas, 14, Brown-street, Manchester (Northern District); Rev. J. Seager, 12, Coburg-road, Montpelier, Bristol (South-Western District); Mr. J. Roles, 34a, Corporation-street, Birmingham (Midland District); Mr. W. Copleston, 4, Burton-road, Thornton Heath, S.E. (London and South-Eastern District). General Secretary, Mr. J. W. Causer. Offices, 14, *Brown-street, Manchester*. Organ, *Sunday Closing Reporter.*

CENTRAL YOUNG MEN'S CHRISTIAN ASSOCIATION, Exeter Hall, Strand, W.C., 186, Aldersgate-street, E.C., and 59 and 60 Cornhill, E.C. Formed 1844. General Secretary, Mr. J. H. Putterill. Financial Secretary, Mr. C. Hooper.

CHILDREN'S AID SOCIETY. Established 1856 (in connection with the Reformatory and Refuge Union). To rescue and to assist to maintain destitute and neglected children. Secretary, Mr. A. J. S. Maddison. Office, 32, *Charing Cross, S.W.*

CHILDREN'S SPECIAL SERVICE MISSION. Instituted 1868. President, Rev. E. A. Stuart, M.A. Treasurer, Mr. J. E. Mathieson. Hon. Children's Evangelists, E. Arrowsmith and J. Spiers, 13A, Warwick-lane, Paternoster-row, E.C., and others. Hon. Sec., T. B. Bishop. Secretary, Mr. H. Hankinson. Office of *Our Own Magazine, The Children's Scripture Union*, and *Golden Bells Hymn Book*, 13a, *Warwick-lane, Paternoster-row, E.C.*

CHINA INLAND MISSION. (Non-denominational.) Directors of the Mission, Rev. J. Hudson Taylor, M.R.C.S., F.R.G.S., Newington Green, N.; Mr. T. Howard, Westleigh, Bickley, Kent. Treasurer, Mr. R. Scott, 12, Paternoster-buildings, E.C. Council: T. Howard, Westleigh, Bickley, Kent, Chairman. W. Hall, 17, St. Faith's-road, West Norwood, S.E.; R. H. Hill, 3, Lombard-court, E.C.; W. Sharp, 13, Walbrook, E.C.; P. S. Badenoch, 108, Newington Green-road, N.; R. Scott, 12, Paternoster-buildings, E.C.; W. B. Sloan. Secretary, W. B. Sloan. Offices of Mission, Newington Green, N. Present Staff of the Mission, 630 missionaries and associates and wives of missionaries, 309 native helpers as pastors, evangelists, colporteurs, Bible-women, &c., and 108 unpaid native helpers. Stations and Out-Stations occupied (in fourteen provinces): Cheh-Kiang Province, 66; Kiang-su Province, 7; Gan-hwuy Province, 20; Hu-peh Province, 3; Kwei-chau, Province, 6; Si-chuen Province, 18; Shan-si Province, 50; Shan-tung Province, 6; Shen-si Province, 18; Ho-nan Province, 6; Yun-nan Province, 6; Kan-suh, 6; Kiang-si, 27; Chih-li Province, 5. Income for 1894, £33,158 1s. Monthly record of information, *China's Millions*. Published by Morgan & Scott, 12, Paternoster Buildings.

CHRISTIAN EVIDENCE SOCIETY. President, The Archbishop of Canterbury. Vice-President, Sir G. G. Stokes, Bart., F.R.S. Secretaries, Rev. C. L. Engström, M.A.; Rev. T. T. Waterman, B.A. Office, 13, *Buckingham-street, Strand, W.C.* Objects:—To declare and defend Christianity as a Divine Revelation. To controvert the errors of Atheists, Agnostics, Secularists, and other opponents of Christianity. To counteract the energetic propagandism of Infidelity, especially among the uneducated. To meet the difficulties and strengthen the faith of the doubting and perplexed. To instruct the young in the Evidences of Christianity. Methods of Operation:—Sermons, lectures, popular controversial addresses, classes, publications, tracts, conversations, and correspondence. It removes serious obstructions which lie in the way of those who preach the Gospel of Christ; and, being catholic in its character, it claims support from all who are interested in the defence of our common Christianity. There is a speciality in the work which is necessitated by the religious unrest and questionings of the times; and the sphere of operation is not occupied by any other organisation whatever.

CHRISTIAN INSTRUCTION SOCIETY. Instituted 1825. President, Sir G. Williams. Treasurer, Mr. T. Dence. Secretary, Rev. R. Mackay. Office, *Memorial Hall, Farringdon-street, E.C.* Object:—To advance evangelical religion by promoting the preaching of the Gospel, the establishment of prayer meetings and Sunday-schools, the circulation of the Scriptures and religious tracts and books, systematic visitation from house to house, by specially qualified Deaconesses, who are affiliated to Churches in different parts of London and the suburbs, and by such other means as the Committee may from time to time approve.

CHRISTIAN LITERATURE SOCIETY FOR INDIA, 7, Adam-street, Strand, W.C. Formed 1858. Secretary, Rev. G. Patterson. Assistant Secretary, W. J. Wintersgill.

CHURCH MISSIONARY SOCIETY, Salisbury-square, Fleet-street. Secretaries, Rev. H. E. Fox, M.A. (Honorary); Rev. B. Baring-Gould, M.A., Rev. F. Baylis, M.A., Rev. G. F. Smith, M.A., Rev. P. I. Jones, M.A., Rev. W. E. Burroughs, B.D., Mr. E. Stock (Editorial), and Mr. D. M. Lang (Lay).

COLONIAL MISSIONARY SOCIETY. (Congregational.) Address, Memorial Hall, Farringdon-street, E.C. Secretary, Rev. D. B. Hooke.

CONGREGATIONAL CHURCH-AID AND HOME MISSIONARY SOCIETY, Memorial Hall, Farringdon-street, London, E.C. Treasurer, Mr. G. N. Ford, Manchester. Secretary, Rev. W. F. Clarkson, B.A. Income (1894), £28,428. The objects of the Society are:—1. To call forth the resources of the Churches for wise and systematic use in Home Mission work. 2. To assist Churches which are unable to meet their financial requirements. 3. To provide for a more adequate remuneration of ministers who are doing good work in necessitous districts. 4. To enlist lay agency for the preaching of the Gospel in villages and remote places, and the establishment and maintenance of Sunday-schools. 5. To form district auxiliaries for gathering information and raising funds for the County Unions. 6. To increase the influence of Free Church principles.

CONGREGATIONAL PASTORS' INSURANCE AID SOCIETY, Memorial Hall, Farringdon-street, E.C. Treasurer, Mr. E. Unwin. Secretary, Rev. F. Sweet. Capital, £5,717. Grants made in 1894-5, £247.

CONGREGATIONAL SCHOOL, Caterham Valley, Surrey. Founded 1811. President and Treasurer, Rev. J. Viney. Secretary, Rev. H. Grainger.

COUNTRY TOWNS' MISSION, 18, New Bridge-street, London, E.C. Treasurer, Mr. H. C. Nisbet. Secretary, Mr. G. H. Mawer.

DISCHARGED PRISONERS' (METROPOLITAN) AID SOCIETY. Established 1864. Aids "short-term" male prisoners from H.M.'s Prison, Pentonville; also from other prisons in town or country on communication from the authorities or friends. Mr. T. R. Price, 10 Freegrove-road, Holloway, N., Secretary. Has a "Home" at 10, Freegrove-road, Holloway, N. Cases assisted in 1894, 1,320; cases assisted since formation, 19,591. Income, 1894, £698 19s. 5d. Agent, Mr. W. Langmaid. Office, 15, *Buckingham-street, W.*

DR. BARNARDO'S HOMES FOR ORPHAN AND DESTITUTE CHILDREN. Founder and Director, Dr. T. J. Barnardo, F.R.C.S.E., 18 to 26, Stepney Causeway, London, E. Treasurer, Mr. W. Fowler. Secretary, Mr. J. Odling. *Eighty-four* separate homes, comprised in fifty-one different Institutions, are now comprehended under this title, in which nearly 5,000 rescued destitute and orphan children are now in residence. The Homes include the following branches:—*Home for Working and Destitute Lads*, 18 to 26, Stepney-causeway, London, E.; *Leopold House Orphan Home for Little Boys*, 199, Burdett-road, E.; *Nursery Home for Very Little Boys*, Teighmore, Gorey, Jersey; *Open-all-Night Refuges for Homeless Boys and Girls*, 6, 8, and 10, Stepney-causeway, London, E.; *Labour House for Destitute Youths*, 622 to 626, Commercial-road, E.; *Village Home for Orphan and Destitute Girls*, Barkingside, Ilford, Essex; *Babies' Castle*, Hawkhurst, Kent; *Her Majesty's Hospital for Waif Children*, 13 to 19, Stepney-causeway, E.; *Servants' Free Registry and Home*, Sturge House, 32, Bow-road, E.; *Shelter for Girls*, Alfred Street, E.; *Factory Girls' Club and Institute*, Copperfield-road, E.; *The "Beehive" Working Home (for Older Girls)*, 273, Mare-street, Hackney, N.E.; *Rescue Home for Young Girls in Danger* (Private Address); *City Messenger Brigade*, Head Offices, 18 to 26, Stepney-causeway, E.; *Union Jack Shoeblack Brigade and Home*, Three Colt-street, Limehouse, E.; *Wood chopping Brigade and Aërated Water Factory*, 622, Commercial-road, E.; *Farm School* (Mr. R. Phipps, J.P.), Bromyard, Worcester; *Burdett Dormitory*, Burdett-road, E.; *Convalescent Seaside Home*, Felixstowe, Suffolk; *Jones Memorial Home for Incurables*, 16, Trafalgar-road, Birkdale, Southport; *Home for Girl Orphans*, 3, Bradninch-place, Exeter; *Children's Free Lodging Houses*, 81, Commercial-street, Spitalfields, and 12, Dock-street, Leman-street, E.; *Emigration Depot and Distributing Homes*: "Hazelbrae," Peterborough, Ontario (for Girls); 214, Farley-avenue, Toronto, Canada (for Younger Boys); Industrial Farm, near Russell, Manitoba (for Young Men); *Boarding-Out Scheme*, Head Offices; *Blind and Deaf Mute Branch*, Head Offices; *Branch for Crippled and Deformed Children*, Head Offices; "*The Children's Fold*," 182, Grove-road, E.; *Shipping Agency*, Head Offices, with branches at Yarmouth and Cardiff; *Free Meal Branch*, Head Offices, and Edinburgh Castle, etc.; *Copperfield-road Schools*, Copperfield-road, E.; *The People's Mission Church*, "Edinburgh Castle," Limehouse, E.; *St. Ann's Gospel Hall*, Limehouse, E.; *Cabmen's Shelter*, Burdett-road, E.; *Edinburgh Castle Coffee Palace*, Rhodeswell-road, E.; *Dublin Castle Coffee Palace*, 39 and 41, Mile End-road, E.; *The East London Tract and Pure Literature Depot*, Rhodeswell-road, E.; *Evangelical Deaconess House*, 403 and 405, Mile End-road, E.; *Dorcas House*, Carr-street, Limehouse, E.; *Earl Cairns Mission Hall*, Salmon's-lane, Limehouse, E.; *Gloucester Place Mission Hall*, Salmon's-lane, E.; "The Institute," 212 Burdett-road, E.; *East London Medical Mission*, 224, High-street, Shadwell, E.; "*An Ever Open Door*," Eight Rescue Branches in Bath, Birmingham, Bristol, Cardiff, Leeds, Liverpool, Newcastle-on-Tyne and Plymouth.

ELMSLIE SCHOLARSHIP FUND.—The death of the Rev. W. G. Elmslie, M.A., D.D., Professor of Old Testament Literature in the Presbyterian College, London, which occurred in November, 1889, gave rise to the formation of a "Memorial Fund," which amounted to about £2,000, contributed chiefly by friends in connection with the Baptist, Congregationalist, and Presbyterian communions. Of this the sum of £1,000 was placed in trust for the benefit of Dr. Elmslie's son, while the remaining £1,000 was placed in trust for the purpose of founding "one or more Elmslie Scholarships for the promotion of Old Testament and Semitic learning among the denominations in England and Wales known as Independents, Baptists, and Presbyterians." The trustees acting under the directions of the Trust Deed have appointed a committee selected from the three denominations named, who have the conduct of the examinations, &c. The committee consists of the Revs. J. Clifford, D.D., J. O. Dykes, D.D., A. M. Fairbairn, D.D., R. H. Roberts, B.A., O. C. Whitehouse, M.A., and John Watson, M.A.; Messrs. A. H. Baynes, F.R.G.S., A. N. Macnicoll, and P. H. Pye-Smith, M.D., together with the trustees Messrs. G. W. Knox, B.Sc., H. M. Matheson, and H. M. Murray, M.D. The scholarships are to be open for competition "to all theological students who shall then be in their last year of study or preparation for the

Holy Ministry at any of the colleges in England or Wales connected with, or from time to time generally understood as connected with, any of the denominations known as 'Independent or Congregational,' 'Baptist,' and 'The Presbyterian Church of England,' to be awarded and held upon such terms and conditions as shall from time to time be directed by the committee. All detailed informations as to the examinations can be obtained from the principals of the various colleges.

EVANGELICAL ALLIANCE, 7, Adam-street, Adelphi, W.C., Formed 1846. General Secretary, Mr. A. J. Arnold; Deputation Secretary, Rev. C. B. Nash.

EVANGELICAL CONTINENTAL SOCIETY, Memorial Hall, Farringdon-street, E.C. Secretary, Rev. G. H. Giddins.

EVANGELIZATION SOCIETY, for employing men of all sections of the Church and of all ranks in life in preaching the Gospel throughout England, Scotland and Wales. Hon. Secretary, Capt. W. E. Smith, 21, Surrey-street, Strand, W.C., and (Scottish Branch) The Secretary, Grove-street Institute, Glasgow.

FEMALE AID SOCIETY AND FEMALE MISSION TO THE FALLEN, OR WOMAN'S MISSION TO WOMEN (in connection with Reformatory and Refuge Union). Established 1858. Upwards of 25,000 have had a fresh start in life. Hon. Sec., Mr. W. T. Paton. Secretary, Mr. A. J. S. Maddison. Office, 32, *Charing Cross, S.W.*

FEMALE SERVANTS' HOME SOCIETY. Formed 1836. Secretary, Mr. C. S. Thorpe, Offices, 79, *Finsbury-pavement, E.C.*

GROTTO HOME FOR DESTITUTE LADS, 55, Paddington-street, W. (in connection with the Reformatory and Refuge Union). Office, 32, *Charing Cross, S.W.*

HOME AND SCHOOL FOR THE SONS AND ORPHANS OF MISSIONARIES, Blackheath, Kent. Established 1842. Head Master, Mr. W. B. Hayward, M.A., late Scholar of Sidney Sussex College, Cambridge. The school is first grade, with alternative classical, modern or commercial courses for boys above fourteen years of age. Pupils must be above six and under twelve years of age on admission. £21 per annum for each boy over ten years of age, and £18 for each boy under that age, are the payments by the parents or guardians, the difference in the cost of maintenance and education being met by subscriptions and donations. There are at present two leaving scholarships, viz., "The Haworth" and "The Basil Memorial," each of the value of £50 per annum for two years, open to sons of missionaries only. Pupils, other than sons of missionaries, are admitted to the school on terms to be obtained direct from the Head Master. Present number 73, of whom 67 are sons of missionaries. Hon. Treasurer, Mr. E. Unwin, Woodcote, Burnt Ash Hill, Lee, S.E. Hon. Secretaries, Rev. R. W. Thompson, London Mission House, 14, Blomfield-street, E.C.; and Mr. A. H. Baynes, Baptist Mission House, 19, Furnival-street, E.C.

HOMES FOR LITTLE BOYS, Farningham and Swanley, Kent. Secretaries, Messrs. A. E. Charles & W. Robson. Offices, 25, *Holborn-viaduct, E.C.*

HOMES FOR WORKING BOYS IN LONDON. Founded 1870. 1. Pelham House, 30, Spital-square, Bishopsgate, E. 2. Hanbury House, 22, Dorchester-place, Blandford-square, N.W. 3. Haddo House, 88, Blackfriars-road, S.E. 4, Rossie House, 35, Lamb's Conduit-street, W.C. 5. Howard House, 14, Fournier-street, Spitalfields, E. 6. Tyndale House, 29, Whitehead's-grove, Chelsea, S.W. 7. Macgregor House, 9, Wine Office-court, E.C. Treasurer, The Hon. T. H. W. Pelham, Deene House, Putney-hill, S.W. Secretary, W. Denham, 18, Buckingham-street, Strand, W.C.

IRISH EVANGELICAL SOCIETY AND CONGREGATIONAL HOME MISSION, Memorial Hall, Farringdon-street, E.C. Secretary, Rev. R. H. Noble.

LADY HEWLEY CHARITY. For assisting poor Congregational, Presbyterian, and Baptist Ministers in the five Northern counties of England, or widows and daughters of such ministers, or ministers disabled from duty who have been located in these northern counties. There are almshouses at York connected with the charity. Clerk to the Trustees, A. Armour, Cereal Court, Brunswick-street, *Liverpool.*

LONDON AGED CHRISTIAN SOCIETY, 32, Sackville-street, W. President, Mr. J. T. Morton. Hon. Secretary, The Rev. Prebendary Webb Peploe, M.A., Secretary, Colonel Hamilton Northcote, R. M. Artillery. Collector, Mr. S. Vaughan. Bankers, Messrs. Drummonds & Co. This Society grants monthly pensions of Ten Shillings to poor members of "The Household of Faith" over 65 years of age, residing within five miles of St. Paul's Cathedral, nominated by Subscribers. Annual Subscribers of £4 4s., or four Annual Subscribers of £1 1s. each, may recommend Candidates.

LONDON CITY MISSION, 3, Bridewell-place, New Bridge-street, E.C. Formed 1835. Treasurer, F. A. Bevan, Esq. Secretaries, Revs. R. Dawson, B.A., and T. S. Hutchinson, M.A. Number of Missionaries, 477.

LONDON CONGREGATIONAL UNION, Memorial Hall, Farringdon-street, E.C. Treasurers, Mr. W. Holborn, and Mr. Edward Spicer, J.P. Secretary, Rev. A. Mearns. Superintendent of Philanthropic Work, Mr. E. W. Gates. Nett Income, Church Aid, Chapel Building and Philanthropic Funds for 1894, £6,258. Objects:—1. To promote the spiritual intercommunion of the Congregational Churches of the Metropolis; to aid such of them as may be weak; to facilitate the expression of their opinions upon religious and social questions, and in general to advance their common interests. 2. To promote the erection or enlargement of Congregational Chapels and Mission Halls, and to secure sites for Chapels and Halls. 3. To raise and distribute a Fund for carrying on philanthropic work, and in other ways to help the sick and destitute poor.

LONDON FEMALE GUARDIAN SOCIETY.—Probational Home, 21, Old Ford-road, Bethnal Green, E.; Training Home, 191, High-street, Stoke Newington, N. Secretary, Mr. W. E. Page.

LONDON FEMALE PREVENTIVE AND REFORMATORY INSTITUTION (known also as "Friendless and Fallen"). Established 1857. Objects:—1. To afford protection to friendless virtuous young women in circumstances of moral danger. 2. To train friendless young girls for domestic service. 3. To seek to reclaim the fallen. Training Home for friendless young girls, 7, Parson's-green, Fulham, S.W.; Homes for respectable young women and friendless girls in moral peril, 459 and 461, Holloway-road, N.; Rescue Homes, 200, Euston-road, N.W.; Milton House, Fernshaw-road, Brompton, S.W.; 35, Eden-grove, Holloway-road, N.; 5, Parson's-green, Fulham, S.W.; Open-all-Night Refuge, for the immediate reception of both classes, 37, Manchester-street, King's Cross, W.C. The inmates are fed, clothed, housed, instructed and placed out in service or otherwise suitably provided for. The benefits conferred are absolutely free. There is no barrier to admission on the ground of creed, class or country. Secretary, Mr. W. J. Taylor, 200 Euston-road, near Gower-street, N.W.

LONDON MISSIONARY SOCIETY, 14, Blomfield-street, London Wall, E.C. Secretaries, Rev. R. W. Thompson (Foreign); Rev. A. N. Johnson, M.A. (Home); and Rev. G. Cousins (Editorial). Treasurer, Mr. A. Spicer, M.P.

LORD'S DAY OBSERVANCE SOCIETY. Established 1831. Secretary, Rev. F. Peake, M.A., LL.D. Office, 20, *Bedford-street, Strand, W.C.*

MIDNIGHT MEETING MOVEMENT. Begun in 1859. Secretary, Mr. C. W. McCree. Office, 8*a*, *Red Lion-square, W.C.*

MILL HILL SCHOOL, LONDON, N.W. This is a public school, not a proprietary school. Founded in the year 1807, it was re-organised under the authority of the Court of Chancery, in 1869, on the model of the great Public Schools; and is conducted on thoroughly unsectarian principles. The inclusive fees for yearly boarders are—under twelve years of age, 22 guineas a Term; under fourteen, 25 guineas; above fourteen, 28 guineas. The sons of Christian ministers are eligible for election by the Governors to "Ministerial Exhibitions," whereby the fees are reduced to forty guineas a year. There are valuable Entrance Scholarships, £30 to £90 a year, tenable so long as the holders remain at the school. The Bousfield Scholarship, founded by the late Mr. Robert Bousfield, of the annual value of £50, is tenable for three years at University College, or, for a ministerial candidate, at New College, London.

Court of Governors—Rev. J. Angus, D.D., Mr. R. W. B. Buckland, Mr. E. S. Curwen, Rev. J. O. Dykes, D.D. Mr. G. Elliott, Mr. E. H. Mayo Gunn, Mr. T. A. Herbert, B.A., LL.B., Mr. J. Howard, Mr. G. W. Knox, B.Sc., Mr. H. Marnham, Mr. N. Micklem, M.A., Mr. S. S. Pawling, Mr. J. Powell, Mr. P. H. Pye-Smith, M.D., F.R.S., Mr. T. Scrutton (Treasurer), Mr. A. Spicer, M.P., and Mr. Percy C. Webb. Head Master, Mr. J. D. McClure, M.A., LL.M., Trinity College, Cambridge. Boarding-House Master, Mr. E. W. Hallifax, M.A. Secretary, Mr. E. Hampden-Cook, M.A., Mill Hill School, N.W.

Ministers' Seaside Home, Morthoe, North Devon. This Home has been established, and is open all through the year, to meet the needs of Ministers of all denominations and their wives, with only limited incomes, who may require seaside change. The scale of payment is graduated according to ministerial stipend. The property is invested in nineteen Trustees. The annual expenses are met by donations and subscriptions. All enquiries and applications for entrance may be addressed to the Warden, the Rev. U. R. Thomas, Redland, Bristol.

National Education Association. President, Right Hon. A. J. Mundella, M.P.; Chairman and Treasurer, Hon. E. L. Stanley; Secretaries, Mr. T. E. Minshall and Mr. B. Whishaw, B.A. Offices, 35 *and* 36, *Outer Temple, London, W.C.* Objects:—1. To promote a system of national education which shall be efficient, progressive and unsectarian, and shall be under popular control; and also to oppose all legislative and administrative proposals having a contrary tendency. 2. To secure the universal establishment of School Boards in districts of suitable area, and having under their control unsectarian schools within reasonable reach of the population requiring them. 3. To secure Free Schools, on the condition that every school receiving a grant in lieu of fees shall be under public representative management during the ordinary school hours. 4. To obtain facilities for the better training of elementary teachers in unsectarian institutions, under public management, in addition to the existing means of training.

National Refuges for Homeless and Destitute Children. Founded in 1843 by the late William Williams. There are eight Homes on shore, in or near London, for Boys and Girls, and the training ships *Arethusa and Chichester*, moored off Greenhithe, Kent. Boys trained from the commencement, 11,285; girls, 2,253. No votes required. Urgent cases admitted *at once*. President, the Rt. Hon. the Earl of Jersey, G.C.M.G.; Chairman and Treasurer, Mr. W. E. Hubbard; Deputy-Chairman, Mr. C. T. Ware; Secretary, Mr. H. B. Wallen; Finance and Deputation Secretary, Mr. H. G. Copeland. Bankers, London and Westminster Bank, 214, High Holborn, W.C. Londonoffice, 164, *Shaftesbury-avenue, W.C.*

National Society for the Prevention of Cruelty to Children (Incorporated by Royal Charter), 7, 8, 9 & 10, Harpur-street, London, W.C. Director and Secretary, Rev. B. Waugh.

Naval and Military Bible Society (1780), 32, Sackville-street, W. Hon. Secretaries, Admiral Sir F. L. McClintock, Colonel F. White. Secretary, Mr. S. Rayson. Bankers, Messrs. Herries, Farquhar & Co.

Nonconformist Grammar School, Bishop's Stortford (an hour's ride from London). Head Master, the Rev. R. Alliott, M.A., with seven Assistant Masters. Fees—14 to 18 guineas per term, inclusive. Seven scholarships tenable in the School. Two Exhibitions tenable at the Universities. Certified Laboratory. Carpentry. New Swimming Bath. Healthy situation. The School is a Centre for Science and Art Examinations. Full Prospectus of the Head Master.

North Africa Mission. This Mission seeks to evangelize the Moslems, Jews, and Europeans in North Africa. Its present sphere embraces five large countries, viz., Morocco, Algeria, Tunis, Tripoli, and Egypt. The Mission Staff consists of eighty-six workers, including five qualified doctors, and several trained nurses. Communications should be sent to the Hon. Sec., E. H. Glenny, 21, Linton-road, *Barking.*

OPEN AIR MISSION, 11, Adam-street, Strand, W.C. Formed 1853. Hon. Secretary, Major G. Mackinlay. Secretary, Mr. F. Cockrem.

ORPHAN HOMES OF SCOTLAND AND DESTITUTE CHILDREN'S EMIGRATION HOMES, Bridge of Weir, Renfrewshire. *City Orphan Home, Working Boys' Home, Children's Night Refuge, Young Women's Shelter, and Mission Hall*, 13, James Morrison-street, Glasgow. *Canadian Distributing Home:* Fairknowe, Brockville, Ont., Canada. *National Consumptive Hospitals for Scotland*, Bridge of Weir. Communications to be addressed to Mr. W. Quarrier, Orphan Homes of Scotland, Bridge of Weir.

ORPHAN WORKING SCHOOL, SENIOR BRANCH, Haverstock-hill, N.W. JUNIOR BRANCH, ALEXANDRA ORPHANAGE, Hornsey Rise, N. CONVALESCENT HOME, Harold Road, Margate. Instituted 1758. Secretary, Mr. A. C. P. Coote, M.A. Offices, 73, *Cheapside, London, E.C.*

PALESTINE EXPLORATION FUND. To obtain Materials for the elucidation of the Scriptures by means of Archæology, Manners and Customs, Topography, Geology, Botany, &c., of the Holy Land. The work proposed for 1895-6 is the continuation of the researches in Jerusalem, Eastern Palestine, &c., and the publication of the work already done. Office, 24, *Hanover-square, W.* Secretary, Mr. G. Armstrong.

PEACE SOCIETY. Secretary, W. E. Darby, LL.D. Office, 47, *New Broad-street, Finsbury, E.C.*

PROTESTANT ALLIANCE. Object: "The Maintenance and Defence of the Scriptural Doctrines of the Reformation against all encroachments of Popery," and for this purpose "to unite Protestants of all Denominations in demanding that the national support and encouragement given to Popery should be discontinued." Secretary, Mr. A. H. Guinness, M.A. Office, 430, *Strand, W.C.*

PROTESTANT UNION. Trustees, Rev. Dr. Angus, Rev. Dr. Kennedy, Mr. J. Spicer, Mr. E. Pye-Smith Reed, Secretary, Rev. F. Sweet. Office, *Memorial Hall, Farringdon-street, E.C.* This Union, which is a ministerial Mutual Assurance Society, was formed in 1798, for the benefit of Protestant ministers of all denominations. Capital, £73,379. Payments to widows, £2,021; to children, £972.

RAGGED SCHOOL UNION, 37 Norfolk-street, Strand. Formed 1844. *Holiday Homes Fund. Poor Children's Aid Society. Ragged Church and Chapel Union.* President, Right Hon. Earl Compton, M.P. Treasurer, Mr. F. A. Bevan. Secretary, Mr. J. Kirk.

REBECCA HUSSEY'S BOOK CHARITY. For making grants of religious and useful books to Parish Libraries, Schools, and other Institutions. Mr. J. M. Clabon, 21, Great George-street, Westminster.

REEDHAM ORPHANAGE, Purley, Surrey. Instituted 1844. Treasurer, Mr. H. C. O. Bonsor, M.P. Secretary, Mr. J. R. Edwards. Office, 35, *Finsbury Circus, E.C.*

REFORMATORY AND REFUGE UNION. Established 1856. Secretary, Mr. A. J. S. Maddison. Office, 32, *Charing Cross, S.W.* Chairman of Committee, Rev. T. Turner.

REFORMATORY AND REFUGE UNION PROVIDENT AND BENEVOLENT FUND. Established 1876. To provide assistance to Widows and Orphans of Officers who have served in Institutions in connection with the Reformatory and Refuge Union; and to the Officers themselves, if through accident or ill-health they become incapacitated. Secretary, Mr. A. J. S. Maddison. Office, 32, *Charing Cross, S.W.*

RELIGIOUS TRACT SOCIETY, 56, Paternoster-row, E.C. Founded in 1799. Treasurer, Mr. E. Rawlings. Hon. Secretaries, The Rev. Canon Fleming, B.D., and Rev. J. Stoughton, D.D. Secretaries, Rev. L. B. White, D.D., and Rev. S. G. Green, D.D. Association Secretaries—England, Rev. C. Williams, Rev. W. J. Wilkins, and Rev. A. Mercer, B.A.; Wales, Hon. Sec., Rev. T. Levi; Scotland, Rev. T. Boyd, M.A.; Ireland, Rev. W. Irwin, D.D.; Continent, Rev. J. Craig, D.D.; Corresponding, Mr. D. J. Legg.

ROYAL NAVAL SCRIPTURE READERS' SOCIETY, 112, St. Martin's-lane. Secretary, Admiral H. Campion, C.B.

SCHOOL OF HANDICRAFTS FOR DESTITUTE BOYS, Chertsey, founded by Dr. Hawksley (in connection with the Reformatory and Refuge Union). Office, 32, *Charing Cross, S.W.*

SEAMEN'S CHRISTIAN FRIEND SOCIETY. Head-quarters, *St. George's-street, London Docks, E.* Office, 255, *Burdett-road, Limehouse, E.* Secretary, Rev. G. J. Hill.

SOCIETY FOR THE LIBERATION OF RELIGION FROM STATE-PATRONAGE AND CONTROL. Treasurers, Mr. A. Illingworth and Mr. B. S. Olding. Parliamentary Chairman, Mr. J. Carvell Williams, M.P. Secretaries, Messrs. J. Fisher and S. Robjohns. Office, 2, *Serjeants'-inn, Fleet-street, E.C.*

SOCIETY FOR PROMOTING FEMALE EDUCATION IN THE EAST. Formed 1834. Secretary, Miss Webb, 267, Vauxhall Bridge-road, S.W.

SOCIETY FOR THE RELIEF OF AGED AND INFIRM PROTESTANT DISSENTING MINISTERS. Treasurer, Mr. P. Cadby. Secretary, Rev. P. G. Scorey, Ellesmere, Venner-road, Sydenham, S.E. Instituted 1818. The persons relieved by this Society are Protestant Dissenting Ministers of the Presbyterian, Independent, and Baptist denominations in England and Wales, accepted and approved by their respective denominations, who have resigned their pastoral office in consequence of incapacity, by age, or other infirmities. Number of cases relieved during the year, 63. The grants amounted to £753. The Society confers on every contributor of £105 the right to nominate one minister to be placed on the list of Annual Recipients.

SOCIETY FOR THE RESCUE OF YOUNG WOMEN AND CHILDREN. Instituted 1853. Secretary, Mr. C. S. Thorpe. Offices, 79, *Finsbury-pavement, E.C.*

STOCKWELL ORPHANAGE FOR FATHERLESS CHILDREN, Clapham-road, London, S.W. Income £11,129 14s. 3d. Expenditure, £13,006 9s. 6d. Trustees and Committee of Management, Rev. J. A. Spurgeon, D.D., (President), Rev. C. Spurgeon, Rev. T. Spurgeon, Mr. T. H. Olney, Mr. C. F. Allison, Mr. W. Higgs, Mr. J. Stiff, Mr. J. Hall, Mr. J. Buswell, Mr. J. E. Passmore, Mr. W. Mills, Mr. F. Thompson, Mr. S. R. Pearce. Master, Rev. V. J. Charlesworth. Secretary, Mr. F. G. Ladds. Fatherless children, boys between the ages of six and ten, girls from seven to ten, are received, when there are vacancies, irrespective of creed and locality, but those of Baptist Ministers are considered specially by the Trustees. Applications, giving full particulars, should be addressed in writing to the Secretary, at the Orphanage.

SUNDAY SCHOOL UNION, 56, Old Bailey, and 57, Ludgate-hill, E.C. Formed 1803. Hon. Secretaries, Messrs. E. Towers, C. Waters, J. Edmunds, and W. H. Groser, B.Sc.

SURREY MISSION SOCIETY. Formed at Tooting, A.D. 1797, for preaching the Gospel in the villages of the County. It embraces Christians of all Evangelical denominations. It has only a small income and a few village chapels. Hon. Secretary, Rev. I. Doxsey, F.S.S., 186, The Grove, Camberwell, S.E.

TRINITARIAN BIBLE SOCIETY (for the circulation of Uncorrupted Versions of the Word of God), 25, New Oxford-street, W.C. Instituted 1831. Clerical Secretary, Rev. E. W. Bullinger, D.D. Hon. Lay Secretary, Mr. H. C. Nisbet, 35, Lincoln's Inn Fields, W.C.

WALTHAMSTOW HALL, SEVENOAKS (Institution for the Education of Daughters of Missionaries). Treasurer, Mr. S. Scott, 66, Widmore-road, Bromley, Kent. Honorary Secretary, Mrs. Pye-Smith, St. Katherine's, Sevenoaks. Cash Secretary, Miss Mary Towne, 28, Walford-road, Stoke Newington, N. Lady Principal, Miss Unwin. Depends for support on payment from pupils, and on private and congregational offerings. The fees are £15 15s. per annum under twelve, and £21 over twelve. A charge of £6 per annum for those under *twelve, and* £9 for those over twelve, if clothing is provided.

WESLEYAN MISSIONARY SOCIETY, 17, Bishopsgate-street Within. Treasurers, Mr. T. M. Harvey, and the Rev. J. H. Rigg, D.D. Secretaries, Revs. G. W. Olver, B.A., F. W. Macdonald, and M. Hartley. Honorary Secretary, Rev. E. E. Jenkins, M.A., LL.D.

WIDOWS' FUND. THE SOCIETY FOR THE RELIEF OF WIDOWS AND ORPHANS OF PROTESTANT DISSENTING MINISTERS of the Three Denominations. Founded in 1733. During the past year 232 widows were helped by grants amounting to £2,772. Treasurer, Mr. W. Edwards. Secretary, Mr. R. Grace, 160, The Grove, Camberwell, S.E.

WORKING MEN'S EDUCATIONAL UNION. Supplies Pictures and Diagrams suitable for popular lectures. Now transferred to the Religious Tract Society, 56, Paternoster-row, where lists may be obtained free.

YOUNG WOMEN'S CHRISTIAN ASSOCIATION. London Office, 16*a*, *Old Cavendish-street, W.* Honorary Secretaries, The Hon. Emily Kinnaird and Miss Morley. Secretary, Mr. H. Kidner.

ZENANA MEDICAL COLLEGE, 58, St. George's-road, S.W. To train ladies to be Missionaries. Lady President, H.R.H. the Duchess of Connaught. Hon. Treasurer, Mr. G. J. Green. Hon. Secretary, Dr. G. de G. Griffith.

K

PART V.

DEATHS OF MINISTERS AND MISSIONARIES

TO NOVEMBER, 1895.

NAME.	FORMERLY AT	AGE	DATE OF DEATH.		
Banks, R. Y.	Egerton Fostal	85	March	24	1895
Bloomfield, J.	Gloucester	76	May	13	1895
Charles, F. A.	Weston-super-Mare, Bristol-rd	57	Jan.	9	1895
Cook, J.	Sutton (Suffolk)	51	March	29	1895
Davies, T. (D.D.)	Haverfordwest, Bethesda	83	March	9	1895
Davis, J.	Dover, Tabernacle	66	March	11	1895
Davis, W. S.	Nottingham, Carrington	55	Dec.	30	1894
Dean, W.	Yarmouth, I.W.	81	Jan.	22	1895
Dearle, G. B.	Pulham St. Mary	67	March	24	1895
Ellis, W. C.	Cutsdean	85	Nov.	7	1895
Evans, H. R.	New Wells	58	May	13	1895
Evans, T. R.	Shepshed	63	June	11	1895
Evans, W.	Cefncymerau	76	June	20	1895
Fishbourne, G. W.	Stratford, The Grove	78	Dec.	22	1894
Foskett, L. R.	Tring, New Mill	37	Dec.	15	1894
Howell, J.	Mountain Ash	47	June	29	1895
Johnson, B.	Raglan	72	April	13	1895
Johnston, R.	Hanley	69	June	19	1895
Jones, D.	Liverpool, Walton	56	Aug.	26	1895
Jones, J.	Speen	85	March	16	1895
Jones, R.	Mochdre	70	July	13	1895
Jones, W.	Fishguard	60	March	24	1895
Jones, W. M. (D.D.)	Finsbury, Seventh Day Baptist	77	Feb.	22	1895
Kitching, H.	Portsmouth, Landport	69	Oct.	21	1895
MacKenna, A.	India (B.M.S.)	63	Aug.	11	1895
Macmaster, R. P.	Darlington	64	March	26	1895
M'Mechan, W. H.	Barnes	52	Nov.	18	1895
Mathias, J. G.	Pontlottyn	55	Feb.	18	1895
Maynard, G. B.	Hatherleigh	79	May	5	1894
Morris, J. S.	Bow, Empson-street	55	Oct.	1	1895
Nicholas, J.	Caersws	83	April	26	1895
Owen, J. T.	Woking	35	Feb.	19	1895
Owen, W.	Narberth	82	Feb.	19	1895
Parkinson, J.	Nuneaton	64	June	12	1895
Passey, T.	Ruardean Hill	24	March	23	1895
Platten, H.	Birmingham, Hagley-road	57	Jan.	11	1895
Reynolds, G.	Kidwelly	72	March	29	1895
Roberts, E. (D.D.)	Pontypridd	75	March	30	1895
Roberts, G. H.	Carmarthen, Priory-street	64	June	7	1895
Roberts, J.	Cefnbychan	54	July	8	1895
Sear, G.	Wem	73	Sept.	17	1895
Speed, R.	Bishop Burton	63	May	17	1895
Stephens, J. M. (B.A.)	Hereford	52	Oct.	6	1895
Taylor, B.	Pulham St. Mary	78	March	29	1895
Taylor, J.	Denholme	76	Jan.	8	1895
Thomas, S.	Howey	82	June	26	1894
Webb, S. R. (M.D.)	Congo (B.M.S.)	28	April	12	1895
Wilkins, H.	Cheltenham, Salem	48	March	3	1895
Wilks, E. D.	Kingsbridge	61	Dec.	25	1894
Williams, J. P. (LL.D.)	Pontlottyn	67	June	20	1895
Williams, W. T.	Gelligaer, Horeb	46	Jan.	20	1895
Wood, J. H.	Monk's Kirby and Pailton	86	May	19	1895
Wyard, G.	Stevenage	63	Aug.	30	1895

MEMOIRS OF DECEASED MINISTERS,

TO NOVEMBER 14TH, 1895.

*** *Memoirs which were not received by November 14th will appear in the Hand-Book for 1897.*

---

1. BANKS, ROBERT YOUNG, the third of four brothers in the ministry, entered into rest 24th March, 1895, at the advanced age of eighty-five. His parents were Baptists, and he was born at Ashford, Kent. When very young he manifested love to the Saviour. Under the preaching of his eldest brother, C. W. Banks, he was brought into the liberty of the Gospel. He then became an earnest student of the Bible, and exercised his gifts in the preaching of salvation by Christ. At the hearty invitation of the Baptist Church at Egerton, Kent, he gave up business in which he had been successful, accepted the pastorate there, and remained for more than thirty years. The truths he preached to his flock he followed in his life. In trouble and joy, in prayer and praise, in private and public, he was the true Christian soldier. His whole life was spent in his native county, and there, where he had lived and laboured, he laid down his armour, and patiently waited the summons calling him away. Grace enabled him to do this, and he often expressed his resignation to the Divine will in Job's words: "All the days of my appointed time will I wait till my change come." It came, and found him ready. His tabernacle dissolved slowly; but strength was given equal to the day of trial, and his spirit returned unto God who gave it. It was on the Lord's Day morning while in prayer that his speech failed him, so that he could not proceed but regaining it he went to the usual service. In reading, it again failed, and he was taken from the pulpit to his home. Though somewhat restored he was not again permitted to preach.

"For ever with the Lord!
Amen, so let it be;
Life from the dead is in that word,
'Tis immortality." —S. J. B.

2. BLOOMFIELD, JOHN, who died on 13th May, 1895, at the age of seventy-six years, was born at Stowmarket, Suffolk, on 13th August, 1818. His long and honourable connection with Gloucestershire commenced when he was quite a young man and held his first pastorate at Bethel Chapel, Cheltenham. He afterwards received and accepted a call to Salem Chapel, Meards Court, London, and subsequently left there for Westgate Chapel, Bradford. Mr. Bloomfield remained in Yorkshire until 1870, when he responded to the invitation of the Gloucester Baptists to become the minister of Brunswick-road Church. His high Christian character, mature experience, and genial kindness eminently qualified him for the large sphere of usefulness which the Church then offered, and from the commencement his ministry proved highly successful. There were crowded congregations and numerous additions to the Church, and it soon became evident that a scheme of extension must be carried out. The schoolroom was taken down and the site used for enlarging the chapel, which became, in the main, a new building. The sitting accommodation was increased from 550 to 1,050, and the work was completed at a cost of about £3,000. The church and congregation threw themselves heartily into the effort made to obtain the requisite funds, and they were led by Mr. Bloomfield, who was personally most successful in obtaining outside assistance towards the object. The Church secured the temporary use of the British Schools for the purposes of the Sunday school until 1884, when the Raikes' Memorial Schools were erected on the site adjoining the chapel, at a total cost, including the land, of £3,500. Mr. Bloomfield commenced his pastorate on 3rd July, 1870. He remained at

Brunswick-road until December, 1886, when he determined to retire from the stated ministry; and he carried with him into his well-earned retirement the respect of all who had the pleasure of his acquaintance. But his retirement did not mean the severance of his connection with Gloucester, for until the last year of his life he continued to evince a lively interest in educational and other matters. He assisted the Brunswick-road Church as far as his strength allowed, both on anniversary and other occasions. He was first Vice-Chairman and then Chairman of the Gloucester School Board, and a member of the Infirmary Committee, and he won the confidence and esteem of his fellow-citizens in other capacities. He attended the meetings of the School Board for the last time on 19th November, 1894. When Mr. Bloomfield's contemplated retirement became known it was proposed by his friends to raise a testimonial in the shape of a fund sufficient to purchase him an annuity, and upwards of £460 was contributed by friends of all denominations from far and near. In politics he was an ardent Liberal, and he was ever ready to assist the cause of progress whenever opportunity offered. At a meeting held at the Corn Exchange in July, 1892, Mr. Bloomfield said: "A man who becomes a religious teacher does not cease to be a citizen, but the responsibilities of citizenship are rendered all the more solemn by the very fact that such a man is a minister of religion. A minister of religion should be concerned for the consolidation of everything that is good, and he should try to get rid of everything that is evil and against the interests of the people." Mr. Bloomfield in due course occupied the presidential chair of the Gloucestershire and Herefordshire Association, and for some years he was on the Committee of the Baptist Missionary Society. The following from the Bishop of Gloucester and Bristol was read at the funeral service:—"I am really greatly grieved that dear, good and kind Mr. Bloomfield has been called from us; yet of no one could it be more truly said that he has verily been called Home. I had a great regard for him, not only for the genial kindness which he ever showed towards me, but from the deep conviction I had of his love and devotion to our dear Lord and Master, and of his faithfulness in all his ministerial work. I greatly grieve that I did not call on him before I left Gloucester, but I knew not that he was in a precarious state. Pray convey to all his friends my sincere condolence and my warm appreciation of his high Christian character and true Christian sympathies. To-day he has been often in my thoughts, and always with the feeling *Requiescat in pace*."—*Abridged from the "Gloucester Journal."*

3. CHARLES, FREDERICK ALDIS, the youngest son of Mr. John Charles, of Broomhall Park, was born in Sheffield, and educated at Chesterfield Grammar School, where he distinguished himself as a scholar. In early life Mr. Charles became a member of Townhead Baptist Church, and there in various ways he sought to further the interests of Christ's Kingdom among men. After leaving school it was intended that he should follow a commercial life, and so he entered his father's business at Kelliam Rolling Mills, Sheffield, in 1852, and there remained until 1858. He thus acquired that keen, practical ability which ever marked his after life as a Christian minister. The desire to help men by preaching the Gospel of the Saviour grew until he determined to obey the Apostle's mandate: "Let no man seek his own, but each his neighbour's good," and, although a promising future opened before him in business, he disregarded pecuniary allurements and rewards, and as one who could honestly have said, "What things were gain to me these have I counted loss for Christ," he steadfastly set his heart upon the work of the ministry. He entered Rawdon College as a lay student under the care of the Rev. S. G. Green, D.D., and there he studied for a year before becoming a ministerial student in 1859. After six years of conscientious preparation, he accepted his first charge at Whitehaven. Thence, in order to be near his father, he removed to Nottingham, and became pastor of a church at Basford. When he resigned that charge, he served the churches in the district for a time by his occasional ministrations. In 1876 Mr. Charles became pastor of the Church at Grange-road, Darlington, and finally he accepted the pastorate at Bristol-road, Weston-super-Mare. His ministry began there on the first Sunday in February, 1885, and was diligently continued until the end of 1894, when in December of that year he resigned owing to ill-health. He survived only a few days, for he died on January 9th, 1895. A local authority says that during his residence in Weston he was for many years secretary to the British Schools, and showed his deep interest in the hospital, not only by frequent visits to *that* institution, but also by the special lecture which he prepared every year on

behalf of its funds. Mr. Charles had for years contributed many articles to several magazines and newspapers. Within a short time before his death he published three booklets which will have more than a transitory interest—"The Preaching for To-day," "The Relationships of Life in the Light of Christianity," and "Charles Kingsley." The last of these has been most favourably reviewed by the Press, and has had a wide circulation. His kindly visitation of the sick and poor, his generosity, his ever-ready help to those in embarrassment, will not soon be forgotten. In writing to a friend a little time before his death, he says, "We disappear one by one—into the dark—but each may throw his comrades a token—before he goes. . . . Take my poor witness. There is one clue—one only—goodness—the surrendered will—everything is there—all faith—all religion—all hope for rich or poor." "Thy will be done."—J. W.

4. COOK, JONATHAN, who died on 29th March, 1895, at the age of fifty-one years, was a member of the church at Waldringfield, and preached in neighbouring churches until he accepted an invitation to the pastorate at Sutton, near Woodbridge, in 1883, where he continued until his death. He was an earnest, devoted, peace-loving, and truthful Christian. All he did was with a whole-hearted desire to glorify God, and he was too unselfish to study his own interests. During his last illness he was happy in the Lord, and peacefully waited the call home. Resting upon the Rock of Ages, he was perfectly ready.—J. A.

5. DAVIES, THOMAS, was born November 12th, 1812, at the Wern Fawr Farm, St. Mellons, three miles from Cardiff, on the way to Newport, Mon. His parents occupied a good position in the world, and were held in great respect in the neighbourhood. All the children became useful, and, in many cases, prominent members of the Baptist Churches after the good example set them by their parents. Thomas received what was, for those times, a good day school education. At the age of sixteen he took a situation at Dowlais. It was during his stay there that he was baptized by Rev. David Saunders, and received into the Church at Zion, Merthyr Tydvil. Soon after, he and some others, united to form the Caersalem Church, Dowlais, now one of the largest in the Principality. In his eighteenth year he returned to his home and joined the Church at Castletown, the pastor of which was the well-known Welsh bard Evan Jones, "Gwrwst." He was one of the founders of the Sunday school at St. Mellons, and soon afterwards he started preaching services in the same place. When, eight years ago, the foundation stone of the present handsome chapel at St. Mellons was laid, Dr. Davies told the large audiences that as a young man—a farmer's son—he had carted most of the stones of the old chapel. In 1831 he removed to Cardiff to study under the direction of the late Rev. William Jones, of Bethany. Among those who signed his application for college training was Christmas Evans, then pastor of the Tabernacle, Cardiff. At the close of the trial sermon the great preacher put his hand on young Thomas Davies' shoulder and said in Welsh, "Well done, my boy: you will make a preacher: I will gladly sign your application." In 1832 he was admitted into Bristol College, under the presidency of the Rev. T. S. Crisp. Among his fellow-students were the Rev. J. T. Brown, Northampton, and the late Doctors Benjamin Davies and F. W. Gotch; the late Dr. F. Trestrail had just left the college. For four years Mr. Davies worked with commendable diligence and success, at the end of which time he accepted an invitation from the English Church, Merthyr Tydvil. He found a small congregation, a small church, and a small and altogether miserable chapel in an out-of-the-way part of the town. There he remained for twenty years accomplishing a really wonderful work. The attendance and the membership grew, well-to-do families were first drawn to the chapel, and then joined the church. The place was soon found to be too small, and in 1843 what was then one of the finest chapels in Wales was erected in the main thoroughfare of the town. This was soon filled and the organizations of the church prospered greatly. "High Street Chapel," Merthyr, and its popular pastor were much talked of throughout the Principality. Mr. Davies threw himself heart and soul into the public movements of the town. During the Chartist riots he used to go fearlessly into the most boisterous meetings, and he never failed to get a hearing. His influence in the town was unique. The present writer was for two years pastor of the same Church, and it is his deliberate conviction that no public man in Merthyr Tydvil ever so completely gained the ear

and the heart of the population as did Thomas Davies. In 1856 Haverfordwest lost David Davies—a man who was equally weighty in character and brilliant as a preacher. Thomas Davies, of Merthyr, was unanimously and cordially invited to succeed him as president of the college and pastor of the Church. To the great joy of all concerned the invitation was accepted, and, in 1857, he entered upon his new duties. The result to the college was a large increase in the income, with a corresponding growth in the number of students. Annual written examinations were introduced, the standard of admission was raised, and many other improvements were effected. In many respects he was an ideal President. His judgment and presence of mind were quite remarkable. He was extremely bright and cheerful in his temperament, and no one could more easily or more pleasantly overcome a difficulty than he could. He was the youngest old man I ever knew, to the last he was as playful as a boy, and as willing to take in new ideas, if they were well-supported, as an ardent youth with his career before him. His shrewdness and common-sense amounted almost to genius, and it was these qualities, rather than large stores of learning, that constituted his strength as teacher and as president. In the sermon class, he would be sure to hit off the principal defects of the sermons, and by mimicry, sarcasm, and wit, make them ridiculous. Like his predecessor, David Davies, though not to the same extraordinary degree, the late Dr. Davies had also much ability in reconstructing a new sermon after he had torn the old one into shreds. His younger days belonged to a period when opportunities for drinking deep of the well of knowledge were few; but his knowledge was wide, and it bore directly upon the work he had to do, and I was always struck with the aptitude and force with which in classroom, in pulpit, and on platform, he could use the knowledge he had. For eleven years it was my pleasure to be classical tutor during his presidency. From 1857 to 1865, the late Rev. T. Burditt, M.A., was Dr. Davies's assistant at the Bethesda Church as well as at the college. From 1865 to 1886, Dr. Davies was sole pastor of the Church. From 1886 to 1894, the Rev. R. O. Johns was co-pastor. Dr. Davies resigned the presidency of the college in 1894, having held the position for thirty-six years. From the time he entered the ministry up to the day of his death he was never out of a pastorate, so that he was in the ministry of the Baptist denomination fifty-nine years. For many years he was Vice-President of the Haverfordwest School Board. In 1874, he occupied the position of President of the Welsh Baptist Union. In 1886, he received a testimonial of £430 in appreciation of his services. In 1889, a beautifully executed oil portrait was presented to him. He was for several years before his death one of the Vice-Presidents of the Bible Society. Of literary work he did practically nothing, though the few articles he wrote and the college reports he issued, show he had great power for concise and pointed writing. He died rather suddenly on 9th March, 1895, leaving behind him a good name and an abiding influence for good.—T. W. D.

6. DAVIS, JAMES, who died 11th March 1895, at the age of sixty-six years, was born in Liverpool, and baptized when only twelve years old in Soho-street Chapel by Rev. R. Lancaster, pastor of the Church. His father had been a deacon, as well as the superintendent of the Sunday school. The immediate occasion of his religious decision was the last sermon preached by the Rev. Moses Fisher (Mr. Lancaster's predecessor), who died shortly afterwards. Starting on a business career in the office of a cotton broker, he did not enter Rawdon (then Bradford) College until he was twenty-one years of age. He was the first *alumnus* of that institution who matriculated at London University, but he was prevented from taking his degree by his early settlement, in 1885, as co-pastor with Mr. Winter, at Counterslip Chapel, Bristol. He subsequently held pastoral charges in Teignmouth, at Banbury for twelve years, and at Dover. He had considerable classical scholarship and acquaintance with modern languages, and his conversational powers were great. As a preacher he found delight in his work. In the sick-room his cheery manner and childlike faith were specially welcome. It is impossible to estimate how much good he did by his custom of quietly and earnestly speaking to people, whenever he had an opportunity, words of spiritual appeal and counsel, and they were generally received with courtesy and gratitude by rich and poor alike. When, a few months before his death, he retired to Weston-super-Mare, into the midst of his happy family circle, and with the longing still to do some work, those who loved him *thought they saw the* brightness of sunset in his life. The Master has called him

THOMAS DAVIES, D.D.

to the highest service, where, to use his own words concerning a brother minister whose sermons he edited for the Press, "No faculty will be left unexercised, no gift will be wasted, and the endowments of the soul will find a scope of action surpassing our grandest conceptions." One of his remarks during his last illness was this: "I am in God's hands, whether it be His will to heal me or to take me to heaven." In this spirit of calm trust and hope he lived and preached, and bore the burden of life (which at times pressed sorely), and died, leaving behind him in the memory of those who knew him the image of a true friend as well as of a happy, earnest, ever-ready servant of the Lord.—M. M. D.

7. DAVIS, WILLIAM STEADMAN, who died at St. Leonards on 30th December, 1894, was born in 1839. He was the third son of the Rev. Joseph Davis, then minister of Blackfriars, London. His boyhood was spent in the village of Arnsby and at Southsea, and he was taught in various schools. He learned the business of cabinet-making in London, during which time he joined his father's old church, under the Rev. William Barker, to whose ministry and kindness he always felt indebted. With other young men he began to write and talk. Encouraged to enter the ministry, he read with his eldest brother before entering college. While at Sabden he was most welcome in the colleges and the school; his picturesque, pathetic, grave, and trenchant style made him acceptable as a preacher, and his industry won him a good place in the entrance examination at Rawdon, which he never lost. He was from childhood a great reader—a devourer of history, biography, and poetry. He was very select in his choice of books, and did not leave a mean one on his shelves. He was never the technical scholar; it was the living nature and human character that attracted him. His preaching was, perhaps, strongest in dealing with ethical and personal topics. He was once fond of John the Baptist; the severity, directness, and picturesqueness of the martyr-prophet touched his sympathies. Before leaving college he was called to the Church at Queen's Park, Manchester, where his ministry was happy and useful, and he was respected and beloved. Thence he moved to Huntingdon. His stay there was cut short by Mrs. Davis' illness, and he removed to Ryde. He afterwards ministered for short periods at Carrington, Nottingham; and at Haslingden. Illness closed his work at both places, but in each of them he is still loved. While at Ryde his most familiar and best-loved brother, Benoni, died at Ventnor. This was a great blow to him, and some think he never quite recovered the shock. Behind his reserved and silent manner there was a well of sincerity and affection for those who tapped it; and, curiously, he was much drawn to those whose personal qualities contrasted most with his own. His intimate friends were not many; it would be hard to find his enemy; he was a man to rely on. His later was not like his earlier preaching; it was weaker in attractive qualities, and stronger in reflection and argument and doctrine and spirituality. This was the result of maturity and of labour. His sermons never cost him nothing, they had to be prepared, and though his temperament was even, their effect was delicately dependent on his surroundings. His life may be best summed up in one phrase; it was a "patient continuance in well-doing." He has the honour and eternal life that follow it.—J. U. D.

8. DEAN, WILLIAM, was born at Chard, Somerset, February 17th, 1814. In early life he was engaged in the boot and shoe trade, and carried on business at Newport, I.W., as a leather cutter for many years, during which he was connected with the Church at Castlehold. He began preaching at Broughton, Hants, where he was very useful, and where his labours are still remembered with thankfulness. Many of the villages around Broughton shared in his earnest and affectionate ministrations. A friend who knew him well during his residence at Newport thus writes of him and his work at that period: "I remember his coming to Newport many years ago. His services as a local preacher were in great demand. The various Nonconformist churches of the island gave him a hearty welcome, and profited greatly by his ministry. One of the foremost in promoting unity, he was ready to serve Independents, Wesleyans, Primitive Methodists, Bible Christians, Free Wesleyans, or Baptists, and as he preached the Gospel in its breadth and fulness, his ministry was equally acceptable to all. I had the privilege of often travelling with him to the west end of the island, where in turn we preached at Freshwater, Colwell, Yarmouth, Wellow, &c. With all his quiet, unassuming manner, he had great resources of spiritual knowledge, and his faith was based on principle and intense

WILLIAM STEADMAN DAVIS.
(From Photograph by A. Debenham, Ryde I.W.)

conviction. He had the 'faith working through love.' As a preacher, he was a 'workman that needeth not to be ashamed.' . . . His spiritual fervour and intense earnestness were highly valued by the village communities. At times his voice would tremble with emotion . . . and his great concern was for the spiritual good of the people. His name is fragrant in all the churches at Roud, Chilleston, Wootton Bridge, Swanmore, St. Helens, Sea View, and Porchfield, as well as in other parts of the island. Always on the side of freedom in politics and in religion, he never failed to promote good feeling and to secure a recognition of the rights of others." The writer's acquaintance with Mr. Dean dates from the year 1879 only, about a year after his settlement at Yarmouth, I.W. This step he took on the recommendation of Dr. Trestrail. There he toiled faithfully, and won the respect of all. He was permitted to serve this Church for fourteen years, when, in 1892, increasing years and infirmities compelled him to resign. He continued, however, to be at least nominally pastor, and took the services one Sunday in the month, when he presided at the Lord's Supper. Even this limited service had eventually to be relinquished, but he preached occasionally as long as his strength permitted. After a protracted and painful illness, born with great patience, he passed away to the presence of the Lord he had so long and conscientiously served, on the 22nd January, 1895.—J. C.

9. DEARLE GEORGE BIRD, was a native of London. His father was a man esteemed for his strict integrity, though he was an avowed Deist. When his son was quite a lad he became deeply impressed, and at the age of sixteen was baptized by Rev. James Nunn at Beulah Strict Baptist Church. From that time he was a most ardent worker in the Sunday school and in other religious institutions connected with the Church. When twenty-six years of age, he left London for Norwich, where for many years he practised as a dentist, and for nearly forty years devoted all his spare time and religious enthusiasm to the service of the Strict Baptist Churches, especially in the Norfolk villages. During this time he was pastor of the Churches at Felthorpe, Shelfanger, and at Pulham St. Mary in which he continued until his death. His home and social life were characterized by deep affection and devotion and a perennial cheerfulness, and his religious and public life was marked by an unswerving fidelity to those truths he held to be in accord with God's Word. He was a bold defender of Strict Baptist principles, fearlessly denouncing the errors he thought other Churches were teaching. As a Nonconformist of a pronounced type, and a Radical in politics, he took great interest in all national questions, believing that the religion of Jesus should have complete sway over the entire life of man. During his residence in Diss, where he spent the last thirteen years of his life, he took an active part in public affairs as a member of the School and Local Boards. His life was in perfect harmony with the truths he loved and taught; and his death, though tragic, was simply the fulfilment of his own desire, for more than once he had been heard to say that if he had any choice about dying, he would prefer to die preaching. On Sunday afternoon, 24th March, 1895, his earthly ministry was abruptly concluded while he was preaching from the text "Lovest thou Me more than these?" (John xxi., 15.) For at 3.15., when the gale, which devastated the Eastern counties, was at its height, without a moment's warning a portion of the roof was blown off, and a chimney and gable end wall were precipitated into the chapel. Tons of brick and mortar came crushing through, striking the pastor violently on the head. Although everything was done that could be done, he never recovered consciousness until the following day, when he was translated to perfect service in the more immediate presence of the King he had so long loved and faithfully served. He was sixty-seven years of age.—R.D.

10. EVANS, HUGH REES, was born at Llanllugan, in the county of Montgomery, about 1837. His parents were in straitened circumstances, and his health, when a child, was very feeble, and never became very strong at any time of his life. His educational advantages were very small, only just enough to enable him to read and write. He spent some years as a farm servant, and when, by an accident, he lost one of his legs, he was apprenticed to a tailor who was a deacon and the leader of the singing at Llanllugan Chapel. Mr. Evans was ardently fond of reading, and out of his scanty means he bought candles, so that he might sit up all night to read *some favourite book*. He was baptized at an early age at Lllanllugan or Llanfair-

Caereinion, and soon after commenced to preach. In 1869 he was invited to take charge of the church at New Wells, and he accepted the invitation, and continued to minister there with much acceptance and success for twenty-five years. His health failed and he resigned in 1894, but he continued to preach occasionally until within a few weeks of his death, which took place in May, 1895. As a man Mr. Evans was quiet, peaceful, and unassuming, and was held in high esteem by all who knew him. As a preacher he was above the average, for his sermons were well thought out, his outlines were clear, and his delivery was marked with great earnestness, pathos, and vigour.—D. E. H.

11. EVANS, THOMAS RHYS, was born at Sirhowy, Monmouthshire, in 1832. His parents were distinguished for their godliness and sterling worth, and very early in life he was received as a member of the Siloh Baptist Church, Tredegar, then under the pastoral care of the Rev. W. Roberts. According to the custom of the Welsh churches he was soon invited to give expression to his religious feelings at the weekly service, which he did in so promising a manner that the church urged him to consecrate his life to the work of the ministry. After he had spent a year at Merthyr Tydfil, under the tuition of Rev. T. Davies, he applied in 1854 for admission to Pontypool College, and was accepted. At the close of an honourable college course, he accepted an invitation to become the pastor of the church at Usk, which he filled successfully for two or three years. About 1861 he removed to Countesthorpe, to assist the venerable Rev. Shem Evans, of Arnsby, who had the oversight of the united churches of Arnsby and Countesthorpe. His relations with the venerable pastor were of the happiest kind, for as a son with a father "he served in the Gospel." But when the new chapel was built at Countesthorpe the two churches became independent of each other, and Mr. T. R. Evans was invited to assume the sole pastorate. For ten years he carried on a vigorous and faithful ministry, and on leaving, in 1872, for Shepshed, he was presented with several valuable presents, and his name is still lovingly remembered in Countesthorpe. At Shepshed, in the maturity of his powers and in the prime of his strength, he unreservedly threw himself into all manner of work. He ungrudgingly gave much strength and time to educational matters, and not deeming political questions as something "common or unclean," he earnestly and boldly advocated the principles of Progressive Liberalism. But his greatest solicitude was for the spiritual welfare of the church. For this he toiled "in season and out of season," and his labours were richly blessed. Towards the end of 1890 his health failed, and he tendered his resignation of the pastorate and removed to Leicester. For a time he rendered valuable service to many churches in the county, until one day he was suddenly smitten with a deadly disease. He died 11th June, 1895.—W. E.

12. EVANS, WILLIAM, of Cefncymerau, passed away on 20th June, 1895, after a brief illness, which lasted for a few hours only. He was the son of Evan Evans, who was for many years pastor of the Church at Garn, Dolbenmaen, Carnarvonshire. William was one of a family of seven children. He was baptized in March, 1840, and about twelve months after he began to preach the Gospel. He was ordained to the ministry at Garn in 1848. About 1850 he settled in Llanbedr, Merionethshire, and took the oversight of the little Church at Cefncymerau. Though he was not a popular preacher, in his quiet way he made his message tell with his hearers all through his long stay. He saw many additions to the Church, so that his ministry showed steady, though slow, growth. Soon after his settlement at Cefncymerau the chapel was rebuilt, and he worked very hard to pay off the debt. A new Church was also started at Harlech, and a neat little chapel was built there, which is now filled. Some years before his death Mr. Evans gave up the charge of the two Churches. He had his share of sorrow, for he buried his only daughter when she was four years old, and his wife was an invalid for many years before her death in January, 1893. Mr. Evans was a man of sterling character, and a thorough Christian. His successor at Cefncymerau testifies to the exceedingly kind, respectful and harmonious spirit in which Mr. Evans worked with him after his resignation of the pastorate.—G. W.

13. FISHBOURNE, GEORGE WILLIAM, who died on 22nd December, 1894, at the age of seventy-eight years, was a resident in London before his admission to Stepney College, and his ministry commenced in 1838. On the 19th January, 1840, he settled as pastor of the Church in Guernsey, and removed to Bow in September,

1846. His ministry at The Grove Chapel, Stratford, E., began in 1853 and terminated in 1866, when he removed to Bognor, and for a time took the oversight of the Congregational church in that town, without, however, ceasing to be a Baptist. West Brighton became his place of residence in 1884, and there he died. He was Financial Secretary of Regent's Park College from 1851 to 1893. His son and all the friends who could have given fuller details of his life have pre-deceased him.—J. A.

14. FOSKETT, LOUIS ROBERT, after a lingering and painful illness, heroically borne, went home early in the morning of 15th December, 1894, at the age of thirty-seven years. He was always bright and hopeful even in the darkest day. Chelsea was his birthplace, and there he was trained in a godly home. When school days were over he commenced work as an electrical engineer. Very soon after his conversion, which took place in September, 1874, he was baptized by the late Rev. John Teall, and became a member of the Strict Baptist Church, worshipping in Queen-street Chapel, Woolwich, where he was a very useful worker, both as a Sunday school teacher and a village preacher. In 1877 he was admitted to the Pastors' College, and continued there three years. His first settlement as pastor was at Shepton Mallet and Croscombe in the Bristol Association, where he remained for seven years. His other pastorate was at New Mill, Tring, in the Hertfordshire Union, also of seven years' duration. There is a coincidence in the fact that the call to his second charge came at the same time of the year and almost on the same date as the first; both were held for the same period. His last duty in the first Church was to receive two new members, and there were also two to be received on the last Sunday of his second pastorate. The work of the ministry was an intense delight to him. Preaching was his chief pleasure, and the wonder is that he did not die in the pulpit, for he told a friend after preaching his last sermon that he had to hold on to the sides of the pulpit as for very life. The thought of being able to leave the membership of the Church at New Mill as large as it was when he undertook the charge was a source of great comfort and joy to him. All that medical skill and affectionate nursing could do for him was most cheerfully done, though with much self-denial on the parts of others. The immediate cause of death was hæmorrhage of the lungs, but for years, inflammation, congestion, pleurisy and influenza had undermined his strength. During the last few hours he had a terrible fight for breath, but the end was calmness and peace. In full possession of all his mental faculties, he turned his face to his beloved wife, and, in a clear voice, he said, "The battle's won." The next moment he had gone to his reward. He was a man of deep conviction, of fearlessness in speech, and one of the most devoted of all the followers of the late President of the Pastors' College.—C. P.

15. HOWELL, JOHN, was a native of Carmarthenshire. His early education was scanty. At Aberdare he worked underground whilst quite a boy. He thirsted for knowledge, and began preaching when very young. In 1870 he entered Pontypool College, and at the close of his course he settled as pastor of the Welsh Church at Cwmpark. He was there for two years, when he was invited to the pastorate of the English Church at Tonypandy. Eighteen months later he was invited to the English Church, Nazareth, Mountain Ash, and there he spent eighteen years in active work. He was a thoughtful and earnest preacher, a painstaking pastor, and an excellent public man. He was foremost in every good movement. The late Lord Aberdare esteemed him very highly, and all regarded him as a leading citizen. He was a member of the Local Board for years, worked hard in connection with the Reading Room and the Hospital; he was one of the most prominent members of the Glamorganshire English Association, and a journalist of much ability. For some years he had not been strong, on account of overwork, but his energy and enthusiasm were unbounded. He died at the early age of forty-seven years, deeply regretted by a large circle of friends, and mourned by a united and loving Church. Three branches in connection with his Church were established by his instrumentality at Miskin, Cefnpenar, and Newtown. He served for years on the Llanwonno School Board, and his work was as effective as it was varied. His lectures on Palestine, Brittany, &c., in which countries he had travelled much, were greatly appreciated. He felt a deep interest in the welfare of Brittany. He was held in the highest esteem for all his work. —W. E.

16. JOHNSON, BENJAMIN, was the son of Edward Johnson, paper manufacturer, Hoarwithy, near Ross, Herefordshire. He was born 17th October, 1822, and was the *youngest of thirteen* children. When he was quite young his parents removed to

Whitebrook, near Monmouth, and it was there he was brought to Christ under the ministry of the Rev. W. Lloyd. He commenced preaching at Llandogo when he was seventeen years of age, and during the pastorate of the Rev. M. Philpin. He served his apprenticeship as a painter and plumber, and worked at that trade for a few years, but feeling that he was called to the work of the Christian ministry he placed himself under the private tuition of the Rev. J. Wright, of Layshill, Herefordshire. In 1845 he was invited to become the pastor of the Church at Garway, near Ross, and in addition to his pastoral work he discharged the duties of schoolmaster in connection with "Gough's Charity." Thirteen years of earnest and faithful toil were spent there, during which he had also under his pastoral supervision the Churches at Norton and Orcop. He preached thrice every Sunday, and his name is still very lovingly remembered by the old members. In 1858 Mr. Johnson removed to Raglan, Monmouthshire, where he toiled diligently and successfully for the long period of thirty-seven years. There also he was schoolmaster as well as pastor, and preached three times regularly every Lord's Day. During his ministry at Raglan, a new chapel was erected (in 1861-2), and through his indefatigible efforts the building was soon free from debt. On the completion of the twenty-fifth year of his pastorate there, he was presented with a handsome testimonial (a purse of money) from his Church and congregation, and about the same time he was elected president of the Monmouthshire English Association. Mr. Johnson was a splendid type of a country pastor, and most loyally, but unostentatiously, did he work for his Master in a Church and Tory-ridden village. He was in reality one of Christ's "good and faithful" servants, and he entered into the "joy of his Lord" on 13th April, 1895. The day after his death Mrs. Johnson died, and, amid many tokens of respect, both were buried the same afternoon at Kingcoed, a preaching station connected with the Church at Raglan. Verily, in "death they were not divided," and their end was peace, accompanied with an abundant "entrance into the everlasting Kingdom of Our Lord and Saviour Jesus Christ."—D. B. J.

17. JOHNSTON, ROBERT, died at his residence, 70, The Avenue, Castle Hill, Ealing, W., on 19th June, 1895. He was born in London in August, 1826, and received his education at the Blue Coat School. A boy of quiet disposition and bookish tastes, he took less than the average schoolboy's interest in sport, and very early in life he was, to use his own familiar phrase, "converted to God." His parents—members of the Church of England—destined him for a commercial life, and he was in the employ of Messrs. Unite, of Edgware Road, W., when, in 1865, he was asked to accept the pastorate of the Baptist Church at Hanley. That position he filled with marked success for two or three years, but, as continued residence in that part of the country was injurious to his health, he returned to London, and resumed his connection with Messrs. Unite, under whom he held a responsible post, until his death. On his retirement from the pastorate at Hanley the church presented him with a handsome clock as a token of its appreciation of his loving and faithful service. For a short time he resided at Shepherd's Bush, and then removed to Ealing. There—in Kirchen Road—he commenced what proved to be his life work. For some time before he left London for Staffordshire he and Mrs. Johnston were in charge of a boys' home in Paddington, and out of that grew a Youths' Christian Association. Soon after he settled in Ealing he founded such an Association there. It began in a very small way—with the gathering of a few youths on Sunday afternoon in one of his rooms. But Mr. Johnston's earnestness and unassumed love for lads soon attracted others, and he found, although he had once or twice enlarged his house for the purposes of the Mission, as it came to be called, that it afforded insufficient accommodation for the Sunday afternoon class, and he therefore built in The Avenue a house with a large comfortable room attached, in which the class met. At one time the Mission numbered nearly 150 members. When Mr. Johnston found that it was competing with the Sunday Schools, he raised the age of admission from twelve to fifteen years. His success must be attributed to his personal character, to the fact that his strong religious convictions were wedded to perfect human sympathy. In other directions he found scope for his burning zeal for the regeneration of mankind. An earnest teetotaller, he often appeared on temperance platforms, and he was an acceptable preacher at the Ealing Dean Primitive Methodist Chapel and elsewhere. He rendered valuable help to the Ealing Branch of the Sunday School Orchestral Band. Mr. Johnston, who was a member of the Ealing Dean Church, lost no opportunity of protesting against

attempts to substitute the dogmas of any Church for personal faith. He wished his "boys," as he lovingly called them, to be connected with some religious organization, but he never attempted to dictate in regard to their choice. By his death Ealing loses one of its notable figures, a man who could ill be spared.—Abridged from *The Middlesex County Times.*

18. JONES, DANIEL, was one of the most brotherly, large-hearted, and helpful of our ministers, and one whose loss must long be felt. Born at Bassaleg 14th November, 1839, he entered Haverfordwest College in 1860. He had been some time in business, and had saved money to pay his college expenses. He was pastor at Shrewsbury from 1864 to 1868, and at Stourbridge from 1869 to 1873. He then removed to Liverpool, and was for some time actively connected with the National Education League. This work secured for him the acquaintance and warm personal esteem of many leading men of different public bodies. He was at that time and until 1879 the pastor of Old Swan Church, for which a chapel was built mainly through his untiring efforts. From there he went to Fabius Chapel, Everton-road, and he continued in that pastorate until 1888. Mr. Jones toiled against great discouragement among a very poor population, but with unfailing energy and hopefulness, and there are many at that place who remember with life-long gratitude his devoted ministry. From 1888 to 1892 he was Deputation for the British Society for the Propagation of the Gospel among the Jews. During the latter part of that time he rendered valuable service to the Walton Church, then without a pastor, and on resigning his post with the Society he became in 1892 pastor of that Church. In 1894 failing health compelled Mr. Jones to resign, and he then left for Sydney in search of health, which seemed at first to be returning to him. He undertook a very hopeful pastorate at Ashfield, N.S.W., when suddenly graver symptoms developed, and he was taken to his rest on 26th August, 1895. In addition to all that has been recounted, he was for some years secretary of the Liverpool Baptist Union, of which he was also chairman; and in all the work of the County Association he took a deep interest, and gave to it valuable help. On his departure from Liverpool many friends of various denominations contributed to raise a fund to defray the expenses of the voyage, and the warm expressions of esteem which accompanied the gifts testified to the worth of Mr. Jones and of his work. "Jesus Christ and Him crucified," was the inspiration of his truly devoted and beautiful life. —J. W. S.

19. JONES, JOHN, was born 10th April, 1810, in the county of Radnor. In his early days he was proficient in athletics, in which he often joined his companions on the Sabbath. Sometimes he felt the stings of conscience, and then he would loiter behind and fall upon his knees under some hedge and cry for pardon. At length God, by His gracious Spirit, wrought the work of saving grace in the young man's heart, whereupon he felt a strong desire to lead his comrades from their follies into the light and joy of salvation. Soon he began to preach and showed much aptitude and zeal in the work. He received, and accepted, a call to settle over the Church at Madley in 1830. Mr. Jones removed to Raglan, thence to Layshill, and, later on, successively to Kidderminster, Oundle, Knighton, Llangwam and Usk. His last charge was at Speen, Buckinghamshire, where he remained ten years and reached his ministerial jubilee. He continued to reside in the place until his death, which occurred 16th March, 1895. After he resigned the pastorate he occasionally conducted services for some of the neighbouring Churches. He was devoted to preaching, and had a fine commanding presence and a good voice. To some he doubtless appeared harsh, but he had a kind heart, and, true to his Divine Master, and severe upon looseness in life or laxity of doctrine, "Christ and his Cross" was all his theme.—C. S.

20. JONES, ROBERT, was born at a farmhouse called Tyn-y-Coed, in the parish of Llanystumdwy, Carnarvonshire, 28th November, 1825. He commenced his religious life with the Independents, by whom he was invited to exercise his gifts as a preacher of the Gospel, and, having done so for some time with much acceptance, he entered Bala College, where he studied for two or three years. After leaving college he was for some time pastor of the Independent Church at Rowen, Carnarvonshire, but having changed his views in regard to Baptism he was baptized at Carnarvon, and in 1866 became the pastor of the Baptist Churches at Newchapel

and Cwmbellan, Montgomeryshire. After he had been there about seven years he resigned. He was then without a pastorate for some time; but the Church at Cwmbellan again invited him to become their pastor in 1875. He did so, and continued until 1878, when he took charge of the Church at Mochdre, in the same county. Advancing age and feeble health compelled him to resign in 1894. He preached occasionally at Mochdre and the churches in the neighbourhood up to the time of his death, which took place on 13th July, 1895. Mr. Jones was a man of unblemished character, an able preacher, and a careful pastor; but of a quiet and retiring disposition. He was not a man to take the lead, but to work quietly out of sight. He was for some years the agent of the Bible Translation Society in his part of the country; and in many other ways he did much unostentatious work for the Master.—J. G.

21. JONES, WILLIAM, was born at Brymbo, Denbighshire, August, 1835. His father, J. R. Jones, was a poet of considerable reputation, and the author of some well-known Welsh hymns. The son was baptized in his eighteenth year by the Rev. R. A. Jones, of Llanfair, and on 25th November, 1855, he commenced to preach. Though his first attempts at preaching did not give any indication of his future eminence, it was evident that he was endowed with talents of no mean order. After the usual course of training at Haverfordwest College, he settled as minister at Penyfron, Flintshire. The Church at Penyfron was small, and not likely confer much distinction on its pastor. The situation was trying, and many a man might have been so influenced by the unfavourable environment as to sink in despair; but he mastered the circumstances, turned his disadvantages to advantage, and made the best possible use of his time in studying the Holy Scriptures and various philosophical writers, and so cultivated the acquaintance of the best society in the form of authors ancient and modern. He would lose himself entirely in the society of Hamilton, Kant, Hegel, and others, whose productions he would read with sympathetic interest, but also with careful discrimination. The Church at Conway enjoyed his ministration for a short period after his removal from Flintshire, and then he removed to Bargoed in Monmouthshire. The Church there was comparatively large, and a wide sphere of usefulness opened before him. Having accepted an invitation from the Church at Fishguard in Pembrokeshire he removed thither in 1870, and there, with the exception of some two years he spent in London as the pastor of the Welsh Church in Castle Street, Oxford Street, he remained until his death, which took place on 24th March, 1895. Mr. Jones was a man of remarkable powers, a profound thinker, and a very eloquent preacher. He read and he thought, and one could wish that he had written as well—but he carefully avoided printers' ink. Even when he filled the chair of the Welsh Baptist Union which he did last year at Morriston—he had not written his carefully prepared address, so that only a fragmentary report of what was acknowledged on all hands to be a very masterly production is ever likely to see the light. Mr. Jones preached a very powerful sermon at Carnarvon, during the sitting of the Welsh Baptist Union, in 1892, on "Eternal Life." Amongst many eloquent passages was one describing the infant waking to consciousness of life. On a certain day the candle is taken from one room to another, the eye of the little one follows it. That is the first time for it to consciously observe any object, but the last time will never come. In addition to the profound thoughts, the apposite illustrations, the rich poetic fancy, and the chaste diction of the preacher, there was an irresistible charm in his manner. He was very conservative in his theological views. He had no interest in conferences or committees, and if by some accident he found himself present at one, he would be most careful to observe the golden rule of silence. He rose to the highest rank of Welsh preachers. His illness was brief, and his transition to the world of fuller knowledge was very sudden.—H. C. W.

22. JONES, WILLIAM MEAD, the son of a physician, was born at Fort Ann, Washington Co., New York, on 2nd May, 1818. In his early years he worked as a farmer, but finding himself called to preach, in 1838 entered Madison University, Hamilton, New York. Ill-health, however, sent him away early in the course. He was ordained pastor in the Mill Creek Church, Huntingdon Co., Pennsylvania, 5th January, 1841. He continued as a pastor and evangelist in Central Pennsylvania until 1844. During this time he travelled 12,000 miles (mostly on horseback) in keeping his appointments. He organized several churches in that State. He entered

enthusiastically into the cause of Emancipation, and encountered the most violent opposition from many of his Baptist brethren on account of his views, some even refusing to have him in their houses. In January, 1845, he was sent by the American Baptist Free Mission Society as a missionary to the freed negroes of the island of Hayti, where he remained for six and a-half years and organized a church at Port au Prince. During a temporary return to the States he became a convert to the observance of the seventh day as the Sabbath. After a few months he severed his connection with the Mission and returned to the States. He entered the Seventh-day Baptist Denomination and became pastor of one of their churches at Shiloh, N.J., which charge he held for two and a-half years. He was then sent by the Seventh-day Baptist Missionary Society to Palestine, and resided for two years at Jaffa, and for five years in Jerusalem. In May, 1859, he baptized in the Pool of Siloam, Youhannah el Karey, a Syrian, of the Greek Church, a native of Nablous, subsequently a student of Regent's Park College, London, and now a missionary at Nablous. On account of ill-health he returned to America in 1860, passing through London. In the States he lectured on Bible lands, and was successively pastor of the Seventh-day Baptist Churches at Walworth, Wis., Scott, N.Y., and Rosenhaym, N.J. In 1872, on the death of the Rev. W. H. Black, F.S.A., he was called to the Seventh-day Baptist Church at Mill-yard, Leman-street, London. Here, buried in a slum, he toiled hard to make known his views of the Sabbath, printed many tracts, and in 1875 started a quarterly journal called "The Sabbath Memorial." This was devoted to the theological, archæological and philological aspects of the question. About 1886 the honorary degree of Doctor of Divinity was conferred upon him by the University of Alfred, N.Y., a Seventh-day Baptist institution. For over ten years Dr. Jones was engaged at the British Museum upon a work which he published under the title of "A Chart of the Week." This consisted of a table comprising the names of the days of the week in 160 languages. In every one of these languages the days of the week appear in the same order, and in 108 of them the Saturday was called "Seventh Day," "Sabbath," or "Rest Day." Dr. Jones was himself responsible for the terms collected from all the Asiatic and African languages, his lengthy residence in the East having made him a master of Hebrew and Arabic, and he was well acquainted with Syriac, Greek, Latin, French and Dutch. He was assisted in his work by H.I.H. the late Prince Louis Lucien Bonaparte, who prepared for him the days of the week in all the European languages.—W.B.

23. KITCHING, HENRY, who passed away on 21st October, 1895, was born at Sheffield on 13th December, 1826, and was in his youth a tool-maker. His pastor, the Rev. J. E. Giles, encouraged him in a desire to devote his life to the ministry. In 1850 he entered Bradford College, where he was known as a singularly diligent student. His first pastorate (at Eye, Suffolk) commenced in 1854, and lasted two years. Thence he removed to Sabden, and in 1859 he accepted an invitation to the church at Lake-road, Portsmouth. At that time the church was in a low estate, but his earnest, thoughtful preaching soon brought about a revival, and the chapel was crowded. A difference arose and a number of the members left with him, who, after worshipping for a short time in a public hall, built a chapel in Herbert-street, Landport. But the church formed there never flourished greatly, and after a while Mr. Kitching accepted the post of chaplain to the Landport Cemetery. He took an active interest in public affairs and showed considerable business ability. He was elected a member of the School Board, and a governor of the Portsmouth Grammar School. Then he removed to the neighbouring village of Waterlooville, where he kept a boarding school, and was pastor of the Baptist church. Eventually he removed to London and took an active part in journalistic work and electioneering. In 1892 he retired to Selsey, Chichester, where his active career came to a peaceful close. He was a man known to but few, though greatly honoured and beloved by such as enjoyed the privilege of his friendship. He was very studious, a good classical scholar, and of refined taste in literature. His sermons were marked by great insight into Scripture, and by elevation of thought, whilst they always had a clear evangelical ring. His preaching failed to be popular through the weakness of his voice. He was characterized by a singular tenderness of disposition, though he was sternly uncompromising in matters of principle. His was a remarkably devout spirit, of the old Puritan type.—J. H. C.

24. MACKENNA, ANGUS, was accepted for foreign mission service in 1856. He found his way before that time to India, and he did Christian work in Calcutta previously to joining the mission. In 1857 he was at Serampore. Subsequently he went to Dinajpore and after that to Chittagong, Barisal, Dacca, and Soory. He was an earnest and affectionate Christian brother and a faithful missionary. He knew and understood the failings and the excellencies of Bengali Christians as perhaps few missionaries did. He was tender, patient, firm and loving in dealing with them as a father among his children. In 1894 his health failed greatly, and the Home Committee would have allowed him to return to England then, but he was unwilling to do so, and he went for a few months to Darjeeling instead. He rallied there somewhat, and returned to Soory before the end of the year, too feeble to do much work himself. There was a slight improvement of health as the cold weather came on, but soon he began to fail again and, as a last hope, he went to Calcutta, where through the kindness of Dr. Crombie he obtained a private room in the General Hospital, and where, attended by Mrs. MacKenna, he received the best medical treatment available. The opinion of the doctor was that the only hope of improvement lay in a speedy departure for a temperate climate, and arrangements were being made for this, when he became so much worse that the doctor said he could not be moved unless he had an accession of strength. He calmly realised the fact that the end was drawing near, and after making the few preparations necessary for his wife and children, quietly trusting the Saviour whom he had so long preached to others, he passed away to the everlasting rest of the saints of God.—G. K.

25. MACMASTER, ROBERT PATON, passed away on 26th March, 1895. He was a Scotchman, the son of an Ayrshire farmer, and was born on 16th October, 1830. His student days were spent in Edinburgh, where he formed the resolution to follow the profession of medicine. Religious convictions, however, turned his thoughts in another direction, and, becoming a Baptist, he soon evinced a desire to enter the ministry of our denomination. His first charge was at Walsall, thence he removed to Coventry (Cow Lane) in 1854. Thereafter, he held successively pastorates at Bristol (Counterslip), Bradford (Hallfield), and Darlington. The last-named post he was compelled to resign in 1883 owing to failure of health. He took a voyage to Australia with his wife, in order to visit a son living there, and with the hope of recovering health and spirits. The loss of his wife, however, on the voyage out was so great a shock to a system already shattered, that he returned to this country scarcely better than when he set out. His physical condition compelled his retirement from the ministry, and he went to Bradford to live with his second son. Throughout his long years of active service Robert Macmaster was a conscientious, earnest toiler in the Master's vineyard. His brethren on two occasions showed their appreciation of his worth by electing him to the Presidency of the Bristol Association, and of the Yorkshire Association (1881). He was also Secretary of Rawdon College from 1874 to 1880. A scholarly, well-read man, his preaching was eminently thoughtful, and always pervaded by a serene spirit. He was one who believed that

"Religion dwells in the depth and not the tumult of the soul."

In his character there was much shrewdness, combined with a kindliness of disposition that made one feel how human he was, and withal, a genial, quiet humour that was refreshing. Common-sense views of things were always characteristic of him. He was also a man of intense sympathy, not of the fussy, boisterous order, but deep and sincere, unobtrusive in manner, yet practically helpful in word and deed. Above all, he was an earnest follower of the Master, with a lofty ideal of Christian possibilities, ever "pressing on." This man, so capable, kindly, vigorous, was laid aside from life's duty in his very prime by a strange, inscrutable Providence, whose ways we cannot understand here. For the last twelve years he was physically disabled by nervous disorders, and unfit for work of any kind, but patient and humble in spirit, never murmuring or complaining, nay, even cheerful and brightly resigned. At first the enforced idleness was irksome, but when he realized what life was thenceforth to be for him, he accepted the Divine will with serenity of spirit. He once said to the writer that his "chief anxiety was to learn the meaning of it for himself, to get the good of it for his own soul." The one bright element in his painful lot was that his mind was always awake, and his interest in the theological and political questions of the day was always keen. He was pre-eminently hopeful, even confident about the issues of human history, as became one who had so closely assimilated the mind and spirit of the Redeemer of mankind.—T. H. M.

26. MAYNARD, GEORGE BLATCHFORD, was born at Northlew, North Devon, 13th August, 1815. He was converted among the Bible Christians when he was about fourteen years of age, and a year later he began to exhort and preach in the open air and in cottages. After some years he was baptized at Inwardleigh, and he then became a local preacher among the Baptists. In 1860 he was appointed pastor at Frithelstock, Buckland, Newton St. Petrock, Shebbear, Halwill, Germansweek, and Muckworthy. After about ten years' faithful service there, he settled at Watchet and Williton as co-pastor with Rev. T. E. Rawlings in 1873. He remained there about three years, and his ministry proved very useful; but his health failed, and, under medical advice, he had to return to his native place. In 1879 he was invited to the church at Hatherleigh, where he ministered for about seven years, and then he retired. He was ill for about four months, and then the end came—very calmly and peacefully—on 5th May, 1894. He was greatly beloved by his friends and neighbours.—C. H. P.

27. MORRIS, JOSEPH STEPHEN, was born at Hackney, 22nd June, 1840. He attended the Sunday School at Mare-street Chapel, and was converted in his sixteenth year. Soon after he was baptized by the Rev. D. Katterns, whose ministry was mainly instrumental in giving him the clear, comprehensive view of Evangelical doctrine which distinguished him in after years. At seventeen he commenced preaching in the streets, and continued active in Christian work until entering the Pastors' College in 1863. He proved a diligent student, and was often asked to preach in different parts of the kingdom. At the close of 1864 the Church at Romney-street, Westminster, appealed to Mr. Spurgeon for help. Mr. Morris was selected to preach, and some elders of the Tabernacle were appointed to co-operate with him. He was elected pastor in 1865, and soon the Church flourished again. In 1875 Mr. Morris was invited to the pastorate of the new chapel erected at Leyton by the London Baptist Association, and in 1876 he left a loving and united people at Romney-street with great regret for that purpose. Soon his thoughtful, vigorous preaching drew around him faithful helpers, who responded readily to his leadership. His wise counsels and administrative ability produced excellent results—a strong Church was gathered, the debt on the building was removed, and a fund was raised for additional schoolrooms. About 1883 the theological lectureship of Harley House Training Institute for Missionaries was vacant, and attention was directed to Mr. Morris, to whom eventually the position was offered. With characteristic modesty he hesitated to accept it; but intimate friends urged him to make the attempt. He soon proved himself equal to the work, and it became increasingly evident that the years of previous training had peculiarly qualified him for the post. He had been a diligent student of the word, and an eager reader of all the critical works to which he could gain access. His lectures were a great success. They attracted and compelled the attention of the students, whose minds they informed and whose views of Divine truth they moulded. For seven years he continued this work in conjunction with his pastorate, but the strain was too severe. Early in 1890 he reluctantly severed his connection with the Church at Leyton, and gave himself entirely to the College. He was installed as principal, and the entire control of the work was committed to him. He discharged the duties of the office faithfully and fearlessly. He was honoured for his quick perception of real worth, and feared for his swift detection of unreality and hypocrisy. He was loved by a wide circle, and his presence was felt to be a tower of strength throughout the College. He was unexpectedly laid aside by a painful illness, and after four months of agonizing pain, borne with Christian fortitude, he entered into rest on 1st October, 1895. It could be said of him, "He was a good man, and feared the Lord above many." In preaching, his exposition of the word would often have a wonderful charm for the attentive hearer because of the bright side-light he was able to throw upon the text. Few present will ever forget the illustration they had of this in the address *he gave at the last* Conference of the Pastors' College Evangelical Association. He

had not the art of appealing to the popular ear and gratifying the popular taste, he could not dazzle by mere rhetorical display; but he was "apt to teach," and the truths he taught will live in those who had the privilege of sitting at his feet. His worth was best appreciated by those who knew him best, and such most feel his loss.—D. R.

28. NICHOLAS, JACOB, was born 23rd April, 1812, at Little Newcastle, in Pembrokeshire. He left that county early in life for "The Hills," as the iron and coal districts of Glamorgan and Monmouth were commonly called, and settled at Rhymney. From the church at Zoar in that town he entered Haverfordwest College, where he was one of the earliest students. In 1844 he was ordained as pastor of the churches of Caersws and Rhydfelen, Montgomeryshire. These churches were then very small and weak, but by his untiring efforts and God's blessing they soon flourished and became comparatively strong for such thinly-populated districts. Mr. Nicholas threw himself heartily into the educational movement, which was beginning to be felt in Wales just at that time. He was the chief promoter of the Caersws British School, and one of its first managers. As a deputation for the Baptist Missionary Society, in the counties of Montgomery and Radnor, for many years, he travelled hundreds of miles over bleak mountains in all kinds of weather. Often he was wet through before reaching his destination for the night, and in order to go to the meeting would be "rigged out" in the clothes of some kind farmer in the neighbourhood. He became a well-known man in all the churches of the Association, and to know him was to love and respect him. His power and influence in the conferences of the Association were soon felt, for his unblemished character, gentle demeanour, and strong common sense combined to give him authority whenever he rose to speak. As he advanced in life, and his health, which was never very robust, became more feeble, he resigned his charge of the churches in 1880, after thirty-six years of faithful and successful service, in recognition of which a testimonial of nearly £100 was presented to him in June, 1881. His health did not permit him to preach often during the remainder of his life. He was seized with an attack of influenza and bronchitis, and he peacefully passed away on 26th April, 1895.—J. G.

29. OWEN, JOHN TOMLINSON, was born at Whitby on 9th of February, 1860. At the age of ten he went to Shields, and after attending school underwent a a training for the teaching profession. He taught for five years in a school at Shields, and finished his training by two years' study at Borough-road College, London. On returning to Shields he became a master in a school at Jarrow, and remained there until he received his "parchment," which would entitle him to accept a position as head-master. He next turned his attention to journalism, and joined the staff of the *Northern Weekly Leader*. Subsequently he occupied the sub-editorial chair of the *Shields Daily Gazette*. After six years of most exacting service, during which period he was also actively engaged in political work as a Liberal of the advanced school, he entered the Ministry, and accepted the pastorate of the Church at Barclay-street, Sunderland. His health broke down, and he went south to recuperate. Whilst staying at Woking in the spring of 1891, he preached at the Baptist Congregational Chapel on one or two occasions, and then, in May of that year, received a hearty call from the Church, which he accepted. His fidelity to his principles and convictions never wavered, and he struggled on against difficulties until he succeeded in making the Church a centre of life and activity. Various organizations sprang up; as, for example, the Pleasant Sunday Afternoon movement, the Mutual Improvement Society, and the Mother's Meeting, and it was his intention to have started a library and reading-room. Always willing to help the poor and suffering, he did much last winter by free breakfasts for children to alleviate distress. One of Mr. Owen's special gifts was his ability to clothe in the most simple, yet beautiful language, the commonest things in nature, and it was this which gave his addresses to children every Sunday a peculiar charm. He entered very heartily into all that concerned the well-being of Woking. The School Board controversy he followed with keen interest, and his sympathies were on the side of the majority of the Board. In the movement for a Local Board he took a prominent part, and his advice was listened to with great attention. He became the first Chairman of the Technical Education Committee, and held that office to the end. In the spring of 1894 he found scope in the Guildford Parliamentary Division for his political energies, for he became the agent of the Liberal party, and carried through the registration work. His health again failed, and on 10th

November, under medical advice, he sailed for the Cape. The previous evening he met the members of his congregation in the school-room, and cheered them with words that showed the sincerity of his affection for them. He was presented with a purse of over £50, and the gift was the more precious to him as it had been made at some sacrifice to the donors, who embraced all classes, and whose subscriptions ranged from 6d. to £10. It was hoped that the parting would only be temporary, and that in May he would again take up his charge, strengthened by the change of climate and rest. Those hopes were not fulfilled. After his arrival at Cape Town he remained there until the 9th January, and, according to his letters, his health seemed to have been benefited by the change. He then left Cape Town for Pretoria. On the way he contracted malarial fever, and, although very ill on his arrival, he preached on Sunday in the Church, and on Monday he paid a visit to a dying person. After that he was confined to his bed, and he died on 19th February, 1895. —*Abridged from the "Surrey Times."*

30. OWEN, WILLIAM, died 19th February, 1895, at the ripe age of eighty-two. He was born in the neighbourhood of Newport, Pembrokeshire. When he was young, he left his home and journeyed as far as Cardiff, which was considered a feat in those days, and there he apprenticed himself as a printer. He soon won the respect and confidence of his master by the rapid progress he made and by his noble and trustworthy character. He acquired a considerable amount of knowledge, and in after years he edited and published "Y Bedyddiwr," a Welsh periodical, which rendered valuable service to the denomination. A volume of sermons by the late Rev. James Rowe, of Fishguard, which is widely read and considered of rare value, was also published by Mr. Owen. He was brought up in a family and in a neighbourhood where religion occupied the most prominent and honoured position, and his character was influenced accordingly from his youth. At Cardiff he joined the Church at the Tabernacle, and made himself very useful in the Sunday school and in the prayer meeting. He was soon asked to preach and consecrate himself to the ministry. He did so, and succeeded in forming a Church at Canton. Receiving an invitation from Felinganol, one of the oldest Churches in his native county, he accepted it with joy and trembling. He laboured there with great acceptance and success for many years. From there he went to Hill Park, Haverfordwest, where his stay was short, but the work he did was great and lasting. After that he settled at Narberth, and there spent the best years of his life, and did the noblest part of his work. Having acquired knowledge and great experience in the ministry, he was able to exercise a considerable influence over the Churches of Pembrokeshire. When he retired from the ministry, he spent the last years of his life preaching as he had opportunity. He was a man of rare qualities, a good organizer, a strict disciplinarian, an enthusiastic supporter of the Missionary Society, and a friend of widows and orphans. In politics he was a staunch, active, and influential Liberal.—J. J.

31. PARKINSON, JAMES, originally of Great Eccleston, was a genuine man, and a most faithful minister of the Gospel of Christ. In youth he was apprenticed by his father in Lancaster with a view to commercial life; but the cherished wish of his mother, whom he greatly revered for her distinctive piety, was that he should enter the Christian ministry, and afterwards this became his own free and deliberate choice. Accordingly, when of age, he relinquished a promising business career, and offered himself as a student to the committee of the college at Bradford, at that time under the presidency of Dr. Acworth. Though he never set himself to achieve academic distinction in his college days, he was a careful and devoted student, and won for himself the admiring friendship of his tutors and fellow students. His ministerial life extended over a period of thirty-six years, during which time he settled over Churches as follows:—In 1858 at Hinckley, in 1866 at Brightside, in 1870 again at Hinckley, in 1874 at New Lenton, Nottingham, in 1879 at Queensbury, and in 1885 at Nuneaton. In each of his pastorates he exerted a gracious influence, and enjoyed the profound respect and warm affection of his people. While an ardent lover of all men, young people had the warmest place in his heart. Among them he found the most congenial department of his ministry, and accomplished the best work of his life. By individual attention and frank dealing, more than by preaching, he induced very many of them to yield to the Saviour and to enter the fellowship of His Church. It was no doubt his practical interest in the young which suggested to his mind the thought of

leaving his library to the students of Rawdon College, an example, by the way, which other ministers might wisely follow. Mr. Parkinson was a lifelong abstainer, and a ready helper of every movement which pertains to the uplifting of the people. As a preacher he was not only careful and sedulous in his preparation for the pulpit, but also conspicuously loyal to evangelical truth, and conscientiously insistent on the necessity of the Holy Spirit's agency to make it vital and saving. His friendship was a sacred thing, and close association with him as a Christian comrade was both an honour and a joy. At Nuneaton, after a protracted illness, Mr. Parkinson devoted himself to re-establish the Baptist cause, which had sadly languished. It was here he finished, through the grace of God, a blameless and truly consecrated life. The number of ministers and crowds of people who attended his interment in Nuneaton Cemetery afforded convincing evidence of the general esteem and affection in which he was held by the public, and showed how his departure had moved the whole town with sorrow and sympathy. Among other words spoken at his funeral in honour and love of his memory were the following by his brother-in-law, the Rev. F. G. Marchant, of the Pastors' College:—"I have known him for more than thirty years, and having regard to all that I remember of him during that period, and judging it from the highest Christian standpoint, I do not think that I ever knew a more consistent and faithful life. His quiet and earnest, yet cheerful and unpretentious goodness has often rebuked me, but I never once felt that he pained me by anything that seemed out of harmony with his position as a minister of Christ. Looking back on all that I have known of him as a man, as my relative by marriage, as a Christian, and as a minister of the Gospel, I do not remember ever to have heard from him any word that I wished he had not spoken, or to have seen him do a thing that I wished he had not done. He was a kindly and patient man, a most considerate and beloved friend and brother, a devout and sincere Christian before us all, an earnest and loving minister of the truth as it is in Jesus, and he was faithful unto death."—J. C.

32. PASSEY, TOM, was born at Ross on 5th December, 1870, and died at Ruardean on 23rd March, 1895. It was his lot to live in the busy little town on the banks of the silvery Wye from birth till early manhood. During this period he certainly enjoyed blessings and advantages, for both his parents were true Christians. His education was not neglected and his Sunday school was most helpful. When he was fifteen years of age, his teacher, a devoted Christain worker, was the means of leading him to the Lord. Soon after, he was baptized and received into the Church. At the age of seventeen he began to preach in the villages, and became so acceptable a "supply" that Baptists and Wesleyans alike constantly sought his assistance. He was full of love for the Lord, and a desire to "rescue the perishing," and many were the fruits of his ministry. By the time he had reached his twentieth year he felt firmly convinced the great Head of the Church was calling him to pastoral work. It was impossible to persuade him to seek a college training. Taking his own course, he resigned his situation and wandered through Herefordshire preaching the Gospel. Concerning these evangelistic tours it may be said he never lacked a home or funds, and his message was blessed to very many. In May, 1891, he accepted an invitation to preach at Woodchester. His services were appreciated, and resulted in a request that he would supply the pulpit for six months. This was followed by a call to the pastorate. Feeling Divinely guided, he accepted the invitation, and for the next two and a-half years he served the Church with much success. The membership and congregation increased considerably. On Easter Sunday, 1894, he undertook the Mission Pastórate at Ruardean Hill, and for twelve months toiled there faithfully. During this brief time he greatly endeared himself to his people, and was used of God in leading a number of people out of darkness into light. The young soldier was, however, soon called to exchange the sword and shield for the crown and palm. He left the battle with startling abruptness. A severe cold, increased by exposure, brought on pneumonia. After a few days of intense suffering, borne with marvellous patience and submission, he "fell asleep" full of confidence and peace. Just before passing away he raised his eyes and appeared to gaze on the glory of Heaven, whilst from his lips there leapt the words:

"O that with yonder sacred throng,
I, at his feet may fall,
Join in the everlasting song,
And crown Him Lord of all."

Not only in Ross, Woodchester, and Ruardean Hill—but also throughout the Forest of Dean, and in many parts of Gloucestershire and Herefordshire, Mr. Passey's memory will remain green. His attractive presence and effective singing, his love and zeal for Christ, his consuming desire and effort to win souls, will not soon be forgotten.—W.A.W.

33. PLATTEN, HENRY, was born at Runton, near Cromer, on 20th May, 1838. His parents were Wesleyans, but on their removal to Yarmouth they joined the Baptist denomination. In 1858 Mr. Platten entered Rawdon College, and while there, showed many signs of the great originality in both methods and thought that characterized his after life. While not a student in the sense of being highly proficient in classics and mathematics, he was a great reader and displayed remarkable powers of sermonizing. It has been told of him that when special seasons of inspiration were upon him, he would remain in his study for days together, admitting only the choice friends who understood his moods and spirit. His absorption in his sermons was complete, and, as we should expect, the criticisms of such a remarkable man in the sermon class were of an uncommon order and highly suggestive. On leaving college in 1862 he accepted the pastorate of the church at Stradbroke, near Ipswich, where he spent, what he often referred to, as the happiest years of his life. Towards the end of 1867 he was invited to the church at Maze Pond, London, and those who enjoyed the privilege of his ministry there speak of it as not simply eloquent, but useful too, in the highest degree. For earnest, thoughtful young men he cleared and widened the ways of truth, and by means of a large and successful Bible class, as well as through his preaching, became a helper of the most valued kind. After a ministry of five years in London, he removed to Derby Road, Nottingham, which pastorate he held for something over three years, until, in 1875, he accepted an invitation from Graham Street, Birmingham, to succeed the late Rev. Charles Vince. Mr. Platten laboured in Graham Street until 1882, when he removed, with part of the congregation, to new and commodious premises in Hagley Road; whilst another portion removed to Handsworth, under the pastoral care of Rev. H. Bonner. For ten years more he occupied the pulpit at the "Church of the Redeemer," closing his ministry in the summer of 1892. Later in the year he declined an invitation to Bournemouth, preferring (chiefly for family reasons) to remain in Birmingham: and shortly afterwards he began to conduct services as an unattached minister. This latter resolve was a source of considerable regret to most of his friends—especially in the ministry—and it is in no spirit of unkindness that they say it was a great mistake, and did not a little to shadow some of the later days of a singularly striking and really beautiful life. Mr. Platten did not take a prominent part in the public affairs of Birmingham, consequently he was not so widely known as his predecessor and some of his contemporaries; but he was a man of fine culture, and of exceptional power as a preacher. It is not easy to describe the charm of Mr. Platten to those who loved him, and less easy, perhaps, to tabulate the results of his ministry. So fascinating was he, and so attractive his preaching, that he was everything to them. To doubters he was a "restorer of paths to dwell in," to the thoughtful and devout a high priest who stood in the very "Holy of Holies," a true voice of God speaking to their souls. The writer of this notice has heard him preach such sermons as he never listened to from any other lips, while his addresses at the Communion of the Lord's Supper have brought him and others face to face with their Lord and Saviour Christ. His preaching was very often mystical in the best sense, and had in it a large measure of the prophetic element. He was a preacher who soared; he dealt with lofty ideas, and he spake like a seer. Some who heard him probably neither saw nor understood this side of him; unsympathetic, hard, mechanical, money-grasping people would perhaps call his preaching unpractical, but it was so only because absorption in material things blinded them to his ideals. Doubtless he saw "visions" and dreamed "dreams," but his visions and dreams were true. It is not to be denied that the duties of a regular pastorate were irksome to him, they fretted him, and, in a way, he was not well fitted for them. Our congregational system does not provide many suitable spheres in which to develop to greatest advantage the peculiar gifts that Mr. Platten possessed; his personality and ministry might have been an incalculable blessing to the churches if he could have preached in much the same way as do the canons of the Episcopal Church, or could have spent a few days together in different districts giving them the results of his

HENRY PLATTEN.

(Reproduced from "Edgbastonia" by permission.)

richest thought and highest inspiration. The personal charm of Mr. Platten to his intimate friends was very great. In fraternal and kindred meetings his presence was eagerly welcomed, and he seldom failed to warm others with the love of his big heart. After association with him, his brethren always felt themselves richer in ideas, their conceptions of the ministry were enlarged, and they came away more anxious to become good ministers of Jesus Christ. Perhaps it is largely true that he was a man of moods, and the faults of moody men, like their virtues, sometimes lie very near the surface. If Mr. Platten was sometimes impetuous to a fault he was also generous to a fault, if impatient sometimes, loveable as a little child at others, and when sorry and repentant sorry and repentant secretly, with a bitterness that colder and more calculating natures never know. There are men to be found who cannot understand the fine abandonment of some noble natures. At the bottom Mr. Platten had the docile heart of the little child, and a simplicity that was deeply touching and beautiful—the apparent roughness was the outside of him; he was gentle and refined within, and with all his affectation of indifference to it, he was dependent upon sympathy to the last degree. Towards the end he became much broken and worn, largely, perhaps, as the result of his detachments and the lack of some former fellowships. It was not surprising, therefore, that when pneumonia assailed an already debilitated constitution it should terminate fatally, and he entered into rest on 11th January, 1895. He was borne to his last resting place by his six sons, to whom the memory of their father's affection is a rich possession. Henry Platten was a child of the Light, and into it he has entered, and he who latterly was often so tired and troubled abides "where beyond these voices there is peace."—R. G.

34. REYNOLDS, GEORGE, was the third son of the late Rev. John Reynolds, the first pastor of the Church at Siloam, Kidwelly. He was born 7th June, 1823. His father baptized him on Whit-Sunday, 1840. He commenced to preach in 1854. After being educated at Derlwyn College, by Dr. Davies, late of Ffrwdvale, he was chosen co-pastor with his father at Salem, Ferryside, and was ordained in 1860. He took charge of the Church at Bethany, Llanstephan, in 1865, and successfully ministered to the two churches for many years. Upon the death of his father in 1878 he removed to Siloam, Kidwelly, and became co-pastor with his brother John, and soon after he gave up the charge of the Churches at Salem, Ferryside, and Bethany, Llanstephan. But at the same time he became pastor of the Churches at Ebenezer, Llandefeilog, and Noddfa, Trimsaran, because they were nearer to Kidwelly. After a few years he restricted his work to Kidwelly on the ground of increasing years, and there he remained until his death. He was not a man of great learning, but of correct judgment and solid piety, and he was an eloquent and evangelical preacher. In 1894 he was the President of the Carmarthenshire and Cardiganshire Association. He lived as he taught others to live, and was very much respected by all classes. After nineteen months' illness he died in peace on 29th of March, 1895.—J. R.

35. ROBERTS, EDWARD, was born at Carrog, in the parish of Corwen, on 11th January, 1820, close to the former residence of Owen Glendower, the renowned Welsh chieftain. His parents were adherents of the Established Church, but owing probably to the influence of some of his early companions, the son was induced when quite a youth to attend a service at the Glyndyfrdwy Baptist Chapel, where he was baptized by Dr. Pritchard, of Llangollen. Soon after, he commenced preaching, and entered Pontypool College. No one made more use of his opportunities than did Mr. Roberts. On leaving the institution, he settled at Pontesbury, Salop. He did a good work in this quiet country town, and left a deep impression on the people. After a few years' work there he returned to his native land, to preach in his native tongue, and was pastor successively of the Churches at Cefnbychan and Rhyl, until he removed in 1869 to Pontypridd, Glamorganshire, and there he remained until his death. He was a man of very varied gifts and accomplishments, but he made all his acquirements subservient to his position as minister of the Gospel. He took a deep interest in political and social questions, and worked hard in the interests of education and temperance, but he allowed nothing to interfere with his study of the Bible. He was successful as an architect of several chapels, was well versed in poetry, and in music. He always paid much attention to Biblical criticism, and went to the fountain head by reading the Old Testament in Hebrew, and the New Testament in Greek. He

possessed a well-balanced mind, strong in judgment and in reasoning, with a retentive memory. Dr. Roberts' sermons gave evidence of hard study, and were often models of Biblical exposition, capable of enlightening the mind and moving the will. He produced more strong meat for men than milk for babes. The diploma of a Doctor of Divinity, which was conferred upon him by the Senate of William Jewell College, Missouri, in 1881, was felt to be an honour fully deserved and worthily worn. His literary productions were extensive and constant. Besides contributing regularly to several periodicals, and acting as editor of *Seren Gomer* for some years, he published a "Grammar of the Welsh Language," completing the work of the late Rev. John Williams, and a "Commentary on the Epistle to the Galatians," in a volume of 464 pages, and, in addition, several pamphlets on various subjects. He was like a little child in humility, and at the same time he was manly and courageous. His attachment to his own denomination was strong and sincere, but he had thorough friends in all denominations. His character was Christ-like. He preached occasionally to the end. He was truly a great man, and those nearest to him were most aware of his greatness.—H. C. W.

36. ROBERTS, GRIFFITH HUMPHREY, was one of the best known ministers in Wales. He was born at Llangybi, Carnarvonshire, 24th April, 1831, and lost both his father and his mother in his childhood. His father was a farmer, but the son when a youth was attracted to a seafaring life, and he was deprived of early educational advantages. Whilst a sailor he was brought to the knowledge of Christ, and was baptized at Penuel, Bangor, in 1851. His heart glowed with love to the Saviour. As he meditated, the fire burned, and the unquenchable longing to save men showed itself two years after his admission to Church membership in his commencing to preach at Tyddynshon. He soon commanded the ear of the people, and the Churches at Capel Gwyn and Bodedeyrn, Anglesey, invited him to the pastorate, which he accepted towards the end of 1853. In this secluded agricultural district he spent three years, faithfully discharging his pastoral duties and studying the theology of the Puritans. In 1858 he removed to Tabor, Dinas, Pembrokeshire. The peace of this church had unfortunately been disturbed, but the advent of Mr. Roberts inaugurated a period of peace and progress. His deep spirituality and sound common sense, under the Divine blessing, restored order, whilst his good preaching and indefatigable efforts outside the pulpit combined to build up a strong church. His health becoming seriously impaired he was advised to seek a change, and he entered upon the pastorate at Penuel, Carmarthen, 8th October, 1874. Although suffering from physical weakness for twenty-one years, he discharged his duties there with marvellous diligence, and received nearly a thousand persons into membership. In addition to his acceptable preaching and proverbially faithful attention to his pastoral work, he took a deep interest in educational matters. While at Tabor he was mainly instrumental in establishing an elementary school in the present schoolroom. This school he successfully piloted through many difficulties. At Carmarthen he was for the last few years a member of the School Board and of the Intermediate Board of Management. He was also invited to occupy positions of honour in the Welsh Baptist Denomination. On one occasion he preached the annual sermon to the students at Haverfordwest, and in June, 1894, he preached to the students at Bangor. He had filled the chair of the Carmarthen and Cardigan Baptist Association, and in the year of his death he was Vice-President of the Welsh Baptist Union. He was also a strenuous advocate of total abstinence from intoxicants. Mr. Roberts was a man of peace, and his end was characterized by a beautiful calmness of spirit. He passed away at noon on 7th June, 1895. For Christ he lived, and he now rests "with Christ, which is far better."—E. U. T.

37. ROBERTS, JOHN, was born at Cefnmawr, Denbighshire, on 21st June, 1841. He never went to school, but was engaged in a coal mine when young. At the age of eighteen years, having keenly felt the need of a Saviour, he was baptized by the Rev. Llewelyn Rees, and a year later, at the urgent request of the Church at Cefnbychan, he commenced preaching. Some years after, his ordination took place at the same church. On 21st December, 1871, he received an invitation to the pastorate of the Churches at Mold and Penyfron, where he became the successor of such eminent men as Rev. H. W. Hughes, Dinas, and the late Rev. W. Jones, Fishguard. Mr. Roberts worked in the mine on Saturday and entered upon his pastorate on Sunday. At Mold he won the affections of all. He toiled hard and

developed considerable power as a preacher of Christ's Gospel. On 19th May, 1874, he received a call to undertake the charge of the newly-formed Church at Brynamman. This became his life work, and it was as "Roberts, Brynamman," that he was known far and wide. During his eighteen years' ministry at Brynamman he baptized upwards of five hundred believers, and was the means of establishing a thriving Church at Cwmgors. Mr. Roberts was popular among the Churches, and was beloved of all. He received several pressing invitations to other spheres, but he declined them all, until he was invited to the pastorate of his mother Church at Cefnbychan, whither he removed in September, 1892, and where he remained until his death on 8th July, 1895. His disposition was genial and sunny. He spent but little time in ordinary public duties, but concentrated his energies on Church and pulpit work. He made up for the loss of early training by greater acquaintance with the Bible, and was never content to advance an argument for Christ without placing it beyond dispute by a verse or passage of Scripture. Mr. Roberts was beautiful in character, kind and loving as a husband and father, firm as a friend, industrious and sympathetic as pastor, and withal an effective preacher of Jesus Christ. He died peacefully at the age of fifty-four years.—E. K. J.

38. SEAR, GEORGE, who died at Wem, Shropshire, on 17th September, 1895, was born at Woburn, Bedfordshire, in February, 1822. His parents attended the Independent Church in that town, and the influence of Mr. Castleton, the pastor, was of the most helpful kind, so that at a very early age Mr. Sear became a preacher of the Gospel, and scarcely remembered the time when he was not anxious to lead others to the knowledge of Christ, which had been blessed to his own salvation. After passing through a course of training at the Borough Road Training College, he became a schoolmaster, and followed that profession until 1862, when, having been baptized by the Rev. T. A. Williams at Haddenham, he became pastor of the Church at Histon, Cambridgeshire. In 1866 he removed to Soham, and in the following year to East Dereham, in Norfolk. In 1870 he became pastor of the Church at Halstead, and during his ministry there took a good deal of interest in the work of the denomination, and also had the privilege of superintending the erection of new schoolrooms, which greatly aided the Church in their work amongst the children. His pastorate at Halstead was a happy one, and during its continuance he secured the esteem of his own people and of the neighbouring churches. In 1876 he undertook the work at Umberslade. There a Church was formed, and in a somewhat limited sphere, good service was rendered to the cause of Christ. During his residence at Umberslade Mr. Sear took great interest in the work of the Midland Association, and for some years acted as one of the District secretaries. The closing years of his life were spent at Wem, where, so long as his strength permitted him, he served the Church as its pastor. The tie which bound him to that Church was broken only by his decease. He served the Shropshire Association for a time as its president and secretary. The last two years of his life were years of intense bodily pain, but his faith failed not. During this period of suffering the members of the Church displayed a large amount of Christian sympathy and love towards him. He had been to them a true Christian pastor and friend, and so won their love that with true gladness of heart they ministered to him in every way possible to them. All through his long life he sought to be true to his Divine calling, and those who knew him best have the pleasure of remembering him as a true Christian friend.—S. H.

39. SPEED, ROBERT, was a native of Bradford, and his early religious life was connected with that stronghold of Baptists, Westgate Chapel, then under the pastorate of the Rev. H. Dowson, of whose ministry Mr. Speed spoke with the utmost veneration and affection. His parents were in humble circumstances, and early in life young Robert entered the employ of Mr. William Peel, a stuff merchant, of Bradford. He was then an earnest and thoughtful youth, attending regularly the classes of the Mechanics' Institute for the study of mathematics, German, &c. He, along with his life-long friend, Mr. Alderman Moulson, and many others, was baptized in 1855. In 1857 Mr. Speed and Mr. Moulson were among those who were dismissed to form the new church at Trinity Chapel, which had been built by Westgate friends as a thank-offering to God for a century of blessing that they, as a church, had enjoyed. Mr. Speed was appointed teacher of the Young Men's Bible Class, a post in which he was privileged to be eminently successful. The Rev. H. J. Betts, the minister of

the new chapel, became much interested in him, and encouraged him to take opportunities of preaching and to give addresses. Mr. Speed entered the Pastors' College in 1863. There his grave, gentle, and earnest character was fully appreciated by his fellow students. He always seemed to live in fear of the sin of presumption, and it appeared to some who valued him highly that that fear was a great restraint to him. Yet no man in the ministry valued the spirit of enterprise and progress more than he did. In due course he began his ministry at Mill Street, Bedford, where he remained many years. He saw the erection of the present chapel, and thence he removed to Milnsbridge; then to Lindsay Road, Sunderland; and finally he settled at Bishop Burton in 1887, where, subjected to clerical opposition and social ostracism, he was enabled to maintain for eight years an earnest evangelical ministry, adorned by a blameless life. About six weeks before his death, on the the Lord's Day morning, he was taken suddenly ill, and was kept from his pulpit engagements for three weeks. The doctor suggested that he should give up preaching and consider that his active work was finished, but he became much better, and a few days before his death remarked to Mr. Alderman Sample at Beverley that he thought he should soon be able to resume his full duties with comfort. On 17th May, 1895, he left home to pay a visit at Walkington, about two miles off. Returning home he had to face a storm of cold north-west wind, and he was found by a labourer, about mid-day, leaning against a hedge, but quite dead. Thus the gentle spirit of Robert Speed was called away to enter into the joy of the Lord he had so quietly and faithfully served.—J. M. M.

40. STEPHENS, JOHN MORTIMER, was born at Bath 15th November, 1843. At nine years of age he was sent to Mill Hill School, where he manifested considerable mental energy and moral courage. He was by nature disposed to argument and intellectual strife, and, perhaps more than most of us, was compelled to fight his way into the citadel of Faith. In this conflict he received great assistance from his mother, a singularly gracious woman, who reasoned and prayed with him so effectively that, in very early days, he was led into a child-like Christian confidence which he steadfastly maintained unto the end. He was baptized at the age of sixteen and joined the Church at Cirencester, of which his father was at that time pastor. On leaving school he became an articled pupil in the laboratory of the late Dr. Voelcker, Professor of Chemistry at the Royal Agricultural College, Cirencester, and so successfully did he make his way that at eighteen years of age he was able to earn his livelihood. At this time he was encouraged to preach at cottage meetings, and his heart was gradually drawn towards the work of the Christian ministry. Much to the regret of his friend, Dr. Voelcker, he left Cirencester for Regent's Park College, and obtained the B.A. degree (London). Before the completion of his college course, he accepted a unanimous call to the pastorate of the united Churches at Naunton and Guiting, in Gloucestershire. After five happy and useful years spent on the Cotswolds he removed to the busy town of Sheffield, and became the first pastor of the Church which was formed at Glossop-road. His position there afforded ample scope for the exercise of his restless energies, and he became deeply attached to the people, but in the year 1877 he received an invitation from the Church at Bewick-street, Newcastle-on-Tyne. He was very happy in his work at Sheffield, and it was a severe trial to leave the town, but the work at Newcastle presented great difficulties, and the difficulties which repel most men always possessed great attractions for him, so he accepted the call. But when the time for parting came the pain of it was so great that those who knew him best said it had added twenty years to his age in less than that number of months. At Newcastle his work soon outgrew his strength. During his ministry there the chapel in Bewick-street was sold, and after amalgamation with the sister Church at Marlborough-crescent it was arranged to build two new churches; one in Westgate-road, the other in Osborne-road, Jesmond. In this work he took a very active and self-denying share. As a pastor he was a capital visitor, and was always welcome in the homes of the people. He has been known to go out before breakfast to seek an enquirer in whom he had been interested the previous evening. Many friends became anxious about him, and early in 1887 he resigned his charge, considerably run down in health and broken in spirit. The following year he felt sufficiently recovered to accept the pastorate of the Church at Hereford, but his strength soon proved unequal to the work. He toiled in that city four years, and then went to Germany for the use of the baths. He remained

JOHN MORTIMER STEPHENS, B.A.

in that country for a year and a-half. Too ill to do much there, he yet displayed a very sympathetic interest in the work of the German Baptists. Feeling a little stronger he returned to England and settled down in Bristol. Occasionally he was able to preach, but his work was almost done. He and his family became associated with the Church at Tyndale Chapel, and much enjoyed the ministry of Dr. Glover. During the last months of his life he was glad to be able to render some service to the Liberation Society in the West of England. It was very affecting to see him with his broken, shattered strength bravely contending for the flag which he had set up in the Lord's name during the days of his youth. He was faithful unto death. Not until within a few weeks of his death did his friends know the real nature of the disease from which he suffered. He received the physician's report with calm fortitude and resignation, his only care being for the wife and family so soon to be left behind. His sufferings at times were intense, but he endured them with Christian heroism. He entered into rest 6th October, 1895. Mr. Stephens was a warm supporter of Foreign Missions. In each of his pastorates the number of subscribers to the Baptist Missionary Society largely increased during his ministry. With almost his last breath he commended the work to those around him. His death, at the comparatively early age of fifty-one, is a great loss to the Churches. His life was one of noble self-denial, and, as one of his deacons described him, he was "a grand man."—C. H.

41. TAYLOR, BENJAMIN, who was pastor at Pulham Mary forty-six years, fell asleep on the very day his successor, Rev. G. B. Dearle was buried, 29th March, 1895. He commenced preaching in a barn at Pulham, and in 1842 the Church was formed of which he continued to be pastor until, in 1886, increasing infirmities compelled him to resign, and from that time he was laid aside from active service. He was an intelligent, earnest preacher, and much beloved. A number of small works which he published had an extensive circulation, and were valued and useful amongst the country folk of Suffolk and Norfolk. He was seventy-eight years of age. —S. K. B.

42. TAYLOR, JOHN, was born in May, 1819, at Longford, near Coventry, where he spent his youth and early manhood. He was baptized, and joined the Church at Longford, under the ministry of the Rev. J. Tunnicliff, of Band of Hope fame. He was soon engaged in Christian work, as Sunday school teacher, local preacher, and "clerk" in the public services of the sanctuary. He was much respected for his amiability of disposition, consistency of character, and willingness to co-operate in Christian and other useful activities. When in his thirtieth year, he was admitted into the college at Leicester, then under the Presidency of the Rev. J. Wallis. Mr. Taylor was a diligent student, affable in his manners, fluent in speech, and a great reader of John Howe, and other seventeenth century theologians. At the close of his college course he entered on his first pastorate at Sandy-lane Chapel, Allerton, where he spent ten happy years, and did useful work. At Wolvey, in Warwickshire, and Sutterton, in Lincolnshire, he also laboured a few years, and then returned to Yorkshire and spent the greater part of his ministerial life at Denholme, near Bradford, first in full pastoral work, and afterwards in retirement. Up to the last he preached occasionally. He was a man of unswerving and uncompromising fidelity, a Christian sincere in his profession, and thoroughly honest in all his activities, and a minister faithful to the trust committed unto him. Though not much of a leader among men, and not of the first order in the pulpit, he still did good work for the Master. His "record is on high," and in the great day of reckoning he will not be without stars in his crown of rejoicing.—W. G.

43. THOMAS, SAMUEL, was born in the parish of Gladestry, Radnorshire. His parents were godly people, and he was baptized by the late Rev. James Jones, of Rock, at Cwmgwillim, Newchurch, in May, 1829. Mr. Thomas soon began to preach the Gospel. A Baptist Church was about that time established at Gladestry, and the young preacher was for a little while under the instruction of the Rev. George Thomas, of Newtown, who was afterwards classical tutor at Pontypool College. His first pastorate was New Wells, near Newtown, his second was at Builth, Brecknockshire, and his third and last pastorate (which commenced in 1854) was at Howey, near Llandrindod Wells, where he was greatly respected. He was a farmer during his

pastorate at Builth, and for many years had a farm near Howey. Mr. Thomas had to devote much time to farming, but he was a diligent and successful pastor. Many were added to the Church under his faithful ministry, and many whom he baptized removed to other places, so that the Church continued small. Mr. Thomas was an energetic preacher. Towards the close of his life Mr. Thomas retired from farming and built a cottage near the chapel. There he lived until the death of his wife. As the infirmities of age came upon him he resigned the pastorate of the Church. Having removed to a farmhouse in Brecknockshire, near Newbridge-on-Wye, he preached occasionally in the houses near him. He was frequently visited by the vicar of the parish. Mr. Thomas died 26th June, 1894, at the age of eighty-two years.—J. J.

44. WEBB, SIDNEY ROBERTS, was born in London on 19th February, 1867. His early boyhood was spent under his father's roof, in that picturesque corner of Hampstead Heath known since the days of Domesday Book as "Wildwood." He was one of a bright and affectionate group of brothers and sisters. Under the Christian influences which surrounded him, and a parental care alike wise, generous, and devout, his character rapidly developed; and at the age of fourteen he was baptized, and became a member of the church at Heath Street. He remained a member there till his death, and if he found help and comfort in its warm and active sympathy with his high purposes, he repaid the debt by the unbroken consistency of his conduct and the inspiration of his example. Sidney Webb was a missionary from the beginning. Almost immediately after his baptism his father received a little note from him, still fondly preserved, in which he says that for six years past he had wished to become a missionary, and asks that he may be educated with that view. The letter led to a conversation, and the conversation to an understanding that his wish was to be recognized, and, if possible, carried out. Sidney himself had never any doubt of the Divine call. Years afterwards he writes from the Congo: "It was Christ's command that prevented me from being at Penmaenmawr this summer. He said, 'Go ye into all the world and preach the Gospel.' He said it to *me* in such a way that I gladly obeyed Him, and came out to Africa." In 1881 he was sent to Mill Hill School, and at the end of his course there, he matriculated in the University of London. A little later he entered on his medical studies at Ediuburgh; he passed his examinations there with credit, and gained his degree of Bachelor of Medicine. The diploma of Doctor was conferred upon him in 1892. After leaving Edinburgh he was for some time resident medical officer at the Mildmay Mission Hospital in Bethnal Green. Through all these stages he showed the same readiness to take up whatever came to his hand to do for Christ, and the same simplicity, directness, and determination in discharging it. But perhaps it was the seaside services for children, into which he was induced to throw himself in 1887, which most excited his ardour, and drew out his peculiar gifts. His letters on this subject, addressed to his friend and comrade, Mr. Howard Staines, show a heart on fire for the personal salvation of the boys and girls with whom he met at these services. Here also the athletic element enters; there are anxious inquiries after "a good pitch for cricket and a good field for sports." He hopes to bring his knowledge of botany into service in the excursions to be made. "But all towards *the great end*," he adds. One by one he sought to get hold of the boys. He corresponded with numbers of them afterwards. He prayed for them continually. "What a crowd of boys," he writes from Wathen in 1893, "whom one has loved and tried to influence, can be recalled in procession by the memory! I should not be so fond of the boys here if it had not been for the practice I had at Worthing and Penmaenmawr." On 1st January, 1893, with his newly-married wife, Dr. Webb was commended to God's care in the midst of the Church at Hampstead, and a few days later sailed from Antwerp for the Congo. Africa had been early laid upon his heart by his intercourse with the Combers, and especially with Mr. Bentley, who had throughout been his adviser. But he was prepared to accept any field to which the Committee might prefer to send him. "I used to say Africa," he writes, "and I had a low idea of all other work; now, thank God, I say anywhere that my Lord and King appoints." Africa, however, was to be the scene of his short two years of missionary service; and Wathen was his allotted post. Dr. and Mrs. Webb were met upon their way by a party of boys from the station with banners and drums and hospitable attentions, and his heart opened to them at once. As

SIDNEY ROBERTS WEBB, M.D.

in England, so upon the Congo—it was the boys with whom he was to find his special opportunities. Medical work was not neglected. Patients multiplied as the skill and kindness of the young doctor became known. He had sometimes as many as 120 in a day; and five of the boys would be assisting him through the long hours of the morning dressing ulcers, while he himself examined into all the cases, dispensed the medicine, and attended to the more serious wounds. He began simple lessons in physiology with the highest classes in the school, and was translating a small hand-book on the same subject for the use of the native evangelists. His medical skill was also in frequent requisition for State officials and other Europeans. But from April, 1893, to March, 1894, he had the entire school at Wathen under his care, comprising from 70 to 110 boys, and it was among them that his directly missionary work was done. There were, first, the regular school lessons to be superintended, and into them the young Englishman plunged with scarcely any knowledge of the native language, but bravely using what he had to "criticise the copies, and explain the mysteries of multiplication and division." There were the games of the boys to be entered into, and all their curious questions to be met. "We are inundated in the evening with boys," he writes soon after his arrival; "they play about the room, look over our shoulders, and watch our writing; and we allow them as much liberty as is good for them." Then, as the language became more familiar, he followed his old plan of individual religious conversation, and gave the address, when his turn came, at the service where all assembled. The first he gave in native speech without assistance was on the last Sunday of 1893. It touched the hearts of many of the boys, and of one in particular, baptized the following year, who traced his decision to its earnest appeals. "We are having good times," he writes home in April, 1894, "and better are coming. There is a spirit of inquiry abroad, and I have begun to try my hand at personal talk with a limited vocabulary. I like the boys," he adds, "as much as I do English boys, and I hardly expected to do this. My twist in the direction of boys holds good for black as well as white." Mrs. Webb's observation is to the same effect. "The boys were fond of him," she says, "and he was passionately fond of them. His longing desire was that they might become Christ's servants and follow Him." It is delightful to know how that desire was gratified before he died. He had himself the joy, on 4th of February, 1895, of baptizing Ntinani and Mabika, and of seeing them engaged in telling out the Gospel to their countrymen. Dr. and Mrs. Webb left Wathen on their homeward journey at the end of March 1895 in good health and spirits. The fatigue and exposure of the long march down the river brought an attack of fever on both of them, and when they reached Underhill they were in a condition that caused intense anxiety. They were tenderly cared for by Mr. and Mrs. Forfeitt and Mr. Pinnock. An English steamer was about to sail for home, and it was thought wisest that they should at once proceed in her. Mrs. Webb gradually rallied, but her husband grew worse, and notwithstanding every effort on the part of the ship's doctor, aided by missionary friends on board, he sank to rest in the early morning of Good Friday, and was buried the same day, according to his own desire, off Ambrigette, in the bosom of "the grand old sea."—W. B.

45. WILKINS, HORATIO, was born 15th January, 1847, in Musbury, South Devon, where he spent his early days. As a child he was very intelligent, and showed a thoughtful interest in sacred things far beyond his years. His parents were members of the Church of England, but when quite young he left home to live with his uncle, who was a Baptist, and under his influence the lad was led to adopt Baptist views, and at the age of fifteen confessed his Saviour by baptism. For some time prior to his conversion he had revealed a strong bent for preaching, and he now found scope for the exercise of his gifts in connection with the village churches. His growing popularity and usefulness furnished unmistakeable proof that God had called him to the work of the ministry, and at the age of twenty he entered the Pastors' College, where by his marked ability, conscientious application and fervent devotion, he won the affection and esteem of the President, the tutors, and all his brethren. While he assiduously cultivated his mental powers, the culture of the devout life was not neglected. His devotion was never obtrusive and demonstrative, but all who knew him knew how genuine it was, and could not fail to be impressed by it. During his college days he preached every Sabbath at a small chapel in Clerkenwell, and in June, 1869, he was ordained to the pastorate of the Church at

HORATIO WILKINS.

Hockliffe-road, Leighton Buzzard, where he spent four useful and happy years. In January, 1873, he received and accepted a call from the Church worshipping in Salem Chapel, Cheltenham, the town which was destined to be the scene of his life's work. There amongst an affectionate and appreciative people he laboured with increasing and multiplying evidences of success for a period of seventeen years. Under his able and devoted ministry the Church grew in spiritual power and usefulness. His amiable disposition, his great tenderness of heart, and his transparent honesty, combined with a deep, fervent, and humble piety, which influenced all he did, endeared him to the hearts of his people and made them feel that he was indeed "a good man and full of the Holy Ghost," while his deep insight into truth and his exceptional power to express his thoughts with ease, felicity, and beauty, are sufficient to account for the attractiveness, efficiency, and helpfulness of his public ministry. Those who had the pleasure of listening to him regularly knew they were listening to a man who had the open vision and who verified the truth of what he taught. His sermons were not only beautiful in conception and diction, but they were also lucid and instructive expositions of Divine truth, showing a strong faith in the infinite goodness of God and a tender sympathy with men in all the sorrows and struggles of their life. He was most at home in enforcing the devotional and practical aspects of religion. His public prayers were remarkable for the qualities of reality, devoutness and helpfulness, and revealed his own close communion with God, in which lay the secret of his power. As a pastor, he was keenly alive to the joys and the sorrows of his people, literally weeping with those who wept and rejoicing with those who rejoiced; and such sympathy as he gave could only be given at great cost to a nature so finely sensitive. He was a true "Son of Consolation." Coming home one day from visiting a family in sorrow, he exclaimed, "Oh, my heart is breaking for my people." It is no wonder that his relations with his Church and Congregation were so cordial and happy. Though quiet and unobtrusive in his habits and disposition he was, nevertheless, a man of public spirit, well qualified to form and express an opinion on the great questions of the day, and his power as a platform speaker secured for him considerable popularity where he was known. He was a leader of Nonconformity in the town, and took an active part in local politics and in all good works. The County Association, the Committee of the Baptist Foreign Missionary Society and the Council of the Baptist Union, received his valued help, and had his life been spared he would doubtless have occupied a prominent position in the denomination. In 1879 his labours were interrupted by a severe affliction which threatened to end his days. He was greatly cheered by the prayerful and practical sympathy of his people, and his restoration to health and work was welcomed by them with deep gratitude and abounding joy. The years following were years of happiness, of deep consecration, of hard and successful work. He ever had a lofty ideal of his pulpit work and pastoral relations, and to the fulfilling of that ideal he offered himself a living sacrifice. In the winter of 1887-8, it became apparent to his intimate friends that his health was slowly giving way under the pressure of his exacting labours, but he struggled on until the first Sunday in April, 1888, when he preached what proved to be his last sermons. On the advice of his deacons, he went away for rest and change, but instead of improving, he broke down completely with nervous exhaustion and bronchial asthma, and for seven years he was a prostrate but patient sufferer. For a time his affliction, working on a mind fond of brooding thought and a temperament keenly susceptible, produced a mental depression which robbed him of the comforts of the Gospel, but the cloud ultimately passed away, and in sweet tranquility and radiant hope he spent the remainder of his days, and entered into his rest on 3rd March, 1895. Those who knew him most intimately loved him dearly, and they thank God for every remembrance of such a good man and faithful servant of Jesus Christ.—F. J. B.

46. WILKS, EDWARD DAVIES: earnest student; instructive and helpful preacher; sympathizing pastor; friend of education at school or college; lover of Missions, Home or Foreign; devout and joyful Christian—all this was the good brother in the Lord whose death occurred on Christmas Day, 1894. He had been staying in Cardiff for a few weeks, at the house of his brother-in-law, making that town the centre of useful work in the interests of the Baptist Missionary Society. The illness of which he died was contracted by overwork and exposure to very trying conditions of labour as a delegate and visitor on behalf of that Society. But he

had no complaint to make. He was far too good a soldier of Jesus Christ to complain of death in the field of battle. He was much more inclined to thank God for giving him "an expected end." Mention is made of this because it was typical of the man in his entire life and character. He was always meek, modest, patient and strong, with a feeling for duty, public or private, which made his path clear from first to last. Born in Swansea in 1833, Mr. Wilks was in his sixty-first year at the time of his death. He was baptized and received into membership at York-place, Swansea, when only twelve years of age. In his boyhood he had the advantage of instruction under Mr. John Jenkins, M.A., head master of an excellent boys' school in the town. At the age of eighteen he was admitted to a three years' course at Pontypool College, whence he proceeded to Bristol, and there he remained four years. His first and longest pastorate was at Oswestry. It began in 1858, and continued twenty-three years. During this time his work as a pastor was solid and lasting in its results, and his reputation for business capacity and scholarship secured him the position of Secretary to the Shropshire Association and to the neighbouring college at Llangollen. The committees of this college and of Pontypool were often indebted to him as Examiner in Classics and Theology. On his removal to Kingsbridge, Devonshire, in 1881, he was again made Association Secretary, and won the esteem of his ministerial associates and lay brethren for his business qualities, but failing health reduced his pastorate in the south to three years. The latter part of his life was spent at Oystermouth (commonly called The Mumbles), near Swansea, where his enforced retirement from pastoral responsibility was turned to account for study and occasional preaching. It was a great joy to him when the Missionary Society asked him to visit the churches of South Wales as their agent and representative. Any kind of Christian work was congenial to him after his long and laborious inactivity. If he had been allowed to make choice of the conditions under which he had to meet and face death, nothing could have been more to his mind than a death-summons which found him with his hands full of work. He was a good preacher, pastor, scholar, friend; one of the men whose very merits stand in the way of their popularity, but who never fail to awaken the esteem and love of those who know them best and are best able to estimate their worth. To men of this sort the Christian Church can never adequately discharge her debt of gratitude.—W. E. W. (V.-D. M.)

47. WILLIAMS, John Penry, was the son of the late Rev. Thomas Williams, of Ebenezer, Llangunnog. He was born on 23rd April, 1828, at Llangunnog, Carmarthenshire, was baptized by his father in 1846, and was soon after encouraged to commence preaching. At the Normal College, Carmarthen, he was a diligent student from 1850 to 1852. On 3rd May, 1853, he was ordained at Ebenezer, Llanelian, Denbighshire. In 1855 Mr. Williams removed to Maesteg, and four years after to Cwmtwrch and Pontardawe. He accepted the pastorate at Zoar, Pontlottyn, in 1861, which he held until the day of his death, a period of thirty-four years. The first nine years of his ministry were only preparatory to the great work of his life. At Pontlottyn he distinguished himself in the cause of public elementary education. He wrote much for the press in English and in Welsh, and he lectured on political and religious topics more than most of his brethren. Mr. Williams was more than once elected chairman of the East Glamorganshire Association. He was secretary of the Committee of the first British school established at Rhymney in 1863, and of another school opened at Pontlottyn in 1865. At that time the Rev. W. Roberts (Nefydd) was an agent of the British and Foreign School Society, and rendered substantial help to Mr. Williams in his efforts to establish and maintain these schools. One of these schools was afterwards transferred to the Bedwellty Board, and the other to the Gelligaer Board. Dr. Williams was a member of the latter from its formation, and was for twelve years its vice-chairman. In 1874 he was elected one of the directors of the Lewis Pengam Endowed School, and three years ago was the chairman of that body. For a considerable time he was a guardian of the poor, a county and a district councillor, &c. Dr. Williams was a strong man all round, and the history of Gelligaer parish could not be written without giving a most prominent place to the noble work which he accomplished on behalf of religion and education. As a minister he was held in the highest respect by his Church and Congregation. His sermons were evangelical and they bore obvious marks of diligent study, but he was not considered one of the most eloquent and effective speakers. He was a man

of strong convictions, and those who could not agree with him never questioned his sincerity and conscientiousness. Many years ago he received the degree of LL.D. from one of the Universities in the United States. After a long and painful illness he gently fell asleep on 20th June, 1895.—T.D.

48. WOOD, JOHN HENRY, was born in 1808 at Lydd, on the Kentish coast, not far from the lighthouse at Dungeness. He received his early education partly at Lydd and partly in a French school across the Channel. Having the misfortune to be "impotent in his feet—a cripple from his mother's womb," he was incapable of physical effort and of any commercial pursuit. He had to support himself by teaching in private boarding schools. He followed the vocation of an usher until he was nearly thirty years old. He then became master of a day school at Melbourne, Derbyshire. With his weekly teaching he combined the work of Sunday preaching, and his services were sought in many of the Midland towns and villages. He also

JOHN HENRY WOOD.

published several small pamphlets on controversial subjects, and in 1847 he completed a volume of nearly four hundred pages, entitled, "The History of the General Baptists." Adam Taylor published his history of the same denomination in 1818, but it was too costly to be reprinted. Mr. Wood ventured on the production of quite a new work, and brought down the history to a much later date, and the entire edition was soon sold. It has not been reprinted, but is of much value as a work of reference. In subsequent years he published treatises on "The Great Propitiatory," and on Popery, as well as such booklets as "The Heavenly Mansions and Joyous Anticipations." His later work was a history of the Martyrs of Kent. Being well known as a preacher and author, he was advised to give up his school and enter the regular ministry. His first sphere was Sutterton, Lincolnshire, and his next was Smarden, Kent. Afterwards he removed to Wolvey, Warwickshire, and, lastly, to Monk's Kirby and Pailton. There he met with a painful accident. On getting out of his pony carriage his crutches became entangled in the reins and he fell to the ground. Both his frail legs were fractured, and a long confinement to his bed ensued. This event, together with approaching old age, compelled him to retire. The means of support in his time of need, and to the end of his days, were providentially offered by the generosity of Colonel Croll, of Reigate, who engaged to make quarterly allowances to twelve aged and disabled ministers. Mr. Wood was thus enabled to return to his birthplace, and spent his closing years in Ebenezer Cottage. Long before the end, his eyesight began to fail, and at length he became totally blind. But as he had ever been one of the best, so was he to the last, one of the happiest of men. In his days of health he was never heard to murmur at his malformation, and when his vision as well as his vigour failed, he did not repine. His faith and hope never failed, and his joy in the Lord was unspeakable and full of glory. He peacefully expired at the age of eighty-six, on 19th May, 1895.—W. U.

49. WYARD, GEORGE, was the eldest son of the Rev. George Wyard, who, for many years, was the honoured and beloved pastor of the church meeting in Soho Chapel, Oxford Street, London. He was born at Richmond, Surrey, in January, 1832, and after receiving a good education, entered upon a business career at the age of fifteen. When fourteen years of age he was brought to the knowledge of the Lord Jesus Christ, was baptized by his father, and admitted to the fellowship of the church. From the time of his conversion he was a diligent reader of the Bible; he took great delight in the means of grace, both public and private, and became not only well grounded in the tenets held by that section of the denomination to which he was attached, but was a devout, earnest and consistent follower of his Lord and Master. When in the prime of his young manhood many of his fellow members, much impressed with his knowledge of the Scriptures, his gift in prayer, and his ability to communicate his knowledge to others, thought they discovered in him gifts for the ministry of the Gospel, and they desired him to exercise those gifts as opportunity arose. This he did with much acceptance, and being solemnly set apart to the work of the ministry, he became the pastor of the church meeting in Providence Chapel, Reading. Leaving Reading, he settled at Irthlingborough, then at Shrewsbury, and subsequently at Brighton, Harlow, and Stevenage. In each place his work was blessed of God, and there are many persons who will be "his joy and crown of rejoicing in the day of Jesus Christ." His life was a chequered one. His trials, sorrows and disappointments were very numerous and heavy, but he endured them with a faith and courage peculiarly his own. As the time of his departure, unexpected by those whom he loved, drew on, his walk with God became close and manifest. His last illness was brief. He preached at Borough Green, in Kent, on the Sunday, returned to his home at Forest Gate on Monday, became exceedingly ill, in two days sank into a state of unconsciousness, and on the morning of 30th August, 1895, he quietly and peacefully breathed his last. "Absent from the body, present with the Lord."—J. S. W.

MEMORABLE NAMES AMONG BAPTISTS.

[*For list of Memorable Names among Baptists, see Baptist Hand-Book*, 1889.]

BAPTIST AUTHORS AND HISTORY, 1527–1800.

By JOSEPH ANGUS, D.D.

I.—Baptist Authors from 1527-1600.

Books and public documents published against Baptists throw more light on the early history of the body in England than any extant Church records.

EARLY NOTICES OF BAPTISTS.

The earliest General Baptist churches of which any history is known were founded about 1611-14 by Thomas Helwisse, in London, Tiverton, Coventry, &c.; and the earliest Particular Baptist church by John Spilsbury, at Wapping, in 1633. There are traditions of earlier churches. The Baptist Society at Shrewsbury is said to have been formed in 1627; that at Bickenhall (now at Hatch), near Taunton, in 1630 (Thompson, quoted by Toulmin, Neal, iii., p. 352). Even in 1457 there is said to have been a congregation of this kind at Chesterton (Robinson's Claude, ii., p. 54). The earliest books in defence of their views were written by John Smyth in 1608-9. More than seventy years earlier, however, literature supplies us with evidence of the existence and activity of Baptists in England. In 1548 John Vernon translated and published Bullinger's "Holesome Antidote against the Pestilent Sect of the Anabaptists." Three years later William Turner, Doctor of Physick, devysed "a Triacle against the poyson—lately stirred up agayn by the furious Secte of the Anabaptists," London, 1551. These are the earliest English Antibaptist books I know. At Bocking and at Faversham ministers and whole congregations were seized by the officers of the law; and Strype notes that these were the first bodies that made separation from the Reformed Church in England. This occurred at least as early as 1548. Within ten years inquiries were made for Anabaptists, as we find from "Articles of Visitation," issued by Bonner in Kent, by Gardiner at Cambridge, and by Dr. Chedsey in Essex. In 1589 Dr. R. Some issued "A Godly Treatise," chiefly against Henry Barrow and John Greenwood, and other Puritans, whom he charges with Anabaptistical errors. Earlier still we have evidence of their activity and numbers in the fires of martyrdom that burnt so fiercely at the beginning of that century. Latimer speaks of 500 of them in one town. In 1538 a commission was issued to the Bishops of the Southern Province to inquire after Anabaptists and to punish them. Froude tells us, with noble indignation, how fourteen were done to death because they "were faithful to their conscience." The members of the "Pilgrimage of Grace" appealed to Henry VIII. that "the heresies of Luther and of the Anabaptists, should be annihilated and destroyed." For a hundred years, therefore, before we hear of Baptist Churches, we read of proclamations against Anabaptists, and of the persecution, banishment, and death, of many in the Southern counties of England, and during the reigns of all the Tudors. These proclamations, it is true, were issued in part against Baptists who came from Holland and Germany, and were thought to hold erroneous doctrines on other points; but, in the Instructions to the Commissioners, they are directed also how to deal with those who denied only infant baptism, and held on other points the common faith.

The following are some of the works which show the wide spread of Baptist sentiment, both in England and on the Continent, before the seventeenth century. Up to the last date no English Baptist is known to have written any defence, nor is there *any* authentic history during the sixteenth century of the existence of English *Baptist Churches.*

In this list: A. means that I have the book; B., that it is in the Bodleian; B.L., in the Baptist Library; B.M., that it is in the British Museum; S, in Sion College; U.C., in the University Library, Cambridge; W., in Dr. Williams' Library; and Y.M., in York Minster.

1527—ZWINGLE, H.: Contra Catabaptistas. Tiguri. B.M.

1535—BULLINGER, H.: Adv. omnia Catabaptistarum Prava Dogmata.. Tig. B.; U.C.

1536—ARTICLES devysed by the Kynge's Highness..to establyshe Christen quietnesse. K.Henry's Creede—agt. Anab. A.; B.M.

1536—THE PILGRIMAGE OF GRACE "To have the heresies of Luther, Wickliffe, the works of Tyndale.. and such other heresies of Anabaptists annulled." Froude ii. 568. A.; B.M.

1546-1640—INIVNCTIONS AND ARTICLES: Contain several cautions and orders for inquiring into Anab. doctrines and practices. See Sparrow's Collns. and separate Articles. A.; B.; B.M.

1548—HORTENSIUS, L.: Tvmvltvvm Anabaptistarum Liber unus. Basil. [The origin of many unfounded charges agt. E. Baptists.] A.; B.M.; B.

1549-1552.—COMMON PRAYER of Ed. VIth. (First and Sec. Edns.) denounces Anab. by name. A.; B.M., &c.

1550-1551—Notes of Interrogatories and Answers before the INQUISITION at Venice, Bologna, Rome, &c., with details of the Beliefs and Practices of Anabaptists in those cities and in other parts of Italy. Published by Emilio Comba, Florence, and tr. by J. T. Betts, Esq. (MS.) A.

1551—BULLINGER, H.: A most sure defence of the baptisme of Children agt. the pestiferous secte of the Anab., tr. by Jno. Veron. A.; B.

1551—TURNER, WM., M.D.: A Preservative or triacle agt. the Poyson of Pelagius lately styrred up agayn by the furious secte of the Anab. devysed by W. Turner, Powles Ch. yard. B.M.; S.; U.C.

1552—THE DUKE OF NORTHUMBERLAND to W. Cecill "..wishes the King would appoint Mr. Knox (John Knox) to the See of Rochester..a whe stone to the Archbp. of Canterbury and a Confounder to the Anabts. lately sprung up in Kent." State Paper Kalendar (Domestic), Rolls Court.

1560—A PROCLAMATION ag. Anabaptisies, given in Arber's Stationers' Co. Register, i., 570.

1560—KNOX, JOHN: An Answer to a great number of Cavillations, by an Anabaptist (it contains the Pamphlet). A.; B.M.; S.

1560—VERON, JNO: An Apology or Defence of Predestination [agt. Anabts. and troublers of the Church]. A.

1562—SIMON MENNO: (First ed. of his treatise on Saving Truth, &c.) A.

1565—DE BRES, G.: La Racine des Anabaptistes avec tres ample refutation, &c. [again in Dutch in 1570, and pub. in America (at Cambridge) in 1688]. W.

1569—A PROCLAMATION agt.dispearsing, buying, and allowing of seditious books; another (1570); another (1573); others (in 1583 and 1588). See Arber's Register, vol. i.

1571—WHITGIFT, JOHN: Answer to a Certain Libell, an admonition to Parlt with Certayne Notes of Anabts. out of Zwingli. W.

1575—DE PÆDOBAPTISTARUM errorum origine per Mart. Czechium (a Polish Author). A.

1588—SOME, R.: A Defence.. and a Refutation of many Anabaptistical absurdities on Magistracie, Baptisme, &c. B.M.; B.; W.

1588—[UDALL, J. &c.]: Martin Marprelate. The Epistle, &c. The beginning of a large Literature. A.; B.M., &c.

1589—SOME, R.: A Godly treatise wherein are examined many execrable Fancies given out by H. Barrow and J. Greenwood; and by other of the Anabt. order. A.; B.L.; Y.M.

FRATRES POLONI:—Socinus, F. (1539-1604); Crallius (1590-1633); Slichtingius (1592-1661); Wolzogenius (1596-1658). The Polish Brethren, as they were called, were Unitarians and Baptists, having defended Believers' Baptism in their works. See indexes in their collected works, 7 vols., fol. 1656. Some have ascribed the existence of the English Baptists to their teaching, but a reference to the above dates shows that there is no ground for this statement. A.

II.—Baptist Authors from 1600-1700.

With the seventeenth century the history of our churches begins. But even during this century, Baptists are known quite as much through the works and persecution of their opponents as from their own writings. Thomas Edwards, in his "Gangræna" (1646), and Daniel Featley, in "The Dippers Dipt; or the Anabaptists ducked and plunged over head and ears at a Disputation in Southwark" (1648), tell us of many faithful workers of whom else we should have known nothing. Edwards speaks of various counties where Baptists abounded, and Featley tells how there had been hundreds of Baptists in Southwark for twenty years or more. In 1589 Dr. Some also reports that there were several congregations of Baptists in London. In 1640 a violent attack in Latin on "Anabaptistes and other Heretics" was translated into English by J. D.; and in 1642 two pamphlets were published in London—one giving "The History of the Anabaptistes in High and Low Germany," and the other warning the English against the entire sect. These publications show how the early Baptists were dreaded and misunderstood.

ANCIENT CONFESSIONS

In the year A. D. 1644 the first English Baptist Confession was published. It was expressly intended to correct mistaken impressions of their faith; and this was followed by other editions, with slight changes or additions, in 1646, 1651, 1652, and 1653 (Leith). In 1656 a Creed of a similar kind was prepared by Thomas Collier, and published in the name of seventeen churches in Somerset and neighbouring counties. Another Creed, based, like the Savoy Confession of the Independents, upon the Westminster Confession of Faith, was published in 1677, 1688, and 1692. Meantime, other Confessions, signed by some of the General Baptists, were published in 1651 by thirty churches in the Midland counties, in 1660, and another in 1678, and in 1691. Fifty years earlier (1611), John Helwisse published a "Declaration of English People" at Amsterdam; and, about the same time, John Smyth, at Amsterdam, drew up a Confession of Faith in Dutch, which has been published in a complete form in English in Evans' History. As an evidence of the spread of Baptist views, and of the hope that they would be counteracted, the French Reformed Church published a "Formulary of Baptisme for those Anabaptists not Baptised"; and this was translated and published in London in 1646. In addition to the usual Articles of Faith, the candidate was required, before he was baptised, to confess his error, and avow his belief in infant baptism. Two of those who signed the Confession of 1646 were French pastors in London.

SEVERITY OF PERSECUTION.

These are indirect proofs of the prevalence of Baptist views; the severity of the persecution of Baptists in the century is another. The men named in the following list held no so-called Mennonite views. They were not prosecuted for civil crime. They were nearly all known as holy, earnest men; and yet nearly all of them suffered for their principles. Three, at least, died in prison—Bampfield, De Laune, and Vavasor Powell. Bunyan and Jennings were each in gaol for a dozen years. John James was executed on a charge of speaking seditious words, but on the scantiest evidence. Samuel Oates was tried for murder, on the ground that he had baptised a convert who died three months after baptism. Keach was put in the pillory for his Catechism; and nearly all were fined or imprisoned, or made to suffer for their faith—a testimony at once to their fidelity, and to the spread of their principles.

PUBLIC DISCUSSIONS.

Two peculiarities distinguish the Baptist history of the seventeenth century. It was the age of public disputation, and ministers devoted a large amount of time to evangelistic work. The former, it is generally admitted, was useless except as calling attention to truth; the latter largely blessed. One dispute was held in Southwark, in 1642, between Dr. Daniel Featley, Mr. William Kiffin, and others; then in London in 1643, where Knollys, Kiffin, and Jessey, took an active part; another at Tirling, in Essex, in 1643, between T. Lamb and others; another at Newport Pagnell, in 1647, between J. Gibbs and R. Carpenter; another at Ashford, in 1649, between S. Fisher and several clergymen; another at Bewdley, in 1649, between Baxter and Tombes; another in London, in 1650, between Dr. Chamberlain and Mr. Bakewell; another at Cork, in 1652; another at Abergavenny, in 1653 between H. Vaughan, Tombes, and J. Craig; the last at Portsmouth, in 1698, "with his Majesty's licence," between W. Russell, M.D., &c., against Samuel Chandler, &c. I have the reports of most of these discussions, and can confirm the judgment that they must have been profitless for conviction. On the other hand, ministers who visited various counties for preaching purposes found many an open door with many adversaries, and formed churches which long prospered, some down to our own day.

LIST OF AUTHORS.

The following list of about one hundred and sixty contains not more than half of those whose names have come down to us as belonging to the seventeenth century. They are the names of men who are best known in our literature. Against most of the names a letter or letters will be found, referring readers who wish to know more of the men to histories which give an account of their life-work and sufferings. These biographical notices are often very touching and instructive.

The references are to the following:—

[B.] BROOK'S (B.) Lives of the Puritans from the Reformation under Elizabeth to the Act of Uniformity, 1662. 3 vols. 1813.

[Ca.] CALAMY'S (E., D.D.) Nonconformists' Memorial: An account of the Lives and Sufferings of 2,000 Ministers ejected in 1662. With S. Palmer's additions. 3 vols. 1802.

[C.] CROSBY'S (T.) History of the English Baptists from the Reformation to the Beginning of the Reign of George I. 4 vols. 1738-1740.

[E.] EVANS' (B., D.D.) Early English Baptists. 2 vols. 1862.

[N.] NEAL'S (D., M.A.) History of the Puritans, or Protestant Nonconformists, from the Reformation in 1517 to the Revolution in 1688. Dr. Toulmin's edition. 3 vols. 1837. Dr. Toulmin himself held Baptist views, and has written a very useful account of the Baptists and Quakers, which is appended to this edition.

[I.] IVIMEY'S (JOS.) History of the English Baptists from the Earliest Times to the Death of George III. 4 vols. 1811-1830.

[T.] TAYLOR'S (A.) History of the English General Baptists from the Beginning of the Seventeenth Century. 2 vols. 1818.

[U.] UNDERHILL'S (Dr. E. B.) Introductory Notices, in the Hansard Knollys' Society's volumes. 1846.

[W.] WILSON'S (WALTER) History and Antiquities of Dissenting Churches and Meeting Houses in London, Westminster, and Southwark, including Lives of their Ministers from the Rise of Nonconformity to the Present Times. 4 vols. 1808-1814.

Brief notices of the more eminent of the names may be found in—

CRAMP'S (J. M., D.D.) Baptist History from the Foundation of the Christian Church to the present time, 1871, and in

WOOD'S (J. H.) History of the General Baptists of the New Connexion. 1847. And in Dr. Cathcart's Baptist Encyclopædia, Philadelphia. 1881.

For the history of ministers in particular districts special notice is due to such works as JOSHUA THOMAS'S History of the Welsh Associations, published in Rippon's Register; DOUGLAS'S History of the Northern Churches; HARGREAVE'S Life of Hirst, 1816; FULLER'S (J. G.) History of Dissent in Bristol, 1840 GOADBY'S Bye-Paths of Baptist History; and Baptists and Quakers in Northamptonshire, 1650-1700, &c.; CATHCART'S Baptist Encyclopædia, Philadelphia. 1881.

Names.	Notice of in
* Adams, R., Leicestershire, Devonshire-square, London, d. 1716	Ca, C. W
* Adis, H., 1661, "A Fanatick's Alarm, by one of the Sons of Zion"	
* Allen, R., White's Alley, d. 1717	C, T, W
* Allen, Will., 1686, author of several works	C
Life of, by Bishop Williams, 1707.	

Names.	Notice of in
Bampfield, F., M.A., b. 1614, d. 1683. London, Wiltshire .. Died in Newgate	Ca, C, W
* Barber, E., Bishopsgate-street, 1641..	B, C, I, T, W
* Barebones, P., 1640 (see Jessey's Life, 7, 11, 83, and Dexter).	
* Barrow, R., "Answer to B. P. in favour of I. B." 1642.	
* Bishop, G., "Election and Reprobation," 1663.	
* Blackett, H., Durham (see Douglas's History).	
* Blackwood, Chr., 1644-1660, Staplehurst, Northumberland, Ireland	B, C, I, T, W
* Bonham, Josiah, Byefield, "The Churches' Glory," 1674 ..	Goadby
Britten, Willm., b. 1608, "The Moderate Baptist," 1654.	
* Brown, T., Scripture Reader, 1673	C
* Brown, R., London, Worcester, 1678, d. Plym	Ca, C
* Bunyan, J., b. 1628; imprisoned from 1660-1672; Biographies..	C, I
* Busher, L., 1614; Plea for Liberty of Conscience, the first book on that subject and On False Translations of N. T.	U
* Caffin, M., Horsham, &c., 1653	T
Camelford, Gab., Furness Fells, d. 1676	Ca, E
* Canne, J., Amsterdam, Bristol, 1640..	B, I, W
* Cary, P., Dartmouth, 1685, d. 1710	I
Chamberlain, Dr. P., London, 1650	U
* Cheare, Abr., Plymouth, 1648..	B, C, I
Clayton, J., Shad Thames, 1660, d. 1689	T
* Coe, C., Bedford (see Bunyan's works).	
* Collet, B., Bourton, 1660	I
* Collier, Thos., Hampshire, &c., 1645	B, C, I
* Collins, H., Wapping (afterwards Prescot-street), 1677, d. 1702	C, I
* Collins, W., Petty France, 1675-1702	W
* Cornwell, F., M.A., Marden, Cranbrook, 1643. First used laying on of hands, T, i., 120	B, I, T
* Cox, B., M.A., 1639, Devon, Coventry, Lon.	B, I, T
* Coxe, N., D.D., Petty France, 1675-1688	C, W
* Danvers, H., near Aldgate, d. 1687	C, I, W
* De Laune, T., Schoolmaster, London. "A Plea for Nonconformity." Died in Prison	I
* Dell, W., M.A., Master of Caius College, Cambridge	Ca, T
* Denne, H., 1643, Fenstanton, &c., Canterbury, London, d. 1660	B, C, E, I, T W
* Denne, J., Lincolnshire	T
* Doe, C., London..	I
Donne, I., Keysoe (K. Coll.), imprisoned with Bunyan	Ca, I
* Drapes, E., London, "Gospel Glory," 1649	I
Du Veil, C.M., D.D., Gracechurch-street	C, I, T, W
* Dyke, D., M.A., b. 1617, Devonshire-square, d. 1688	B, C, W
* Ewer, S., on Baptism	W
Ewins, T., d. 1670, Broadmead	Ca, I
* Everard, R., recommended by Marsom	T
* Field, H., Burnham, 'Last Legacy" of	T
* Fisher, S., Ashford, 1649	Ca, C
Forty, H., London, Abingdon, d. 1692	C, I
Frewen, Paul, Warwick	Ca, C
Gibbs, J., Newport Pagnell, Olney	Ca, C, I
Gifford, A., Bristol, b. 1649, d. 1721	C, I
* Gifford, J., Bedford, 1650, Bunyan's "Evangelist"	B, I
* *Gosnold, Jno., Pembroke* Hall, London, d. 1678	Ca, C, E, I

Names.	Notice of in
* Grantham, T., b. 1634, Linc., Norf., d. 1692	B, C, I, T
* Griffiths, I., Bishopsgate-street, d. 1702	C, W
* Haggar, H., Stafford, baptised Danvers	C
* Hammond, G., Biddenden, 1648	I, T
Hardcastle, Thomas, Shadwell; Broadmead, Bristol	Ca, C
* Harrison, Major-General. "Head of the Baptists in England"	E, U
* Harrison, T., Petty France, 1689-1699	W
Head, Josh., Bourton-on-W.	Ca
* Helwisse, Thos., London, 1615, d. 1620, Founder of the first General Baptist Church	B, E, T, W
* Hobson, Paul, Crutched Friars, Northumberland, &c.	Ca, C, W
* Hooke, Jos., Bourn, "Apology for Believers' Baptism," 1701	T
Horrockes, T., Essex, see Davids' History of Nonconformity in Essex	Ca, E
* How, S., "Cobbler," Deadman Place, 1639, warmly praised by Roger Williams	W
* Hutchinson, E., "On the Covenants and Baptism," 1676	C, I
* Hutchinson, Col., and Mrs. (see Memoirs, and Toulmin's Neal, iii.)	
* Ives, Jer., Old Jewry, 1655-1674	C, T, W
* James, Jno., Whitechapel, 1661, executed	B, C, E, T
* Jeffry, W., b. 1616, Bessels Green	B, C, I, T
Jennings, Jno., Bishopsgate, 1675, was imprisoned twelve years	C, I, T
* Jessey, H., b. 1601, bap. 1645, d. 1663, Founder of an open Communion Church, urged a revision of the authorised version	Ca, C, I, W
* Keach, B., b. 1640, Horselydown, 1668-1704	C, I, W
* Keach, Elias, Hymns, 1696, in the Huth Library	C, I
* Kiffin, W., b. 1616, Devonshire-square, 1644-92, d. 1701, imprisoned. See Orme's Life	C, I, W
Killcop, Th.	
* King, D., near Coventry, 1650, Southwark	I
* Kingsworth, R., Staplehurst	
* Knollys, Hans., b. 1598, London, d. 1691. See Kiffin's Life, 1692	B, C, E, W
* Knutton, Immanuel.	
* Lamb, Thos., Colchester, Colman-street, b. 1640, d. 1672	B, C, E, I, T, W
Lamb, Is. (son of above), Ratcliffe Highway, often preached before Blake and Penn, d. 1691. T. Oates became one of his members	C, I
* Laurence, H., Sec. of Council of State, Milton's friend	C, E
* Lilburne, Jas., Col., Devonshire-square, &c.	
* Loveday, S., East Smithfield, 1660, d. 1685	T
* Ludlow, E., "Head of Baptists in Ireland"	E
Maisters, Jos., b. 1640, London, d. 1717	Ca, I
* Marlow, Is., Maze Pond. Wrote against singing, answered by Keach, 1692. One of the Treasurers of the Fund.	
Marsden, Jer. (called Ralphson from his father's name). Imprisoned with Bampfield	B, Ca, E
Marsom, J., Luton, 1675. Imprisoned with Bunyan, d. 1726.	I.
* Milton, John, b. 1608, d. 1674. See Masson's Life; he held Baptist Views.	
* Minge, Thomas, "Gospel Baptist," 1700.	
* Monk, T., Buckingham, author of Creed of 1678	T
* Morton, J., Lon., 1610, Colchester. A Colleague of John Smyth's	B, C, E, T

	Names.	Notice of in
	Mulliner, Abr., Bishopsgate-street, b. 1671, d. 1739. Mentioned by D'Assigny, 1709	C, T
	Myles, I., Ilston, Founded 1st Welsh Church at Swansea, 1649	Thomas
*	Nicholas, J. St., Lutterworth, d. 1698	C, I
*	Norcott, J., the successor of Spilsbury, at Wapping, d. 1675	I
*	Oates, Sam., Co-pastor with Lamb, Coleman St., Essex, 1646, d. 1666. Tried on charge of murder for baptizing a convert	B, C, I, W
*	Oates, Titus, He was a Baptist, was excluded, then became a clergyman, and afterwards a Roman Catholic	C, I
	Page, Edw., Bristol	
*	Palmer, Ant., Bourton and London, 1678. Leominster, Worcester	Ca, I
*	Pardoe, W., "Ancient Christianity Reviewed," written in Leicester and Worcester Prisons	I, T
*	Patients (or Patience), Thos., assistant of Kiffin, Devonshire Square, Dublin, 1644, d. 1666	B, C, I, U, W
*	Pendarves, J., B.A., b. 1622, Abingdon, 1652, d. 1657	C, I
*	Piggott, John, London	I, T
*	Piggott, Thomas, Amsterdam (see Barclay).	
*	Plant, Thomas, London	I, T
	Plimpton, J., Dublin, 1696-1698.	
*	Porter, J., Dispute at Ellesmere, 1656.	
*	Powell, Vavasor, the Apostle of Wales, died in prison, 1671	Ca, C, E, I
*	Prince, Thos., against Kiffin, 1649.	
	Prudhom, C., Bridlington, 1698.	
*	Purnell, R., Bristol, 1652-1659.	
	Quarrel, T., Llangwm. (See J. Thomas's History of Associations in Wales)	Ca
*	Richardson, S., Colleague of Spilsbury, 1647	I
*	Rider, W., first Pastor of Keach's Church, 1652	C, I
*	Robotham, J., Upminster.	
*	Russell, W., M.D., d. 1701, Northamptonshire, Portsmouth, &c.	C
*	Sharpe, I., Frome, d. 1740. A Convert of Bunyan's.	
	Sickelmore, Jno., 1640, Portsmouth and Chicester	B, C. T
*	Simpson, Jno., London, 1650, d. 1662	B
	Sims, John, Southampton, 1646 (Edwards' Gangræna)	B, C, I
*	Smith, F., Bookseller, imprisoned by Judge Jeffries, d. 1691.	T
	Smith, W., Welton	T
*	Smyth, Jno., Amsterdam, Lincolnshire, d. 1610	B, C, E, I, W
*	Spilsbury, Jno., Wapping, 1633. Founder of the 1st Particular Baptist Church (?)	B, C, W
*	Spittlehouse, J.	
*	Stanley, F., East Haddon, Northamptonshire, d. 1696	C T
*	Steed, Robt., Dartmouth, 1640, and co-pastor of Hansard Knollys	C, I
*	Stennett, Ed., Wallingford	C, I
*	Stennett, Joseph, b. 1663. Pinners' Hall, 1690 to 1713. Suc. Bampfield	C, I
*	Stennett, Joseph, D.D., Little Wild-street	C, I
*	Sturgion, John, 1661. Plea for Toleration	C, U
	Terrill, Ed., Schoolmaster and Minister, Bristol, b. 1635, d. 1686 Laid foundation for Bristol Academy	I
	Thomas, W., d. 1693, Bristol, trained ministers	I
	Tillam, T., Hexham, &c.	

* Tombes, J., b. 1603, d. 1676. Temple, Bewdley, &c. .. .. Ca, C, I
* Tredwell, J., Suffolk, 1692 I
Tuthill H.

* Vane, Sir Henry.
Vaughan, H., Olchon, Radnorshire, 1633-1653, Pastor of first Baptist Church in Wales (see Myles) .. .. B, C

* Walwyn, R., Herts.
* Walwyn, W., London
Whinnell, T., Taunton I
* Wilcox, T., b. 1622, d. 1687. Often imprisoned. Cannon-street and Southwark. "A Choice drop of Honey," &c. .. .. C, I
Wilkinson, Jno., 1619 .. .. B
* Williams, Roger, b. 1599, d. 1683. Founder of first Baptist Church in America (See Biography of) .. .. B, W
Wise, Laurence, Chatham, Goodman's Yard .. .. .. Ca, E, I
Woodward, W., Harlow, 1662-1712 and Davids' *Essex* .. .. Ca, C, I
Woolwich, Hez.
Wright, Jos., b. 1623, Maidstone. Twenty years in prison ..I, T, W
*Wyke, A. (see Edward's Gangræna).
*Wyles, N., Colchester.

REMARKS ON THIS LIST.

I.

Of the whole number, more than fifty, and these among the most eminent, had received a University education. Biographical notices of seven-and-twenty of them are given in Brook's "Puritans," and of three-and-twenty more who were ejected at the Restoration, in Calamy. Several others, whose names are not found in Brook or Calamy, were also members of one of the universities, like Dr. N. Coxe and Dr. Chamberlain. Some, like Samuel How and John Bunyan, were, as Baxter says of himself, "of no University"; but more than are generally supposed were trained men; and proved by their history the extent of their learning and the strength of their principles.

II.

In consequence of the amalgamation of General and Particular Baptists in 1891, the distinctive designations are omitted; but it may be well to remark that both sections of the body as they formerly existed are included in this list. In the early part of the seventeenth century, the Particular and the General Baptists were more closely agreed than in the eighteenth, and were nearly equal in numbers and influence. The earliest Creeds (1644, 1646, &c.), and the first Creed of 1677, which is based on the Westminster Confession, are Calvinistic. The Creed of 1660 is Arminian; and the Creed of 1670 is claimed by both, though perfectly acceptable to neither. Both were earnest and evangelical, nor is it always easy to distinguish between them; "however, the seeds of decay had taken deep root," towards the close of the century, in the General Baptist churches (Taylor's History, i. 355), nor did they regain their old vigour and faith till after the formation of the New Connexion in 1770.

III.

I have not included Welsh Baptists in the above list, except the names of Vavasor Powell and two others. About twelve Welsh clergymen are said to have been ejected at the Restoration who became Baptist ministers, and others had left the Established Church before. In a touching narrative of the condition of Wales given by Vavasor Powell and prefixed to "The Bird in the Cage" (London, 1662), he tells us that at the beginning of the Civil War there were but one or two gathered congregations in all Wales, and in some counties scarce any that made profession of godliness; but that when he wrote "there were above twenty gathered churches with, in some two, in some three, in some four or five hundred members." These were the beginnings of dark days. The noble and sainted man died, in 1670, in the fifty-third year of his age, and in the eleventh year of his imprisonment.

IV.

Of this list of 156 authors I have one or more works of 117 of them, marked (*). This is an increase of 30 Baptist ministers, and of one or more of the works of 40, as compared with the list as issued some years ago.

V.

I shall be specially glad to hear of copies of works by Allen (R.), Blackwood (C.) Britten, Chamberlain (Dr. W.), Doe (C.), Edwards (Dublin), Gifford (Dr. A.), Gosnold (J.), Hammon (G.), Haggar (H.), Helwisse (T.), Ives (Jer.), Keach (B.) (I have 30 works of his out of 45), Knollys (H.), Lamb (Thos.), Monk (Thos.), Pendarves (J.), Richardson (S.), Russell (Dr. W.), and Smith (John and William), of Welton, and any Works of authors in the preceeding list which have no asterisks prefixed.

III.—Baptist Authors from 1700-1800.

In the following list each author has the name of the place appended, whereby he may be most easily identified. The number after the name indicates how many works of his I possess; and the dates indicate when or between what times the works were published.

Name and Field of Labour.	No. of Works.	Date of Publications.
Acton, S., Nantwich	3	1710-1741
Allen, John, Petticoat-lane	9	1752-
Anderson, W., Grafton-street	1	1757
Applegarth, Mr. R., Kent	1	1789
Ash, John, LL.D., Pershore	6	1763-1778
Ashdowne, W., MSS. and books	4	1763-1791
Austin, A., S. Colefield	2	1790-1808
Auther, J., Waltham Abbey	2	1731-1762
Backus, Is., Boston, U.S.A.	4	1754-1792
Bailey, N., LL.D., London	10	1726-1768
Beatson, T., Hull, &c.	(w)	1779
Beddome, B., Bourton	6	1734-
Beddome, B., Jun.	1	1777
Belbin, B., Reading	2	1732
Bicheno, Jas., Newbury	3	1798-1806
Biggs, Jas., Devizes	2	1795
Birt, W., London	3	1746
Bligh, Michael, Sevenoaks	1	1764
Booth, Ab., Prescott-street	40	1769-1796
Booth, P., Lincolnshire	1	1718
Boyce, Gilbert, Coningsby	1	1787
Bradford, John	6	1787-1800
Braidwood, W., Edinburgh	6	1796-1799
Braithwaite, G., Devonshire-square	3	1733-1737
Brine, Jno., Curriers Hall	50	1743-1765
Bristol College, Rep. and Ser.	14	1770-1784
Brittain, T., Luton, London—MSS.	(wanted)	
Brown, J., Kettering	3	1758-1777
Bulkley, C., Old Jewry	8	1735-1771
Burnham, R., Grafton-street	9	1787-1807
Burroughs, Jas., Paul's-alley	1	1733

Name and Field of Labour.	No. of Works.	Date of Publications.
Burroughs, Jos., Joiners' Hall	19	1713-1761
Burt, Job	1	1737
Butterworth, J., Birmingham	1	1774-1781
Butterworth, L.	1	1771
Buttfield, W., Dunstable	1	1778
Button, W., Dean-street	3	1785-1787
C. J., Sevenoaks	1	
Cameron, H. (Scots Bt.)	2	1806-1808
Carey, Wm. (D.D.)	2	1792
Clark, Jas., Lincoln	1	1804
Clark, J., Trowbridge	10	1784-1804
Clarke, Aug., Redcross-street	5	1781-1789
Clarke, W. N. (M.A.), Unicorn-yard	6	1768-1784
Cole, C., Whitchurch	1	1782
Collett, J., Bourton	3	1734-1744
Collins, W. Petticoat-lane	1	1748
Cornthwaite, R., Boston, &c.	1	1740
Crabtree, W. Bradford	2	1780-1789
Craven, J., Redcross-street	6	1744-1771
Crossley, D., London, Tottlebank	2	1744
Dafforne, M. J., MSS.	1	1788-1803
Davison, J., Trowbridge	1	1704
Davye, T., Leicester	1	1719
Day, R. (M.A.), Wellington	1	1799
Deacon, S., Barton	15	1786-1803
Dobel, D., Cranbrook	1	1755
Dobel, Jos., Kent	1	1807
Dore, Jas., Maze-pond	35	1784-1814
Dore, W., Cirencester	1	1779
Dowars, W., Spitalfields	10	1757-1795
Dunkin, J., London	1	1783
Dunscombe, T., Aston	1	1792
Dutton, Anne	5	1735-1748
De Foe, D. } With details about Baptists.		
Dunton, John, London } With details about Baptists.		
Dyer, Geo., Cambridge } With details about Baptists.		
Edwards, M., Rye	1	1761
Edwards, Morgan	1	1792-
Edwards, Peter, Portsea	7	1779-1805
Elwall, Edw., Mill-yard	7	1723-1736
Evans, Caleb (D.D.), Bristol	30	1766-1790
Evans, Hugh	2	1773
Evans, John Abingdon	7	1778-&c.
Evans, J. (LL.D.), Worship-street	35	1793-1811
Fall, Jas., Watford	3	1746-1756
Fanch, Jas., Ramsey	4	1763-1768
Fawcett, Jno., (D.D.), Hebden Bridge	14	1774-1810
Feist, P., Beverley	1	1795
Fellows, J., Bromsgrove	13	1771-1779
Filkes, J. D., Wilts	2	1718-1737
Fisher, S., Norfolk	8	1767-1802
Flower, B., Harlow	3	1796-1804
Foot, W., Bristol	6	1739-1766
Foskett, B., and H. Evans, Bristol, MSS.	..	1755-1756

Name and Field of Labour.	No. of Works.	Date of Publications.
Foster, Jas. (D.D.), London	12	1720-1735
Francis, Benj., Shortwood	10	1771-1799
Fuller, A., Kettering, various editions	40	1784-1815
Fund, Baptist—Rules, Orders, and Reports from beginning	..	1791-&c.
Gale, Jno. (M.A., D.D.), Barbican	8	1713-1724
Garner, J., MSS., Oulton, Cumberland	2	
Garratt, J. Northampton	1	1723
General Baptist New Connexion formed	..	1770
General Baptist Magazine—3 vols.	..	1798-1800
General Baptist Repository	6	1802
Gibbs, P., Plymouth	1	1786
Gifford, A. (D.D.), Eagle-street	5	1733-1746
Giles, W., Kent	6	1771-1799
Gill, Jno. (D.D.), Works	45	1732-
Gillard, D., Folkestone and Hammersmith	2	1784-1787
Gould, Js., Harlow	1	1776
Graham, W., Carlisle	3	1741-1784
Grosvenor, B., (D.D.), baptised by Keach	11	1710-1735
Gurney, Mr. J., London	1	1795
Gurney, Mr. T., London	4	1755-1770
H. J., London	1	1729
Hague, W., Scarborough	1	1792, &c.
Hall, Chr., Leicester and London	2	1769
Hall, E., Boston	2	1817-1719
Hall, R., Sen., Arnsby	7	1771-1776
Harrison, Amos, Croydon	3	1724-1743
Harrison, R.	2	1759-1761
Harrison, T., Loriner's Hall	1	1700
Harrison, Thos., Jun., Little Wild-street	5	1715-1729
Hartley, Jno., Haworth	2	1755-1774
Hassell, Thos., Newcastle	1	1779
Hatch, Thos., London	1	1804
Haydon, J., Sen.	1	1724
Haydon, J., Jun., Shortwood	5	1745-1780
Hewley, Lady: Her "Charity" and its History	1	1710-1840
Hews, Fr., Dunstable	1	1798
Hinton, Jas., M.A., Oxford	6	1792-1820
Hodges, N., Paul's-alley	1	1713
Holden, Jas.	1	1775
Hollis, Thos., Mr., London	6	1730-1736
Howard, John, Mr., Cardington and London	2	1780
Hughes, John, London	1	1768
Hill, T., Carleton	1	1771
Hupton, Job	4	1800
Hutchinson, R., Rotherhithe	1	1773
Hutton, J., Broughton	1	1781
Hymns, Collection of—		
Ash and Evans	..	1769-
Burnham, R.	..	1783
Clark, J., Trowbridge	..	1799
Clarke, W. A., Bunhill-row	..	1788-1801
Cole, C., Whitchurch	..	1789-1792
Deacon, S.	..	1785-1797
Fawcett, J.	..	1782-
Fellowes, J.	..	
Franklin, Jonathan, Croydon	..	1801

Name and Field of Labour.	No. of Works.	Date of Publications.
Gifford, Dr. A.		1766
Hupton, John		
Keach, Benjamin		1700
Keach, Elias		1700
Medley, Sam		1789
Middleton, Jos.		1793
Needham, J.		1768
Rippon, John, D.D.		1782
Ryland, John, D.D.		1773, &c.
Steele, Anne		1760, &c.
Stennett, Joseph		1705-1712
Swaine, Jos., Walworth		1796
Taylor, Dan		1772
Turner, D., Abingdon		1745
Wallin, Benjamin, Maze Pond		1750
Westlake, T.		1789
Wyles, N., Colchester		1700
Inglis, H. D., Edinburgh		1791-1860
Jackson, Alvery, Yorkshire	2	1752
James, Sam	2	1766-1768
Jenkins, Jos., Duke-street	5	1706
Jenkins, Jos., D.D., Walworth	15	1781-1815
Johnson, John, Liverpool	12	1758-1796
Job, David	1	1803
Keeble, J., Blandford-street	1	1805
Killingworth, Grant, Norwich	8	1736-1757
Kimber, Is., Nantwich	1	1756
Kingsford, J., Deal, Portsmouth	1	1795-
Kingsford, Mr. W. M., Canterbury	2	1789-1812
Knott, J., Eythorne	1	1794-
Lacey, J., Portsea	3	1741-1781
Ladson, J., Needingworth	1	1802-
Langdon, J., Hebden Bridge	4	1802-1804
Liddon, J., Hampstead	8	1781-1816
Liele, Geo., Jamaica	1	1796-
Littlewood, T., Rochdale	6	1790-1806
Llewellyn, Thos., LL.D., Prescott-street	1	1747-
Lloyd, J., Tenterden, Colnbrook	6	1768-1799
Lovegrove, R. S., Wallingford	1	1794-
Lyon, W., Dundee	1	1794-
Macgowan, J., Devon square	20	1768-1713
Macgregor, R., London	7	1758-1773
McLean, A., Works	20	1791-1822
Maisters, Jos., Joiners' Hall	11	1717-
Marsom, John F., London	1	1795-
Martin, John, Keppel-street, MSS.	35	1771-1820
Matthews, N., London	1	1742-
[Maurice, M.]	1	1726-
Medley, S., Watford and Liverpool, MSS.	5	1779-1800
Medley, Sarah	1	1807-
Messer, B., Grafton-street	2	1769-1773

N

Name and Field of Labour.	No. of Works.	Date of Publications
Middleton, Jos., Lewes	2	1786-
Miller, John, Pulham Market	1	1720-
Moore, J., Northampton	1	1722-
Moore, W., Redcross-street	3	1793-1796
Morgan, Abel	1	1747-
Morris, Jos., Weston	2	1743-1757
Morris, J. W., Clipstone	5	1792-
Neale, Miss	4	1796-
Needham, J., Hitchin	2	1742-1753
Newton, Jas., Bristol	3	1766-1782
Noble, D., Mill-yard		1761-1781
Northamptonshire History of Churches		1700-1800
Price, H., Liverpool	3	1796-1815
Palmer, T., Hull	1	1750
Parsons, R., Bath	1	1774
Parsons, T., Wilts	2	1791
Pearce, S., Birmingham	9	1796-1806
Pendered, W., Hull	1	1797
Piggott, J., Wild-street	8	1702-1713
Randall, W., Chichester and London	[2w]	1747
Reed, B., Exeter	2	1714-1715
Rees, D., Limehouse	8	1726-1748
Reynolds, J., Curriers' Hall	1	1782
Rhudd, J., Devonshire-square	3	1733-1734
Rhudd, S., M.D., Turners' Hall	4	1732-1742
Richards, W., Lynn	11	1781-1806
Richardson, S., Chester	1	1796
Richardson, T., Pinners' Hall	1	1729
Rippon, John, D.D., London	11	1784-1836
Rippon, Mr. Thos., London	1	1791
Robinson, R., Cambridge	25	1777-1799
Rogers, J., Eynsford	1	1802
Rowles, S., Canterbury, Colnbrook	3	1781-1809
Rutherford, J., Dublin	1	1758
Ryland, J. C., Warwick	32	1757-1792
Ryland, J., D.D., Works, Bristol	50	1769-1825
Sharp, John, Frome	2	
Sheraton, J., Jun., Stockton	1	1782
Shoveller, J., Portsea	1	1803
Sing, J., Bridgnorth	2	1738
Skepp, T., Cripplegate	1	1722-1751
Slee, J., Haworth	3	1779
Smith, Jas., Islington	1	1804
Stanford, J., Hammersmith	1	1784
Stanger, J., Kent	2	1785-1789
Stanford, Jno., D.D., from Maze Pond	1	
Staughton, S., Coventry, Washington	1	
Steele, Anne, Broughton	3	1780-
Stennett, Jos., Pinners' Hall	10	1695-1713
Stennett, Dr. J., Exeter, Little Wild-street	14	1738-1754
Stennett, Dr. S., Little Wild-street	28	1760-1797
Stevens, J., Horsleydown	6	1755-1767
Stewart, T., Windmill-street	1	1803
Stinton, B., MSS. and works	3	1714

Name and Field of Labour.	No. of Works.	Date of Publications
Sutcliffe, John, Olney	6	1783-1808
Swaine, J., Walworth	10	1792-1814
Swanston, A. (Scotch Bt.)	1	1800
Symonds, Joshua, Bedford	1	1767
Taylor, Dan	50	1809
Taylor, Is., Calne	3	1778-1807
Thomas, John (Missionary)	1	1793-1800
Thomas, Joshua, Leominster	5	1786-1794
Tommas, John, Bristol	2	1774-1790
Toms, J., Chard, M.S.	1	
Tomlinson, J., D.D., Taunton, &c.	9	1741-1802
Trivett, Edward, Norwich	1	1770
Tucker, William, Chard	..	1798-1814
Turner, D., M.A., Abingdon	34	1747-1803
Twining, J., Trowbridge	3	1775-1790
Upton, James, London	5	1795-1802
Wallin, B., Maze Pond	20	1748-1782
Wallin, G., Colne	3	1723-1733
Walton, T., Colne	1	1803
Ward, J., LL.D., Gresham Professor	6	1744-1762
Ward, Thomas, Melksham	1	1799
Watt, Dr. James, Glasgow	2	
Weatherley, W., Pinners' Hall	2	1750-1801
Whiston, W. (member of Foster's and Stennett's Church)	50	1702-1745
Whitfield, C., Hamsterley	7	1778-1801
Wilks, M., Norwich	3	1791-1818
Williams, B., Salisbury	1	1780
Williams, T., Ryeford	1	1787
Wilson, S., Prescott-street	20	1732-1750
Winterbotham, W., Plymouth	7	1793-1796

This list of the last century contains 270 authors, and I have about 1,500 of their works. I shall be glad to hear of other authors, and of additional works by authors whose names I have already. There are volumes, and especially single sermons, which would prove very welcome.

CREEDS.

The following are the Baptist CONFESSIONS and CATECHISMS generally accepted as setting forth Baptist doctrine and practice. I have copies of them all.

A CONFESSION OF THE FAITH of the remainder of SMYTH'S Company (Evans) 1611

HELWYS' Declaration of the Faith of the English people at Amsterdam (Barclay) 1611

CONFESSION of the Faith of THE SEVEN CHURCHES in London falsely called Anabaptists 1644

Do., 2nd Edition corrected January, 1645 .. .. ·1646

CONFESSION of Churches in Somerset (partly by Thos. Collier).. .. 1646-1656

Do., Appendix to, by Benj. Cox 1646

N 2

The FAITH AND PRACTICE of thirty Congregations in Beds., Northamptonshire, &c. (G. B.). 1651

3rd Edition of LONDON CONFESSION, with Heart Bleedings 1651

4th Edition.. 1652

5th Edition, Leith 1653

A BRIEF DECLARATION of Faith by Anabaptists met in London. (G. B.) .. 1660

An ORTHODOX CREED, or A PROTESTANT CONFESSION OF FAITH (partly G. and partly P. Baptist) 1679

A CONFESSION of Faith based on the Westminster Assembly's Confession. 1st Edition 1677

A CONFESSION OF FAITH of many Congregations in General Assembly, with Appendix on Baptism and Communion.. 1688

Part of the Edition recommended by the Messengers 1689

GENERAL ASSEMBLY of 1689, Proceedings of, with a General Epistle to the Churches 1689

CONFESSION ordered to be translated into Latin. [Was this done?] 1693

A THIRD EDITION was published in 1699; 4th and 5th in 1719-20; and a Philadelphia Edition in 1742. There are many later Editions as at Manchester, 1851. Many Associations described themselves, up to comparatively recent times, as accepting this Confession.

ARTICLES OF FAITH owned as Orthodox by the Baptist Congregations, and subscribed by their Ministers at Quarter Sessions 1704

(This is based largely on the doctrinal articles of the English Church, and was required under the Toleration Act, and to the exclusion of Popery and Unitarianism.)

Besides these General Confessions some Ministers and some Churches framed Creeds for themselves.

BUNYAN'S Reasons for his Faith and Practice may be found in his Works.

VAVASOR POWELL'S Creed in his LIFE AND DEATH, p. 20; and BENJ. KEACH framed a CONFESSION for the Church over which Dr. Gill afterwards presided.

CATECHISMS.

A Soul-searching Catechism, by CHR. BLACKWOOD, 2nd Edition 1653

Do., do., for Lancashire 1652

B. KEACH'S Primer, Child's Instructors, &c. (for which he was pilloried) .. 166[illegible]

V. POWELL'S Catechism and Concordance. 5th Edition 1673

H. JESSIE'S Catechism for Children 1673

J. S. The Christian Doctrine. A Short Catechism approved by Elders of Baptist Churches 1680

THE BAPTIST CATECHISM, on the basis of the Shorter Catechism prepared by William Collins, and ordered by the Assembly to be printed 1693-4

THE BAPTIST CATECHISM, with Keach's portrait, and often called by this name. 16th Edition 1764

Do., edited by Dr. Rippon, and corrected 1794

Other Editions are:—The 17th, Horselydown; Bristol, 1775; American Edition, Philadelphia, 1751; the Sunday School Union, &c.; in all which Scripture proofs are added.

"THE BAPTIST CATECHISM" was also published by B. BEDDOME, with Scripture expositions, at London, pp. 188, in 1752; and in Bristol, pp. 192, in 1776; and elsewhere. It is based in part on Henry's.

Though "THE BAPTIST CATECHISM" is a common title, the contents differ.

Keach's and Beddome's were best known in the last century.

All these Creeds were prepared in the first instance for explanatory and defensive purposes, and to show in a general way the sentiments of the Body. When adopted by any Church all Sister Churches were left free; and in the Churches adopting them as much freedom was allowed as was consistent with a substantial agreement in the same general truth. (See quotations from Baptist authors in *Schaff's History of the Creeds of Christendom*, Lond., p. 853-4). J. A.

PART VI.

ASSOCIATIONS, CHURCHES AND CHAPELS.

I.—ASSOCIATIONS.

NAME.	When formed.	No. of Churches.	President.	Vice-President.	Treasurer.	Secretaries.
ENGLAND.						
Bedfordshire Union of Christians*	1797	30	Rev. John Brown, D.D.	.. .. ..	Mr. R. Goodman, jun.	Rev. G. H. Jones, Sandy (for Baptist Sub-Committee).
Berkshire	..	20	Rev. J. Cave	Rev. G. J. Knight ..	Mr. Philip Davies ..	,, J. Cave, Wokingham.
Bristol	1640	50	Rev. C. Griffiths ..	Rev. H. Knee.. ..	Mr. Samuel Iles ..	,, G. Jarman, Knowle, Bristol, and Mr. Edward Parsons, 24 Nicholas-street, Bristol.
Buckinghamshire	1867	27	Rev. H. J. Lester ..	Rev. W. Dorey ..	Mr. S. Adcock ..	,, W. Coombs, 180, Cambridge-road, Aylesbury.
Cambridgeshire	1877	28	Rev. J. Carvath ...	Mr. J. Johnson ..	Mr. R. J. Moffat, F.S.S.	,, J. Carvath, Willingham.
Cornwall	1850	8	Rev. C. T. Johnson	Rev. E. Osborne ..	Mr. T. Stocker ..	,, M. L. Gaunt, Helston.
Devonshire	1852	57	Rev. J.F.Toone, B.A.	Rev. G. McFadyean	Mr. W. Hawkes, J.P.	,, E. C. Pike, B.A., Exeter.
East Midland	1892	153	Mr. H. Ashwell, J.P.	Rev. J. Thew	Mr. W. B. Clark ..	,, W. Woods, 11, Winslade-road, Brixton, London, S.W.
Essex Union	1869	31	Rev. E. Dyer	Rev. A. Curtis ..	Mr. S. Young	,, W. Walker, Brentwood.
Gloucestershire and Herefordshire	1841	40	Rev. J. George ..	Rev. E. Davis ..	Mr. H. Rogers, J.P.	,, J. Meredith, Hereford.
Hertfordshire Union ..	1878	25	Mr. J. Bowden ..	Rev. A. E. Jones ..	Mr. J. Marnham, J.P.	,, C. M. Hardy, B.A., Lemsford-road, St. Albans.
Home Counties	1877	56	Mr. J. Corpe	Rev. C. Spurgeon ..	Rev. E. H. Brown ..	,, E.W.Tarbox, Netherwood, Epsom-road, Guildford.
Huntingdonshire†	1861	13	Mr. J. McNish ..	.. .. ..	Mr. W. R. Todd ..	,, Hy. Bell, Houghton, Huntingdon.
Kent and Sussex	1835	55	Rev. W. Townsend	Rev. E. J. Edwards	Mr. G. H. Dean, J.P.	,, N. Dobson, Deal.

* Comprising Union, Baptist, and Congregational Churches. The latter are not included in the number of Churches given.
† There are 13 Churches in the Hunts Association—5 are Baptist, 7 Union, and one Independent.

ASSOCIATIONS—*continued.*

NAME.	When formed.	No. of Churches.	President.	Vice-President.	Treasurer.	Secretaries.
Lancashire and Cheshire	1837	148	Rev. S. W. Bowser, B.A.	Mr. Alderman G. Shepherd, J.P.	Mr. H. Stevenson ..	Rev. C. Williams, Accrington.
London	1865	146	Rev. G. P. MacKay	Rev. F. A. Jones ..	Mr. H. Marnham ..	" J. Fletcher, 322, Commercial-road, E.
Metropolitan Strict ..	1871	62	Mr. C. Wilson ..	Rev. E. Mitchell ..	Mr. C. Wilson ..	" J. Box, 26, Flodden-road, Camberwell, S.E.
Norfolk	1663	32	Rev. J. Jackson ..	Mr. H. P. Gould ..	Mr. J. J. Colman, J.P.	" T. A. Wheeler (Hon.), and Rev. J. M. Hamilton, Lowestoft (Gen.)
Northamptonshire	1764	50	Mr. R. Cleaver, J.P.	Rev. T. Phillips, B.A.	Mr. J. Campion ..	" W. Fidler, Towcester.
Northern	1690	32	Mr. W. Goode Davies	Rev. C. G. Jones ..	Mr. S. B. Burton ..	Mr. J. M. Bartlett, Benwell View, Newcastle-on-Tyne.
Oxfordshire	1802	27	Mr. J. F. Maddox, J.P.	Rev. T. Bentley ..	Mr. I. Alden	Rev. F. E. Blackaby, Stow-on-the-Wold.
Shropshire	1808	17	Rev. H. Reid	Mr. T. Roberts ..	Mr. James Jones ..	" A. Lester, Dawley.
Southern	1823	57	Rev. C. Joseph ..	.. .. ..	Mr. J. H. Blake ..	" J. Hasler, Andover.
Suffolk and Norfolk ..	1829	31	Rev. A. J. Ward ..	.. .. ..	Mr. J. E. Hitchcock	" S. K. Bland, Warrington-rd, Ipswich.
Suffolk and Norfolk Union	1809	19	Rev. G. Cobb	.. .. ..	Mr. James Collier ..	" T. M. Morris, Paget-road, Ipswich.
Western	1823	26	Rev. Levi Palmer ..	Rev. C. H. M. Day	Mr. T Penny and Mr. T. S. Penny	" A. MacDonald, Chard.
West Midland	1892	70	Rev. W. B. Bliss ..	Mr. D. Lewis	Mr. H. P. Chapman	" R. Gray, Valentine-road, King's Heath, Birmingham.
Wilts and East Somerset	1862	31	Rev. F. Pugh	Mr. S. T. Rawlings	Mr. H. J. Deacon ..	" W. H. J. Page, Calne.
Worcestershire	1836	21	Rev. E. J. Crofts ..	Mr. T. T. Allen ..	Rev. J. Lord	" J. Lord, Droitwich.
Yorkshire	1837	127	Mr. William Hirst..	Rev. W. Jones ..	Mr. William Best	" A. P. Fayers, Yeadon, Leeds, and Rev. R. Howarth, Bradford.
WALES AND MONMOUTHSHIRE.						
Baptist Union of Wales ..	1867	..	.. .. ..	Mr. D. Davies, C.C. (Merthyr Tydvil)	Mr. O. Lewis	" W. Morris, Treorky.
Anglesey	1845	35	Rev. W. Price.. ..	.. .. ..	Mr. O. Hughes ..	Mr. E. W. Lewis, Brynteg, Menai Bridge, Anglesey.
Breconshire	1864	29	Mr. M. P. Jones..	Rev. T. Harries ..	Mr. D. Evans ..	Rev. J. L. Evans, Llanfihangel Nantbran.

ASSOCIATIONS—*continued.*

NAME	When formed.	No. of Churches.	President.	Vice-President.	Treasurer.	Secretaries.
Carmarthenshire and Cardiganshire	1832	102	Rev. J. Williams ..	Rev. J. Reynolds ..	Mr. Isaac Phillips ..	Rev. R. H. Jones, St. Clears, Carm.
Carnarvonshire	1845	36	Mr. O. R. Hughes	Rev. D. Davies ..	Mr. R. Williams ..	" J. G. Jones, Penrhyn-deudraeth.
Denbigh, Flint, and Merioneth	1779	104	Mr. R. Edwards ..	Rev. D. Williams ..	Mr. R. Roberts (Ponkey)	" E. K. Jones, Ael-y-bryn, Brymbo, Wrexham.
Glamorganshire East ..	1884	106	Rev. R. O. Jones	Mr. Evan Owen, J.P.	Mr. W. G. Howell and Mr. E. Owen	" T. Davies, Aberaman.
Glamorganshire West ..	1832	80	Rev. T. V. Evans ..	Mr. C. Jones, J.P. ..	Mr. James Williams (Ystalyfera)	Mr. D. Griffiths, 37, Park Terrace, Swansea.
Glamorgan and Carmarthen (English)	1860	82	Rev. E. E. Probert	Rev. J. W. Williams, D.D.	Mr. R. G. Roberts (Swansea)	Rev. W. G. Davies, Penarth, Cardiff.
North Wales English Union	1879	12	Rev. S. Morris, M.A.	.. .. ..	Mr. R. Beck	" J. Raymond, Llandudno.
Old Welsh	1770	43	Mr. D. Davies ..	Mr. T. Edmunds ..	Mr. J. Kinsey ..	" J. Griffiths, Llanidloes, Mont.
Pembrokeshire	1832	62	Mr. D. Richards	Rev. W. Davies ..	Mr. J. Rowlands ..	" W. Griffith, Clynderwen, Pembs.
Monmouthshire English	1857	44	Rev. W. Powell ..	Rev. J. D. Rees ..	Mr. E. Cooke	" D. Bevan Jones, Caerleon, Mon.
Monmouthshire Welsh ..	1831	71	Mr. W. Davies J.P.	Rev. J. Parrish ..	Mr. T. Phillips, J.P. (Abertillery)	" W. Jones, 5, Brynderwyn-road, Maindee, Newport, Mon.
SCOTLAND.						
Baptist Union of Scotland	1869	100	Mr. G. W. Elmslie	Rev. A. Wylie, M.A.	Mr. G. W. Elmslie	" Geo. Yuille, Stirling.
IRELAND.						
Baptist Union of Ireland	..	28	Rev. R. Clark ..	Mr. D. Crosthwaite, LL.D.	Mr. W. Irwin	" J. D. Gilmore, Brannoxtown.

Further details may be found in the Reports by the Associations.

II.—CHURCHES.

N.B.—(1) A List of Churches in Membership with the Baptist Union will be found at page 9.

(2) (U.) denotes a Union Church, composed of Baptists and Pædobaptists with equal rights under the Trust Deed.

(3) (Sc.) "Scotch Baptist."

(4) (C.) after a Minister's Name indicates that he is a Congregationalist.

(5 Places in *Italics* are subordinate stations. Places where Cottage Meetings only are held are not given.

(6) In England and Wales the population of MUNICIPAL BOROUGHS, according to the census of 1891, is inserted where such population is not less than 10,000.

(7) The statistics which follow will in almost all cases be found to agree with those given in the latest annual Reports of the various Associations. In the very few cases, however, where the Associations have not yet found it to be practicable to adopt the Baptist Union form for statistics, the Editor has, whenever possible, obtained Returns direct from the Churches. Churches not in any Association have also been communicated with direct.

(8) ***A List of CHAPELS not connected with Associations, and from which returns cannot be obtained, will be found at page 294. In some of these cases it is known that the Churches have ceased to exist.***

England.

(Aggregate Population, exclusive of Monmouthshire, 27,231,074.)

(Monmouthshire will be found at page 264.)

BEDFORDSHIRE (*Pop.*, 160,704).

(B., Beds Union.)

Churches.	Date.	Chapel seats	No. of Members.	Sunday School Teachers.	No. of Scholars.	Local Preachers.	Pastors.	When settled.	Associations.
Ampthill (U.)	1882	350	98	18	160	3	J. H. Kelly	1890	B.
Bedford (28,023):—									
Bunyan Meeting (U.)	1650	1100	..	..	..	..	J. Brown, D.D. (C.)	1864	B.
Stagsden	..	200							
Goldington	..	200							
Elstow	..	150							
Kempston	..	300							
Mill-street	1793	700	222	34	300	7	W. Turner	1889	B.
Rothsay-road	1830	600	..	..	130	6	J. W. Wren.. ..	1877	
Biggleswade:—									
Old Meeting	1771	600	108	26	295	4	H. G. Stembridge	1888	B.
Dunton	..	120	..	3	60				
Blunham, Old Meeting.	1724	350	40	10	100	..	G. Goodwin.. ..	1895	B.
Carlton	1688	600	70	8	65	1	D. Flavel	1891	B.

BEDFORDSHIRE—*continued.*

Churches.	Date.	Chapel seats.	No. of Members.	Sunday School Teachers.	No. of Scholars.	Local Preachers.	Pastors.	When settled.	Associations.
Cotton End	1776	500	70	9	95	2	W. H. Smith ..	1890	B.
Cardington									
Cranfield :—									
East End	1660	120	50	7	57	..	S. McAlister ..	1871	B.
Dunstable :—									
West-street	1836	650	80	20	109	3	E. A. Smith ..	1895	B.
Heath & Reach	1842	180	20	10	50	1	G. Durrell of Leighton	1878	B.
Hinwick (see Northamptonshire)									
Houghton Regis	1760	500	139	34	253	6	J. T. Frost	1886	B.
Sundon	..	100							
Streatley..	..	70							
Keysoe, Brookend ..	1652	500	101	14	130	..	T. Varley	1887	B.
Leighton Buzzard :—									
Hockliffe-street ..	1835	850	154	29	224	3	G. Durrell	1875	B.
Lake-street	1775	400	52	13	101	1	F. E. Robinson, B.A., B.D.	1894	B.
Ledburn..	..	80							
Luton (30,006) :—									
Castle-street (U.) ..	1836	1050	460	50	468	15	H. Collings	1866	B.
Caddington	1837	225	..	..	82				
Perry Green	1841	300	..	..	170				
Park-street	1689	1000	640	50	759	22	Frank Thompson	1892	B.
Pepperstock	..	300	..	21	142				
Limbury..	..	130	..	8	65				
Stopsley	..	140	..	10	100				
Wellington-street ..	1846	900	498	50	691	16	G. D. Hooper ..	1893	B.
Woodside	1862	110	26	16	60				
Maulden (U.)	1768	400	84	12	118	..	J. R. Andrews ..	1894	B.
Renhold	1873	150	25	6	42	..	.. ..	..	B.
Ridgmount	1701	500	132	11	114	1	J. Palmer	1891	B.
Riseley	1839	270	9	5	36	..	.. ..	..	B.
Sandy	1858	550	134	20	234	2	G. H. Jones.. ..	1891	B.
Shefford (U.)..	1829	350	54	9	90	2	L. Humby	1895	B.
Stondon	1865	200	9						
Staughton, Little.. ..	1766	450	50	8	75	..	C. B. Warren ..	1872	
Stevington	1655	400	36	7	50	..	S. Williams.. ..	1894	B.
Stotfold	1832	250	33	11	104	..	J. Hart	1889	B.
Thurleigh	1837	250	62	8	68	..	G. Chandler ..	1866	B.
Keysoe-Row	..	100	..	7	48				
Toddington	1816	200	..	..	..	..	H. C. Field	1891	B.
Wootton, High-street ..	1826	200	53	7	70		J. H. Readman ..	1870	B.

BERKSHIRE (*Pop.*, 238,709).
(B., Berks.)

Churches.	Date.	Chapel seats.	No. of Members.	Sunday School Teachers.	No. of Scholars.	Local Preachers.	Pastors.	When settled.	Associations.
Abingdon, Ock-street..	1652	650	113	17	128	27	W. H. Doggett ..	1894	B.
Cothill									
Drayton									
Fyfield									
Marcham									
Ascot	1886	120	31	5	45		.. ..	..	B.
London Road ..	..	..	..	2	45				
Beech Hill	1796	140	24	4	29		Alfred Ward ..	1880	
Bourton (Shrivenham)	1851	250	39	4	44		R. W. Mansfield..	1867	B.
Bracknell	1886	200	31	5	60		.. ..	..	H.C.
Brimpton	1843	140	24	5	41	3	J. G. Skelly.. ..	1891	B.
Faringdon	1576	250	69	8	113	9	H. Smith	1889	B.
Buscot	1880	100	..	5	30				
Kingston Lisle ..	1790	80	..		12				
Little Coxwell ..	1880	100							
Maidenhead (10,607):—									
Marlow-road	1873	240	120	17	186	6	H. J. Preece ..	1888	B.
Boyn Hill	..	..	..	8	51				
Moreton, South	1834	70	8	2	20		G. Russell ,. ,.	1895	
Newbury (11,002):—									
North Brook-street..	1640	500	316	48	419	16	G. J. Knight ..	1889	B.
Headley	1836	120							
Long-lane	1813	120							
Berries Bank.. ..	1822	100							
Ashmore-green ..	1869	100							
Ramsdale									
Reading (60,054):—									
King's-road	1640	920	395	36	418	20	F. Jackson, M.A...	1896	B.
Silver-street	1860	200	..	20	266				
Hurst	1849	120	26	10	82				
Sherfield..	1831	130							
East Ilsley	1864	150	18	5	42				
Ashampstead.. .	1840	100	18	4	20				
Compton..	1851	100	3						
Streatley	1858	120	13						
West Ilsley	1866	100	18		24				
Oxford-road	1859	500	77		100	3	W. H. Rose.. ..	1886	
Knowl Hill									
Carey	1866	700	166	28	230	6	W. A. Findlay ..	1888	B.
Calcot									
Wycliffe	1881	600	253		425	9	W. G. Hailstone..	1887	B.
Grovelands	1887	350	112	30	284		R. M. Hunter ..	1895	B.
Sandhurst	1884	130	20	6	40		.. ..	..	B.
Sunningdale	1828	130	61	7	38	2	.. ..	..	B.
Wallingford :—									
Thames-street	1794	350	85	12	60	3	H. R. Salt	1883	B.
Roke	1798	100	..	2	45				
Cholsey	1825	150	..	3	20				
Wantage	1648	300	55	10	110	2	G. A. Ambrose ..	1892	B.
Garston-lane.. ..									
Windsor, New (12,327):									
Victoria-street	1838	350	154	24	200	8	J. Aubrey	1893	B.
Wokingham	1774	550	167	18	135	3	J. Cave..	1885	B.
Sindlesham	..	180	..	6	33				
Finchampstead ..	..	150							
New Mill	..	120							

BUCKINGHAMSHIRE (*Pop.*, 185,284).

(B., Bucks. H., Herts Union. H.C., Home Counties. N., Northamptonshire.)

Churches.	Date.	Chapel seats.	No. of Members.	Sunday School Teachers.	No. of Scholars.	Local Preachers.	Pastors.	When settled.	Associations.
Amersham:—									
Lower Meeting ..	1782	450	120	20	127	2	J. W. Colley ..	1894	B.
Aylesbury :—									
Walton-street	1801	220	6[illegible]	10	90	2	D. Witton	1893	
Bierton (Aylesbury) ..	1851	200	30	12	82	3			
Buckland Common (Tring) ..	1860	150	12	9	60	3			
Chenies	1789	200	40	5	33		.. ..	..	H.
Chesham :—									
Broadway	1706	850	335	56	520	23	W. B. Taylor ..	1883	B.
Ashley Green	..	80							
Charteredge	..	100							
Vale	..	60							
Lower	1714	500	183	42	195	10	L. G. Carter ..	1890	B.
Hyde Heath	..	120							
Ley Hill	..	80	..	14	70				
Whelpley Hill ..	..	50							
London-road, Zion ..	1868	500	178	31	221	10	H. Trueman ..	1890	B.
Cuddington	1831	140	24	5	38		.. ..	..	B.
Dinton	1847	120	15	6	55		.. ..	..	B.
Drayton Parslow ..	1805	150	34	8	53		} J. A. Andrews ..	1893	B.
Mursley	1838	150	73	14	92				
Newton Longville ..	1812	160	23	6	26	2			
Farnham Common ..	1874	60	..	2	25		H. Stone	1874	
Fenny Stratford	1800	750	160	24	225	4	H. S. Smith	1880	B.
Ford (Aylesbury)	1716	250	..		..		.. ..	..	B.
Gold-hill (Chalfont) ..	1774	450	76	12	85	4	.. ..	..	B.
Seer Green	1843	140	41	9	70	3			
Haddenham	1810	500	151	2	182	8	J. Edwards	1891	B.
Chearsley	1854	100							
Hanslope, Long-street (see Northamptonshire.)									
Ickford (Thame)	1825	120	..		..		.. ..	..	B.
Kingshill, Little	1814	300	60	13	85		J. Robinson	1886	B.
Lee Common	1854	100	17	8	74	4			
Long Crendon	1799	480	66	25	258		J. L. Cooper ..	1894	B.
Loosley Row	1862	230	57	16	100		.. ..	..	B.
Marlow, Gt., Glade-rd.	1855	250	46	10	60	2	J. E. Joynes ..	1895	
Marsworth (See Hertfordshire)									
Missenden, Great ..	1778	370	85	10	85		W. Dorey	1888	D.
Olney	1694	500	89	16	160	3	M. Joslin	1893	N.
Lavendon	..	140	..	7	90				
Ravenstone	..	80	..	3	30				
Weston Underwood	..	80							
Princes Risborough ..	1707	600	125	17	..	10	.. ..	..	B.
Longwick	..	100							

BUCKINGHAMSHIRE—*continued*

Churches.	Date.	Chapel seats.	No. of Members.	Sunday School Teachers.	No. of Scholars.	Local Preachers.	Pastors.	When settled.	Associations.
Quainton	1817	200	47	12	100	2	H. J. Lester ..	1880	B.
Slough	1894	150	32	5	26	..	A. E. Phillips ..	1894	H.C.
Speen (P. Risborough)	1813	400	88	23	110	..	W. Harrison ..	1892	B.
Stantonbury	1856	200	37	14	120	1	.. ..	..	N.
Stony Stratford and Loughton	1656	400 / 100	163	29	230	13	S. Cheshire.. ..	1893	N.
Cosgrove..	..	..	15						
Towersey (Thame) ..	1837	130	..	..	..	..	.. ..	..	B.
Wendover	1683	200	78	12	..	..	J. Wilkins	1893	B.
Weston Turville (U.) ..	1855	170	37	8	53	..	G. Barnes	1891	B.
Winslow, Tabernacle..	1864	450	47	11	60	1	H. K. Byard ..	1892	B.
Swanbourne	1809	250	18	4	32	..			
Wooburn Green	1833	130	10	4	30	..	F. Tilbury	1889	
Wraysbury (Staines) ..	1868	180	35	6	76	..	.. ..	..	H.C.
Wycombe (13,435):—									
Bridge-street, Zion ..	1680	400	65	14	200	3	J. Morling	1891	
Union Church	1845	550	210	23	240	10	C. Hobbs.. ..	1895	B.
Holmer Green ..	1877	150	39	12	57				
Wycombe Marsh ..	..	120	..	20	99				

CAMBRIDGESHIRE (*Pop.*, 188,961).

(C., Cambridgeshire. E.M., East Midland.)

Churches.	Date.	Chapel seats.	No. of Members.	Sunday School Teachers.	No. of Scholars.	Local Preachers.	Pastors.	When settled.	Associations.
Aldreth	..	200	46	7	50	..	C. W. Dunn.. ..	1866	
Burwell :—									
North-street	1851	500	75	14	120	..	H. A. Fletcher ..	1892	C.
Cambridge (36,983):—									
Eden	1823	700	124	31	189	1	J. Jull	1879	
St. Andrew's-street..	1721	750	638	43	394	19	T. Graham Tarn	1879	C.
Cambridge-place ..	..	200							
Mill-road	1881	450	..	34	530				
Nelson-street	..	200							
Zion	1837	900	398	36	592	6	H. Frank Griffin	1884	C.
Newmarket-road ..	1889	150	..	21	180				
Caxton	1842	300	54	12	71	2	W. Kelsey	1891	C.
Longstowe									
Chatteris :—									
West Park-street ..	1783	500	72	19	200	9	W. K. Bryce ..	1894	C.
Forty Foot Bank ..	1860	100	4	3	50	..			
Park-street, Zion ..	1819	900	90	25	190	..	H. M. Winch ..	1895	

CAMBRIDGESHIRE—*continued.*

Churches.	Date.	Chapel seats.	No. of Members.	Sunday School Teachers.	No. of Scholars.	Local Preachers.	Pastors.	When settled.	Associations.
Chesterton	1844	300	90	17	140	..	T. T. Ball	1889	C.
Chittering	1858	120	17	7	60	..	Mark Wyatt	1879	C.
Cottenham:—									
Old Meeting	1780	750	174	29	176	1	C. T. Allen	1894	C.
Ely, Zion	1820	250	13						
Gamlingay, Old Mtng.	1710	500	92	18	215	..	H. J. Milledge	1885	C.
Haddenham	1814	500	159	..	182	..	W. Higgins	1892	C.
Harston	1786	337	89	13	160	..	F. Potter	1890	C.
Histon	1858	325	89	24	191	4	R. Smith	1895	C.
Milton	1865	150							
Isleham:—High-street	1812	450	153	31	215	4	S. B. Newling	1892	C.
Isleham Fen	1875	150							
Pound-lane (U.)	1693	450	72	12	95	..	J. A. Wilson	1872	C.
Landbeach	1828	320	36	..	60	..	..	..	C.
March:—									
Centenary Church	1700	750	156	40	320	6	I. L. Near	1894	C.
Whittlesea-road	1845	80							
Chain Bridge	1859	120							
Providence	1835	750	155	24	310	3	B. J. Northfield	1889	
Melbourn	1675	600	77	6	60	1	R. A. Belsham	1894	C.
Over	1737	350	40	9	90	..	F. S. Reynolds	1891	
Prickwillow	1815	400	98	10	80	4	..	..	C.
Shelford, Great	1825	410	108	13	135	..	D. Bruce	1890	C.
Soham	1752	500	127	15	170	2	F. W. Dunster	1889	C.
Swavesey:—									
Main Road	1789	400	45	5	50				
Bethel	1840	400	57	11	92	4	B. G. Knight	1892	C.
Thetford (Ely)	..	150	26	4	60	1	F. W. Dunster, of Soham	1889	C.
Tydd St. Giles	1792	120	..	..	..	..	..	..	E.M.
Waterbeach, High-st.	1660	600	111	26	143	2	H. Jenner	1894	C.
Willingham, Tabernacle	1873	600	165	20	165	..	J. Carvath	1891	C.
High Street	1662	800	..	12	70	..	W. Gill	1893	
Wisbech:—									
Ely Place	1665	850	121	13	160	4	A. G. Everett	1892	C.
West Walton	..	150	..	4	40				
Upper Hill-street	1792	600	211	..	..	..	J. Cockett J. W. Campbell	1862 1886	C.
North Brink									
Norwich-road, Walsoken									
Victoria-road	1857	60							
Witchford (Ely)	1871	135	9	..	..	..	..	..	C.

CHESHIRE (*Pop.*, 730,058).

L.C., Lancashire and Cheshire. D.F.M., Denbigh, Flint, and Merioneth.)

Churches.	Date.	Chapel seats.	No. of Members.	Sunday School Teachers.	No. of Scholars.	Local Preachers.	Pastors.	When settled.	Associations.
Alderley Edge, Brook-lane (U.)	1890	160	17	10	60	3	.. ..	..	L.C.
Altrincham, Tabernacle	1887	450	104	12	130	..	F. C. Lloyd	1893	L.C.
Audlem	1814	120	28	3	22	..	J. F. Matthews ..	1890	L.C.
Birkenhead (99,857):—									
Grange-road	1858	620	212	49	600	7	S. W. Bowser, B.A.	1881	L.C.
Cathcart-street ..	1878	270	92	23	326	4	E. Peake	1894	
Jackson-street	1868	550	62	16	190	1	R. Frame	1894	L.C.
Woodlands (W.) ..	1839	300	146	12	113	1	J. Davies	1884	DFM
Chester (37,105):—									
Grosvenor-park ..	1871	400	146	20	243	7	J. B. Morgan ..	1889	L.C.
Milton-st., Ebenezer	1877	800	95	20	230	3	W. Povey.. ..	1895	
Hoole									
Northgate-st. (W.) ..	1860	200	46	5	41	..	M. F. Wynne ..	1889	DFM
Crewe (28,761):—									
Victoria-street	1849	350	126	26	160	2	W. Hughes	1890	L.C.
Underwood-lane ..	1878	300	..	8	60				
Union-street	1883	640	89	16	160	2	J. Thomas	1893	L.C.
Disley, Wycliffe Hall ..	1893	200	25	10	65	2	J. Lister	1893	L.C.
Egremont, Liscard-road (U.)	1864	500	215	23	215	..	A. Gordon, M.A..	1888	L.C.
Frodsham	1889	300	25	20	150	..	A. H. Sayers (C.)	1894	L.C.
Haslington (Crewe) ..	1884	200	46	11	82	..	.. ..	..	L.C.
Hill Cliff (Warrington)	1522	300	47	16	96	..	J. S. Hughes ..	1893	L.C.
Hyde (30,670)	1869	325	52	16	101	..	.. ..	..	L.C.
Latchford (Warrington)	1852	300	83	15	135	..	C. Andrew ..	1895	L.C.
Little Leigh (Wrringtn)	1820	200	35	4	46	..	J. Aldis, Jun. ..	1895	L.C.
Macclesfield (36,009):—									
St. George's-street ..	1822	550	137	14	171	2	E. A. Hobby ..	1891	L.C.
Nantwich	1862	350	62	30	260	1	J. R. Mitchell ..	1894	L.C.
Willaston	1878	150							
New Brighton	1894	364	44	8	103	..	E. Morley	1894	
Onston	1849	200	34	7	50	1	.. ..	..	L.C.
Poynton	1862	180	31	9	64	1	G. Walker	1862	L.C.
Sale (Manchester) ..	1875	350	106	16	149	1	.. ..	..	L.C.
Seacombe, Brighton-st. (W.)	1877	Hall	19	2	12	..	.. ..	..	DFM
Stalybridge (26,783):—									
Cross Leech-street..	1838	500	62	22	130	2	A. Bowden	1886	L.C.
Wakefield-road ..	1808	750	233	31	263	1	C. Rushby	1881	L.C.
Dukenfield	..	..	..	17	102				
Stockport (70,263):—									
Greek-street	1838	920	284	20	280	8	.. ..	..	L.C.
Thomson-street ..	..	..	15	15	200				
Grove-lane Cheadle Hulme..	1840	..	12	5	44	1			
Brook-lane Alderley									
Tarporley	1717	200	57	10	55	1	.. ..	..	L.C.
Warford and..	1600	120	23	2	25	..	J. Davenport ..	1879	
Bramhall	1856	180							
Wheelock Heath.. ..	1823	250	57	8	98	1	.. ..	..	L.C.

CORNWALL (*Pop.*, 322,571)

(C., Cornwall. D., Devon.

Churches.	Date.	Chapel seats.	No. of Members.	Sunday School Teachers.	No. of Scholars.	Local Preachers.	Pastors.	When settled.	Associations.
Calstock and..	1816	220	92	24	175	4	A. Pidgeon	1886	D.
Metherill	..	150							
Falmouth :—									
Market-street	1772	900	272	31	542	4	C. T. Johnson ..	1888	C.
Hayle	1856	300	31	18	73	2	M. L. Gaunt, of Helston, and F. W. Reynolds, of Redruth	..	C.
Helston, Wendron-st...	1804	400	32	10	81		M. L. Gaunt ..	1893	C.
Launceston	1876	130	22	8	31	6	H. Smart, *See also Devon*	1891	D.
Greystone :.. ..	1850	80	15	4	15				
Liskeard, Dean-street..	1876	350	61	20	165		G. F. Payn ..	1895	C.
Newquay, Ebenezer ..	1822	100	14						
Penzance (12,432) :—									
Clarence-street.. ..	1802	600	..		..		.. ..	..	C.
Redruth, Ebenezer ..	1802	400	35	9	75		F. W. Reynolds ..	1894	C.
St. Austell, Ebenezer..	1833	400	78	33	290		E. Osborne	1893	C.
Saltash	1790	400	87	15	130		G. McFadyean ..	1879	D.
Burraton									
Carkele									
Truro (11,131)	1789	500	68	17	248	4	.. ..	..	C.

CUMBERLAND (*Pop.*, 266,549).

(L. C., Lancashire and Cheshire.)

Churches.	Date.	Chapel seats.	No. of Members.	Sunday School Teachers.	No. of Scholars.	Local Preachers.	Pastors.	When settled.	Associations.
Broughton, Gt.	1648	200	39	6	70		A. Greer	1887	L.C.
Carlisle (39,176)	1880	450	82	15	113		F. C. Haggart ..	1890	L.C.
Maryport, Trinity ..	1808	700	183	55	480	2	W. H. Elliott ..	1889	L.C.
Grasslot									
Furnau-road	..	150	23						
Millom	1879	280	66	3	150	2	J. Hodgson	1894	L.C
Workington (23,490) ..	1882	400	170	34	382	5	J. H. Brooksbank..	1894	L.C.
Marsh Side	..		..	6	40				

DERBYSHIRE (*Pop.*, 528,033).

(E. M., East Midland. Y., Yorkshire.)

Churches.	Date.	Chapel seats.	No. of Members.	Sunday School Teachers.	No. of Scholars.	Local Preachers.	Pastors.	When settled.	Associations.
Belper	1818	600	..	..	..	..	.. ..	..	E.M.
Birches-lane (Alfreton)	1864	200	24	10	80				
Cauldwell (see Staffordshire)									
Chellaston	1868	100	..	..	..	..	.. ..	..	E.M.
Chesterfield (22,009) ..	1861	350	99	24	204	8	R. I. Mesquitta ..	1886	E.M.
Clay Cross	1863	210	42	14	150	..	.. ..	..	E.M.
Cotmanhay (see Nottinghamshire)									
Crich	1838	250	54	9	104				
Derby (94,146):—									
Green Hill, Trinity..	1795	400	194	24	352	6	W. F. Harris ..	1884	E.M.
Osmaston-road.. ..	1831	900	529	44	794	..	J. Mursell	1891	E.M.
Pear Tree	1873	180	..	28	455				
St. Mary's-gate ..	1797	1200	386	47	311	13	A. Mills	1889	E.M.
Willington	..	120	27	7	40				
Littleover	..	200	42	6	70				
Junction-street ..	..	400	132	30	900	..	P. A. Hudgell ..	1895	
Boyer-street	..	250	12	10	160				
Watson-street	1867	200	102	20	300	6	.. ..	..	E.M.
Dronfield	1846	300	159	22	300	1	C. J. Rendell ..	1892	Y.
Duffield	1810	200	40	7	72	2	.. ..	..	E.M.
Heanor	1861	450	90	28	360	..	G. D. Jeffcoat ..	1895	E.M.
Ilkeston (19,744):—									
Queen-street	1784	500	53	13	150	1			
South-street	1881	200	91	19	222	3			
Kilbourne	1832	130	41	7	75	..	.. ..	..	E.M
LangleyMill(nr.Nottm.)	1837	300	50	18	260	..	.. ..	..	E.M
Long Eaton:—									
Station-street	1877	450	111	29	202	1	.. ..	..	E.M.
Chapel-street	1887	room	92	26	150	1	E. Webb	1893	E.M.
Loscoe	1783	400	78	28	206	3	.. ..	..	E.M.
Measham and	1811	500	126	34	223	8	W. S. Lord	1891	E.M.
Netherseal..	1840	200							
Melbourne and	1750	450	162	38	290	8	D. Chinnery ..	1894	E.M.
Ticknall	..	..	9	1	40				
Milford	1849	150	19	6	50	..	.. ..	..	E.M.
New Whittington.. ..	1862	350	..	..	..	..	.. ..	..	Y.
Riddings and..	1806	400	68	16	130	3	W. C. Sage, M.A., B.D.	1894	E.M.
Swanwick	1796	500	67	20	190	3			
Ripley	1833	450	143	26	413	3	S. S. Allsop.. ..	1895	E.M.
Sawley	1783	270	96	26	160	..	.. ..	..	E M.
Smalley	1785	300	68	17	80	1	E. Hilton	1884	E.M.
Stonebroom (Alfreton)	1877	250	38	13	113	..	.. ..	..	E.M.
Swadlincote	1867	500	158	24	367	8	K. H. Bond	1890	E.M.
Hartshorne	..	..	3	4	23				
Wirksworth	1818	300	144	29	223	10	B. Noble	1889	E.M.
Shottle	1812	150							
Bonsall	1823	150							

DEVONSHIRE (*Pop.*, 631,808).

(D., Devon.)

Churches.	Date.	Chapel seats.	No. of Members.	Sunday School Teachers.	No of Scholars.	Local Preachers.	Pastors.	When settled.	Associations
Appledore	1823	400	76	20	168	2	W. L. Crathern ..	1888	D
Westward Ho!	1887	140							
Ashwater	1820	80	96	45	170	13	.. ..	..	D.
Halwill	..	200							
Germansweek	..	120							
Halwill Station	1885	110							
Muckworthy	1886	80							
Bampton	1690	300	30	11	95	3	E. Scott ..	1876	D.
Shillingford	..	100	..	2	40				
Barnstaple (13,058):—									
Boutport-street	1833	800	203	31	370	1	G. R. Hern ..	1894	D.
Bideford	1821	500	185	26	328	10	F. Durbin ..	1894	D.
Abbotsham	1852	120	..	6	38				
Bishop's Teignton	1885	150	18	4	30	..	G. Duckett..	1891	
Bovey Tracey	1772	500	37	9	84	3	W. H. Payne ..	1895	D.
Lustleigh	..	..	..	1	18				
Bradninch	1814	270	75	16	142	2	R. C. Lemin ..	1892	D.
Brayford	1815	140	..	..	..	..	T. Breewood ..	1895	D.
Bratton Fleming	1850	150							
Stowford	..	100							
Brixham	1797	600	198	46	610	2	W. A. Barker ..	1891	D.
Broad Clyst	1880	210	26	..	..	..	G. Keen, of Thorverton	1893	D.
Budleigh Salterton	1844	300	32	5	25	2	.. ..	..	D.
Chudleigh	1848	200	27	12	70	2	C. Stovell ..	1889	D.
Combmartin	1850	300	144	10	109	..	W. Ewens ..	1885	D.
Kentisbury	1850	150							
Croyde and	1824	150	20	7	65	3	W. Leyshon ..	1889	D.
Georgeham	1884	120	20	7	41	1			
Cullompton	1745	270	86	19	210	5	J. Horne ..	1892	D.
Ashill	1832	100							
Dartmouth	1600	350	53	15	146	1	J. G. Scott ..	1894	D.
Devonport (54,803):—									
Hope Chapel	1852	850	110	21	136	..	Albert Braine ..	1883	D.
Morice-square	1798	650	158	24	290	2	H. N. Mitchell ..	1890	D.
Pembroke-street	1789	430	54	17	169	2	*Colporteur* ..	..	D.
Dolton	1839	200	49	6	37	5	G. J. Whiting ..	1892	D.
Beaford	..	120	..	2	33				
Kingscote	..	120	..	2	18				
Exeter (37,404):—									
Bartholomew-street	1817	800	68	15	120	3	E. Francis ..	1894	D.
South-street	1656	700	258	41	410	13	D. P. McPherson, B.D.	1894	D.
Christow	..	..	18						
Dunsford	..	..	19						
Wonford	..	60							
Exmouth	1891	Hall	29	..	..	..	R. A. Good ..	1895	D.
Frithelstock	1833	150	15	6	42	9	A. O. Shaw ..	1891	D.
Newton	1830	80	7	6	35				
Caute	1840	70	12	6	30				
Tythecott	1840	60	8						

DEVONSHIRE—*continued.*

Churches.	Date.	hapel seats.	No. of Members.	nday School Teachers.	No. of Scholars.	Local Preachers.	Pastors.	When settled.	Associations
Hatherleigh	1835	250	46	10	50	12	C. L. Gordon ..	1892	D.
Sheepwash	..	120	28	2	15				
Inwardleigh	..	100	20	12	22				
Hemyock and	1833	200 }	53	4	58	6	J. L. Smith	1886	D.
Saint Hill	1803	150 }							
Bolham Water ..	..	60							D.
Honiton	1817	350	181	19	156	3	A. Stock, B.A., B.D.	1887	D.
Luppitt	1859	120	..	6	70				
Awliscombe	1869	130							
Ilfracombe, High-street	1851	550	166	14	160	4	T. Philpot	1894	D.
Kilmington & Loughwd	1650	340	58	12	69	5	R. Bastable	1876	D.
Kingsbridge	1640	350	119	17	131	4	W. T. Adey	1893	D.
Lifton	1850	200	14	..	..	4	Henry Smart (*see also Cornwall*)	1891	D.
Thornecross	1881	100	7	5	30	1			
Sprytown									
Malborough and	1839	200	48	10	84	2	} G. W. Ball ..	1894	D.
Salcombe	1867	290	32	8	77	..			
Modbury	1791	260	103	12	110	2	E. Spanton	:891	D.
Lupridge	1873	60							
St. Ann's	1888	60	..	4	18				
Moretonhampstead ..	..	140	15	2	16	..	.. ..	..	D.
Newton Abbot, East-st.	1819	500	113	32	360	3	S. Lyne	1884	D.
Denbury									
Okehampton and	1882	180	90	13	102	10	} E. C. Monk ..	1895	D.
Sourton	1860	120	30	10	40	3			
Ottery St. Mary	1874	350	..	..	..	..	H. Davis	1876	D.
Paignton	1886	300	90	11	101	8	W. F. Price	1892	D.
Stoke Gabriel ..	1823	200	..	6	40				
Plymouth (84,248) :—									
George-street	1640	1000	547	45	638	13	S. Vincent	1883	D.
Car-green	..	100	41	8	51	..	} *A. T. Head* ..	1878	
Ford	..	200	90	23	247	..			
Hooe	..	100	13	10	60	..			
Lower-street	1849	200	..	17	500	..			
Mutley	1876	860	276	53	603	7	{ Benwell Bird .. { H. Henderson ..	1876 1894	} D.
Buckland Monachorum	1850	150	16	2	12				
Meavy	1840	150	10						
Millbrook	1821	150	22						
West Hill									
South Molton	1841	250	12	..	..	..	.. ..	..	D.
Stonehouse, Ebenezer	1873	280	24	..	..	2	W. Trotman ..	1879	
Teignmouth	1865	380	50	7	85	7	S. J. Thorpe ..	1894	D.
Shaldon	1883	150	9	2	16				
Thorverton	1832	165	35	7	60	..	G. Keen	1893	D.
Bramford Speke ..	..	120							
Tiverton (10,892) ..	1607	860	210	36	506	6	J. F. Toone, B.A.	1888	D.
Ash Thomas	1890	80	..	2	20				
Butterleigh									

DEVONSHIRE—*continued*.

Churches.	Date.	Chapel seats.	No. of Members.	Sunday School Teachers.	No. of Scholars.	Local Preachers.	Pastors.	When settled.	Associations.
Torquay (25,534) :—									
Upton Vale	1832	1000	359	33	379	10	W. Emery	1885	D.
Barton	..	130	..	2	15				
Compton	..	100	..	6	63				
Hele	..	180	..	6	56				
Torrington, Great ..	1820	400	103	25	245	5	G. F. Owen	1891	D.
Totnes, Fore-street ..	1873	250	144	19	263	8	G. D. Evans ..	1891	D.
Little Hempstone ..	1874	90	..		32				
Tuckenhay	1874	120							
Uffculme and Prescott	1743	400	69	10	80	4	W. Gillard	1889	D.
Lamb	1885	50							
Culmstock	1889	150							
pottery, Newhouse ..	1655	200	43		45	..	W. Gliddon	1894	D.
Churchinford ..	..	100							
Yarcombe	1829	140	29	4	..	..	J. Powell	1874	

DORSETSHIRE (*Pop*., 194,517).

(W., Western. W. E. S., Wilts and East Somerset. S., Southern.)

Churches.	Date.	Chapel seats.	No. of Members.	Sunday School Teachers.	No. of Scholars.	Local Preachers.	Pastors.	When settled.	Associations.
Bridport	1830	300	119	16	165	..	.. ..	..	W.
Buckland Newton ..	1862	150	24	5	27	..	.. ..	..	W.
Dorchester Dorford ..	1648	300	66	7	65	..	R. B. Clare	1891	W.
Gillingham	1840	400	81	12	122	4	T. Hayden	1876	W.E.S
East Stour	..	100							
Fifehead	..	100							
Iwerne Minster	1831	150	22	3	40	..	J. E. Evans.. ..	1892	W.E.S
Lyme Regis, Silver-st.	1655	350	57	10	80	..	E. Marks	1881	W.
Harcombe	..	50							
Parkstone, Upper	1888	418	77	17	175	4	R. B. Morrison ..	1891	S.
Poole (15,438) :—									
Hill-street	1805	400	194	20	202	8	R. Walker	1881	S.
Corfe Mullen	1813	140	..	4	61				
Heatherland	1877	240	..	16	195	..	S. Flemington ..	1892	
Sherborne	1884	200	58	6	56	..	F. J. Walkey ..	1894	W.
Weymouth (13,866) :—									
Bank-buildings	1813	500	168	34	263	..	G. Robinson ..	1890	W.
Putton	1862	200							
Wimborne, Grove-road	1882	180	..	..	..	..	.. ..	..	S.
Mission Stations :—									
Piddletrenthide ..	..	300	..	..	..	..	*Evangelist*	..	W.
WinterbourneAbbas	..	100	..	..	..	..			
Muckleford	..	130	..	..	..	..			

DURHAM (*Pop.*, 1,016,559).

(N., Northern. D. F. M., Denbigh, Flint, and Merioneth.)

Churches.	Date.	Chapel seats.	No. of Members.	Sunday School Teachers.	No of Scholars.	Local Preachers.	Pastors.	When settled.	Associations.
Bishop Auckland.. ..	1873	300	35	8	67	2	A. Westwood ..	1893	N.
Witton-park	1857	200	11	4	35				
Consett, Front-street ..	1870	300	65	10	120		T. Durant	1885	N.
Crook	1892	220	43	14	171		A. G. Barton ..	1890	N.
Darlington (38,060):—									
Grange-road	1846	650	248	31	272		J. Duncan, M.A...	1889	N.
Gateshead (85,692):—									
Durham-road	1877	850	300	24	390	8	D. P. Packer ..	1894	N.
Oakwellgate	..		..	20	220				
Cato-street	..		..	5	50				
Hamsterley	1652	200	39	6	47		W. H. Rowling ..	1890	N.
Hartlepool (21,271) ..	1845	500	83	20	260		C. W. Vaughan ..	1890	N.
Hartlepool, W. (42,710)	1862	550	144	20	298		A. W. Curwood ..	1889	N.
Middleton-in-Teesdale	1827	260	102	16	130	8	J. Charter	1880	N.
Egglesburn	1873	120							
Forest	1833	130							
Rowley and Blackhill ..	1652	450	208	35	253	12	E. W. Jenkins ..	1878	N.
Shotley Field									
Shields, South (78,391):									
Imeary-st., Emanuel	1893		162	9	202	2	E. Mason	1893	
Laygate-lane, Tabernacle	1841	900	192	47	450	4	D. A. Spence ..	1894	N.
Westoe-road	1821	750	128	42	480		W. H. Gorham ..	1892	N.
Anderson's-lane ..									
Percy-street									
Spennymoor..	1876	250	49	12	100	4	.. ..	..	N.
Spennymoor (Welsh) ..	..	Sch.	34	12	60		W. Hughes	1874	D F M
Stockton (49,708):—									
Wellington Street ..	1741	500	373	27	380	4	T. L. Edwards ..	1884	
Northcote-street ..	1887	250	161	25	293	4	D. Ross	1890	N.
St. Ann's-road (W.)..	1864	450	..		..		.. ..	..	D F M
Sunderland (131,015):—									
Lindsay-road	1790	750	124	26	268		H. C. Bailey ..	1889	N.
Monkwearmouth:									
Barclay-street ..	1834	750	77	8	152	4	G. Wilson	1890	N.
Waterhouses..	1871	200	180	38	350	18	.. ..	..	N.
Langley Park ..	1881	60							
Ushaw Moor.. ..	1882	60							
Langley Moor ..									
Wolsingham..	1830	250	46	2	110		.. ..	..	N.

ESSEX (*Pop.*, 785,445).

For other Churches in Essex see "METROPOLITAN," pp. 233—241.

(E., Essex Union. C., Cambs. H. C., Home Counties. M., Metropolitan.)

Churches.	Date.	Chapel seats.	No. of Members.	Sunday School Teachers.	No. of Scholars.	Local Preachers.	Pastors.	When settled.	Associations.
Ashdon	1809	300	90	7	63		.. ..	..	C.
Radwinter	..	150							
Barking, Linton-road ..	1850	640	265	24	415		D. H. Moore ..	1892	E.
Blackmore	1843	150	15	4	30		G. Stevens	1883	
Braintree :—									
Coggeshall-road ..	1550	550	..		..		A. Curtis	1890	E.
Brentwood	1886	300	65	13	95		W. Walker	1886	E.
Burnham-on-Crouch ..	1673	350	80	17	178	2	C. D. Gooding ..	1877	E.
Althorne..	1834	20	..	5	30				
Chelmsford (11,008) :—									
London-road	1803	370	109	10	80				
Clacton-on-Sea (U.) ..	1887	500	78	8	126	2	C. J. Gayler (C.)..	1890	E.
Coggeshall	1829	400	39	6	60	2	G. H. F. Jackman	1889	E.
Colchester (34,559) :—									
Eld-lane	1689	700	285	35	420	7	E. Spurrier	1866	E.
Parson's Heath ..	1879	150	..	9	130				
St. John's Green ..	1872	220	51	15	127	3	W. Chisnall.. ..	1895	
Elmstead Heath ..	..		12	3	24				
Dunmow, The Ark ..	1823	100	13						
Earl's Colne	1786	750	..		..		.. ..	..	E.
Colne Engain ..	..	50							
Farnham (*See Hertfordshire*)									
Grays :—									
The Grove	1878	200	15	5	19		.. ..	..	M.
Tabernacle	1885	550	138	28	310	6	T. Heywood ..	1892	E.
Tilbury Docks ..	..	100	..	3	50				
Purfleet	..	150	..	6	70				
Halstead :—									
North-street	1678	550	119	20	195	5	A. B. Preston ..	1893	E.
Harlow	1662	500	83	9	90		J. W. Butcher ..	1893	E.
Harlow, Potter-street ..	1662	300	22	5	90		A. P. McKenzie ..	1888	E.
Hornchurch	1882	220	64	10	130		A. W. Holden ..	1894	E.
Langham	1754	400	62	9	65		W. Crosby	1892	E.
Stratford S. Mary									
Langley	1828	256	..		..		W. Franklin ..	1892	E.
Mensden (*Herts*) ..									
Leigh	1893	150	27	5	35		A. C. Sidey ..	1893	H.C.
Maldon :—									
Crown-lane	1872	320	67	7	103		F. C. Morris ..	1892	E.
Manor Park	1890	350	87		125		F. D. Robbins ..	1890	E&HC
Mark's Tey	1824	150	30		..		H. G. Polley ..	1892	
Matching Green	1885	180	22	7	75		J. K. Walker ..	1888	E.
Fyfield	..		..	2	32				
Rayleigh	1796	400	38	10	100	3	.. ..	..	E.
Romford	1836	400	..		..		J. M. Steven ..	1879	E.
Saffron Walden:—									
High-street	1774	560	173	20	201	7	A. Rollason	1874	E.
Sewards End ..	..	100	..	7	63				
Sampford, Great ..	1805	360	65	13	125	2	G. Hider	1891	E.
New Sampford ..									

ESSEX—*continued.*

Churches.	Date.	Chapel seats.	No. of Members.	Sunday School Teachers.	No. of Scholars.	Local Preachers.	Pastors.	When settled.	Associations.
Southend (12,333):—									
Clarence-road ..	1883	400	120	12	116	3	F. A. Hogbin ..	1888	E.
Hamlet-rd. Tabernacle	1876	530	128	18	190	3	E. Dyer	1889	E.
Thaxted, Park-street ..	1832	400	88		60	1	W. Goacher ..	1887	E.
Theydon Bois	..	100	25	8	60	2			
Thorpe-le-Soken	1802	330	39	5	46	..	.. ..	..	E.
Waltham Abbey, Fountain-place, Ebenezer	1824	20	55		100	..	.. ..	..	M.
Walthamstow:—									
Higham Hill	1894	220	85	17	250				
Maynard-road	1874	150	31	7	93	..	.. ..	..	M.
Woodford, George-lane	1883	620	130	16	150	3	J. R. Cox	1886	H.C.

GLOUCESTERSHIRE (*Pop.*, 599,947).

(G. H., Gloucestershire and Herefordshire. O., Oxfordshire. B., Bristol.)

Churches.	Date.	Chapel seats.	No. of Members.	Sunday School Teachers.	No. of Scholars.	Local Preachers.	Pastors.	When settled.	Associations.
Arlington (Fairford) ..	1839	200	..		..		.. ..	..	O.
Avening	1819	320	82	16	185	3	W. E. Frost.. ..	1879	B.
Leighterton	1828	80							
Blakeney	1818	320	77	14	159	2	S. J. Robins.. ..	1895	G.H.
Bourton-on-the-Water	1650	320	135	36	288	8	.. ..	..	O.
Aston	..		..		58				
Clapton	..		..	4	30				
Rissington									
Slaughter	..		..	2	25				
Bristol (221.578):—									
Bedminster:									
Philip-street	1856	800	245	22	626		H. Moore	1886	B.
East-street	1884	750	251	32	527		T. Davies	1893	B.
Broadmead	1640	500	1011	44	633	15	D. J. Hiley	1893	B.
City-road	1835	900	478	4	447		J. T. Briscoe ..	1895	B.
Clifton, Buckingham	1847	476	184	16	167	3	T. R. Williams ..	1893	B.
Cotham-grove	1872	500	245	27	269	10	R. Richard	1887	B.
Freestone-road ..	1880	..	..	29	366				
Counterslip:—									
Victoria-street ..	1804	850	403	35	505	12	H. Knee	1883	B.
Tower-street ..	1878	90	28	21	310				
Horfield	1893	40	129	2	200	4	R. C. Griffin ..	1895	B
Hotwells:—									
Buckingham Hall	1886	430	129	41	614	3	W. Tucker	1871	B.
Old King-street ..	1650	1000	579	29	256	6	J. M. Logan ..	1891	B.
Maudlin-street (W.)	1820	300	..		..		.. ..	..	B.
Redland, Tyndale ..	1869	620	307	7	189	6	R. Glover, D.D. ..	1869	B.
Deanery-road ..	1881	400	100	45	479				
St. George's, Mount Pleasant	1872	250	69	5	141		R. H. Coe	1891	B.
Stapleton-road, Kensington	1832	1000	282	36	460	5	C. Griffiths	1881	B.
Totterdown	1881	600	265	24	425	4	G. Jarman	1881	B.

GLOUCESTERSHIRE—*continued.*

Churches.	Date.	Chapel seats.	No. of Members.	Sunday School Teachers.	No. of Scholars.	Local Preachers.	Pastors.	When settled.	Associations.
Bristol *(contd.)*—									
Stations of the Bristol Baptist Itinerant Society:									
Backwell	..	200							
Barrow Gurney ..	..	140							
Bedminster, Victoria Park, John's Lane									
Blagdon	1850	200							
Breach Hill	1845	50							
Charlton	1858	100							
Chew Magna	1829	190							
Dundry	1828	300	356	96	1141				
Eastville	1889	70							
Hallen	1850	100							
Littleton	1889	80							
Nempnett	1842	100							
Patchway	1888	220							
Rickford	1854	200							
Ridgehill	1851	85							
St George	1846	150							
Winford	1824	150							
Chalford, Tabernacle ..	1740	500	224	29	280	7	D. R. Morgan ..	1871	G.H.
Frampton Mansel	..	100							
Charlton Kings	1875	250	53	10	102	..	.. ..	..	G.H.
Cheltenham (42,914):—									
Cambray	1843	1000	432	27	397	15	H. A. B. Phillips..	1895	G.H.
Elmstone	..	100							
Birdlip	1833	140							
Uckington									
Clarence-parade, Salem	1836	1300	620	39	357	12	R.G.Fairbairn,B.A	1890	G.H.
Brockhampton ..	..	120	..	7	78				
Gas-green	..	280	..	29	350				
Leckhampton ..	..	160	..	12	145				
Naunton-parade, Providence	1870	300	26	..	..	..	W. Brooke	1890	
St. James'-square ..	1746	650	25	8	70	1			
Chipping Campden ..	1780	300	40	7	88	..	P. Lewis	1895	O.
Broad Campden ..									
Chipping Sodbury ..	1656	270	61	22	155	3	A. Lemon	1885	B.
Acton-lane	1873	80							
Cinderford	1843	920	413	66	1580	8	J. George	1890	G.H.
Steam Mills	..	280							
Greenbottom ..	..	100							
Cirencester, Coxwell-st.	1635	400	86	14	137	..	.. ..	..	G.H.
Coleford	1799	800	261	33	450	19	W. Ross	1891	G.H.
Joyford									
Symonds Yat ..									
Downend	1893	250	37	10	73	..	G. A. Webb.. ..	1893	B.
Eastcombe (Stroud) ..	1801	630	132	18	130	4	J. Evans	1890	G.H.
Fairford	1700	250	..	..	..	..	A. R. Morgan ..	1890	O.
Kempsford	1876	150							
Maiseyhampton ..									
Fishponds (Bristol) ..	1841	420	145	24	291	..	T. S. Campbell ..	1890	B.

GLOUCESTERSHIRE—*continued.*

Churches.	Date.	Chapel seats.	No. of Members.	Sunday School Teachers.	No. of Scholars.	Local Preachers.	Pastors.	When settled.	Associations.
Gloucester (39,444) :—									
Brunswick-road ..	1813	1100	294	76	783	15	W. E. Rice	1894	G.H.
Little Witcombe ..									
Barton-terrace ..									
Suffolk-street ..									
South End									
Corn Exchange ..	1893	Hall	138	..	320	2	J. E. Barton ..	1893	G.H.
Hanham . ..	1714	350	108	16	150	1	P. H. Michael ..	1890	B.
Hillsley (Wotton) ..	1730	350	..	..	..	..	.. ..	..	B.
Kingstanley	1640	400	119	24	192	5	.. ..	..	G.H.
Lechlade	1819	250	..	..	..	..	W. J. McKittrick	1886	O.
Longhope, Zion	1846	220	35	10	140	2	.. ..	..	G.H.
Lydbrook	1857	450	107	16	275	3	A. W. Latham ..	1883	G.H.
Lydney	1834	350	93	14	180	2	E. Davis	1881	G.H.
Bowlash									
Minchinhampton ..	1824	650	98	15	180	1	H. J. Wicks.. ..	1889	B.
Nailsworth, Shortwood	1715	700	266	35	299	2	A. M. Nickalls ..	1890	B.
Nymphsfield	1760	160							
Naunton and Guiting..	1800	400	80	12	123	4	.. ..	..	O.
Nupend	1827	200	70	19	102	..	.. ..	..	G.H.
Old Sodbury..	1835	150	46	8	60	3	A. J. Parker ..	1888	B.
Little Sodbury ..	..	120							
Codrington	..	80							
Parkend	1860	150	30	14	90	4	S. J. Elsom, of Yorkley ..	1891	G.H.
Ruardean Hill	1845	350	30	8	120	3	G. Neighbour ..	1895	G.H.
Slimbridge (Stonehouse)	1834	120	14	6	50	..	G. Steele	1864	
Stapleton	1890	..	27	8	80	..	J. E. D. Beresford	1890	B.
Stow-on-the-Wold ..	1660	350	90	16	262	10	F. E. Blackaby ..	1881	O.
Donnington									
Stroud :—									
John-street	1824	750	163	26	190	5	C. A. Davis ..	1895	G.H.
Painswick	1832	150	19	..	..	..			
Pagan Hill	..	..	..	10	55				
Tetbury	1720	320	19	5	48	..	T. N. Smith ..	1895	G.H.
Tewkesbury	1655	400	87	21	150	3	J. E. Brett	1890	G.H.
Twyning									
Thornbury	1780	300	85	27	219	8	G. Rees	1872	B.
Morton	1839	100							
Tytherington ..	1842	140							
Woodford	..	70							
Uley	1820	400	..	..	..	..	.. ..	..	G.H.
Wickwar	1863	200	30	7	67	3	.. ..	..	B.
Yate Rocks	1881	50	10	4	36				
Winchcombe	1874	230	24	12	175	..	T. Whittard.. ..	1873	
Winstone	1822	150	19	..	..	..	J. Evans, of Eastcombe ..	1890	G.H.
Woodchester	1833	250	66	7	60	..	.. ..	..	G.H.
Wotton-under-Edge ..	1717	450	80	13	120	3	S. Mann	1891	B.
Yorkley	1860	230	54	13	150	2	S. J. Elsom	1887	G.H.

HAMPSHIRE (*Pop.*, 690,974).

(S., Southern. B., Berks. H. C., Home Counties.)

Churches.	Date.	Chapel seats.	No. of Members.	Sunday School Teachers.	No. of Scholars.	Local Preachers.	Pastors.	When settled.	Associations.
Aldershot	1883	450	66	14	120		E. P. Connor ..	1893	H.C.
Ash Vale (*Surrey*)	1860	250	9	6	50				
Allbrook	1894	65	20		..		.. ..	..	S.
Andover	1824	450	97	24	125	6	.. ..	..	S.
Smannell	1828	100	..	8	45				
Ashley (Lymington) ..	1817	250	63	3	92		E. Edginton ..	1892	S.
Beaulieu Rails	1817	300	38	5	63		H. New..	1887	S.
Blackfield Common (Fawley)	1833	300	60	10	75		.. ..	..	S.
Boscombe	1875	300	128	9	174		W. V. Robinson, B.A. ..	1891	S.
Bournemouth (37,781):									
Lansdowne	1875	650	255	15	233	5	W. C. Minifie ..	1893	S.
West Cliff Tabernacle	1880	560	216	16	207	9	G. Wainwright ..	1888	S.
Brockenhurst	1841	200	26	10	95	3	.. ..	..	S.
Broughton	1655	200	51	8	50	3	H. A. Tree.. .. (Broughton, Winterslow, Stockbridge)	1894	S.
Winterslow, Wilts ..	1866	100	10		..				
Stockbridge ..	1885	100	..		65				
Christchurch..	1875	200	48	7	62	3	.. ..	..	S.
Cosham, East	..	200	24	8	80		W. H. Barham ..	1889	
Cove	1856		3						
East Parley	1827	20	25	4	30		.. ..	..	S.
Emsworth	1848	230	35	12	121	2	A. G. Barley ..	1893	S.
Prinstead	1852	50	..	5	35				
Fleet	1846	300	48	9	80		T. S. Fidge.. ..	1895	
Gosport:—									
Avenue-road	1883	550	142	15	202	8	J. S. Wyard .. (Avenue-road, Grove-road)	1890	S.
Grove-road, Hardway	1860	20	29	9	92	4			
Brockhurst	1858	250	33	9	75		B. French	1876	S.
Forton	1811	350	55	12	135		J. S. Haggett ..	1894	S.
Stoke-road (U.) ..	1865	250	..		..		J. Pitman.. ..	1894	S.
Hartley Row..	1807	200	10	5	40				
Isle of Wight:—									
Colwell	1836	150	21	8	70		.. ..	..	S.
Cowes, West	1866	300	111	22	104		G. Sparks	1867	S.
Newport (10,216):—									
Castlehold	1809	650	..	30	212		A. E. Johns.. ..	1890	S.
Niton	1835	230	88		95	3	J. Bateman	1891	S.
Roud	1830	20	15	3	32				
Ryde (10,952):—									
George-st., Christ Church	1849	550	178	8	153		E. B. Pearson ..	1888	S.
Oddfellows' Hall	1890	250							
Park-road	1866	400	100	14	84	2	E. Haggis	1893	S.
Oakfield	1881	40							
Sandown	1882	300	69		67		A. G. Short.. ..	1889	S.
Ventnor	1866	350	49	8	40		J. N. Rootham ..	1887	S.
Wellow	1804	200	50	10	68		.. ..	..	S.
Yarmouth	1821	100	10		..		.. ..	..	S.

HAMPSHIRE—*continued.*

Churches	Date.	Chapel seats.	No. of Members.	Sunday School Teachers.	No. of Scholars.	Local Preachers.	Pastors.	When settled.	Associations.
Lockerley, Ebenezer ..	1750	200	69	13	62	..	.. ..	..	
Lockerley Green ..	1879	50							
Mottisfont	1860	100	..	15	76				
Lymington	1688	620	145	22	198	2	J. Collins	1879	S.
Lyndhurst	1700	50	32		85		T. W. Scamell ..	1890	S.
Milford	1816	300	51	3	18		G. R. Tanswell ..	1891	S.
Tiptoe, Jireh	1820	100	..	7	48				
Odiham	1877	60	24	4	26	3	J. T. Lane	1891	B.
Portsmouth (159,251):—									
Southsea—									
Elm-grove	1854	950	505		..	5	J. P. Williams ..	1882	S.
Denmead (Cosham)	1881	150	34	6	45	3			
Castle-road,									
Immanuel	1892	300	238	20	135		J. Kemp	1892	S.
Wellington-street	1893	200	..		83				
Landport,									
Commercial-road	1798	550	139	26	349		J. Harrison	1891	
Portsea, Kent-street	1704	800	167	8	200		.. ..	..	
Lake-road	1818	1250	895	51	851		C. Joseph	1889	
Alfred-street	1870	200	..	3	256				
London-road	1894	250	..	30	466		D. B. Griggs ..	1895	
Westbourne	1889	100							
Poulner (Ringwood) ..	1840	120	21	7	70	1	E. Diffey	1892	S.
Romsey, Bell-street ..	1750	250	87	11	94	8	.. ..	..	S.
Ashfield	1889								
Sholing	1879	200	..	3	34		.. ..	..	S.
Southampton (65,325):									
Carlton	1861	700	186	25	246		N. T. Jones-Miller	1890	S.
East-street	1689	600	145	16	142	6	B. J. Gibbon ..	1892	S.
Portland	1840	750	312	33	320	12	Carey Bonner ..	1895	S.
Eastleigh	1888	250	70	13	110		C. A. Fellowes ..	1895	
Shirley (U.)	1852	300	107	3	333		E. R. Pullen ..	1889	S.
Sway	1827	100	11	5	47		.. ..	..	S.
Waterlooville (Cosham)	1856	350	32		..		C. H. Thomas ..	1885	S.
Whitchurch	1690	220	41	8	74		.. ..	..	S.
St. Mary Bourne ..	1842	100							
Winchester (19,073):—									
City-road	1861	300	101	16	111	7	A. W. Wood ..	1893	S.

HEREFORDSHIRE (*Pop.*, 115,949).

(G. H., Gloucestershire and Herefordshire. B., Breconshire.)

(M. E., Monmouthshire English.)

Churches.	Date.	Chapel seats.	No. of Members.	Sunday School Teachers.	No. of Scholars.	Local Preachers.	Pastors.	When settled.	Associations.
Ewias Harold	1862	220	30	3	30		T. Williams ..	1876	G.H.
Foothog (Cymyoy, nr. Abergavenny), Tabernacle	1837	200	18	1	10		J. N. Smith (*see also* pp. 267 and 285)	1890	B.
Fownhope, Old Way ..	1826	200	44	5	54	3	W. Pontifex.. ..	1893	G.H.
Common Hill.. ..	..	100							
Garway and	1817	130	60	10	90	4	J. Hook	1887	G.H.
Orcop	1820	200							
Gorsley	1831	465	186	16	110		E. Ashton	1881	G.H.
Crowhill..	1837	165	..	8	60				
Kempley	1856	100	..	5	20				
Four Oaks									
Hereford (20,267):—									
Commercial-road ..	1829	650	216	21	294		J. Meredith	1892	G.H.
Kington	1805	500	59	10	70	4	W. B. Nichols ..	1893	G.H.
Lyonshall	1862	200							
Ledbury..	1836	280	23	4	27		J. Harper	1893	G.H.
Leominster	1656	300	57	6	60		J. Cole	1892	G.H.
Kingsland	..	..	14						
Longtown, Salem ..	1843	150	37	4	30	3	.. ..	..	M.E.
Peterchurch	1820	250	93	2	57	3	J. Beard	1864	G.H.
Bredwardine.. ..	..	150							
Preston-on-Wye ..	..	120							
Ross, Broad-street ..	1819	550	157	15	157	2	J. J. Knight ..	1894	G.H.
Layshill	1832	150	20	..	..				
Ryeford (Ross)	1662	350	82	8	60		E. Watkins	1876	G.H
Whitestone (Withington)	1817	200	26	3	35		W. Price	1884	

HERTFORDSHIRE (*Pop.*, 220,162).

For other Churches in Hertfordshire, see "METROPOLITAN," pp. 233—241.

(H. U., Herts Union. M., Metropolitan.)

Churches.	Date.	Chapel seats.	No. of Members.	Sunday School Teachers.	No. of Scholars.	Local Preachers.	Pastors.	When settled.	Associations.
Bedmond	1854	120	35	7	38	1	W. Wood	1874	
Berkhamsted	1678	650	190	30	260	8	J. F. Smythe ..	1883	H.U.
Frithsden	1835	100							
Bishop's Stortford ..	1819	300	103	30	250	5	W. Walker	1893	
Farnham (U.) (*Essex*)	1879	150							
Bovingdon	1872	350	40	10	70	3	*Evangelist*	..	H.U.
Boxmoor	1826	500	214	33	367	2	F. J. Flatt	1894	H.U.
Breachwood Green ..	1825	400	159	28	184	3	M. Ashby	1889	H.U.
Chipperfield	1820	400	84	12	83	..			
Flaunden (U.)	1836	125	23	1	21	..	} J. Pringle	1886	H.U.
Hemel Hempstead ..	1679	750	250	28	250	6	W. W. Robinson	1895	H.U.
Leverstock-green ..	1841	150	..	6	60				
Hitchin:—									
Mount Zion	1856	350	7	6	40				
Tilehouse-street ..	1669	700	208	24	300	8	C. S. Hull	1894	H.U.
Preston	..	150							
Stondon	..	160							
Wymondley	..	120							
Datchworth	1893	140	..	..	..	..	*Evangelist*		
Walsworth-road ..	1869	567	215	16	163	11	T. H. Smith ..	1890	H.U.
Whitwell	..	150	..	8	129				
King's Langley	1875	150	60	12	78	3			
Abbotts Langley ..	1893	120	23	5	39		} D. Macmillan ..	1881	H.U.
Bedmond	1891								
Long Marston	1862	150	19	6	40	8			
Markyate Street	1813	500	75	18	150	..	J. S. Bruce	1888	H.U.
Mensden (*see Essex*) ..									
Mill End	1799	250	..	6	80	..	J. W. Thomas ..	1894	
Northchurch..	1841	100	50	9	53	1	.. ..	..	H.U.
Aldbury									
Redbourn Tabernacle	1870	250	20	8	83	..	.. ..	..	H.U.
Rickmansworth	1843	350	60	15	145	2	W. Fisk	1893	
St. Albans (12,898):—									
Dagnall-street	1675	450	250	31	418	7	C. M. Hardy, B.A.	1886	H.U.
London Colney ..	1797	150	..	7	104	..			
Park-street	1813	120	..	11	150	..			
Tittenhanger	1858	80	..	4	57	..	} *Evangelist*		
Sopwell Lane	1889	150	..	6	45	..			
Essendon	1885	140	..	..	..	..	*Evangelist*		
Tabernacle	1880	500	..	..	..	..	H. W. Taylor ..	1880	H.U.
Verulam-road	1853	100	51	4	47	..	H. J. Wileman ..	1894	M.
Sarratt	1844	300	48	10	80	..	.. ..	..	H.U.
Tring:—									
Akeman-street.. ..	1808	850	120	24	200	4			
Aldbury	..	120							
Wigginton	..	80							
Wilstone	..								
High-street	1750	450	133	15	140	2	C. Pearce	1876	H.U.
New Mill	1655	600	149	24	187	5	H. J. Martin ..	1895	H.U.
Marsworth (*Buckinghamshire*) ..	..	120							
Waltham Cross	1895	170	18	12	90	1			

HERTFORDSHIRE—*continued.*

Churches.	Date.	Chapel seats.	No. of Members.	Sunday School Teachers.	No. of Scholars.	Local Preachers.	Pastors.	When settled.	Associations.
Watford :—									
Beechen Grove ..	1707	850	552	82	583	12	J. Stuart	1880	H.U.
Hunton Bridge ..	..	150							
Leavesden		135							
New Bushey	1870	550	160	27	300	6	H. T. Spufford ..	1878	H.U.
Derby-road, Tabncle	1868	550	84	20	240	2	G. W. Thomas ..	1892	M

HUNTINGDONSHIRE (*Pop.*, 57,761).

(H., Hunts.)

Churches.	Date.	Chapel seats.	No. of Members.	Sunday School Teachers.	No. of Scholars.	Local Preachers.	Pastors.	When settled.	Associations.
Bluntisham	1787	500	155	15	120	..	W. S. Rowland, [M.A.	1893	H.
Earith	1841	50							
Colne	1870	100							
Bythorn (see Northamptonshire)									
Catworth, Great	1834	250	15	9	48	..	S. Burkitt	1890	
Fenstanton (U.)	..	300	..	21	100	..	H. G. Lewis, B.A. (C.)	1893	H.
Gidding, Great	1792	300	19	8	43	..	C. Thew	1894	
Godmanchester :—									
Silver-street (U.) ..	1862	250	..	..	..	..	.. ..	..	H.
Gransden, Great	1732	280	20	11	76	..	J. Morton	1887	
Hail Weston..	1668	450	35	4	50	1	W. E. Davies ..	1883	H.
Houghton (U.)	..	300	..	..	..	..	H. Bell (C.) ..	1875	H.
Broughton	..	150							
Hemingford	..	150							
Huntingdon Trinity(U.)	1823	850	27.	34	348	15	R. F. Guyton ..	1890	H.
Brampton	..	300	..		..	..	J. Parr (C.)	1892	
Buckden	..	250	..		..	..			
Offord d'Arcy ..	1844	170	..		..	..	*G. Brown*	1879	
Hartford	..	120	..		..	..			
Little Stukeley ..	..	250	..		..	..	*Evangelist.*		
Perry	..	200	..		..	..			
Staughton, Gt. ..	..	200	..		..	..	*Evangelist.*		
Wistow	..	00							
Kimbolton (U.)	1692	300	50		20	..	T. G. Gathercole	1889	H.
New Fletton (see Northamptonshire)									
Ramsey :—									
Great Whyte	1810	350	..		..	..	S. H. Firks	1893	H.
Mereside	1833	20							
High-street, Salem ..	1887	500	40	13	120	..	J. N. Throssell ..	1892	
St. Ives, Free Church (U.)	1844	800	..		..	..	D. Macfadyen B.A. [(C.)	1891	H.
Winwick	..	200							
Wistow									
Woodhurst									
St. Neots :—									
East-street	1866	300	26	6	28				
New-street	1800	700	103	2	145		J. Clark..	1891	
Somersham, Old Mtg..	1818	350	22	9	70		G. Sneesby	1895	
Stanground (see Northamptonshire)									
Spaldwick (U.)	1692	350	26	4	30		B. J. Holland ..	1886	
Warboys..	1829	600	13	30	300		J. Lambourne ..	1868	
Yelling	1831	200			..		.. ..	..	H.

KENT (*Pop.*, 1,142,324).

For other Churches in Kent, see "METROPOLITAN," pp. 233—241.

(K. S., Kent and Sussex. M., Metropolitan.)

Churches.	Date.	Chapel seats.	No. of Members.	Sunday School Teachers.	No. of Scholars.	Local Preachers.	Pastors.	When settled.	Associations.
Ashford :—									
Marsh-street	1653	650	278	38	310	6	J. Whitaker	1887	K.S.
Bessels Green	1770	210	75	15	125	7	J. Cattell	1876	
Goathurst Common	1892	..	..	6	120				
Borough Green	1804	450	60	15	140				
Brabourne	1818	250	67	9	87	..	A. F. Cotton	1895	K.S.
Elmsted	1858	100		3	15				
Brasted	1877	264	115	27	240	9	W. Burnett	1877	K.S.
Brasted Chart	1882	90							
French-street	..	40							
Hawley Corner	1887	90							
Moorhouse	..	100							
Broadstairs, Providence	1844	250	22	..	..	..	J. W. Carter	1878	
Canterbury (23,062) :—									
Burgate Lane	1845	..	25	2	12	..	J. House	1892	
St. George's-place	1823	650	310	31	262	9	W. Townsend	1883	K.S
Tyler Hill	..	100							
Chatham (31,657) :—									
Clover-street, Zion	1644	800	260	102	1164	18	W. Osborne	1892	K.S.
Blue Bell Hill	..	80							
Luton Road	..								
Borstal	..								
Best Street	..								
Nelson Road, Enon	1842	200	34	8	65				
Crockenhill (U.)	1801	200	80	20	140	1	J. H. Marshall	1889	
Deal, Victoria-road	1814	600	192	38	380	8	N. Dobson	1873	K.S.
Ripple									
Dover (33,300) :—									
Pentside	1820	500	62	6	65	..	W. E. Palmer	1892	
Biggin-street, Salem	1839	700	337	45	504	20	E. J. Edwards	1877	K.S.
Ewell	1876	140	..	6					
Ewell Minnis	1878	70							
St. Margaret's	1880	70							
Priory-rd. Tabernacle	1873	320	..	..	..	..	W. A. Martin	1890	K.S.
Down (Farnborough)	1851	100	18						
Eden Bridge	1847	360	181	24	280	9	R. H. Powell	1882	K.S.
Marlpit Hill	..	150							
Haxted		50							
Eltham, High-street	..	..	14	3	38	..	.. ..	..	M.
Erith, Bexley-road	1859	120	28	9	88	1	.. ..	..	M.
Eynsford	1792	340	115	10	70	1	.. ..	1892	K.S.
Kingsdown	1860	140	..	5	36				
Eythorne	1550	600	198	55	342	9	G. Stanley	1880	K.S.
Adisham	..	80							
Ashley	..	125							
Barfrestone	..	50							
Barnswell	..	150							
Eastry									
Woodnesborough	..	80							
Woolwich Green	..	100							
Farnborough, Beulah	1846	250	39	..	..	..	Isaac Ballard	1866	M.
Pratt's Bottom	..	100							

KENT—*continued.*

Churches.	Date.	Chapel seats.	No. of Members.	Sunday School Teachers.	No. of Scholars.	Local Preachers.	Pastors.	When settl.d.	Associations.
Faversham (10,478) ..	1867	350	97	22	275	1	T. T. Minchin ..	1895	K.S
Brents									
Folkestone (23,905) ..	1750	800	380	47	540	7	R. F. Jeffrey ..	1881	K.S
Uphill (U.)	..	..	66	9	74				
North Street	..	..	..	11	130				
Foot's Cray	1836	400	99	23	231	1	E. A. Tydeman ..	1890	K.S.
Goudhurst	1864	200	44	16	180	4	J. J. Kendon ..	1861	K.S.
Gravesend (23,876) :—									
Peacock-street	1847	250	107	9	79	3			
Hawkhurst	1891	238	45	8	121	..	S. J. Henman ..	1891	K.S.
Headcorn	1675	140	47	7	35	1	J. Watmough ..	1888	
Herne Bay	1879	420	71	7	75	7	A. D. Brown ..	1895	K.S.
Lessness Heath	1805	100	10	5	41	..	.. ..	..	M.
Loose (Maidstone) ..	1880	280	38	10	60	1	.. ..	..	K.S.
Maidstone (32,145) :—									
Providence	1820	300	43	7	56				
Union-street	1833	450	161	..	..	8	G. Walker	1875	K.S.
Leeds	..	..	11	3	30				
Margate (18,417):—									
Mount Ephraim ..	1875	160	21	10	60				
New Cross-street ..	1762	700	216	26	306	2	B. Brigg	1891	K.S.
Meopham	1832	250	92	14	75	3	A. B. Hall	1888	
Ash	1843	100							
New Brompton	1879	638	283	42	531	6	W. W. Blocksidge	1881	K.S.
New Romney	1888	240	58	14	130	4	C. A. Ingram ..	1895	K.S.
Lydd									
Orpington	1849	300	176	23	362	10	W. Usher, M.D...	1893	K.S.
Ford Croft	..	..	..	9	70				
Crofton	..	..	..	6	50				
Plumstead, East, Station-road	1880	500	163	37	714	2	T. Henson	1886	
Ramsgate (24,733):—									
Ellington (U.)	1873	300	72	14	125	..	W. J. S. Wall ..	1892	K.S.
Cavendish	1840	750	290	24	222	4	T. Hancocks ..	1892	K.S.
St. George's Hall ..									
Reading-st. (St. Peter's)	1871	120	19	6	43	..	C. Denniss	1871	K.S.
Rochester (26,290) ..	1888	300	139	16	155	10	G. A. Miller.. ..	1889	K.S.
Strood									
St. Mary Cray, Zion ..	1887	200	36	7	76	..	R. W. Clark.. ..	1891	
St. Peter's	1710	300	84	15	90	1	J. T. Castle	1894	K.S.
Sandhurst	1730	400	130	14	118	1	T. G. Atkinson..	1888	K.S.
Sevenoaks	1748	580	167	20	120	3	C. Rudge	1885	K.S.
Seal									
Sheerness-on-Sea :—									
Strode-crescent ..	1868	370	69	6	60	..	J. R. Hadler ..	1895	K.S.
Halfway	1870	150	..	2	40				
Sittingbourne	1866	750	351	56	588	4	J. Doubleday ..	1882	K.S.
Bayford-road ..	..	..	..	10	80				
Milton		..	..	5	86				
Bapchild	..	..	..	4	45				
Smarden, Zion	1744	350	..	..	..	..	G. E. Ausden ..	1893	K.S.
Sutton-at-Hone	1842	140	22	4	41	..	.. ..	..	M.
Deane Bottom ..	1879	40							

KENT—*continued.*

Churches.	Date.	Chapel seats.	No. of Members.	Sunday School Teachers.	No. of Scholars.	Local Preachers.	Pastors.	When settled.	Associations.
Tenterden :—									
High-street, Zion ..	1767	270	85	13	136	..	J. Glaskin	1881	K.S.
Biddenden	..	100	..	7	99				
Tunbridge :—									
High-street	1868	450	142	22	250	5	J. H. Blake	1892	K.S.
TunbridgeWells(27,895)									
Calverley-rd., Tabernacle	1874	650	361	32	250	10	J. Smith	1881	K.S.
Rusthall (U.)									
Frant	..	..	10	4	30				
West Malling	1837	270	87	18	164	3	D. Mace	1889	K.S.
Whitstable	1869	350	40	18	130	..	H. R. Passmore ..	1891	K.S.
Woolwich :—									
Anglesea-road ..	1852	800	120	19	200	2			
High-street, Enon ..	1754	250	124	27	204	..	E. White	1891	M.
Queen-street	1786	500	155	38	300	..	T. Jones	1877	
Yalding	1892	350	55	6	30	5	D. C. Chapman ..	1892	K.S.
Wateringbury ..									

LANCASHIRE (*Pop.*, 3,926,760).

(L. C., Lancashire and Cheshire. D. F. M., Denbigh, Flint, and Merioneth.)

Churches.	Date.	Chapel seats.	No. of Members.	Sunday School Teachers.	No. of Scholars.	Local Preachers.	Pastors.	When settled.	Associations.
Accrington (38,603) :—									
Cannon-street	1760	1900	588	51	484	20	C. Williams .. F. J. Kirby	1851 1895	L.C.
Huncoat	..	..	..	21	127				
Royds-street	..	..	..	38	500				
Barnes-street	1858	700	112	29	244	1	.. ..	..	L.C.
Ashton-under-Lyne (40,463) :—									
Welbeck-street	1836	500	132	36	218	2	E. Hopkins	1893	L.C.
Atherton	1833	580	154	31	415	2	H. V. Thomas ..	1890	L.C.
Dangerous Corner ..	1891	270	36	13	150	1	.. ..	..	L.C.
Bacup (23,498) :—									
Acre Mill	1889	500	143	34	445	1	G. Charlesworth ..	1895	L.C.
Doals, Weir-terrace ..	1867	350	119	33	253	3	A. Harrison ..	1893	L.C.
Ebenezer	1710	1000	300	100	553	5	F. Overend	1884	L.C.
New Gate	..	..	..	1	68				
Irwell-terrace	1821	800	177	31	350	4	T. B. Field	1892	L.C.
Lane Head-lane ..	1880	300	62	18	77	4			
South-street	1851	300	51	11	90	2	.. ..	..	L.C.
South-st., Providence	1851	350	40	10	75				
Zion	1821	850	240	45	425	2	.. ..	..	L.C.

LANCASHIRE—*continued.*

Churches.	Date.	Chapel seats.	No. of Members.	Sunday School Teachers.	No. of Scholars.	Local Preachers.	Pastors.	When settled.	Associations.
Barrow-in-Furness (51,712):—									
Abbey-road	1875	920	168	35	502	2	.. ..	..	L.C.
Blackburn (120,064):—									
Islington	1726	200	60	..	200				
Leamington-street ..	..	800	..	20	150	..	W. A. Mursell ..	1895	L.C.
Montague-street ..	1853	550	238	50	550	5	.. ..	..	L.C.
Blackpool (23,846) ..	1858	700	111	15	181	4	.. ..	..	L.C.
Bolton (115,002):—									
Claremont	1821	1000	380	35	441	3	Chas. Cole	1892	L.C.
Astley Bridge	1845	550	150	33	320	2	G. Williams.. ..	1878	L.C.
St. John-street, Zion	1883	300	93	20	180	3	W. L. Williams ..	1890	L.C.
Farnworth..	1886	240	69	20	200	3	S. Jones	1890	L.C.
Briercliffe, Hill-lane ..	1840	350	147	14	180	..	A. Gray	1895	L.C.
Burnley (87,016):—									
Enon	1850	750	248	35	348	4	J. Heath	1893	L.C.
Mount Olivet	1893	300	40	11	20	1	.. ..	..	L.C.
Yorkshire-street ..	1828	700	173	24	333	6	T. A. Plant, B.A.	1892	L.C.
Colne-rd., Ebenezer	1787	750	415	48	753	6	S. C. Allderidge..	1893	L.C.
Mount Pleasant ..	1868	650	160	23	328	2	J. P. Newman ..	1895	L.C.
Haggate (Sc.)	1767	850	456	24	423	1	R. Shoesmith ..		
Angle-street	..	..	..	55	527				
Brierfield	..	..	..	17	121				
Bury (57,212):—									
Knowsley-street ..	1845	300	149	24	166	2	B. Bowker	1885	L.C.
Chesham	1881	160	157	14	154	1	F. J. Greening ..	1894	L.C.
Church (Accrington) ..	1870	750	235	43	438	1	E. M. Durbin ..	1895	L.C.
Clayton-le-Moors ..	1888	300	100	31	270	..	S. Caldwell	1887	L.C.
Clitheroe (10,815).. ..	1888	200	43	25	160	2	R. A. Boothman..	1891	L.C.
Cloughfold	1675	750	254	40	279	..	W. C. Davies, B.A.	1887	L.C.
Clowbridge (Burnley)	1844	500	78	17	195	3	.. ..	..	L.C.
Colne	1769	760	204	38	440	6	.. ..	..	L.C.
Coniston	1836	300	13	7	48	3	.. ..	..	L.C.
Dalton-in-Furness ..	1878	350	77	15	136	2	J. G. Anderson ..	1878	L.C.
Darwen (34,192)	1858	480	157	26	245	..	.. ..	..	L.C.
Edgeside (Manchester)	1853	650	119	28	166	2	R. Heyworth ..	1882	L.C.
Garston, Tabernacle ..	1893	350	73	22	170	..	J. Thomas	1893	L.C.
Goodshaw (Rawtenstall)	1753	780	205	30	436	1	T. Thomas	1884	L.C.
Goodshawfold (Rawtenstall	1854	172	19	26	134	2			
Haslingden (18,225):—									
Bury-road	1842	410	166	38	358	..	M. Gledhill	1895	L.C.
Chapel-st., Adullam	1855	200	25	5	50	2			
Trinity	1811	830	376	46	560	..	.. ..	..	L.C.
Haydock	1845	250	16	8	90				
Heywood (23,185):—									
Rochdale-road	1831	500	133	24	292	1	I. H. James.. ..	1891	L.C.
Horwich	1890	240	63	9	120	4	.. ..	..	L.C.
Hurstwood (Burnley)	1876	150	37	4	42	..	.. ..	..	L.C.
Inskip (near Preston)	1815	250	61	7	50	1	O. Maden	1892	L.C.
Great Eccleston ..	1872	150							
Lancaster (31,038) ..	1862	320	132	20	188	8	J. Baxandall ..	1873	L.C.
Caton	..	80							
Leigh	1872	520	..	20	200	1	G. W. Brooker ..	1890	L.C.
Littleborough	1861	500	69	18	132	..	E. Towler	1894	L.C.

LANCASHIRE—*continued*.

Churches.	Date.	Chapel seats.	No. of Members.	Sunday School Teachers.	No. of Scholars.	Local Preachers.	Pastors	When settled.	Associations.
Liverpool (517,980) :—									
Bootle (49,217) :—									
Brasenose-rd. (W.)	1868	175	155	16	166	..	J. H. Hughes ..	1888	D F M
Derby-road	1846	585	95	11	90	..	E. Moore	1894	L.C.
Bousfield-street (W.)	1840	500	131	13	100	..	P. Jones	1893	D F M
Byrom Hall	1861	1000	152	11	160	6	F. G. West	1892	L.C.
Cottenham-street and Empire-street ..	1875 1886	350 250	117	..	..	7	.. ..	..	L.C.
Edge-lane (W.) ..	1858	200	65	5	50	..	.. ..	..	D F M
Everton Village (W.)	1815	650	194	12	110	1	D. Powell	1889	D F M
Everton-road, Fabius	1863	560	159	22	185	4	C. R. Green ..	1888	L.C.
Kensington	1825	1300	416	43	700	7	E. E. Walter ..	1872	L.C.
Old Swan									
Kirkdale, Stanley-pk.	1875	550	263	25	400	6	H. Cordon	1875	L.C.
Knowsley-rd. (W.) ..	1869	Hall	..	..	..	..	L. W. Lewis ..	1876	D F M
Myrtle-street	1800	1800	527	71	610	..	J. Thomas, M.A. ..	1893	L.C.
Solway-street ..	1867	260							
Mill-street	1849	260							
Spekefields	1878	70	47	19	236				
S. Helens, Park-rd.	1869	500	112	20	220	5	.. ..	..	L.C.
Earlestown	1875	303	97	20	200	2	F. E. Miller.. ..	1894	L.C.
Brynn	1887	200	61	15	224				
Aughton	1874	200	40	10	70				
Golborne	..	..	23						
Pembroke	1838	1150	380	24	209	3	C. F. Aked	1890	L.C.
Walnut-street ..	1850	150	..	18	147				
Prince's Gate	1881	1000	188	30	350	..	R. Lewis	1885	L.C.
Richmond	1865	900	399	54	590	..	J. H. Atkinson ..	1883	L.C.
Leadenhall-street ..	..	..	..	18	300				
Toxteth Tabernacle	1869	1200	600	40	550	10	S. J. Jones	1895	
Miller-street ..	..	400		18	180				
Mill-street	..	250		24	210				
Tue Brook	1876	250	44	20	250	5	J. C. Elder	1894	L.C.
Walton, Carisbrooke	1875	450	152	24	320	..	W. Bathgate ..	1875	L.C.
Walton, Rice-lane ..	1878	450	37	5	80	..	C. F. Perry	1895	L.C.
Windsor-st. (Welsh)	1830	380	143	10	112	1	W. Samuel	1878	D F M
Lumb (Rossendale) ..	1828	800	265	33	514	2	B. T. Davies ..	1895	L.C.
Manchester (505,368):—									
Brighton-grove ..	1874	200	29	4	25	..	.. ..	..	L.C.
Broughton, Gt. Clowes-street	1880	400	136	21	239	..	J. D. Bray	1893	L.C.
Coupland-street ..	1886	800	146	27	237	6	J. O'Neill Campbell	1893	L.C.
Eccles (29,633) Peel-st.	1878	270	80	18	130	2	E. K. Everett ..	1886	L.C.
Gorton, West, Birch-street	1878	600	94	34	750	..	.. ..	..	L.C.
Clowes-street (U.)	1868	600	73	34	552	..	W. A. Livingstone	1895	L.C.
Gorton, Wellington-street	1861	550	122	23	262	1	T. Armstrong ..	1893	L.C.
Grosvenor - street, Chorlton	1845	750	182	21	256	3	E. B. Woods, B.A.	1894	L.C.
Hamer-street	1894	300	60	10	230	..	J. A. Jamieson ..	1889	L.C.
Longsight, Rushford Bar	1888	250	46	12	160	4	.. ..	..	L.C.

LANCASHIRE—*continued.*

Churches.	Date.	Chapel seats.	No. of Members.	Sunday School Teachers.	No. of Scholars.	Local Preachers.	Pastors.	When settled.	Associations.
Manchester (*contd.*):—									
Moss Side	1818	850	563	67	944	35	A. W. H. Streuli	1891	L.C.
Hall-street	1885	250							
Openshaw, Higher ..	1873	200	100	20	180	1	L. M. Thomas ..	1894	L.C.
Oxford-road (U.) ..	1842	1360	646	26	352	6	A. Maclaren, D.D.	1858	L.C.
Wilmott-street ..	1870	860	..	54	679		J. E. Roberts, M.A., B.D.	1890	
Rusholme, Nelson-st	..	..	..	18	140				
Pendleton, Nursery-street	1873	300	114	19	108	1	J. G. Skemp, M.A.	1884	L.C.
Queen's Park (U.) ..	1854	700	176	37	630	1	T. W. Thomason	1879	
Salford (198,139), Gt. George-st	1840	600	128	25	230	..	J. J. Hargreaves..	1893	L.C.
Stretford, Edge-ln(U.)	1865	325	98	16	130	2	G. N. Williams ..	1888	
Up. Medlock-st(W.)	1830	350	132	10	60	1	.. ..	..	D F M
Upper Brook-street, Emmanuel	1891	550	84	13	123	2	W. Owen	1892	L.C.
Withington	1892	Hall	50	6	55				
Middleton (22,162) ..	1862	300	84	15	220	..	C. Deal..	1894	L.C.
Millgate (Rochdale) ..	1876	750	73	28	309	..	J. Evans	1893	L.C.
Mills-hill (Chadderton)	1853	350	67	24	260	..	.. ..	..	L.C.
Morecambe	1875	260	60	9	58	..	H. C. Wagnell ..	1895	L.C.
Nelson (22,700), Carr-rd.	1874	500	280	37	555	5	D. McCallum ..	1889	L.C.
Ogden	1783	630	233	42	350	1	W. S. Llewellyn..	1880	L.C.
New Hey									
Oldham (131,463):—									
Pitt-street	1876	560	150	30	390	..	W. Hughes	1881	L.C.
King-street	1816	1000	449	45	415	..	.. ..	..	L.C.
Manchester-street ..	1863	500	121	18	145	..	L. Morris	1891	L.C.
Hollinwood, Beulah	1891	324	73	10	250	..	T. Smedley	1891	L.C.
Oswaldtwistle	1840	700	177	39	419	1	A. Woodward ..	1895	L.C.
Cockerbrook	..	150	..	12	40				
Padiham, Burnley-road	1852	350	54	20	65	..	.. ..	..	L.C.
Pendle-street	1866	400	71	22	200	2	J. Lee	1894	L.C.
Preston (107,573):—									
Ashton-on-Ribble ..	1881	212	74	17	141	..	B. A. Evans ..	1891	L.C.
Fishergate	1783	500	116	20	200	1	W. H. Harris ..	1879	L.C.
Pole-street	1854	450	136	13	150	2	A. Priter	1895	L.C.
St. George's-road ..	1877	200	21	14	118	2	John Snalam ..	1877	L.C.
Radcliffe	1880	350	75	20	402	..	Isaac Watson ..	1892	L.C.
Ramsbottom	1851	500	350	55	570	4	J. McCleery	1889	L.C.
Bank-lane	1865	300							
Rawtenstall (29,507) ..	1872	300	79	18	143	..	.. ..	..	L.C.
Rochdale (71,401):—									
Drake-street	1863	650	38	25	160	..	S. H. Taylor ..	1893	L.C.
Newbold, Milnrow-rd	1887	700	276	46	400	3	D. O. Davies ..	1883	L.C.
West-street	1773	900	346	54	667	10	.. ..	..	L.C.
Cutgate	..	250	..	21	115				
Shaw									
Castleton									
Royton:—									
Oldham-road	1875	220	95	26	280	2	.. ..	..	L.C.
Rochdale-road	1775	350	25	24	142	..	W. B. Suttle ..	1889	
Sabden	1798	600	161	40	238	..	.. ..	..	L.C.
Billington	1882	120	20	6	40				

LANCASHIRE—*continued.*

Churches.	Date.	Chapel seats.	No. of Members.	Sunday School Teachers.	No. of Scholars.	Local Preachers.	Pastors.	When settled.	Associations.
St. Anne's-on-the-Sea	1884	350	49	7	70	..	J. W. Varley ..	1894	L.C.
St. Helen's (71,288):—									
Boundary-road, Jubilee	1885	400	137	12	147	..	N. Macleod.. ..	1893	L.C.
Hall-street	1888	300	109	15	245	2	W. Holroyd.. ..	1888	L.C.
Park-road (*See Liverpool.*)									
Southport (41,406):—									
Hoghton-street.. ..	1861	750	319	21	158	..	J. J. Fitch	1883	L.C.
Princes-street	1876	200	9						
Scarisbrick New-rd.	1887	950	320	25	300	3			
Sunnyside (Rawtenstl.)	1847	500	139	28	240	..	A. Tildsley	1894	L.C.
Tottlebank	1669	200	34	4	47	..	T. Taylor .. .. A. M. Riddell ..	1841 1894	L.C.
Tyldesley (W.)	..	Hall	28	10	110	..	J. Lewis	1890	D F M
Ulverston	1871	400	48	8	100	..	R. L. Houston ..	1894	L.C.
Vale, near Todmorden	1851	750	158	30	291	1	.. ..	..	L.C.
Warrington (52,743):—									
Golborne-street ..	1869	350	56	18	120	..	.. ..	..	L.C.
Waterbarn (Stacksteads)	1847	700	324	60	786	2	.. ..	..	L.C.
Waterfoot	1854	600	152	38	447	1	A. D. Garrow ..	1895	L.C.
Widnes	1871	250	56	18	150	3	E. L. Jones.. ..	1893	L.C.
Wigan (55,013):—									
King-street	1826	550	169	24	400	3	G. J. Cliff	1895	L.C.
Scarisbrick-street ..	1796	550	137	22	270	1	F. G. Kemp ..	1886	L.C.
Bottling Wood ..	..	..	..	3	35				

LEICESTERSHIRE (*Pop.*, 373,584).

(E.M., East Midland.)

Churches.	Date.	Chapel seats.	No. of Members.	Sunday School Teachers.	No. of Scholars.	Local Preachers.	Pastors.	When settled.	Associations.
Appleby	1820	200	15	2	27	..	W. S. Lord, of Measham ..	1893	E.M.
Arnsby	1667	500	93	8	92	2	G. Hirst	1885	E.M.
Bruntingthorpe ..		80							
Saddington	..	60	..	2	14				
Ashby-de-la-Zouch .. and Packington ..	1807 ..	500 250	180	45	180	1	J.D.T.Humphreys	1893	E.M.
Barrow-on-Soar	1820	300	47	14	120	..	J. D. Alford.. ..	1896	E.M.
Barton Fabis(Nuneaton) *Bagworth* .. .. *Barlestone* .. .. *Bosworth* .. .. *Congerstone* .. .. *Desford* .. .. .. *Newbold Verdon* ..	1745	400 300 250 100 100 288 120	263	37	383	17	J. R. Godfrey .. G. E. Payne ..	1885 1888	E.M
Billesdon:—									
Back-street	1813	160	30	6	30	..	J. B. Field	1887	
West-lane	1846	150	4						
Blaby .. .. *Whetstone*	1807 1855	500 270	190	48	450	3	Geo. Barker ..	1879	E.M.

LEICESTERSHIRE—*continued*.

Churches.	Date.	Chapel seats.	No. of Members.	Sunday School Teachers.	No. of Scholars.	Local Preachers.	Pastors.	When settled.	Associations.
Castle Donington (Derby)	1774	500	130	..	..	3	..	..	E.M.
Weston									
Coalville :—									
London-road	1835	600	205	35	450	4	F. Pickbourne	1882	E.M.
Ashby-road	1879	650	130	18	250	5	J. H. Grant	1895	E.M.
Countesthorpe	1836	350	69	22	122	..	E. Yemm	1881	E.M.
Earl Shilton (Hinckley)	1758	320	57	18	180	..	..	..	E.M.
Foxton	1716	200	40	6	35	..	..	..	E.M.
Hathern	1840	150	48	12	90	1	..	..	E.M.
Hinckley	1766	600	215	40	561	..	Price Williams	1892	E.M.
Hose, Chapel-street	1850	210	79	16	65	4	..	..	E.M.
Long Clawson	1845	120	8	10	30				
Hugglescote	1798	625	195	45	450	2	Chas. Barker	1889	E.M.
Coleorton	1823	200							
Husband's Bosworth	1793	200	28	12	90	..	B. Dickins	1894	E.M.
Walton	1833	100							
North Kilworth	1856	80							
Ibstock	1878	320	114	26	295	2	A. E. Johnson	1895	E.M.
Kegworth and Diseworth (Derby)	1760	500	170	27	240	6	T. Adamson	1892	E.M.
Leicester (174,624) :—									
Archdeacon-lane	1790	950	412	59	959	3	W. Bishop	1869	E.M.
Smeeton	..	150							
Belgrave (U.)	1875	500	..	..	..	..	R. Y. Roberts	1879	E.M.
Belgrave-rd. Tabncle.	1869	600	128	24	328	..	W. Priestnall	1888	E.M.
Belvoir-street	1760	1300	515	47	660	..	J. Thew	1872	E.M.
Abbey Gate	1878	250	..	30	310				
Aylestone	..	200	..	7	70				
Harvey-lane	1864	700	195	39	382	8	J. Cornish	1885	E.M.
Huncote	1876	150	..	6	44				
Cropstone	1850	70	6	4	36				
Carley-street	1876	520	211	30	365	1	J. C. Forth	1875	E.M.
Charles-street	1831	800	318	35	323	8	R. Caven, B.A.	1875	E.M.
West Humberstone	1876	250	..	14	150				
Clarendon Hall	1894	1000	119	25	400	2	F. J. Feltham	1892	E.M.
Dover-street	1823	750	345	36	314	4	W. Evans	1871	E.M.
Friar-lane	1665	1000	330	34	401	8	J. Evans	1890	E.M.
Fleckney	..	130	65	13	126				
Croft	..	100	9	10	68				
Melbourne Hall	1878	1250	743	196	2113	7	W. Y. Fullerton	1894	E.M.
Paradise-place	1879	180							
Christow-street									
Palmerston-street									
New Park-street, Emanuel (U.)	1873	800	158	35	495	..	G. S. S. Saunders (C.)	1894	E.M.
Victoria-road	1866	1100	312	39	325	4	J. G. Greenhough, M.A.	1879	E.M.
Long Whatton	1799	230	34	14	78	..	..	..	E.M.
Loughboro' (18,196) :—									
Baxter-gate	1770	1250	462	50	652	9	E. Stevenson R. F. Handford	1842 1893	E.M
Moira-street	..	..	..	12	80				
Wymeswold	..	400	22	13	45				

LEICESTERSHIRE—*continued.*

Churches.	Date.	Chapel seats.	No. of Members.	Sunday School Teachers.	No. of Scholars.	Local Preachers.	Pastors.	Whe settled.	Associations.
Loughboro' (*contd.*):—									
Wood-gate..	1846	830	352	46	360	4	S. P. Carey, M.A.	1893	E.M.
Market Harborough ..	1830	300	80	18	132	3	C. A. Slack	1892	E.M.
Melton Mowbray.. ..	1867	400	53	9	85	..	J. Ney	1891	E.M.
Mount Sorrel	1820	300	54	20	145	..	.. ..	..	E.M.
Oadby	1795	224	88	18	174	1	W. G. Branch ..	1892	E.M.
Overseal (*see Staffordshire.*)									
Quorndon	1770	400	56	12	102	..	.. ..	..	E.M.
Rothley	1800	300	35	8	65	..	.. ..	..	E.M.
Shepshed, Charnwood-road	1695	550	126	19	233	2	E. M. Andrews..	1890	E.M.
Belton-street	1822	250	81	39	219	..	.. ..	..	E.M.
Sileby	1800	90	..	..	..	..	.. ..	..	E.M.
Sutton-in-the-Elms ..	1650	350	94	10	56	..	W. Bull, B.A. ..	1857	E.M.
Cosby	1830	160	..	13	90				
Syston	1869	200	80	14	120	1	W. Maynard ..	1895	E.M.
Thurlaston (Hinckley)	1787	200	23	4	26	..	.. ..	..	E.M.
Whitwick	1832	300	44	13	180	2	.. ..	..	E.M.
Woodhouse Eaves ..	1807	260	53	10	47	..	.. ..	..	E.M.

LINCOLNSHIRE (*Pop.*, 472,878).

(E.M., East Midland. Y., Yorkshire.)

Churches.	Date.	Chapel seats.	No. of Members.	Sunday School Teachers.	No. of Scholars.	Local Preachers.	Pastors.	When settled.	Association
Boston (14,593):—									
High-street	1653	600	186	43	294		C. Waterton ..	1888	E.M.
Witham Green ..									
Liquorpond-st., Salem	1770	350	86	8	75	2	W. Sexton	1880	E.M.
Cowbridge	..	100	..	2	20				
Holland Fen	..	120	..		60				
Bourne	1646	450	224	54	456	12	G. H. Bennett ..	1882	E.M.
Dyke	..	150							
Hacconby	..	100							
Morton	..	200							
Gedney Hill	1820	150							
Stainfield									
Burgh & Monksthorpe	1669	350	21	4	50		G. F. Pitts	1893	
Coningsby (Boston) ..	1651	200	28	7	40		A. Evans	1894	E.M.
Crowle (Doncaster):—									
Mill-road	1599	150	45	15	150		W. Rowton-Parker	1887	Y.
Epworth & Butterwick	1599	400	41	15	40	7	G. Camp	1894	E.M.
Fleet, Hargate-street ..	1681	450	100		104		W. F. Dart	1893	E.M.
Gedney Broadgate	..	20	..	6	60				
Gosberton	1666	21	42	8	96		F. Todd	1894	E.M.
Grantham (16,746):—									
Wharf-road	1859	500	97	21	178	4	G. B. Bowler ..	1866	E.M.
Bottesford	1789	150							

LINCOLNSHIRE—*continued.*

Churches.	Date.	Chapel seats.	No. of Members.	Sunday School Teachers.	No. of Scholars.	Local Preachers.	Pastors.	When settled.	Associations.
Grimsby (51,934):—									
Victoria-street ..	1826	1100	320	40	510	8	J. Edmonds.. ..	1894	
Freeman-st., Zion ..	1868	700	85	22	141	..	R. C. Ford, M.A.	1894	E.M.
New Clee	1880	150	35	10	200	6			
Holbeach	1879	230	24	3	18	..	.. ..	..	E.M.
Horncastle	1767	250	21	6	25	..	.. ..	...	E.M.
Kirton-in-Lindsey ..	1663	230	59	12	110	4	W. Smith	1895	E.M.
Lincoln (41,491):—									
Thomas Cooper Memorial	1652	600	140	22	243	2	F. A. Jackson ..	1895	E.M.
Mint-street	1767	590	105	25	168	1	A. A. Saville ..	1894	E.M.
Monk's-road	1881	400	166	28	185	..	.. ..	..	E.M.
Long Sutton	1840	380	..	..	..	..	.. ..	..	E.M.
Louth (10,040):—									
Northgate	1802	500	131	18	112	4	E. H. Jackson ..	1877	E.M.
Asterby	..	100							
Donnington	1761	75							
Eastgate	1849	375	80	10	80	..	F. Norwood.. ..	1887	E.M.
Maltby-le-Marsh ..	1696	120	4						
Lutton, Chapel Bridge..	1700	120	13	2	23	..	W. J. Pond	1890	
Skegness	1894	500	40	6	90	5	G. Goodchild ..	1893	E.M.
Spalding	1646	650	297	68	530	17	J. C. Jones, M.A..	1846	E.M
Podehole	..	160							
Spalding Common	..	200							
Sutterton	..	340	27	9	50	1	J. Britton	1895	E.M.
Sutton St. James.. ..	1813	250	42	14	120	3	A. E. Cawdron ..	1894	E.M.
Tydd St. Giles ..	1792	120	4						

METROPOLITAN.

INCLUDES ALL CHURCHES WITHIN THE LIMITS OF THE METROPOLITAN POSTAL DISTRICT, AND ALSO CHURCHES OUTSIDE THAT DISTRICT WHICH ARE CONNECTED WITH THE LONDON BAPTIST ASSOCIATION.

(*Population of Administrative County of London, including the City*, 4,232,118.)

(L., London. M., Metropolitan. E., Essex Union. H. U., Herts Union. H. C., Home Counties. C. C., Carmarthenshire and Cardiganshire.)

Churches.	Date.	Chapel seats.	No. of Members.	Sunday School Teachers.	No. of Scholars.	Local Preachers.	Pastors.	When settled.	Associations.
Acton, Church-road	1865	700	215	30	293	4	W. A. Davis.. ..	1885	L.
Acton-lane Tabernacle ..	1888	200	28	7	50		W. Archer	1885	M.
Alperton (Sudbury)	1853	220	89	6	100		A. J. W. Back ..	1892	L.
Balham, Ramsden-road ..	1874	750	136	23	210		T. Greenwood ..	1895	L.
Barnes :—									
Stanton-road	1868	300	..		..		.. ..	..	L.
Roehampton									
Barnet, New	1873	387	185	23	220	4	A. E. Jones.. ..	1888	L. & H.U
Henry Road									
Battersea :—									
York-road	1736	900	200	42	485		W. Hamilton ..	1885	L.
Battersea Pk. Tabernacle	1870	1200	327	46	560		W. Stott	1892	L.
Raywood-street School ..	..	..	..	20	180				
Beckenham, Elm-road ..	1884	400	152	22	194		R. S. Fleming, M.A.	1892	L.
Belle Isle	1877	550	..		..		J. Benson	1872	L.
Blundell-street	1879	300							
Belvedere	1863	240	..		..		A. C. Chambers..	1891	L.
Bermondsey :—									
Drummond-road	1866	668	399	38	703		H. A. Burleigh ..	1892	L.
Lynton-road	1813	400	63	17	190		B. T. Dale	1892	
Abbey-street	1878	450	75	15	210		A. V. G. Chandler	1894	L.
Spa-road	1845	300	40	5	80		.. ..	..	M.
Bethnal Green, Norton-street	1854	250	94	9	120	2	G. W. Shepherd..	1892	M.
Bexley Heath, Trinity ..	1823	460	113	22	250		G. K. Smith.. ..	1877	L.
Blackheath :—									
Shooter's-hill-road	1866	400	227	17	185	4	W. L. Mackenzie..	1894	L.
Bloomsbury	1849	1440	..		..		J. Baillie	1886	L.
Meard-street, Soho ..									
Keppel-street	1795	650	103	21	190		H. T. Chilvers ..	1895	M.
Bow :—									
Bow Road	1785	1000	223	34	500		.. ..	..	L.
Drift Mission	..	130							
Burdett-rd., East London Tabernacle	1861	3200	2388	101	1542		A. G. Brown ..	1866	
Marnham Hall									
Devonport-street	1881	350							
Tryphena Hall									
Empson-street	1888	800	219	70	1060		.. ..	..	L.

METROPOLITAN—*continued.*

Churches.	Date.	Chapel seats.	No. of Members.	Sunday Schol Teachers.	No. of Scholars.	Local Preachers.	Pastors.	When settled.	Associations.
Bow Common	1867	700	..	..	..	..	T. J. Hazard	1889	L.
Blackthorn-street	..	650							
Workmens' Home									
Brixton:—									
Barrington-road, Gresham	1869	650	198	40	409	..	F. G. Wheeler	1894	L.
Solon-road	1885	950	308	40	550	..	J. Douglas, M.A.	1884	
Cornwall-road Hall	..	500							
Stockwell-road Tabernacle	1884	600	105	10	100	2	C. Cornwell	1871	M.
Wynne-road	1875	700	292	21	214	..	Z. T. Dowen, M.D.	1887	L.
Brixton Hill:—									
New Park-road	1840	500	240	25	235	..	W. Pettman	1889	L.
Long-lane, Southwark.	1880	400	..	18	200				
Raleigh Park	1889	400	50	10	70	..	A. Dickerson	1895	H.C.
Brockley-road	1867	870	459	44	365	3	J. Lewis	1889	L.
Creek-street, Deptford	1878	400	..	33	343				
New-street	1879	150	..	8	140				
Trinity Hall									
Brompton:—									
Onslow	1852	650	224	31	273	2	J. Garden	1889	L.
Bromley, Kent:—									
Park-road	1863	500	156	22	143	2	R. Silvey	1895	L.
Sherman's-road									
Brondesbury	1879	780	303	45	635	..	C. W. Vick	1893	L.
Camberwell:—									
Camberwell New-road, Clarendon	1865	900	139	26	300	8	W. B. Haynes	1892	L.
Cottage-green	1854	350	196	38	575	1	J. A. Brown	1883	L.
Denmark-place	1823	720	470	57	672	..	W. R. Skerry	1889	L.
Edmund-street	..	..	..	10	200				
Leipsic-road	..	..	..	14	120				
Dugdale-street	1835	520	85	14	150	..	J. Waite	1894	
Mansion House-square	1880	600	136	13	147	1	G. W. Linnecar	1880	
Camberwell-gate, Arthur-st.	1824	820	534	37	583	..	R. A. Elvey	1893	L.
Camden-road	1854	1100	478	40	420	..	G. Hawker	1885	L.
Goodinge-road	1884	120							
Camden Town (168, Camden street), High Schools	..	..	41	12	143	..	..	..	M.
Canning Town, Shirley-street	1878	120	12	2	12	..	..	..	M.
Catford-hill	1878	365	295	23	267	6	W. J. N. Vanstone	1895	L.
Bell Green	1883	230	..	30	431				
Chadwell Heath	1846	130	22	14	140	1	..	..	L.&E.
Chalk Farm, Berkley-road	1870	550	87	23	205	..	..	..	L.
Chelsea, Lower Sloane-st.	1817	960	302	27	206	9	J. Spence	1894	L.
Child's-hill	1877	400	115	27	254	..	J. S. Poulton	1894	L.
Clapham:—									
Bedford-road	1858	150	38	4	37	..	..	..	M.
Courland-grove	1841	300	83	9	106	..	H. Dadswell	1893	M.
Grafton-square	1787	1000	140	22	220	4	T. Hanger	1886	L.
Clapham Junction, Meyrick-road	1876	350	78	16	300	..	R. E. Sears	1895	M.

METROPOLITAN—*continued.*

Churches.	Date.	Chapel seats.	No. of Members.	Sunday School Teachers.	No. of Scholars.	Local Preachers.	Pastors.	When settled.	Associations.
Clapton :—									
Downs Chapel	1869	1008	526	90	799	8	E. Medley, B.A...	1891	L.
Rendlesham Rooms ..	1872	240							
Waterloo Rooms	1877	80							
Chatsworth-road Tabernacle	1864	800	203	23	353	5	W. Moxham ..	1887	
Clerkenwell :—									
Chadwell-street	1851	500	255	20	240		E. Mitchell	1889	M.
Spencer-place, Goswell-rd	1815	1000	150	25	350	2	P. Gast..	1861	L.
Commercial-road East ..	1653	629	284	21	264		J. Fletcher	1874	L.
Crayford, Kent	1810	360	..		..		.. ..	..	L.
Saw Mills	1885	150							
Dartford Heath									
Wilmington									
Croydon (102,695) :—									
South Croydon, Croham-road (U.)	1893	500	72	10	92		A. J. Reid ..	1896	L.
West Croydon	1869	850	441	67	983		J. A. Spurgeon, D.D.	1869	L.
Boston-road	..	300	..	14	200				
Memorial Hall	..	300	..	16	221				
Dalston :—									
Queen's-road	1831	750	47	14	276		.. ..	..	L.
Dalston Junction, Ashwin-street	1871	1250	550	5	670		R. O. Johns ..	1895	L.
Dartford, Highfield-road ..	1867	350	148	25	210	2	H. Spendelow ..	1892	L.
Deptford :—									
Octavius-street..	1863	580	268	33	480		D. Honour	1867	L.
New Cross-road Zion ..	1842	650	265	36	398	2	T. Jones	1894	M.
Dulwich, Lordship-lane ..	1870	570	260	37	469		E. T. Mateer ..	1891	L.
Barry-road..	1876	320	..		..		A. J. Grant	1882	L.
Ealing Dean..	1864	400	180	32	355		W. L. Gibbs ..	1893	H.C.
Ealing, Haven-green	1881	824	326	24	220		Evan Thomas ..	1893	L.
Edmonton, Lower	1859	400	272	29	321	7	D. Russell	1863	L.
Marsh Side	..	..	..	6	70				
Enfield Highway :—									
Totteridge-road	1868	400	99	9	280		A. W. Welch ..	1895	L.
Enfield, Tabernacle	1867	417	274	30	250	7	G. W. White ..	1870	L.
Erith, Queen-street	1875	650	236	24	320	5	J. E. Martin ..	1875	L.
Northumberland Heath	..	..	..	22	175				
Finchley, North	1868	400	175		..		A. B. Middleditch	1888	L.
Dale-grove	..	..	..	2	205				
Finchley, East, High-road	1877	250	105	10	120	2	J. J. Bristow ..	1894	L.
Finsbury, Eldon-street (W.)	1822	450	111	3	20		.. ..	..	C.C. & L.
Do. do. Seventh-Day Baptist (*late Millyard*)	1617	..	19						
Forest-gate, Woodgrange ..	1883	800	274	49	578		J. H. French ..	1882	L. & E.
Forest-hill, Sydenham ..	1858	500	163	26	190	4	J. C. Foster.. ..	1885	
Fulham, Dawes-road	1889	700	175	38	472		R. C. Evill	1893	
Lillie-road, Ebenezer ..	..	100	41	7	80	2	H. D. Sandell ..	1894	

METROPOLITAN—*continued.*

Churches.	Date.	Chapel seats.	No. of Members.	Sunday School Teachers.	No. of Scholars.	Local Preachers.	Pastors.	When settled.	Associations.
Greenwich:—									
Lewisham-road	1838	600	157	30	280	..	.. ..	..	L.
South-street	1879	950	640	60	1300	2	C. Spurgeon ..	1879	H.C.
East Greenwich:—									
Azof-street	1892	250	69	17	250	..	W. E. Wells ..	1892	H.C.
Gunnersbury	1887	650	70	11	90	..	J. P. Clark, M.A.	1892	L.
Hackney:—									
Mare-street	1798	1100	489	89	989	..	J. E. Bennett, B.A.	1894	L.
Ann's-place	1882	200							
Lauriston-road, Hampden	1825	450	160	25	300	2	J. Hillman	1881	L.
Oval	1840	250	56	6	70	..	H. Myerson.. ..	1861	M.
Hammersmith, West End..	1793	750	258	47	504	4	W. Page, B.A. ..	1875	L.
Hampstead:—									
Heath-street	1860	700	456	36	508	..	W. Brock	1860	L.
New End	1827	250	31						
Hanwell (U.)..	1867	600	126	26	230	4	G. R. Lowden ..	1867	
Greenford	..	..	..	..	..	..	*Evangelist*		
Horsington	..	..	..	..	..	..			
Northolt..	..	..	..	..	..	..			
Yeading	..	..	..	..	..	..			
Harlesden, Acton-lane ..	1890	827	176	26	283	4	B. Thomas	1894	L.
Harlington	1798	550	105	19	280	1	W. F. Edgerton ..	1895	L.
Harringay, Emmanuel ..	1888	400	108	13	120	6	W. Frith	1888	H.C.
Harrow-on-the-Hill	1810	250	95	9	130	4	W. Dyson	1889	L.
Hendon, Finchley-lane ..	1874	600	242	24	250				
New Hendon	1884	200	20	5	100				
Highbury-hill	1871	1050	251	36	350	2	W. Stevenson ..	1892	L.
Riversdale-road	..	..	..	6	50				
Highgate, Southwood-lane	1812	335	84	12	124	..	J. H. Barnard ..	1864	L.
Archway-road	1894	702	129	18	120	..	A. F. Riley ..	1894	L.
Highgate-road	1878	850	683	56	709	..	J. Stephens, M.A.	1878	
Falkland-road	1882	..	..	9	70				
Holborn:—									
Kingsgate-street	1735	800	148	26	230	4	H. Thomas	1892	L.
Little Wild-street	1867	1000	..	..	..	..	.. ..	..	L.
Brooke-street, Holborn									
Drury-lane									
Earl-street, Seven Dials									
Neal-street, Long Acre									
Prison Ground, Holloway									
Prison Ground, Wandsworth									
Caledonian-road									
John-st., Theobald's-rd.	1818	1300	252	49	490	1	.. ..	..	L.
Holloway, Hornsey-road ..	1893	300	31	6	30	..	E. Smart	1893	H.C.
Holloway, Upper..	1868	1340	918	60	730	13	J. R. Wood	1874	L.
Rupert-road	1878	300	..	30	254				
Holloway, Tollington-park	1880	..	21	6	50	..	J. J. Cooler	1894	M.
Homerton-row	1820	350	78	10	100	..	S. T. Belcher ..	1891	M.
Honor Oak, Mundania-road	1890	650	155	26	305	..	G. H. Heynes ..	1892	L.
Hornsey:—									
Ferme Park-road	1889	630	390	18	224	..	C. Brown	1890	L.
Campsbourne-road ..	1875	250	..	29	350				

METROPOLITAN—*continued.*

Churches.	Date.	Chapel seats.	No. of Members.	Sunday School Teachers.	No. of Scholars.	Local Preachers.	Pastors.	When settled.	Associations.
Hornsey Rise :—									
Elthorne-road	1864	350	44	7	114	..	.. ..	..	M.
Hazellville-road	1871	500	..	..	..	..	R. D. Darby ..	1895	L.
Ilford, High-street	1801	500	139	19	200	..	J. Parker, M.A. ..	1892	L.
Islington :—									
Cross-street	1840	650	296	38	450	..	F. A. Jones	1878	L.
Salters' Hall, Baxter-rd.	1821	850	..	..	..	..	A. Bax	1876	L.
Wall-street									
Highbury-place	1850	600	214	14	230	3	P. Reynolds ..	1880	
Wilton-square	1857	400	..	..	..	..	W. Flack	1857	M.
Kentish Town, Bassett-st.	1862	270	67	16	164	..	M. H. Wilkin ..	1869	
Kilburn, Canterbury-road ..	1865	569	119	32	286	2	H. B. Murray ..	1889	L.
Kings Cross :—									
Arthur-street	1646	750	..	..	..	..	J. Love..	1895	L.
Vernon-square	1861	1300	..	..	..	..	J. T. Mateer ..	1888	L.
Handel-st. (Henrietta-st.)	1819	400	65	10	130	..	G. Curtis	1895	L.
Lambeth :—									
Lambeth-road, Upton ..	1785	800	626	40	500	..	W. Williams ..	1877	L.
Oakley-street	..	..	..	8	180				
Waterloo-road	..	..	..	8	100				
Ethelred-street, Regent ..	1821	500	57	18	170	1	D. Henderson ..	1895	H.C.
Lee :—									
High-road	1855	400	140	22	306	..	F. G. French ..	1894	
Burnt Ash, Bromley-road	1877	200	132	22	200	8	J. W. Davies ..	1886	H.C.
Summerfield-street ..									
Hither Green									
Dacre-pk., Kingswood-pl.	1851	350	87	12	105	..	J. H. Lynn	1894	M.
Lewisham, College Park .	1873	200	52	12	130	..	J. Crook	1890	M.
Leyton, Vicarage-road ..	1876	400	220	20	300	5	G. T. Bailey ..	1890	L.
Lea Bridge Mission ..	1887	150	..	10	120				
Leytonstone, Fairlop-road	1878	650	430	38	363	10	J. Bradford	1878	L.&E.
Ashville Hall	..	..	..	15	200				
Cann Hall-road	1887	700	333	71	1000	..	.. ..	..	L.
Edith-road	..	250	..	15	200				
Limehouse, East India-rd.									
Pekin-st., Elim	1870	300	100	12	170	4	F. C. Holden ..	1878	M.
Loughton (U.)	1817	425	187	24	223	3	J. A. Jones	1889	L.&E.
Marylebone :—									
Church-street	1831	650	140	14	136	..	J. Tucker	1895	L.
Hill-st., Dorset-square ..	1826	600	319	27	353	..	.. ..	..	M.
John-street, Trinity ..	1800	800	200	25	241	..	J. C. Carlile ..	1894	L.
John-street	1869	300	45	15	138	..	W. T. Russell ..	1871	
Shouldham-street	1870	500	128	10	118	1	E. Beecher	1890	M.
Oxford Market, Castle-street, (W.)	1859	450	322	..	120	..	R. E. Williams ..	1890	L. & C.C.
Kensal-road									
Willoughby-road									
Newington :—									
Metropolitan Tabernacle	1719	4880	4965	451	3660	130	T. Spurgeon ..	1894	H.C.
Twenty-two Mission Stations	..	3905							
Twenty-eight Sunday and Ragged Schools ..	..	..	..	208	4787				

METROPOLITAN—*continued.*

Churches.	Date.	Chapel seats	No. of Members.	Sunday School Teachers.	No. of Scholars.	Local Preachers.	Pastors.	When settled.	Associations
Norwood, West, Chatsworth-road	1878	1100	232	27	195	..	J. L. Stanley	1892	
Gipsy-road	1877	900	..	..	..	..	Walter Hobbs	1880	L.
Auckland-hill	1878	200	16	5	56	..	..	..	M.
Norwood, South, Holmesdale-road	1887	400	133	16	186	..	J. Chadwick	1887	L.
Norwood, Upper:—									
Central-hill	1852	480	..	..	..	..	S. A. Tipple	1854	L.
Notting-hill:—									
Ladbroke-grove Chapel, Cornwall-road	1865	850	..	..	..	..	J. F. Shearer	1894	L.
Notting-hill-gate:—									
Kensington-place	1866	250	94	8	57	..	..	..	M.
Nunhead, Edith-road	1871	500	170	30	480	1	C. P. Sawday	1893	L.
Old Kent-road, Maze Pond	1692	1000	208	26	580	..	..	..	L.
Paddington:—									
Westbourne-park Praed-street Bosworth-road	1836	1050 600 400	1162	131	1344	8	J. Clifford, M.A., D.D. J. Briggs J. Heap	1858 1895 1895	L.
St. Peter's Park	1871	300	69	12	150	..	J. M. Cox	1871	
Peckham:—									
Peckham Park-road	1854	800	412	51	692	..	F. James	1894	L
66, Peckham Park-road	..	..	..	9	171				
Rye-lane	1818	1000	750	45	825	..	J. W. Ewing, M.A.	1896	L.
Sumner-road	1880	80							
Relf-road	1882	90							
S. London Tabernacle	1880	800	438	46	566	5	E. Roberts	1887	L.
Linnell-road	..	..	..	8	108				
Heaton-road	1878	350	39	10	75	..	H. S. Boulton	1894	M.
James Grove	1870	360	43	21	193	..	G. S. Read	1895	
Peckham Rye Tabernacle	1887	1250	112	17	230	1	H. J. Knight	1895	
Penge, Maple-road	1866	1130	624	45	600	5	J. W. Boud	1881	L.
Pimlico:—									
Westbourne-street	1830	400	70	11	50	1	J. Kingston	1893	M.
Princes-row	1871	175	21	..	..	..	..	..	M.
Plaistow Barking-road Tab.	1871	500	..	..	..	..	G. T. Edgley	1893	L.
Plumstead:—									
Conduit-road	1861	400	..	..	..	..	..	..	L.
Park-road	1885	300	84	19	197	1	J. W. Cole	1885	L.
Ponder's End	1877	500	..	..	..	..	..	..	L.
Poplar & Bromley Tabncle	1888	1212	..	..	..	..	W. K. Chaplin	1888	L.
Poplar:—									
Cotton-street	1805	750	205	17	380	2	W. Joynes	1893	L.
High-street, Bethel	1855	300	33	8	110	2	H. F. Noyes	1882	M.
Potter's Bar	1795	250	42	8	75	..	Jesse Dupée	1883	L.
Putney:—									
Werter-road	1877	800	186	26	259	5	S. H. Wilkinson	1892	L.

METROPOLITAN—*continued.*

Churches.	Date.	Chapel seats.	No. of Members.	Sunday School Teachers.	No. of Scholars.	Local Preachers.	Pastors.	When settled.	Associations.
Regent's-pk., Park-sq. East	1855	1500	718	46	393	..	E. G. Gange, F.R.A.S.	1893	L.
Drummond-street Hall	..	..	..	33	340				
Richmond (22,684):—									
Duke-street	1870	320	120	14	120	..	E. Matthews ..	1892	L.
Rotherhithe:—									
Bush-road, Midway-place	1835	200	80	21	230	1	H. E. Inman ..	1889	L.
Rotherhithe New-road ..	1882	320	..	..	..	..	.. ..	..	H.C.
Shepherd's Bush-road ..	1890	470	140	25	266	..	G. W. Pope	1890	L.
Shoreditch Tabernacle ..	1835	2000	897	132	1740	4	W. Cuff..	1872	L.
Kingsland-road	1880	150							
Shap-street	1880	100							
Gibraltar-walk	1883	500							
Sidcup	1890	..	72	12	71	1	G. Simmons ..	1889	L.
Silvertown	1887	350	105	32	320	..	.. ..	..	H.C.
Soho:—									
Shaftesbury Avenue ..	1791	400	157	18	165	..	J. Box	1875	M.
Southgate, Chase-side ..	1886	250	65	9	50	1	.. ..	..	H.C.
Southgate, New	1863	300	303	25	380	6	G. Freeman ..	1892	L. & H.C
Pembroke-road, Muswell Hill	..	120	..	13	200				
Southwark:—									
Borough-road	1673	700	197	23	245	8	F. C. Hughes ..	1893	L.
Stepney, Wellesley-street..	1831	300	31	8	140	..	J. Parnell	1895	M.
Stockwell:—									
South Lambeth-road ..	1866	1100	..	..	..	..	A. Mursell	1887	L.
Stoke Newington:—									
Bouverie-road	1838	300	49	9	70	..	W. Mitchell.. ..	1895	H.C.
Stoke Newington-road (Devonshire-square) ..	1638	1050	792	84	780	..	G. P. McKay ..	1891	L.
St. John's Wood, Abbey-rd.	1863	1250	..	..	..	..	H. E. Stone.. ..	1891	L.
Henry-street, Portland Town	..	200							
St. Luke's, James-street ..	1850	130	51	..	..	..	W. H. Chillman..	1891	L.
Stratford:—									
The Grove	1854	520	103	17	180	..	W. H. Stevens ..	1895	L.
Gurney-road	1870	470	142	22	430	..	E. Marsh	1893	M.
Carpenter's-road	1877	820	..	..	..	..	.. ..	..	L.& E.
Major-road	1885	400	142	24	350	..	T. Maycock.. ..	1885	H.C.
West Ham-lane	1844	240	75	17	250	..	.. ..	..	M.
Streatham, Lewin-road ..	1866	761	..	..	..	..	J. Ewen	1891	L.
Lonesome Mission Hall	..	..							
Stroud-green, Stapleton Hall-road	..	475	..	..	..	..	.. ..	..	L.
Surbiton-hill, Oaklands ..	1874	500	113	8	80	..	W. Baster	1874	L. & H.C.
Sutton	1869	550	190	24	329	4	G. Turner	1893	L.
Tooting, Lwr, Longley-road	1880	340	100	21	280	..	G. H. Rumsey ..	1888	H.C.
Tooting Upper, Trinity-road	1870	550	132	27	285	2	H. Oakley	1895	L.
Tottenham:—									
High-road	1827	700	260	42	566	..	W. W. Sidey ..	1885	L.
West-green	1868	450	248	40	520	..	E. H. Howard ..	1893	L.

METROPOLITAN—*continued.*

Churches.	Date.	Chapel seats.	No. of Members.	Sunday School Teachers.	No. of Scholars.	Local Preachers.	Pastors.	When settled.	Associations
Tottenham *(contd.)*:									
Napier-road, Philip-lane	1887	230	..	8	120	..	T. House	1885	
Westerfield-road	1887	300	38	12	140	2	R. H. Eastty ..	1887	H.C.
Upton, Upton Cross	1883	350	128	20	200	..	J. Wilkinson ..	1883	L.
Vauxhall, Kennington-lane	1864	700	173	28	350	1	C. Pummell ..	1895	H.C.
Victoria-park:—									
Grove-road	1868	793	..	..	..	..	W. Thomas.. ..	1887	L.
Green-street									
Wallington	1876	600	206	28	250	6	J. E. Jasper.. ..	1880	L.
Bandon Hill..	..	70	..	6	50				
Waltham Abbey, Paradise-row	1729	500	141	21	153	12	G. H. Kilby.. ..	1892	L.
Victoria Hall, Honey-lane	..	70	..	2	40				
Walthamstow:—									
Wood-street (U.)	1851	600	200	35	440	5	W. Hetherington	1889	L.
Boundary-road	1876	550	270	29	500	..	W. Murray	1892	L.& E
Walworth-road	1805	800	542	34	492	4	W. J. Mills	1882	L.
Victory-place Institute	1884	400	..	36	432				
,, *Ragged School*	..	..	..	20	380				
Walworth, East-street ..	1791	387	121	20	250	..	E. T. Davis.. ..	1895	L.
Wandsworth:—									
East Hill	1859	900	542	41	476	5	.. ..	..	L.
Onward Mission	..	..	..	14	130				
Northcote-road	1875	1000	490	41	497	4	J. Felmingham ..	1892	L.
Honeywell-road	..	..	..	11	54				
West Hill	1821	350	86	9	70	..	.. ..	..	M.
Wandsworth-road (Vict.)	1873	950	427	85	1020	..	E. Henderson ..	1873	L.
Renshaw-street Hall ..									
Westbourne Grove	1853	1460	300	25	211	7	John Tuckwell ..	1881	
Westminster, Romney-st. ..	1807	600	150	24	180	1	G. Davies	1886	L.
Whitechapel:—									
Commercial-street	1633	600	132	6	50	..	.. ..	..	L.
Little Alie-street	1753	500	108	10	92	..	.. ..	..	M.
Willesden Green:—									
Huddleston-road	1882	250	62	..	..	4	W. J. Sears.. ..	1894	L.
Wimbledon, Queen's-road..	1871	400	333	31	507	19	C. Ingrem	1880	L. & H.C.
Morden	1885	80	..	10	62				
Merton	1886	200	..	14	190				
Wood-green:—									
Finsbury-road	1870	420	359	54	780	10	W. W. Haines ..	1883	L.
Bowes Park	1884	220							
Green Lanes	1886	80							
Park Ridings, Mayes-road	..	250	43	9	98	..	J. E. Flegg	1893	M.

METROPOLITAN—*continued.*

Churches.	Date.	Chapel seats.	No. of Members.	Sunday school Teachers.	No. of Scholars.	Local Preachers.	Pastors.	When settled.	Associations.
Woodberry Down	1883	900	559	56	543	..	G.H.Morgan B.Sc.	1890	L.
Woolwich, Parsons-hill ..	1873	700	1254	65	1127	9	J. Wilson	1877	L.
New Beckton	..	300	..	15	205				
Joseph-street	..	200	..	15	185				
North Woolwich									

For Churches around London which are not within the Metropolitan Postal District, nor connected with the London Baptist Association, see the various Home Counties.

MIDDLESEX.—Beyond the Metropolitan Postal District.

(Pop. for the whole county, 3,251,671.*)*

For other Churches in Middlesex, see "METROPOLITAN," pp. 233—241.

(H. U., Hertfordshire Union. H. C., Home Counties. M. Metropolitan.)

Churches.	Date.	Chapel seats.	No. of Members.	Sunday school Teachers.	No. of Scholars.	Local Preachers.	Pastors.	When settled.	Associations.
Barnet, Tabernacle ..	1891	300	113	14	80	2	P. J. Smart	1893	H.C.
Bedfont	1881	100	19	8	80	.	J. E. Johnson ..	1881	H.C.
Brentford, Old, North-rd	1819	300	89	22	420	.	R. Mutimer	1893	M.
Brentford, New, Park Ch	1802	500	95	23	350	.	T. G. Pollard ..	1895	H.C.
Chiswick, Annandale-rd,	1866	300	152	24	295	3	A. G. Edgerton ..	1892	H.C.
Feltham	1894	100	13	..	..	.	J. W. Avis	1894	H.C.
Hayes, High-road ..	1847	150	15	13	120	.	.. ..	..	M.
Hounslow :—									
Providence	1871	300	79	13	175	8	J. E. Barnes ..	1894	H.C.
Staines-road	1864	200	67	12	130	.	J. Curtis	1878	M.
Pinner and	1863	180	} 51	6	45		T. Antill	1892	H.U.
Harefield	1834	120							
Ponders End, Eden ..	..	100	14	6	42		.. ..	..	M.
Southall	1889	250	35	18	112	.	T. G. Williams ..	1894	H.C.
Teddington	1883	600	201	20	160	.	R. J. Williamson	1892	H.C.
Twickenham Green ..	1852	250	190	{ 25	450	} 4	E. H. Brown ..	1889	H.C.
and St. Margaret's ..	..	140		10	..				
Uxbridge	1885	200	37	6	30	.	J. R. Scoones ..	..	H.C.
Wealdstone	1875	200	84	22	216	.	J. G. Wells	1894	H.C.

NORFOLK (*Pop* 454,516).

(N., Norfolk. S. N., Suffolk and Norfolk Association. S. U., Suffolk and Norf Union)

Churches.	Date.	Chapel seats.	No. of Members.	Sunday School Teachers.	No. of Scholars.	Local Preachers.	Pastors.	When Settled.	Associations.
Attleborough	1825	350	42	12	108	..	E. J. Burrows ..	1894	N.
Aylsham	1780	450	99	13	77	3	.. ..	..	N.
Bacton	1822	250	38	11	72	2	G. Pilgrim	1878	N.
Buckenham, Old	1831	300	50	7	50	..	A. K. Davidson ..	1887	S.U.
Buxton Lamas	1796	300	31	4	30	..	.. ..	..	N.
Carleton Rode (Attlboro)	1812	500	59	6	45	1	H. W. Clabburn..	1894	N.
Bunwell Low Comn									
Claxton	1750	650	51	10	80	..	T. L. Sapey ..	1893	
Cossey and	1822	150 }	25	7	101	..	A. E. Saxby ..	1894	N.
Drayton	1847	130 }							
Dereham, E., High-st..	1784	650	106	16	128	..	R. J. Layzell ..	1891	N.
Diss, Denmark-street..	1788	650	214	19	120	10	J. Easter	1890	N.
Dickelburgh	1882	230							
Downham Market ..	1800	325	66	17	80	6	S. Howard	1874	N.
Stowbridge	1817	100	..	7	55				
Ellingham, Great ..	1699	300	23	6	39	..	T. H. Sparham ..	1893	N.
Fakenham	1801	350	61	12	41	2	A. J. Causton ..	1886	N.
Tittleshall									
Felthorpe	1831	180	35	4	48	1	.. ..	..	N.
Foulsham	1820	350	33	9	77	2	H. Vince	1882	N.
Kenninghall	1810	400	42	5	40	..	.. ..	..	S.N.
Lynn (18,360) :—									
Stepney	1689	800	178	25	185	10	T. Perry	1890	N.
West Lynn.. ..	..	120	..	5	50				
Magdalen	1817	..	..	..	14				
Union..	1856	550	70	21	175	.	C. Houghton ..	1889	N.
Martham	1800	250	24	6	65	2	G. Bass	1894	N.
Mundesley	1850	400	58	10	67	3	T. R. Matthews ..	1889	N.
Knapton									
Neatishead (Norwich)..	1809	400	47	9	40	.	C. B. Chapman ..	1894	N.
Necton	1789	250	58	7	45	.	J. Porter	1893	N.
Norwich (100,970) :—									
Gildencroft	1877	400	182	22	430	5	T. Bullimore ..	1877	N.
Orford-hill	1833	600	120	14	80	.	.. ..	..	S.N.
St. Clement's	1670	800	..	..	..	.	W. Ruthven ..	1890	N.
St. Mary's	1669	800	449	51	473	14	J.H.Shakespeare, M.A.	1883	N.
Sayer-st. Heigham..	..	200	95	26	305	.	G. Pring	1890	
Pottergate-street ..	1778	150	..	14	205				
Unthank's-road ..	1788	650	131	23	320	.	H. H. Youlden ..	1895	N.
Pulham St. Mary ..	1841	250	42	2	20	.	.. ..	..	S.N.
Saxlingham (Thorpe)..	1802	300	20	2	16				
Shelfanger	1765	400	42	2	24		A. J. Jarrett ..	1893	
Bressingham	..	100							
Stalham..	1653	450	122	22	109	7	B. V. Bird	1894	N.
Ludham	1821	100	17	5	35				
Palling	1860	130	..	5	25				

NORFOLK—*continued.*

Churches.	Date.	Chapel seats.	No. of Members.	Sunday School Teachers.	No. of Scholars.	Local Preachers.	Pastors.	When settled.	Associations.
Swaffham	1822	550	207	19	231	..	.. ..	..	N.
Castleacre	..	250							
Pentney	..	80							
Sporle	..	100							
Thetford, King-street..	1859	280	40	10	50	..	W. Fitch	1894	S.U.
Upwell	1840	350	68	14	112	2	A. C. Batts	1888	N.
Worstead	1717	600	85	10	86	1	J. Jackson	1880	N.
Wymondham	1800	200	45	10	97	..	.. ..	..	N.
Yarmouth (49,334):—									
Tabernacle, Wellesley-road	1754	500	46	10	80	..	T. B. Curry	1884	N.
The Park	1861	565	311	30	856	11	J. H. Jones	1892	N.
Ormesby St. Margaret	1876	132	14	10	74	..			
York-road	1841	250	23	6	72	..	J. Muskett	1881	

NORTHAMPTONSHIRE (*Pop.*, 302,183).

(E.M., East Midland. N., Northamptonshire. O., Oxfordshire.)

Churches.	Date.	Chapel seats.	No. of Members.	Sunday School Teachers.	No. of Scholars.	Local Preachers.	Pastors.	When settled.	Associations.
Aldwinckle	1822	365	44	6	40		O. Thompson ..	1887	N.
Blisworth	1825	340	112	24	155		H. Wyatt	1893	N.
Braunston	1710	250	29	7	40		T. Brimley	1886	N.
Braybrooke	1796	200	17	2	18		.. ..	..	N.
Brington	1825	280	39	8	91		J. H. Bath	1894	N.
Buckby, Long	1759	600	160	30	220		A. C. G. Rendell	1890	N.
Bugbrook	1805	275	98	13	58	2	W. Adams	1891	N.
Heyford	..	150	..	8	40				
Bulwick Lodges	1881	80	23	2	..		W. Gays	1888	N.
Burton Latimer	1744	420	83	42	420	3	T. Collings	1885	N.
Clipston	1778	520	136	15	80	2	.. ..	..	N.
Oxendon	..	60							
Sibbertoft	..	80							
Deanshanger	..		34	7	62	2	.. ..	..	N.
Desborough	1848	350	82	26	350	3	Isaac Near	1891	N.
Earl's Barton	1793	300	86	34	294		H. A. Hunt	1891	N.
Ecton	1815	100	18	7	60		J. Field..	1864	N.
Gretton	1786	300	45	5	70	2	.. ..	..	N.
Guilsborough	1778	500	55	4	36	2	.. ..	..	N
Hollowell	..	100							
Cold Ashby									

NORTHAMPTONSHIRE—*continued.*

Churches.	Date.	Chapel seats.	No. of Members.	Sunday School Teachers.	No. of Scholars.	Local Preachers.	Pastors.	When settled.	Associations.
Hackleton	1781	270	124	8	86	3	W. V. Phillips ..	1891	N.
Brayfield	..	100	..	5	32				
Cooknoe	..	100	..	9	65				
Denton	..	180	..	6	31				
Harpole	1822	200	45	13	53	2	A. Parker	1888	N.
Irthlingborough	1723	450	40	20	191				
Kettering :—									
Fuller Chapel	1696	1035	560	125	1462	14	T. Phillips, B.A..	1891	N.
Oakley Street									
Nelson-street	..	500	108	35	350	2	D. John	1894	N.
King's Sutton	1846	250	74	14	140	1	J. Churchill.. ..	1891	O.
Kingsthorpe	1823	400	130	28	326	1	G. W. Robert ..	1891	N.
Kislingbury	1810	350	75	15	87	3	R. T. Lewis.. ..	1894	N.
Rothersthorpe ..	..	..	..	3	30				
Middleton Cheney ..	1740	400	83	10	57	1	C. Saville	1894	N.
Milton	1825	250	41	4	26	..	E. R. Broom ..	1873	N.
Moulton, Carey	1783	300	85	17	152	..	F. C. Watts.. ..	1891	N.
Pitsford	1802	180							
Northampton(61,012):—									
College-street	1693	1200	659	105	1749	16	P. H. Smith ..	1894	N.
Barrack-road ..	..	200							
Compton-street									
Duston	..	200							
Great Houghton ..	..	100							
Hardingstone ..	..	180							
Harlestone	..	180							
Far Cotton	1893	200	84	39	270	..	R. A. Selby.. ..	1893	N.
Grafton-street	1840	340	93	17	360	1	S. Needham.. ..	1885	N.
Mount Pleasant ..	1872	600	326	39	702	9	F. T. Smythe ..	1889	N.
Market Street ..	..	..	..	5	50				
Kingsley Park ..	..	..	..	4	52				
Princes-street	1834	700	297	30	420	6	A. A. Morgan ..	1894	N.
St. Michael's-rd. (U.)	1884	1066	120	..	..	..	H. Bradford.. ..	1884	N.
Pattishall	1838	150	43	..	70	..	.. ..	..	N.
Peterborough(25,171):—									
Queen-street	1653	800	675	100	995	14	T. Barrass .. .. J. H. Jackman ..	1852 1895	E.M
Sergeant-street Hall	..	250	..	..	..	..	G. W. Elliott ..	1894	
New Fletton, Hunts	..	250							
Stanground, Hunts	..	200							

NORTHAMPTONSHIRE—*continued.*

Churches.	Date.	Chapel seats.	No. of Members.	Sunday School Teachers.	No. of Scholars.	Local Preachers.	Pastors.	When settled.	Associations.
Raunds :—									
Rotten-row	1801	400	57	25	104	..	H. E. Sadler ..	1894	N.
Ringstead	1714	300	70	18	113	3	J. Bates..	1893	N.
Roade	1688	450	50	6	40	..	F. G. Masters ..	1893	N.
Hanslope (Bucks), Long-street ..	1845	100	13	8	81				
Rushden :—									
Old Chapel	1727	600	261	65	560	4	W. J. Tomkins ..	1885	N.
Chelveston	..	..	..	3	37				
Hinwick (Beds.) ..	..	60							
Spratton and	1840	200	10	4	56	..	} R. W. Ayres ..	1895	N.
Ravensthorpe	1819	160	16	6	44	..			
Stanwick	1842	200	41	..	36	..	.. ..	..	N.
Sulgrave	1835	200	53	17	125	5	W. J. Young ..	1889	N.
Helmdon..	..	200							
Culworth	..	180							
Thrapston	1797	500	80	14	140	3	H. E. Roberts ..	1894	N.
Bythorn (Hunts) ..	1810	250	..	2	12	1			
Towcester	1784	310	96	17	120	4	W. Fidler	1871	N.
Duncote	..	100							
Walgrave, Gold-street..	1700	250	26	6	62	..	F. Cunliffe	1890	N.
Wellingboro', Taber'cle	1863	450	104	24	150	1	F. G. Burgess ..	1894	
West Haddon (Rugby)..	1821	300	63	10	80	1	E. E. Lovell ..	1888	N.
Weston-by-Weedon ..	1681	300	84	7	35	2	J. T. Schofield ..	1894	N.
Wood End	1814	150	} ..	12	55				
Morton Pinkney ..	1837	100							
Wollaston, Zion	1835	290	45	13	180	1	A. Hewlett	1892	
Woodford (Thrapston)	1822	350	75	10	83	2	J. Tyrrell	1872	N.
Great Addington ..	1874	150							

NORTHUMBERLAND (*Pop.*, 506,030).

(N., Northern.)

Churches.	Date.	Chapel seats.	No. of Members.	Sunday School Teachers.	No. of Scholars.	Local Preachers.	Pastors.	When settled.	Associations.
Alnwick	1884	200	47	7	45	1	W. W. Wilks ..	1892	N.
Rosebrough									
Berwick (13,377) :—									
Castlegate	1808	330	165	14	80	10	J. L. Harvey ..	1895	N.

NORTHUMBERLAND—*continued.*

Churches.	Date.	Chapel seats.	No. of Members.	Sunday School Teachers.	No of Scholars.	Local Preachers.	Pastors.	When settled.	Associations.
Broomhaugh and Broomley	1652	100	24	4	30	..	.. ..	..	N.
Ford Forge	1806	100	..	..	..	..	.. ..	..	N.
Newcastle (186,300):—									
Westgate-road ..	1650	850	452	76	1049	13	.. ..	..	N.
Elswick									
Osborne-rd. Jesmond	1650	450	250	30	332	3	T.D.Landels, M.A.	1892	N.
Denmark-st., Byker	..	220	..	..	..	..	B. Gawthrop ..	1894	
Rye-hill	1817	1200	187	35	369	..	W. Walsh	1888	N.
N. Shields, Howard-st.	1799	420	182	22	180	4	C. Stanley	1893	N.
Stephenson-street ..									

NOTTINGHAMSHIRE (*Pop.*, 445,823).

(E.M., East Midland.)

Churches.	Date.	Chapel seats.	No. of Members.	Sunday School Teachers.	No of Scholars.	Local Preachers.	Pastors.	When settled.	Associations.
Arnold	1822	600	70	30	280	2	.. ..	..	E.M.
Beeston, Nether-street	1804	400	128	25	253		R. Pursey	1884	E.M.
Boughton (Newark) ..	1827	100	..		..		S. Skingle, of Retford ..	..	E.M.
Carlton (nr. Nottingm.)	1876	110	53	30	180		.. ..	..	E.M.
Collingham	1670	250	32	3	11		E. B. Shepherd, of Newark	1887	E.M.
East Leake	1700	450	28	6	100	2	J. J. Berry	1894	E.M.
Wysall	..		2						
Eastwood	1876	450	27	15	150		.. ..	..	E.M.
Hucknall Torkard ..	1849	800	276	62	562	3	T. Cutts	1891	E.M.
Kimberley	1878	20	17	10	76		.. ..	..	E.M.
Kirkby-in-Ashfield ..	1820	200	48	16	77		.. ..	..	E.M.
Kirkby, East	1873	600	203	42	401	7	.. ..	..	E.M.
Mansfield (15,925) ..	1820	450	222	40	440	10	A. Firth	1880	E.M.
Mansfield Wdhouse.	1874	150							
Newark (14,457):—									
Albert-street	1810	400	106	19	162		E. B. Shepherd ..	1876	E.M.
Carlton-le-Moorland	1788	250	17		..		.. ..	..	E.M.
Newthorpe	1828	350	28	17	185				

NOTTINGHAMSHIRE—*continued*.

Churches.	Date.	Chapel seats.	No. of Members.	Sunday School Teachers.	No. of Scholars.	Local Preachers.	Pastors.	When settled.	Associations.
Nottingham(213,817):—									
Arkwright-street ..	1775	500	265	30	350	3	W. R. Jones.. ..	1892	E.M.
Basford, Old—									
High-street	1857	700	218	52	358	1	R. Jenkins	1893	E.M.
Queensbury-street	1890	350	134	34	450	1	.. ..	..	E.M.
Basford, New—									
Chelsea-street ..	1861	350	165	48	469	..	E. E. Coleman ..	1888	E.M.
Palm-street . ..	1829	270	80	26	210	1	C. G. Croome ..	1895	E.M.
Broad-street	1818	515	260	21	175	..	J. Douglas, B.A.	1891	E.M.
Edwin-street ..	..	200	69	20	200	5			
Daybrook	1847	209	99	32	209	2			
Redhill	..	..	..	12	120				
Bulwell	1862	750	195	33	552	..	W. Slater	1891	E.M.
Carrington..	1846	500	139	36	275	2	J. F. Makepeace..	1892	E.M.
Derby-road	1847	800	373	55	423	6	G. Hill, M.A. ..	1893	E.M.
Radford, Independent-street	1875	200	..	21	229				
George-street	1740	700	246	24	302	3	L. C. Parkinson, [B.A.	1895	E.M.
Woodborough ..	1832	200	..	7	30				
Hyson-green	1878	500	175	40	300	1	R. Silby	1881	E.M.
Lenton, New,									
Church-street ..	1851	500	94	30	220	1	.. ..	..	E.M.
Mansfield-road ..	1849	600	167	9	52	..	G. M. McElwee, M.A., B.Sc.	1887	E.M.
Leen Side	..	..	..	13	230				
Radford, Prospect-pl.	1868	220	111	22	140	2	.. ..	..	E.M.
Tabernacle	1868	2200	756	99	994	20	J. Clark	1891	E.M.
Herbert-street ..	1880	240							
Cross-street, Arnold	1840	400							
Cotmanhay, Derbyshire	..	300							
Woodborough-road..	1875	980	276	40	379	5	G. H. James.. ..	1881	E.M.
Retford (10,603) and Gamston	1692	400	80	16	104	1	S. Skingle	1881	E.M.
Ruddington	1823	250	40	17	110	..	.. ..	..	E.M.
Southwell, Park-street..	1811	270	70	12	68	..	J. H. Plumbridge	1876	E.M.
Calverton	1832	200	20	7	26	..			
Stanton-hill (Mansfield)	1876	300	40	15	96	1	A. Firth, of Mansfield ..	..	E.M.
Stapleford	1875	300	74	18	140	..	.. ..	..	E.M.
Sutton Bonnington ..	1704	100	15	8	73				
Sutton-in-Ashfield,									
Eastfield Side	1770	250	35	14	145	..	M. Fox..	1889	E.M.
Wood-street	1811	300	132	39	351	2	J. Cornish, of Leicester.	1893	E.M.
Sutton-on-Trent	1818	250	24	3	40	..	E. B. Shepherd, of Newark	1887	E.M.

OXFORDSHIRE (*Pop.*, 185,669).

(O., Oxfordshire. B., Berkshire.)

Churches.	Date.	Chapel seats.	No. of Members.	Sunday Sch. Teachers.	No. of Scholars.	Local Preachers.	Pastors.	When settled.	Association.
Banbury (12,768):—									
Bridge-street	1840	420	126	21	210	6	Isaac Watts.. ..	1895	O.
Bloxham	1808	200	17	8	62	..	J. Churchill, of King's Sutton	1893	O.
Milcombe	..	60							
Burford	1700	250	37	6	38	5	W. Clarke	1892	O.
Shilton	1830	80							
Caversham, Free	1872	600	145	20	198	2	S. H. Case, M.A.	1888	
Chadlington and	1842	250	44	6	45	2	R. Parkin	1892	O.
Charlbury	1866	250	34	7	44	..			
Chipping Norton.. ..	1694	500	196	26	260	..	T. Bentley	1869	O.
Great Rollright ..	..	70							
Coate	1657	400	116	27	232	24	J. Stanley	1895	O.
Aston	1805	150							
Bampton	..	200							
Buckland	..	150							
Ducklington	1865	120							
Standlake	1832	170							
Henley-on-Thames ..	1876	300	27	6	35	6	.. ..	..	B.
Boyn Hill	..	..	..	..	51				
Hook Norton	1645	300	50	10	78	2	C. E. Shearman..	1895	O.
Leafield (Witney) ..	1875	250	43	..	..	..	.. ..	..	O.
Little Tew and	1778	150	58	13	79	..	R. B. Wallace ..	1888	O.
Cleveley	1864	80							
Milton (C. Norton) ..	1837	250	100	30	240	2	G. W. Davidson..	1884	O.
Ascott	..	120							
Shipton	..	120							
Lyneham									
Oxford (45,742):—									
Commercial-road ..	1867	500	95	11	132	..	H. B. Case	1890	O.
New-road	1600	500	643	100	1000	45	J. Dann	1882	O.
Littlemore	1804	100							
Headington	1805	120							
Osney	1883	100							
Wolvercote	1884	150							
Charlton..	1843	160							
Eynsham	1815	150							
Hinchsey									
Botley									
St. Thomas's ..									
Sydenham	1826	200	14	3	30				
Thame	1825	350	12	10	60				
Woodstock	1827	220	88	8	40	..	C. Duxbury.. ..	1893	O.
Thrupp	1876	80							

RUTLANDSHIRE (*Pop.*, 20,659).

(E. M., East Midland. N., Northamptonshire.)

Churches.	Date.	Chapel seats.	No. of Members.	Sunday School Teachers.	No. of Scholars.	Local Preachers.	Pastors.	When settled.	Associations.
Belton (Uppingham) ..	1843	120	30	4	34	..	.. ..	..	E.M.
Morcott and Barrowden	1710	300	37	8	55	2	.. ..	..	E.M.
Oakham :—									
Melton-road	1770	280	66	11	100	1	H. J. A. Suter ..	1892	N.
Langham	1854	200	..	8	100				

SHROPSHIRE (*Pop.*, 236,339).

(S., Shropshire. D. F. M., Denbigh, Flint, and Merioneth. O. W., Old Welsh.)

Churches.	Date.	Chapel seats.	No. of Members.	Sunday School Teachers.	No. of Scholars.	Local Preachers.	Pastors.	When settled.	Associations.
Aston-on-Clun	1830	60	6	1	8	1	.. ..	..	S.
Bettws	1803	100	8	2	7	1	W. G. Mansfield of Velindre, Rdnr.	1891	O.W.
Bridgnorth	1700	600	88	13	101	10	J. J. Griffiths ..	1894	S.
Chorley	1878	150	..	5	50				
Brockton and Rowley..	1876	200	10	2	20	..	.. ..	..	S.
Broseley, Birch Meadow	1803	300	36	10	100	2	A. Shinn	1887	
Ironbridge									
Coxall	1870	130	36	5	48	2	W. Williams, of Knighton, Radnorshire ..	1879	O.W.
Craven Arms	1872	150	15	4	35	..	M. Matthews ..	1872	O.W.
Dawley	1846	500	109	22	260	4	A. Lester	1892	S.
Lord's-hill, Snailbeach	1818	500	89	14	80	3	W. L. Jones ..	1892	S.
Tankerville	1879	200							
Bromlow	..	..	5						
Madeley, High-street..	1857	250	6	..	..	..	*Evangelist*	..	S.
Shifnal, Zion	1891	300	9	..	..	..			
Broseley, Old Chapel	1749	300	6	..	..	..			
Market Drayton	1817	260	51	18	150	..	T. Clark	1861	S.
Oakengates	1866	200	21	10	60	2	*Evangelist*	..	S.
Donnington Wood	1820	200	17	3	40				
Oswestry :—									
Salop-road..	1806	500	86	11	107	9	.. ..	..	S.
Sweeney	1831	70	2						
Maesbrook	1844	80	10						
Llandrinio	1829	100	3						
Castle-street, (W.) ..	1860	150	84	7	76	..	D. Rees	1893	D F M
Pontesbury	1828	250	48	8	60	2	T. Evans	1866	S.
Shrewsbury (26,967):—									
Claremont..	1620	600	206	14	160	..	W. Maurice.. ..	1891	S.
Wellington	1807	320	94	17	160	2	H. Reid	1889	S.
Wem	1815	280	60	12	90	..	.. ..	..	S.
Whitchurch	1808	250	67	9	72	9	S. T. Williams ..	1893	S.
Ightfield	1843	140	7	2	14				
Prees Heath	1856	..	..	2	17				

SOMERSETSHIRE (*Pop.*, 484,337).

For Stations of Bristol Itinerant Society, see "GLOUCESTERSHIRE."

(B., Bristol. W., Western. W. E. S., Wilts and East Somersetshire.

Churches.	Date.	Chapel seats.	No. of Members.	Sunday School Teachers.	No. of Scholars.	Local Preachers.	Pastors.	When settled.	Associations.
Banwell	1892	150	28	7	45	..	.. ..	..	B.
Bath (51,844):—									
Lower Bristol-road ..	1840	400	55	15	150	..	E. Carr..	1893	
Manvers-street ..	1752	634	394	30	308	..	H. F. Gower ..	1887	B.
Dunkerton	1828	250	11	2	12	..	.. ..	..	B.
Walcot, Bethesda	1883	150	..	13	126				
Hay-hill	1871	560	161	23	156	5	T. R. Dann	1890	B.
Beckington	1786	350	73	12	94	..	.. ..	..	W E S
Boroughbridge	1837	230	73	19	150	..	A. Sprague	1884	W.
Northmoor Green	1836	100							
Stathe	1887	100							
Bridgwater (12,436):—									
St. Mary's-street ..	1600	520	282	45	718	..	C. H. M. Day ..	1886	W.
Union Street									
Burnham	1845	350	146	14	130	4	H. V. Hobbs ..	1893	B.
Burton (Stogursey) ..	1833	150	31	8	83	..	W. S. Wyle	1892	W.
Whitnell	1837	100							
Stolford	1885	80							
Chard, Holyrood-street	1653	500	195	42	348	..	A. MacDonald ..	1881	W.
Blind Moor	..	80							
Marsh	..	90							
Talworth	..	110							
Wadeford	..	80							
Cheddar..	1832	300	185	53	435	14	J. W. Padfield ..	1895	B.
Allerton	..	150							
Crickham	..	150							
Rooksbridge	..	100							
Rodney Stoke	..	130							
Rowberrow	..	100							
Winscombe	..	180							
Clewer	..	70							
Crewkerne, North-street	1820	500	120	29	302	..	J. Cruickshank ..	1877	W.
Misterton	1866	160							
Fivehead (Taunton) and Isle Abbots	1868 1808	220 180	84	14	115	..	E. S. Hadler ..	1895	W.
Frome :—									
Badcox-lane	1669	600	210	41	346	5	J. S. Paige	1894	W E S
Lock's Lane									
Sheppard's Barton ..	1705	500	243	36	380	3	J. Walker	1877	W E S
Hatch Beauchamp ..	1742	250	89	9	102	..	E. Curtis	1861	W.
Curry Mallett ..	1874	200							
Windmill Hill ..	1883	150							
Highbridge, Hope ..	1817	300	33	10	79	1	.. ..	..	B.
Keynsham, Ebenezer..	1807	340	68	14	131	..	W. Mann	1884	B.
Merriott (U.)..	1883	200	28	12	106	..	T. Hawkins.. ..	1888	W.
Minehead	1817	200	51	11	60	..	W. Burton	1894	W.
Montacute	1824	300	95	13	128	..	H. Hardin	1870	W.
Odcomb	..	100							

SOMERSETSHIRE—*continued.*

Churches.	Date.	Chapel seats	No. of Members.	Sunday School Teachers.	No. of Scholars.	Local Preachers	Pastors.	When settled.	Associations.
North Curry and.. ..	1828	300	62	8	69		B. W. Osler..	1894	W.
Stoke St. Gregory ..	1869	230	45	9	85				
Paulton	1655	370	128	31	250	5	J. Kempton.. ..	1872	B.
Welton	..	150	..	11	106				
Pill	1815	200	57	15	159	1	J. Culross, M.A., D.D.	..	B.
Radstock	1844	254	63	18	160	1	W. H. Buller ..	1882	B.
Road	1783	300	30	8	41				
Rudge (Frome)	1845	80	23	4	40		.. ..	..	W E S
Shepton Mallet	1875	120	20	6	24	5	.. ..		B.
Shirehampton	1890	200	14	4	30		.. ..	..	B.
Stogumber	1680	170	27	11	72		F. T. White ..	1895	W.
Crowcombe	1890	60							
Street	1813	200	39	6	83		J. Bartlett	1891	W.
Taunton (18,026) :—									
Albemarle	1875	500	115	18	805		L. Palmer	1877	W.
Silver-street	1814	700	230	34	358		J. P. Tetley ..	1874	W.
Creech St. Michael	1831	172	45	7	65				
Twerton-on-Avon ..	1828	350	96	24	146	2	B. Oriel	1891	B.
Watchet and Williton	1808	450	98	29	273		W. White	1894	W.
Doniford	1883	50							
Wedmore	1600	230	60	13	105	3	W. W. Reed ..	1893	B.
Mark	..	150					[B.A.		
Wellington, South-st.	1739	650	402	113	1019		G. W. Humphreys,	1862	W.
Rockwell Green ..	1890	400	..	..	..		O. R. Gibbon ..	1895	
Holywell Lake ..	..	120	..	..	..				
Holcombe Rogus ..	..	100	..	..	..				
Sampford Moor ..	1871	80	..	..	..				
Wells, Union-street ..	1814	450	49	10	52	4	W. Owen	1891	B.
West Horrington ..	1875	60							
Wookey	1870	110							
Weston-super-Mare :—									
Bristol-road	1866	600	22	12	100		W. P. Davies ..	1895	B.
Wadham-street ..	1847	850	229	33	396	4	T. J. Longhurst..	1895	B.
Puxton	1890	120							
Wincanton	1829	360	66	24	123		J. Brown	1887	W.
Bourton	1834	200							
Brewham	1870	80							
Charlton Musgrove	1830	60							
Holton	1873	50							
Yeovil, South-street ..	1688	800	222	44	500		S. Newnam.. ..	1883	W.
Tintinhull	1862	60							

STAFFORDSHIRE (*Pop.*, 1,083,408).

(W. M., West Midland. E. M., East Midland. L. C., Lancashire and Cheshire. D. F. M. Denbigh, Flint, and Merioneth.)

Churches.	Date.	Chapel seats.	No. of Members.	Sunday School Teachers.	No. of Scholars.	Local Preachers.	Pastors.	When settled.	Associations.
Baddeley Edge	..	80	3	2	12				
Bilston :—									
Broad-street	1859	250	26	10	100	..	D. Smith	1882	
Wood-street	1798	550	110	15	200	..	.. ..	..	W.M.
Brierley-hill, South-st.	1776	400	59	20	216	..	W. B. Bliss	1880	W.M.
Burslem (31,999) ..	1806	370	81	16	160	..	J. C. Taylor ..	1892	L.C.
Burton-on-Trent (46,047) :—									
Station-street	1792	630	..	..	..	..	.. ..	..	E.M.
Walton-on-Trent ..	1877	100							
Castle Gresley ..	1877	200							
Derby-street	1871	600	150	27	250	..	J. Askew	1874	E.M.
New-street	1824	840							
Cauldwell (*Derbyshire*)	1785	100	263	40	360	..	J. Porteous ..	1891	E.M.
Overseal (*Leicestershire*)	1854	120	35	8	65	..			
Butt Lane	1880	150	50	8	93	4	.. ..	..	W.M.
Chadsmoor (Cannock)	1879	200	34	15	150	..	.. ..	..	W.M.
Coseley :—									
Darkhouse	1783	750	90	24	499	2	.. ..	..	W.M.
Providence	1809	500	123	29	298	..	.. ..	..	W.M.
Ebenezer	1857	400	19	12	190	1	.. ..	..	W.M.
Cradley Heath	1834	250	74	15	160	..	.. ..	..	W.M.
Croxton (Eccleshall) ..	1860	120	13	2	12	..	J. Shelley	1860	
Fenton	1881	370	27	10	90	..	P. Miller	1894	W.M.
Hanley (54,946) :—									
New-street	1789	350	87	16	145	2	G. Buckley	1892	W.M.
Gt. York-street (W.)	1855	100	37	5	35	..	J. Williams	1882	D F M
Eastwood Vale.. ..	1877	200	..	..	..	..	.. ..	..	W.M.
Latebrook (Stoke-on-Trent)..	1877	100	12	7	60				
Longton (34,327)	1853	600	250	15	310	3	.. ..	..	W.M.
Newcastle-under-Lyme (18,452)	1872	220	60	18	180	2	.. ..	..	W.M.
Prince's End (Tipton)	1846	540	81	..	..	..	J. C. Whitaker ..	1870	W.M.
Smethwick (*see Birmin gha m*)									
Stafford (20,270) :—									
Water-street	1858	450	128	25	214	..	W. Springthorpe ..	1894	W.M.
Stoke-on-Trent (24,027)	1841	500	137	20	304	2	F. Samuels	1893	W.M.
Tamworth, Tabernacle	1821	260	39	14	120	3	.. ..	..	W.M.
Walsall (71,789) :—									
Goodall-street	1831	400	..	16	230	..	B. A. Millard ..	1890	
Stafford-street	1845	700	270	37	370	5	G. Barrans	1884	W.M.
Vicarage-walk	1881	675	256	36	470	8	A. H. Lee	1880	W.M.
Dudley-street ..	..	..	..	10	100				

STAFFORDSHIRE—*continued.*

Churches.	Date.	Chapel seats.	No. of Members.	Sunday School Teachers.	No. of Scholars.	Local Preachers.	Pastors.	When settled.	Associations.
Wednesbury (25,347) ..	1856	500	86	22	310	..	W. Williams ..	1892	W.M.
W. Bromwich (59,474):—									
High-street	1835	500	154	36	205	1	A. W. Oakley ..	1886	W.M.
Willenhall :—									
Little London	1792	900	54	24	265	..	G. Banks	1884	
Lichfield-street ..	1871	650	82	26	240	..	.. ..	..	W.M.
Wolverhampton (82,662) :—									
Waterloo-road	1830	800	153	16	220	..	F. C. Player, B.A.	1894	W.M.
Cannon-street ..	..	300	..	8	100				

SUFFOLK (*Pop.*, 371,235).

(S N., Suffolk and Norfolk Association. S. U., Suffolk and Norfolk Union. N., Norfolk.)

Churches.	Date.	Chapel seats.	No. of Members.	Sunday School Teachers.	No. of Scholars.	Local Preachers.	Pastors.	When settled.	Associations.
Aldeburgh	1822	430	37	7	107	..	L. E. Bartlett ..	1894	S.U.
Aldringham	1812	400	47	16	68	3	.. ..	..	S.N.
Aldeburgh	1812	120							
Leiston	1880	80							
Bardwell	1824	300	105	6	72	3	G. F. Wall	1883	S.U.
Beccles, Martyrs' Mem.	1808	800	155	18	172	4	.. ..	..	S.N.
Bildeston	1737	400	128	15	128	..	F. W. Walter ..	1893	S.U.
Blakenham	1870	200	26	3	24	..	.. ..	..	S.N.
Bradfield St. George ..	1844	250	72	6	51	1	W. Dixon	1877	S.N.
Hessett	1890	150							
Brandon	1866	350	48	26	245	..	W. T. Lea	1888	S.U.
Brockley	1841	250	19	5	60	..	W. Rumsey.. ..	1891	
Bungay	1846	310	64	9	36	..	J. D. Bowtell ..	1889	S.N.
Bures St. Mary	1831	400	124	10	98	4	G. Monk	1881	S.U.
Lamarsh	..	130							
Bury St. Eds. (16,630):—									
Garland-street	1800	900	534	45	450	15	S. J. Baker	1895	S.U.
Barton									
Higham									
Whepstead									
Westgate-road, Rehoboth	1840	150	24	8	60	1	W. Tooke	1895	
Charsfield	1804	400	40	12	87	..	.. ..	..	S.N.
Clare	1803	400	90	16	111	..	A. B. Tettmar ..	1894	
Cransford	1838	400	36	5	31	..	.. ..	..	S.N.
Earl Soham(Wkm.Mkt.)	1821	400	69	8	62	..	.. ..	..	S.U.
Eye	1810	500	81	13	130	1	F. E. Cossey .	1891	S.U.

SUFFOLK—*continued*.

Churches.	Date.	Chapel seats.	No. of Members.	Sunday School Teachers.	No. of Scholars.	Local Preachers.	Pastors.	When settled.	Associations.
Framsden	1835	230	25	5	40	..	E. Ward	1880	S.U.
Fressingfield	1839	700	50	6	38	..	..	..	S.N.
Friston	1830	350	62	10	77	..	R. Frankland	1891	S.N.
Glemsford :—									
Ebenezer	1830	350	66	20	145	1			
Hunts Hill	1859	400	34	10	80	..	R. Page	1878	
Gorleston (Yarmouth)	1868	350	60	23	180	..	A. A. Savage	1893	N.
Brenston									
Grundisburgh	1798	800	112	16	116	..	H. D. Tooke	1894	S.N.
Halesworth	1819	274	35	..	..	..	H. B. Berry	1892	S.N.
Hadleigh	1815	400	77	11	90	..	A. Morling	1891	S.N.
Hadleigh Heath	1823	200							
Haverhill	1870	200	6	4	20	..	G. Firbank	1881	
Horham	1799	700	146	11	80	2	J. R. Debnam	1879	
Hoxne	1843	500	61	11	78	..	W. J. Denmee	1895	S.N.
Ipswich (57,360) :—									
Burlington	1856	1020	418	53	654	10	T. M. Morris	1858	S.U.
Washbrook	1883	160							
David-street, Zoar	1841	400	154	14	130	..	R. C. Bardens	1891	
Fonnereau-road, Bethesda	1829	800	225	23	174	..	W. Kern	1877	S.N.
Stoke-green	1757	800	283	40	435	4	R. E. Willis	1889	S.U.
Rushmere	..	200							
Witnesham	..	250							
Turret-green, Silent-st	1842	800	345	41	470	10	C. E. P. Antram	1896	S.U.
Levington	..	..	..	4	20				
Laxfield	1808	800	172	19	200	..	A. J. Ward	1893	S.N.
Little Stonham	1858	600	20	4	35	..	J. Grimwood	1875	
Lowestoft (23,347) :—									
London-road	1813	450	152	23	288	4	J. M. Hamilton	1887	N.
Tonning-st.	1894	300	22	6	75	2	D. Bennett, B.A.	1894	S.N.
Mendlesham Green	1839	400	41	10	85	..	D. Dickerson	..	S.N.
Mildenhall	1875	300	28	6	50	..	H. M. Burt	1877	S.U.
Norton	1834	300	35	4	30	..	H. Alexander	1893	S.N.
Occold	1832	300	42	6	50	..	S. H. Haddock	1893	S.N.
Otley	1800	500	112	19	160	..	F. J. Harsant	1893	
Rattlesden	1813	300	95	11	75	..	W. H. Evans	1890	S.N.
Rishangles	1849	480	66	8	37	1	G. Harris	1849	S.N.
Somersham	1815	400	50	8	80	..	W. H. Ranson	1888	S.N.
Stowmarket, Bury-st.	1795	580	69	10	58	3	..	..	S.N.
Stoke Ash	1805	600	172	17	101	..	C. Hill	1849	S.N.
Stradbroke	1817	450	80	12	78	1	F. W. Rumsby	1895	S.U.
Sudbury :—									
Church-street	1834	567	222	35	469	3	Robt. Jones	1885	S.U.
Borley									
Cross-street									
Ebenezer	1851	300	..	2	20				
Sudbourne	1860	150	46	13	112	..	W. Large	1863	
Sutton	1810	300	28	4	37	..	..	..	S.N.
Tunstall Common	1804	550	110	10	100	..	W. Glasgow	1883	S.N.
Boyton	1876	120							
Eyke	1880	100							
Waldringfield	1823	300	40	8	47	..	..	..	S.N.
Walton	1808	420	97	10	71	3	T. Evans	1884	S.U.
Wattisham	1763	500	87	8	85	..	J. Hazelton	1893	S.N.
West Row (Mildenhall)	1804	400	100	22	178	6	C. J. Fowler	1892	S.U.

SURREY (*Pop.*, 1,731,343).

For other Churches in Surrey, see "METROPOLITAN," pp. 233—241.

(B. Berks. H. C. Home Counties. K. S., Kent and Sussex. M., Metropolitan. S., Southern.)

Churches.	Date.	Chapel seats.	No. of Members.	Sunday School Teachers.	No of Scholars.	Local Preachers.	Pastors.	When settled.	Associations.
Addlestone	1828	330	112	22	294	..	H. Bayley	1888	H.C.
Stone Hill	..	..	..	5	60				
Alfold	1883	270	..	6	70	2	F. Joseph	1885	
Burningfold	1886	..	..	5	50				
Dunsfold	1892	150							
Ash Vale (see Hampshire)									
Cheam	1862	150	111	11	73	..	T. G. Griffiths ..	1895	H.C.
Claygate..	1861	125	16	8	80	..	T. Rush	1895	M.
Cranleigh Common ..	1826	250	48	12	140	2	C. B. Barringer ..	1870	
Croydon (102,695):—									
Derby-road	1876	..	32	12	300	..	J. Copeland.. ..	1892	M.
Tamworth-road ..	1722	350	70	13	160	..	E. Wilmshurst ..	1892	
Croydon, South—									
Brighton-road ..	1894	650	139	38	390	3	R. E. Chettleborough ..	1893	
Croydon, West—									
Windmill-road ..	1881	250	41	8	61	..	W. Horton	1885	M.
Dorking	1869	250	83	12	89	..	T. F. Waddell ..	1892	H.C.
Esher, Park-road.. ..	1852	200	57	8	70	1	T. G. Head	1893	H.C.
Oxshott	1873	100	..	6	48				
Godstone	1882	250	12	3	45	..	.. ..	..	H.C.
Guildford (14,316):—									
Castle-street	1689	200	74	14	115				
Commercial-road ..	1824	220	80	12	100	4	J. Rankine	1879	H.C.
Chiddingfold	1889	120	26	5	49				
Horley	1881	320	71	12	120	1	B. Marshall.. ..	1878	K.S.
Fern-hill	1880	200	..	5	53				
Horsell, Anthonys ..	1888	100	25	4	70	1	E. W. Tarbox ..	1890	H.C.
Kingston (27,059).. ..	1790	760	270	32	330	..	G. Wright	1883	H.C.
Hampton Wick ..	..	100							
Richmond-road ..	..	150	51	13	166	..	.. ..	..	M.
Lingfield:—									
Dorman's Land ..	1792	400	42	8	61	..	R. Wilson	1891	H.C.
Malden, New	1862	350	86	14	150	..	S. H. Moore ..	1883	H.C.
Mitcham, Upper	1882	200	69	15	120	..	J. T. Figg	1891	H.C.
Molesey, East	1885	300	58	9	50	..	G. Wright, of Kingston ..	1893	H.C.
Norbiton, London-st...	1856	160	27	2	22	2	.. ..	..	M.
Bunyan	1882	850	254	34	400	15	D. Thompson ..	1892	H.C.
Outwood (Redhill) ..	1879	150	20	6	48	..	T. Green	1863	H.C.
Redhill and Reigate (22.646):—									
London-road(Redhill)	1864	500	190	16	150	13	G. Davies	1890	H.C.
Richmond (22,684):—									
Salem, Parkshot ..	1861	174	40	11	76	..	R. Sampson.. ..	1895	M.
Tadworth	1822	150	10	2	25	..	.. ..	..	M.
Thornton Heath	1888	300	155	33	273	..	T. Lardner	1892	H.C.
Woking, Goldsworth-rd	1879	350	73	23	130	..	E. J. Page	1895	S.
York Town	1813	250	84	18	170	2	J. M. Bergin ..	1895	B.

SUSSEX (*Pop.*, 550.446).
(K. S., Kent and Sussex.)

Churches.	Date.	Chapel seats.	No. of Members.	Sunday School Teachers.	No. of Scholars.	Local Preachers.	Pastors.	When settled.	Associations.
Battle	1780	350	41	10	54	..	G. B. Richardson	1895	K.S.
Brighton (115,873):—									
Florence-road	1894	524	49	7	60	..	D. J. Llewellyn ..	1894	K.S.
Holland-road	1887	900	339	29	240	..	D. Davies	1887	K.S.
Mighell-street	1878	400	30	10	100	..	G. Virgo	1892	
Queen's-square ..	1856	424	232	17	115	..	J. S. Geale	1880	K.S
Beaconsfield-road ..									
Upper Gardner-st. ..	..	..	..	12	160				
Sussex Street	1863	400	114	24	175	..	T. S. Burros ..	1894	K.S.
West Brighton, Providence	1878	120	39	10	103	..	W. S. Turner ..	1887	
Burgess Hill	1874	230	34	7	73	2	E. Standing ..	1879	K.S.
Crawley:—									
Station-terrace ..	1883	335	63	15	150	2	J. McAuslane ..	1883	K.S.
Temperance Reading Room									
Crowborough:—									
Forestfold	1845	280	47	10	100	2	E. Littleton	1868	
Withyham, Motts Mill									
South View, Gethsemane	1871	200	19	13	100	..	J. Whatford	1868	
Cuckfield, Zion	1845	100	16	5	40				
Eastbourne (34,969):—									
Ceylon-place	1870	650	193	20	187	2	W. J. Harris ..	1894	K.S.
Forest Row	..	..	36	9	73	..	.. ..	..	K.S.
Hailsham	1795	340	65	..	..	1	J. Nunn	1860	
Magham Down ..									
Handcross	1887	220	15	9	90				
Hastings (52,223):—									
Wellington-square ..	1838	750	293	34	260	6	W. R. Peacock ..	1889	K.S.
Halton	1871	200							
Heathfield	1850	340	57	10	120	..	G. Mockford ..	1860	
Horsham	1895	Hall	36	7	36	1	.. ..	..	H.C.
Lamberhurst	1851	200	18	..	..	..	W. Boorman ..	1881	
Lewes (10,997):—									
Eastgate	1781	400	88	28	172	4	W. K. Armstrong, [B.A.	1879	K.S.
Portslade-by-Sea ..	1872	400	79	14	245	..	H. J. Dyer	1893	K.S.
Rye:—									
Mermaid-street ..	1750	220	32	8	60	..	E. Compton ..	1882	
Shoreham	1870	350	73	11	118	..	.. ..	..	K.S.
St. Leonards:—									
Chapel Park-road ..	1880	500	97	13	105	..	H. Rodger	1895	K.S.
Uckfield	1792	250	29	5	35	..	H. Gardner	1894	
Wadhurst, Shover's Grn.	1816	300	23	6	50	..	A. Boorman ..	1883	
Wivelsfield	1763	200	30	3	30	..	G. Virgo, of Brighton	1873	
Worthing (16,606) ..	1879	500	187	29	347	4	A. W. L. Barker ..	1895	K.S.
Arundel	1843	180							
Small Dole	1880	130							

WARWICKSHIRE (*Pop.*, 805,072).

(W.M., West Midland. E.M., East Midland. W., Worcestershire. D. F. M. Denbigh, Flint, and Merioneth.)

Churches.	Date.	Chapel seats.	No. of Members.	Sunday school Teachers.	No. of Scholars.	Local Preachers.	Pastors.	When settled.	Associations.
Alcester	1640	380	90	19	160	5	E. J. Crofts	1884	W.
Attleborough	1840	260	78	19	220	..	W. Satchwell ..	1887	W.M.
Austrey (Atherstone) ..	1808	500	12	4	20	1	J. R. Godfrey, of Barlestone, Leicestershire	1895	E.M.
Bedworth	1884	350	..	..	..	..	.. ..	..	W.M.
Birmingham (478,113):–									
Aston-park, Christ Church	1866	900	457	58	625	14	W. A. Wicks ..	1894	
Victoria-road, Handsworth ..	1884	200	..	14	150				
Burlington-street, Aston	1884	250	..	55	667				
Bevington-road ..	..	..	..	4	60				
Balsall Heath-road ..	1872	350	118	18	200	..	S. Nield	1892	W.M.
Bristol-road, Wycliffe	1861	950	203	48	619	..	.. ..	..	W.M.
(Cannon-street), Graham-street	1737	1700	551	90	810	27	W. Hackney, M.A.	1887	W.M.
Alvechurch	1828	200							
Anderton Street ..									
King's Norton ..	1842	150							
Shirley	1845	80							
Slade-lane	1888	100							
Colmore-row, No. 116 (W.)	1870	room	19	..	..	..	M. Morgan	1895	D F M
Erdington	1878	500	169	19	197	2	J. Dawson	1881	W.M.
Great King-street ..	1848	550	281	59	678	5	.. ..	..	W.M.
Guildford-street ..	1881	250	70	24	320	5	J. Bradford	1883	W.M.
Hagley-road	1828	1000	383	101	989	7	J. M. G. Owen ..	1895	W.M.
Carter-lane	..	200	..	8	60	..	G. Dunnett, of Halesowen, Worcestershire	1895	
Ellen-street, Brookfields	..	250	..	30	400				
Handsworth, Hamstead-road	1882	780	156	59	915	..	H. Bonner	1883	W.M
Harborne	1854	390	123	28	350	..	W. W. B. Emery	1888	W.M.
Beech-lanes	..	150	..	9	83	..	G. Dunnett, of Halesowen, Worcestershire	1895	
Heneage-street ..	1842	750	390	60	673	4	G. West	1884	W.M.
Highgate Park	1775	700	207	22	253	6	E. W. Cantrell ..	1882	W.M.
Alcester-street ..	..	200	..	..	50				
Little Sutton ..	..	120	..	..	40				
Lodge-road	1858	500	135	23	214	3	D. E. Evans	1880	W.M.
Longmore-street ..	1882	300	141	20	200	..	C. Beaumont ..	1895	

WARWICKSHIRE—*continued.*

Churches.	Date.	Chapel seats.	No. of Members.	Sunday School Teachers.	No. of Scholars.	Local Preachers.	Pastors.	When settled.	Associations
Birmingham (*contd.*):—									
Moseley, Oxford-rd	1835	570	282	39	460	..	R. Gray	1874	W M
King's Heath		300				..	J. Collett	1888	
Newhall-street	1814	300	56	19	136	4	.. ..	..	W.M.
Saltley	1893	..	51	18	350	3	.. ..	..	W.M.
Selly Park..	1878	400	69	17	145	..	F. C. Fuchs.. ..	1894	W.M.
Small Heath :—									
Coventry Road	1873	750	178	25	350	10	.. ..	..	W.M.
Victoria-street ..	1891	450	100	29	491	2	J. Dowse	1891	W.M.
Smethwick	1866	830	157	27	260	2	H. Singleton ..	1894	W.M.
Sparkbrook, Stratford-road	1880	1000	315	85	800	10	J. Hulme	1880	W.M.
Spring-hill	1887	700	198	32	422	2	T. E. Titmuss ..	1892	W.M.
Warwick-street ..	1869	300	97	22	300	2	S. W. Martin ..	1869	W.M.
Penn-street	..	..	..	8	85				
Yates-street	1859	250	104	21	300	..	F. M Young ..	1886	W.M.
Elkington-street ..	..	..	..	15	219				
Coventry (52,724):—									
Queen's-road	1626	1000	440	140	2024	4	W.E. Blomfield, B.A., B.D.	1895	W.M.
Cow-lane	..	700							
Lord-street	..	400							
Wolston	1814	300							
Gosford-street	1822	708	..	..	..	..	.. ..	..	W.M.
St. Michael's	1855	700	235	36	376	..	P. Morrison ..	1895	W.M.
Dunchurch (Rugby) ..	1844	200	14	4	20	..	.. ..	..	W.M.
Henley-in-Arden	1688	200	40	6	45	3	E. Edginton ..	1892	W.
Yarningale	1873	60	..	1	20				
Leamington (26,930):—									
Clarendon (U.) ..	1859	500	102	15	220	4	G. A. Willis.. ..	1884	W.M.
Radford	..	..	12	6	100				
Warwick-street ..	1830	650	208	15	137	4	A. Phillips	1892	W.M.
Satchwell-street ..									
Longford :—									
Salem	1773	830	250	40	336	1	J. Spanswick ..	1889	W.M.
Walsgrave-on-Sowe	1830	100	40						
Union-place	1826	400	..	..	..	..	.. ..	..	W.M.
Monk's Kirby & Pailton	1817	300	32	3	18	1	E. Gilbert	1884	E.M.
Nuneaton	1846	460	100	19	263	1	.. ..	..	W.M.
Polesworth	1828	350	59	11	120	5	.. ..	..	W.M.
Rugby	1808	350	118	15	120	9	J. Young	1894	E.M.
Draycott	1884	103	..	3	23				
Hillmorton	1682	150	..	6	31				
Stratford-on-Avon ..	1832	350	149	19	202	9	.. ..	..	W.
Temple Grafton ..	1841	150	..	3	16				
Preston-on-Stour	1867	100	..	3	33				
Studley	1848	250	101	19	150	..	J. Read..	1893	W.
Umberslade	1877	200	55	8	64	..	J. Mann	1888	W.M.
Hockley Heath ..	1877	80							
Warwick (11,903):—									
Castle Hill	1640	400	60	11	75	..	H. W. Meadow ..	1890	W.M.
Wolvey (Hinckley) ..	1815	400	50	12	110				
Wyken-sq. (Coventry)	1817	200	69	13	45	15	.. ..	..	W.M.
Shilton	..	..	..	6	14				

WESTMORLAND (*Pop.*, 66,098).

(N., Northern.)

Churches.	Date.	Chapel seats.	No. of Members.	Sunday School Teachers.	No. of Scholars.	Local Preachers.	Pastors.	When settled.	Associations.
Kirkby Stephen	1890	150	83	18	146	10	C. G. Jones.. ..	1888	N.
Crosby Garrett	1856	100							
Brough	1834	200							
Great Asby	1839	100							
Winton	1864	150							

WILTSHIRE (*Pop.*, 264,997).

(W. E. S., Wilts and East Somerset. B., Bristol. S., Southern.)

Churches.	Date.	Chapel seats.	No. of Members.	Sunday School Teachers.	No. of Scholars.	Local Preachers.	Pastors.	When settled.	Associations.
Bearfield (Bradford) ..	1858	100	15	8	80				
Bradford-on-Avon :—									
Conigre, Zion	1844	480	80	25	220	2	E. E. Smith.. ..	1890	B.
Bratton (Westbury) ..	1667	300	167	26	162	6	W. Fry	1894	W E S
Coulstone	..	110							
Steeple Ashton ..	..	110							
Tinhead	..	120							
Great Cheverill ..	..	120							
Bromham	1828	200	12	10	60	..	.. ..	..	W E S
Calne :—									
Castle-street	1660	350	102	20	125	9	W. H. J. Page ..	1893	W E S
Yatesbury	1874	100							
Ralford Bridge ..	1887	..	..	4	40				
Chapmanslade	1788	140	23	4	40	..	*Evangelist*	..	W E S
Chippenham :—									
Station Hill	1857	300	51	13	120	2	J. E. Tranter ..	1892	W E S
Corsham :—									
Priory-street	1823	350	240	46	312	6	J. Smith	1891	B.
Biddestone	1832	150							
Moor Green	1833	150							
Velley	1857	120							
Atworth	1860	120							
Corton	1827	150	38	6	48	2	.. ..	..	W E S
Crockerton	1669	200	27	5	26	1	*Evangelist*	..	W E S
Damerham	1828	140	11	7	70	2	L. Earney	1895	S.
Rockbourne	1802	100	..	4	40				
Devizes :—									
Maryport-street ..	1649	300	60	14	120	1	C. Hemington ..	1871	
Sheep-street	1649	650	130	26	290	2	J. Day	1895	W E S
Stert	1887	80	..	3	35				
Pewsey	..	100							
Marden	..	70							

WILTSHIRE—*continued*

Churches.	Date.	Chapel seats.	No. of Members.	Sunday School Teachers.	No of Scholars.	Local Preachers.	Pastors.	When settled.	Associations.
Downton :—									
South-lane	1735	350 }	100	19	135	..	W. Evans	1892	S.
Gravel Close	1666	120 }							
Redlynch	1858	100	..	8	68				
Grittleton (Chippnhm.)	1720	200	5						
Hilperton (Trowbridge)	1806	88	25	6	34				
Imber	1839	180	29	6	97	1	.. ..	..	W E S
Limpley Stoke	1889	130	20	5	25	..	.. ..	..	B.
Littleton Panell (Devizes) ..	1848	150	25	10	93	1	.. ..	..	W E S
Melksham :—									
Broughton-road ..	1669	380	177	25	300	12	Wm. Smith	1891	W E S
Forest	1839	150							
Beanacre	1840	100							
North Bradley	1775	500	144	26	82	3			
Salisbury (15,533) :—									
Brown-street	1657	600	272	33	341	10	G. Short, B.A. ..	1868	S.
Coombe Bissett ..	..	150	..	6	30				
Porton	1665	100	..	5	39				
Bodenham	1860	100	..	4	40				
Semley	1817	250	68	9	50	1	T. Yauldren ..	1895	W E S
Sherston Magna	1837	150	18	2	16	1	A. J. Parker, of Old Sodbury, Glos.	1892	B.
Shrewton, ...	1812	500	80	10	85	2	}		
Tilshead	1851	130	26	6	60	..	}	..	W E S
Chitterne	1859	120	27	5	45	1	}		
Southwick (Trowbridge)	1655	300	68	22	104	..	.. ..	..	W E S
2nd Church	1860	..	60	24	110				
Stratton, Upper	1861	200	58	17	160	7	.. ..	..	W E S
Stratton Green	1750	100	12	4	40	..	R. W. Mansfield, of Bourton, Berks.	1892	W E S
Swindon :—									
Tabernacle	1855	1000	394	58	750	8	F. Pugh	1877	W E S
Cambria	1882	250							
Gorse Hill	1878	200							
Trowbridge :—									
Back-street	1736	860	479	63	362	10	.. ..	..	W E S
Studley Green ..	1850	110	..	10	80				
Westwood, Lower ..	1865	90	..	9	65				
Yarnbrook	1874	230	..	7	42				
Bethesda	1821	700	253	40	320	..	H. Sanders	1890	W E S
Zion	1813	700	165	32	220				
Warminster, North-row	1811	370	74	12	92	5	G. W. Roughton ..	1890	W E S
Upton Scudamore ..									
Westbury :—									
Leigh	1662	500	139	17	151	4	W. Price	1889	W E S
Stormore	1826	120							
Penknap, Providence	1810	500	141	17	156	2	.. ..	..	W E S
West End	1825	350	104	17	130	1	W. P. Laurence ..	1876	W E S
Whitbourne (Corsley)	1811	200	45	8	60	..	*Evangelist*	..	W E S
Winterslow, *(See Broughton, Hants)*									

WORCESTERSHIRE (*Pop.*, 413,760).
(W., Worcestershire. W.M., West Midland. O., Oxfordshire.)

Churches.	Date.	Chapel seats.	No. of Members.	Sunday School Teachers.	No. of Scholars.	Local Preachers.	Pastors.	When settled.	Associations.
Astwood Bank	1813	700	..	66	505	..	J. R. Russell ..	1895	W.
Atch Lench and ..	1825	165	117	10	110	3	C. Chrystal ..	1888	W.
Dunnington	..	200					G. Towler ..	1895	
Harvington	1886	180							
Bewdley..	1649	260	30	10	97	2	F. J. Aust	1891	W.
Blockley	1820	320	69	26	160	..	E. G. Lovell.. ..	1894	O.
Draycott..	..	50							
Paxford	..	75							
Bromsgrove, New-road	1666	500	167	30	298	12	J. Ford	1893	W.M.
Catshill	1830	100	28	12	120	3			
Dodford	1865	100	..	8	55				
Cinderbank	1820	400	108	33	450	4	T. Lewis	1872	W.M.
Cookhill (Alcester) ..	1841	200	74	20	100	3	J. R. Russell (*see above*).	1895	W.
Cutsdean	1839	150	49	10	..	4	C. Sirett	1884	O.
Stanton	1842	100							
Droitwich, Hill End ..	1874	180	34	7	50	1	J. Lord..	1891	W.
Dudley (45,740):—									
New-street..	1772	400	109	15	165	..	E. Milnes	1893	W.M.
Evesham, Cowl-street	1732	550	144	52	505	12	.. ..	..	W.
Aldington	1881	120							
Ashton	1881	200							
Bengeworth	1874	150							
Offenham	..	60							
Bretforton	..	100							
Charlton	..	120							
Goose-hill (Droitwich)	1866	50	11	..	..	..	.. ..	..	W.
Halesowen	1878	170	26	9	100	2	G. Dunnett .. *see* also p. 257.	1895	W.M.
Inkberrow District Mission	1889	..	..	6	40	..	*Evangelist*	..	W
Kidderminster (24,803):									
Church-street	1808	600	274	31	375	1	T. Fisk	1862	W.
							L. T. Harry ..	1892	
Milton Hall	1890	400	..	20	270				
Malvern, Great	1886	300	69	5	30	3	W. J. Povey, M.A.	1889	W.
Netherton:—									
Ebenezer	1864	500	50	32	240	1	.. ..	..	W.M.
Sweet Turf	1803	200	60	15	200	3	A. Griffiths	1895	W.M.
Pershore, Broad-street	1658	550	102	21	170	3	J. H. Feek	1873	W.
Bishampton									
Redditch, Ipsley-street	1862	280	165	28	180	5	E. W. Berry ..	1886	W.
Web Heath	..	70	..	7	68				
Shipston-on-Stour ..	1781	200	44	10	89	4	J. Butler	1895	O.
Stretton-on-Fosse..	..	60							
Stourbridge, Hanbry-hl.	1837	365	71	19	160	..	T. Woodhouse ..	1892	W.M.
Stourport	1875	300	69	14	150	3	R. Evans	1877	W.
Tenbury, Cross-street..	1816	200	18	3	24	1	.. ..	..	W.
Upton-on-Severn.. ..	1693	460	52	10	40	..	W. T. Shepherd..	1894	W.
Naunton..	1863	100	..	5	50				
Westmancote	1779	180	50	5	60	..	E. Balmford ..	1889	W.
Worcester (42,908):—									
Sansome-walk	1641	850	397	91	889	10	.. ..	..	W.
Kempsey..	1860	200							
Red Hill..	1879	85							
Rainbow Hill ..	1881	200							

YORKSHIRE (*Pop.*, 3,208,828)

(Y., Yorkshire. N., Northern. L.C., Lancashire and Cheshire. D. F. M., Denbigh Flint and Merioneth.)

Churches.	Date.	Chapel seats.	No. of Members.	Sunday School Teachers.	No. of Scholars.	Local Preachers.	Pastors.	When settled.	Associations.
Armley, Carr Crofts ..	1848	600	149	40	248		W. Sumner	1884	Y.
Barnoldswick	1661	588	137	25	305		.. ..	..	Y.
Bethesda	1661	600	145	24	430		.. ..	..	Y.
Barnsley (35,427):—									
Parker-street	1894	150	44	28	294	4	W. R. Ponton ..	1893	Y.
Sheffield-road	1845	500	172	45	500		John Young ..	1881	Y.
Batley (28,719):—									
Park-road	1877	400	57	17	116		F. Wynn	1895	Y.
Bedale	1836	230	27	8	45		.. ..	..	Y.
Beverley (12,539):—									
Well-lane	1833	500	145	33	304	9	.. ..	..	Y.
Woodmansey	..	100							
Bingley:—									
Park-road	1760	680	121	37	204		E. R. Lewis	1893	Y.
Birchcliffe (Hebden Bg)	1763	700	352	78	367		J. Gay	1894	Y.
Bishop Burton	1764	250	46	4	40		.. ..	..	Y.
Blackley (Elland) ..	1793	750	178	30	240		R. Briggs	1874	Y.
Boroughbridge	1822	160	27	3	24		*Evangelist*	..	Y.
Dishforth									
Bradford (216,361):—									
Allerton, Bethel ..	1824	500	123	24	226		.. ..	..	Y.
Central	1873	488	128	32	183		A. T. Walker ..	1892	I.
Girlington	1882	1000	254	55	617		R. Evans	1888	Y.
Hallfield	1863	950	143	27	216		T. G. Hunter ..	1894	Y.
Heaton	1862	360	180	35	250	3	R. Howarth	1877	Y.
Infirmary-st., Bethel	1850	200	76	22	105		.. ..	..	Y.
Leeds-road	..	825	352	60	643		R. Herries	1892	Y.
Marshfield	1892	350	..		..		G. Edmondson ..	1892	Y.
Ripley-street, Eben.	1867	714	233	33	478		A. C. Perriam ..	1891	Y.
Sion Jubilee	1824	1200	511	67	850		G. C. Williams ..	1894	Y.
Caledonia-street ..	..		..	29	319				
Tetley-street	1832	600	222	27	218		S. Kent	1889	Y.
Trinity	1857	800	273	37	367	2	C. Rignal	1881	Y.
Westgate	1753	840	380	32	360	4	C. W. Skemp ..	1881	Y.
Bramley:—									
Zion	1774	650	196	41	273		.. ..	..	Y.
Salem	1878	450	77	20	120		.. ..	..	Y.
Brearley, Luddenden-foot	1846	400	100	20	112		F. Allsop	1883	Y.
Bridlington	1698	500	40	2	94		J. Scilley	1892	Y.
Clayton	1828	750	222	47	358		J. W. Hambly ..	1881	Y.
Cononley	1861	240	37	11	70	2	.. ..	..	Y.
Cowlinghill	1744	400	41	13	60		.. ..	..	Y.
Middleton Cowling									
Crigglestone	1879	250	23	10	70		.. ..	..	Y.
Cullingworth	1836	400	62	6	140		J. Davis	1892	Y.
Denholme (Bradford) ..	1851	430	83	24	174		.. ..	..	Y.
Dewsbury (29,847):—									
Leeds-road	1865	410	143	33	260		C. Payne	1892	Y.

YORKSHIRE—*continued.*

Churches.	Date.	Chapel seats.	No. of Members.	Sunday School Teachers.	No. of Scholars.	Local Preachers.	Pastors.	When settled.	Associations.
Doncaster (25,933) :—									
Chequer-road	1889	300	101	16	140	3	J. F. Porteous ..	1890	Y.
Driffield	1786	440	47	9	60	..	F. D. Tranter ..	1893	Y.
Cranswick	1876	140							
Earby-in-Craven	1819	650	234	42	400	5	W. Wynn	1893	Y.
Eccleshill, Undercliff-rd	1885	220	44	12	120	..	T. E. Rawlings, of [Idle	1889	Y.
Elland	1863	450	91	30	226	1	.. .. ..	..	Y.
Farsley	1777	1050	319	84	405	3	H. Ellis, M.A. ..	1890	Y.
Calverley	1874	140							
Gildersome	1707	700	124	20	200	3	J. Haslam	1862	Y.
Golcar	1835	1150	303	73	445	1	W. Gay	1882	Y.
Leymoor	1884	170	..	19	67				
Guiseley	1884	250	39	21	110	..	R. Scott	1895	Y.
Halifax (89,832) :—									
North-parade	1774	668	300	42	298	5	C. Hood	1888	Y.
Lee Mount	1892	600	167	36	399	1	J. H. Robinson ..	1893	Y.
Pellon-lane	1755	600	239	34	273	2	F. Slater	1895	Y.
Pellon	1840	350	..	45	273				
Trinity-road	1851	1000	320	45	375	2	H. Davis	1892	Y.
Harrogate (13,917) ..	1880	600	145	16	118	1	.. ..	..	Y.
Haworth :—									
West-lane	1752	500	209	32	172	1	D. Arthur	1889	Y.
Hawksbridge ..	..	200	..	48	178				
Hebden Bridge	1777	1000	264	40	379	..	W. Jones	1891	Y.
Hellifield	1833	200	19	10	68	2	.. ..	..	Y.
Heptonstall Slack ..	1807	550	220	29	183	7	J. K. Archer ..	1895	Y.
Broadstone	..	300	83	24	67				
Blakedean	..	80	11	..	16				
Horkinstone (Ox'nhope)	1837	200	42	46	72	..	.. ..	..	Y.
Horsforth, Cragg Hill ..	1802	500	141	30	227	1	.. ..	..	Y.
Huddersfield (95,420) :—									
New North-road ..	1846	800	315	35	268	6	F. J. Benskin ..	1884	Y.
Birkby	1879	120	..	16	184				
Lindley	1864	670	157	31	480	3	W. H. Holdsworth, M.A.	1895	Y.
Lockwood..	1795	720	245	61	462	2	G. Archer	1893	Y.
Rehoboth	1835	..	42	30	230	1			
Primrose Hill	1889	700	75	27	196	..	W. J. Dyer	1893	Y.
Hull (200,044) :—									
George-street	1795	500	219	15	152	4	J. E. Shephard ..	1895	Y.
Hedon									
South-street	1736	800	134	22	196	1	J. M. Murphy ..	1892	Y.
Beverley-road	1885	450	122	13	215	3	.. ..	..	Y.
Idle	1808	850	169	34	230	1	T. E. Rawlings ..	1889	Y.
Keighley (30,810) :—									
Albert-street	1810	700	322	71	522	1	J. Alderson	1886	Y.
Worth	1873	250							
Leeds (367,505) :—									
Blenheim	1848	720	259	25	238	1	P. T. Thomson, M.A.	1895	Y
Camp-road	1877	300	..	26	306	..	J. H. McKeracher	1895	
Burley-road	1877	650	209	34	390	3	.. ..	..	Y.
Kirkstall	1877	300	..	8	30				

YORKSHIRE—*continued.*

Churches.	Date.	Chapel seats.	No. of Members.	Sunday School Teachers.	No. of Scholars.	Local Preachers.	Pastors	When settled.	Associations.
Leeds (*contd.*):—									
Hunslet Tabernacle	1837	700	320	47	530	8	A. E. Greening ..	1880	Y.
North-street	1844	550	118	25	246		F. W. W. Pugh ..	1894	Y.
South-parade	1779	900	507	104	697	5	.. ..	..	Y.
Meanwood-road ..	1834	200	..	..	..		G. W. Bonell ..	1888	
Beeston Hill	1874	200	..	..	..				
Wintoun-street ..	1850	600	30	10	60		A. E. O. Jones ..	1895	Y.
York-road	1861	750	102	31	346		C. Riseborough ..	1894	Y.
Lineholme, (Todmorden)	1818	500	164	34	285	2	G. M. Rice	1890	L.C.
Long Preston	1833	200	11	4	20		.. ..	..	Y.
Lydgate (Todmorden) ..	1859	300	137	30	204	2	W. L. Stevenson	1884	Y.
Malton, Wells-lane ..	1822	350	74	10	120	2	J. O. Ogilvy.. ..	1894	Y.
Masham	1815	200	37	9	30		.. ..	..	Y.
Meltham	1814	560	160	32	178		F. Oliver	1893	Y.
Middlesboro' (75,532):—									
Brentnall-street (W.)	1876	350	..	..	..		.. ..	..	D F M
Linthorpe-road ..	1849	250	58	15	220		R. Ensoll	1894	Y.
Marton-road	1886	520	135	24	260	5	J. R. Fawcett ..	1887	N.
Newport-road	1856	1000	276	63	756		C. E. Stone.. ..	1892	N.
North Ormesby ..	1884	400							
Milnsbridge	1843	800	262	51	350		A. J. Davies ..	1892	Y.
Mirfield	1825	750	168	33	180		J. Kitchener ..	1887	Y.
Morley (21,068):—									
Commercial-street ..	1872	400	129	42	370	3	C. Welton	1888	Y.
Nazebottom (Hebden Bridge)	1872	300	40	16	152		.. ..	..	Y.
Norland	1864	120	18	14	76		.. ..	..	Y.
Normanton	1878	750	78	20	300	2	J. T. Heselton ..	1885	Y.
Northallerton	1845	250	8	1	25		*Evangelist*	..	Y.
Brompton									
Ossett (10,984)	1834	400	64	24	130	2	E. Greenwood ..	1882	Y.
Ossett, Central	1894	..	19	6	30		.. ..	..	Y.
Polemoor	1790	640	219	98	320	3	.. ..	..	Y.
Clough Head.. ..	..	300							
Outlane	..	300							
Pudsey	1848	200	67	22	141		F. W. Turner ..	1893	Y.
Queensbury (Bradford)	1773	550	204	50	332	3	A. C. Carter ..	1885	Y.
Rawdon	1715	500	200	34	242	2	A. P. Fayers ..	1883	Y.
Redcar	1889	320	20	2	15		J. Horn	1893	Y.
Rishworth	1803	350	96	23	142		.. ..	..	Y.
Rodley	1892	350	51	18	50		.. ..	..	Y.
Rotherham (42,061):—									
Westgate	1837	500	115	..	..		J. Collinson ..	1888	Y.
Salendine Nook (Huddersfield)	1743	900	324	125	458	4	D. W. Jenkins ..	1895	Y.
Salterforth (Barnldswk)	1861	250	77	16	120		.. ..	..	Y.
Scapegoat Hill	1871	240	176	60	247		T. R. Lewis.. ..	1889	Y.
Scarboro' (33,776):—									
Albemarle	1865	670	226	44	440	4	R. Wood	1892	Y.
West Gate (Eben)	1771	450	68	13	117	2	J. H. P. Smith ..	1887	Y.
Burniston	..	..	9	6	36				

YORKSHIRE—*continued.*

Churches.	Date.	Chapel seats.	No. of Members.	Sunday School Teachers.	No. of Scholars.	Local Preachers.	Pastors.	When settled.	Associations.
Sheffield (324,243) :—									
Attercliffe	1874	750	175	38	470	3	J. G. Williams ..	1887	Y.
Treeton	1885	60	..	6	70				
Cemetery-road ..	1839	680	271	44	330	4	E. Carrington ..	1883	Y.
Glossop-road	1871	800	284	35	273	2	.. ..	..	Y.
Hillsborough	1893	350	79	20	200	1	.. ..	..	Y.
Port Mahon	1834	600	364	46	520	4	H. Trotman ..	1893	Y.
Townhead-street ..	1813	650	236	31	170	3	Isaac A. Ward ..	1887	Y.
Walkley	1880	250	102	30	320	2	A. G. Haste.. ..	1893	Y.
Shipley :—									
Bethel	1758	500	209	22	257	1	.. ..	..	Y.
Charlestown	1890	200	39	17	64	..	.. ..	..	Y.
Rosse-street	1866	1000	304	..	..	2	.. ..	..	Y.
Shore (Todmorden) ..	1777	750	214	31	218	2	J. F. Archer ..	1894	L.C
Skipton, Otley-street ..	1850	350	91	30	208	..	W. Judge	1878	Y.
Belmont	1890	180	42	13	130	1	J. S. Griffiths ..	1892	Y.
Slack-lane (Keighley)..	1819	650	161	45	160	3	H. Davies	1888	Y.
Slaithwaite (Hddrsfld) :									
Providence	1816	470	62	22	126				
Zion	1886	450	30	20	220	..	E. Evans	1886	Y.
South Bank, Normanby-road	1877	300	89	16	200	2	D. M. Pryse ..	1894	N.
Sowerby Bridge	1884	300	28	17	79	..	.. ..	..	Y.
Staincliffe	1821	300	100	15	158	..	J. Rigby	1893	Y.
Stanningley, Salem ..	1828	500	122	25	251	2	.. ..	..	Y.
Steep-la. (Sowerby Bge)	1779	600	151	50	290	..	W. Haigh	1864	Y.
Sunny Bank (Golcar) ..	1883	250	41	34	107	1	.. ..	..	Y.
Sutton-in-Craven.. ..	1741	850	382	70	525	4	F. W. Pollard ..	1892	Y.
Glusburn	1875	100	..	32	160				
Thornaby-on-Tees (15,637)	1881	400	84	15	155	..	H. W. H. Winsor	1881	N.
Todmorden :—									
Wellington-road ..	1845	450	243	48	274	2	T. Cotes	1888	Y.
Roomfield	1808	750	254	47	420	3	H. Briggs	1871	Y.
Wainsgate (Hebden Bridge)	1750	420	126	30	140	..	.. ..	..	Y.
Wakefield (33,146) :—									
George-street	1838	500	134	18	121	..	J. Cottam	1894	Y.
West Vale, near Halifax	1871	500	106	33	210	..	D. R. Lewis ..	1895	Y.
York (67,004) :—									
Priory-street	1862	650	151	20	140	1	C. Pates	1895	Y.

Wales and Monmouthshire.

(Aggregate Population, 1,771,451.)

The letter (E.) in brackets after the name of a Church signifies that the service is in English.

An asterisk prefixed to the name of a Pastor indicates that he is Pastor of more than one Church.

ANGLESEY (*Pop.*, 50,098).

(A., Anglesey. N.W., North Wales English Union.)

Churches.	Date.	Chapel seats.	No. of Members.	Sunday School Teachers.	No. of Scholars.	Local Preachers.	Pastors.	When settled.	Associations.
Amlwch, Salem	1796	500	146	18	140	..	G. Williams ..	1895	A.
Llaneilian, Bethania	..	100	20	5	30	1			
Beaumaris	1784	195	42	5	38	1	T. Hughes	1881	A.
Belan	1833	150	58	10	36	1	.. ..	..	A.
Bodedeyrn	1824	120	40	8	61	1	.. ..	..	A.
Ainon	..	100	28	..	39	..	.. ..	..	A.
Bontripont	1828	250	55	..	55	..	.. ..	..	A.
Brynsiencyn Tab'nacle	1804	140	14	4	26	..	J. G. Williams ..	1895	A.
Caerceiliog, Siloh ..	1848	240	67	..	90	1	.. ..	..	A.
Capel Gwyn	1796	100	48	7	40	..	.. ..	..	A.
Capel Newydd, Peny-graigwen	1796	122	33	..	38	..	*J. C. Rees	1893	A.
Cemaes, Bethlehem ..	1823	150	33	7	34	..	.. ..	..	A.
Gaerwen, Moriah	1850	300	40	7	50	..	*T. E. Williams ..	1891	A.
Garegfawr	1815	120	24	..	6	..	.. ..	..	A.
Gwalchmai	1889	..	9	4	25	..	.. ..	..	A.
Holyhead :—									
Edmond-st., Bethel ..	1790	1060	333	33	350	6	T. M. Rees	1892	A.
Porthyfelin, Salem	1865	150	..	10	60				
Hebron	1862	201	91	12	100	..	W. Price	1887	A.
New Park - street, (Newry-street) (E.)	1862	250	58	11	120	..	G. Evans	1894	N.W.
Siloh	1844	350	58	22	52	3	.. ..	..	A.
Llandegfan, Seion ..	1815	250	50	7	23	1	.. ..	..	A.
Llanddeusant :—									
Horeb	1816	185	45	..	35	..	.. ..	..	A.
Llanerchymedd	1818	350	53	13	90	..	H. Edwards	1891	A.
Llanfachreth	1796	400	80	13	70	..	.. ..	..	A.
Llanfaethlu, Zoar ..	1820	200	77	10	55	2	*D. Lloyd	1894	A.
Llanfair-Math	1782	250	35	6	30	..	*E. W. Lewis ..	1895	A.
Llangefni, Ebenezer ..	1779	300	140	18	145	2	T. Frimston ..	1893	A.
Pisgah	1875	150							
Llangoed, Jerusalem ..	1804	150	43	..	50	..	.. ..	..	A
Llanwenllwyfo, Sardis	1833	193	48	8	30	..	*J. C. Rees	1893	A.
Menai Bridge	1884	250	37	..	..	..	.. ..	..	A.
Newburgh	1849	200	7	..	12	1	.. ..	..	A.
Pencarneddi	1784	200	38	8	60	2	*T. E. Williams ..	1891	A.
Pensarn	1837	400	88	12	70	1	*J. C. Rees	1893	A.
Rhosybol, Bethel	1841	250	56	9	50	..	E. E. Jones	1875	A.
Rhydwyn	1791	400	79	..	119	..	*D. Lloyd	1894	A.
Traethcoch	1816	124	6	3	14	..	*E. W. Lewis ..	1895	A.
Valley	1868	131	38	7	50	..	.. ..	..	A.

BRECKNOCKSHIRE (*Pop.*, 57,031).

(B., Breconshire. M., Monmouthshire Welsh. M.E., Monmouthshire English G.C.E., Glamorganshire and Carmarthenshire English.)

Churches.	Date.	Chapel seats.	No. of Members.	Sunday School Teachers.	No. of Scholars.	Local Preachers.	Pastors.	When settled.	Associations.
Beaufort, Zoar (W. & E.)	1853	700	90	8	127	1	D. S. Jones	1890	M.
Siloam (E.)	1862	140	20	5	40	..	A. Tovey	1892	M.E.
Brecon :—									
Watergate	1819	350	172	10	120	1	D. B. Edwards ..	1868	B.
Kensington (E.) ..	1817	500	114	16	244	..	S. Jones	1893	G C E
Brynmawr :—									
King-street, Calvary	1837	500	160	14	190	2	John Williams ..	1876	M.
Tabor .. .. [(E.)	1835	800	120	12	150	..	H. J. Evans.. ..	1892	M.
Zion	1846	700	27	5	45	..	J. L. Bowen ..	1895	M.
Builth, Ebenezer (E.)..	1787	300	163	11	100	..	H. Evans	1892	B.
Capel y Ffin (E.)	1663	150	13	2	16	..	*J. N. Smith (*see also* pp. 220 & 285)	1890	B.
Crickhowell	1839	300	128	12	116	..	.. ..	..	B.
Cwmdwr (nr. Trecastle), Horeb	1820	140	28	2	20	..	.. ..	..	B.
Erwood, Hephzibah ..	1829	200	52	5	68	..	John Morgan ..	1885	B.
and Ramah	1855	150	16	2	15	..			
Garth, Pisgah	1827	260	71	3	30	..	*T. Harries	1889	B.
Gilwern (E.), Hope ..	1861	200	61	7	120	..	S. Howells	1890	M.
Glasbury (E.) and ..	1862	350	71	4	30	1	J. Lloyd Williams	1892	B.
Penyrheol (E.)	1819	250	58	2	24	..			
Hay (E.), Salem	1815	400	69	9	74	1	C. Morgan	1895	B.
Bronith									
Llanelly :—									
Bethlehem (W. & E.)	1837	560	40	4	25	..	.. ..	..	M.
Darrenfelen (W. & E.)	1842	500	55	10	70	..	.. ..	..	M.
Nazareth (E.)	1853	250	41	10	130	..	.. ..	..	M.
Llanfihangel, Zoar ..	1827	250	32	4	24	..	J. L. Evans ..	1861	B.
Bethel Lower	1841	200	35	4	30	1			
Sardis	1824	150	48	4	25	..	.. ..	..	B.
Llanfrynach, Mizpah ..	1834	200	48	3	28	..	.. ..	..	B.
Llangamarch, Salem ..	1847	150	36	3	22	..	*J. W. Humphreys	1888	B.
Llangorse	1823	140	39	3	30	..	*T. Harries	..	B.
Llangynidr, Sardis ..	1812	400	116	8	70	..	W. Llewellyn ..	1895	B.
Llanwrtyd, Zion	1863	200	73	6	60	1	*J. W. Humphreys	1888	B.
Sugar Loaf	..	..	..	2	20				
Maesyberllan	1700	350	124	6	70	..	G. H. Llewelyn ..	1872	B.
Nantyffin (Ystradgynlais)	1796	200	61	10	90	..	*D. H. Jones.. ..	1871	B.
Colbren	..	..	..	6	55				
Pantycelyn	1806	200	72	6	40	..	S. Thomas	1885	B.
Pontestyll	1819	150	16	2	14	..	.. ..	..	B.
Senny Bridge	1843	150	19	2	9	..	*D. H. Jones.. ..	1887	B.
Talgarth, Tabernacle ..	1836	350	89	8	70	..	J. B. Thomas ..	1895	B.
Trevil (See Monmouthshire.)									
Ynysfelin, Bethel.. ..	1798	150	25	2	20	..	.. ..	..	B.

CARDIGANSHIRE (*Pop.*, 62,630).

(C.C. Carmarthenshire and Cardiganshire.)

Churches.	Date.	Chapel seats.	No. of Members.	Sunday School Teachers.	No. of Scholars.	Local Preachers.	Pastors.	When settled.	Associations.
Aberayron	1881	300	28		30		J. Davies	1894	C.C.
Aberystwyth :—									
Baker-street	1789	750	272		250		J. A. Morris.. ..	1873	C.C.
Alfred-place (E.) ..	1870	400	70	6	40		T. Williams, B.A.	1893	C.C.
Moriah	1829	240	36	4	20		.. ..	..	C.C.
Capel Gwndwn (Cardigan)..	1844	120	11		.		*R. Jones	1895	C.C.
Cardigan :—									
Bethania	1799	900	524		250	..	J. Williams	1880	C.C.
Blaenwenen	1838	200	69	5	40	..	.. ..	..	C.C.
Mount Zion (E.) ..	1881	300	57	10	75	2	G. Hughes	1881	C.C.
Cwmsymlog, Taberncle	1865	300	74	10	60	..	} I. Thomas	1894	C.C.
Goginan, Jezreel	1821	350	45	5	40	..			
Lampeter :—									
Silian, Bethel	1829	200	..	3	30		{ *H. James (*see Aberduar, Carm.*) }	1880	C.C.
Caersalem..	1873	350	97	9	59				
Llanrhystid	1821	20	16	3	35		.. ..	..	C.C.
Llandyssil, Ebenezer ..	1832	250	80	6	60		.. ..	..	C.C.
Llwyndafydd..	1796	300	50		47		*R. Jones	1895	C.C.
New Quay, Bethel ..	1854	260	55	6	40				
Penrhyncoch..	1788	500	111		129		.. ..	..	C.C.
Penyparc (Cardigan) ..	1780	600	223		84		W. T. Francis ..	1894	C.C.
Pontrhydfendigaid ..	1835	350	75	6	50	1	} T. R. Morgan ..	1887	C.C.
Swyddffynnon, Bethel	1821	20	41	9	37	..			
Talybont (Glandovey),									
Tabernacle	1817	600	140	15	145	..	E. R. Williams ..	1895	C.C.
Siloh, Pontprengeifr	..	60	..	..	..				
Verwig (Cardigan) ..	1796	500	118	..	73	..	.. ..	..	C.C.

CARMARTHENSHIRE (*Pop.*, 130,566).

(C. C., Carmarthenshire and Cardiganshire. G. C. E., Glamorganshire and Carmarthenshire English. W.G., West Glamorganshire.)

Churches.	Date.	Chapel seats.	No. of Members.	Sunday School Teachers.	No. of Scholars.	Local Preachers.	Pastors.	When settled.	Associations.
Aberduar	1742	500	314	..	168	..	*H. James (*see Cardiganshire*)	1880	C.C.
Ammanford, Ebenezer *Dorwen*	1848	500	320	..	370	..	T. F. Williams ..	1867	C.C.
Brynamman	1873	600	278	27	232	..	J. L. Davies.. ..	1893	W.G

CARMARTHENSHIRE—*continued*

Churches.	Date.	Chapel seats.	No. of Members.	Sunday School Teachers.	No. of Scholars.	Local Preachers.	Pastors	When settled.	Associations.
Brynhafod (Llanybyther)	1861	250	52	6	60	..	*E. Phillips	1880	C.C.
Bwlchyrhiw and	1817	84	123	..	81	..	.. ..	..	C.C.
Seion	1827	200							
Caio, Bethel	1741	740	130	5	50	..	J. E. Thomas ..	1891	C.C.
Salem			122	..	93	..			
Carmarthen (10,300):—									
Tabernacle	1763	800	418	30	400	1	E. U. Thomas ..	1892	C.C.
Felinwen	1834	300	50	..	40	..	J. C. Griffiths ..	1890	C.C.
Priory-street, Penuel	1763	800	480	48	480	..	.. ..	..	C.C.
Talog, Bethany ..	1839	250	92	..	60	..	*D. Roberts	1879	C.C.
Lammas-street (E.)	1868	400	153	11	110	..	A. F. Mills	1892	G C E
Cross Hands, Tabor ..	1871	300	80	7	65	..	*D. M. Morgan ..	1871	C.C.
Bethel Tumble ..	1893	150	40	4	30				
Cwmdu (Talley)	1779	350	109	9	75	2	*J. M. Pughe.. ..	1874	C.C.
Cwmduad	1871	450	172	10	100	..	D. Richards.. ..	1881	C.C.
Cwmfelin	1798	500	161	..	108	..	*D. S. Davies ..	1871	C.C.
Cwmifor..	1774	400	90	8	60	..	*D. J. Davies ..	1894	C.C.
Cwmsarnddu..	1814	200	70	4	30	..	*D. W. Waters ..	1893	C.C.
Drefach (Llandyssil) ..	1793	550	277	..	200	..	W. E. Davies ..	1887	C.C.
Elim Park	1850	150	59	6	52	..	*T. Thomas	1891	C.C.
Felingwm, Sittim ..	1816	250	83	8	60	..	*J. Herbert	1889	C.C.
Ferryside, Salem.. ..	1806	500	110	12	132	..	W. A. Williams	1887	C.C.
Llandefeilog, Ebenezer ..	1868	140	46	5	33	..			
Ffynnonhenry	1737	600	209	12	85	..	*T. John	1882	C.C.
Foelcwan, Noddfa ..	1881	250	87	7	57	..	*D. Roberts	1881	C.C.
Cwm Mydrim ..	..	180	32	5	36				
Glanamman, Bethesda	1844	500	220	19	170	2	H. Jones	1894	W.G.
Kidwelly, Siloam.. ..	1834	550	136	12	105	1	J. Reynolds.. ..	1879	C.C.
Llandilo-vawr:—									
Ebenezer	1831	450	169	15	152	1	*D. James	1877	C.C.
Llandovery	1844	350	137	10	65	1	D. P. Evans.. ..	1892	C.C.
Llandybie, Saron.. ..	1814	500	*260	..	140	..	D. S. Davies ..	1892	C.C.
Carmel	1859	300	88	6	60	..	*D. M Morgan ..	1876	C.C.
Llandyfan, Zoar	1818	314	107	6	30	1	*M. Jones	1878	C.C.
Llandyssil, Hebron ..	1831	300	130	11	80	..	Joseph Jones ..	1895	C.C.
Penybont	1776	180	120	10	70	..			
Pencader	..	..	..	5	30				
Llanedi, Sardis	1849	300	61	4	45	..	.. ..	..	C.C.
Llanelly:—									
Bethel..	1840	800	606	..	500	..	T. Idwal Jones ..	1894	C.C.
Caersalem..	1894	800	259	35	230	2	R. B. Jones	1895	C.C.
Calfaria	1881	860	327	34	280	2	R. M. Humphreys	1891	C.C.
Emmanuel (E.) ..	1894	..	91	15	119	1	E. George	1894	C.C.
Felinfoel	1700	900	757	31	400	..	B. Humphreys ..	1889	C.C.
Greenfield (E.).. ..	1858	700	..	..	..	..	R. Evans	1874	G C E
Horeb..	1832	350	88	6	80	..	*Owen John	1887	C.C.
Llwynhendy, Soar ..	1830	900	584	50	550	..	J. R. Evans.. ..	1889	C.C.
Salem, Spitty ..	1870	250							
Tabor, Bryn.. ..	1874	200							
Moriah	1872	1000	615	36	400	2	J. Rowlands, D.D.	1873	C.C.
New Dock, Bethany	1870	800	298	26	314	..	W. T. Jones ..	1893	C.C.
Zion	1822	1500	790	45	625	..	J. R. Morgan, D.D.	1855	C.C.
Cwmbach	1846	200							

CARMARTHENSHIRE—*continued.*

Churches.	Date.	Chapel seats.	No. of Members.	Sunday School Teachers.	No. of Scholars.	Local Preachers.	Pastors.	When settled.	Associations.
Furnace									
Llanfynydd	1829	170	..		..		*J. M. Pughe ..	1885	C.C.
Llangadock, Zion ..	1805	250	62		35		*D. J. Davies ..	1894	C.C.
Llangendeirn, Bethel	1797	360	245	14	120		R. P. Thomas ..	1892	C.C.
Bankffosfelen ..	1874	70							
Llangennech, Salem ..	1840	300	245	25	260		P. Phillips	1864	C.C.
Llangunog, Ebenezer..	1791	250	146	7	67		E. Watkins	1889	C.C.
Llannon, Hermon ..	1850	400	98	3	32		.. ..	..	C.C.
Llanstephan	1833	200	60	8	45		D. Williams ..	1895	C.C.
Maescanner	1864	500	225	20	220		.. ..	..	C.C.
Meinciau(Llangennech)	1865	300	320		226		E T. Jones	1895	C.C.
Carway, Siloh ..	1891	250							
Pedairheol	1870	510							
Mydrim, Salem	1795	450	169	10	90		*D. Williams ..	1850	C.C.
Bryn Llangining ..	1868	100							
Newcastle Emlyn :—									
Graig	1775	450	278	16	160		O. M. Pritchard ..	1889	C.C.
Rehoboth	1696	500	120		80		.. ..	..	C.C.
Clawddcoch	1867	100							
New Court, Sion	1820	250	83	7	80		*E. Phillips	1880	C.C.
Pembrey :—									
Tabernacle	..	800	367	22	300		W. E. Watkins ..	1873	C.C.
Board School ..	..		22	6	50				
Penrhiwgoch	1799	275	72	6	50		*T. Thomas	1891	C.C.
Pontbrenaraeth, (Llandilo) Bethel	1822	200	24	2	21		*D. James	1883	C.C.
Ponthenry, Bethesda ..	1836	450	143	9	100		*Owen John	1887	C.C.
Porthyrhyd :—									
Bethlehem	1818	550	119		65		*J. Herbert	1889	C.C.
Smyrna	1835	120	67	3	30		*D. W. Waters ..	1893	C.C.
Pwll (Llanelly):—									
Bethlehem	1838	600	187	24	160		.. ..	..	C.C.
Rhydargaeau	1720	250	65	7	53		*T. John	1883	C.C.
Rhydwilym	1668	500	245		167		J. J. Evans	1889	C.C.
St. Clears :—									
Ænon	1847	300	..	5	47		*D. Williams ..	1879	C.C.
Bwlchgwynt	1765	210	105		40		*Daniel Jones ..	1885	C.C.
Bwlchnewydd and..	1803	140	80	7	70		L. Davies	1872	C.C.
Laugharne, Bethel..	1861	140	70	6	70	1			
Zion	1849	450	155	10	100		R. H. Jones.. ..	1878	C.C.
Trimsaran, Noddfa ..	1879	140	36	10	52		L. R. Williams ..	1894	C.C.
Waunclyndaf	1798	400	51		20		*M. Jones	1895	C.C.
Whitland, Nazareth ..	1851	400	180	14	140		*Daniel Jones ..	1885	C.C.
Login, Calvaria ..	1873	500	211	16	189		*D. S. Davies ..	1871	C.C.

CARNARVONSHIRE (*Pop.*, 118,204)

(C., Carnarvonshire. N.W., North Wales English Union.)

Churches.	Date.	Chapel seats.	No. of Members.	Sunday School Teachers.	No. of Scholars.	Local Preachers.	Pastors.	When settled.	Associations.
Bangor :—									
Penuel	1812	800	221	..	300	16	Edwd. Evans	1894	C.
Hirael, Calvaria	1880	200							
Kyffin-square									
Penrallt-road (E.)	1875	220	59	10	76	1	W. R. Saunders	1878	C. & N.W
Bethesda, near Bangor	1835	700	122	25	131	..	T. P. Davies	1877	C.
Caellwyngrydd, Bethel	1885	250							
Capel y Beirdd	..	220	48	11	60	..	..	..	C.
Carnarvon	1815	750	263	..	250	..	Owen Davies, D.D.	1877	C.
Clwtybont, Libanus	1877	200	34	..	60	..	..	..	C.
Conway, Bethesda	1846	200	..	..	..	..	W. Edwards	1891	C.
Dinorwic, Sardis	1820	180	69	10	82	..	..	..	C.
Galltraeth	..	100	18	..	..	..	*C. Roberts	1892	C.
Garn (Dolbenmaen)	1786	500	141	21	145	1	..	..	C.
Ainon	1862	90	10	..	..	..	..	..	C.
Gilfach (Bangor)	1820	220	31	6	40	..	*John Griffiths	1881	C.
Glanadda	1862	200	66	..	80	..	..	..	C.
Glanwydden	1799	350	95	..	140	..	J. Thomas	1893	C.
Groeslon (Llandwrog)	1884	350	36	..	45	..	..	..	C.
Pisgah	1878	350	19	..	32	..	*J. Frimston	1889	C.
Llanaelhaiarn	1790	350	78	..	84	1	*H. Hughes	1888	C.
Llanberis, Coed-y-Ddol Sion	1869	400	67	10	59	3	..	..	C.
Llandudno :—									
Tabernacle	1818	750	256	..	350	2	D. Davies	1888	C.
Gt. Orme's Head, Horeb									
Adelphi-st., Salem									
Mostyn-street (E.)	1876	700	85	5	90	..	J. Raymond	1878	N.W
Llanfairfechan, Libanus	1878	250	75	12	84	..	*John Griffiths	1878	C.
Penmaenmawr	..	200							
Llangian	1784	200	23	..	19	..	*C. Roberts	1892	C.
Llanllyfni	1826	250	65	..	80	..	*J. J. Williams	1888	C.
Llithfaen	..	150	24	..	21	1	*H. Hughes	1888	C.
Nevin, Sion	1750	400	77	10	85	1	..	..	C.
Penygroes, Calvaria	1878	250	71	13	70	2	*J. J. Williams	1888	C.
Pontllyfni	1822	160	20	4	22	..	..	..	C.
Port Dinorwic, Salem	1862	300	53	..	55	..	..	..	C.
Port Madoc, Zion	..	300	..	..	..	..	..	..	C.
Berea (Sc.)	1800	150	24	4	21	..	Stephen Jones	1884	
Porthynlleyn	1854	160	38	..	30	..	..	..	C.
Pwllheli and	1816	420	128	25	116	..	S. P. Edwards	1888	C.
Tyddynshon	1784	140	48	10	55	..			
Roshirwaen	1835	250	29	5	35	1	W. Evans	1891	C.
Roewen (Conway)	1785	96	9	2	10	..	..	..	C.
Talysarn, Salem	1862	500	118	20	130	..	*J. Frimston	1888	C.
Tyndonen (Pwllheli)	1797	220	19	4	24	..	*C. Roberts	1892	C.

DENBIGHSHIRE (*Pop.*, 117,872).

(D.F.M., Denbigh, Flint, and Merioneth. N.W., North Wales English Union. S., Shropshire.)

Churches.	Date.	Chapel seats.	No. of Members.	Sunday School Teachers.	No. of Scholars.	Local Preachers.	Pastors.	When settled.	Associations.
Abergele	1870	300	70	12	90	..	T. Roberts	1889	D F M
Bodgynwch	1866	150	..	..	..	..	..	..	D F M
Bontnewydd (St. Asaph)	1826	130	17	3	25	..	..	..	D F M
Brymbo	1836	500	171	26	388	..	E. K. Jones	1891	D F M
Penrhos	..	..	..	4	35				
Lodge (E.)	1860	160	..	..	..	..	..	..	D F M
Cefnbychan	1786	250	68	10	90	..	..	..	D F M
Cefnmawr, Ebenezer (E.)	1862	178	..	..	..	..	..	..	D F M & N W
Acrefair									
Sion	1805	500	249	30	234	7	..	..	D F M
Tabernacle	1860	800	171	25	200	2	R. E. Williams	1894	D F M
Codau	1886	220	41	7	60	..	..	..	D F M
Coedpoeth :—									
Tabernacle	1864	212	50	11	100	..	W. A. Jones	1894	D F M
Bethesda	1891	200	39	8	62	1	..	..	D F M
Colwyn, Old (E.)	1891	200	12	4	12	..	J. B. Brasted	1893	N.W.
Colwyn, Calfaria	1862	350	93	13	108	..	..	..	D F M
Colwyn Bay	1888	466	78	12	81	1	..	..	D F M
Colwyn Bay (E.)	1890	300	37	5	52	..	H. T. Cousins	1894	D F M & N W
Denbigh	1812	500	77	12	96	..	B. Williams	1893	D F M
Dolywern	..	180	66	10	80	..	..	..	D F M
Egiwysbach	..	150	28	4	25	..	..	..	D F M
Fforddlas, Glan Conway	1786	200	70	12	70	3	..	..	D F M
Fron (Llangollen),									
Carmel	1830	230	121	23	190	2	*T. Morris	1893	D F M
Garth	1850	350	50	17	105	..	*T. Morris	1893	D F M
Gefailyrhyd	1831	100	20	4	24	..	..	..	D F M
Glynceiriog	1750	600	212	21	230	..	J. L. Jones	1895	D F M
Garth	..	..	..	5	40				
Nantyr	..	..	..	3	15				
Pandy	..	..	..	7	64				
Groes (E.)	1874	150	..	..	..	..	*D. H. Jenkins	1895	N.W.
Llanddulas, Bethesda	1836	200	38	12	74	1	..	..	D F M
Llanddoget, Soar	1861	200	45	8	68	..	O. Jones	1894	D F M
Llandyrnog	1836	200	22	4	28	..	..	..	D F M
Llanelian	1832	300	40	8	31	..	..	..	D F M
Llanfair Dyffryn Clwyd,									
Zion	1873	100	15	1	5	..	..	..	D F M
Llanfairtalhaiarn	1862	200	54	..	..	..	..	..	D F M
Llangernyw	1830	140	33	7	38	..	..	..	D F M
Llangollen :—									
Castle-street	1815	550	233	32	305	..	D. Williams	1881	D F M
Penybryn (E.)	1861	310	60	8	70	1	H. Rees	1894	N.W.
Llannefydd	1815	200	81	8	68	1	..	..	D F M
Llanrhaiadr	1855	120	11	3	12	..	..	..	D F M
Llanrwst	1790	220	55	10	60	..	..	..	D F M
Llansanan	1828	100	36	8	50	..	..	..	D F M
Llansilin	1832	150	45	8	45	1	..	..	D F M
Llysfaen, Tabor	1884	150	46	9	35	..	..	..	D F M

DENBIGHSHIRE—*continued.*

Churches.	Date.	Chapel seats.	No. of Members.	Sunday School Teachers.	No. of Scholars.	Local Preachers.	Pastors.	When settled.	Associations.
Moelfre (Oswestry) ..	1829	120	36	7	40	..	.. ..	..	D F M
Moss, Salem (Wrexham)	1850	200	70	16	106	1	J. Pritchard.. ..	1894	D F M
Penycae, Salem	1791	400	195	28	400	2	W. B. Jones ..	1895	D F M
Ponkey, Zion	1881	250	156	25	185	2	E. Mitchell	1884	D F M
Ponkey (E.)	1889	250	..	..	..	..	*D. H. Jenkins ..	1895	D F M & N W
Ruabon	1894	150	29	7	49	..	W. Jones	1894	D F M
Rhosllanerchrugog ..	1815	700	275	35	600	..	E. Williams.. ..	1894	D F M
Ruthin	1795	400	90	15	135	1	Isaac James ..	1873	D F M
Wrexham (12,552):—									
Chester-street (E.) ..	1630	350	136	17	197	3	J. H. Thomas ..	1892	S.
Holt	1827	200	13	8	125				
Rhos-ddu (W.)	1872	200	131	23	220	3.	Isaac James ..	1892	D F M

FLINTSHIRE (*Pop.* 77,277).

(D.F.M., Denbigh, Flint, and Merioneth. N.W., North Wales English Union.)

Churches.	Date.	Chapel seats.	No. of Members.	Sunday School Teachers.	No. of Scholars.	Local Preachers.	Pastors.	When settled.	Associations.
Axtyn (Holywell).. ..	1821	200	15	3	15		.. ..	..	D F M
Bagillt	1854	200	51	9	60		.. ..	..	D F M
Bodffari	1848	80	..		..		*T. Davies	1894	D F M
Buckley (E.)	1876	200	32	10	80		W. Jenkins ..	1892	D F M & N W
Nantmawr	1890	150	22	8	57	1			
Caerwys	1890	160	24	5	42		*T. Davies	1894	D F M
Coedllai	1868		12	4	18		.. ..	..	D F M
Flint	1870	280	17	6	33		.. ..	..	D F M
Ffynongroew	1890	200	20	6	56		.. ..	..	D F M
Helygen	1827	200	28	6	40		E. Bellis	1889	D F M
Holywell	1820	450	85		..		.. ..	..	D F M
Leeswood (Mold) ..	1863	200	12	5	24				
Lixwm (Holywell) ..	1813	120	27	8	51	2	.. ..	..	D F M
Maesglas (Holywell) ..	1894		15	7	79		.. ..	..	D F M
Milwr	1846	100	7	3	11		.. ..	..	D F M
Mold	1827	300	63	10	117		T. Morgan	1894	D F M
Penyfron (Mold)	1823	50	14	4	26		.. ..	..	D F M
Penygelli	..		19	4	20		*T. Davies	1894	D F M
Rhuddlan, Zion	1824	350	58	17	90		B. Evans	1876	D F M
Rhyl:—									
Water-street	1856	500	92	16	120		T. Shankland ..	1891	D F M
Brighton-road	1890		29	6	50		E. T. Davies ..	1893	D F M
Sussex-street (E.) ..	1869	400	59	6	40		D. G. Lewis.. ..	1892	N.W.
St. Asaph	1821	150	28	4	25		.. ..	..	D F M
Treuddyn, Berea.. ..	1861	250	17	6	45		.. ..	..	D F M

GLAMORGANSHIRE (*Pop.*, 687,218).

(C.C., Carmarthenshire and Cardiganshire. E.G., East Glamorganshire. W.G., West Glamorganshire. G.C.E., Glamorganshire and Carmarthenshire English. M., Monmouthshire Welsh.)

Churches.	Date.	Chapel seats.	No. of Members.	Sunday School Teachers.	No. of Scholars.	Local Preachers.	Pastors.	When settled.	Associations.
Aberavon :—									
Ebenezer	1784	850	310	34	315	4	D. Griffiths	1887	W.G.
Water-street (E.) ..	1872	200	78	9	110	..	W. Jones	1894	G C E
Abercanaid	1841	500	173	20	210	..	H. J. Harris ..	1895	E.G.
Aberdare :—									
Aberaman	1853	900	262	25	250	1	T. Davies	1875	E.G.
Aberaman (E.)	1884	350	74	12	100	2	.. ..	..	G C E
Abercwmboye	1860	400	89	14	109	1	H. N. Richards ..	1895	E.G.
Abernant, Bethel ..	1863	600	263	26	271	1	J. Mills..	1876	E.G.
Calvaria	1813	1200	518	35	400	1	J. Griffiths	1889	E.G.
Carmel (E.)	1856	700	302	23	300	..	T. Jones	1873	G C E
Cwmdare, Nebo ..	1858	750	106	13	100	..	W. Thomas.. ..	1882	E.G.
Cwmbach	1844	700	334	31	250	1	D. Thomas	1888	E.G.
Gadlys	1866	700	265	26	195	..	B. Evans	1876	E.G.
Trecynon, Mill-street	1855	1000	386	50	380	1	W. Harris	1862	E.G.
Aberdare Junction ..	1894	..	..	..	..	..	*W. D. Nicholas ..	1894	G C E
Aberdulais (Neath) ..	1856	400	134	20	225	..	E. Parry	1892	W.G.
Aberfan, Smyrna ..	1891	150	70	7	70	..	D. Rees	1892	E.G.
Abergwynfi (Maesteg)									
Caersalem	1881	500	129	16	160	..	W. G. Jones.. ..	1883	W.G.
Abergwynfi (E.)	1887	70	..	..	..	..	D. Thomas	1894	G C E
Barry District :—									
Barry, Bethel	1891	400	133	13	140	..	H. J. Horn	1894	G C E
Barry Dock, Holton-road	1892	300	215	28	430	1	T. P. John	1893	G C E
Cadoxton, Mount Pleasant..	1887	300	70	*23	250	2	.. ..	..	G C E
Cadoxton, Philadelphia	1814	..	66	8	65	1	M. Isaac	1892	E.G.
Barry Dock, Salem ..	1890	..	..	..	..	..	.. ..	..	E.G.
Berthlwyd (Treharris)	1851	500	148	12	160	..	.. ..	..	E.G.
Bettws (Bridgend) ..	1839	250	48	5	41	..	*W. Griffiths ..	1891	W.G.
Birchgrove, Ainon ..	1884	250	95	16	100	1	*J. E. Griffiths ..	1883	W.G.
Blaenclydach, Noddfa	1891	750	300	30	230	1	O. W. James ..	1892	E.G.
Blaenclydach	1894	..	39	9	65	1	.. ..	..	G C E
Blaengarw	1887	720	205	20	180	1	W. Morgan	1887	W.G.
Blaenrhondda	1885	140	82	10	120	..	G. Matthews ..	1888	E.G.
Blaenycwm	1868	800	192	26	230	..	.. ..	..	E.G.
Zoar	1890	500	86	14	150	..	.. ..	..	E.G.
Bridgend :—									
Blackmill, Paran ..	1823	300	58	8	60	1	*W. Griffiths.. ..	1889	W.G.
Ruamah	1789	500	112	13	115	1	G. James	1877	W.G.
Hope (E.)	1850	350	146	32	250	..	J. S. Johns	1892	G C E
Brithdir, Siloh	1859	250	..	..	..	..	.. ..	..	E.G.
Brithdir	1875	..	62	12	100	2	*R. Owen (*see Rhymney, Mon.*)	1894	M.
Briton Ferry :—									
Jerusalem (E.)	1863	500	102	15	240	..	Rees Powell ..	1895	G C E
Rehoboth	1848	1000	288	34	340	..	H. Hughes	1883	W.G.
Salem	1875	550	127	14	140	1	.. ..	..	W.G.
Bryncethin, Nazareth..	1877	70	23	5	50	..	D. C. Evans ..	1895	W.G.
Bryntroedgam (Cmvn.)	1852	200	18	5	35	..	.. ..	..	W.G.

GLAMORGANSHIRE—*continued.*

Churches.	Date.	Chapel seats.	No. of Members.	Sunday school Teachers.	No. of Scholars.	Local Preachers.	Pastors.	When settled.	Associations.
Caerphilly, Tonyfelin..	1784	600	126	15	140	..	J. P. Davies.. ..	1878	E.G.
Caerphilly, Mt. Carmel (E.)	1874	400	69	10	100	1	J. G. Hopkins ..	1890	G C E
Cardiff (128,915):—									
Bethany (E.)	1806	943	434	28	286	3	W. E. Winks ..	1876	G C E
Bute Docks, Mount Stuart-sq., Siloam	1860	600	141	14	95	1	D. E. Roberts ..	1884	E.G.
Bethel (E.)	1855	750	163	24	389	3	T. Davies	1878	G C E
Canton (W.)	1859	600	130	17	150	1	Z. H. Lewis.. ..	1891	E.G.
Hope (E.)	1858	600	303	40	436	4	T. W. Medhurst..	1889	G C E
Grange-Town (E.) ..	1881	500	128	29	673	2	J. Williams.. ..	1893	G C E
Longcross-st., Zion..	1883	600	..	..	..	..	W. T. Lee	1895	G C E
Riverside (E.)	1886	320	154	21	290	3	T. L. Evans.. ..	1895	G C E
Roath, Salem	1861	650	351	18	200	..	T. T. Jones.. ..	1881	E.G.
Pearl-st., Ebenezer	1882	450	47	11	160	..	.. ..	..	G C E
Splott-road (E.) ..	1884	1100	275	28	501	..	C. H. Watkins ..	1893	G C E
Tabernacle	1822	950	512	45	250	7	C. Davies	1888	E.G.
Tredegarville (E.) ..	1861	1000	557	35	350	12	.. ..	..	G C E
Maindy	1879	270	..	7	140				
Rumney	1882	60	..	9	85				
Llanishen									
Merthyr-street ..	..	..	..	6	120				
Walker's-road, Ainon	1894	300	159	17	180	1	T. Morgan	1895	E.G.
Woodville-road (E.)	1881	800	293	41	551	3	C. Griffiths	1883	G C E
Cefncribwr	1848	450	88	10	80	..	.. ..	..	W.G.
Cilfynydd (Pontypridd)									
Rehoboth	1890	..	189	24	150	..	.. ..	..	E.G.
English	1889	200	..	..	..	..	.. ..	..	G C E
Clydach, Calvaria ..	1844	750	381	32	377	2	T. V. Evans.. ..	1882	W.G.
Colwinstone (Cowbridg)	1852	300	28	3	25	..	.. ..	..	W.G.
Corntown	1839	250	35	5	25	..	.. ..	..	W.G.
Cowbridge, Ramoth ..	1820	800	180	24	190	..	O. Jones	1884	E.G.
Craig Cefn Park, Elim	1880	373	164	16	140	1	Rhys Lewis.. ..	1889	W.G.
Croesyparc (Cardiff) ..	1777	500	62	8	50	..	.. ..	..	E.G.
Cwmaman, Zion	1861	750	213	37	218	..	T. Humphreys ..	1868	E.G.
Cwmavon, Penuel ..	1845	1000	378	27	250	..	R. S. Morris ..	1894	W.G.
Cwm Clydach, Calvaria	1880	750	248	17	211	..	W. E. Davies ..	1880	E.G.
Cwmfelin, Salem	1834	800	175	18	170	3	W. Morton	1891	E.G.
Cwmgarw, Tyle-gwyn..	1843	300	107	15	130	..	T. B. Phillips ..	1895	W.G.
Cwmgors	1894	..	70	10	60	..	J. E. Thomas ..	1894	W.G.
Cwmpark, Bethel.. ..	1874	600	222	20	230	..	D. C. Jones	1876	E.G.
Cwmtwrch, Beulah ..	1834	500	222	44	237	2	B. James	1894	W.G.
Cymmer..	1893	335	45	7	50	..	.. ..	..	W.G.
Cymmer (Porth), Pisgah	1893	400	109	20	250	..	J. M. Lewis.. ..	1895	E.G.
Deri, Tabernacle.. ..	1866	350	144	22	132	..	H. B. Thomas ..	1892	E.G.
Dowlais:—									
Beulah (E.)	1856	700	212	26	266	3	J. Williams	1874	G C E
Pantyscallog	1877	150							
Caersalem..	1829	800	262	20	250	2	.. ..	..	E.G.
Hebron	1849	1000	301	35	250	1	W. C. Thomas ..	1890	E.G.
Moriah	1857	830	348	48	300	..	B. Davies	1888	E.G.
Pontsticill	1878	150	18	10	50				
Evanstown (Gilfach Goch)..	1894	..	68	10	95	..	*W. Griffiths.. ..	1895	E.G.

GLAMORGANSHIRE—*continued*

Churches.	Date.	Chapel seats.	No. of Members.	Sunday School Teachers.	No. of Scholars.	Local Preachers.	Pastors.	When settled.	Associations.
Ferndale, Nazareth ..	1867	600	223	24	240	2	T. Humphreys ..	1891	E.G.
Bethel (E.)	1871	450	115	10	110	..	.. ..	..	G C E
Salem Newydd.. ..	1878	800	309	15	210	1	Isaac Jones.. ..	1881	E.G.
Fochriw	1881	260	99	20	90	..	L. John	1890	E.G.
Gelligaer, Horeb	1849	250	59	7	50	..	.. ..	..	E.G.
Gilfach Goch	1872	700	89	12	87	..	J. Jenkins	1885	E.G.
Glais, Peniel	1891	200	91	15	98	..	.. ..	..	W.G.
Glancynon	1888	900	122	14	140	..	J. F. Williams ..	1892	E.G.
Gwaelodygarth	1863	350	68	11	84	..	.. ..	..	E.G.
Glyncorrwg	1868	350	..	..	..	..	James L. Jones ..	1876	W.G.
Glyn Neath :—									
Bethel..	1849	700	166	20	180	..	T. C. Harries ..	1893	W.G.
Gorseinon	1890	500	182	18	140	1	J. S. Hopkin ..	1891	W.G.
Hengoed	1650	600	119	16	150	..	R. Evans	1878	E.G.
Clawr-yr-Ystrad ..									
Hirwain, Ramoth	1831	600	269	30	200	..	D. Collier	1892	E.G.
Killay, Siloam	1832	240	113	10	80	1	J. Davies	1872	W.G.
Knelstone (E.)	1858	130	35	3	30	..	S. Jones	1872	G C E
Laleston, Bethel	1892	200	33	4	40	..	.. ..	..	W.G.
Lancarvan (Cowbridge)	1822	200	55	6	60	..	.. ..	..	E.G.
Landocha	1861	300	17	4	40	..	.. ..	..	E.G.
Lantwit-major, Bethel	1823	400	74	9	90	..	Owen Davies ..	1884	E.G.
Lantwit-vardre, Salem	1853	750	68	12	100	..	T. Richards.. ..	1889	E.G.
Lisvane (Cardiff)	1831	400	107	15	135	..	D. Davies	1881	E.G.
Capel Gwilym ..	1836	100							
Llangyfelach :—									
Salem	1779	600	125	8	96	..	B. Lewis	1889	W.G.
Gerizim	1830	140	90	9	96	..	Danl. Davies ..	1887	W.G.
Llansamlet, Adullam ..	1859	600	221	26	186	..	J. D. Harries ..	1878	W.G.
Llantrissant :—									
Tabor	1859	300	106	14	135	1	J. Jones	1894	E.G.
Llwynypia, Jerusalem	1872	800	474	34	320	..	E. T. Jones	1892	E.G.
Loughor, Penuel	1850	750	219	20	175	2	T. M. Reed	1892	W.G.
Llwydcoed	1876	200	110	11	70	..	D. Jones	1876	E.G.
Maerdy, Zion	1878	650	180	24	180	..	J. Evans	1887	E.G.
Maesteg :—									
Bethania	1827	1000	412	45	416	..	E. Jones	1894	W.G.
Bethel (E.)	1848	500	121	14	150	..	I. Lloyd	1888	G C E
Caersalem	1890	500	95	20	190	..	J. C. Williams ..	1893	W.G.
Calvaria	1877	650	190	15	150	..	R. Allen	1893	W.G.
Castle-street, Zion ..	1883	600	150	19	130	..	W. Harries	1889	G C E
Salem	1850	1150	300	37	329	..	D. C. Howells ..	1892	W.G.
Noddfa Blaencaerau	..	300							
Tabernacle	1864	600	124	17	120	2	J. Williams	1893	W.G.
Melincrythan (Neath) ..	1882	450	39	9	160	2	T. W. George ..	1886	G C E
Merthyr Tydvil :—									
George Town, Bethel	1860	200	189	18	200	1	H. I. Jenkins ..	1894	E.G.
Ainon (E.)..	1856	400	92	14	160	..	H. Jenkins	1893	G C E
Cefncoedycymmer, Carmel	1856	..	112	12	170	..	W. B. Griffiths ..	1890	E.G.

GLAMORGANSHIRE—*continued.*

Churches.	Date.	Chapel seats.	No. of Members.	Sunday School Teachers.	No. of Scholars.	Local Preachers.	Pastors.	When settled.	Associations.
MerthyrTydvil *(contd.)*:									
Ebenezer	1793	800	132	15	110	..	J. Lewis	1892	E.G.
Pentreback									
High-street (E.) ..	1839	750	227	24	250	..	A. Hall	1894	G C E
Morlais	1885	400	194	17	200	..	E. G. Thomas ..	1893	G C E
Tabernacle	1856	1500	364	32	370	..	D. Price	1893	E.G.
Zion	1791	1200	325	32	330	1	W. A. Jones ..	1892	E.G.
Merthyr Vale, Zion (E.)	1876	700	156	20	280	..	H. P. Jones	1884	G C E
Calfaria	1885	240	150	14	151	..	E. H. Evans ..	1895	E.G.
Mountain Ash (Rhos) ..	1855	950	470	51	382	3	T. T. Hughes ..	1893	E.G.
Cefnpennar									
Ffrwd									
Nazareth (E.)	1866	600	319	48	710	2	.. ..	..	G C E
Mishin									
Mumbles, W. Cross (E.)	1843	240	74	11	120	1	T. Davis	1885	G C E
Nantymoel, Saron ..	1878	650	205	27	200	..	J. Hughes	1881	W.G.
Horeb (E.)	1879	500	113	31	280	..	T. D. Matthias ..	1885	G C E
Navigation, Mount Zion	1893	350	35	6	70	..	.. ..	..	E.G.
Neath (11,113) :—									
Bethany	1789	800	260	19	220	..	D. W. Hopkins ..	1895	W.G.
Christchurch	1884	500	60	9	70	..	W. Davies	1895	
Orchard-place (E.) ..	1855	750	168	20	295	..	E. R. Evans	1893	G C E
Ogmore Vale :—									
Calvary (E.)	1877	290	28	8	61	..	.. ..	..	G C E
Pantywaen (Dowlais) ..	1870	229	30	8	70	..	M. Jones	1894	E.G.
Penarth, Tabernacle (E.)	1868	1000	237	25	344	2	W. G. Davies ..	1882	G C E
Penuel	1878	200	51	5	40	1	.. ..	..	E.G.
Stanwell-road (E.) ..	1886	300	86	16	123	..	I. O. Stalberg ..	1889	G C E
Penclawdd, Trinity ..	1814	450	138	16	190	1	John Thomas ..	1874	W.G.
Pengam	1881	350	98	13	90	..	J. M. Jones	1895	E.G.
Penprysg, Penuel ..	1862	150	87	7	60	1	.. ..	..	W.G.
Penrhiwceiber, Bethesda (E.)	1885	300	94	9	115	2	D. Howells	1894	G C E
Tynte Town	..	..	..	2	20				
Jerusalem	1885	700	152	20	193	..	W. R. Jones	1894	E.G.
Penrhiwfer, Zion	1884	200	69	7	50	..	.. ..	..	E.G.
Pentre :—									
Moriah	1875	2000	247	30	250	..	.. ..	..	E.G.
Zion (E.)	1878	500	157	21	240	2	D. G. Morris ..	1895	G C E
Pentyrch, Penuel ..	1838	600	92	12	90	..	J. Jenkins	1890	E.G.
Penydarren, Elim ..	1856	620	346	49	380	2	Jason James ..	1885	E.G.
Penyfai (Bridgend) ..	1706	400	81	13	112	..	W. E. Harries ..	1894	W.G.
Penygraig, Dinas	1831	900	333	30	255	3	.. ..	..	E.G.
Pontardawe, Adullam	1849	550	153	14	95	1	E. R. Evans ..	1888	W.G.
Elim	1887	144	69	7	56	..	D. Davies	1893	W.G.
Pontarddulais	1871	450	253	26	230	1	D. D. Hopkins ..	1888	W.G.
Hendy, Calfaria ..	1885	600	140	20	150	..	J. Y. Jones	1892	C.C.
Pontbrenllwyd (Abdre.)	1823	400	56	7	52	..	.. ..	..	E.G.
Pontllyw, Carmel	1843	251	129	14	130	..	S. F. Roberts ..	1895	W.G.
Pontlottyn, Bethel (E.)	1870	200	..	..	..	..	.. ..	..	G C E
Zoar	1837	850	218	21	256	..	.. ..	..	E.G.

GLAMORGANSHIRE—*continued.*

Churches.	Date.	Chapel seats.	No. of Members.	Sunday School Teachers.	No. of Scholars.	Local Preachers.	Pastors.	When settled.	Associations.
Pontrhydycyff (near Maesteg), Ainon ..	1887	150	30	6	36	..	.. ..	..	W.G.
Pontrhydyfen	1856	400	59	12	90	..	.. ..	..	W.G.
Argoed	..	..	3	2	20				
Pontyclun (E.)	1876	250	48	7	80	1	L. T. Evans ..	1895	G C E
Pontycymmer, Noddfa	1884	700	340	35	340	..	T. Davies	1884	W.G.
Zion	1887	500	75	15	120	..	J. Lamb	1888	G C E
Pontygwaith	1877	560	372	42	400	3	J. D. Hughes ..	1885	E.G.
Tylorstown	..	..	29	7	70				
Pontypridd:—									
Carmel (E.)	1868	750	251	27	298	1	E. E. Probert ..	1888	G C E
Coedpenmaen	1887	600	100	15	200	..	Joshua Thomas ..	1890	G C E
Rhondda	1862	800	186	20	200	..	W. Rees	1893	E.G.
Tabernacle	1813	..	301	20	250	..	J. R. Jones	1889	E.G.
Temple	1888	450	63	13	140	1	G. G. Cule	1889	G C E
Vestry Hall	1895	..	68	10	88	..	.. ..	..	E.G.
Porth, Salem..	1855	950	563	52	473	..	Dan Davies.. ..	1891	E.G.
Tabernacle (E.) ..	1874	600	213	21	340	1	O. Owens	1880	G C E
Porthcawl	1868	500	..	..	88	..	J. H. Miles ..	1893	W.G
Port Talbot, Smyrna ..	1866	400	112	15	133	1	D. D. Davies ..	1883	W.G
Pyle, Pisgah	1860	500	72	12	60	..	.. ..	..	W.G.
Resolven, Bethania ..	1854	700	81	17	118	1	D. C. Davies ..	1889	W.G.
Sardis	1876	130	48	7	90	..	.. ..	..	G C E
Rhydfelen, Bethlehem..	1858	300	71	12	100	..	J. S. Morgan ..	1894	E.G.
Seven Sisters	1895	..	20	3	32	..	*D. J. Davies ..	1895	W.G.
Skewen, Horeb	1869	550	182	20	200	..	G. A. Hague ..	1894	W.G.
Bethlehem	1895	..	103	17	160	..	*J. E. Griffiths ..	1895	W.G.
St. Brides Major, Horeb	1864	200	13	1	10	..	.. ..	..	W.G.
Swansea (90,349):—									
Bethesda	1649	1150	476	29	391	1	E. Edmunds ..	1887	W.G.
Brynhyfryd	1881	856	312	25	265	..	D. B. Richards ..	1890	W.G.
Caersalem Newydd..	1840	850	504	44	500	..	I. Thomas	1871	W.G.
Capel Gomer	1878	1000	479	15	235	3	J. G. Lewis, D.D.	1878	W.G.
Carmarthen-road (E.)	1875	600	116	11	150	1	.. ..	..	G C E
Cwmbwrla, Libanus..	1866	650	307	53	360	..	.. ..	..	W.G.
Danygraig	1883	300	78	18	280	..	W. E. Prince ..	1894	G C E
Foxhole	1843	300	46	9	60	..	D. R. Davies ..	1874	W.G.
Gorse-lane	1892	450	102	22	288	..	C. E. Shipley ..	1892	G C E
Gowerton, Bethania..	1874	500	109	17	125	..	W. J. John	1895	W.G.
Herbert-place (late St. James)	1891	..	43	..	..	2	A. W. Pay	1894	G C E
Landore, Salem ..	1884	300	164	15	220	..	.. ..	..	G C E
Dinas Noddfa ..	1846	840	277	38	360	..	W. P. Williams ..	1876	W.G.
Morriston, Sion ..	1846	1400	..	..	..	..	R. Roberts	1874	W.G.
Ainon	1880	200	103	10	140	..	D. Samuel	1893	G C E
Calfaria	1888	700	311	22	200	3	J. W. Lewis.. ..	1892	W.G.
Clydach Road ..	1888	200	41	10	100	2	W. John	1888	G C E
Tabernacle	1886	300	148	14	158	..	E. G. Thomas ..	1890	W.G.
Mount Pleasant (E.)..	1825	1150	549	66	805	3	J. Owen	1870	G C E
Hafod									
Mount Zion (E.) ..	1866	500	134	11	160	2	D. Thomas	1892	G C E
Newtown	1888	180	..	..	..	..	.. ..	..	G C E
Philadelphia	1862	800	211	16	160	3	B. O. James.. ..	1894	W.G.

GLAMORGANSHIRE—*continued.*

Churches.	Date.	Chapel seats.	No. of Members.	Sunday School Teachers.	No. of Scholars.	Local Preachers.	Pastors.	When settled.	Associations.
Swansea (*contd.*):—									
Raven Hill, Calfaria..	1862	550	157	30	200		E. Evans	1886	W.G.
St. Helen's..	1873	380	82	26	251		J. W. Causton ..	1893	G C E
York-place (E.).. ..	1830	650	165	24	420		D. B. Davies ..	1893	G C E
Walter's-road, Memorial (E.)	1873	900	254	25	220		J. W. Williams, D.D.	1893	G C E
Tirphil, Tabernacle (E.)	1869	300	124	14	160		H. G. James.. ..	1894	E.G.
Tondu (Bridgend) Jerusalem	1849	200	134	16	130		R. John	1883	W.G.
Carey (E.)	1876	250	109	17	120	5	W. W. Richards..	1885	G C E
Cefn..	1877	50	12	4	50				
Tongwynlais, Salem (E.)	1880	500	126	18	200		C. Rees	1893	G C E
Ainon	1838	650	86	15	120		R. A. James ..	1895	E.G.
Tonypandy (E.), Bethel	1870	650	265	20	240	3	Daniel Davies ..	1884	G C E
Tonyrefail, Ainon ..	1861	650	117	23	200		J. Prichard	1877	E.G.
Tonystrad, Hebron ..	1868	900	343	50	350		E. W. Davies ..	1889	E.G.
Gelly, Siloam	1887	700	142	14	120		S. G. Bowen ..	1889	E.G.
Trealaw, Bethlehem ..	1877	750	201	25	180		.. ..	..	E.G.
Treforest:—									
Calvary (E.)	1859	350	75	2	182		Evan Lewis ..	1895	G C E
Libanus	1858	400	88	15	130		Samson Jones ..	1891	E.G.
Trehafod	1884	650	142	12	135		T. Davies	1890	E.G.
Treharris, Bethel (E.)..	1877	260	122	15	211		*W. D. Nicholas ..	1889	G C E
Brynhyfryd	1880	850	296	25	250	2	W. Jones	1885	E.G.
Treherbert Bethany (E.)	1868	500	170	17	185		.. ..	..	G C E
Libanus	1849	800	294	40	360		H. Harries	1889	E.G.
Hope	1890	350	84	13	120		.. ..	..	E.G.
Treorky, Noddfa	1869	1500	606	65	769	5	W. Morris	1869	E.G.
Ainon	..		..	20	251				
Horeb (E.)	1870	450	146	10	150		E. D. Lewis ..	1895	G C E
Troedyrhiw:—									
Bethel (E.)	1886	600	125	14	135		W. Thomas.. ..	1893	G C E
Carmel	1852	600	209	2	190		W. G. Owen ..	1894	E.G.
Troedrhiwfuwch	1874	300	33		75		.. ..	..	E.G.
Twynyrodyn (Cardiff)..	1843	500	33	6	40		.. ..	..	E.G.
Tynewydd (Ogmore Vale), Bethlehem ..	1872	650	156	24	170		J. A. Humphreys	1894	W.G.
Wattstown	1894	600	115	18	190		E. O. Parry ..	1894	E.G.
Waunarlwydd:—									
Zion	1860	650	154	22	150		T. J. Davies ..	1895	W.G.
English	1873	150	53	10	100	2	.. ..	..	G C E
Wauntrodau, Ararat ..	1828	350	116	15	150	2	J. Bevan	1885	E.G.
Bethel (E.)..	1867	280	46	9	94		.. ..	..	G C E
Ynyshir, Ainon	1884	750	115	18	130	2	.. ..	..	E.G.
English	1885	365	60	10	100		J. H. Lamb ..	1893	G C E
Ynyslwyd	1862	750	235	22	240		Robt. E. Williams	1878	E.G.
Ynystawe, Moriah ..	1888	550	198	25	240		R. D. Phillips ..	1890	W.G.
Ynysybwl, Zion (E.) ..	1887	350	80	14	140		W. Parry	1891	G C E
Noddfa	1886	800	148	18	150	5	J. Williams	1895	E.G.
Ystalyfera, Caersalem	1857	600	126	17	130		J. Evans	1865	W.G.
Zoar	1849	800	123	15	150		W. Jones	1890	W.G.
Ystrad, Nebo	1785	750	258	25	250		A. Williams ..	1879	E.G.
Tabernacle (E.) ..	1874	300	34	8	120		M. H. Jones ..	1877	G C E
Ystrad-gynlais	1849	250	124	15	115		*D. J. Davies.. ..	1892	W.G.

MERIONETHSHIRE (*Pop.*, 49,212).

(D.F.M., Denbigh, Flint, and Merioneth. C., Carnarvonshire.)

Churches.	Date.	Chapel seats.	No. of Members.	Sunday School Teachers.	No. of Scholars.	Local Preachers.	Pastors.	When settled.	Associations.
Bala	1839	260	40	7	55	..	*R. R. Jones	1893	D F M
Barmouth	1877	220	70	7	86	2	T. J. Roberts ..	1894	D F M
Cefncymerau (Llanbdr)	1829	250	30	10	90	..	.. ..	..	D F M
Corwen	1865	350	77	15	135	..	} H. C. Williams..	1868	D F M
Cynwyd	1832	160	46	10	90	..			
Trerddol	1865	100	..	..	..	..			
Dolgelly, Capel Judah	1820	500	116	17	156	..	.. ..	..	D F M
Llwyngwril	..	..	..	2	14				
Festiniog, Sion	1860	750	192	29	270	2	M. Roberts	1892	D F M
Calfaria	..	300	103	20	166	..	A. Morris	1895	D F M
Moriah	1877	250	23	7	46	..	.. ..	..	D F M
Glyndyfrdwy	..	180	54	9	90	..	*W. G. Owen ..	1890	D F M
Harlech (Sc.), Rehoboth	..	400	46	11	48				
Engedi	..	106	23	9	42				
Ainon	1872	120	78	13	86	..	†D. Davies	1895	D F M
Llanelidan	1845	200	54	9	75	..	*W. T. Davies ..	1870	D F M
Llanfrothen:—									
Brondanw, Ramoth (Sc.)	1794	100	34	7	45	..	*S. Pierce	1882	
Llansantffraid, Salem..	1853	140	54	13	105	..	*W. G. Owen ..	1890	D F M
Llanuwchllyn	..	..	8	2	12	..	*R. R. Jones.. ..	1893	D F M
Pandyr'capel	1826	180	82	12	120	1	*W. T. Davies ..	1870	D F M
Penrhyndeudraeth	1879	180	26	..	30	..	.. ..	..	C.
Bryngwyn (Sc.)	..	160	42	7	45	1	*S. Pierce	1882	
Ragged Schools	..	..	..	3	30				
Towyn	1887	60	15	2	10	..	.. ..	..	D F M

† Also pastor of Talsarnau (*page* 297).

MONTGOMERYSHIRE (*Pop.*, 58,003).

(O.W., Old Welsh. D.F.M., Denbigh, Flint, and Merioneth. C.C., Carmarthenshire and Cardiganshire.)

Churches.	Date.	Chapel seats.	No. of Members.	Sunday School Teachers.	No. of Scholars.	Local Preachers.	Pastors.	When settled.	Associations.
Beulah (E.) nr Llanidloes	1851	140	73	5	55	..	*T. D. Jones, *see Radnorshire*	1894	O.W.
Caersws (E.)	1824	220	90	8	80	2	.. ..	..	O.W.
Cwmbelan	1824	150	56	5	50	1	*D. E. Hughes ..	1884	O.W.
Kerry (E.)	1840	150	68	7	70	..	J. Harrison	1885	O.W.
Llanfair-Caereinion ..	1823	270	51	9	85	1	.. ..	..	O.W.
Llanllugan	1840	90	9	..	..	..	.. ..	..	O.W.
Llanfyllin	1836	150	39	8	66	2	} W. H. Jones ..	1893	D F M
Bethel	1826	130	27	7	50	1			
Llanidloes	1808	650	190	33	272	1	J. Griffiths	1885	O.W.
Caenycoed									
Machynlleth, Bethesda	1800	250	64	7	68	..	D. H. Hughes ..	1893	C.C.
Mochdre (E.)	1830	110	60	4	40	..	*J. Roberts	1894	O.W.
Newchapel (E.)	1796	250	101	4	60	..	*D. E. Hughes ..	1886	O.W.

MONTGOMERYSHIRE—*continued.*

Churches.	Date.	Chapel seats.	No. of Members.	Sunday School Teachers.	No. of Scholars.	Local Preachers.	Pastors.	When settled.	Associations.
Newtown (E.)	1736	1250	320	40	410	1	T. E. Williams ..	1892	O.W.
New Wells (E.)	1838	200	39	3	30	1	*J. Roberts	1894	O.W.
Pontllogell (near Llanfyllin)	..	100	14	2	12	..	.. ..	..	D F M
Rhydfelin (E.)	1791	112	16	3	16	..	.. ..	..	O.W.
Sarn (E.)	1786	200	90	11	125	..	A.G. Jones, Ph.D.	1895	O.W.
Cwm (E.)	..	80	90	..	..	..			
Staylittle and Tanlan..	1805	198	102	12	110	..	.. ..	..	O.W.
Dylife	1813	120	17	4	21	..			
Talywern, Sion	1824	350	86	8	62	1	.. ..	..	C.C.
Welshpool (E.)	1837	250	51	6	76	..	T. Rowson	1892	O.W.

PEMBROKESHIRE (*Pop.* 89,133).

(P., Pembrokeshire. G.C.E., Glamorganshire and Carmarthenshire English.)

Churches.	Date.	Chapel seats.	No. of Members.	Sunday School Teachers.	No. of Scholars.	Local Preachers.	Pastors.	When settled.	Associations.
Blaenconin Clynderw'n	1846	500	250	17	186		.. ..	..	P.
Blaenffos	1785	800	328	18	190		A. Morgan	1892	P.
Bethabara	1827	500	155	8	98		*W. J. Lewis.. ..	1891	P.
Blaenllyn and	1842	250	236	5	130		Theo. John	1873	P.
Newton	1862	210							
Blaenywaen	1745	800	..		..		Hugh Jones ..	1894	P.
Bethsaida	..	650	..		..				
St.Dogmell's, Gerizim	..	250	101	8	40				
Broadhaven, Hephzibah (E.)	1841	180	72	8	106		T. R. Lewis.. ..	1892	P.
Camrose (E.)	1838	250	76	6	75		*J. Williams	1889	P.
Cemaes, Penuel	1824	200	122	12	130		.. ..	..	P.
Cilfowyr	1704	600	214	14	137		W. C. Williams ..	1895	P.
Cilgerran, Penuel.. ..	1820	250	165	15	100		.. ..	..	P.
Clarbeston, Carmel ..	1804	300	96	8	70		J. D. Thomas ..	1895	P.
Gelly	1858	200	135	8	86				
Cold Inn (E.)	1861	250	121		122	2	T. Gravell	1888	P.
Cresswell Quay Pisgah (E.)	1820	300	126		110		J. Roberts	1895	P.
Croesgoch	1816	600	332	16	120		D. Phillips	1857	P.
Trevine									
Dinas Cross, Tabor ..	1798	600	373	19	152		J. W. Maurice ..	1885	P.
Eglwyswrw, Ebenezer	1768	600	169	9	103		*W. J. Lewis.. ..	1891	P.
Ffynnon (Narbeth) and	1779	400	118	6	110		.. ..	..	P.
Glanrhyd	1811	250	54	5	67				
Fishguard, Hermon ..	1807	640	521	40	350		.. ..	..	P.
Goodwick	1873	360							
Lower Fishguard..									
Scleddy	1859	200							
Haverfordwest :—									
Bethesda (E.)	1769	950	340	18	226	2	O. D. Campbell, M.A.	1895	P.
Machpelah (E.) ..	1842	100							
Prendergast									
Hill Park (W. & E.)..	1857	550	228	27	186		John Jenkins ..	1871	P.

PEMBROKESHIRE—*continued.*

Churches.	Date.	Chapel seats.	No. of Members.	Sunday School Teachers.	No. of Scholars.	Local Preachers.	Pastors.	When settled.	Associations.
Honeyborough :—									
Hephzibah (E.) ..	1840	250	167	6	130		D. Lewis	1895	P.
Lanteague, Zoar (E.) ..	1854	120	19	2	15		.. ..	..	P.
Letterston, Saron ..	1828	500	292	20	121		B. Thomas	1865	P.
LittleNewcastle, Beulah	1817	400	100		70		Jacob John	1885	P.
Llanfyrnach, Hermon	1808	400	197	14	170		.. ..	..	P.
Llangloffan	1745	750	239	8	132		E. Davies	1874	P.
St. Nicholas, Bethel	1866	200							
Mathry, Nebo ..									
Llangwm, Galilee (E.)	1833	250	90	2	95		W. Davies	1883	P.
Llanychllwydog (Cwmgwaen), Jabez	1801	400	204	22	174		*J. Ll. Morris ..	1883	P.
Maenclochog, Horeb ..	1864	400	152	14	107		*W. Davies	1875	P.
Manorbier, Penuel (E.)	1850	300	37	5	50		J. Harrington ..	1888	G C E
Marloes (E.)	1821	350	104	5	50		*D. T. Richards ..	1891	P.
Martletwy (Narberth) (E.)	1840	400	103	9	120		W. Reynolds ..	1890	P.
Middlemill	1794	1000	293	20	150		W. Roberts ..	1890	P.
Milford, North-road (E.)	1828	600	115	13	140		W. H. Prosser ..	1891	P.
Moleston (Narberth) (E.)	1667	350	132	8	120		T. Evans	1879	P.
Loveston (E.)	..	20	..	8	60				
Mynachlogddu, Bethel	1794	450	200	18	150		W. Griffith	1867	P.
Narberth (E.)	1816	600	307	20	220		J. A. Thomas ..	1894	P.
Nevern, Caersalem ..	1841	400	206	13	100		*J. Ll. Morris ..	1853	P.
Newport :—									
Bethlehem	1793	600	462	20	160		J. Jenkins	1852	P.
Newtonpants :—									
Bethlehem	1820	300	132	5	80		D. O. Edwards ..	1878	P.
Salem	1827	50	94	8	52				
Neyland, Bethesda (E.)	1863	250	144	17	220		B. C. Evans	1894	P.
Sardis (E.)	1822	250	118		120		*E. Lawrence ..	1895	P.
Pembroke (E.) (14,978)	1830	600	284	23	230	3	E. Thomas	1875	P.
Cosheston	1840	150							
Pembroke Dock :—									
Bush-st., Bethel (E.)	1843	750	188	22	180		R. C. Roberts ..	1876	P.
High-st., Bethany (E.)	1818	650	292	30	330	5	J. D. Jones	1880	P.
Pennar, Gilgal (E.) ..	1862	450	158	24	206		D. Davies	1894	P.
Pencaer, Harmony ..	1828	320	218		100		W. Rees	1887	P.
Penybryn (Cilgerran) ..	1808	290	94	7	60		.. ..	..	P.
Pope Hill, Horeb (E.) ..	1817	200	58	6	35		*E. Lawrence ..	1895	P.
Puncheston, Smyrna ..	1827	350	186	2	100		*W. Davies	1875	P.
Roch Castle, Penuel (E.)	1822	250	52	4	30		.. ..	..	P.
St. David's, Zion	1840	300	150	8	70		J. S. Jones	1890	P.
Sandyhill (E.)	1812	250	66	4	30		*D. T. Richards ..	1891	P.
Saundersfoot, Hebron (E.)	1854	200	64	7	46		.. ..	..	P.
Southdairy (E.)	1832	200	24	3	17		.. ..	..	P.
Star	1831	350	120	0	79		.. ..	..	P.
Sutton (E.) (Haverfordwest)	1834	180	49	5	40		*J. Williams	1895	P.
Tenby (E.), South-parade	1830	600	160	16	195		.. ..	..	P.
Thornton (E.) (Milford Haven)	1867	16	20	2	20		.. ..	..	P.

RADNORSHIRE (*Pop.*, 21,791).

(O W., Old Welsh. B., Brecknockshire.)

Churches.	Date.	Chapel seats.	No. of Members.	Sunday School Teachers.	No. of Scholars.	Local Preachers.	Pastors.	When settled.	Associations.
Bwlchysarnau (E.) ..	1829	230	125	5	60	..	*D. S. Evans.. ..	1892	O.W.
Cascob	1860	..	25	2	16	1	.. ..	..	O.W.
Cefnpole (E.)	..	170	42	2	7	..	*D. S. Evans	1892	O.W.
Dolau, Nantmel (E.) ..	1761	250	71	4	45	..	.. ..	..	O.W.
Dolau, Llanfihangel (E.)	1872	200	79	5	60	..	*W. D. Young ..	1889	O.W.
Evenjobb (E.)	1841	250	53	4	40	..	}		
Gladestry (E.)	1840	200	62	5	60	2	} G. P. Edwards ..	1895	O.W.
New Radnor	1860	200	40	5	40		}		
Franksbridge (E.) ..	1824	200	160	5	60	1	} C. Harris	1895	O.W.
Glascwm (E.)	1867	50	11	..	..	..	}		
Glyn-Elan, Bethany ..	1834	150	49	6	47	..	T. Rees..	1887	B.
Gravel, Llanbister-road, (E.)	1844	200	61	6	80	..	*W. D. Young ..	1889	O.W.
Howey(E.), Llandrindod	1853	150	61	3	30	..	.. ..	..	O.W.
Knighton (E.)	1864	400	212	24	240	6	*W. Williams .. (*see Shropshire*)	1878	O.W.
Llandilo, Moriah (E.)..	1830	250	41	4	50	..	*T. James	1886	O.W.
Llandrindod Wells (E.)	1876	350	114	6	60	..	J. Jones	1876	O.W.
Maesyrhelem (E.) ..	1801	250	248	17	235	1	D. Davies	1876	O.W.
Nantgwyn (E.)	1766	300	129	6	81	..	*T. D. Jones (*see Montgomeryshire*)	1893	O.W.
Newbridge-on-Wye (E.)	1727	350	137	6	62	..	H. C. Edwards ..	1895	O.W.
Painscastle, Adullam(E)	1836	350	55	5	50	1	*T. James	1886	O.W.
Presteign (E.)	1824	400	158	20	169	..	} W. Skinner ..	1893	O.W.
Stan-batch	1861	150	..	..	..	..	}		
Rhayader (E.)	1840	200	51	3	30	..	.. ..	..	O.W.
Rock (Penybont) (E.)..	1721	300	119	11	134	1	D. Thomas	1895	O.W.
Velindre (E.)..	1852	200	76	5	62	..	*W. G. Mansfield.. (*See Shropshire.*)	1891	O.W.

MONMOUTHSHIRE (*Pop.*, 252,416)

(M., Monmouthshire Welsh. M.E., Monmouthshire English. E.G., East Glamorganshire. B., Breconshire.)

Churches.	Date.	Chapel seats.	No. of Members.	Sunday school Teachers.	No. of Scholars.	Local Preachers.	Pastors.	When settled.	Associations.
Abercarn (E.)	1876	750	371	27	361	1	.. ..	..	M.
Abercarn (W.)	1847	650	158	14	140	..	T. A. Thomas ..	1884	M.
Chapel of Ease ..	1895	..	76	10	160	..	.. ..	..	M.
Abergavenny :—									
Frogmore-street (E.)	1807	750	250	26	283	8	T.E.Cozens Cooke	1883	M.E.
Bethany (E.)	1828	380	123	13	130	1	S. R. Young ..	1856	M.E.
Abersychan (E.)	1827	400	189	23	350	..	J. O. Hughes ..	1893	M.E.
Noddfa (W. & E.) ..	1846	500	108	10	195	..	.. ..	..	M.
Abertillery :—									
King-street (E.) ..	1852	500	168	19	180	..	T. Griffiths	1878	M.
Blaina Gwent(W.&E.)	1660	500	324	25	350	1	T. T. Evans ..	1882	M.
Workmen's Hall ..	..	..	..	9	80				
Ebenezer (E.)	1877	800	278	31	285	1	D. Hussey	1890	M.
Argoed (W. & E.)	1818	450	147	26	210	2	Evan George ..	1879	M.
Holly Bush	1884	125							
Bargoed, Caersalem (W.)	1852	650	205	30	245	1	.. ..	..	M.
Cwmsyfiog, Bethania	1860	200							
Bassaleg, Bethel (W. & E.)	1831	532	150	13	140	..	W. Morgan	1894	M.
Bethesda (E.)	1742	600	239	26	300	..	T. G. James ..	1892	M.
Bedwas (W.)..	1851	450	167	20	150	..	Morgan James ..	1873	M.
Blackwood, Libanus (W)	1835	250	35	5	40	2	.. ..	..	M.
Mount Pleasant (E.)	1876	600	158	15	190	..	.. ..	..	M.E.
Blaenavon :—									
Horeb (E.)	1823	600	282	29	420	..	J. Johns	1894	M.
Blaenycwm	1870	150							
Ebenezer (E.)	1825	500	136	15	130	1	Ioan Meredyth ..	1894	M.
Broad-street (E.) ..	1846	650	141	15	220	2	T. Phillips	1895	M.E.
Forge Side, Zion (E.)	1875	350	111	11	214	..	.. ..	..	M.
King-street (E.) ..	1878	500	160	26	300	1	W. E. Stephens ..	1895	M.
Blaina, Salem (W. & E.)	1841	800	297	31	400	1	J. Gimblett	1894	M.
Caerleon (E.)	1771	400	90	12	100	..	D. B. Jones	1866	M.E.
Caerwent (Chepstow) (E.)	1816	150	28	3	33	..	*J. Berryman ..	1888	M.E.
Castletown (Cardiff) (W. & E.)	1823	700	203	15	202	..	R. Lloyd	1861	M.
Chepstow (E.)	1816	350	67	16	132	3	C. Thomas	1892	M.E.
Bowlash									
Cross Keys (Newport) (E.)	1882	700	244	36	600	3	W. Evans	1894	M.
Cwmbran, Siloam, (Newport) (W. & E.)	1839	300	71	12	112	..	.. ..	..	M.E.
Cwm, Tirzah (E.).. ..	1879	150	64	11	140	1	J. J. Young	1894	M.
Cwmnera	1856	140	28	4	40	..	*B. Davies	1892	M.
Ebbw Vale :—									
Briery-hill, Zion (E.)	1841	500	153	26	350	1	W. Powell	1880	M.E.
Brynhyfryd (W. & E.)	1853	700	159	19	190	1	L. M. Roberts, M.A	1886	M.
Newtown, Providence (E.)..	1860	300	54	12	130	..	E. Edwards.. ..	1888	M.
Nebo (W.)	1827	800	135	13	120	1	J. A. Evans	1893	M.
Victoria, Caersalem (W. & E.)	1845	550	192	20	300	1	T. Thomas	1895	M.

MONMOUTHSHIRE—*continued.*

Churches.	Date.	Chapel seats.	No. of Members.	Sunday School Teachers.	No. of Scholars.	Local Preachers.	Pastors.	When settled.	Associations.
Glascoed (Pontypl.) (E.)	1817	200	54	2	30	..	.. ..	..	M.
Goytrey, Sharon (W.&E.)	1826	250	46	6	50	1	.. ..	..	M.
Griffithstown, Newport (E.)	1876	400	..	..	..	..	.. ..	..	M.E.
Henllan (E.), Cwmyoy, near Abergavenny ..	1878	100	26	3	24	..	*J. N. Smith (*see also* p.p. 220 *and* 267) ..	1890	B.
Henllys, Zoar (W. & E.)	1843	300	52	8	60	..	R. L. Morris ..	1894	M.
Llanddewi Rhydderch (E.)	1828	250	66	9	70	..	W. Rees	1892	M.
Llanfihangel Crucorney Zoar (E.)	1837	150	58	5	40	..	.. ..	..	M.E.
Llanfihangel Ystern Llewern (E.)	1829	150	9	3	18	..	*T. C. Powell ..	1871	M.E.
Llangibby (E.)	1837	200	23	..	..	..	*B. Davies	1892	M.E.
Llangwm (Usk) (E.) ..	1772	400	49	6	30	..	*B. Davies	1892	M.
Llanhilleth (W. & E.) ..	1837	350	123	13	120	..	J. Lloyd	1880	M.
Llantarnam (E.)	1862	500	136	14	212	1	W. E. Robinson ..	1892	M.
Llanvaches, Bethany (E)	1809	120	25	4	40	..	.. ..	..	M.E
Llanwenarth (W. & E.)	1696	400	132	13	167	..	T. H. Williams ..	1884	M.
Pwlddu									
Machen, Siloam (W.&E.)	1830	700	137	10	100	..	.. ..	..	M.
Maesycwmmer (E.) ..	1863	300	82	9	130	..	T. Batstone.. ..	1880	M.E.
Magor (Newport) (E.) ..	1816	300	99	18	101	..	O. Tidman	1893	M.E.
Michaelstone - y - Vedw (Cardiff), Tirzah (E.)	1861	300	94	5	90	1	.. ..	..	M.
Monmouth, Monnow-street (E.)	1818	200	63	3	30	..	.. ..	..	M.E.
Nantyglo :—									
Hermon (W.)	1830	1000	179	29	249	..	H. Williams ..	1879	M.
Bethel (E.)	1871	500	83	8	173	..	John G. Williams	1890	M.E
Bethlehem (E.)	1880	..	110	13	235	..	D. Lewis	1880	M.
Nash (E.)	1821	140	31	3	30	1	T. Delahaye ..	1872	M.E.
Liswerry		250	34	10	130				
Newbridge (E.)	1864	550	368	35	370	2	J. M. Jones	1884	M.
Crumlin	..	300	..	11	130				
Beulah (W.)	1823	500	319	30	250	1	J. Edwards	1891	M.
Newport (54,707) :—									
Alexander-road (E.)	1884	500	90	12	277	..	.. ..	..	M.E.
Alma-street (E.) ..	1866	500	200	26	300	1	J. P. Thomas ..	1866	M.E.
Charles-street (E.) ..	1817	500	139	9	128	1	Daniel Davies ..	1880	M.
Commercial-st. (E.) ..	1829	1000	251	24	230	..	.. ..	..	M.E.
Commercial-road (E.)	1861	850	444	30	570	1	G. Evans	1895	M.
Duckpool-road (E.) ..	1875	800	394	24	395	2	A. T. Jones.. ..	1876	M.E.
Maindee, Durham-road ..									
East Usk-road	1889	150	52	8	144	..	A. Purnell	1889	M.E.
Maindee (E.)	1862	600	213	35	409	1	G. H. Cook	1876	M.E.
St. Mary-street (E.) ..	1868	660	307	39	508	9	C. Ayliffe	1870	M.E.
Stow Hill (E.)	1860	1000	176	24	170	..	H. Abraham ..	1886	M.E.
Temple (W.)	1842	800	58	4	30	..	D. Evans	1895	M.
New Tredegar, Saron (W.)	1860	500	167	14	141	..	W. Williams ..	1890	E.G.

MONMOUTHSHIRE—*continued.*

Churches.	Date.	Chapel seats.	No. of Members.	Sunday School Teachers.	No. of Scholars.	Local Preachers.	Pastors.	When settled.	Associations.
Norton (E.) (Skenfrith)	1841	150	26	6	50	2	J. Hook, of Garway (p. 220)	1889	M.E.
Penalt (Monmouth) (E.)	1838	130	9	7	40	..	*T. C. Powell ..	1879	M.E.
Penheolybadd (Cwmbran) (E.)	1883	200	41	7	70	..	*T. Cocker	1883	M.E.
Peterstone (W. & E.) ..	1874	100	28	4	14	..	.. ..	..	M.
Ponthir (E.)	1800	400	175	9	142	..	W. I. James ..	1891	M.E.
Pontllanfraith, Elim (W. & E.)	1892	200	42	6	50	..	D. Lewis	1894	M.
Pontnewydd (E.)	1877	300	75	13	186	..	*T. Cocker	1877	M.E.
Pontnewynydd (E.) ..	1877	350	169	14	343	..	J. G. Watts	1886	M.E.
Zion Hill	1881	200	20	9	121	1	O. Jenkins	1886	M.
Pontrhydyryn (E.) ..	1815	600	196	20	180	..	J. D. Rees	1880	M.E.
Pontypool:—									
Crane-street (E.) ..	1836	600	213	19	320	8	J. Williams	1878	M.E.
Penygarn Tabernacle (E.)	1720	700	207	20	406	1	.. ..	..	M.
Bridge-street, Trosnant (E.)	1776	680	123	18	312	..	D. R. Jenkins ..	1893	M.
Raglan, Usk-road (E.)	1818	300	79	11	87	..	.. ..	..	M.E.
Kingcoed	1845	80							
Redwick (E.)..	1830	100	27	3	32	..	*J. Berryman ..	1891	M.E.
Rhymney:—									
Penuel (W.)	1828	1200	340	43	390	..	G. Griffiths	1882	M.
Tafarnaubach (W.)..	1856	280	73	11	80	..	D. E. Davies ..	1893	M.
Jerusalem (W.).. ..	1844	800	198	12	126	..	W. Saunders ..	1895	M.
Beulah (E.)	1861	800	..	..	..	..	*R. Owen (*See Brithdir, Glam.*)	1889	M.
Risca, Moriah (W. & E.)	1835	950	321	41	490	..	J. O. Jenkins ..	1893	M.
Cwmynant	1870	150							
Risca, Bethany (E.) ..	1855	1000	449	32	794	1	T. Thomas	1874	M.
Sirhowy:—									
Carmel (W.)	1836	700	173	14	130	1	D. Mathias	1894	M.
Tabernacle (W & E)	1847	500	39	6	60	..	.. ..	..	M
St. Bride's (Newport) (W. & E.)	1843	150	46	4	50	..	.. ..	..	M.
St. Mellon's (Cardiff) (W. & E.)	1843	450	109	12	80	..	.. ..	..	M.
Talywain, Pisgah (W. & E.)	1828	600	126	19	274	..	J. Morgan	1892	M.
Tintern (E.)	1884	200	15	3	25	..	C. Thomas, of Chepstow ..	1894	M.E.
Tredegar:—									
Church-street (E.) ..	1833	500	250	18	300	4	W. Evans	1894	M.E.
Shiloh (W.)	1798	1200	299	40	250	..	P. Williams ..	1886	M.
Trevil, Breconshire	..	100							
George Town, Bethel (E.)	1868	450	145	19	271	1	M. H. Matthews..	1895	M.
Armageddon	1859	250	25	10	80	..	.. ..	..	M.
Twyngwyn (W. & E.)..	1829	300	70	10	100	..	.. ..	..	M.
Usk (E.)..	1840	300	70	8	80	..	.. ..	..	M.E
Whitebrook & Llandogo (E.)	1839	400	30	7	50	1	.. ..	..	M.E.

Scotland.

(Aggregate Population, 4,025,647.)

(B. U. S., Baptist Union of Scotland.)

N.B.—The populations of towns and cities of over 10,000 inhabitants are either for the Parliamentary or Police burghs.

ABERDEENSHIRE (*Pop.*, 281,332).

Churches.	Date.	Chapel seats.	No. of Members.	Sunday School Teachers.	No. of Scholars.	Local Preachers.	Pastors.	When settled.	Associations.
Aberdeen (121,623) :—									
Academy-street ..	1803	280	53	8	40	1			
Crown-terrace	1821	388	344	18	153	..	W. S. Chedburn ..	1879	B U S
Gilcomston Park ..	1886	600	265	16	240	..	A. Bisset, M.A. ..	1883	B U S
Longacre	..	..	..	10	63				
Union Grove	1892	300	75	13	160	..	S. G. Woodrow ..	1893	B U S
Fraserburgh	1840	300	90	9	100	..	E. Hughes	1895	B U S
Peterhead (12,195) :—									
King-street	1859	300	123	9	87	4	A. J. Payne	1891	B U S

ARGYLLSHIRE (*Pop.*, 75,003).

Churches.	Date.	Chapel seats.	No. of Members.	Sunday School Teachers.	No. of Scholars.	Local Preachers.	Pastors.	When settled.	Associations.
Dunoon	1883	360	106	9	70	..	D. Macgregor ..	1885	B U S
Lochgilphead	1815	250	40	2	12	..	John Knox	1880	B U S

AYRSHIRE (*Pop.*, 226,283).

Churches.	Date.	Chapel seats.	No. of Members.	Sunday School Teachers.	No. of Scholars.	Local Preachers.	Pastors.	When settled.	Associations.
Ayr (23,826)	1886	500	44	2	25	..	H. D. Brown ..	1892	B U S
Irvine, Bank-street ..	1808	320	36	8	41	..	A. Kerr	1894	B U S
Kilmarnock (28,447) :—									
Fowlds-street	1866	300	118	14	130	..	W. Donald	1884	B U S
Old Cumnock	1875	200	28	3	28	4	J. Adair	1894	B U S
New Cumnock ..	..	..	..	15	124				

BANFFSHIRE (*Pop.*, 64,190).

Churches.	Date.	Chapel seats.	No. of Members.	Sunday School Teachers.	No. of Scholars.	Local Preachers.	Pastors.	When settled.	Associations.
Aberchirder	1806	200	30	..	..	2	.. ..	..	B U S

BERWICKSHIRE (*Pop.*, 32,406).

BUTESHIRE (*Pop.*, 18,404)

Churches.	Date.	Chapel seats.	No. of Members.	Sunday School Teachers.	No. of Scholars.	Local Preachers.	Pastors.	When settled.	Associations.
Millport	1836	150	12	6	25	..	J. Black, M.A. ..	1895	B U S
Rothesay, Ardbeg ..	1855	450	75	8	40	..	S. Crabb	1869	B U S

CAITHNESS-SHIRE (*Pop.*, 37,177).

Churches.	Date.	Chapel seats.	No. of Members.	Sunday School Teachers.	No. of Scholars.	Local Preachers.	Pastors.	When settled.	Associations.
Keiss	1750	260	..	5	51	..	J. McPherson ..	1893	B U S
Freswick	..	..	..	5	47				
Scarfskerry	1868	300	55	5	60	1	Jas. Scott	1883	B U S
Stroma	..	..	15	2	14				
Wick	1809	400	84	14	179	..	W. H. Millard ..	1893	B U S

CLACKMANNANSHIRE (*Pop.* 28,432).

Churches.	Date.	Chapel seats.	No. of Members.	Sunday School Teachers.	No. of Scholars.	Local Preachers.	Pastors.	When settled.	Associations.
Alloa (10,711)	1838	500	193	11	85	..	J. D. Robertson..	1895	B U S
Tillicoultry	1893	..	77	12	105	3	J. Holden	1893	B U S

DUMBARTONSHIRE (*Pop.*, 94,495).

Churches.	Date.	Chapel seats.	No. of Members.	Sunday School Teachers.	No. of Scholars.	Local Preachers.	Pastors.	When settled.	Associations.
Clydebank	1891	350	99	19	161	2	J. Burns	1891	B U S
Dalmuir									
Dumbarton (16,908) ..	1876	500	78	12	120	4	P. McLeod	1891	B U S
Helensburgh	1881	280	67	7	37	..	G. A. Wilson ..	1883	B U S
Kirkintilloch	1887	250	136	14	101	5	W.B.Nicolson,M.A	1890	B U S

DUMFRIES-SHIRE (*Pop.*, 74,221).

Churches.	Date.	Chapel seats.	No. of Members.	Sunday School Teachers.	No. of Scholars.	Local Preachers.	Pastors.	When settled.	Associations.
Dumfries (17,821) ..	1872	430	52	5	40	..	A. Bremner.. ..	1889	B U S

EDINBURGHSHIRE (*Pop.*, 434,159).

Churches.	Date.	Chapel seats.	No. of Members.	Sunday School Teachers.	No. of Scholars.	Local Preachers.	Pastors.	When settled.	Associations.
Dalkeith	1852	150	106	4	40		H. McLean.. ..	1891	B U S
Edinburgh (261,225):—									
Bristo-place	1765	570	562	38	354	3	W. Grant .. .. A. Cromar	1870 1888	
Potterrow	..	..	..	10	66				
Dublin-street	1810	850	..	21	161		J. T. Forbes, M.A.	1895	B U S
Canon Mills	1883	150		15	253				
Duncan-street	1779	350	128	8	50		P. Fleming	1894	B U S
Marshall-street ..	1846	650	228	14	125		A. Wylie, M.A. ..	1880	B U S
Morningside	1894	600	40	4	27	2	J. C. Brown.. ..	1894	B U S
Rose-street, Charlotte-square	1806	500	217	3	143		T. W. Way	1888	B U S
Leith (67,700):—									
North Leith, Madeira-street	1868	500	145	16	160		W. Richards ..	1895	B U S
South Leith	1891	500	247	2	221		David Tait	1891	B U S

FIFESHIRE (*Pop.*, 187,346).

Churches.	Date.	Chapel seats.	No. of Members.	Sunday School Teachers.	No. of Scholars.	Local Preachers.	Pastors.	When settled.	Associations.
Anstruther	1860	430	116	30	235		H. Edwards ..	1893	B U S
Pittenweem									
Cowdenbeath	1875	250	141	2[illegible]	98	9	J. M. Munro ..	1893	B U S
Cupar	1816	500	87	6	29		.. ..	..	B U S
Dunfermline (19,647):—									
Viewfield-place ..	1842	600	331	30	330		J. T. Hagen.. ..	1875	B U S
Kirkcaldy (17,304):—									
Whyte's Causeway ..	1852	500	287	32	234	6	W. J. Hunter ..	1893	B U S
Thistle-street ..									
Mill-street									
Largo	1868	160	40	7	60	3	W. Pulford	1893	B U S
Buckhaven	..		34	8	128				
Leslie	1880	400	108	8	60	2	D. Kerr	1893	B U S
Leven	1892	250	51	7	59	2	A. Piggot	1893	B U S
St. Andrews	1841	200	61	10	83	1	S. Hirst	1890	B U S

FORFARSHIRE (*Pop.*, 277,773).

Churches.	Date.	Chapel seats.	No. of Members.	Sunday School Teachers.	No. of Scholars.	Local Preachers.	Pastors.	When settled.	Associations.
Arbroath (22,800):—									
Market-place	1810	300	103	14	92	13	G. Menzies	1893	B U S
Broughty Ferry	1876	250	54	11	75	..	G. P. Craise.. ..	1891	B U S
Dundee (153,051):—									
Ward-road..	1874	650	417	24	172	4	D. Clark	1889	B U S
Wellgate Hall ..	..	..	..	14	100				
Rattray-street	..	500	379	15	120	4	T. W. Lister ..	1890	
Millers Pend ..	..	..	..	6	50				
Forfar (12,057)	1872	400	83	9	79	4	G. Lauder	1891	B U S
Lochee	1865	330	130	25	174	..	.. ..	..	B U S

HADDINGTONSHIRE (*Pop.*, 37,485).

INVERNESS-SHIRE (*Pop.*, 89,317).

KINCARDINESHIRE (*Pop.*, 35,647).

KINROSS-SHIRE (*Pop.*, 6,280).

KIRKCUDBRIGHTSHIRE (*Pop.*, 39,985).

LANARKSHIRE (*Pop.*, 1,046,040).

Churches.	Date.	Chapel seats.	No. of Members.	Sunday School Teachers.	No. of Scholars.	Local Preachers.	Pastors.	When settled.	Associations.
Airdrie (15,133):—									
Graham-street	1842	430	155	24	200		**W. Macintosh** ..	**1892**	**B U S**
Bellshill	1894	..	37	..	..		**J. Bruce**	**1894**	
Cambuslang	1881	500	262	29	248		**A. A. Milne** ..	**1892**	**B U S**
Coatbridge (30,034) ..	1868	500	150	12	103	4	**H. Gunn**	**1890**	**B U S**
Glasgow (564,981):—									
Adelaide-place ..	1829	1000	489	45	546		**T. H. Martin** ..	**1888**	**B U S**
St. Clair-street ..									
Brown-street ..									
Bridgeton, Sister-st.	1886	450	408	25	285		**W. J. Millar..** ..	**1884**	**B U S**
Cambridge-street ..	1862	450	380	26	233	12	**E. Last..**	**1891**	**B U S**
John Knox-street ..	1845	630	311	40	404		**P. J. Rollo**	**1879**	**B U S**
North Frederick-st.	1851	700	321	54	480		**E. Aubrey**	**1895**	**B U S**
Hillhead	1883	800	474	30	225	17	**F. H. Robarts** ..	**1883**	**B U S**
Partick	..	..	..	22	267				
Port Dundas ..	..	..	..	16	206				
Hutchesontown ..	1883	..	90	17	200		**T. Collins**	**1895**	**B U S**
North John-street ..	1768	450	347	20	378	12	**R. Watson** .. .. **G. McCrie** .. ***R. Coats*** .. .. ***J. Todd***	**1870** **1885** **1895** **1895**	
Shiloh Hall									
Queen's-park	1878	575	239	25	235	6	**H. Wright**	**1892**	**B U S**
South Side (Gorbals)	1876	450	291	11	220	6	**J. McLean**	**1890**	**B U S**
Govanhill	..	..	..	12	80				
Springburn	1892	..	117	23	249		**J. Horne**	**1892**	**B U S**
Govan (61,363)	1872	650	284	27	336		**J. Coats, M.A.** ..	**1872**	**B U S**
Hamilton (24,859) ..	1886	450	75	9	86	5	**J. R. Chrystal, [M.A., B.D.**	**1886**	**B U S**
Motherwell (18,726) ..	1887	372	59	8	69	3	**J. Connor**	**1888**	**B U S**
Rutherglen	1892	Hall	57	11	95		**J. Young**	**1894**	**B U S**
Wishaw (15,252)	1872	300	265	17	150		**G. Whittet**	**1876**	**B U S**

LINLITHGOWSHIRE (*Pop.*, 52,808)

MORAYSHIRE (*Pop.*, 43,453).

Churches.	Date.	Chapel seats.	No. of Members.	Sunday School Teachers.	No. of Scholars.	Local Preachers.	Pastors.	When settled.	Associations.
Elgin, Reidhaven-street	1808	400	133	10	60	4	R. E. Glendening	1884	B U S
Forres	1860	240	..	..	..	..	.. ..	..	B U S
Grantown	1805	250	..	9	50	..	W. H. Davies ..	1891	B U S
Lossiemouth	1861	360	149	14	155	..	B. J. Cole	1892	B U S
Hopeman									

NAIRN (*Pop.*, 10,019).

PEEBLES-SHIRE (*Pop.*, 14,761).

Churches.	Date.	Chapel seats.	No. of Members.	Sunday School Teachers.	No. of Scholars.	Local Preachers.	Pastors.	When settled.	Associations.
Peebles	1889	..	15	3	20	..	A. M. Crooks ..	1889	B U

PERTHSHIRE (*Pop.*, 126,199).

Churches.	Date.	Chapel seats.	No. of Members.	Sunday School Teachers.	No. of Scholars.	Local Preachers.	Pastors.	When settled.	Associations.
Crieff	1881	120	31	4	35	4	W. R. Simpson ..	1889	B U S
Perth (29,899):—									
Tay-street	1808	1200	287	18	180	..	J. A. G. Robinson, [M.A.	1890	B U S
Pitlochry	1881	286	70	1	10	..	J. W. Kettle ..	1895	B U S
Tullymet	1806	320	69	4	25	..	L. S. Steedman ..	1894	B U S

RENFREWSHIRE (*Pop.*, 290,798).

Churches.	Date.	Chapel seats.	No. of Members.	Sunday School Teachers.	No. of Scholars.	Local Preachers.	Pastors.	When settled.	Associations.
Greenock (63,096):—									
George-square	1884	500	101	15	115		W. H. Griffith ..	1894	B U S
Orangefield-place ..	1806	650	266	19	175	12	A. Corbet	1887	B U S
Paisley (66,418):—									
Thomas Coats' Memorial	1795	1000	319	26	329		.. ..	..	B U S
George-street	1795	450	95	26	105		J. Farquhar, M.A.	1887	B U S
Victoria-place	1866	500	283	33	224		J. Crouch	1866	B U S
Barr-street ..									

ROSS AND CROMARTY (*Pop.*, 77,810).

ROXBURGHSHIRE (*Pop.*, 53,741).

Churches.	Date.	Chapel seats.	No. of Members.	Sunday School Teachers.	No. of Scholars.	Local Preachers.	Pastors.	When settled.	Associations.
Hawick (19,204)	1846	300	142	22	132	3	W. Seaman	1880	B U S
Jedburgh	1886	Hall	34	6	50	..	J. McKean	1886	B U S
Kelso	1878	340	45	5	36	2	W. Shearer	1893	B U S

SELKIRKSHIRE (*Pop.*, 27,353).

Churches.	Date.	Chapel seats.	No. of Members.	Sunday School Teachers.	No. of Scholars.	Local Preachers.	Pastors.	When settled.	Associations.
Galashiels (17,252) :—									
Victoria-street	1804	300	152	20	116	4	A. Thomson ..	1852	
							Henry Fleming ..	1881	
							D. Craighead ..	1894	
Stirling-street	1804	350	297	36	273	7	J.B. Johnston, M.A	1887	B U S
***Brewery Hall* ..**	..		..	7	60				
Selkirk	1880	160	74	9	54	4	J. Brown	1880	B U S

STIRLINGSHIRE (*Pop.*, 125,608).

Churches.	Date.	Chapel seats.	No. of Members.	Sunday School Teachers.	No. of Scholars.	Local Preachers.	Pastors.	When settled.	Associations.
Alva	1882	200	56	15	140	4	D. W. Laing ..	1882	B U S
Falkirk (16,620)	1867	375	132	12	96	..	A. Paterson, M.A.	1889	B U S
Stirling (16,776)	1805	400	162	10	81	..	G. Yuille	1870	B U S

SUTHERLANDSHIRE (*Pop.*, 21,896).

WIGTOWNSHIRE (*Pop.*, 36,062).

ORKNEY ISLES (Post-town, Kirkwall) (*Pop.*, 30,453).

Churches.	Date.	Chapel seats.	No. of Members.	Sunday School Teachers.	No. of Scholars.	Local Preachers.	Pastors.	When settled.	Associations.
Burray	1826	170	49	4	31	..	S. Lindsay	1895	B U S
Eday	1827	150	..	..	..	..	.. ..	..	B U S
***Sanday* .. ..**									
Westray..	1803	230	45	5	45	..	J. Yeomans.. ..	1895	B U S

SHETLAND ISLES (Post-town, Lerwick) (*Pop.*, 28,711).

Churches.	Date.	Chapel seats.	No. of Members.	Sunday School Teachers.	No. of Scholars.	Local Preachers.	Pastors.	When settled.	Associations.
Dunrossness	1861	400	193	8	100	2	J. McCallum ..	1893	B U S
***Burra Isle* .. ..**	..		42	3	40				
Lerwick	1840	350	87	13	70		C. J. Jackman ..	1894	B U S
Lunnasting and	..	150	33		..		T. Young	1859	B U S
Sandsting	..	20	51	2	36				
***West Burrafirth* ..**									

WESTERN ISLES (*Populations included in the counties*).

Churches.	Date.	Chapel seats.	No. of Members.	Sunday School Teachers.	No. of Scholars.	Local Preachers.	Pastors.	When settled.	Associations.
Colonsay	1818	150	26	2	12	2	Alex. Macdougall	1891	B U S
***Port Charlotte* (Islay)**	..		15						
***Gortan* .. .. (Islay)**									
***Kilchoman* .. (Islay)**									
***Kilnave* .. .. (Islay)**									
Islay :—									
Bowmore	1819	400	62	10	10		D. Ross	1881	B U S
Mull :—									
Bunessan	1822	200	47	3	37		A. Brown	1892	B U S
Tobermory	1816	250	33	5	25		D. Bell	1886	B U S
Skye :—									
Broadford	1828	200	24		.		Allan Macdougall	1886	B U S
Tyree	1816	300	87	2	20	1	D. M'Farlane ..	1879	B U S

Ireland.

(Aggregate Population, 4,704,750.)

(I., Baptist Union of Ireland.)

ANTRIM (*Pop.*, 428,128).

Churches.	Date.	Chapel seats.	No. of Members.	Sunday School Teachers.	No. of Scholars.	Local Preachers.	Pastors.	When settled.	Associations.
Ballymena, Hill-street..	1859	500	69	5	58	5	T. Whiteside ..	1881	I.
and Clough	1872	200	40	5	30	..			
Belfast :—									
Great Victoria-street	1847	500	153	11	135	..	A. Walker	1893	I.
Mount Pottinger ..	1891	500	174	15	164	6	R. Clark	1891	I.
Ballyhackamore ..									
Regent-street	1867	500	374	44	387	30	C. S. Donald ..	1891	I.
Fairfax-street ..									
Carrickfergus	1862	200	61	5	36	..	M. V. F. Dawson, [M.A.	1895	I.
Grangecorner	1811	200	80	4	30	2	H. Phillips	1879	I.

ARMAGH (*Pop.*, 143,289).

Churches.	Date.	Chapel seats.	No. of Members.	Sunday School Teachers.	No. of Scholars.	Local Preachers.	Pastors.	When settled.	Associations.
Fivemile Hill	1890	..	65	6	80	3	.. ..	..	I.
Lurgan	1885	150	58	4	46	4	J. H. Boyd	1891	I.
Poyntz Pass	1894	150	32	4	34	4	A. Jardine	1895	I.
Tandragee	1864	250	85	5	40	2	J. Taylor	1863	I.

CORK (*Pop.*, 438,432).

Churches.	Date.	Chapel seats.	No. of Members.	Sunday School Teachers.	No. of Scholars.	Local Preachers.	Pastors.	When settled.	Associations.
Cork	1890	240	44	4	20	..	W. L. Tweedie ..	1894	I.

DERRY (*Pop.*, 152,009).

Churches.	Date.	Chapel seats.	No. of Members.	Sunday School Teachers.	No. of Scholars.	Local Preachers.	Pastors.	When settled.	Associations.
Coleraine, Meeting House-street	1795	220	103	6	50	4	P. H. Blaikie ..	1895	I.
Cool Hill	..	..	16						
Tubbermore	1805	400	222	13	138	..	G. Marshall ..	1894	I.

DONEGAL (*Pop.*, 185,635).

Churches.	Date.	Chapel seats.	No. of Members.	Sunday School Teachers.	No. of Scholars.	Local Preachers.	Pastors.	When settled.	Associations.
Letterkenny	1810	150	12	6	110	1	J. Storey	1859	I.

DOWN (*Pop.*, 267,059).

Churches.	Date.	Chapel seats.	No. of Members.	Sunday School Teachers.	No. of Scholars.	Local Preachers.	Pastors.	When settled.	Associations.
Ballykeel	1891	120	39	5	19	1	James Hodge ..	1891	I.
Banbridge	1846	260	87	8	90	4	J. Bennett	1895	I.
Derryneil	1864	300	37	2	16	..	G. Rock	1891	I.

DUBLIN (*Pop.*, 419,216).

Churches.	Date.	Chapel seats.	No. of Members.	Sunday School Teachers.	No. of Scholars.	Local Preachers.	Pastors.	When settled.	Associations.
Dublin :—									
Harcourt-street ..	1640	800	401	21	210	22	H. D. Brown, [M.A., B.L.	1887	I.
Lower Gardiner-st.	..	140	..	5	50				
Dundrum									
Phibsboro'-avenue ..	1891	200	62	4	55	..	Fenton E. Bury..	1891	I.

KILDARE (*Pop.*, 70,206).

Churches.	Date.	Chapel seats.	No. of Members.	Sunday School Teachers.	No. of Scholars.	Local Preachers.	Pastors.	When settled.	Associations.
Brannoxtown	1873	120	50	3	30	..	J. D. Gilmore ..	1893	I.

LIMERICK (*Pop.*, 158,912).

Churches.	Date.	Chapel seats.	No. of Members.	Sunday School Teachers.	No. of Scholars.	Local Preachers.	Pastors.	When settled.	Associations.
Limerick, Military-road	1891	210	26	2	7	..	Alex. G. Gibb, M.A.	1892	I.
TYRONE (*Pop.*, 171,401).									
Dungannon	1884	Hall	17	..	..	..	A. Patterson ..	1884	I.
Lisnagleer (Donaghmore)	1866	160	63	6	68	1	J. W. Pearce ..	1891	I.
Knockconny	1807	200	42	7	100	..	M. Simpson ..	1884	I.
Mullycar									
WATERFORD (*Pop.*, 98,251).									
Waterford, Catherine-street	1652	150	27	9	84	1	J. Lloyd	1895	I.
WESTMEATH (*Pop.*, 65,109).									
Athlone, Scotch-parade	1825	120	52	..	..	2	J. S. Flook	1895	I.
and Moate	1650	120							
Ferbane									

Channel Islands.

(*Population* 92,234.)

(S., Southern.)

Churches.	Date.	Chapel seats.	No. of Members.	Sunday School Teachers.	No. of Scholars.	Local Preachers.	Pastors.	When settled.	Associations.
Jersey:—									
St. Helier, Vauxhall	1864	700	130	20	170		.. ..	..	S.
Guernsey:—									
St. Peter's Port ..	1888	420	100	13	90		J. Gard	1893	S
St. Saviour's, Bethlehem	1829	250	50	40	140	10	C. J. Bougourd	1880	
Castel, St. Luke's ..	1884	100	12	15	85	10		1883	

Isle of Man.

(*Population* 55,608.)

(L.C., Lancashire and Cheshire.)

Churches.	Date.	Chapel seats.	No. of Members.	Sunday School Teachers.	No. of Scholars.	Local Preachers.	Pastors.	When settled.	Associations.
Douglas	1893	300	..	..	..	..	F. T. B. Westlake ..	1893	L.C.

III.—LIST OF CHAPELS

Not connected with Associations, and from which returns cannot be obtained. *See* note on page 201.

Where it is *known* that a Church does not exist, an asterisk is prefixed to the name of the Chapel.

The figures indicate the sitting accommodation.

ENGLAND.

Bedfordshire.

Biggleswade:—
Providence 300
Blunham: Providence 150
Clifton 500
Cranfield: Church End 100
Dunstable: St. Mary-st 300
Eaton Bray (Dunstable) 350
Luton: Dumfries-st .. 500
Potton 400
Sharnbrook:—
Bethlehem.. 150
High-street 420
Southill .. ..
Westoning .. ..
Wilden 300

Berkshire.

*Sutton Courtney .. 120
Swallowfield.. 50
Wallingford: Wood-st. 200

Buckinghamshire.

Amersham:—
Upper Meeting .. 200
Askett (Princes' Risborough) 300
Aston Clinton 200
Brickhill, Great 100
Chalkshire 100
Chesham: Townfield.. 350
Colnbrook 275
Long Ford 100
Datchet 50
Ivinghoe 350
Linslade.. 150
Nash (Stony Stratford) 140
Newport Pagnel 150
Northall (Dunstable) .. 272
Olney: 2nd Church .. 150
Penn: Beacon Hill .. 200
Prestwood (Missenden) 300
Waddesdon Hill 200
Waddesdon 100
Wycombe: Bridge-st... 400

Cambridgeshire.

Bottisham Lode 400
Chatteris:—
Hive-lane .. ..
Cottenham: Rook's-lane 700
Dry Drayton.. 150
Elsworth 250
Kirtling .. ..
Littleport .. ..
Mepal (U.) 150
Oakington 230
Stretham (Ely) 350
Sutton (Ely) 400
Whittlesea:—
Gracious-street .. 350
Windmill-street .. 300
Wilburton 220

Cheshire.

Birkenhead, Clifton-park..
Cheadle Hulme, Grove-lane 250
Chester:—
Hamilton-place .. 300
Lymm:—
Cherry-lane 150
Higher-lane 150
Millington .. .. ..

Derbyshire.

Charlesworth (Manchester) 300
Windley.. 100

Devonshire.

Ashburton .. ..
Atherington (Barnstple) 120
Aveton Gifford .. .. ..
*Brent, South 50
Harbeton Ford, Zion's-hill 100
Littlehill (Chapelton).. ..
Plymouth: York-street 300
Swimbridge 50
Tawstock .. ..
Eastcombe .. .. ..
Hiscott .. ..
Lovacott .. .. ..

Durham.

Jarrow, Grange-road .. 750
Hebburn, New Town ..

Essex.

Billericay .. ..
Braintree: Albert-road 200
Chesterford 200

LIST OF CHAPELS—*continued.*

Epping 100
Halstead: Head-street 250
Harwich, King's Head-street 350
Mersea, East .. .. ..
Saffron Walden:—
London-road 350
Sible Hedingham:—
Old Chapel 400
Swan-street 300
Newtown .. .. ..
Southminster 200
Tillingham 200
White Colne 150
Witham 250
Yeldham, Great 300

GLOUCESTERSHIRE.

Acton Turville 90
Bristol: West-street .. 130
Cubberley: Ebenezer.. 200
Hawkesbury Upton .. 200
Maiseyhampton 120
Nailsworth Tabernacle 380

HAMPSHIRE.

*Barton Cliff (U.) (Lymington) 220
Basingstoke 150
Hedge End (Botley) .. ..
Long Parish .. ..
Portsmouth: Salem .. 200
Wallop 200
Grateley 100
Yateley: Cricket Hill.. 100

HERTFORDSHIRE.

Hertford: Park-street.. 270
Hitchin:—
Queen-street, Bethel ..
Redbourne: Zion .. 200
Stevenage 300
Tring: Chapel-street.. 300
Walkern 120
Ware: New-road.. .. 50
Watford, Queen's-road, Mount Zion 210

HUNTINGDONSHIRE.

Alconbury Weston .. 150
Ellington, Jireh 220
Godmanchester:—
Cambridge-street .. 500
Needingworth 350
St. Ives:—
Crown-yard 350
Woodhurst 230
Yaxley (U.) 250
Jireh 150

KENT.

Ashford: Norwood-st.. 120
Bethersden (U.) .. .. ..
Cranbrook 100
Egerton Fostal 200
Gravesend, Windmill-street 750
Hadlow 200
Halling 107
Matfield Grn. (Brenchley) 400
Pembury (U) 209
Alders .. ..
Ramsgate:—
Camden-road 350
Ryarsh (Maidstone) .. 125
Sellinge (Hythe) .. .. ..
Sheerness-on-Sea:—
Mile Town, Russell-st. 200
Minster 250
Smarden, Tilden.. .. 330
Staplehurst 400
Sturry (Canterbury) .. ..
Tenterden: 2nd Church ..
Tunbridge Wells:—
Hanover-road 400

LANCASHIRE.

Accrington:—
Blackburn-road, Zion 300
Frederick-street .. 300
Peel-street, Ebenezer ..
Burnley:—
Boot-street, Jireh .. 200
Freetown (Bury) 400
Heywood:—
*Starkye-street .. 250
Hindley (Wigan) .. 150
Liverpool:—
Cazneau-street.. .. ..
Kirkdale, Sharon Hall 850
Shaw-street 600
Waterloo .. ..
Love Clough (Rawtenstall)
Manchester:—
Patricroft, Byron-st... 150
Rochdale-road.. .. 900
Nateby (Garstang) .. 200
Pemberton (Wigan) .. 150
Pendlebury (Manchester)..
Preston, Vauxhall-rd. 350
Rochdale, Hope 700
Fishwick-street .. .. ..
Warrington, Leigh-st. 250

LEICESTERSHIRE.

Cropstone .. ..
Knipton (Grantham) .. 100
Leicester:—
Erskine-street, Zion ..
Newark-street 400
St. Peter's-lane .. 400
*Lutterworth .. .. ..
Quenlborough 100
Wigston Magna 80

LINCOLNSHIRE.

*Billingboro': Bridge-st. 150
Billinghay .. ..
Boston:—
Liquorpond-st., Eben. 170
Whyberton .. .. ..
Deeping Market .. .. ..
Eckington, Bank-st .. 100
Pinchbeck 300
Quadring 150
Sleaford, New .. .. ..
Sleaford, Old 150
Swineshead 200

METROPOLITAN.

Bethnal Green-road .. 850
Hope Town Hall .. ..
Bishopsgate:—
Artillery-street.. .. 300
Bow, Botolph-road .. 225
Brixton: St. Anne's-rd. ..
Brompton:—
Grove Chapel .. ..
Camden Town:—
Pratt-st, Avenue .. ..
Clapham:—
Wirtemberg-st 350
Clerkenwell:—
Spencer-street 150
*Clerkenwell-road .. 350
Euston-sq, Gower-st .. 800
Hoxton:—
Newton-street 150
Kilburn Vale, Ebenezer 200
King's-cross:—
Lavina-grove 120
Marylebone:—
Riding House-street, Rehoboth .. .. ..

LIST OF CHAPELS—*continued.*

Nunhead Green .. ..
Paddington:—
Harrow-road, Beulah 120
Peckham:—
Gordon-road 200
Tooting-grove:—
Providence 120
Tottenham, Manor-road 100
Victoria-park:—
*Parnell-road .. 450
Whitechapel:—
Zoar 600
Winchmore-hill 90

MIDDLESEX.

*Cranford 250
Enfield Highway:—
Pulteney-road 150
Hayes:—
*Woodend Green .. 300
Staines 180
West Drayton, Money-lane 150

NORFOLK.

Brooke .. ..
Moulton 150
Forncett.. 120
Salhouse (Norwich) .. 250
Wortwell 150

NORTHAMPTONSHIRE.

Earl's Barton:—
Rehoboth 200
Northampton:—
Abington-street .. 550
Oundle, Zion .. .. ..
Rushden, Succoth .. 450
Towcester:—
North End.. 280

NOTTINGHAMSHIRE.

Broughton and Willoughby 340
Kirkby Woodhouse .. 170
Normanton .. ..
Nottingham:—
Whitemoor, Basford 200

SHROPSHIRE.

Ludlow .. ..

SOMERSETSHIRE.

Bath:—
Widcombe.. 750
Frome:—
*Naish's-st.. Ebenezer 400
Horsington 300
Laverton 120

STAFFORDSHIRE.

*Chesterton 200
Coseley: Coppice .. 350
Gornal .. ..
Rowley Regis .. .. ..
*Tunstall, Market-sq... 200
Willenhall: New-road ..
Wolverhampton:—
Temple-street 200

SUFFOLK.

Barton Mills 500
Crowfield 220
Kedington 250
Saxmundham 200
Walsham-le-Willows .. 450

SURREY.

Brockham-green 200
Croydon:—
West-street 500
Farnham:—
Park-lane 200
Hungry-hill 100
Haslemere 130
Horley, Victoria-road.. 150
Horsell Common.. .. 150
Leatherhead.. 100
Lingfield:—
Plaistow-street.. .. 150
*Merstham 250
Redhill:—
Station-road 300
Reigate-road 260
Richmond: Rehoboth 150
Ripley 120
Ripley-green 100

SUSSEX.

Balcombe 60
Brighton:—
Bond-street, Salem.. 830
Richmond-st., Ebenzr 600

Dane Hill 100
Eastbourne:—
South-street .. .. ..
Hastings: East Hill .. 600
Horsham, New-street.. 150
Mayfield 160
*Midhurst 200
Southwick .. ..
Wadhurst:—
Pell Green.. .. .. ..

WARWICKSHIRE.

Birmingham:—
*Hope-street 450
Coventry: Rehoboth .. 300
*Kenilworth .. ..

WILTSHIRE.

Aldbourne 80
Avebury (Calne) .. .. ..
Blunsden .. ..
Bradford: 1st Church 600
Broughton Gifford .. ..
Calne: Zion.. .. .. ..
Chippenham:—
High-street 300
Clack (Lyneham) .. ..
Colerne 200
Corsham: 2nd Church ..
Crudwell (Cirencester) 100
Dauntsey .. ..
Devizes, Salem 450
Enford .. ..
Hillmarton (Calne) .. ..
Langley Fitzurse .. 150
Hullavington .. 150
Marlborough 85
Malmesbury 300
Netheravon 300
Ogbourne 150
Rushall 100
Salisbury:—
*Harcourt 280
Sandy-lane 120
Studley (Calne) 120
Upavon .. ..
Wootton Bassett 200

WORCESTERSHIRE.

Bromsgrove:—
Worcester-street .. 250
*Buckridge Forest, Rock, near Bewdley 50
*Cradley, High-street .. 200

LIST OF CHAPELS—*continued.*

Dudley: Salop-street ..
Oldbury 400
Wythall Heath 200

YORKSHIRE.

Beverley:—
Dyer-lane (Sc.) .. 250
Bradford:—
Darfield-street 200
Halifax:—
Butts Green 126
Siddal 500
Haworth: Hall Green 500
Kilham 300
Leeds: St. James's-st. 250
Masborough 250
Newbald .. ..
•South Bank .. .. ..
Thornhill (Dewsbury).. 240

WALES.

GLAMORGANSHIRE.

Cardiff:—
Windsor-road, Zoar ..

Swansea:—
•Tontine-street .. 300
Tirphil.. .. ..

MERIONETHSHIRE.

Llanfair, Caersalem (Sc.) 90
Talsarnau (Sc.) 100
Tanygrisiau (Sc.) .. 250
Trawsfynydd (Sc.) .. 120

MONMOUTHSHIRE.

Caldicot 200

SCOTLAND.

ABERDEENSHIRE.

St. Fergus 80

ARGYLLSHIRE.

Lismore .. ..

FIFESHIRE.

Newburgh 280
Tayport 100

KINCARDINESHIRE.

•Luthermuir 60

PERTHSHIRE.

•Blair Athol 120
•Glenlyon .. ..

RENFREWSHIRE.

•Johnstone .. ..

CHANNEL ISLANDS.

GUERNSEY.

Catel Landes 325
St. Martin Fosse .. 25c

SUMMARY OF STATISTICS FOR ENGLAND, WALES, SCOTLAND, IRELAND, CHANNEL ISLANDS, ETC.

These figures include the Statistics from ONLY SUCH BAPTIST CHURCHES—associated and non-associated—AS HAVE SENT RETURNS for the year 1895, except that the Chapels and Sittings on pages 294—297 are given here.

ENGLAND (excluding Monmouthshire).

Counties.	Chrchs.	Chapels.	Sittings in Chapels.	Members	Sunday-School Teachers	Sunday Scholars.	Local Prchrs.	Pastors	Baptisms.
Bedfordshire ...	30	61	21,175	3,509	551	5,715	95	26	123
Berkshire	21	54	10,250	2,416	404	3,795	118	17	113
Buckinghamshire	41	79	18,367	3,036	636	4,705	127	24	113
Cambridgeshire ...	36	64	22,777	3,991	608	6,005	73	30	129
Cheshire	32	46	13,399	2,867	551	5,231	52	23	147
Cornwall	12	16	4,930	807	189	1,825	23	8	43
Cumberland ...	6	8	2,180	563	129	1,235	9	5	52
Derbyshire	33	45	14,210	3,549	724	8,219	89	15	192
Devonshire	55	118	26,105	5,446	970	9,764	213	46	206
Dorsetshire	11	20	4,708	866	150	1,451	16	9	79
Durham	22	34	10,650	2,804	491	5,158	74	18	203
Essex	39	67	18,366	2,815	448	4,721	52	27	205
Gloucestershire ...	82	125	36,141	10,211	1,453	17,859	243	48	633
Hampshire	54	78	22,125	5,575	802	7,700	113	38	290
Herefordshire ...	15	24	5,630	1,122	121	1,164	33	13	36
Hertfordshire ...	31	59	15,997	3,400	595	5,524	100	21	127
Huntingdonshire	19	46	13,190	913	189	1,510	18	13	8
Kent	61	127	29,416	7,296	1,249	12,390	206	49	391
Lancashire	141	189	84,196	21,892	3,805	40,913	304	103	957
Leicestershire ...	53	90	31,197	7,948	1,482	14,977	117	36	286
Lincolnshire ...	27	54	14,112	2,463	300	4,228	79	22	124
Metropolitan ...	225	336	157,339	49,695	6,444	78,045	463	190	2,2[illegible]5
Middlesex	16	23	5,320	1,254	242	2,705	19	14	121
Norfolk	41	61	19,242	3,469	555	5,532	84	31	113
Northamptonshire	51	82	24,021	5,874	1,148	11,810	118	44	264
Northumberland	8	12	3,870	1,307	188	2,085	31	6	81
Nottinghamshire	42	55	20,894	5,609	1,168	10,697	86	21	411
Oxfordshire	18	41	8,070	1,845	312	2,834	94	12	55
Rutlandshire ...	3	4	900	133	31	289	3	1	2
Shropshire	21	32	7,140	1,179	191	1,715	47	11	49
Somersetshire ...	51	88	22,320	4,797	964	9,565	57	36	186
Staffordshire ...	35	46	17,285	3,165	623	6,928	35	20	138
Suffolk	59	81	29,691	5,744	805	7,340	82	47	215
Surrey	31	54	12,739	2,435	463	4,658	46	25	109
Sussex	29	46	13,093	2,374	375	3,398	24	23	168
Warwickshire ...	48	79	29,371	7,167	1,535	17,573	168	34	357
Westmorland ...	1	5	700	83	18	146	10	1	3
Wiltshire	41	96	20,213	3,974	763	6,170	102	17	161
Worcestershire ...	26	53	12,800	2,387	630	5,750	80	22	143
Yorkshire	136	172	78,449	20,670	4,426	34,241	192	93	765
Totals ...	1,704	2,770	902,588	216,650	36,928	375,570	3,895	1,239	10,033

WALES AND MONMOUTHSHIRE.

Counties.	Chrchs.	Chapels.	Sittings in Chapels.	Members	Sunday-School Teachers	Sunday Scholars.	Local Prchrs.	Pastors	Baptisms.
Anglesey	36	38	8,981	2,117	277	2,313	23	13	77
Brecknockshire ...	36	40	11,040	2,402	232	2,431	8	20	81
Cardiganshire ...	22	23	8,070	2,192	102	1,594	5	11	78
Carmarthenshire	77	91	35,233	14,250	868	10,851	33	50	560
Carnarvonshire ...	37	43	12,476	2,539	207	2,881	29	16	110
Denbighshire ...	50	56	13,736	3,685	595	5,422	32	21	209
Flintshire	24	24	4,540	746	153	1,099	5	8	47
Glamorganshire...	257	278	135,966	41,371	4,808	47,551	179	195	1,943
Merionethshire ...	20	27	5,526	1,213	221	1,846	6	9	88
Montgomeryshire	22	23	5,420	1,653	186	1,758		9	65
Pembrokeshire ...	63	75	27,836	10,422	797	7,468	22	39	443
Radnorshire ...	25	25	5,750	2,179	159	1,718	13	14	112
Monmouthshire ...	107	118	51,517	14,858	1,662	20,086	75	71	641
Totals ...	776	861	326,091	99,627	10,267	107,018	441	476	4,454

SUMMARY OF STATISTICS—*continued.*

SCOTLAND.

Counties.	Chrchs.	Chapels.	Sittings in Chapels.	Members	Sunday-School Teachers	Sunday Scholars.	Local Prchrs.	Pastors	Baptisms.
Aberdeenshire ...	6	8	2,248	950	83	843	5	5	48
Argyllshire	2	3	610	146	11	82	...	2	9
Ayrshire	4	5	1,320	226	42	348	4	4	11
Banffshire	1	1	200	30	...	...	2	...	...
Buteshire	2	2	600	87	14	65	...	2	...
Caithness-shire ...	3	5	960	154	31	351	1	3	2
Clackmannanshire	2	2	500	270	23	190	3	2	18
Dumbartonshire	4	5	1,380	380	52	419	11	4	45
Dumfries-shire ...	1	1	430	52	5	40	...	1	...
Edinburghshire ...	9	11	4,820	1,673	164	1,600	5	10	124
Fifeshire	9	15	3,670	1,256	150	1,316	23	8	94
Forfarshire	6	7	2,430	1,166	118	862	25	5	83
Kincardineshire ...	...	1	60	...	...	...	...	...	...
Lanarkshire... ...	20	24	8,707	4,811	513	5,295	65	23	377
Morayshire	4	5	1,250	282	33	265	4	3	15
Peebles-shire ...	1	1	...	15	3	20	...	1	4
Perthshire	4	6	2,046	457	27	250	4	4	35
Renfrewshire ...	5	7	3,100	1,064	119	948	12	4	47
Roxburghshire ...	3	2	640	221	33	218	5	3	17
Selkirkshire ...	3	3	810	523	72	503	15	5	27
Stirlingshire ...	3	3	975	350	37	317	4	3	14
Orkney Isles ...	3	4	550	94	9	76	...	2	...
Shetland Isles ...	4	6	1,020	406	26	246	3	3	9
Western Isles ...	6	10	1,500	294	22	204	4	6	13
Totals ...	105	137	39,826	14,907	1,587	14,458	195	103	992

IRELAND.

Counties.	Chrchs.	Chapels.	Sittings in Chapels.	Members	Sunday-School Teachers	Sunday Scholars.	Local Prchrs.	Pastors	Baptisms.
Antrim	7	9	2,600	951	89	860	43	5	120
Armagh...	4	4	550	240	19	200	13	3	51
Cork	1	1	240	44	4	20	...	1	7
Derry	2	3	620	341	19	188	4	2	25
Donegal	1	1	150	12	6	110	1	1	...
Down	3	3	680	163	15	125	5	3	6
Dublin	2	4	1,140	463	30	315	22	2	43
Kildare	1	1	120	50	3	30	...	1	4
Limerick	1	1	210	26	2	7	...	1	2
Tyrone	3	3	360	122	13	168	1	3	4
Waterford	1	1	150	27	9	84	1	1	...
Westmeath	1	3	240	52	...	...	2	1	6
Totals ...	27	34	7,060	2,491	209	2,107	92	24	268

CHANNEL ISLANDS.

Counties.	Chrchs.	Chapels.	Sittings in Chapels.	Members	Sunday-School Teachers	Sunday Scholars.	Local Prchrs.	Pastors	Baptisms.
Jersey	1	1	700	130	20	170	1	...	18
Guernsey	3	5	1,345	162	68	315	21	2	30
Totals ...	4	6	2,045	292	88	485	22	2	48

ISLE OF MAN.

Counties.	Chrchs.	Chapels.	Sittings in Chapels.	Members	Sunday-School Teachers	Sunday Scholars.	Local Prchrs.	Pastors	Baptisms.
Isle of Man	1	1	300	...	...	...	...	1	...

TOTALS.

Counties.	Chrchs.	Chapels.	Sittings in Chapels.	Members	Sunday-School Teachers	Sunday Scholars.	Local Prchrs.	Pastors	Baptisms.
England	1,704	2,770	902,588	216,650	36,928	375,570	3,895	1,239	10,033
Wales and Monmouthshire ...	776	861	326,091	99,627	10,267	107,018	441	476	4,454
Scotland	105	137	39,826	14,907	1,587	14,458	195	103	992
Ireland	27	34	7,060	2,491	209	2,107	92	24	268
Channel Islands...	4	6	2,045	292	88	485	22	2	48
Isle of Man	1	1	300	...	...	...	...	1	...
Totals of Reporting Churches ...	2,617	3,809	1,277,910	333,967	49,079	499,638	4,645	1,845	15,795

(See next page for Grand Totals.)

COMPARATIVE TABLE, 1886-95.

NOTE.—The Editor does not vouch for more than approximate correctness in the Statistics. Since the year 1885, figures have not appeared in the tables (pages 201-293) opposite the names of those Churches which have failed to send returns. Where these Churches are non-associated and no information can be gained respecting them, they have been included in a separate list (page 294). An estimate gives 300 Churches, about 20,000 members, 1,400 teachers, 14,000 scholars, and 90 Pastors as the totals for the non-reporting Churches for the year 1895. These additional figures are included in the following table:

	Churches.	Chapels.	Chapel Seats.	Members.	Sunday-school Teachers.	Sunday Scholars.	Local Preachers.	Pastors in Charge.	Baptisms.
*1886	2,742	3,737	1,192,274	302,615	47,170	456,694	4,041	1,868	—
*1887	2,764	3,701	1,198,027	304,385	46,786	458,200	4,118	1,860	—
†1888	2,770	3,745	1,221,823	324,498	48,977	482,167	4,138	1,865	—
†1889	2,786	3,781	1,227,476	329,126	48,339	483,796	4,082	1,881	—
†1890	2,802	3,781	1,223,526	330,163	48,132	482,892	4,000	1,874	—
†1891	2,812	3,798	1,225,097	334,163	47,784	483,921	4,155	1,841	—
†1892	2,803	‡3,754	‡1,237,612	337,409	47,927	487,801	4,369	1,858	15,184
†1893	2,825	‡3,777	‡1,242,038	342,507	47,969	495,284	4,534	1,881	18,006
†1894	2,871	‡3,793	‡1,264,017	349,688	49,099	506,094	4,643	1,913	17,626
†1895	2,917	‡3,809	‡1,277,910	353,967	50,479	513,638	4,645	1,935	15,

* *Reporting Churches only.* † *Reporting Churches and estimates for non-reporting Churches.*

‡ *Including those shown in the list at page 294.*

PART VII.

ARCHITECTURAL.

I.—DESCRIPTIONS AND ILLUSTRATIONS OF NEW CHAPELS, &c.

ILDERTON ROAD CHAPEL, BERMONDSEY, S.E.

THIS is the Chapel for 1894 of the London Baptist Association, and is situated in the midst of a dense population, mainly of the working classes. The internal dimensions are 49 feet wide by 59 feet long, including two front entrance lobbies to the ground floor and two side entrances and staircases to the galleries on three sides of the chapel. The total seating accommodation is for over 700. The roof is in three spans, and the central span is carried up higher than the sides, with clerestory windows and an open timber roof. The front has two bold arched doorways surmounted by stone moulded pediments, and flanked by two pilasters carried up as pinnacles on either side of the central gable, which has a bold two light stone tracery window in the centre, with a single light on each side. This gable is flanked by staircase wings with return gables at the sides. All the gables have moulded brick cornices finished with stone coping. The contract was let to Messrs. Battley, Sons & Holness for £3,777. The architect is Mr. George Baines, F.R.I.B.A., 4, Great Winchester-street, London, E.C.

HEATON CHAPEL, BRADFORD.

Minister—R. HOWARTH.

THE site for the new chapel was secured and paid for so far back as 1886. Plans were subsequently obtained by open competition, and about a dozen Bradford architects and several from a distance sent in designs. In September, 1893, the old chapel was removed, and from the foundation, some stone of good colour, suitable for the outside walls of the new building, was quarried. The cost of the new building, exclusive of land and some material supplied by the trustees, is about £3,500. The contracts, including boundary walls, flagging, &c., have been let for £3,447. Towards this sum the Building Committee have had promised or have received £1,200. The property is very valuable, comprising nearly 10,000 square yards of land, and including the burial-ground, the Sunday school, and the chapel. The new building is in the Gothic style of architecture. It was designed by Mr. John Jackson, of Bradford, and is of commanding aspect. It is at the junction of Highgate and Leylands-lane, and the architect has specially sought to keep the whole of the rooms above the level of the street. On the ground floor there is a mortuary chapel, with a minister's vestry and a mortuary for use in connection with the cemetery. On the same floor there are also two large general

class-rooms, two cloak-rooms, a young men's class-room and a young women's class-room, a heating chamber, and stairs for access to the chapel floor level. The chapel is 60 feet long, 44 feet wide, and the height about 32 feet. There are a large front entrance, a vestibule, and a gallery over the vestibule, with staircases in the wings. The seating of the chapel is on the circular principle. On one side there is a minister's vestry, and on the other side a deacons' vestry, and there are men's and women's vestries for use at baptisms. All the interior wood-work is of pitch pine, stained and varnished, with an open timber roof. The building is of stone, with ashlar dressings. The contracts were let as follows:—Mason's work, Mr. Thomas Patefield, Manningham; joiner's work, Messrs. Foster & Fortune, Ingrow; plumber's work, &c., Mr. Job Wood; slater's work, Mr. James Smithies; plasterer's work, Messrs. C. Howroyd & Sons; painter's work, Mr. Walker Priestley, Allerton.

SPLOTT ROAD CHAPEL, CARDIFF.

Pastor—C. H. WATKINS.

THIS chapel has been recently erected in a very commanding position at the corner of Splott-road and Railway-street, Splottlands, Cardiff. It is in what is chiefly a working-class district, very thickly populated and increasing rapidly. For some years the congregation had been worshipping in a schoolroom now at the rear of the new chapel. Messrs. Habershon & Fawckner, of 39, Bloomsbury-square, London, W.C., and Pearl-street, Cardiff,

prepared plans and specifications in June, 1894. The tender of Messrs. Lattey & Co. was accepted at £4,378, but subsequently it was decided to add some additional classrooms, which increased the cost. The building is in the Gothic style of architecture, and is of local stone faced with Bath stone. Two turrets carried up on either side of the main entrance form the principal feature. The seating capacity is 1,100, *i.e.*, for 616 on the ground floor, and 484 in the gallery, which is on three sides of the chapel. At the opposite end from the entrances is a handsome rostrum with a baptistery in front, which is supplied with hot and cold water. The chapel is heated throughout with hot water. There is a lecture hall to seat 150, a minister's vestry and eight classrooms. Provision is also made for an organ at the back of the rostrum.

WALKER'S ROAD CHURCH, CARDIFF.

Minister—T. Morgan.

The new chapel, the contract price of which is £2,560, will accommodate 800 worshippers. Messrs. Habershon & Fawckner are the architects, and Mr. George Haywood, Moorland-gardens, is the contractor. The building

will be mainly of blue local stone, with Bath stone dressings. An octagonal turret at the junction of the two streets in which the building will have frontages, will be an attractive feature.

ANNADALE ROAD CHURCH, CHISWICK.

Pastor.—A. G. EDGERTON.

THE new church is to be erected on the site now occupied by the iron building. Unfortunately it is restricted, and therefore the schools and class-rooms must be in the basement. Accommodation can be provided in the church for 493 adults, or a mixed congregation of 625 persons, and in the

schools and classrooms for 300 children. The buildings will consist of church, assembly room, two vestries, and five classrooms, together with lavatories, &c., &c. The material to be used is brick, with stone dressings, and the internal fittings are to be of pitch pine. The church will have a gallery at one end and on the two sides, with the choir gallery on a lower level behind the pulpit. The organ will be placed in a corner with arched openings into the choir gallery and into the side gallery, an arrangement very effective in appearance and in saving of space. The cost is estimated to be £2,750, exclusive of architect's fees. The architect is Mr. John Wills, F.S.Sc., Derby and London.

WEST STREET SCHOOLS, CREWE.

Pastor.—W. Hughes.

These buildings are erected on part of a site in West-street, where it is proposed ultimately to erect a chapel for the use of the Victoria-street congregation. The plan allows of the opening of two rooms (a lecture room and a classroom), one on each side of the rostrum, into the assembly room, while all the other rooms are entirely separated by brick walls. This ensures perfect isolation and quietness—conditions necessary to successful Sunday School work. There are an assembly room, a lecture room, six classrooms,

a library, a kitchen and a lavatory, together with the usual offices, and ample accommodation is provided for 550 scholars. The premises are light and airy, and are warmed with hot water. Special provision is made for ingress and egress. The boys can assemble apart from the girls, and the junior separately from the senior scholars. There is direct communication between every room and the porches and lobbies, and thence to the street. The cost, exclusive of architect's fees, is £1,350. The architect is Mr. John Wills, F.S.Sc., of Derby and London, and the builder is Mr. Gresty, of Willaston, Nantwich.

WOOLWICH LOWER ROAD CHAPEL, EAST GREENWICH.

Pastor—W. E. Wells.

This chapel is now being erected upon a corner site in Woolwich Lower-road. Its internal dimensions are 48 feet wide by 68 feet long, including front entrance lobbies and two staircases to the galleries which are on three sides of the chapel. It will accommodate about 520 persons on the ground floor, and 410 in the galleries; total, 930. The roof will be in a single span. There will be bold three-light windows at the sides of the chapel, under and over the galleries, and the upper windows are to be semicircular-headed. In the front gable there will be a handsome stone three-light window, with a single light on either side of it, and bold pilasters terminating in pinnacles. Each window will have tinted leaded lights. The staircase roofs will have

East Greenwich Baptist Church and Schools.

GEORGE BAINES, F.R.I.B.A., Architect,
4, Great Winchester Street, London, E.C.

battlemented parapets. The main entrances are in the centre of the front gable and consist of two boldly-arched double doors, between pilasters, and surmounted by a moulded pediment with carved spandrel. The baptistery will be lined with white glazed tiles. The facing of the chapel will be of stock bricks, with stone bands and dressings, and the building will be surrounded by dwarf walls, with wrought-iron railings and gates. There are two vestries, a kitchen, and a heating chamber. The heating will be by hot-water pipes, and the chapel will be well ventilated. The contract is taken by Mr. I. Barden, of Maidstone, at £3,790. The architect is Mr. George Baines, F.R.I.B.A., 4 Great Winchester-street, London, E.C.

CAMPSBOURNE MISSION CHAPEL, HORNSEY, N.

Minister—C. Brown.

This freehold chapel (which is in connection with the Ferme Park Church) is built at the corner of the Campsbourne and Pembroke-roads. The total length of the building is 66 feet by 29 feet wide, and accommodation is

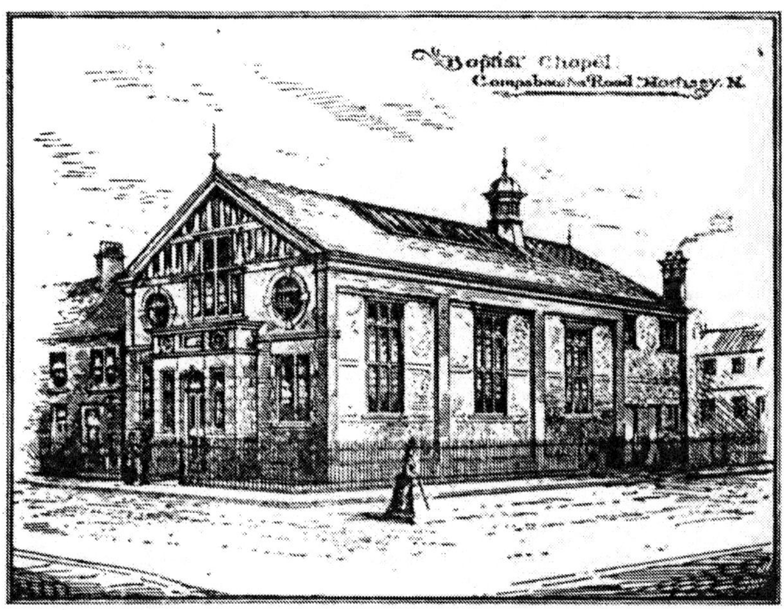

provided in the body of the chapel for 250, and in the gallery for fifty, worshippers. The back of the gallery can be curtained off and used as a class-room, 23 feet by 15 feet. There is another classroom of similar size at the opposite end of the building, to seat fifty persons, and beneath it (on the ground floor) are a minor classroom, a vestry, and a kitchen. The building is well lighted by means of large windows at the sides, and also from the roof. The ventilation is by inlet tubes on the Tobin principle, with hinged lids or valves for closing, and an "exhaust" in the roof. The premises are efficiently warmed on Neville's patent high-pressure system with small bore pipes. The internal faces of the walls are plastered, the roofs are boarded and stained, and the windows are filled in with tinted lead glazing; the gallery front, vestibule, and other pannelled woodwork are painted in suitable tones, and the floor is of pitch-pine wood-block paving. There is a large central light, and there are wrought iron ornamental gas brackets on the walls, &c. The seats, whch are of pitch-pine, are movable. Ample cupboard and other fittings are provided. The exterior of the building is of red brick and stucco, finished with stone dash, and the roofs are covered with green slate The principal front has a stone entrance porch, and the gable is filled in with timber framing. The whole has a pleasing effect, and, although possessing no strikingly ornate architectural features, everything accords with the purpose for which the building is designed. The architect is Mr. G. A. Foster, of Tottenham, under whose supervision the work has been carried out by Messrs. John Willmott & Sons, of Hornsey and Hitchin, at a total cost of £1,300. A friend has lent £700, free of interest, for seven years, and the balance has been almost extinguished by donations and by an amount which had accumulated for the purchase of the freehold, before the work passed into the hands of the Church at Ferme Park.

CLUMBER STREET CHAPEL, LONG EATON.

Minister—E. Webb.

This building consists of chapel 50 ft. by 32 ft. and 26 ft. high, two classrooms, two vestries, lobby, platform and baptistery under the platform, with necessary outbuildings. It is of the modern style of architecture, and is faced with red dressed brick and stone dressings, and slated roof. The inside is similarly treated, and is picked out in white brick. There is an open roof with framed principals. A wood dado to window-sill level is continued round the inside of the chapel. The woodwork and the fittings are of rich stained deal. The lighting is effected by means of large square-headed windows filled in with obscure glass. There are also four dormer windows in the roof. This building will eventually be used as a schoolroom, as further ground has been reserved for a chapel on a more extensive scale. The building was designed by Mr. Ernest R. Ridgway, of Long Eaton, and Mr. Youngman was the contractor.

LONDON ROAD CHURCH, LOWESTOFT.

Pastor—J. M. Hamilton.

A commanding site facing London-road, has been purchased on which it is proposed to erect the new chapel from the designs of Mr. George Baines, F.R.I.B.A., 4 Great Winchester-street, London, E.C. The building will seat 450 persons on the ground floor, and about 150 in the gallery over the front end of the chapel and the choir gallery behind the pulpit. The seats will be arranged in a semi-circular plan, so that the whole congregation will directly face the minister. There will be a nave and aisles divided by columns and brick arches, with clerestory windows above. Two spacious entrances will be provided in the front, and in the rear there will be an entrance to the lecture hall and the two vestries on the ground floor, with stairs to the choir, the organ gallery, and two classrooms above. There will also be a classroom over one and a cloak-room over the other, front lobby. The internal dimensions of the chapel are 49 feet wide by 59 feet long, with 15 feet additional length for the organ-chamber which will be open to the chapel under a bold moulded arch. The baptistery is to be lined with white glazed tiles, and the heating will be by hot-water pipes. Fresh air inlet flues and foul air exit ventilators will be provided. The estimated cost is £3,100. The front will be of split flints, with red brick dressings and stone sparingly used. The style is decorated Gothic, simply treated.

WARWICK STREET CHURCH, LEAMINGTON.

Minister—A. PHILLIPS.

THE improvements and additions recently carried out were elaborate and extensive. The schoolroom, which has been urgently needed for years, is a handsome structure. The open wooded roof and sides are lined with varnished pitch pine. The length is 45 ft., and the width 16 ft. On the ground floor at the south end of the schoolroom is the infants' classroom, 21 ft.

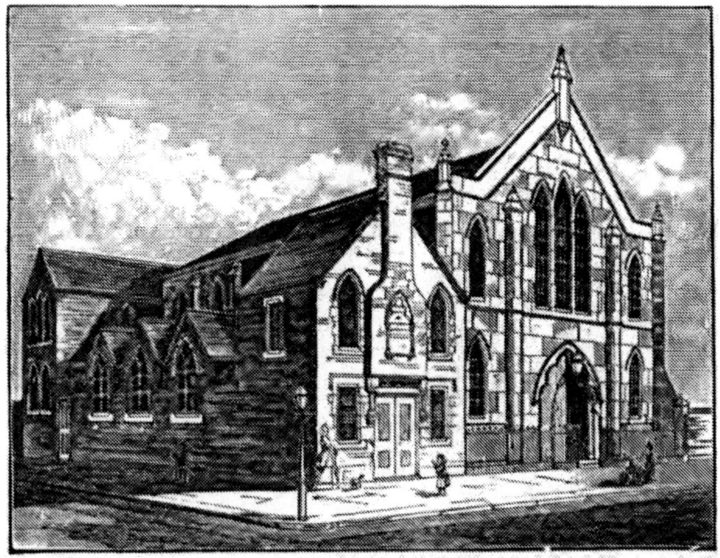

in length and 13 ft. in width. Adjoining this, ladies', deacons', and minister's vestries have been built. These, with the exception of the minister's, have been arranged for baptismal purposes. In the basement a new kitchen, lavatories, and heating chambers have been constructed, while upstairs, on either side of the organ chamber, are the church vestry and the ladies' vestry. Internally, the chapel has been almost reconstructed. A handsome apse has been built at the south end of the building, in which the organ and the choir stalls have been placed. Formerly the organ faced the preacher and blocked up the principal window. About one hundred additional sittings, which were greatly needed, have been provided, and also new gas-fittings. The interior has been decorated with bright and cheerful tints. The whole of the premises is heated with a high-pressure hot-water system. Messrs. Ingall & Son, Birmingham, were the architects, and Messrs. Smallwood & Co., of Woolen, Wawen, were the builders. The total cost was about £1,735, and the present debt is about £850.

PRITCHARD MEMORIAL CHURCH, LLANGOLLEN.

Pastor—H. Rees.

The new building, which occupies a very commanding site near the railway station, is designed in the Early Gothic style. It is built of Ruabon brick, with Monk's Park stone dressings. It is 54 feet 6 inches long and 30 feet 8 inches wide inside, and seats 233 adults or a mixed congregation of 310 persons. A schoolroom, which opens into the church at right angles, provides a hundred

additional sittings, or a total of 410. The plan of the church consists of nave with chancel and organ chamber. In the chancel is placed the baptistery. It is open, lined with marble, and fenced with pitch pine Gothic balustrading. The pews are of pitch pine with solid bench ends. The pulpit is also of pitch pine. The roof is partially open, with arched timbering, and a pitch pine ceiling. The front has a gable with a four-light window and tracery, flanked on one side with tower and spire rising to 70 feet. There is one doorway in the tower and one in the opposite flank, and at the sides of the church there are single light-pointed windows. The windows throughout are of cathedral glass, in special designs, and all are memorial gifts. There are two vestries and lavatories, and there is space at the rear for a caretaker's lodge. The plan for this is drawn, but the cost is not included in the present contract, which is for £1,900, exclusive of architect's fees. The architect is Mr. John Wills, F.S.Sc., of Derby and London, and the builder is Mr. W. H. Thomas, of Oswestry.

GRACEY MEMORIAL CHURCH, NEW SOUTHGATE N.

Pastor—G. FREEMAN.

THE style of the new building will be Gothic, and the material, brick with stone dressings. The front will have a main gable and a handsome four-light window with geometrical tracery. This will be flanked on the left with a dwarf tower and on the right with a tower and spire, each containing a main entrance door, porch, and stairs to gallery. The spire will terminate at eighty feet above the street level. The plan of the church is cruciform, with nave, transepts and chancel. In addition to an organ chamber, there are two large vestries with lavatories, &c. There is a gallery at one end, and the total accommodation will be for 647 adults, or for a mixed congregation of 860 persons. The roof is partially open, with arched timbers and a ceiling of pitch pine. The chancel arch is richly moulded and supported with carved corbels. The side windows will be pointed and the chancel window will be circular with geometrical tracery, and the windows throughout will be glazed with rolled cathedral glass in leadwork of special design. The seating and the pulpit will be of pitch pine. The cost, exclusive of architect's fees, is expected to be £3,000. The architect is Mr. John Wills, F.S.Sc., of Derby and London.

WOODBOROUGH ROAD CHURCH, NOTTINGHAM.

Minister—G. H. JAMES.

THE general style of the new building may be described as arch-round Gothic. The chapel is erected over the schoolrooms built seventeen years

ago. Consequently the old lines have governed, and to some extent hampered, the planning of the new structure. But the difficulties of fitting the new work to the old structure have been successfully overcome without sacrificing in any way the convenience of either the school or the chapel, and the result, so far as the plan is concerned, is a nave of seven bays, divided from aisles of slightly unequal width by iron columns which support a semicircular arcade and clerestory. One end, that next to Alfred-street, is a portion of a many-sided polygon, and the other is a semi-octagon containing the choristry and platform, with the pulpit in the centre and the organ behind. The choir is slightly elevated on either side of the pulpit, and there is room for about forty persons. The roof of the choristry is circular. The pulpit is of wood, and just in front is the baptistery. There is rather a novel feature about the baptistery, in that there is a passage into the dressing-rooms through a door beneath the pulpit, and therefore no need for candidates to ascend into the open chapel. There are galleries over the aisles and one at the end opposite the pulpit which provide 284 sittings. Five new class-rooms have been added in connection with the school, and three of the old class-rooms have been enlarged and improved. In length the chapel occupies the

whole site and is 109 feet, and the width inside is 49 feet. It will accommodate 990 worshippers. There are ample exits and staircases of fireproof construction. The main entrances are from the corner of Woodborough-road and from Alfred-street. All the doors open outwards, and each entrance leads to every department of the church. The main ceilings are boarded and stained and varnished, as is also the interior woodwork. The walls inside are of red brick, relieved with blue and buff bricks in bands. Nearly all the windows will have small squares of glass of suitable tints in lead work. Those over the Woodborough-road side gallery are of stone tracery having iron casements. The windows on the opposite side, facing the Co-operative Stores, are not so elaborate. The principal feature of the exterior is an octagonal tower about ninety feet high at the juncture of the four roads, four sides of which are occupied by a clock face in the upper part. Red brick relieved with blue brick bands is used for the exterior, but the plinth is of rock-faced Derbyshire stone with terra cotta bands. The roof is of red tiling. At the Alfred-street end is a lobby connecting the two principal entrances. The entrance to the school is by a flight of steps at the corner of the two roads. The light in the school is provided as before, and additional light is obtained from Alfred-street. There are nine class rooms altogether, besides minister's and deacons' vestries. The plans have been prepared by Mr. Watson Fothergill, of Clinton-street.

FAR COTTON CHAPEL, NORTHAMPTON.

Minister—R. A. Selby.

This chapel, which will be an ornament to the district, was built from plans prepared by Mr. Stevenson and Mr. Dorman, A.R.I.B.A., Derngate, Northampton. New Duston stone, from Mr. Goldby's quarries, has been used. Including the windows and tracery, the style is Perpendicular Gothic. A view of the building suggests an English parish church, minus the tower and steeple. The main entrance fronts Abbey-road, from which the chapel is recessed a few feet, and protected by a dwarf wall and ornamental iron railing. Above the entrance is a gallery; the platform over the baptistery and the pulpit and organ chamber are at the other end. Two choir galleries flank the organ, and on one side is a second gallery for members of the congregation. The floor, laid with solid wood blocks, slopes towards the pulpit end, and gives the worshippers a fuller and more comfortable view of the preacher. The windows are glazed in lead, with tinted cathedral glass, and the open timbered roof is tiled. By the side are the schoolrooms, including a large assembly room, and a number of classrooms. This part of the building is treated like the chapel, though it is not so ornate. The classrooms for the boys and girls are all on the first floor, the infants' classrooms are on the ground floor behind the chapel. In all, eight classrooms are provided. The floors of the large hall are laid with solid blocks, and this portion of the building will be practically fireproof. There are also kitchens and other offices, and the place will be heated with hot water. The chapel—the internal dimensions of which are 70½ ft. by 37 ft.—will seat about five hundred worshippers, the hall measures 40 ft. by 21½ ft., and the schools will accommodate about six hundred children. Mr. William Heap is the builder, and the cost, including site, is about £3,500.

PLASSEY STREET CHAPEL, PENARTH.

Minister—W. G. Davies.

This chapel is in the Italian Renaissance style of architecture. The dressings are of Box ground Bath stone, with intermediate spaces of Newbridge paving cuts. The floor is approached by two flights of steps above the pavement, and the building is entered by three sets of teak doors. The porch is divided from the chapel with a wood-panelled screen, and the upper panels are fitted with ornamental glass. Adjoining the porch are two cloak-rooms, on each side of which are staircases to the galleries. The interior of the chapel has a

FAR COTTON CHAPEL NORTHAMPTON.

gallery on each side and one on the front. The three large front windows are fitted with stained glass lead lights designed specially to suit the style of architecture. The galleries are supported by cast-iron columns with carved ornamental caps, above which are semicircular arches supporting the clerestory. The clerestory is lighted by a series of semicircular windows with panelled pilasters dividing them. The building is ventilated by means of ornamental perforated centre flowers connected with extracting ventilators on the roof, and is decorated with richly-moulded plaster arches, friezes, and panelled work. A bold arch, 23 ft. diameter, divides the chapel from the orchestra (the ceiling of which forms a dome), in which is placed a large organ. The seating is framed in figured pitch pine, with panelled sloping backs. Foot rests, hat rails and book casing, with solid worked ends, are provided. The baptistery is on a raised platform in front of the rostrum, and is built of white glazed bricks with marble steps, and fitted with hot and cold water. The rostrum is richly designed, and made of teak and figured pitch pine; it will accommodate twelve persons in addition to the minister. On each side of the orchestra are vestries and lavatories. The chapel will accommodate a thousand persons and the orchestra will accommodate seventy singers. Underneath the chapel there are a large schoolroom and lecture hall, fifteen classrooms, library, kitchen, storeroom and room for heating apparatus. The kitchen is fitted up with every requisite for large or small tea meetings. The schoolroom is paved with wood block flooring, and together with the classrooms it will accommodate 700 scholars. The premises are heated by means of low-pressure hot-water pipes, supplemented with fireplaces in vestries and classrooms. The buildings were designed and carried out under the supervision of Messrs. Jones & Thomley, St. Mary-street, Cardiff, and Mr. D. G. Price, of Hickman-road, Penarth, was the contractor.

STANWELL ROAD CHAPEL, PENARTH.

Pastor—I. O. Stalberg.

On 11th September, 1895, the memorial stone of the new building was laid by Mr. F. H. Jotham, C.C. The chapel is built of blue stone with Bath stone dressings, in the perpendicular Gothic style of architecture, and was designed by Messrs. J. P. Jones, Richards and Budgen, Cardiff. The principal features of the front elevation are the entrance lobby and a large cusped window over the lobby, occupying nearly the whole of the gable, which is flanked by buttresses carried up above the roof and terminating in octagonal turrets surmounted with crocketted finials. At each side of the front gable are boldly conceived hipped wings slightly receding from the face of the lobby with a range of windows lighting the gallery. Internally the chapel is 49 ft. wide by 65 ft. long, excluding the choir chamber. There are 490 sittings on the ground floor: and a minister's vestry, men and women's retiring rooms, small lecture room, lavatories, &c., are arranged at the rear. The gallery is across the front, over the entrance lobbies, and has ninety-four sittings. The total accommodation is therefore 584 sittings. The building of side galleries is deferred for the present. The roof is in one span with open framed trusses and chamfered collar beams, purlins, &c., and is ceiled with matchboarding. The aisles are laid with wood blocks and the lobbies with tiles. The former are on an incline from the entrance to the platform, in order that every person may easily see the minister. The chapel and lobbies are warmed by hot-water pipes. The baptistery is situated under the floor of the platform and is lined with glazed bricks in two colours. The retiring rooms are on the same level. The windows are glazed with cathedral glass in

PLASSEY STREET CHAPEL, PENARTH.

neutral tints, and the various shades in combination have a very pretty effect. Special attention has been given to the ventilation; the fresh air is brought into the building by means of tubes built up in the walls, and the vitiated air

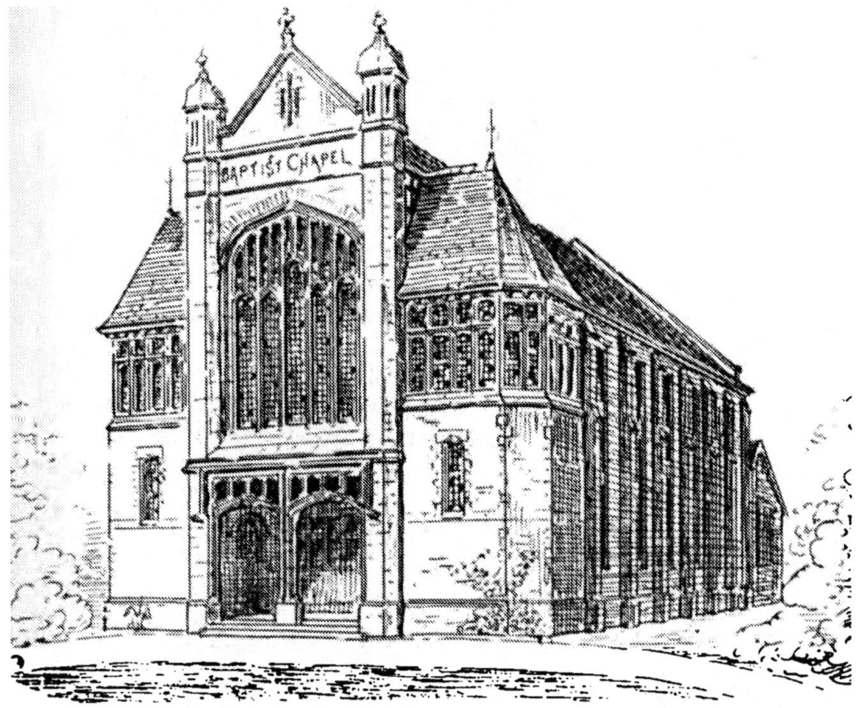

is extracted by Banner's cowls fixed on the roof. At an angle of the site is a neat cottage for the caretaker. At the rear of the new chapel is the Sunday schoolroom, erected in 1887, with class-rooms added in 1889 and 1893, at a total cost of £1,222, which has been defrayed. Before the erection of the chapel the schoolroom was used for public worship. The whole of the building operations in connection with the new chapel have been very satisfactorily carried out by Mr. Thomas Bevan, Contractor, Penarth. The cost of the chapel buildings, caretaker's cottage, front railings, heating apparatus, &c., is £3,328, so that the value of the whole property is £4,550. Towards this new effort the church and congregation had contributed, raised and promised, up to October 1895, about £1,500, of which £1,000 is already in hand. The site is one of the best in the town, on a main road, in a commanding position, within sight of the railway station. The immediate neighbourhood is a rapidly rising one, and comprises high-class private residences and the new Intermediate School, as well as a very promising populous quarter; and it is believed that the provision of a commodious and comfortable Baptist Chapel will meet with general acceptance on the part of the residents and of the increasing number of visitors to this attractive *seaside town.*

SOUTH WOODFORD CHAPEL, ESSEX

Minister—J. R. Cox.

The site is in front of the existing School-Chapel in George-lane. The building will be in the Gothic of the thirteenth century, and will consist of a nave 62 ft. long, 35 ft. 6 in. wide, inside; transepts, each measuring 13 ft. 6 in. by 20 ft., and a chancel arrangement containing baptistery, &c., and on one side

of the chancel an organ chamber. The chancel will be separated from the rave by a richly moulded arch and carved corbels. The front of the church will have a gabled central doorway, over which will be a handsome four-light tracery window flanked with buttresses, terminating with octagonal pinnacles. There will be entrances at the sides and rear, so that the provision for ingress and exit is very complete. The pewing will be all of pitch pine, with solid bench ends. There will be a gallery at the front end, with a pitch pine panel and cusped front. The windows throughout will be glazed with rolled cathedral tinted glass in squares and margins, with a special design for the chancel window, which is circular. There will be two vestries at the rear. The church will seat 464 adults or a mixed congregation of 620 persons. The cost of the undertaking, including the builder's contract and architect's fees, will be £2,550. The architect is Mr. John Wills, of Derby and London; the builder is Mr. Samuel J. Scott, of South Woodford.

HAWTHORN ROAD CHAPEL, HILLSBOROUGH, SHEFFIELD.

THIS chapel has recently been erected in the centre of the rapidly increasing population of Hillsborough, and occupies a prominent position at the corner of Hawthorn and Taplin roads. As the area of the site is limited, the building has been designed for two floors, the school to occupy the ground floor and

the chapel the first floor. It is the lower portion which has just been completed. The floor is rather below the level of the roads in order that the floor of the proposed chapel, which will be approached by two broad external flights of stone steps, may not be too elevated. The present building is used for both school and chapel purposes. It is in the form of a square, measuring internally 46 feet by 46 feet, with the angles next the entrances cut off so as to form a semi-octagonal end. In front, and opposite the angle formed by the two roads is a vestibule 30 feet by 6 feet, at each end of which is an entrance door. In the rear are two vestries communicating with the chapel by means of two doors, one on each side of the rostrum and the baptistery. From one of them there is communication also with a lobby and a back entrance. There are also a kitchen with tea boiler, a heating chamber, and the necessary offices. The building provides accommodation on loose benches and chairs for 450. It is faced externally with Crooke's "rockies" with Grenoside stone dressings, and is in a free Renaissance style of architecture. It has been erected from the designs and under the superintendence of Messrs. Hemsoll & Paterson, of Norfolk-row, Sheffield, and Mr. Thos. Roper, of Broomhill, was the contractor. The cost, exclusive of site, is £1,000

WESTWARD HO! MISSION CHAPEL.

Pastor—W. Crathern, Appledore.

This chapel is the only Nonconformist place of worship at this seaside resort. It is a substantial structure of well-dressed local stone, with an open roof of pitch pine polished, as are also the platform, pulpit and other fittings. The chapel will seat over two hundred, and is supplied with very comfortable chairs. It is declared to be an ornament to the locality. Mr. A. Lander, of

Barnstaple, is the architect, and Mr. J. Tamlin, of Appledore, the builder. The entire cost is £400. The stone was given by the gentleman from whom the freehold was purchased. The chapel was opened on 31st July, 1895, by the president of the Devon Association.

CALLOW LAND CHAPEL, WATFORD.

Minister—J. Stuart.

This chapel, now in course of erection, is the outcome of a desire on the part of the minister and members of the Church worshipping at Beechen-grove, Watford, to take their due share in providing for the spiritual necessities of a rapidly increasing industrial population which has sprung up within the last five or six years on the N.E. side of the town in consequence of the removal from Leighton Buzzard to Watford by the London and North-Western Railway Company of the staff of workmen employed upon the maintenance of their permanent way and station buildings south of Rugby. The railway company built a large number of houses, and a still larger number was built by private speculators, so that the present population is estimated at upwards of 2,500. The new chapel occupies a prominent position in Leavesden-road at its junction with Garfield-street, and it is anticipated that it will be opened early in the new year, at a cost for land, buildings, and fittings of about £1,600. There is also a site for a school, but for the present the chapel will be used for

BERESFORD STREET TABERNACLE, WOOLWICH.

school purposes, and, consequently, only seats with reversible backs are provided. The style of architecture is Early English Gothic, freely treated, and the structure is of brick, with roof of Broseley tiles. The internal dimensions are 59 feet by 31 feet 6 inches, in addition to the minister's vestry, classroom, &c., at the rear. The exterior is faced with Leverstock Green (grey) bricks, and the interior, above the panelled dado, with Beart's (Arlesey) white facing bricks, whilst the arches and reveals of doors and windows and the angles of buttresses, quoins, &c., are of red Leverstock Green facing bricks. The roof is open timbered in five bays, and has pitch pine trusses with arched ribs terminating on stone corbels. The windows are filled with quarried lights in subdued tints, popularly known as cathedral glazing. Due provision has been made for the ventilation of the chapel, and also for heating by hot water pipes on the low pressure system. The work is being carried out by Messrs. Andrews & Sons, builders, of Watford, under the superintendence of Mr. K. J. Beecham, architect, of Bushey. It is an interesting fact that architect and builders are all members of the Church at Beechen-grove.

WOOLWICH TABERNACLE.

Minister—J. Wilson, M.L.S.B.

This building is now being erected in Beresford-street, Woolwich. The Building Committee experienced considerable difficulty in securing a site, and eventually obtained one which permits of the building fronting on to both Beresford-street and Ropeyard Rails. The accompanying sketch, which is a reduced copy of the architect's drawing, exhibited in this year's Royal Academy, shows the front to Beresford-street, and is a bold and ornate treatment in the Georgian style of architecture. The front is to be erected in best red bricks, with Monk's Park Bath stone dressings, cornices, &c. The Chapel, which will seat 2,000 people, is raised some seven feet above the level of the pavement, and the main entrance to it is approached by an arcade vestibule, with entrances from both streets. Beneath the chapel there is a large schoolroom or lecture hall to seat 1,200 people, which is partially below the level of the pavement. The gallery is reached by separate entrances and surrounds the interior of the building in the form of an amphitheatre. There is a large church parlour, which can be used as a separate room or thrown into the chapel by the raising of revolving shutters. In addition, there are vestries, classrooms, &c., to the number of six, all well lighted and ventilated. The roof inside the chapel is formed of open woodwork in pitch pine, with bold curved trusses projecting below the panelling of the roof, and the appearance is elegant. The walls are to be treated inside with pale straw-coloured facing bricks, and bands and patterns are to be in red and brindled bricks. All the pews are to be of best pitch pine, stained and varnished. The glazing of the windows will be in leaded lights, and cathedral glass of various designs will be used. The heating and ventilation have been well considered by the architect, and the system adopted will be by extract tubes and cowls fixed in the ridge of the roof, with Tobin tubes for the admission of fresh cold air in summer and ventilating radiators for the admission of warm fresh air in winter. It is proposed to heat the building by hot water under ordinary low-pressure, with pipes and radiators dispersed about the building at regular intervals. The electric light will be used, and pendants will be suspended from the roof, wall brackets, &c. The chapel floor and staircases are of fire-proof construction, and all the doors are arranged to open outwards, so as to be easily used in case of emergency. The building, exclusive of the site, is to cost £11,000. The builders are Messrs. James Smith and Sons, South Norwood, and the architect is Mr. W. H. Woodroffe, A.R.I.B.A., 214, Great Dover-street, London, S.E.

II.—NEW CHAPELS.

County.	Place.	Sittings.	Cost.
ENGLAND.			£
Berkshire	Newbury, North Brook-street—Mission Chapel in Long-lane	120	450
Devonshire	Thorverton—Mission Chapel at Bramford Speke	120	250
Essex	South Woodford, George-lane.. ..	620	2,550
Gloucestershire .. .	Stroud, John-street—Mission Chapel at Pagan Hill	..	170
Hampshire .. .	Portsmouth, Lake-road—Mission Hall in London-road	250	2,500
	Southsea, Elm Grove — Mission Chapel at Denmead	150	135
Hertfordshire .. .	Bishop's Stortford—Mission Hall at Farnham (*Essex*)	150	175
Huntingdonshire.. .	Ramsey, Great Whyte	350	850
Lancashire .. .	Blackburn, Leamington-street ..	800	5,263
	Liverpool: Bootle, Derby-road (Temporary Iron Building)	200	200
Metropolitan .. .	Leytonstone, Cann Hall-road—Mission Hall in Edith-road	250	643
	Silvertown..	350	1,100
Northamptonshire .	Rushden, Old Chapel — Mission Chapel at Hinwick (*Beds.*)	60	50
Nottinghamshire	Nottingham, Woodborough-road ..	980	5,000
Sussex	Burgess Hill	230	1,100
Wiltshire	Salisbury, Brown-street — Mission Chapel at Coombe Bissett	150	350
WALES AND MONMOUTHSHIRE.			
Anglesey	Holyhead, Edmond-street	1,060	2,700
Carmarthenshire	Foelcwan, Noddfa—Mission Chapel at Cwm Mydrim	180	420
	Llanelly, Caersalem	800	2,200
Carnarvonshire	Llanfairfechan—Mission Chapel at Penmaenmawr..	200	1,035
Denbighshire	Llangollen, Penybryn	310	2,300
Glamorganshire	Cardiff, Splott-road	1,100	4,700
	Cymmer (Porth), Pisgah	400	868
	Glancynon	900	2,000
	Penarth, Tabernacle	1,000	3,000
	Pontypridd, Rhondda	800	—
	Tonyrefail	650	1,520
	Troedyrhiw, Bethel	600	1,800
	Wattstown	600	2,000
	Wauntrodau, Bethel	280	1,025

County.	Place.	Sittings.	Cost.
			£
Pembrokeshire	Cemaes, Penuel	200	500
	Llangloffan—Mission Chapel at Mathry	..	280
Monmouthshire	Ebbw Vale, Providence	300	—
	Newbridge (E.)—Mission Chapel at Crumlin..	300	—
SCOTLAND.			
Forfarshire	Dundee, Ward-road	650	4,300
Lanarkshire	Cambuslang	500	2,500
	Coatbridge	500	1,250
	Hamilton	450	850
Shetland Isles	Lerwick	380	1,070
IRELAND.			
Limerick	Limerick	210	2,500
	TOTALS	17,150	59,604

III.—CHAPEL IMPROVEMENTS, NEW SCHOOL ROOMS, CLASS ROOMS, &c.

County.	Place.	Work done.	Cost.
ENGLAND.			£
Bedfordshire ..	Cotton End..	New Schoolroom	450
Berkshire.. ..	Reading, Wycliffe.. ..	New Infants' Schoolroom	210
Buckinghamshire	Chesham, Broadway ..	New Schoolroom	1,129
	Wendover	New Schoolroom	442
Cambridgeshire ..	March, Centenary Church	Renovation and Enlargement of Chapel.. ..	300
	Waterbeach	Renovation of Chapel ..	450
Cheshire	Altrincham..	Improvement to Chapel Premises	30
Cornwall	St. Austell	Enlargement of Schoolroom	100
Derbyshire ..	Sawley	Enlargement of Schoolroom	50
Devonshire ..	Ashwater	New Schoolroom	100
	Bideford	Enlargement of Classrooms	46
	Croyde	Enlargement of Schoolroom	90
	Totnes	Renovation of Chapel, and Enlargement of Vestry and Infants' Schoolroom	120
Durham	Waterhouses	Enlargement of Chapel ..	220
Essex	Grays, Tabernacle ..	Enlargement of Schoolroom	40
	Rayleigh	Renovation of Chapel ..	40
Gloucestershire ..	Bristol, Old King-street ..	Restoration of Chapel, &c.	2,500
	Hanham	Enlargement of Chapel ..	220
Hampshire ..	Blackfield Common ..	Improvements to Chapel	35
	Emsworth	New School and Classrooms	300
	Poulner	New Windows	4
Hertfordshire ..	St. Albans, Verulam-road	Enlargement of Chapel, &c.	250
Huntingdonshire	Huntingdon, Trinity (U.)	Enlargement of *Hartford* Chapel, and reseating of Chapel at *Little Stukeley*	249
Kent	Gravesend, Peacock-street	Renovation of Chapel ..	62
	Sittingbourne	New Mission Room at *Bapchild*	—
Lancashire ..	Blackburn, Montague-street	New Organ..	450
	Clayton-le-Moors	Erection of Gallery and alteration to Classrooms	120
	Manchester, Moss Side ..	Enlargement of Chapel ..	—
Leicestershire ..	Hinckley	New Schoolroom	1,000
Lincolnshire ..	Burgh and Monksthorpe	Cleaning and Repairing Chapel	25

County.	Place.	Work done.	Cost.
			£
Metropolitan ..	Blackheath, Shooter's Hill-road..	Enlargement of Chapel ..	220
	Camberwell, Cottage-green	Renewal of Heating Apparatus	25
	Catford Hill	Purchase of additional land	196
	Leytonstone, Fairlop-road	New Classrooms and Institute	950
	Tottenham, Westerfield-rd.	Purchase of Hall	—
	Wood Green, Finsbury-rd.	Improvements to Chapel	200
Norfolk	Stalham	New Manse	500
Northamptonshire	Kettering, Fuller Chapel	Purchase of land	400
	Northampton, College-street	Enlargement of *Compton Street* Schoolroom ..	320
	St. Michael's-road (U.)	New Schoolroom	600
Nottinghamshire	Kirkby, East	Acquisition of new Property	300
	Nottingham: Lenton, New	Restoration of Chapel ..	100
	Woodborough-road ..	Enlargement of Schoolroom	—
Rutlandshire ..	Oakham, Melton-road ..	New Schoolrooms ..	500
Somersetshire ..	Pill	Enlargement of Chapel ..	309
Staffordshire ..	Burton-on-Trent, New-st.	Enlargement of Schoolroom, additional work, &c...	500
Suffolk	Bury St. Edmund's, Garland-street	New Schoolroom at *Whepstead*	65
	Gorleston	New Schoolroom	300
	Ipswich, Burlington ..	New Classrooms	—
Sussex	Brighton, Florence-road..	New Schoolroom (used for Worship at present) ..	—
	Crawley	Enlargement of Schoolroom	120
	Worthing	Enlargement of Chapel ..	300
Warwickshire ..	Leamington, Warwick-st.	Enlargement of Chapel and New Schoolroom ..	1,747
Wiltshire	Bratton	New Baptistery	60
Worcestershire ..	Inkberrow	New American Organ, and porch to chapel.. ..	29
	Kidderminster	Renovation of Church-st. chapel and new organ for *Lorne street*	592
Yorkshire ..	Blackley	Renovation of Chapel and new Organ	750
	Cullingworth	New Classrooms	30
	Ossett	New Schoolroom	570
	Polemoor	Purchase of property for extension of Burial Ground	450
WALES AND MONMOUTHSHIRE.			
Anglesey	Holyhead, Edmond-street	New Schoolroom	—
Brecknockshire ..	Brynmawr, King-street ..	New Porch to Chapel ..	22
Cardiganshire ..	Lampeter—Silian, Bethel	New Schoolroom	150
Carmarthenshire	Landovery	Renewal of front of Chapel, &c...	28
	Llanelly, Caersalem ..	New Schoolroom	500

County.	Place.	Work done.	Cost.
Carnarvonshire ..	Port Madoc, Berea (Sc.)..	Enlargement of Chapel ..	130
Denbighshire ..	Llangollen, Penybryn ..	New Schoolroom	—
	Penycae	New Gallery to Chapel ..	—
	Rhosllanerchrugog ..	New Minister's House ..	400
Flintshire	Axtyn (W.)	Repairs to Chapel ..	3
Glamorganshire..	Aberdare, Abernant ..	Enlargement of Chapel and Schoolroom ..	1,920
	Abergwynfi, Caersalem ..	Enlargement of Chapel ..	96
	Cardiff, Tabernacle (W.)..	Renovation of Chapel, &c.	250
	Hengoed	New Schoolroom at *Llanbradach*	400
	Maesteg, Bethania ..	New Schoolroom	610
	Merthyr Tydvil, Cefn Coed	Renovation of Chapel ..	—
	Neath, Bethany	Repairs to Chapel ..	11
	Penydarren..	Boundary wall and repairs to Chapel	90
	Pontllyw	Enlargement of Schoolroom	—
	Pontrhydycyff (Maesteg)..	Repairs to Chapel ..	22
	Pontrhydyfen	Alterations to Chapel ..	122
	Wauntrodau, Ararat ..	Enlargement of Burial Ground	105
Pembrokeshire ..	Fishguard, Hermon ..	Enlargement of Schoolroom at *Lower Fishguard*	80
Radnorshire ..	Nantgwyn	New Vestry	100
Monmouthshire	Cross Keys (Newport) ..	Purchase of house for Minister	800
	Newport, St. Mary-street	New Classrooms	425
	Stow Hill	New Organ, &c.	172
SCOTLAND.			
Ayrshire	Ayr	Improvements to Baptistery	4
Lanarkshire ..	Cambuslang	New Schoolroom	—
Perthshire ..	Crieff	Enlargement of Schoolroom	53
Shetland Isles ..	Lerwick	New Schoolroom	—
		TOTAL	£25,658

IV.—CHAPEL DEBTS PAID OFF OR DIMINISHED.

Place.	Amount.
ENGLAND.	
BEDFORDSHIRE—	£
Ampthill (U.)	40
Bedford, Rothsay-road	200
Luton, Wellington-street	200
Stevington	30
BERKSHIRE—	
Maidenhead	50
Newbury, North Brook-street	379
Reading, King's-road	70
BUCKINGHAMSHIRE—	
Fenny Stratford	228
Newton Longville	5
Olney	102
Quainton	21
Stony Stratford and Loughton	30
Wendover	306
Wycombe, Union Church	20
CAMBRIDGESHIRE	
Histon	97
March, Centenary Church	220
Waterbeach	350
CHESHIRE—	
Crewe, Union Street	40
New Brighton	20
CORNWALL—	
Calstock and Metherill	4
Hayle	10
Launceston	20
CUMBERLAND—	
Carlisle	30
Millom	20
DERBYSHIRE—	
Crich	7
Derby Watson-street	10
Heanor	20
Ilkeston, Queen-street	10
South Street	10
Long Eaton, Station-street	18
Measham and Netherseal (*Manse*)	120
Ripley	20
Swadlincote	20
Swanwick	20
DEVONSHIRE—	
Ashwater	20
Bideford	320
Bovey Tracey	5
Devonport, Pembroke-street	10
Ilfracombe	62
DEVONSHIRE (*contd.*)—	£
Okehampton	15
Sourton	5
Stonehouse	10
Torrington, Great	60
Totnes	7
DURHAM—	
Bishop Auckland	35
Crook	37
Hartlepool, West	12
South Shields, Tabernacle	30
Sunderland, Lindsay-road	50
Waterhouses	220
ESSEX—	
Barking	85
Brentwood	20
Clacton-on-Sea (U.)	250
Coggeshall	75
Colchester, Eld Lane	170
Grays, Tabernacle	40
Saffron Walden	90
Southend, Clarence-road	50
GLOUCESTERSHIRE—	
Cirencester	134
Coleford	30
Longhope, Zion	65
Lydbrook	20
Old Sodbury: *Codrington*	139
Stroud, John Street	110
Thornbury: *Tytherington*	60
HAMPSHIRE—	
Aldershot	100
Andover	10
Boscombe	45
Bournemouth, Lansdowne	55
West Cliff Tabernacle	460
Cosham, East	5
Fleet	25
Gosport, Avenue-road	75
Brockhurst	25
Isle of Wight: Ryde, Park-road	30
Ventnor	28
Odiham	3
Portsmouth: Landport, Commercial-road	25
Southsea, Castle-road	10
Elm-grove	350
Denmead	113
Southampton, Portland	50

Place.	Amount.
HEREFORDSHIRE—	£
Hereford Commercial-road..	263
Leominster	10
HERTFORDSHIRE—	
Breachwood Green	15
King's Langley	250
St. Albans, Verulam-road ..	170
HUNTINGDONSHIRE—	
Bluntisham	190
Bythorn	10
KENT—	
Brabourne	8
Hawkhurst	25
Herne Bay	30
Loose	20
New Brompton	275
St. Peter's	50
Sheerness, Strode-crescent ..	22
Yalding	140
LANCASHIRE—	
Blackburn, Montague-street..	200
Burnley, Colne-road	300
Mount Pleasant	50
Clayton-le-Moors	40
Dalton-in-Furness	30
Edgeside	25
Garston	30
Heywood	60
Hurstwood	20
Leigh	575
Liverpool:	
Myrtle-street:	
Earlestown	129
St. Helen's, Park-road ..	17
Prince's Gate	250
Nelson, Carr-road	40
Oldham	
Hollinwood, Beulah ..	20
King-street	210
Preston Ashton-on-Ribble ..	52
Pole-street ..	30
Southport, Scarisbrick New-road	1,100
St. Helen's, Boundary-road ..	30
Hall-street	120
Tyldesley (W.)	18
Vale, near Todmorden ..	100
Widnes . ..	15
Wigan, Scarisbrick-street ..	140
LEICESTERSHIRE—	
Barrow-on-Soar	25
Coalville, Ashby-road.. ..	40
London-road	200
Earl Shilton	25
Hathern..	10
Hinckley	300
Hose	10
Hugglescote	85
Ibstock	250
LEICESTERSHIRE (*contd.*)—	£
Leicester:	
Belgrave-road Tabernacle..	220
Belvoir-street:	
Harvey-lane:	
Cropstone	105
Huncote	12
Carley-street..	30
Clarendon Hall	2,000
Loughborough, Baxter Gate..	15
Mount-Sorrel	15
Shepshed, Belton-street ..	36
Charnwood-road	20
Syston	20
LINCOLNSHIRE—	
Fleet	60
Gt. Grimsby Victoria-street..	70
Louth, Eastgate	10
Sutterton	100
METROPOLITAN—	
Battersea:	
Battersea Park Tabernacle	300
York-road	37
Beckenham	100
Blackheath, Shooter's Hill-rd.	100
Brixton, Barrington-road ..	150
Stockwell-road Tabernacle	100
Brixton Hill, New Park-road	138
Bromley (Kent), Park-road ..	100
Brondesbury	280
Camberwell:	
Camberwell New-road, Clarendon	127
Mansion House-square ..	20
Catford-hill	850
Clapham Junction, Meyrick-road	140
Ealing, Haven-green	1,000
Erith, Queen-street	162
Finchley, North	400
Forest-hill, Sydenham Ch. ..	30
Hackney, Lauriston-road ..	50
Hanwell (U.)	40
Harlesden	50
Hendon, Finchley-road ..	97
Holloway, Upper	200
Honor Oak	50
Lee, Bromley-road	240
Leyton, Vicarage-road ..	30
Leytonstone, Cann Hall-road	100
Fairlop-road	450
Limehouse: East India-road, Pekin-street	100
Nunhead, Edith-road.. ..	475
Peckham, South London Tabernacle	50
Penge, Maple-road	50
Plumstead, Park-road ..	30
Putney Werter-road	125
Richmond, Duke-street ..	150

Place.	Amount.
METROPOLITAN (*contd.*)—	
Sidcup	100
Silvertown	200
Upton, Upton Cross	15
Wallington	50
Wandsworth, Northcote-road	200
Wood Green, Finsbury-road:	
Bowes Park	50
NORFOLK—	
Carleton Rode (Attleboro')	10
Lynn, Union Chapel	20
Swaffham	90
NORTHAMPTONSHIRE—	
Brington	20
Burton Latimer	170
Kingsthorpe	130
Northampton: College-street,	
Compton-street	193
Mount Pleasant	156
Towcester	20
Walgrave	10
NORTHUMBERLAND—	
Newcastle, Jesmond:	
Byker	30
NOTTINGHAMSHIRE—	
Arnold	15
Eastwood	10
Hucknall Torkard	40
Kimberley	13
Kirkby, East	20
Newark	26
Nottingham:	
Basford, New, Chelsea-st.	20
Hyson Green	40
Radford	10
Woodborough-road	3,210
Retford	20
Stapleford	15
Sutton Bonnington	5
Sutton-in-Ashfield:	
Eastfield-side	30
Wood-street	20
OXFORDSHIRE—	
Oxford New-road	50
SHROPSHIRE—	
Whitchurch	15
SOMERSETSHIRE—	
Bath, Hay-hill	90
Highbridge	25
Pill	154
Twerton-on-Avon	100
STAFFORDSHIRE—	
Brierley-hill	20
Burslem	120
Coseley, Ebenezer	4
Tamworth	15
Wednesbury	50
West Bromwich	200
Willenhall, Little London	50
SUFFOLK—	£
Bury St. Edmunds, Westgate-rd	31
Gorleston	240
Ipswich, Burlington	850
SUSSEX—	
Brighton, Queen's-square	40
St. Leonards	60
WARWICKSHIRE—	
Birmingham:	
Aston Park, Christ Church	50
Great King-street	50
Hagley-road	82
Handsworth, Hamstead-road	300
Highgate-park	37
Small Heath, Coventry-road	77
Smethwick	30
Nuneaton	10
Stratford-on-Avon	20
WILTSHIRE—	
Devizes, Sheep-street	67
Limpley Stoke	8
Swindon, Tabernacle	133
WORCESTERSHIRE—	
Kidderminster	212
Netherton, Ebenezer	10
Stourbridge	15
YORKSHIRE—	
Armley, Carr Crofts	65
Barnoldswick	80
Barnsley, Sheffield-road	60
Batley	25
Blackley	300
Bradford, Infirmary-street	12
Ripley-street	400
Clayton	80
Doncaster	140
Driffield	150
Earby-in-Craven	200
Elland	100
Gildersome	135
Huddersfield, New North-rd.	450
Hull, Beverley-road	70
Leeds, Blenheim	226
Burley-road	170
York-road	20
Lydgate	80
Middlesbro', Marton-road	50
Nazebottom	5
Polemoor	200
Rodley	50
Scarborough: West Gate,	
Ebenezer	20
Sheffield, Attercliffe	75
Hillsborough	560
Walkley	15
Skipton, Belmont	220
Slaithwaite, Zion	450
Stanningley	90
Thornaby-on-Tees	20

Place.	Amount.	Place.	Amount.
WALES AND MONMOUTHSHIRE.		GLAMORGANSHIRE (*contd.*)—	£
		Blaenclydach	135
		Bridgend, Ruamah	50
		Bryncethin	10
		Cardiff:	
BRECKNOCKSHIRE—	£	Canton (W.)	12
Hay	20	Grange Town	20
Talgarth	50	Tabernacle	150
CARDIGANSHIRE—		Woodville-road	50
Aberystwyth, Alfred-place ..	270	Clydach, Calvaria	70
Lampeter:		Craigcefnparc, Elim	66
Silian, Bethel	100	Croesyparc (Cardiff)	12
Llanrhystid	100	Cwmaman	190
CARMARTHENSHIRE—		Cwmavon	40
Cwmsarnddu	25	Cwm Clydach, Calvaria ..	100
Foelcwan, Noddfa:		Cwmfelin	30
Cwm Mydrim	5	Cwmgors	40
Llanelly, Caersalem	100	Cwmpark	190
Pwll (Llanelly), Bethlehem ..	75	Deri, Tabernacle	50
CARNARVONSHIRE—		Dowlais, Beulah	70
Bangor, Penrallt-road ..	80	Caersalem	90
Galltraeth	4	Hebron	40
Garn, Horeb	10	Moriah	90
Llandudno, Mostyn-street ..	300	Ferndale, Salem Newydd ..	122
Llanfairfechan, Libanus ..	15	Fochriw	35
Penmaenmawr	635	Gilfach Goch	25
Penygroes	20	Glais, Peniel	25
DENBIGHSHIRE—		Glyn Neath, Bethel	40
		Lantwit-vardre	30
Coedpoeth, Bethesda	5	Maesteg, Bethel	50
Tabernacle	10	Caersalem	80
Colwyn, Calfaria	18	Calvaria	20
Glynceiriog	39	Zion	30
Llangollen, Castle-street (W.)	400	Merthyr Tydvil, Ainon ..	26
Penybryn	850	George Town	30
Llanrwst	102	Zion	100
Moss, Salem	20	Merthyr Vale, Calfaria ..	50
Ponkey, Zion	10	Zion	200
Rhosllanerchrugog	100	Mountain Ash (Rhos)	50
Wrexham, Chester-street ..	5	Nantymoel, Horeb	500
Rhos-ddu	281	Penarth, Penuel	85
FLINTSHIRE—		Penrhiwceiber, Jerusalem ..	15
Caerwys	30	Pentre, Moriah	100
Lixwm (Holywell)	5	Zion	30
Rhuddlan	3	Penydarren	75
Treuddyn	12	Penygraig	206
GLAMORGANSHIRE—		Pontardawe, Elim	34
Aberavon, Ebenezer	170	Pontllyw	30
Water-street	30	Pontrhydycyff (Maesteg) ..	20
Aberdare:		Pontrhydyfen	42
Aberaman (W.)	70	Pontycymmer, Noddfa ..	20
Abercwmboye	55	Pontypridd, Rhondda	100
Abernant	320	Porth, Salem	242
Cwmbach	130	Tabernacle	100
Trecynon, Mill-street ..	50	Resolven, Bethania	22
Aberfan	50	Swansea:	
Barry District:		Caersalem Newydd ..	215
Barry, Bethel	30	Cwmbwrla	50
Bettws (Bridgend)	10	Danygraig	25
Birchgrove	50	Landore, Salem	30

Place.	Amount
GLAMORGANSHIRE (*contd.*)—	
Swansea (*contd.*)—	£
Mount Pleasant	158
Philadelphia	96
York Place	250
Tongwynlais, Ainon (W.) ..	70
Salem	15
Tonyrefail	347
Treharris, Bethel	110
Brynhyfryd	337
Treorky, Noddfa	265
Horeb..	28
Tynewydd (Ogmore Vale) ..	15
Wauntrodau, Ararat	90
Ynyshir, Ainon	110
Ynyslwyd	90
Ynysybwl, Noddfa	90
Ystalyfera, Caersalem ..	25
Zoar	10
Ystrad, Nebo	220
Tabernacle	20
MERIONETHSHIRE—	
Bala	7
Barmouth	25
Festiniog:	
Calfaria	29
Moriah	14
Sion	44
Glyndyfrdwy	40
Harlech, Ainon	6
MONTGOMERYSHIRE—	
Caersws	15
Newtown	2,000
PEMBROKESHIRE—	
Creswell Quay, Pisgah ..	36
Fishguard: Hermon, *Lower Fishguard*	50
Llangloffan, *Mathry*	200
Maenclochog	87
Marloes	80
Pembroke Dock, Bush Street	75
High Street	120
Pennar	50
RADNORSHIRE—	
Presteign	5
MONMOUTHSHIRE—	
Abercarn (W.)	90
Abergavenny, Frogmore-st.	450
Blackwood, Mount Pleasant..	50
Blaenavon	
Broad-street	50
Horeb..	5
Ebbw Vale, Newtown ..	5
Goytrey, Sharon	25
Machen, Siloam	15
Nash	10
Newport, St. Mary-street ..	275
New Tredegar (W.)	60
Penheolybadd	10
Pontnewynydd (E.)	38
MONMOUTHSHIRE (*contd.*)—	£
Pontypool, Bridge-street ..	20
Sirhowy (W.)	20
St. Mellon's	50
Tredegar, George Town ..	15
SCOTLAND.	
ABERDEENSHIRE—	
Aberdeen, Gilcomston-park..	202
Union-grove	30
ARGYLLSHIRE—	
Lochgilphead	65
AYRSHIRE—	
Irvine	30
Kilmarnock	5
DUMBARTONSHIRE—	
Clydebank	40
Kirkintilloch	17
FIFESHIRE—	
Cowdenbeath	8
Kirkcaldy, Whyte's Causeway	120
Leven	70
FORFARSHIRE—	
Dundee, Ward-road	4,096
LANARKSHIRE—	
Airdrie	40
Cambuslang	1,700
Glasgow:	
Bridgeton	16
John Knox-street	45
Queen's Park	30
Springburn	42
MORAYSHIRE—	
Elgin	30
PERTHSHIRE—	
Perth	50
RENFREWSHIRE—	
Greenock, Orangefield-place	75
Paisley:	
George-street	400
Victoria-place	45
ROXBURGH SHIRE—	
Hawick	10
SELKIRKSHIRE—	
Selkirk	45
SHETLAND ISLES—	
Lerwick	529
WESTERN ISLES—	
Mull, Bunessan	9
CHANNEL ISLANDS.	
JERSEY—	
St. Helier	62
TOTAL	£57,392

PART VIII.

LIST OF BAPTIST MINISTERS IN THE BRITISH ISLES.

FOR THE YEAR COMMENCING JANUARY 1, 1896.

. NAMES ARE PLACED ON THIS LIST BY AN ANNUAL VOTE OF THE COUNC OF THE BAPTIST UNION. THE COUNCIL REQUIRE RECOMMENDATIONS EITHER (1) BY TUTORS OF COLLEGES, OR (2) BY COMMITTEES OF ASSOCIATIONS, OR (3) BY THREE MEMBERS OF THE COUNCIL. SUCH RECOMMENDATIONS MUST BE IN THE HANDS OF THE SECRETARY NOT LATER THAN SEPTEMBER 15TH.

THE NAMES OF EVANGELISTS ARE NOT INCLUDED IN THIS LIST UNLESS THEY HAVE SERVED PREVIOUSLY AS PASTORS.

IN CASES WHERE THE PASTOR DOES NOT LIVE IN THE TOWN OR VILLAGE IN WHICH HIS CHAPEL IS SITUATED, THE NAME OF THE CHURCH IS INSERTED IN BRACKETS AFTER THE POSTAL ADDRESS, IN ORDER TO FACILITATE REFERENCE TO THE LIST OF CHURCHES (PAGES 201—293). THE NAME OF THE CHURCH IS INSERTED ALSO IN THE CASE OF EACH PASTOR IN THE "METROPOLITAN" SECTION (PAGES 233—241).

THE SAME INSTITUTION IS IN EACH CASE COMPRISED IN THE "COLLEGE" COLUMN UNDER THE DESIGNATIONS:—(1) "STEPNEY" AND "REGENT'S PARK"; (2) "BRADFORD" AND "RAWDON"; (3) "BURY" AND "MANCHESTER"; (4) "CHILWELL," "NOTTINGHAM" AND "MIDLAND"; (5) "LLANGOLLEN" AND "BANGOR"; (6) "PONTYPOOL" AND "CARDIFF"; AND (7) "BAP. TH. IN. EDIN.," "B.U.S.," AND "BAP. TH." (GLASGOW); THE LAST-NAMED PLACES BEING THE PRESENT LOCATIONS.

"METROPOLITAN" MEANS PASTORS' COLLEGE, METROPOLITAN TABERNACLE.

Name and Postal Address.	College.	Ministry commenced
ABBOTT, W., 25, Argyle-street, Bedford..		1844
Abraham, Harry, 35 York-place, Newport, Mon.	Metropolitan	1877
Acomb, Wm. Jas., 26 Welford-road, Handsworth, Birmingham	Metropolitan	1871
Adams, William, Bugbrook, Weedon	Metropolitan	1891
Adamson, Thomas, Derby-road, Kegworth, Derby	Metropolitan	1889
Adey, William Thomas, 41, Fore-street, Kingsbridge	Regent's Park	1864
Aikenhead, Robert, 203, Mary-street, Balsall Heath, Birmingham	Bradford	1847
Aitken, James Richmond, M.A. (GLAS.), Siriol House, Olney, *S.O., Bucks.*	Reg. Pk., Edin. U. & Glas. U.	1893

Name and Postal Address.	College.	Ministry commenced
Aked, Charles Frederic, 53, Bedford-street North, Liverpool	Midland	1886
Alderson, James, 52, Devonshire-street, Keighley	Manchester	1873
Aldis, John, Beckington, Bath	Bradford	1830
Aldis, John, jun., Little Leigh, near Warrington	Bristol	1862
Aldridge, Stephen Robinson, B.A., LL.D. (DUBLIN), 32, Lethbridge-road, Southport	Reg. Pk. & Tr. Coll., Dub.	1877
Alford, James Drewitt, Barrow-on-Soar, Loughborough		1864
Allderidge, Saml. Charles, 17, Lawn-street, Thursby-square, Burnley	Midland	1887
Allen, Charles Thomas, Cottenham, Cambridge	Metropolitan	1883
Allen, Robert, Maesteg, Bridgend		1879
Allsop, Frederick, Brearley, Luddendenfoot, via Manchester	Rawdon	1883
Allsop, Solomon Smithee, Ripley, Derby		1860
Almy, John Thomas, Vectis Villa, Brixham R.S.O., S. Devon	Metropolitan	1873
Ambrose, George Arthur, Wantage	Metropolitan	1892
Anderson, John George, Crossgates House, Dalton-in-Furness S.O., Lancs.	Metropolitan	1878
Anderson, Wm. Milroy, The Grange, Epworth, Doncaster	Bap. Th. In. Edin.	1851
Andrews, Edgar Manning, Shepshed, Loughborough	Regent's Park	1890
Andrews, James A., Drayton Parslow, Bletchley Station		1869
Andrews, John, 106, Spring-road, Ipswich		1859
Andrews, John R., Maulden, Ampthill	Regent's Park	1894
Angus, Joseph, M.A. (EDIN.), D.D. (U.S.), 5, Ellerdale-road, Hampstead, London, N.W.	Step. & Edin. Un.	1839
Antill, Thomas, Pinner S.O., Middlesex		1885
Antram, Charles Edward Potts, Ipswich	Rawdon	1890
Archer, George, Thornton Lodge-road, Lockwood, Huddersfield	Manchester	1882
Archer, John Kendrick, Heptonstall Slack, Manchester	Midland	1891
Archer, John Francis, Shore Manse, near Todmorden	Midland	1889
Archer, William Elisha, 4, Warwick-place, Leeds	Bradford	1841
Armstrong, Thomas, 848 Hyde-road, Gorton, Manchester	Metropolitan	1881
Armstrong, Wm. Kingo, B.A. (GLAS.), Newcastle Ho., Lewes	Brad. & Glas. Un.	1851
Arthur, David, Haworth, Keighley	Glas. U. & B.U.S.	1887
Ashby, Martin, Breachwood Green, Welwyn, Herts	Metropolitan	1889
Ashdown, Eli, 43, Endwell-road, Brockley, London, S.E. (*Zoar, Whitechapel*)		1881
Ashton, Edward, Gorsley, near Ross, Herefordshire	Metropolitan	1881
Askew, John, 80, Derby-street, Burton-on-Trent	Metropolitan	1870
Atkinson, Henry Clapham, 47, Otley-road, Bradford	Manchester	1871
Atkinson, James Hudson, 3, Oakfield, Anfield, Liverpool	Midland	1866
Atkinson, Thomas George, Sandhurst, Hawkhurst		1860
Aubrey, Edwin, 34, Garthland-drive, Dennistoun, Glasgow	Haverfordwest	1882
Aubrey, Jesse, 10, St. Mark's-road, Windsor	Metropolitan	1885
Aust, Francis John, Severn View, Bewdley	Metropolitan	1876
Avery, William J., 19, Furnival-street, London, E.C. (*Baptist Union*)	Chilwell	1877
Ayliffe, Charles, York-place, Newport, Mon.		1870
Ayres, Richard Willie, Ravensthorpe, Northampton	Metropolitan	1874
BAILEY, George Thomas, 2, Florence-villas, Grange Park-road, Leyton, Essex (*Vicarage-road, Leyton*)	Metropolitan	1876
Bailey, Henry Charles, 1, Athol-terrace, Sunderland	Bristol	1878
Bailey, John, B.A. (LON.), 44, Dover-road, Sheffield	Regent's Park	1872
Baily, Robert, Cranbrook, Boston-road, Brentford	Metropolitan	1891
Baillie, James, 67, Oakley-square, London, N.W. (*Bloomsbury*)	Bristol	1877
Baker, Stephen James, Brown-road, Bury St. Edmunds	Metropolitan	1888
Baker, Thomas, B.A. (LON.), 62, Western-road, Lewes	Bristol	1854
Baker, Thomas, Llandaff-yard, Cardiff	Haverfordwest	1875
Ball, George Woodvine, Devon-road, Salcombe, Kingsbridge	Metropolitan	1889
Ballard, Isaac, Beulah Villa, Farnborough R.S.O., Ken		1844

Name and Postal Address.	College.	Ministry commenced.
Balmford, Edward, Westmancote, Tewkesbury	Rawdon	1871
Banfield, James Hawkey, 50, Hamfrith-road, Stratford, London, E. (*Stratford-grove*)	Metropolitan	1875
Banks, George, 11, Cemetery-road, Willenhall, Wolverhampton	..	1879
Banks, Samuel James, Craig Fernie-terrace, Lisburn-road, Belfast	..	1857
Bardens, R. C., 36 Palmerston-road, Ipswich	..	1891
Bardwell, Henry Bagley, Orwell House, Chippenham, Wilts	Metropolitan	1866
Barker, A. W. Leighton, 6, Montague-place, Worthing	Metropolitan	1884
Barker, Charles, Belvoir-road, Coalville, Leicester (*Hugglescote*)	Midland	1875
Barker, George, Blaby, near Leicester	Bristol	1870
Barker, William Alfred, Braeside, Brixham R.S.O., Devon	Regent's Park	1884
Barley, A. G., Emsworth	Metropolitan	1886
Barnard, John H., 119, North Hill, Highgate, London, N. (*Southwood-lane, Highgate*)	Metropolitan	1862
Barnes, George, 63 Castle-street, Great Berkhamsted (*Weston Turville*)	..	1891
Barnes, J. E., Bristow-road, Hounslow	Metropolitan	1894
Barrans, George, 11, Westbourne-street, Walsall	Rawdon	1867
Barrass, Thomas, Peterborough	Midland	1850
Barringer, Charles Barclay, The Cottage, Cranleigh, Guildford	..	1870
Bartlett, James, Street S.O., Somerset	..	1891
Bartlett, Lewis, Hartington Villas, Aldburgh	Bristol	1889
Barton, Alexander Graham, Crook R.S.O., co. Durham	..	1885
Barton, Joseph Edwin, Tuffleigh-avenue, Gloucester	..	1871
Bastable, Richard, Kilmington, Axminster, Devon	..	1872
Baster, William, Mayfield, Southborough, Surbiton (*Surbiton Hill*)	Metropolitan	1874
Bateman, John, Niton, Isle of Wight	Metropolitan	1867
Bates, John, Ringstead, Thrapston	..	1884
Bathgate, Walter, 19, Carisbrooke-road, Walton, Liverpool	..	1875
Batstone, Thomas, Oakley House, Maesycwmmer, near Cardiff	..	1880
Batts, Arthur C., Upwell, Wisbech	Metropolitan	1884
Bax, Alfred, 23, Burma-road, Stoke Newington, London, N. (*Salter's Hall, Islington*)	Metropolitan	1861
Baxandall, John, 68, Parkfield-terrace, Lancaster	Rawdon	1862
Bayley, Henry, Oakside, Addlestone, Surrey	Regent's Park	1861
Bayly, Richard Howard, Blackpool	Bradford	1855
Beard, Joseph, Peterchurch, Hereford	..	1859
Beecliff, R. J., 52 Tredegar-road, Bow, London, E.	Metropolitan	1867
Bell, Donald, Tobermory R.S.O., Argyllshire	Glas. U. & B.U.S.	1881
Bell, John, 50, Bank Side-street, Roundhay-road, Leeds	..	1870
Bellis, Edward, Halkin, Holywell	..	1889
Belsham, Richard A., Melbourn, Cambridge	Metropolitan	1889
Bennett, Daniel, B.A. (CANTAB.), 3 Beach-road, Lowestoft	Camb. Univ.	1894
Bennett, George Henry, Bourne, Lincolnshire	Midland	1882
Bennett, John Ebenezer, B.A. (ROY. UN. I.), 54, King Edward-road, Hackney, London, N.E. (*Mare-street, Hackney*)	..	1884
Benskin, Frederick John, 3, Belmont-street, Huddersfield	Metropolitan	1870
Benson, Joseph, 55, Hilldrop-road, London, N. (*Belle Isle*)	..	1872
Bentley, Thomas, Chipping Norton	Rawdon	1864
Bentley, William, 227a, Brooke-road, Upper Clapton, London, N.E.	Stepney	1853
Beresford, James E. D., Stapleton, Bristol	..	1890
Bergin, J. Marmaduke, Yorktown, Camberley	Regent's Park	1867
Berry, Edward William, Mount Pleasant, Redditch	Metropolitan	1886
Berry, Herbert B., Halesworth	..	1884
Berry, John James, East Leake, Loughborough	..	1858
Berryman, James, Caerwent, Chepstow, Mon.	Pontypool	1872
Betts, Henry John, The Elms, Thurmaston, Leicester	..	1847
Betts, Thomas, 5, Hosier-street, Reading	..	1875

Name and Postal Address.	College.	Ministry commenced
Bevan, James, 1 Brook-villas, Whitchurch, Cardiff (*Wauntrodau*)	.. ..	.. 1870
Billings, Daniel Dunneley, 13, Little Francis-street, Bloomsbury, Birmingham	.. ..	.. 1836
Birch, Charles Boardman, 10, Sampson-road, Sparkbrook, Birmingham	Rawdon ..	.. 1891
Bird, Benwell, Wychbury, Mannamead, Plymouth	.. ..	.. 1861
Bird, Benwell Vernon, Stalham S.O., Norfolk..	Midland..	.. 1893
Birt, Isaiah, B.A. (LON.), 20, The Crescent, Hertford-road, Lower Edmonton	Bristol ..	.. 1856
Bishop, William, 110, Laurel-road, Leicester	Midland ..	.. 1867
Bisset, Alexander, M.A. (ABERDEEN), 24, Osborne-place, Aberdeen	Aber. & Edin. U.	1872
Black, James, M.A. (EDIN.), Windsor-terrace. Millport R.S.O., Buteshire	Reg. Pk. & B.U.S.	1895
Blackaby, Frederick Edward, Stow-on-the-Wold S.O., Gloucestershire..	Metropolitan	.. 1881
Blaikie, Peter Hatton, Coleraine..	Metropolitan	.. 1881
Blake, James Henry, Salisbury Villa, Tunbridge	.. ..	.. 1852
Blake, Joseph, 68, Nightingale-road, Clapton, London, N.E.	Metropolitan	.. 1858
Bland, S. K., Warrington-road, Ipswich	.. ..	.. 1853
Blinkhorn, Rayner Rootham, 56, Alpha-road, Chesterton, Cambridge	.. ..	.. 1842
Bliss, William B., South-street, Brierley Hill, Staffordshire..	Stepney ..	.. 1848
Blocksidge, Walter William, 26, Green-street, New Brompton, Chatham..	Metropolitan	.. 1881
Blomfield, William Ernest, B.A. (LON.), B.D. (ST. ANDREW'S), Regent-street, Coventry	Regent's Park	.. 1884
Bloom, William Knighton, 331, West Green-road, South Tottenham	Metropolitan	.. 1865
Bond, Kenneth Herbert, Swadlincote, Burton-on-Trent ..	Midland..	.. 1890
Bonell, George W., 118, Beeston-road, Leeds	Rawdon ..	.. 1888
Bonner, Carey, Oakfield, Wilton-avenue, Southampton ..	Rawdon ..	.. 1884
Bonner, Henry, 122, Hamstead-road, Handsworth, Birmingham	Rawdon ..	.. 1873
Booth, Samuel Harris, D.D. (U.S.), (*Secretary Baptist Union*), 19, Furnival-street, London, E.C.	Stepney ..	.. 1848
Bosher, Alexander, Oak Cottage, Shotley-bridge R.S.O., co. Durham	Regent's Park	.. 1882
Boud, John Wesley, 28, Jasmine-grove, Anerley, London, S.E. (*Penge*)	.. ..	.. 1871
Boulsher, George, 48, Hawthorne-road, Bootle, Liverpool ..	Metropolitan	.. 1867
Bourgourd, Charles John, Les Hubits, St. Martin, Guernsey	.. ..	.. 1877
Bourn, Henry Hugh, 24, Claremont-road, Tunbridge Wells..	.. ..	.. 1849
Bowden, Andrew, Stalybridge-road, Ashton-under-Lyne (*Stalybridge*)	Bradford	.. 1856
Bowen, Samuel Glannedd, 14, Alexandria-street, Gelli, Pentre, R.S.O. Glam. (*Tonystrad*)	Llangollen	.. 1885
Bowker, Benjamin, 199, Rochdale-road, Bury, Lancs. ..	Bury ..	.. 1873
Bowler, George Benson, Dudley-road, Grantham	Metropolitan	.. 1863
Bowman, William Robert, B.A. (LON.), 44, Langdon Park-road, Highgate, London, N.	U. Col. Lond. and Cheshunt	.. 1884
Bowser, Sidney William, B.A. (LON.), 19, Alfred-road, Birkenhead	U. Col. Lond. and Regent's Park	1879
Bowtell, James Daniel, Bungay	.. ..	.. 1873
Box, John, 26, Flodden-road, Camberwell, London, S.E. (*Shaftesbury Avenue, Soho*)	.. ..	.. 1872
Boyd, James H., 5, Marion-terrace, Hill-street, Lurgan ..	.. ..	.. 1891
Bradford, Henry, Kingsley-road, Northampton	Metropolitan	.. 1868
Bradford, John, Ivy Bank, Leytonstone, London, N.E. (*Fairlop-road, Leytonstone*)	Metropolitan	.. 1878
Braine, Albert, 23, Trafalgar-place, Stoke, Devonport ..	Bristol ..	.. 187[illegible]

Name and Postal Address.	College.	Ministry commenced
Branch, William George, Oadby, Leicester	Midland	.. 1892
Brandon, Alfred, 101, Beaufort-street, Chelsea, London, S.W. (*Grove, Brompton*)	.. ..	.. 1852
Brasted, John Bangley, Mount Clear, Old Colwyn R.S.O., Denbighshire	.. ..	.. 1850
Bray, John Dyer, 164, Great Clowes-street, Broughton, Manchester	Rawdon..	.. 1889
Breewood, Thomas, Brayford, South Molton	Metropolitan	.. 1876
Bremner, Alexander, Castle Braes, Dumfries	.. ..	.. 1889
Brett, John Edward, 69 Barton-street, Tewkesbury	Metropolitan	.. 1869
Bridge, Isaac, 184, Brooke-road, Clapton, London, N.E. ..	Metropolitan	.. 1864
Brigg, Benjamin, Saltwood House, Hawley-square, Margate	Metropolitan	.. 1881
Briggs, Henry, Roomfield, Todmorden	Manchester	.. 1871
Briggs, James, 23, Honiton-road, Kilburn, London, N.W. (*Praed-street, Paddington*)	Metropolitan	.. 1883
Briggs, Roger, Blackley, Elland, Yorks	Bury ..	.. 1874
Bright, Henry, 77, Hanley-road, Crouch-hill, London, N. (*Evangelist*)	.. ..	.. 1872
Brimley, Thomas, Braunston, Rugby	.. ..	.. 1886
Briscoe, John Thomas, 26, Woodstock-road, Redland, Bristol	.. ..	.. 1868
Bristow, John James, Rushton Villa, Leicester-road, East Finchley, N. (*East Finchley*)	Metropolitan	.. 1894
Brock, William, 16, Ellerdale-road, Hampstead, London, N.W. (*Heath-street, Hampstead*)	Edinburgh Univ.	1860
Brooker, G. Whitfield, 45, Church-street, Leigh, Lancs. ..	Manchester	.. 1890
Broom, Edward Richard, Milton, near Northampton ..	Rawdon ..	.. 1873
Broome, Caleb, Bridge-street, Stowmarket	.. ..	.. 1861
Brown, Alexander, Bunessan, Oban	Glasgow Univ..	. 1892
Brown, Archibald Geikie, 22, Bow-road, London, E. (*East London Tabernacle, Bow*)	Metropolitan	.. 1863
Brown, Charles, 25, Ridge-road, Hornsey, London, N. (*Ferme Park, Hornsey*)	Bristol ..	.. 1882
Brown, Edward Heath, Brathay Lodge, The Green, Twickenham	.. ..	.. 1873
Brown, Edwin, St. Anne's-on-the-Sea, Preston	Rawdon ..	.. 1865
Brown, George, Mill-road, Offord D'Arcy, Huntingdon ..	.. ..	.. 1879
Brown, Henry David, Carrick View, Ayr	Rawdon ..	.. 1872
Brown, Hugh Dunlop, M.A., B.L. (DUBLIN), Glengyle, Rathgar, Dublin	Dublin Univ.	.. 1884
Brown, J. Cumming, 3, Marchiston Bank-avenue, Edinburgh	Reg.Pk.& Edin.U.	1859
Brown, James, 4, Hallidays-park, Selkirk	.. ..	.. 1880
Brown, James Jones, Church-street, Cromer	.. ..	.. 1856
Brown, John, High-street, Wincanton, Bath	Bristol ..	.. 1869
Brown, John Alexander, Coombe Lodge, Peckham, London, S.E. (*Cottage Green, Camberwell*)	Metro. & Edin..	. 1866
Brown, John Jenkyn, 3, Priory-road, Edgbaston, Birmingham	Bristol ..	.. 1844
Brown, John Turland, Lebanon, Kingsley-road, Northampton	Bristol ..	.. 1838
Brown, Joseph, Upwell, near Wisbech	Melksham	.. 1849
Brown, Walter, 1, Mersea-road, Colchester	.. ..	.. 1874
Bruce, David, Great Shelford, Cambridge	Metropolitan	.. 1876
Bruce, Francis William Clark, 22, Connaught-road, Kensington, Liverpool	.. ..	.. 1862
Bruce, Joseph Stevens, 17, Adolphus-road, Finsbury Park, London, N. (*Markyate-street, Herts*)	Metropolitan	.. 1878
Bryan, Wyndham Colin, Hunstanton R.S.O., Norfolk ..	Metropolitan	.. 1883
Bryce, W. Kirk, West Park-street, Chatteris, S.O. Cambs. ..	Metropolitan	.. 1894
Buchanan, William J., 5, Lion-terrace, Portsea, Portsmouth	Regent's Park	.. 1892
Buckley, George, 33, Rectory-road, Shelton, Stoke-on-Trent (*Hanley*)	Manchester	.. 1892
Bull, William, B.A. (LON.), Sutton-in-the-Elms, near Rugby	Bris. & U.C. Lon.	1857
Buller, William Hutchings, Radstock, Bath	.. ..	.. 1868

Name and Postal Address.	College.	Ministry commenced
Bullimore, Thomas, Montrose House, Hellesdon-road, Norwich	..	1877
Burbridge, R., 9, Eaton-terrace, St. John's Wood, London, N.W. (*Avenue, Pratt-street, Camden Town*)	..	1884
Burgess, Frederick George, Park-road, Wellingborough	..	1870
Burnett, William, Brasted S.O., Kent	..	1874
Burnham, John, Fern Bank, Brentford (*Evangelist*)	Metropolitan	1874
Burns, Dawson, M.A., D.D. (U.S.), 12, Foxmore-street, Battersea, London, S.W.	Midland	1851
Burns, Joseph, Crescent-place, Dalmuir, Glasgow (*Clydebank*)	..	1891
Burrell, George, 48, Gladstone-road, Watford	..	1869
Burrows, Edward John, London-road, Attleborough, Norfolk	Metropolitan	1894
Burrows, Robert Alanson, 12, Almond-street, Farnworth R.S.O., Lancs.	Manchester	1886
Burton, William, Minehead R.S.O., Som.	Bristol	1857
Burt, Henry Matthew, Mildenhall S.O., Suffolk	Metropolitan	1877
Bury, Fenton Ernest, Rockefeller House, Harcourt-street, Dublin	Dublin Univ.	1891
Butcher, Joseph William, Harlow	Regent's Park	1871
Butlin, James, M.A. (OXON.), 15, Beauchamp-avenue, Leamington	Oxford Univ.	1879
Butterworth, Joseph Croucher, M.A. (EDIN.), Surbiton T.S.O., Kingston-on-Thames	Bristol	1842
Byard, Henry Kerby, Winslow	Metropolitan	1892
CALDWELL, Stuart, Clayton-le-Moors, Accrington	Manchester	1887
Callaway, Joseph Hall, Wendover, Tring	Richmond (Wes.)	1877
Camp, George, Epworth, Doncaster	Midland	1883
Campbell, John, 32½, King-street, Dundee	..	1875
Campbell, John O'Neill, 60, Fernleaf-street, Moss Side, Manchester	Metropolitan	1885
Campbell, John W., Queen's-road, Wisbech	Metropolitan	1882
Campbell, Owen D., M.A. (CANTAB.), The Grove, Haverfordwest	Rawdon & Camb. Univ.	1877
Campbell, Thomas Simpson, Fishponds, Bristol	Glas. U. & B. U.S.	1887
Cantrell, Edwin Wykes, 34, Claremont-road, Sparkbrook, Birmingham	Midland	1867
Carey, Samuel Pearce, M.A. (LON.), 11, Gregory-street, Loughborough	Regent's Park	1887
Carlile, John Charles, 37, Reverdy-road, Bermondsey, London, S.E. (*Trinity, John-street, Marylebone*)	Metropolitan	1884
Carrington, Elijah, 8, Grange Crescent-road, Sharrow Sheffield	Midland	1881
Carryer, Thomas Haddon, 2, St. Stephen's-road, Highfields, Leicester	Bradford	1863
Carson, Robert Haldane, Tubbermore, co. Derry	..	1845
Carter, Arthur Charles, Queensbury, near Bradford	Midland	1885
Carter, Edwin Alfred, Oreston, Bolingbroke-grove, Wandsworth-common, London, S.W.	Metropolitan	1882
Carter, Frederick, 173, Brixton-hill, London, S.W. (*Raleigh-park, Brixton-hill*)	Metropolitan	1889
Carter, James William, 7, Belmont-road, Broadstairs R.S.O., Kent	..	1861
Carter, Lawrence George, 81 Waterside, Chesham R.S.O., Bucks	Rawdon	1868
Carvath, James, Willingham R.S.O., Cambs.	Shebbear B.C.	1886
Carver, Thomas Albert, 29, Thurleigh-road, Wandsworth Common, London, S.W.	Metropolitan	1880
Case, Harry B., 5, Stockmore-street, Oxford	Metropolitan	1890
Case, Sydney Henry, M.A. (OXON.), Caversham, Reading	Bris. & Ox. Univ.	1877
Castle, John T., 28, Osborne-road, Broadstairs, R.S.O. Kent, (*St. Peters*)	Metropolitan	1894

Name and Postal Address.	College.	Ministry commenced
Cattell, James, Park Lodge, Bessels Green, Sevenoaks	.. .. ..	1865
Causton, Alfred James, Fakenham, Norfolk	.. .. ..	1870
Causton, John William, 4, St. Helen's-crescent, Swansea	Bristol ..	1893
Cave, James, Oxford House, Wokingham	Regent's Park	1867
Caven, Robert, B.A. (LON.), 56, St. Peter's-road, Leicester	Regent's Park	1859
Chadwick, John, Holmesdale, Tennison-road, South Norwood, London, S.E. (*Holmesdale-road, South Norwood*)	Metropolitan	1866
Chambers, Arthur Clarence, Lyndhurst, Woolwich-road, Belvedere (*Belvedere*)	Metropolitan	1884
Chambers, Clarence, 172, Choumert-road, Peckham, London, S.E.	Metropolitan	1863
Chambers, William, 22, Queen's-place, Shoreham, Sussex	Metropolitan	1878
Chandler, George, Thurleigh, Bedford	.. .. ..	1866
Chaplin, W. Knight, 26, Venne-street, South Bromley, London, E. (*Poplar and Bromley Tabernacle*)	.. .. ..	1881
Chapman, Charles Bell, Neatishead, Norwich	.. .. ..	1878
Chapman, David Charles, Yalding, near Maidstone	Metropolitan	1875
Chapman, William, 3, Northwick-terrace, Cookham-road, Maidenhead	Midland ..	1843
Chappelle, J. K., Roughton, Horncastle	Manch. (Ind.)	1862
Charlesworth, G., Newchurch-road, Stacksteads, Manchester (*Acre Mill, Bacup*)	.. .. ..	1869
Charlesworth, Vernon J., Orphanage, Stockwell, London, S.E.	.. .. ..	1864
Charter, John, Middleton-in-Teesdale, via Darlington	.. .. ..	1862
Chedburn, William Stewart, 86, Beech-grove-terrace, Aberdeen	Edin. Univ. & Rawdon	1868
Chenery, Richard, 19, Greame-street, Moss Side, Manchester	Bap. Evan. Soc.	1849
Cheshire, Stephen, The Green, Stony Stratford	Regent's Park	1885
Chettleborough, Robert Edward, Chelsham-road, South Croydon	Metropolitan	1878
Chinnery, David, Melbourne, Derby	Metropolitan	1886
Chrystal, Colin, Dunnington, Alcester, Redditch	Bristol, Glas. U. and B.U.S.	1884
Chrystal, James Robert, M.A., B.D. (ST. ANDREW'S), Almada Grange, Hamilton	St. And. & Glas. U.	1886
Clare, Robert Bone, Dorchester	.. .. ..	1866
Clark, Charles, St. Kilda, Durdham-park, Bristol	Midland ..	1862
Clark, David, 4, Airlie-terrace, Dundee	Pont. & Glas. U.	1889
Clark, Henry, M.A. (EDIN.), Durley Dean Mansions, Bournemouth	Stepney ..	1844
Clark, James, New-street, St. Neots	.. .. ..	1858
Clark, John Pearce, M.A. (EDIN.), Gunnersbury, London, W. (*Gunnersbury*)	Edin. & Bristol	1877
Clark, Joseph, Mountford-house, Carrington, Nottingham	Metropolitan	1882
Clark, Robert, 7, Ravenscroft-avenue, Connswater, Belfast	.. .. ..	1889
Clark, Thomas, 9, Hardinge-road, Ashford, Kent	.. .. ..	1851
Clark, Thomas, Market Drayton, Salop	Pontypool	1861
Clark, William, Brooke, Norwich	.. .. ..	1882
Clarke, Charles, B.A. (LON.), Ashby-de-la-Zouch	Bradford	1858
Clarke, James Bosworth, 9, Connaught-avenue, Mutley, Plymouth	.. .. ..	1885
Clarke, William, Burford R.S.O., Oxon.	.. .. ..	1892
Cliff, George James, 3, Colinfield, Douglas-road, Wigan	Rawdon ..	1891
Clifford, John, M.A., LL.B., B.Sc. (LON.), D.D. (U.S.), F.G.S. 50, St. Quintin's-avenue, N. Kensington, London, W. (*Westbourne Park, Praed-street, and Bosworth-road, Paddington*)	Midland & Lon. U.	1858
Coats, Jervis, M.A. (GLAS.), 8, Ibrox-terrace, Govan	Glas. U. & B.U.S.	1872
Cobb, George, 4, Queen's-road, Bury St. Edmunds	.. .. ..	1860
Cocker, Thomas, Redland House, Pontnewydd, Newport, Mon.	Pontypool	1867

Name and Postal Address	College.	Ministry commenced
Cockerton, Frederick Murfit, Limpsfield S.O., Surrey ..	Metropolitan ..	1857
Cockett, John, The Chestnuts, Walsoken, Wisbech (*Wisbech*)	.. .. ..	1859
Cole, Benjamin James, Lossiemouth	Metropolitan ..	1892
Cole, Charles, 157, Park-road, Bolton	Metropolitan ..	1882
Cole, John, Leominster	Haverfordwest ..	1869
Cole, John William, 44, Macoma-road, Plumstead, London, S.E. (*Park-road, Plumstead*)	.. .. ..	1859
Cole, Thomas John, 41, St. Marys-road, Peckham, London, S.E..	.. ..	1853
Coleman, Edward Ernest, 87, Burford-road, Nottingham ..	Rawdon	1878
Collett, James, Woodfield-road, King's Heath, Birmingham	Rawdon	1888
Colley, John William, Hope House, High-street, Amersham	Metropolitan ..	1887
Collier, David, Hirwain, Aberdare	Pontypool and Cardiff U.C. ..	1892
Collier, John Thomas, 1, Cranbourne Villas, Wilton-road, Salisbury	Bristol	1847
Collings, Harry, Lawn House, Castle-street, Luton	Bristol	1880
Collings, Thomas, Burton Latimer, near Kettering	.. .. ..	1885
Collins, John, Ingleside, Lymington	Metropolitan ..	1863
Collins, Thomas, 99, St. Andrews-road, Pollockshields, Glasgow	Glas. U. & Free Church Coll.	1895
Collinson, James, 6, Broom Bank-villas, The Broom, Rotherham	Rawdon	1882
Colls, Lazarus Henry, Tring	.. .. ..	1884
Colman, Robert, J.P., Leehurst, Wyndham Park, Salisbury..	Regent's Park ..	1870
Colsell, T., 18, Lower Ford-street, Coventry	.. .. ..	1868
Comfort, Jabez Ambrose, Witney College, Witney, Oxon ..	Regent's Park ..	1861
Compton, Edward, 9, Wellington-square, Hastings (*Rye*) ..	Metropolitan ..	1863
Connor, E. Poole, Cambridge-road, Aldershot..	.. .. ..	1893
Connor, John, Cathcraig, Motherwell	Glasgow Univ...	1888
Cook, George H., 31, Summer Hill-road, Maindee, Newport, Mon.	Bristol	1876
Cook, George Smith, 82, Tredegar-road, Bow, London, E.	.. .. ..	1847
Cooke, John Hunt, Ramleh, Coolhurst-road, Crouch End, London, N.	Stepney	1856
Cooke, Thomas Edward Cozens, Western-road, Abergavenny	Regent's Park ..	1865
Coombs, William, 180, Cambridge-road, Aylesbury	Metropolitan ..	1860
Cooper, James Lewitt, Long Crendon, Thame	Bristol	1876
Cooper, John, Smeeth, Ashford	.. .. ..	1877
Corbet, Alexander, 85, Finnart-street, Greenock	Metropolitan ..	1887
Cordon, Henry, 61, Rockfield-road, Anfield, Liverpool ..	.. .. ..	1875
Cork, Daniel, Marengo-villa, Budleigh Salterton S.O., Devon	.. .. ..	1868
Cornish, Joseph, 19, Hastings-street, Leicester	Regent's Park ..	1885
Cornwell, Charles, Brixton Tabernacle, Stockwell-road, London, S.W. (*Stockwell-road, Brixton*)	.. .. ..	1863
Cossey, Francis Edward, Eye, Suffolk	Bury	1869
Cotes, Thomas, 24, Byrom-street, Todmorden	Glas U. & Midland	1888
Cottam, James, 5, Newstead-road, Wakefield	Metropolitan ..	1883
Cotton, Arthur Frederic, Brabourne, Ashford, Kent.. ..	Metropolitan ..	1878
Cousins, Henry Thomas, Abergele-road, Colwyn Bay R.S.O., Denbighshire	E. London Inst...	1880
Cowdy, Samuel, LL.D. (U.S.), 26, Lorn-road, Brixton, London, S.W.	.. .. ..	1840
Cowell, Josiah, Coriantum, Rushton-crescent, Bournemouth	.. .. ..	1849
Cox, James Mitchell, 108, Shirland-road, London, W. (*St. Peter's Park, Paddington*)	Metropolitan ..	1866
Cox, James R., 2, Lincoln-villas, Cleveland-road, South Woodford, Essex	.. .. ..	1867
Crabb, Samuel, Glen Islay Villa, Ardmory-road, Rothesay, Bute	Metropolitan ..	1865
Craise, George Philp, Caenlochan-terrace, Broughty Ferry R.S.O., Forfarshire	Regent's Park ..	1887
Crassweller, Harris, B.A. (LON.), 21, Hermon-hill, Dundee ..	Stepney	1853

Name and Postal Address.	College.	Ministry commenced
Crathern, William Luke, 8, Alpha-place, Appledore R.S.O., Devon		1878
Crofts, Edmund James, Alcester, Redditch	Rawdon	1884
Croome, Charles George, Highfield, Wiverton-road, Sherwood Rise, Nottingham	Metropolitan	1882
Crouch, John, Janefield-place, Paisley	Metropolitan	1866
Cruickshank, James, Crewkerne, Somerset	Metropolitan	1867
Cuff, William, Amesbury House, Lordship-road, Stoke Newington, London, N. (*Shoreditch Tabernacle*)	Metropolitan	1865
Cule, George Griffiths, Dynevor House, Pontypridd	Llangollen	1883
Culross, James, M.A., D.D. (St. Andrew's), *Joint President*, The College, Stokes Croft, Bristol	St. Andrew's & Edinburgh Univ.	1850
Cunliffe, Frederick, Walgrave, Northampton	Midland	1885
Curry, Thomas Burton, Apsley House East, Britannia-road, Great Yarmouth	Metropolitan	1884
Curtis, Alfred, Coggeshall-road, Braintree	Metropolitan	1890
Curtis, Edward, Hatch Beauchamp, near Taunton	Rawdon	1861
Curtis, George, 41, Acton-street, Gray's-inn-road, London, W.C. (*Handel-street [Henrietta-street], King's Cross*)	Metropolitan	1889
Curtis, James, Ashburton Villa, Uxbridge-road, Hanwell, London, W. (*Staines-road, Hounslow*)		1878
Curwood, Alfred William, Hylton-terrace, South-parade, West Hartlepool	Metropolitan	1889
Cutts, Thomas, 64, Derbyshire-lane, Hucknall Torkard, Nottingham		1861
DANN, James, 3, Tackley-place, Oxford		1865
Dann, Thomas Ruffell, Oriel Villa, Bloomfield-avenue, Bath	Rawdon	1890
Darby, R. D., 17, Harberton-road, Whitehall Park, London, N. (*Hazellville-road, Hornsey Rise*)		1886
Dart, William Francis, Fleet, Holbeach		1875
Davidson, Alfred Knight, Old Buckenham, Attleboro', Norfolk	Metropolitan	1871
Davidson, George W., Milton, Chipping Norton	Metropolitan	1884
Davies, Alfred Jones, Cowlersley House, Milnsbridge, Huddersfield	Manchester	1883
Davies, Benjamin, 12, Kemeys-street, Griffithstown, Newport, Mon. (*Cwmmera*)	Pontypool	1887
Davies, Benjamin, 19, Bryntirion-street, Dowlais	Haverfordwest	1882
Davies, Benjamin, 29, Richard-street, Pontypridd	Haverfordwest	1854
Davies, Benjamin, 85, Belgrave-road, Darwen	Manchester	1888
Davies, Benjamin T., Lumb, Manchester	Haverfordwest	1882
Davies, Charles, 31, Glynrhondda-street, Cardiff	Llangollen	1870
Davies, Dan, Porth R.S.O., Glam.	Pontypool	1879
Davies, Daniel, 9, Ombersley-road, Newport, Mon.	Haverfordwest	1864
Davies, Daniel, 2, Gellydeg Cottages, Tonypandy, Llwynpia R.S.O., Glam.	Pontypool	1866
Davies, Daniel, 24, Stepney-place, Llanelly, Carm.		1841
Davies, Daniel, Felinfoel, Llanelly, Carm. (*Llangyfelach, Glam.*)		1885
Davies, Daniel James, Ivor Towy, Manordilo R.S.O., Carm. (*Cwmifor*)		1873
Davies, David, Brook Cottage, Llanbister, Penybont R.S.O., Radnorshire (*Maesyrhelem*)		1876
Davies, David, Lisvane, near Cardiff	Haverfordwest	1867
Davies, David, Oakhurst, Llandudno	Llangollen	1874
Davies, David, Laws-street, Pembroke Dock	Pontypool	1853
Davies, David, 63, Wilbury-road, Hove, Brighton	Bristol	1872
Davies, David, Harlech R.S.O., Merioneth		1886
Davies, David Burwyn, 23, Cradock-street, Swansea	Pontypool	1886
Davies, David Charles, Resolven, Neath	Haverfordwest	1889
Davies, David Dyvan, Bryndilo, Port Talbot, Glam.	Pontypool	1866

Name and Postal Address.	College.	Ministry commenced
Davies, David James, Gough-buildings, Ystradgynlais, Swansea	Llangollen	1892
Davies, David Morgan, B.A. (LON.), Rhiw-road, Colwyn Bay R.S.O., Denbighshire	Pontypool and Bristol	1885
Davies, David Owen, 89, Milnrow-road R.O., Rochdale	Manchester	1881
Davies, David Rees, Brynhyfryd T.S.O., Swansea	.. .. ..	1868
Davies, David Saunders, Pleasant View, Llanboidy, Whitland R.S.O., Carm. (*Whitland*)	Pontypool	1867
Davies, David Stephen, Saron, Llandybie R.S.O., Carm.	Pontypool	1863
Davies, Evan, Peny-Bryn House, near Monmouth	Haverfordwest	1847
Davies, Evan, Llangloffan, Letterston R.S.O., Pem.	Haverfordwest	1865
Davies, Evan Thomas, 4, Church-street, Rhyl	Llangollen	1873
Davies, Evan Wicliffe, 9, Church-street, Ton Pentre, Pentre R.S.O., Glam. (*Tonystrad*)	Haverfordwest	1881
Davies, George, 164, Grosvenor-road, Westminster, London, S.W. (*Romney-street, Westminster*)	Metropolitan	1886
Davies, George, 1, Prospect-villas, Ridgeway-road, Redhill	.. .. ..	1890
Davies, Gethin, D.D. (U.S.), *Principal*, The College, Bangor	Bristol	1870
Davies, Hugh, Slack lane, Keighley	Manchester	1875
Davies, James Phillips, Mill-road, Caerphilly, Cardiff	Haverfordwest	1863
Davies, James Waite, 2, Bromley-road, Lee, London, S.E. (*Burnt Ash, Lee*)	Metropolitan	1886
Davies, John, Alban-square, Aberayron R.S.O., Card.	.. .. ..	1852
Davies, John, Killay, Swansea	Haverfordwest	1867
Davies, John Lee, Brynamman R.S.O., Carm.	Pontypool	1893
Davies, Joseph, 11, Lowwood-grove, Birkenhead	Llangollen	1873
Davies, Joseph Morlais, M.A. (LON.), *Classical Tutor*, The College, Cardiff	Pont., Reg. Pk., & U. Coll. Lond.	1885
Davies, Lewis, Roger's Well, St. Clear's, Carm.	.. .. ..	1872
Davies, Owen, D.D. (U.S.), Cefnfaes, Carnarvon	Llangollen	1865
Davies, Owen, Greenfield House, Llantwit Major, Cowbridge	Pontypool	1884
Davies, Richard, Stanley House, Morley, Leeds	Haverfordwest	1863
Davies, T. J., Waunarlwydd, Gowerton R.S.O., Glam.	.. .. ..	1883
Davies, T. Witton, B.A. (LON.), M.R.A.S., *Principal*, Midland Baptist College, Nottingham	Pont., Reg. Pk., U. Coll. Lond. & Berlin Univ.	1879
Davies, Thomas, Hafod, Pontypridd (*Trehafod*)	Pontypool	1890
Davies, Thomas, 3, Windsor Esplanade, Cardiff	Bristol	1878
Davies, Thomas, 29, Glamorgan-street, Aberaman, Aberdare	.. .. ..	1867
Davies, Thomas, Bridgend-road, Pontycymmer, Bridgend	Haverfordwest	1884
Davies, Thomas, 10, Helfa, Treforest R.O., Pontypridd	.. .. ..	1886
Davies, Thomas Philip, Bethesda, near Bangor	Hav. & Rawdon	1877
Davies, Thomas, West End, Coronation-road, Bristol	Bristol	1893
Davies, Thomas Cynog, 2, Pulteney-gardens, Bath	Manchester	1885
Davies, Walter P., Glenroy, Arundel-crescent, Weston-super-Mare	Llangollen	1885
Davies, Walter Embrey, High-street, St. Neots (*Hail Weston*)	.. .. ..	1875
Davies, William Collins, B.A. (LON.), Cloughfold, near Manchester	Haverfordwest & Regent's Park	1882
Davies, William, Rosedale, Llangwm, Haverfordwest	Pontypool	1866
Davies, William, Tufton, Letterston R.S.O., Pemb. (*Puncheston*)	Haverfordwest	1875
Davies, William, Oak-villas, Briton Ferry R.S.O., Glam. (*Neath*)	Pontypool	1862
Davies, William Elvad, 64, Wern-terrace, Clydach Vale, Pontypridd	.. .. ..	1880
Davies, William Evan, Drefach, Llandyssil	Haverfordwest	1887
Davies, William Gershom, 32, High-street, Penarth	Haverfordwest	1882
Davies, William Henry, Grantown	Pontypool	1884
Davies, William Thomas, Pandyr-capel, Llanelidan, Ruthin R.S.O., Denbighshire	Pontypool	1862
Davis, Charles Alfred, Berkshire House, Stroud	Metropolitan	[illegible]

Name and Postal Address.	College.	Ministry commenced
Davis, Ebenezer Tamsett, Arnsby, Crescent-road, Sidcup R.S.O., Kent (*East-street, Walworth*)	.. ..	.. 1869
Davis, Edwin, High-street, Lydney, Gloucestershire	.. ..	.. 1881
Davis, Henry, Ottery St. Mary, Devon	Metropolitan	.. 1874
Davis, Henry, 18, Elmfield-terrace, Savile Park, Halifax ..	Manchester	.. 1888
Davis, John, Farleigh, Manor-park, Redland-road, Bristol ..	Bristol ..	.. 1857
Davis, John, Cressingham-villas, Cullingworth, Bradford, Yorks.	Metropolitan	.. 1889
Davis, Joseph Upton, B.A. (LON.), Northwold, Moss Hall-grove, Finchley, London, N...	Stepney ..	.. 1859
Davis, Thomas, 16, Bay-street, Mumbles, Swansea	.. ..	.. 1885
Davis, William Alfred, 44, Burlington-gardens, Acton, London, W. (*Acton*)	Metropolitan	.. 1878
Dawson, Joseph, Naerodal, Woodend-road, Erdington, Birmingham	.. ..	.. 1879
Day, C. H. Marsack, Causeway-villas, Wembdon, Bridgwater (*Bridgwater*)		
Day, Joseph, 18, Long-street, Devizes	Regent's Park	.. 1892
Deal, Charles, 22, Greenhill, Middleton Junction, near Manchester	Metropolitan	.. 1891
Deane, Joseph James, 4, Rydal-street, Gateshead	Metropolitan	.. 1868
Dearing, James, Needham Market, (*Crowfield*)	.. ..	.. 1859
Debnam, Joseph Risk, Horham, Wickham Market, Suffolk	.. ..	.. 1870
Delahaye, Thomas, 28, Oxford-street, Maindee, Newport, Mon. (*Nash*)	.. ..	.. 1872
Denmee, William John, Cross-street, Hoxne, Scole	.. ..	.. 1874
Denniss, Charles, Reading-street, St. Peter's, Broadstairs R.S.O., Kent	.. ..	.. 1871
Dickerson, Daniel, Mendlesham-green, Stowmarket		
Dickins, Butlin, Husbands Bosworth, Rugby	Regent's Park	.. 1859
Dixon, W., 109, Risbygate-street, Bury St. Edmunds (*Bradfield*)	.. ..	.. 1875
Dobson, Nicholas, Gilsland House, Deal	Metropolitan	.. 1873
Dodwell, Jabez, The Croft, Haddenham, Thame	Metropolitan	.. 1869
Doggett, William Harold, Ock-street, Abingdon	Metropolitan	.. 1892
Donald, Charles Smith, 13, Allworthy-avenue, Belfast ..	Glasgow Univ..	.. 1883
Donald, William, Kay Park Crescent, Kilmarnock	Glasgow Univ..	.. 1871
Dorey, William, Gt. Missenden S.O., Bucks	.. ..	.. 1888
Doubleday, John, Ingleside, Sittingbourne	Metropolitan	.. 1881
Douglas, James, M.A. (GLAS.), 48 Lambert-road, Brixton Hill, London, S.W. (*Solon-road, Brixton*)	Glas. U. & B.U.S.	1871
Douglas, John, B.A. (ROY. UN. I.), 111, Waterloo-crescent, Nottingham	Regent's Park	.. 1874
Douglas, John, Avondale, Hermosa-road, Teignmouth ..	Dublin ..	.. 1861
Dove, Henry Howe, Waltham Chase, Bishop's Waltham, S.O., Hants	.. ..	.. 1860
Dowen, Z. T., M.D. (U.S.), 22, Burton-road, Brixton, London, S.W. (*Wynne-road, Brixton*)	Metropolitan	.. 1873
Doxsey, Isaac, F.S.S., 186, The Grove, Camberwell, London, S.E.	Dublin ..	.. 1843
Drew, Joseph, 41, Magdalen-road, St. Leonard's-on-Sea ..	.. ..	.. 1845
Duncan, James, M.A. (ABER.), 3, Cleveland-parade, Darlington	Aberdeen & Edin.	1878
Dunckley, James, 54, Victoria-road, Clapham Common, London, S.W.	Accrington	.. 1849
Dunington, Henry, 12, West-square, St. George's-road, London, S.E.	Metropolitan	.. 1870
Dunkley, Henry, Eynsford, Kent	.. ..	.. 1883
Dunlop, J., 96, Great Russell-street, London, W.C. (*Jews' Society*)	Glasgow Univ..	.. 1863
Dunn, Charles Walter, Aldreth, Haddenham, Ely	.. ..	.. 1860
Dunn, Stephen, 7, Hickman-road, Sparkbrook, Birmingham	.. ..	.. 1841
Dunnett, George, Quinton, Birmingham (*Halesowen, Worc.*)	Metropolitan	.. 1876

Name and Postal Address.	College.	Ministry commenced
Dunster, Fred Wheaton, Churchgate-sreet, Soham	Metropolitan	1889
Dupée, Jesse, Laurel Villa, Southgate-road, Potter's Bar (*Potter's Bar*)	Metropolitan	1883
Durant, Thomas, 9, Templetown, Consett R.S.O., Co. Durham	Bap. Evan. Soc.	1862
Durbin, Frank, 9, Westcroft-terrace, Bideford	Metropolitan	1887
Durrant, Henry James, Ceylon House, Palmerston-road, Sparkbrook, Birmingham	Bristol	1883
Durrell, George, Beau Desert House, Leighton Buzzard	Bristol	1868
Duxbury, C., Woodstock	.. ..	1888
Dyer, Edward, The Grange, St. Vincent's-road, Southend-on-Sea	Metropolitan	1883
Dyer, Henry John, 1, St. Leonard's-road, Aldrington, West Brighton	Metropolitan	1876
Dyer, William John, 45, Newsome-road, Huddersfield	Metropolitan	1875
Dyson, Watson, West-street, Harrow-on-the-Hill (*Harrow-on-the-Hill*)	Bradford	1859
EARNEY, Henry, Whitsbury, near Salisbury	.. ..	1852
Easter, James, Swiss Cottage, Victoria-road, Diss	Metropolitan	1880
Edgerton, Arthur George, 15, Homefield-road, Chiswick	Metropolitan	1892
Edgerton, William Frew, Harlington, Hounslow (*Harlington*)	Metropolitan	1868
Edginton, Edwin, Henley-in-Arden, Birmingham	.. ..	1870
Edginton, Ernest, Ashley, Lymington	.. ..	1892
Edgley, G. T., 68, Selwyn-road, Plaistow, London, E. (*Barking-road Tabernacle, Plaistow*)	Metropolitan	1867
Edmonds, John, Sunnyside, Pelham-terrace, Gt. Grimsby	Metropolitan	1894
Edmondson, George, 83, Parkside-road, Bradford	.. ..	1867
Edmunds, Edwyn, 26, Cradock-street, Swansea	Pontypool	1884
Edwards, David Bowen, The Avenue, Brecon	Haverfordwest	1852
Edwards, David Oliver, Treffgarne R.S.O., Pem. (*Newton-pants*)	Carmarthen	1859
Edwards, Eliasaph, 9, Brick-avenue, Willowtown, Ebbw Vale R.S.O., Mon.	.. ..	1879
Edwards, Elijah John, 11, Laureston-place, Dover	Metropolitan	1872
Edwards, Evan, Springleton, Torquay	Pontypool	1838
Edwards, Frederic, B.A. (LON.), Harlow	Bris., Edin. Univ. & Reg. Pk.	1857
Edwards, George Philip, Evenjobb, Kington, Hereford	Metropolitan	1892
Edwards, Harri, Anstruther, Fife	Pontypool	1891
Edwards, Henry C., Newbridge-on-Wye R.S.O., Radnorshire	Pontypool	1892
Edwards, Hugh, Llanerchymedd R.S.O., Anglesey	.. ..	1889
Edwards, John, Haddenham, Thame	Pontypool	1883
Edwards, John, Ffynnon, Narberth, Pemb.	Haverfordwest	1848
Edwards, John, Glen View-terrace, Newbridge, Newport, Mon.	Pontypool	1891
Edwards, Thomas Llewellyn, 4, Richmond-road, Stockton-on-Tees	Metropolitan	1875
Edwards, Sylvanus Peter, 6, Bay View-terrace, Pwllheli	Pontypool	1871
Edwards, William, B.A. (LON.), D.D. (U.S.), *President*, The College, Cardiff	Pont. & Reg. Pk.	1872
Edwards, William, Berkerley House, Llandudno (*Conway*)	Llangollen	1882
Eland, Francis Greville, 9, Abercorn-street, Belfast (*Evangelist*)	.. ..	1891
Elliott, G. W., 129, Lincoln-road, Peterborough	Metropolitan	1894
Elliott, W. H., 6, Curzon-street, Maryport	Metropolitan	1873
Ellis, David Francis, Meirion House, Aberystwith	Pontypool	1871
Ellis, Herbert, M.A. (OXON.), Farsley, Leeds	Man. & Oxford Univ.	1890
Ellis, James Joseph, 119, Earlsfield-road, Wandsworth Common, London, S.W.	Metropolitan	1878
Elliston, William Delf, 30, Hockcliffe-road, Leighton Buzzard	Stepney	1856
Elsom, Sidney Jones, Yorkley, Lydney	.. ..	1887

Name and Postal Address.	College.	Ministry commenced
Elvey, Ralph Allsworth, Glen Roy, Bushey Hill-road, Camberwell, London, S.E. (*Arthur-street, Camberwell Gate*) ..	Regent's Park ..	1893
Emery, William, Rowton, Torquay	.. .. ..	1856
Emery, Wm. W. B., 12, Wellington-road, Harborne, Birmingham	Rawdon	1888
English, Amos, 124, Nightingale-road, Hitchin	.. .. ..	1862
Ennals, George Thomas, Mavisbank, Upminster, Romford	Metropolitan ..	1867
Ensoll, Robert, 45, Granville-road, Middlesborough	Metropolitan ..	1875
Etheridge, Benjamin Copeland, 156, Ramsden-road, Balham, London, S.W.	.. .. ..	1843
Etherington, William Duke, M.A. (CANTAB.), Belgrave-road, Torquay	Bris. & Camb. Univ. ..	1863
Evans, B., 46, Gadlys-road, Aberdare	Haverfordwest ..	1871
Evans, Benjamin, Rhuddlan R.S.O., Flintshire	Llangollen ..	1874
Evans, Benjamin Arberth, 7, Rose-terrace, Ashton-on-Ribble T.S.O., Preston	Manc. & Cardiff U. C. ..	1891
Evans, Daniel Ebenezer, 58, Holly-road, Handsworth, Birmingham	Metropolitan ..	1868
Evans, Daniel Philip, Queen-street, Llandovery R.S.O., Carm.	Bangor	1892
Evans, David, Newport, Mon.	Pontypool ..	1890
Evans, David Samuel, Bwlchysarnau, Rhayader	Manchester ..	1892
Evans, Edward, 8, Penrallt-road, Upper Bangor	Haverfordwest ..	1874
Evans, Edward Raven Hill, Swansea	Llangollen ..	1880
Evans, Elias, Claremont, Hill Top, Slaithwaite, Huddersfield	Pontypool ..	1879
Evans, Ernest Rowe, 14, Alfred-street, Neath	.. .. ..	1886
Evans, Evan Robert, Pontardawe, Swansea	Pontypool ..	1888
Evans, George, 13, Ruperra-street, Newport, Mon.	Haverfordwest ..	1893
Evans, George David, 3, Dart Villas, Totnes	Metropolitan ..	1863
Evans, Gomer, Brynllawen, Holyhead	Bangor	1894
Evans, Henry, 7, Victoria-terrace, Builth R.S.O., Breconshire	Manc. & Cardiff U.C.	1892
Evans, Henry J., Alma-street, Brynmawr R.S.O., Breconshire	Haverfordwest ..	1892
Evans, Hugh, 11, Pantdu-cottages, Penygroes, near Carnarvon	.. .. ..	1876
Evans, James, Millgate, near Rochdale	Manchester ..	1875
Evans, John, Eastcombe, Stroud	Haverfordwest ..	1871
Evans, John, Penylan, Springfield-road, Stoneygate, Leicester	Regent's Park ..	1890
Evans, John, Gough-road, Ystalyfera, near Swansea	.. .. ..	1844
Evans, John Arthur, Willow Town, Ebbw Vale R.S.O., Mon.	Haverfordwest ..	1888
Evans, John Jenkin, Glanrhydwilym, Clynderwen R.S.O., Pemb. (*Rhydwilym, Carm.*)	Haverfordwest ..	1889
Evans, John Lewis, Llanfihangel Nantbran, near Brecon ..	Haverfordwest ..	1861
Evans, John Rees, Llwynhendy, Llanelly, Carm.	Pontypool ..	1882
Evans, Joseph Mardy, Ferndale, R.S.O. Glam.	Pontypool ..	1872
Evans, Richard, Hengoed, Cardiff	Pontypool ..	1878
Evans, Richard, Sandringham Villa, Llanelly, Carm. ..	Accrington ..	1842
Evans, Richard, Farm Bed, Stourport	.. .. ..	1877
Evans, Rowland, Bryntirion, Daisy-hill, Manningham, Bradford	Manchester ..	1882
Evans, Thomas, Pontesbury, Shrewsbury	Haverfordwest ..	1861
Evans, Thomas, 1, Gordon-villas, Walton, Ipswich	Pontypool ..	1872
Evans, Thomas, Molleston House, Narberth, Pemb. (*Moleston*)	Haverfordwest ..	1879
Evans, Thomas Lodwig, 108, King's-road, Canton, Cardiff ..	Haverfordwest ..	1875
Evans, Thomas Towy, Blaina Gwent, Cwmtillery R.S.O., Mon. (*Abertillery*)	Pontypool ..	1882
Evans, Tom Valentine, Clydach, near Swansea	Pontypool ..	1882
Evans, William, Downton, Salisbury	Bristol	1876
Evans, William, 2, Lincoln-street, Leicester	Midland	1864
Evans, William, 73, Church-street, Tredegar	Llangollen ..	1881
Evans, William, Crosskeys, Newport, Mon.	Haverfordwest ..	1881
Evans, William, Rhoshirwaen, Carnarvon	Llangollen ..	1869
Evans, William Henry, Rattlesden, Bury St. Edmund's ..	.. .. ..	1861

Name and Postal Address.	College.	Ministry commenced
Everett, Arthur George, Woodland Villa, Clarkson-road, Wisbech	Metropolitan	1882
Everett, Edward Knight, The Grove, Eccles, Manchester		1869
Everett, Edwin, Markyate-street, Dunstable		1870
Everett, Geo., Pulham St. Mary, Harleston, Norfolk		1846
Evill, Reginald C., 18, Brondesbury-villas, Kilburn, London, N.W. (*Dawes-road, Fulham*)	Metropolitan	1893
Ewen, John, Althorpe, Tankerville-road, Streatham, London, S.W. (*Streatham*)	Bristol	1879
Ewens, William, Combmartin, Ilfracombe	Metropolitan	1876
Ewing, John William, M.A. (LON.), Sainte Marguerite, Grove-park, Camberwell, London, S.E. (*Rye-lane, Peckham*)	Metropolitan	1886
Eyres, John, 11, Britannia-road, Southsea	Bristol	1835
FAIRBAIRN, Robert Gordon, B.A. (ROY. UN. I.), 22, Clarence-square, Cheltenham	Bristol	1890
Farquhar, Joseph, M.A. (GLAS.), 3, Lylesland-terrace, Paisley	Glas. U. & B.U.S.	1887
Fawcett, James Richardson, 2, Woodlands-terrace, Borough-road East, Middlesborough	Rawdon	1883
Fayers, Arthur P., Yeadon, Leeds (*Rawdon*)	Regent's Park	1876
Feek, Julius Harnwell, Pershore, Worcestershire	Rawdon	1867
Felce, John Thomas, 7, Mount-street, Nuneaton		1861
Fellowes, Charles A., Eastleigh, Southampton	Metropolitan	1878
Felmingham, John, 15 Kyrle-road, New Wandsworth, London, S.W. (*Northcote-road, Wandsworth*)		1890
Feltham, Frederick Joseph, Cotham House, Clarendon Park-road, Leicester	Metropolitan	1878
Fergusson, A., Springland Villa, Drayton Green-road, Ealing, London, W.		1865
Fidler, William, Towcester		1869
Field, Henry Cowles, Market-square, Ampthill, Beds. (*Toddington*)	Metropolitan	1873
Field, John, 30, Lorrimore-square, Walworth, London, S.E.	Metropolitan	1864
Field, John, Ecton, Northampton		1864
Field, John Bryant, Back-street, Billesdon, Leicester	Metropolitan	1862
Field, Thomas Boulanger, Thorne House, Bacup	Metropolitan	1879
Figg, J. Thorold, Sandown Villas, Grove-road, Mitcham	Metropolitan	1891
Findlay, William Alexander, 201, Sydney-terrace, Oxford-road, Reading	Regent's Park	1888
Firks, Samuel H., Ramsey, Huntingdon	Regent's Park	1871
Firth, Alfred, Mansfield	Midland	1877
Fisk, Ebenezer Edward, 52, Holgate-terrace, York	Metropolitan	1868
Fisk, Thomas, High Cliffe, Kidderminster	Bristol	1862
Fisk, William, West End Villa, Rickmansworth		1857
Fitch, John James, Ivyholme, Leyland-road, Southport	Metropolitan	1876
Fitch, W., 34, King-street, Thetford	Metropolitan	1894
Flack, William, Wilton-square, Islington, London, N. (*Wilton-square, Islington*)		
Flatt, Frederick Joseph, Boxmoor, Hemel Hempstead	Metropolitan	1883
Fleming, Henry, Galashiels		1881
Fleming, Peter, 8, Burgess-terrace, Edinburgh		1894
Fleming, Robert Stewart, M.A. (GLAS.), 7, Manor-road, Beckenham (*Beckenham*)	Glasgow Univ.	1887
Flemington, Samuel, Upper Parkstone R.S.O., Dorset		1874
Fletcher, Henry Alais, Burwell, Cambridge	Metropolitan	1871
Fletcher, Joseph, 322, Commercial-road, London, E. (*Commercial-road*)	Midland	1868
Float, William Thomas., Douglas House, Longbridge-road, Barking		1877
Flory, Joseph, 12, Stanley-road, Manor-park, Essex		1837
Foote, William Evans, Victoria-road, Bridport	Bristol	1850

Name and Postal Address.	College.	Ministry commenced
Forbes, Finlay, Fishponds, Bristol	Bap. Th. In. Edin.	1848
Forbes, John Thomas, M.A. (GLAS.), 7, Royal-crescent, Edinburgh	Glas. & Edin. Unvs. & B.U.S.	1886
Ford, James, The Crescent, Bromsgrove	Rawdon	1882
Ford, Reuben Chambers, M.A. (EDIN.), New Heneage-street, Great Grimsby	Midland & Edin. Univ.	1888
Forth, Jacob Coupland, 317½, Humberstone-road, Leicester	Metropolitan	1865
Foster, John C., 37, Westbourne-rd, Forest Hill, London, S.E. (*Forest Hill*)	Metropolitan	1878
Foster, William Rands, 12 Flaxen-gate, Lincoln	Metropolitan	1885
Foston, Tom, Hathern, near Loughborough	Bristol	1864
Fowler, Charles John, West Row, Mildenhall S.O., Suffolk	Metropolitan	1885
Frame, Robert, 79, The Woodlands, Birkenhead	Manchester	1894
Francis, Edward, Cambridge Villa, Queen's-road, St. Thomas, Exeter	Bristol	1874
Francis, William Thomas, Penyparc, near Cardigan	Llangollen	1891
Frankland, Robert, Friston, Saxmundham	.. ..	1891
Freeman, George, Logan Bank, Beaconsfield-road, New Southgate, London, N. (*New Southgate*)	Metropolitan	1889
French, Benjamin, 95, North-street, Gosport	.. ..	1869
French, Frederic Goldsmith, 2, Quentin-road, Blackheath, London, S.E. (*High-road, Lee*)	Midland	1891
French, John Henry, 96, Hampton-road, Forest Gate, London, E. (*Forest Gate*)	Regent's Park	1882
Frimston, John, Glasfryn-terrace, Talysarn, Penygroes R.S.O., Carnarvonshire	Llangollen	1889
Frimston, Thomas, Llangefni R.S.O., Anglesey	Llangollen	1879
Frith, William, 91, Burgoyne-road, Harringay, London, N. (*Emmanuel, Harringay*)	.. ..	1861
Frost, John T., Houghton Regis, Dunstable	Metropolitan	1883
Frost, William E., Mount Pleasant, Avening, near Stroud	.. ..	1879
Fry, William, Bratton, Westbury, Wilts	.. ..	1871
Fuchs, Frederick C., Hurlstone Villa, Selly Park, Birmingham	Bristol	1894
Fuller, Frederick, Aylesbury-lodge, Rothsay-road, Bedford	.. ..	1868
Fullerton, William Young, Boscombe, Springfield-road, Leicester	Metropolitan	1879
GANGE, Edwin Gorsuch, F.R.A.S., Regent's Park Chapel, Park-square East, London, N.W. (*Regent's Park*)	Metropolitan	1863
Garden, John, 24, Elmstone-road, Fulham, London, S.W. (*Onslow, Brompton*)	Manchester	1884
Gardiner, Thomas, 1, Lanoweth-road, Penzance	Rawdon	1876
Garnon, Thomas, High-street, Fishguard, Pembrokeshire	Haverfordwest	1876
Gast, Philip, 12, Noel-street, Islington, London, N. (*Spencer-place, Goswell-road, Clerkenwell*)	Bristol	1858
Gathercole, Thomas George, Kimbolton, St. Neot's	Metropolitan	1870
Gaunt, M. Lister, Wendron-street, Helston	Rawdon	1893
Gawthrop, Benjamin, 91, Cardigan-terrace, Heaton, Newcastle-on-Tyne (*Byker*)	Rawdon	1894
Gay, Joseph, Birchcliffe, Hebden Bridge, *via* Manchester	Manchester	1894
Gay, William, Golcar, Huddersfield	.. ..	1872
Geale, John S., 19, York-villas, Prestonville, Brighton	Metropolitan	1872
Genders, John William, Park View House, Ilfracombe	Metropolitan	1859
George, Elias, The Croft, Ockbrook, Derby	Metropolitan	1876
George, Enos, 4, New-street, Llanelly New Dock, Carm.	Pontypool	1871
George, Evan, Argoed, Newport, Mon.	Pontypool	1879
George, John, Cinderford, Newnham	Pontypool	1862
George, Thomas William, 19, Queen-street, Neath (*Melincrythan*)	Bristol	1881
Gibb, Alexander Grant, M.A. (ABERDEEN), 5, Victoria-terrace, Limerick	Aber. & Edin. Us.	1892

Name and Postal Address.	College.	Ministry commenced.
Gibbon, Benjamin John, Rothay, Gordon-avenue, Southampton	Metropolitan	1892
Gibbon, Oscar Rees, 2 Trinity-place, Wellington, Som.	Metropolitan	1895
Gibbs, W. Leonard, 40, Arlington-road, Ealing, London, W. *(Ealing Dean)*	Metropolitan	1893
Gilbert, Edward, 243, Clarendon Park-road, Leicester (*Monk's Kirby*)		1881
Gill, William, Willingham, Cambs.		1865
Gillard, William, The Square, Uffculme, Cullompton	Metropolitan	1880
Gillmore, Horatio, 7, Ellenbro' Park, Weston-super-Mare		1862
Gilmore, John Dinnen, Brannoxtown, co. Kildare	Metropolitan	1883
Gimblett, Joseph, Blaina R.S.O., Mon.	Pontypool	1887
Glasgow, William, Tunstall Common, near Wickham Market		1865
Glaskin, John, High-street, Tenterden, Kent		1849
Glass, David, M.A. (EDIN.), *Classical Tutor*, The College, Rawdon, Leeds	Edin. U., B.U.S. & Reg. Park	1891
Gledhill, Morton, East Bank, Haslingden, Manchester	Manchester	1895
Glendening, Robert Ernest, Fife Park-villa, Elgin	Metropolitan	1884
Gliddon, William, Newhouse, Upottery, Honiton		1880
Glover, Richard, D.D. (EDIN.) 15, Westfield Park, Bristol	Ed. U. & King's & Pres. Colls., Lon.	1861
Goacher, William, Thaxted, Dunmow, Essex	Metropolitan	1877
Godfrey, John Rufus, Barlestone, Nuneaton	Midland	1871
Golding, William Randles, 155, Belle Vue-road, Leeds		1880
Goodchild, George, 4, Edinburgh-avenue, North-parade, Skegness, R.S.O. Lincs.	Metropolitan	1880
Gooding, Charles Denham, Burnham S.O., Essex	Metropolitan	1877
Goodman, William, B.A. (LON.), 7 Manor-terrace, Leigh-road, Highbury, London, N.	Stepney	1847
Goodman, William Ebenezer, 2, Nemoure-road, Acton, London, W.	Bradford	1851
Gordon, Alexander, M.A. (GLAS.), 26, Falkland-road, Egremont, Birkenhead	Glas. Univ.	1888
Gordon, Charles Leicester, Hatherleigh R.S.O., N. Devon	Metropolitan	1867
Gorham, William Henry, 16, Ravensbourne-terrace, South Shields		1892
Gould, G. P., M.A. (GLAS.), (*Tutor, Regent's Park College*), 47, Gloucester-road, London, N.W	Glas. & Berlin	1876
Gower, Harry F., Manvers Cottage, Bloomfield, Bath	Metropolitan	1883
Graham, Arthur, Pembury, Tunbridge Wells	Metropolitan	1886
Grant, Alfred James, Denford House, Atkins-road, Clapham Park, London, S.W. (*Barry-road, Dulwich*)		1875
Grant, John Hugh, Coalville, near Leicester	Metropolitan	1882
Grant, John King, "Northern Ensign" Office, Wick	Bradford	1859
Grant, Peter William, Inveraven Bank, Perth	St. And., Glas. U. & Theo. Acad.	1844
Grant, William, 22, Blackford-road, Edinburgh	Edin. U. & Free Church Coll.	1845
Gravell, Thomas, Cold Inn, near Tenby	Haverfordwest	1888
Gray, Archibald Campbell, Orange House, College-park, Lewisham, London, S.E.	Edin. Univ.	1856
Gray, Robert, Valentine-road, King's Heath, Birmingham	Rawdon	1874
Gray, Samuel, 15, Gladstone-terrace, Brighton		1873
Gray, William, 69, Clare-road, Halifax	Midland	1850
Green, Charles Richard, 60, Aubrey-street, Everton, Liverpool	Regent's Park	1878
Green, Samuel Gosnell, D.D. (U.S.), Northcourt, Mount Ephraim-road, Streatham, London, S.W.	Stepney	1843
Green, Samuel Walter, M.A. (LON.), (*Tutor, Regent's Park College*), Aldhurst, Leigham Court-road West, Streatham, London, S.W.	Rawdon	1878
Green, Thomas, Outwood, Redhill, Surrey		1864

Name and Postal Address.	College.	Ministry commenced
Greenhough, John Gershom, M.A. (LON.), Stoneygate-road, Leicester	Rawdon ..	.. 1869
Greening, Alfred Edward, 22, Wakefield-road, Stourton, Leeds	Bury ..	.. 1870
Greening, F. J., 10, York-terrace, Bury, Lancs.	.. .. ..	.. 1862
Greenwood, Edwin, Spa-street, Ossett R S.O., Yorks. ..	Rawdon ..	.. 1878
Greenwood, Thomas, 182, Bedford-hill, Balham, London, S.W. (*Ramsden-road, Balham*)	Metropolitan	.. 1878
Greer, Alexander, Great Broughton, Cockermouth	Metropolitan	.. 1874
Griffin, Henry Frank, 1, Petersfield, Cambridge	.. .. ..	.. 1868
Griffin, Richard Clark, Downside, Maurice-road, St Andrew's Park, Bristol	Bristol ..	.. 1895
Griffith, James, 12, Riles-road, Plaistow, London, E. ..	.. .. ..	.. 1859
Griffith, William, Brynarthur, Clynderwen R.S.O., Pembrokeshire (*Mynachlogddu*)	Carm. Pres.	.. 1867
Griffith, William Hussey, 4, Ardgowan-square, Greenock ..	Regent's Park	.. 1894
Griffiths, Caradoc, 1, Llanishen-street, Cathays, Cardiff ..	Haverfordwest ..	1883
Griffiths, Cornelius, Twinfield House, Easton-road, Bristol..	Pontypool	.. 1857
Griffiths, David, Pentyla, Aberavon R.O., Port Talbot, Glam.	Pontypool	.. 1864
Griffiths, George, Bryn Villa, Rhymney R.S.O., Mon. ..	Llangollen	.. 1884
Griffiths, James, 2, Clifton-street, Aberdare	Pontypool	.. 1882
Griffiths, James Simon, 28, Gladstone-street, Skipton-in-Craven	Llangollen	.. 1892
Griffiths, John, New-street, Llanidloes, Mont...	Pontypool	.. 1876
Griffiths, John, Plas Newydd, Llanfairfechan R.S.O., Carn.	Llangollen	.. 1878
Griffiths, John Edward, Skewen, Neath	Llangollen	.. 1870
Griffiths, John Josiah, Laura Villa, Bridgnorth	Cardiff ..	.. 1894
Griffiths, Philip, 2, Heyworth-road, Clapton, London, N.E...	Stepney & H'wst	1850
Griffiths, Thomas, Scranton Villa, Castle-street, Abertillery R.S.O., Mon.	Haverfordwest ..	1878
Griffiths, Thomas Gough, Alfred-road, Sutton, Surrey (*Cheam*)	Haverfordwest ..	1862
Griffiths, W. B., Cefncoedycymmer, Merthyr Tydvil.. ..	Pontypool	.. 1881
Grigg, Henry T., 41, Marmora-road, Honor Oak, London, S.E.	.. .. ..	.. 1850
Griggs, David Barnes, 51 St. George's-sq., Portsea, Portsmouth	Metropolitan	.. 1894
Gunn, Hugh, 1, Lugar-street, Coatbridge	.. .. ..	.. 1886
Guyton, Robert Firth, 36, High-street, Huntingdon	Bristol ..	.. 1871
HACKING, James, West Villa, Brighton-road, Horley, Surrey (*Southminster*)	.. .. ..	.. 1892
Hackney, Walter, M.A. (OXON.), 275, Birchfield-road, Handsworth, Birmingham, and Barnt Green S.O., Worcestershire	Metro. & Ox. Un.	1878
Haddock, Edgar, Barking Tye, near Stowmarket	.. .. ..	.. 1876
Hadler, Edward Samuel, Fivehead, Taunton	Metropolitan	.. 1879
Hadler, John Robert, 13 Maple-street, Sheerness	Metropolitan	.. 1868
Haggart, F. C., 40, Petteril-street, Carlisle	Regent's Park	.. 1882
Hagen, John Thomas, Viewfield-place, Dunfermline ..	Bury ..	.. 1870
Haggett, John S., 4, Moreland-terrace, Gosport	Western Congl.	1885
Haggis, Edward, Eastnor, Melville-street, Ryde, Isle of Wight	.. .. ..	.. 1889
Haig, James, 15, Broughton-place, Edinburgh..	Edin.U.&Theo.I.	1856
Haigh, William, Steep-lane, Sowerby Bridge	.. .. ..	.. 1864
Hailstone, William George, Edenhurst, Hamilton-road, Reading	Metropolitan	.. 1870
Haines, William Winston, 19, Park-avenue, Wood Green, London, N. (*Wood Green*)	Metropolitan	.. 1874
Hall, Alfred, Baydonfield, Penydarren Park, Merthyr Tydvil	Metropolitan	.. 1881
Hall, Alfred B., Woodland Villa, Meopham, Gravesend ..	.. .. ..	.. 1873
Hall, Joseph Greves, 12, East-street, St. Neots	.. .. ..	.. 1864
Hall, Richard, B.A. (LON.), 14, Warwick-row, Coventry ..	Stepney ..	.. 1846
Hall, Simon, Congo-terrace, Hindley-green, Wigan	.. .. ..	.. 1854
Hambly, Joseph Whendon, 69, Oakleigh-road, Clayton, Bradford	Rawdon ..	.. 1881

Name and Postal Address.	College.	Ministry commenced
Hamilton, John Miller, London-road, Lowestoft	Regent's Park	1883
Hamilton, William, 7, Louvaine-road, New Wandsworth, London, S.W. (*York-road, Battersea*)	Metropolitan	1876
Hancock, Charles, Sturry, Canterbury	.. ..	1859
Hancocks, Thomas, Albert-road, East Cliff, Ramsgate	Metropolitan	1877
Handford, Reuben F., Beacon-road, Loughborough	Rawdon	1878
Hanger, Thomas, 9, Liston-road, Clapham, London, S.W. (*Grafton-square, Clapham*)	.. ..	1866
Hanson, John, Henshaw, Yeadon, Leeds	Bradford	1843
Hanson, Walter, 34, Salmon-street, South Shields	Bradford	1859
Harcourt, James, 160, Rockleigh, London-road, Leicester	.. ..	1843
Harcus, Henry, Ronaldshaw Villa, Ayr	.. ..	1843
Hardin, Henry, Montacute S.O., Somerset	Regent's Park	1861
Harding, R., Haslemere S.O., Surrey	.. ..	1861
Hardy, Charles Millice, B.A. (LON.), Lemsford-road, St. Albans	Regent's Park	1881
Hargreaves, John James, 84, Sussex-street, Lower Broughton, Manchester	Rawdon	1893
Harmer, Augustus Arthur, 2, Beulah-road, Thornton-heath, Surrey (*Evangelist*)	Metropolitan	1880
Harper, John, Newbury Park, Ledbury	Rawdon	1864
Harrald, Joseph William, 7, Beauchamp-road, Grange-road, Upper Norwood, London, S.E.	Metropolitan	1870
Harries, Henry, Treherbert, Pontypridd	Pontypool	1860
Harries, John Dyfnold, Bonymaen, Swansea (*Llansamlet*)	Haverfordwest	1878
Harries, Thomas, Garth R.S.O., Breconshire	Pontypool	1889
Harries, Thomas C., Glyn Neath, Neath	Haverfordwest	1893
Harries, W. E., Penyfai, Bridgend, Glam.	Manchester	1894
Harries, William, 11, Cavan-row, Maesteg, Bridgend	Haverfordwest	1874
Harrington, Joseph, Manorbier R.S.O., Pem.	Regent's Park	1879
Harris, George, Rishangles, near Eye, Suffolk	.. ..	1845
Harris, George H., 21, Bedford-grove, Eastbourne	Metropolitan	1885
Harris, William, 4, Park-lane, Trecynon, Aberdare	Haverfordwest	1855
Harris, William Frederick, 61, Wilson-street, Derby	Metropolitan	1879
Harris, William Herbert, 1, Stanley-terrace, Preston	Q. Col. Liverpool	1879
Harris, William J., 21, Bedford-grove, Eastbourne	Metropolitan	1882
Harrison, Arthur, 18, Wesley-terrace, Doals, Bacup	Manchester	1875
Harrison, John, Sherwood House, Derby-road, Portsmouth	Midland	1861
Harrison, John, Llanidloes-road, Newtown, Mont. (*Kerry*)	.. ..	1865
Harry, Lewis Thomas, 117, Chester-road, Kidderminster	Bristol	1892
Hart, Josiah, Stotfold, Baldock	Metropolitan	1869
Harvey, John Lamb, 40, Ravensdown, Berwick	Glas. U. & B.U.S.	189[illegible]
Haslam, John, Turton Hall, Gildersome, Leeds	Rawdon	1862
Hasler, Joseph, 41, East-street, Andover, Hants	Bradford	1857
Haste, Alfred George, Old Park View, Providence-road, Walkley, Sheffield	Metropolitan	1889
Hatton, George E., 31, Beulah-road, Tunbridge Wells	.. ..	1867
Hawker, George, Broadlands, Anson-road, Tufnell-park, London, N. (*Camden-road*)	Bristol	1877
Hawkes, Samuel, 6, Sandon-road, Seacombe, Liverpool	Regent's Park	1862
Hayden, Thomas, Gillingham, Dorset	.. ..	1860
Hayman, Jabez John, Hope House, New Southgate, London, N.	Metropolitan	1875
Haynes, Samuel, St. Ives, Hunts	.. ..	1860
Haynes, William B., 81, Grosvenor Park, Camberwell, London, S.E. (*Camberwell New-road*)	Metropolitan	1874
Hazelrigg, G., Leicester	.. ..	1849
Hazzard, T. J., 52, Addington-road, Bow, London, E. (*Black-thorn-street, Bow Common*)	.. ..	1875
Head, Albert T., Oxford Villa, Ford, Devonport	.. ..	1873
Head, Theophilus G., Millbourn-lane, Esher	.. ..	1876

Name and Postal Address.	College.	Ministry commenced.
Heap, John, 30, Fulham-place, Harrow-road, London, W. (*Westbourne Park, Paddington*)	Midland ..	.. 1895
Heath, John, 6, Brunshaw-road, Burnley	Mid.and ..	.. 1890
Heath, Noah, Buckhurst-hill S.O., Essex	Metropolitan	.. 1865
Hemington, Charles, Castle Grounds, Devizes	.. ..	.. 1857
Henderson, Ebenezer, 21, Victoria-road, Clapham, London, S.W. (*Victoria, Wandsworth-road*)	Metropolitan	.. 1873
Henderson, Hugh, 6, Hartley-avenue, Compton, Plymouth	Glas. U. & Bris..	.. 1886
Henderson, W. T., 36, Dunsmure-road, Stoke Newington, London, N.	Stepney ..	.. 1851
Henderson, William John, B.A. (LON.), *Joint President*, The College, Stokes Croft, Bristol	Rawdon ..	.. 1868
Henman, Sydney James, Hawkhurst	Regent's Park	.. 1891
Henson, Thomas, 92, Woodland-terrace, Old Charlton S.O., Kent (*East Plumstead*)	.. ..	.. 1854
Herbert, Job, Porthyrhyd, Carmarthen	Pontypool	.. 1889
Hern, G. Roberts, Ashleigh-road, Barnstaple	Bristol ..	.. 1892
Herries, Robert, 31, Southey-place, Bradford	Metropolitan	.. 1877
Heselton, James Tranmer, Elm-villas, Normanton, Yorks ..	Rawdon ..	.. 1885
Hester, Giles, 83, Charlotte-road, Sheffield	Stepney ..	.. 1858
Hetherington, William, 5, Addison-road, Walthamstow (*Wood-street, Walthamstow*)	Metropolitan	.. 1874
Hewitt, Charles, 12, York-terrace, Nag's Head-road, Ponder's End	Metropolitan	.. 1865
Hewlett, Alfred, Wollaston, Wellingborough	Metropolitan	.. 1877
Hewson, John Morris, 4, The Avenue, Acre-lane, Brixton, London, S.W. (*Baptist Total Abstinence Association*) ..	New Coll., Edin.	1861
Heynes, George Hugo, 8, Marmora-road, Honor Oak, London, S.E. (*Honor Oak*)	Bristol ..	.. 1883
Heywood, Thomas, 47, London-road, Grays	Metropolitan	.. 1892
Heyworth, Richard, 34, New Crescent, Newchurch, Manchester (*Edgeside*)	.. ..	.. 1882
Hider, George, Great Sampford, Braintree	.. ..	.. 1864
Higgins, William, Haddenham, Ely	Metropolitan	.. 1877
Hiley, David John, 45, Alma-road, Clifton, Bristol	Metropolitan	.. 1882
Hill, Charles, Brockford, Stonham, Suffolk (*Stoke Ash*) ..	.. ..	.. 1845
Hill, George, M.A. (OXON.), Clare Valley Lodge, The Park, Nottingham	Met. & Oxn. Un.	1870
Hill, William, 9, St. Julian's-road, Kilburn, London, N.W. (*Baptist Missionary Society*)	Midland ..	.. 1856
Hillman, John, 51, St. Thomas's-road, South Hackney, London, N.E. (*Hampden, Hackney*)	Metropolitan	.. 1867
Hilton, Edward, Prospect House, Smalley, near Derby ..	.. ..	.. 1872
Hirst, George, Arnsby, via Leicester	Rawdon ..	.. 1880
Hirst, Sim, Lade Braes Villas, St. Andrews	Rawdon ..	.. 1881
Hitchon, George, Rochdale-road, Heywood	Bradford	.. 1854
Hobbs, Charles, High Wycombe	Bristol ..	.. 1882
Hobbs, Henry Vincent, Burnham, R.S.O., Somerset	Bristol ..	.. 1876
Hobbs, Walter, Haddon, Salter's Hill, Norwood, London, S.E. (*Gipsy-road, West Norwood*)	Metropolitan	.. 1875
Hobbs, William Ayers, 16 Selborne-place, Minehead R.S.O., Somerset	.. ..	.. 1859
Hobby, Edward Arthur, James-street, Macclesfield	Metropolitan	.. 1888
Hockey, John S., Henfield R.S.O., Sussex	Metropolitan	.. 1870
Hodge, James, Ballykeel, Dromara, co. Down	.. ..	.. 1891
Hodges, Samuel, Bristol-road, Nailsworth, Stroud	.. ..	.. 1845
Hogbin, Frederick Albert, Normanhurst, York-road, Southend-on-Sea	Metropolitan	.. 1888
Holden, Frederick Cooper, 42, Wallwood-street, Burdett-road, Limehouse, London, E. (*Pekin-street, Limehouse*)	.. ..	.. 1868
Holden, Jonathan, Tillicou try R.S.O., Clackmannanshire ..	Manchester	.. 1890
Holland, Burdwood J., Spaldwick, Huntingdon	Metropolitan	.. 1868

Name and Postal Address.	College.	Ministry commenced
Holroyd, William, 159, North-road, St. Helen's, Lancs.	Manchester	1888
Holyoak, Thomas Henry, 27, Greame-street, Alexandra-park Manchester	Bristol	1865
Honour, David, 18, Shardeloes-road, New Cross, London, S.E. (*Octavius-street, Deptford*)	Metropolitan	1867
Hood, Carey, 124, Lister-lane, Halifax	Metropolitan	1876
Hook, John, Garway, Ross, Herefordshire		1867
Hooper, George Downs, Oakthorpe, Hart Hill, Luton	King's Coll. Lon.	1860
Hopkin, John Salem, Gorseinon R.S.O., Glam.	Haverfordwest	1888
Hopkins, D. W., Rugby-road, Neath	Llangollen	1888
Hopkins, Daniel D., Prospect-pl., Pontardulais R.S.O., Glam.	Pont. & Cdf. U.C.	1888
Hopkins, Esaiah, Taunton-road, Ashton-under-Lyne	Pont. & Reg. Pk.	1893
Hopkins, John G., Caerphilly, Cardiff	Pont. & Cdf. U.C.	1890
Horn, James, 15, Turner-street, Coatham, Redcar	Rawdon	1868
Horne, John, High-street, Cullompton	Horton	1858
Horne, John, 228, Meadow-park-street, Glasgow	Metropolitan	1886
Horton, William, 67, Sydenham-road, Croydon		1876
Houghton, Charles, 3, Burns-villas, Whitefriars-road, King's Lynn	Nottm. Cong.	1880
Houston, Robert Lyle, Townbank-road, Ulverston	Glas. U. & B.U.S.	1894
Howard, Ernest Henry, 30, Summerhill-road, South Tottenham (*West Green, Tottenham*)	Metropolitan	1893
Howard, Samuel, Downham Market, Norfolk	Bristol	1872
Howarth, Richard, Wilmer-villas, Heaton, Bradford	Manchester	1877
Howe, George, 102, Burnt Ash-hill, Lee, London, S.E.	Bristol	1840
Howells, David, Penrhiwceiber, Mountain Ash	Manchester	1885
Howells, David Christmas, Rose Cottage, Maesteg, Bridgend	Pontypool	1892
Howes, John, 10, Whitefriars-road, Hastings		1869
Hudgell, George, Oriel-villa, Bloomfield-avenue, Bath		1863
Hudgell, Philip Augustus, 5 Elm Tree-terrace, Uttoxeter-road, Derby	Metropolitan	1889
Hughes, B., B.A. (U.S.), North-road, Milford Haven	Rochester, U.S.A.	1876
Hughes, D. E., Llanidloes R.S.O., Montgomery (*Cwmbelan*)		1882
Hughes, Daniel Hugh, Machynlleth		1889
Hughes, David, Maesteg, Bridgend	Llangollen	1881
Hughes, E., Fraserburgh	Manchester	1892
Hughes, Frederick Charles, 68, Tremadoc-road, Clapham, London, S.W. (*Borough-road, Southwark*)	Bristol	1887
Hughes, George, 9, St. Mary-street, Cardigan	Pontypool	1869
Hughes, Henry, 37, Ritson-street, Briton Ferry	Llangollen	1879
Hughes, Hugh, Llanaelhaiarn, Chwilog R.S.O., Carnarvonshire	Llangollen	1870
Hughes, James Owen, Pear Tree-pl., Abersychan, Pontypool	Pont. & Cdf. U.C.	1886
Hughes, James Samuel, 20, Cliffe View, Stockton Heath, Warrington (*Hill Cliff*)	Manchester	1877
Hughes, John, Nantymoel R.S.O., Glam.	Pontypool	1876
Hughes, John David, Pontygwaith, Ferndale R.S.O., Glam.	Llangollen	1882
Hughes, John Henry, 91, Bedford-road, Bootle, Liverpool	Llangollen	1884
Hughes, Thomas, Llanddona, Beaumaris, Anglesea		
Hughes, Thomas Tower, Austin-street, Mountain Ash	Haverfordwest	1890
Hughes, William, Congo Institute, Colwyn Bay R.S.O., Denbighshire	Llangollen	1882
Hughes, William, 246, Waterloo-street, Oldham	Manchester	1877
Hughes, William, Middleston Moor, Spennymoor, co. Durham		1874
Hughes, William, 13, Heathfield-avenue, Crewe	Llangollen	1890
Hull, Charles Summerford, Tilehouse-street, Hitchin	Metropolitan	1889
Hulme, John, 96, Anderton-road, Sparkbrook, Birmingham	Rawdon	1872
Humby, Leonard, Shefford R.S.O., Beds.	Metropolitan	1881
Humphreys, Benjamin, Felinfoel, Llanelly, Carm.	Llangollen	1878
Humphreys, George Ward, B.A. (LON.), Wellington, Somerset	Bristol	1857
Humphreys, J. A., Tynewydd, Ogmore-vale R.S.O., Glam.	E. Lond. Inst.	1891
Humphreys, James W., Llanwrtyd R.S.O., Breconshire	Pontypool	1888

Name and Postal Address	College.	Ministry commenced
Humphreys, John David Thomas, Packington-road, Ashby-de-la-Zouch	Llangollen ..	1891
Humphreys, Richard Machno, 15, Coldstream-terrace, Llanelly, Carm.	Llangollen ..	1877
Humphreys, Thomas, Cwmaman, Aberdare	Haverfordwest ..	1868
Humphreys, Thomas, Ferndale, Pontypridd	.. .. ..	1882
Hunt, Horace Augustus, Earls Barton, Northampton ..	.. .. ..	1886
Hunter, R. M., Beecham-road, Reading	Metropolitan ..	1895
Hunter, Thomas George, 26, Hallfield-road, Bradford ..	Rawdon	1894
Hunter, William J., Preston Villa, Wemyssfield, Kirkcaldy ..	Rawdon	1884
Huntley, John, Shunem-villa, Bath	.. .. ..	1860
Hussey, David, Milford House, Abertillery R.S.O., Mon. ..	Haverfordwest ..	1877
Huxham, Richard Ash, 15, Childer-road, Stowmarket ..	.. .. ..	1842
IBBERSON, William Henry, 53, Granville-terrace, Frizinghall, Bradford	Bury	1868
Ince, Edward George, 15, Lucretia-road, Lower Kennington-lane, London, S.E.	Metropolitan ..	1879
Ingram, Christopher Austin, New Romney S.O., Kent ..	Metropolitan ..	1875
Ingrem, Charles, Arnewood, Griffiths-road, South Wimbledon (*Wimbledon*)	Metropolitan ..	1880
Isaac, Morris, Bryn Glas Villa, Cadoxton, Cardiff	Haverfordwest ..	1890
JACKMAN, George Henry Francis, Coggeshall, Kelvedon ..	Metropolitan ..	1889
Jackson, Edward Hall, 38, Broad Bank, Louth, Lincs. ..	.. .. ..	1861
Jackson, Forbes, M.A. (GLAS.), Reading	Glas. U., B.U.S., & Bristol ..	1885
Jackson, Frederick Arthur, Holme View, West Parade, Lincoln	Metropolitan ..	1887
Jackson, John, Worstead, near Norwich	Bury	1873
Jackson, John, Scottiswoode House, Sevenoaks	Metropolitan ..	1863
James, Benjamin, Cwmtwrch, near Swansea	Haverfordwest ..	1884
James, Benjamin Owen, 21, Verig-street, Manselton, Swansea	Pontypool ..	1894
James, David, Walk Villa, Llandilo, Carmarthen	Llangollen ..	1872
James, Frank, 16, Cicely-road, Peckham, London, S.E. (*Peckham Park-road, Peckham*)	Metropolitan ..	1887
James, George, Park-street, Bridgend	Haverfordwest ..	1863
James, George Howard, 4, Gorsey-road, Nottingham	Regent's Park ..	1881
James, Henry, Duar Villa, Llanybyther, Carmarthenshire (*Aberduar*)	Pontypool ..	1880
James, Isaac, Ruthin R.S.O., Denbighshire	Pontypool ..	1864
James, Isaac, Bradley-road, Wrexham	Llangollen ..	1885
James, Ivor Hael, 88, Manchester-road, Heywood	Haverfordwest ..	1886
James, Jason, Penydarren, Merthyr Tydvil	.. .. ..	1885
James, Jeremiah, Pontardulais R.S.O., Glam.	Llangollen ..	1865
James, Morgan, Bedwas, via Cardiff	Pontypool ..	1868
James Owen Waldo, Blaenclydach, Llwynypia R.S.O., Glam.	Llangollen ..	1865
James, Thomas, Painscastle, Erwood R.S.O., Breconshire ..	Llangollen ..	1884
James, Thomas Gwynfab, Tydu, near Newport, Mon. (*Bassaleg*)	Pont. & Cardiff U. C. ..	1890
James, William Ingli, Ponthir, Newport, Mon.	Haverfordwest ..	1887
Jardine, Alexander, Drummond, Jerrettspass, Newry (*Pontz Pass*)	.. .. ..	1891
Jarman, George, Knowle, Bristol	Bristol	1868
Jasper, James Edward, Fernilea, Clifton-road, Wallington, Surrey (*Wallington*)	Metropolitan ..	1880
Jeffcoat, George Dean, 6 Jackson-avenue, Ilkeston R.S.O., Derbyshire	Midland	1895
Jefferson, John, Lime Grove, Rawtenstall, Manchester ..	Accrington ..	1849
Jeffrey, Robert Foster, 9, Connaught-road, Folkestone ..	Metropolitan ..	1874
Jenkins, David Rhys, Brynheulog, Wainfelin-road, Pontypool	Pontypool ..	1867

Name and Postal Address.	College.	Ministry commenced
Jenkins, David Witton, Marsh, Huddersfield (*Salendine Nook*)	Manchester	1881
Jenkins, Edwin William, Carey-cottage, Black-hill R.S.O., Co. Durham	Haverfordwest	1878
Jenkins, Henry, 148, Twynrodyn, Merthyr Tydvil	Rawdon	1890
Jenkins, J., Pentyrch, Cardiff	Haverfordwest	1890
Jenkins, James, Castle Hill, Newport, Pemb.	Haverfordwest	1852
Jenkins, Jenkin, Gilfach Goch, near Bridgend, Glam.	..	1866
Jenkins, John, Prendergast, Haverfordwest	Haverfordwest	1871
Jenkins, John Onfel, Shelley House, Risca, Newport, Mon.	Llangollen	1880
Jenkins, Rhys, Monsal Villas, High-street, Old Basford, Nottingham	Pontypool	1887
Jenkins, W., Buckley, Chester	..	1873
Jenner, Harry, Waterbeach, Cambridge	Metropolitan	1893
Jennings, Daniel, 18 West-sreet, Stratford-on-Avon	..	1839
Jermine, Thomas, 5, Bethel-terrace, Tredegar, Mon.	Haverfordwest	1866
John, David, Carrington-street, Kettering	Llangollen	1892
John, Jacob, Ambleston, Treffgarne R.S.O., Pemb. (*Little Newcastle*)	Haverfordwest	1885
John, John, Llanbrynmair, Mont.	Llangollen	1878
John, Owen, Ponthenry, Llanelly, Carm.	Haverfordwest	1868
John, Richard, Maesteg-road, Tondu, Bridgend, Glam.	Pontypool	1883
John, Theophilus, Brynsiriol, Wolf's Castle, Haverfordwest (*Blaenllyn*)	Haverfordwest	1873
John, Thomas, Llanpumpsaint R.S.O., Carm. (*Ffynnonhenry*)	Haverfordwest	1860
John, Thomas Pandy, Barry Dock, Glam.	Haverfordwest	1883
John, W. J., Glanyrafon, Gowerton, Swansea	E. London Inst.	1885
John, William, 119, Woodfield-street, Morriston, Swansea	..	1855
Johns, Alfred E., Landsdown, Newport, I.W.	Metropolitan	1890
Johns, James, Pencoed-terrace, Blaenavon, Mon.	Haverfordwest	1874
Johns, John Syllio, Hope Villa, Bridgend	Haverfordwest	1882
Johns, Roger Owen, 18, Queensdown-road, Clapton, London, N.E. (*Dalston Junction*)	Pont. & Reg. Pk.	1888
Johnson, A. E., Ibstock, Ashby-de-la-Zouch	Metropolitan	1872
Johnson, Alfred, 58, Bishop-street, Whalley Range, Manchester	Bristol	1878
Johnson, C. T., 38, Kimberley Park-road, Falmouth	Metropolitan	1868
Johnson, Francis, Usk, Newport, Mon.	Pontypool	1879
Johnson, John, Pound-lane, Isleham, Soham (*Barton Mills*).	..	1874
Johnston, J. Bell, M.A. (Edin.), Galashiels	Edin. U. & Pres. Theo. Hall	1887
Johnson, John E., 9, Winifred-road, Manor Park, Essex (*Bedfont, Middlesex*)	..	1880
Jones, Alfred Emlyn, Hascombe Villa, Warwick-road, New Barnet (*New Barnet*)	Regent's Park	1880
Jones, Alfred Thomas, Emlyn House, Morden-road, Maindee, Newport, Mon.	..	1876
Jones, Christopher George, Riddlesay, Kirkby Stephen	..	1888
Jones, D., Lwydcoed, Aberdare		
Jones, D. C., Cwmpark, Treorky R.S.O., Glam.	Haverfordwest	1876
Jones, Daniel, Whitland, Carm.	Haverfordwest	1885
Jones, Daniel Leonard, 4, Park-terrace, Oxford	Bristol	1890
Jones, David Havart, Nantyffin, Ystrad-gynlais, Swansea	..	1867
Jones, David S., Beaufort R.S.O., Mon.	E. Lond. Inst.	1890
Jones, Dewi Bevan, Caerleon, Newport, Mon.	Pontypool	1865
Jones, Edmund Edward, Greenfield House, Pencoed, near Bridgend	..	1850
Jones, Edward, Milford Cottage, Maesteg R.S.O., Glam.	Haverfordwest	1860
Jones, Edward, Ivy Cottage, Castle-street, Maesteg R.S.O., Glam.	Llangollen	1877
Jones, Emmanuel Lewis, 3, Highfield-place, St. Paul's, Llanelly, Carm.	Haverfordwest	1880

Name and Postal Address.	College.	Ministry commenced
Jones, Evan Evans, Rhosybol, Anglesey	Llangollen ..	1875
Jones, Evan Kenffig, Ael-y-bryn, Brymbo, Wrexham ..	Pont. & Cardiff U.	1889
Jones, Evan Talfryn, Llwynypia R.S.O., Glam.	Llangollen ..	1881
Jones, Frederick A., 23, Douglas-road, Canonbury, London, N. (*Cross-street, Islington*)	Metropolitan ..	1878
Jones, G. H., Sandy	Regent's Park ..	1883
Jones, Henry Powell, 10, Nixon-villas, Merthyr Vale R.S.O., Glam.	.. .. ..	1884
Jones, Hugh, Blaenywaen, St. Dogmell's, Cardigan	Pontypool ..	1881
Jones, Hugh, Glanamman R.S.O. Carm.	Bangor	1894
Jones, Isaac, 41, Dyffryn-street, Ferndale, Pontypridd ..	Llangollen ..	1869
Jones, J. D., Prospect House, Pembroke Dock	Haverfordwest ..	1876
Jones, J. M., Newbridge, Newport, Mon.	Haverfordwest ..	1876
Jones, J. R., Springfield Villa, Pontypridd, Glam.	Llangollen ..	1866
Jones, James L., Glyncorwg, Cymmer R.S.O., Glam. ..	Haverfordwest ..	1876
Jones, James Albert, 14, Henri-street, Peterborough	Midland	1847
Jones, James Young, Hendy, Pontardulais R.S.O., Glam. ..	Llangollen ..	1875
Jones, John, 4, Glyn-terrace, Llantrissant, Glam.	Pontypool ..	1868
Jones, John, 2, Mont-villas, Llandrindod Wells	Pontypool ..	1847
Jones, John Arthur, Loughton S.O., Essex (*Loughton*) ..	Regent's Park ..	1885
Jones, John Chatwin, M.A. (GLAS.), Charnwood, Spalding..	Mid. & Glasgow	1846
Jones, John Gwyndud, Eirianfa, Penrhyndeudraeth, Merioneth	.. .. ..	1862
Jones, John Haslam, 13, Paget-road, Great Yarmouth ..	Bristol	1885
Jones, John Lewis, Glynceiriog, Ruabon	Pontypool ..	1880
Jones, John Samuel, St. David's R.S.O., Pemb.	.. .. ..	1887
Jones, Joseph, Llandyssil, Carm...	Haverfordwest ..	1888
Jones, Morgan Howell, Talbont, Llanrwst R.S.O., Denbighshire	Bangor	1893
Jones, Morgan Humphrey, Watts Town, Porth R.S.O., Glam. (*Ystrad*)	Haverfordwest ..	1872
Jones, Moses, Llandyfan, Llandilo R.S.O., Carm.	Llangollen ..	1873
Jones, Owen, Broadway Villa, Cowbridge, Glam.	Llangollen ..	1875
Jones, Peter, 10, Rockfield-road, Stanley Park, Liverpool ..	Bangor	1893
Jones, Robert, Rydal House, Sudbury, Suffolk	Rawdon	1885
Jones, Robert, Llanllyfni, Penygroes R.S.O., Carnarvonshire	.. .. ..	1832
Jones, Robert Henry, St. Clear's, Carm.	Llangollen ..	1878
Jones, Rhys B., 3, Marsh-street, Llanelly, Carm.	Pontypool ..	1893
Jones, Samuel, Claremont, Camden-road, Brecon	Haverfordwest ..	1880
Jones, Samuel, 23a, Darley-street, Farnworth R.S.O., Lancashire	Metropolitan ..	1888
Jones, Silvanus, Knelstone, Gower, Swansea	Haverfordwest ..	1872
Jones, Stephen, 17, Belmont-terrace, Aberaman, Aberdare ..	Pontypool ..	1861
Jones, Sydney Jenkins, 47, The Elms, Prince's-park, Liverpool	Metropolitan ..	1890
Jones, T. T., 7, Longcross-street, Roath, Cardiff	Haverfordwest ..	1881
Jones, Theophilus, Halkin-street, Flint	.. .. ..	1871
Jones, Thomas, 3, Highland-place, Aberdare	Pontypool ..	1869
Jones, Thomas, 69 Endwell-road, Brockley, London, S.E. (*New Cross-road, Deptford*)	.. .. ..	1881
Jones, Thomas, 5, Little Heath Villa, Old Charlton S.O., Kent (*Queen-street, Woolwich*)	Manchester ..	1877
Jones, Thomas Decimus, Pantydwr, Rhayader (*Nantgwyn*)..	Llangollen ..	1876
Jones, Thomas Idwal, 44, High-street, Llanelly, Carm. ..	Llangollen ..	1890
Jones, Watkin, 16, Gething-street, Aberavon T.S.O., Port Talbot	Metropolitan ..	1894
Jones, William, Hope House, Hebden Bridge, via Manchster	.. .. ..	1882
Jones, William, 67, Havod-terrace, Swansea	.. .. ..	1852
Jones, William, 1, Windsor-place, Treharris R.S.O., Glam...	Llangollen ..	1872
Jones, William, 5, Brynderwyn-road, Maindee, Newport, Mon.	Pontypool ..	1865
Jones, William, Alltgrug-road, Ystalyfera, Swansea	Llangollen ..	1890
Jones, William Aerus, 3, Fair View-terrace, Merthyr Tydvil	Llangollen ..	1887
Jones, William Barker, Penycae, Ruabon	Pontypool ..	1889
Jones, William Corden, 146, Acre-lane, Brixton, London, S.W.	Metropolitan ..	1866

Name and Postal Address.	College.	Ministry commenced
Jones, William Gwynfi, Commercial-street, Abergwynfi R.S.O., Glam.	Pontypool	1883
Jones, William Henry, Llanfyllin (Mont.), near Oswestry	.. ..	1888
Jones, William Lewis, Lord's Hill, Minsterley, Salop	Pontypool	1879
Jones, William Rufus, 2, Elm Tree-avenue, West Bridgford, Nottingham	Pontypool	1885
Jones, William Trevor, 9, Rope Walk-road, Llanelly, Carm.	Llangollen	1889
Jones-Miller, N.T., Hillsley, New Alma-road, Southampton	Metropolitan	1877
Joseph, Charles, Teesdale, St. David's road, Southsea	Metropolitan	1876
Joseph, Frederick, Alfold, Billingshurst R.S.O., Sussex	.. ..	1877
Joslin, Morten, High-street, Olney S.O., Bucks	Regent's Park	1893
Judd, Thomas Allen, 146, Peckham Park-road, London, S.E.	Metropolitan	1879
Judge, William, Otley-street, Skipton-in-Craven, Yorkshire	Manchester	1878
Judson, Josephus, Rose Hill, Wellington, Salop	Bradford	1856
Jull, John, Eden Lodge, Causeway, Cambridge	.. ..	1860
KEEN, Charles Thomas, 7, North-terrace, Cambridge	.. ..	1846
Kelly, James Henry, Ampthill	Shebbear	1882
Kelsey, William, Caxton, Cambridge	.. ..	1874
Kemp, Foster Greening, 7, Mariebonne-place, Wigan	Metropolitan	1882
Kemp, John, Coombe Lodge, Castle-road, Southsea	Metropolitan	1873
Kempton, John, Paulton, near Bristol	.. ..	1865
Kendon, Joseph James, Goudhurst S.O., Kent	.. ..	1858
Kent, Sandy, 42, Peel-square, Bradford	Owen's	1884
Kern, William, Bethesda Lodge, Fonnereau-road, Ipswich	.. ..	1871
Kerr, Archibald, Irvine	Free Ch. Coll. Edinburgh	1894
Kerr, David, Douglas-road, Leslie R.S.O., Fifeshire	Free Ch. Coll. Edinburgh	1893
Kettle, John William, Pitlochry	Regent's Park	1890
Keys, John Lewis, 45, Beckenham-road, Penge, London, S.E.	Metropolitan	1869
Kidner, Henry, 4, West End Mansions, West Hampstead, London, N.W.	Metropolitan	1874
Kilby, George Henry, Paradise-row, Waltham Abbey (*Paradise Row, Waltham Abbey*)	Metropolitan	1887
Kilgour, J., Newburgh, Fife	.. ..	1869
King, Samuel, Bank Bottom, Luddenden, via Manchester	.. ..	1868
King, William Henry, 3, Cromwell-avenue, Highgate, London, N.	Bristol	1864
Kirby, F. J., 5, Bank-terrace, Manchester-road, Accrington	Bristol	1895
Kitchener, Jabez, Providence House, Mirfield, Yorks	Metropolitan	1874
Knee, Henry, 5, Ashley-road, Bristol	Metropolitan	1878
Knight, Benjamin George, Swavesey, St. Ives, Hunts	Metropolitan	1888
Knight, George James, Nascott, Newbury	Metropolitan	1870
Knight, James Joseph, The Mount, Ross	Metropolitan	1880
Knox, John, Lochgilphead, Argyllshire	Glas. U. & B.U.S.	1880
LADBROOK, Ebenezer Springate, B.A. (LON.), Serampore, New Malden S.O., Surrey	Regent's Park	1871
Laing, David W., Mount Hope Cottages, Bridge of Allan (*Alva*)	Metropolitan	1882
Lamb, John, 4 Pant-street, Pontycymmer, Bridgend	E. London Inst.	1888
Lambourne, John, Warboys, Huntingdon	.. ..	1858
Landels, Thomas Durley, M.A. (LON.), 5, Jesmond-gardens, Newcastle-on-Tyne	Reg. Pk., U. Coll. Lond., Ox. U. & Edin. U.	1884
Landels, William, D.D., 10, Bellvue-terrace, Edinburgh	.. ..	1846
Lane, John Thomas, Odiham, Winchfield	Hackney	1861
Lang, William Lang, 2, Pitville-lawn, Cheltenham	Metropolitan	1868
Lardner, Thomas, 85, The Chase, Clapham Common, London, S.W. (*Thornton Heath*)	Metroplitan	1871
Large, William, Butley, Wickham Market, Suffolk (*Sudborne*)	.. ..	1845
Last, Edward, 39 Blytheswood-drive, Glasgow	Metropolitan	1888
Latham, Arthur William, Lydbrook, Ross, Herefordshire	Metropolitan	1883

Name and Postal Address.	College.	Ministry commenced
Latimer, Robert Sloan, Mayfield, Ashcombe-road, Weston-super-Mare	Metropolitan	1878
Lauder, George, Blytheswood Cottage, Rosebank, Forfar	Glasgow Univ.	1886
Laurence, William Paul, Westbury, Wilts		1869
Lawrence, Edward, Pope-hill, Haverfordwest	Haverfordwest	1893
Lawton, John, Scout-road, Mytholmroyd, via Manchester	Midland	1848
Layzell, Robert John, 26, Norwich-terrace, East Dereham	Metropolitan	1871
Lea, Walter Thomas, Brandon, Suffolk	Regent's Park	1888
Lee, Alfred Hampden, Highgate-road, Walsall	Midland	1880
Lee, Job, Laycock, Keighley		1855
Lee, Jonas, West Bank, Padiham, Burnley	Man. & Owen's	1878
Lemin, R. C., Bradninch, Cullompton	Regent's Park	1892
Lemon, Aquila, Chipping Sodbury	Bristol	1880
Lemon, George Heath, The Nook, Huntspill, Bridgwater		1876
Leonard, Henry Charles, M.A. (LON.), 10, Gordon-road, Clifton, Bristol	Reg. Pk. & Lon. U.	1858
Le Page, Eleazar Daniel, Cauchibué, Vale Parish, Guernsey		1878
Le Riche, Edward Mildred, Parkhurst-road, Bexley, Kent		1864
Lester, Arthur, Dawley R.S.O., Salop	Metropolitan	1887
Lester, Henry James, Britannia-street, Aylesbury (*Quainton*)		1870
Levinsohn, Isaac, 5, Bromley-road, Lee, London, S.E. (*Jews' Society*)	Metropolitan	1880
Lewis, B., Llangyfelach, Swansea	Llangollen	1889
Lewis, David, Nantyglo R.S.O., Mon.		1880
Lewis, David, Honeyborough, Pemb.	Pontypool	1863
Lewis, David, Abersychan, Pontypool	Haverfordwest	1865
Lewis, David Glyn, Plas Merllyn, Dyserth-road, Rhyl	Manchester	1882
Lewis, David R., West Vale, Halifax	Manchester	1895
Lewis, Ebenezer, 38, Albert-street, Merthyr Tydvil		1853
Lewis, Evan, 85, Wood-road, Treforest, Pontypridd	Haverfordwest	1892
Lewis, Evan David, Treorley R.S.O., Glam.	Llangollen	1890
Lewis, Evan Robert, Thornfield, Bingley	Manchester	1888
Lewis, John, 52, Manor-road, Brockley, London, S.E. (*Brockley-road*)	Regent's Park	1884
Lewis, John, 36, Manchester-road, Tyldesley, Manchester	Haverfordwest	1890
Lewis, John Maldwyn, Cymmer, Porth R.S.O., Glam.	Haverfordwest	1878
Lewis, John, 7, Hawthorn-terrace, Merthyr Tydvil	Pontypool	1891
Lewis, John Gomer, D.D. (U.S.), Belle Vue-street, Swansea	Haverfordwest	1867
Lewis, John William, 38, Martin-street, Morriston, Swansea	Haverfordwest	1872
Lewis, Lewis W., 20, Nevada-street, Bootle, Liverpool	Llangollen	1869
Lewis, Philip, Chipping Campden S.O., Glos.	Rawdon	1867
Lewis, Robert, 12, Croxteth Grove, Liverpool		1865
Lewis, Robert Thornton, Kislingbury, Northampton	Metropolitan	1867
Lewis, Thomas, Cinderbank, Netherton, near Dudley		1872
Lewis, Thomas, 74, Morden-road, Newport, Mon.	Pontypool	1848
Lewis, Thomas Richard, Broadhaven, Pembs.	Pontypool	1886
Lewis, Thomas Roberts, Scapegoat Hill, Golcar, Huddersfield	Manchester	1889
Lewis, W., 12, Common-road, Pontypridd	Haverfordwest	1888
Lewis, William, The Moor, St. Ishmaels, Milford Haven	Pontypool	1855
Lewis, William John, Court, Eglwyswrw R.S.O., Pemb.	Pontypool	1891
Lewis, Zechariah Henry, 43, Alexandra-road, Cardiff	Cardiff Univ.	1891
Lewitt, James, 14, Pittville-lawn, Cheltenham	Midland	1844
Leyshon, William, Georgeham, Braunton R.S.O., N. Devon		1884
Lindsay, Samuel, Burray, St. Margaret's Hope, R.S.O., Orkney	Glas. U. & B.U.S.	1892
Linnecar, George William 56, Hackford-road, Brixton, London, S.W. (*Mansion House-square, Camberwell*)	Metropolitan	1874
Lister, Thomas Whitson, 1, Blackness-crescent, Dundee		1880
Littleton, Ebenezer, Forest Fold, Crowborough, Tunbridge Wells		1868
Livingstone, Alexander Lismore		1852

Name and Postal Address.	College.	Ministry commenced
Livingstone, W. A., 124, Clowes-street, West Gorton, Manchester	Manchester	.. 1895
Llewellyn, David John, 85, Southdown-road, Preston Park, Brighton	Bris. & H'west	.. 1881
Llewelyn, George Henry, Maesyberllan, Brecon	Pontypool	.. 1859
Llewellyn, William S., Rock-villa, New Hey, near Rochdale (*Ogden*)	Metropolitan	.. 1874
Lloyd, David, Rhydwyn, Valley R.S.O., Anglesey	Bangor ..	.. 1894
Lloyd, Frederick Cowell, Hale-road, Bowdon, Altrincham (*Altrincham*)	Regent's Park	.. 1893
Lloyd, Isaac, Queen-street, Maesteg, Bridgend	Pontypool	.. 1877
Lloyd, John, Aberbeeg, near Newport, Mon. (*Llanhilleth*) ..	Pontypool	.. 1880
Lloyd, Robert, Castletown, via Cardiff	Haverfordwest	.. 1862
Logan, James Moffat, St. David's, Belmont-road, Bishopston, Bristol	Rawdon ..	.. 1883
Loinaz, Diego, 2, Cromwell-villas, Cromwell-street, Hounslow	Metropolitan	.. 1890
Longhurst, Caleb Mark, Fairmount, Gillott-road, Birmingham	Bristol ..	.. 1869
Longhurst, T. J., Cardigan Villa, Connaught-place, Weston-super-Mare	Metropolitan	.. 1883
Lord, John, St. Peter's-walk, Droitwich	.. .. ..	.. 1891
Lord, Walter Smith, Measham, Atherstone	Rawdon ..	.. 1891
Lovell, Edward Ebenezer, West Haddon, Rugby	Bristol ..	.. 1884
Lovell, Ernest George, Blockley S.O., Worcestershire ..	Metropolitan	.. 1894
Lowden, George Rouse, F.R.G.S., Hanwell, London, W. (*Hanwell*)	King's College	.. 1856
Lowe, Richard, Welford, Rugby	.. .. ..	.. 1860
Lydiatt, Thomas, 8, Brookland-road, Woodlands, Birkenhead	.. .. ..	.. 1868
Lyne, Samuel, 1, Brunswick-villas, Newton Abbot	Metropolitan	.. 1880
Lynn, John Hunt, 10, Gilmore-road, Lewisham, London, S.E. (*Dacre-park, Lee*)	.. .. ..	.. 1864
McALISTER, Stewart, Cranfield, Newport Pagnell	Metropolitan	.. 1871
Macalpine, Charles Scott, M.A., B.D. (GLAS.), 44, High-street, Oxford-street, Manchester	Glas Univ.&U.P. Coll. Edin.	.. 1880
McAuslane, James, Crawley, Sussex	Metropolitan	.. 1883
M'Caig, Archibald, B.A., LL.D. (ROY. UN. I.) (*Tutor, Pastors' College*), 175, Brixton-hill, London, S.W.	Metropolitan	.. 1874
McCallum, Duncan, 54, Lomeshaye-road, Nelson, Burnley ..	Glasgow Univ.	.. 1863
McCleery, James, Oak Bank, Ramsbottom, Manchester ..	Man. & Owen's	1889
McCracken, S. A., 17, Artesian-road, Bayswater, London, W.	.. .. ..	.. 1889
M'Crie, George, 61, Cecil-street, Hillhead, Glasgow	.. .. ..	.. 1885
MacDonald, Alexander, Hillside House, Chard, Somerset ..	.. .. ..	.. 1855
Macdougall, Alexander, Colonsay, Greenock	Metropolitan	.. 1866
McDougall, Allan, Broadford, Skye	.. .. ..	.. 1873
Mace, Daniel, 20, Patrick-street, Market Harborough ..	.. .. ..	.. 1875
Mace, David, West Malling S. O., Kent	Metropolitan	.. 1866
McElwee, George Munro, M.A., B.Sc. (GLAS.). 19, Larkdale-street, Nottingham	Glas. Univ. & B. U. S.	.. 1885
McFadyean, Gavin, 1, Windsor-ter., Saltash R.S.O., Cornwall	Bristol ..	.. 1879
M'Farlane, Duncan, Baugh, Tyree, Oban	.. .. ..	.. 1858
Macgregor, Duncan, Dunoon	Glasgow Univ.	.. 1868
Macintosh, William, 96, Hallcraig-street, Airdrie	Rawdon ..	.. 1878
McKay, George Peter, 33, Northwold-road, Stoke Newington, London, N. (*Devonshire-square, Stoke Newington*)	.. .. ..	.. 1879
McKean, John, Queen-street, Jedburgh	.. .. ..	.. 1886
McKenzie, Arthur Philip, Potter-street, Harlow	Regent's Park	.. 1878
Mackenzie, W. Lomax, Hervey-road, Blackheath, London, S.E. (*Shooter's Hill-road, Blackheath*)	Metropolitan	.. 1889
McKeracher, John Hunter, 11, Exmouth-street, Camp-road, Leeds	Glas. U. & B.U.S.	1890
Mackey, Henry O., 61, St. Augustine's-road, London, N.W.	Metropolitan	.. 1876
McKittrick, William James, Lechlade, Glos.	E. London Inst.	1880

Name and Postal Address.	College.	Ministry commenced
McLaren, Alexander, B.A. (LON.), D.D. (EDIN.) 1, Carill-drive, Fallowfield, Manchester	Stepney ..	.. 1846
McLean, Hector, 15, Muir-park, Dalkeith	Glasgow Univ. ..	1884
McLean, John, 18, Montgomery-ter., Mount Florida, Glasgow	Glasgow Univ. ..	1884
M'Lellan, John, 8, Oxford-drive, Kelvinside, Glasgow ..	.. .. ..	1861
Macleod, Norman, 24, City-gardens, St. Helens	Glasgow Univ. ..	1886
McLeod, Peter, West Bridge-end, Dumbarton	.. .. ..	1891
McMichael, George, B.A. (LON.), Clarendon, Cowleigh-road, North Malvern, Malvern	Stepney ..	.. 1853
Macmillan, Daniel, King's Langley R.S.O., Herts	Metropolitan	.. 1881
McNab, James, 13, Brunswick-street, Carlisle	Metropolitan	.. 1877
McPherson, Duncan P., B.D. (U.S.), 4, St. James-place, Exeter	Woodstock (Canada) Chicago & Edin. U.	.. 1883
Maden, James, St. David's-rd., St. Annes-on-the-Sea, Preston	Midland ..	.. 1858
Makepeace, John Foster, 21, Waldeck-road, Carrington, Nottingham	Regent's Park	.. 1873
Mann, James, Umberslade, Hockley Heath, Birmingham ..	Regent's Park	.. 1883
Mann, Robert William, Smarden, via Staplehurst, Kent ..	.. ..	.. 1862
Mann, Samuel, Wotton-under-Edge, Glos.	Bristol ..	.. 1862
Mann, Walter, Greenhill Villa, Keynsham R.S.O., Somerset	Metropolitan	.. 1880
Mansfield, Robert William, Bourton, Shrivenham	.. ..	.. 1867
Mansfield, William George, Velindre, Knighton	.. ..	.. 1884
Manton, Thomas Cavit, 16, Cyril-street, Northampton ..	.. ..	.. 1869
March, William, 94, Anderton-road, Sparkbrook, Birmingham	Midland ..	.. 1867
Marchant, Frederick G. (*Tutor, Pastors' College*), 56, Denmark-villas, West Brighton	Metropolitan	.. 1864
Markham, John, 2 Matlock-terrace, Shefford R.S.O., Beds	Metropolitan	.. 1869
Marks, Edward, Lyme Regis, Dorset	.. ..	.. 1867
Marsh, Ebenezer, 41, Borthwick-road, Stratford, London, E. (*Gurney-road, Stratford*)	.. ..	.. 1879
Marshall, Benjamin, Horley S.O., Surrey	Metropolitan	.. 1878
Marshall, George, Tubbermore, co. Derry	Metropolitan	.. 1891
Marshall John Turner, M.A. (LON.) (*Classical Tutor, Baptist College, Manchester*), Sunnyside, Fallowfield, Manchester	Manchester & Owen's.	
Martin, Henry J., Hillden Villa, New Mill, Tring	Metropolitan	.. 1883
Martin, John Eastwood, Queen's-road, Erith, Kent (*Erith*) ..	Metropolitan	.. 1875
Martin, Samuel Wythes, 226, Bradford-street, Camp Hill, Birmingham	.. ..	.. 1869
Martin, Thomas Henry, 46, Bentinck-street, Glasgow ..	Regent's Park	.. 1878
Martin William Alfred, 4, De-Burgh-terrace, Dover	Metropolitan	.. 1887
Mason, Edwin, 78, Dorothy-road, Lavender-hill, London, S.W.	Metropolitan	.. 1874
Mason, Ernest, 7, Marine-approach, South Shields	Rawdon ..	.. 1887
Masters, Frederick George, Roade, Northampton	Bristol ..	.. 1867
Mateer, Edward Thomas, 261, Friern-road, East Dulwich, London, S.E. (*Lordship-lane, Dulwich*)	E. London Inst.	1880
Mateer, John Thomas, 23, Highbury-terrace, London, N. (*Vernon, King's Cross*)	Metropolitan	.. 1888
Mathams, Walter John, 20, Strensham-road, Moseley, Birmingham	Regent's Park	.. 1878
Mathews, John, Stantonbury, Wolverton R.S.O., Bucks ..	Bristol ..	.. 1841
Mathias, David, 18, Alexandra place, Sirhowy, Tredegar ..	Haverfordwest ..	1860
Matthews, Aaron, 8, Swinburne-place, Newcastle-on-Tyne ..	Nott. Cong. Inst.	1872
Matthews, John Francis, Audlem, Nantwich	Midland ..	.. 1890
Matthews, Matthew, Newton, Craven Arms R.S.O., Salop ..	.. ..	.. 1860
Matthias, Thomas D., 19, Llewellyn-street, Nantymoel R.S.O., Glam.	.. ..	.. 1850
Maurice, John William, Dinas Cross, Pembrokeshire ..	Haverfordwest ..	1862
Maurice, William, 1, Deptford-villas, Cannon-street, Shrewsbury	Pontypool	.. 1875

Name and Postal Address.	College.	Ministry commenced
May, John Shakespeare, Yew Tree Villa, Featherstone-road, King's Heath, Birmingham		1884
Maycock, Thomas, 11, Station-road, Leyton, Essex (*Major-road, Stratford*)	Metropolitan	1883
Mayers, Walter John, Abbotsthorpe, Wallington, Surrey	Metropolitan	1870
Maynard, William, Syston, Leicester	Metropolitan	1889
Meadow, Henry Wooster, 4, Church-street, Warwick	Metropolitan	1865
Medhurst, Thomas William, 199, Severn-road, Cardiff	Metropolitan	1856
Medley, Edward, B.A. (LON.), 10, Warwick-road, Upper Clapton, London, N.E. (*Downs, Clapton*)	Regent's Park	1869
Medley, William, M.A. (LON.), *Classical Tutor*, Rawdon College, Leeds	Regent's Park	1869
Meeres, James Lane, 79, Spa-road, Bermondsey, London, S.E.		1845
Menzies, George, Hays Well-road, Arbroath	Metropolitan	1893
Meredith, John, Derlton Villa, Aylestone-hill, Hereford	Pontypool	1877
Meredyth, Ioan, Blaenavon, Mon.	Llangollen	1882
Mesquitta, Richard Isaac, Avondale-road, Chesterfield	Metropolitan	1869
Meyer, Frederick Brotherton, B.A. (LON.), Christ Church, Westminster Bridge-road, London, S.E.	Regent's Park	1870
Miall W., 236, Richmond-road, Dalston, London, N.E.		1839
Michael, Peter Hall, Hanham, Bristol	Bristol & Glas. U.	1890
Middleditch, Alfred Bradley, 4, Melita-villas, Finchley, London, N. (*North Finchley*)	Nottingham	1884
Miles, J. H. Porthcawl, R.S.O., Glam.	Pontypool	1882
Millar, William Johnston, 9, Roslea Drive, Glasgow	Glasgow Univ.	1882
Millard, Benjamin Albert, 40, Emery-street, Walsall	Regent's Park	1889
Millard, William Henry, West Bank, Wick	Metropolitan	1893
Milledge, Henry Josiah, Gamlingay, Sandy	Metropolitan	1885
Miller, Frank Edward, 120, Wargrave-road, Earlestown, Newton-le-Willows, Lancs.	Midland	1889
Miller, George Anderson, 17, Rochester-avenue, Rochester	Metropolitan	1886
Miller, William, Stanley-avenue, Chesham R.S.O., Bucks	Midland	1845
Mills, Abraham, 70, Uttoxeter New Road, Derby	Metropolitan	1878
Mills, Andrew Fuller, 4, Esplanade, Carmarthen	Pontypool	1870
Mills, John, 34, Windsor-terrace, Abernant, Aberdare	Llangollen	1874
Mills, William J., 13, Grosvenor-park, Camberwell, London, S.E. (*Walworth-road*)	Bristol	1874
Milne, A. A. Cambuslang, Glasgow	Glas. U. & B.U.S.	1886
Milnes, Edward, 87, Himley-road, Dudley	Metropolitan	1893
Minifie, William Charles, Ivy Glen, Christchurch-road, Bournemouth	Metropolitan	1890
Mitchell, E., 2, Victoria-terrace, Rhos, Ruabon (*Ponkey*)		1884
Mitchell, Edward, 25, Calabria-place, Highbury-place, London, N. (*Chadwell-street, Clerkenwell*)		1878
Mitchell, Henry Nettleton, 17, St. Hilary-terrace, Stoke, Devonport		1882
Mitchell, John R., 146, Hospital-street, Nantwich	Manchester	1894
Mockford, G., Heathfield S.O., Sussex		1856
Monk, George, Bures St. Mary, Suffolk	Metropolitan	1867
Monti, Francis B., Oak Lodge, Acton, London, W.		1885
Moore, David Henry, 17, Church-road, Barking	Metropolitan	1892
Moore, Edward, 91, Brook-road, Bootle, Liverpool	Manchester	1881
Moore, George James, 56, Colwyn-road, Northampton	Metropolitan	1879
Moore, Henry, Porlock House, Coronation-road, Bedminster, Bristol	Metropolitan	1869
Moore, John Henry, 10, Warnborough-road, Oxford	Regent's Park	1880
Moore, Sydney Herbert, Cambridge-road, New Malden S.O., Surrey	Manchester	1883
Morgan, Aaron, Blaenffos R.S.O., Pemb.	Llangollen	1878
Morgan, Arthur Alfred, 20 Thenford-street, Northampton	Regent's Park	1884
Morgan, David Mathry, Cross Hands, Llanelly, Carm.	Haverfordwest	1871
Morgan, David Richard, Chalford, Stroud	Pontypool	1865

Name and Postal Address.	College.	Ministry commenced
Morgan, Edward, Skipton-road, Colne, Lancs..	Pontypool	.. 1860
Morgan, George Hay, B.Sc. (LON.), 17, West Bank, Amhurst-park, London, N. (*Woodberry Down*)	Pontypool, Cardiff U.C., and Lond. U.C..	.. 1890
Morgan, John, Erwood R.S.O., Breconshire	Pontypool	.. 1869
Morgan, John, Talywain, Pontypool	Pontypool	.. 1862
Morgan, John, Rhys, D.D. (U.S.), West End, Llanelly, Carm.	Pontypool	.. 1845
Morgan, John Symlog, Rhydfelen, Pontypridd	E. London Inst.	1888
Morgan, Joseph Brown, 2, Exton-park, Parkgate-road, Chester	.. .. ..	1880
Morgan, Maurice, 3, Clarence-villas, Harborne, Birmingham	Haverfordwest ..	1852
Morgan, Thomas, 6, Moorland-gardens, Cardiff	Pontypool	.. 1878
Morgan, Timothy Richard, Tynlon, Ystrad Meurig R.S.O., Cardigan (*Pontrhydfendigaid*)	Haverfordwest ..	1887
Morgan, William, 5, Brynbedw-terrace, Blaengarw R.S.O., Glam.	Llangollen and Bangor U.C..	.. 1887
Morgan, William, St. Brides, Castleton, via Cardiff	.. .. ..	.. 1862
Morgan, William, Newbridge, Newport, Mon.	.. .. ..	.. 1866
Morgan, William, Bassaleg, Newport, Mon.	Manchester	.. 1891
Morley, Edmund, 11, Sandfield-road, Liscard T.S.O., Liverpool (*New Brighton*)	Metropolitan	.. 1867
Morling, Abner, Hadleigh R.S.O., Suffolk	.. .. ..	.. 1891
Morling, Josiah, 7, London-road, High Wycombe	.. .. ..	.. 1867
Morris, Alfred, Dorvil-road, Blaenau Festiniog (*Festiniog*)..	Aberystwyth	.. 1895
Morris, David, Cowley House, Albert Town, Haverfordwest	Haverfordwest..	1865
Morris, David G., 51, Gelli-road, Pentre R.S.O., Glam. ..	Pontypool ..	.. 1893
Morris, David William, 64, Gorse-lane, Swansea	Haverfordwest ..	1850
Morris, Fred Charles, 46, Farnbridge-road, Maldon	Metropolitan	.. 1892
Morris, John Alban (*Theological Tutor, Aberystwyth College*), 13, Queen's-terrace, Aberystwyth	Haverfordwest ..	1868
Morris, John Llewellyn, Jabez, Newport, Pemb. (*Llanychlluydog*)	Haverfordwest ..	1879
Morris, Lewis, 67, Eldon-street, Oldham	Llangollen	.. 1891
Morris, Richard, 1, Trinity-place, Aberystwyth	Brad. & H'west..	1848
Morris, Robert Seiriol, Cwmavon, Port Talbot	Llangollen	.. 1892
Morris, Silas, M.A. (LON.), *Tutor*, The College, Bangor ..	Pont. & Bangor..	1886
Morris, Thomas, Fron, Llangollen	.. .. ..	.. 1886
Morris, Thomas Mew, Paget-road, Ipswich	Brad.& Edin. Un.	1855
Morris, William, Glyn Villa, Treorky R.S.O., Glam... ..	Pontypool	.. 1869
Morrison, Peter, Fern Bank, Middleborough-road, Coventry	Regent's Park ..	1883
Morton, William, Cwmfelin, Brynmawr R.S.O., Breconshire	Haverfordwest..	1878
Mostyn, John, 100, London-road, Ipswich	Bradford	.. 1856
Mowbray, Henry, 8, Cawdor-road, Fallowfield, Manchester	.. .. ..	.. 1881
Moxham, William, 27, Powerscroft-road, Clapton, London, N.E. (*Chatsworth-road, ClaptonPark*)	Metropolitan	.. 1884
Munns, Charles Oliver, Fleet (Hants.), Winchfield	Regent's Park ..	1863
Munns, John William, 5, Mountfield-road, Grove-hill, Tunbridge Wells	.. .. ..	.. 1858
Munro, J. M., Cowdenbeath R.S.O., Fifeshire	Toronto ..	.. 1877
Murphy, John Michael, 84, Linnæus-street, Hull	Metropolitan	.. 1865
Murray, Henry Beckett, 2, Plympton-avenue, Kilburn, London, N.W. (*Canterbury-road, Kilburn*)	.. .. ..	.. 1883
Murray, John, Perth-street, Edinburgh..	Edinburgh Univ.	1872
Murray, W., 2, Clarendon-road, Walthamstow (*Boundary-road, Walthamstow*) .. :	Metropolitan	.. 1892
Mursell, Arthur, Kintore, The Chase, Clapham Common, London, S.W. (*South Lambeth-road, Stockwell*)	Bristol ..	.. 1857
Mursell, James, Charnwood-street, Derby	Rawdon&Edin.U.	1885
Mursell, Walter A., 78, Park View-terrace, Blackburn ..	Regent's Park ..	1892
Muxworthy, Daniel, Fern Royd, Padiham, Burnley	.. .. ..	.. 1881
Myers, John, 22, Grove-street, Longwood, Huddersfield ..	Bradford	.. 1858
Myers, John Brown, Clarendon-road, Watford (*Association Secretary, Baptist Missionary Society*)	Bristol ..	.. 1867

Name and Postal Address.	College.	Ministry commenced
Myerson, Henry, 96, Bonner-road, Victoria-park, London, N.E. (*Oval, Hackney*)	.. ..	.. 1858
NEALE, Eppa Secundus, 5, Maidstone-villa, Knight's Hill, West Norwood, London, S.E.	Metropolitan	.. 1860
Near, Isaac, Desborough, Market Harborough	Metropolitan	.. 1874
Near, Isaac L., Lyndhurst, March	Metropolitan	.. 1894
Needham, George, 66, Toothill-road, Loughborough	Midland ..	.. 1848
Needham, Samuel, 8, St. Paul's-road, Northampton	Metropolitan	.. 1885
Neighbour, George, Ruardean-hill, Mitcheldean R.S.O., Glos.	.. ..	.. 1892
Neighbour, John, Chesterton, Cirencester	Bristol ..	.. 1893
New, Harry, Forest View, Beaulieu, Southampton	.. ..	.. 1887
Newell, William, Cleve Villa, Downend, Bristol	Melksham	.. 1847
Newling, Samuel Boyce, Isleham, Soham	.. ..	.. 1892
Newman, Joseph Price, 90, Belvedere-road, Burnley	Manchester	.. 1882
Newnam, Samuel, Yeovil	Dunstable	.. 1849
Newton, F. Horace, 18, Ribblesdale-road, Hornsey, London, N. (*Baptist Building Fund*)	Bury & Owen's ..	1870
Newton, John, Southborough, Tunbridge Wells	.. ..	.. 1867
Ney, John, North-street, Melton Mowbray	Metropolitan	.. 1877
Nicholas, John, Hanerch Isaf, Crumlin R.S.O., Mon. ..	Pontypool	.. 1864
Nicholas, W.D., Sunnybank, Treharris R.S.O., Glam. ..	Pontypool and Cardiff U.C. ..	1889
Nichols, William Frederick, 20, Beauchamp-street, Stockport	Manchester	.. 1885
Nichols, Walter Benjamin, Kington, Herefordshire	Metropolitan	.. 1888
Nicolson, William Browne, M.A. (EDIN.), Kirkintilloch, Glasgow	Edin.U. & B.U.S.	1886
Nickalls, Arthur Mastin, Glenmore, Nailsworth, Stroud ..	Bristol ..	.. 1887
Nield, William, 13, New Cateaton-street, Walmersley-road, Bury, Lancs.	.. ..	.. 1882
Noble, Balmforth, Wirksworth, Derby	Midland ..	.. 1883
Northfield, Benjamin John, Beville House, High-street, March	.. ..	.. 1880
Norwood, Frederick, Louth, Lincs.	Midland ..	.. 1885
Nunn, Joseph, Hailsham S.O., Sussex	.. ..	.. 1859
OAKLEY, Arthur William, Park Villas, West Bromwich ..	Rawdon ..	.. 1883
Oakley, Henry, 22, Ouseley-road, Balham, London, S.W. (*Upper Tooting*)	Regent's Park	.. 1888
O'Dell, John, 233, Spring-bank, Hull	Bradford	.. 1858
Ogilvy, John Ogilvy, East Mount, Malton	Rawdon ..	.. 1894
Oldman, C., 24, Hall-road, Lakenham, Norwich	.. ..	.. 1882
Oldring, George Wright, Gedney-road, Long Sutton, Wisbech	Metropolitan	.. 1861
Oliver, Frederick, Broadlands, Meltham, Huddersfield ..	Manchester	.. 1890
O'Neill, Arthur George, 55, Hall-road, Handsworth, Birmingham	Glasgow Univ. ..	1840
Oriel, Benjamin, Twerton, Bath	Bristol ..	.. 1891
Orton, William, 257, Humberstone-road, Leicester	Midland ..	.. 1844
Osborne, Alfred Thomas, 4, Exton's-road, King's Lynn ..	Regent's Park	.. 1867
Osborne, Edwin, The Lawn, St. Austell	Metropolitan	.. 1871
Osborne, William, 14, Albany-terrace, Ordnance-place, Chatham	Metropolitan	.. 1866
Osler, Benjamin Williams, North Curry, Taunton	.. ..	.. 1868
Overend, Frederick, Blackthorn House, Bacup	Manchester	.. 1880
Owen, David Richard, Kingsthorpe, Northampton	Haverfordwest ..	1870
Owen, George Frankling, Great Torrington	Bristol ..	.. 1886
Owen, J. M. Gwynne, 7, Vernon-road, Edgbaston, Birmingham	Bristol & Glas. U.	1878
Owen, James, Miramor Villa, Swansea	H'west & Bristol	1860
Owen, Richard, Grove-villa, Rhymney R.S.O., Mon.	Haverfordwest ..	1884
Owen, William, Gordon-villas, Wells, Somerset	Haverfordwest ..	1871
Owen, William, 13, Derby-street, Moss Side, Manchester ..	Manchester	.. 1892
Owen, William G., Carrog, Corwen (*Llansantffraid*)	Llangollen	.. 1890
Owen, William Griffith, Troedyrhiw R.S.O., Glam.	Llangollen	.. 1892

Name and Postal Address.	College.	Ministry commenced
Owens, Owen, Mona Villa, Porth R.S.O., Glam.	Pontypool ..	1880
Owers, John Thomas, 55, Eleanor-street, Grimsby	Metropolitan ..	1869
PACKER, Daniel Powell, 6, Woodhouse-terrace, Gateshead ..	Midland	1889
Packer, William James, Willow Bank, South-street, Rochdale	Abdn. U. & Bris.	1877
Page, Ernest Judson, Haroldene, Bath-road, Woking ..	Regent's Park ..	1887
Page, Robert, Cavendish R.S.O., Suffolk (*Glemsford*).. ..	.. ..	1878
Page, W. H. J., Hilfield House, Calne	Metropolitan ..	1866
Page, William, B.A. (LON.), Upper Mall, Hammersmith, London, W. (*West End, Hammersmith*)	Regent's Park ..	1864
Paige, James Somerville, 7, Weymouth-road, Frome.. ..	Metropolitan ..	1877
Palmer, John, Ridgmount, Bletchley Station	Metropolitan ..	1872
Palmer, Josiah, Offord D'Arcy, Huntingdon	.. .. ..	1858
Palmer, Levi, Beulah, Staplegrove, Taunton	Metropolitan ..	1874
Palmer, William Ervy, 1, Charlton Villas, Charlton-green, Dover	.. .. ..	1869
Parker, Alfred, Harpole, Northampton	Metropolitan ..	1880
Parker, Arthur James, Old Sodbury, Chipping Sodbury ..	Metropolitan ..	1883
Parker, Edward, D.D. (U.S.), *President*, Baptist College, Manchester	Bap. Evan. Soc.	1857
Parker, George, Mursley, near Winslow, Bucks	.. .. ..	1860
Parker, James, M.A. (U.S.), Elgin House, Richmond-road, Ilford (*Ilford*)	Mad. U., U.S.A.	1862
Parkin, Richard, Chadlington, Charlbury S.O., Oxon. ..	.. .. ..	1865
Parkinson, Louis C., B.A. (CANTAB), Arthur-street, Nottingham	Camb. Univ., Regent's Pk., & Univ.Coll.Lond.	1893
Parnell, Jabez, 7, Trigon-road, Clapham-road, London, S.W. (*Wellesley-street, Stepney*)	.. .. ..	1868
Parrett, Charles Henry, Carisbrooke, Boscombe, Bournemouth	.. .. ..	1884
Parrish, John, Bargoed, via Cardiff	Llangollen ..	1869
Parry, Abel Jones, Cefnmawr, Ruabon	Pontypool ..	1858
Parry, Edmund Owen, Wattstown, Porth R.S.O., Glam. ..	Haverfordwest ..	1882
Parry, Edward, Aberdulais, Neath	Llangollen ..	1869
Parry, William, 31, Taff-street, Pontypridd (*Ynysybwl*) ..	Bristol	1864
Passmore, Henry Robert, Melbourne House, West Cliff-road, Whitstable S.O., Kent..	Metropolitan ..	1882
Pates, Charles, 29, East Mount-road, York	Metropolitan ..	1867
Paterson, Alexander, M.A. (GLAS.), Comely-park, Falkirk	Glasgow Univ...	1889
Payn, G. F., Liskeard	Rawdon	1895
Payne, Arthur James, Peterhead	Metropolitan ..	1891
Payne, Charles, 4, Hope-street, Dewsbury	Midland	1865
Payne, George Edward, Barton Fabis, Nuneaton	Midland	1885
Payne, William Henry, Bovey Tracey R.S.O., South Devon	Regent's Park ..	1862
Peacock, Samuel, Castle-street, Todmorden	.. .. ..	1873
Peacock, William Richard, 8, Belgrave-terrace, Baldslow-road, Hastings	Regent's Park ..	1889
Peake, Edward, 16, Halcyon-road, Birkenhead	.. .. ..	1891
Pearce, Charles, Tring	Metropolitan ..	1874
Pearce, Frederick, 24, Wingfield-road, Trowbridge	.. .. ..	1842
Pearce, James William, Donaghmore, co. Tyrone (*Lisnagleer*)	.. .. ..	1890
Pearce, Joseph, 97, Cowick-street, St. Thomas, Exeter ..	.. .. ..	1860
Pearson, Edward Bruce, Clevehurst, Ryde, Isle of Wight ..	Metropolitan ..	1882
Peden, Robert James, Ivy-villa, First-avenue, Enfield ..	Metropolitan ..	1888
Perkins, William Henry, M.A. (ABERDEEN), Englehome, Boscombe, Bournemouth	Raw. & Abdn.Un.	1868
Perriam, Arthur C., 28, Ryan-street, West Bowling, Bradford	.. .. ..	1876
Perrin, John Edward, Laxfield, Hamilton-road, Reading ..	.. .. ..	1856
Perry, Charles F., 12, Chepstow-street, Walton, Liverpool ..	Midland	1890
Perry, Thomas, 11, St. John's-terrace, King's Lynn	Metropolitan ..	1883
Peters, Thomas Oliver, Hill Side, Bushey, Watford	Stepney	1852

Name and Postal Address.	College.	Ministry commenced
Pettman, Wallace, 95, Tierney-road, Streatham-hill, London, S.W. (*New Park-road, Brixton-hill*)	Metropolitan	1876
Phillips, Alfred, Lindenfield, Leamington Spa	Metropolitan	1885
Phillips, David, Brynhyfryd, Letterston R.S.O., Pemb. (*Croesgoch*)	Haverfordwest	1857
Phillips, Evan, New Court, Llanybyther R.S.O., Carm.	Llangollen	1877
Phillips, George, 52, New-road, Newtown, Mont.	Haverfordwest	1858
Phillips, Henry, Kilnock House, Randalstown R.S.O., co. Antrim (*Grange Corner*)	..	1862
Phillips, Henry Arthur Beynon, Belvedere Villa, Carlton-street, Cheltenham	Metropolitan	1889
Phillips, John, Trevasser, Fishguard, Pemb.	Pontypool	1873
Phillips, Philip, Dafen, Llanelly, Carmarthenshire (*Llangennech*)	Pontypool	1864
Phillips, Rees David, Ynystawe, Swansea	Haverfordwest	1890
Phillips, Thomas, Broad-street, Blaenavon R.S.O., Mon.	Cardiff	1895
Phillips, Thomas, B.A. (LON.), Avalon, Kettering	Llangollen	1891
Phillips, Thomas Brisil, Pontyrhyl, Bridgend (*Cwmgarw*)	Cardiff U.C.	1885
Phillips, Walter Vaughan, Preston Deanery, near Northampton (*Hackleton*)	Pontypool	1891
Philp, Christopher, 55, Shaftesbury-road, Gosport	..	1867
Philpot, Thomas, 13, Oxford-grove, Ilfracombe	Metropolitan	1888
Pickbourne, Frederick, Coalville, near Leicester	Midland	1882
Pickering, John, Towyn R.S.O., Merioneth	Llangollen	1867
Pickles, Alfred, 10, Oppidan's-road, Primrose-hill, London, N.W.	Bury	1869
Pidgeon, Alfred, Calstock, Tavistock	Metropolitan	1874
Pierce, Samuel, Bank-place, Penrhyndeudraeth, Merioneth	Llangollen	1875
Piggot, Alexander, Leven, Fife	Metropolitan	1885
Piggott, William, 16, Courtenay-street, St. Paul's, Cheltenham	..	1860
Pike, E. C., B.A. (LON.), Exeter	Regent's Park	1861
Pilgrim, George, Bacton, North Walsham, Norfolk		
Pilling, Samuel, 100, The Rye, Peckham, London, S.E.	Metropolitan	1868
Pitts, George Francis, Burgh R.S.O., Lincolnshire	..	1878
Plant, Thomas Arthur, B.A. (LON.), 17, Fair View Road, Burnley	Mid. & Glas. U.	1889
Player, Frederick Charles, B.A. (LON.), 3, Brighton-terrace, Merridale-road, Wolverhampton	Bristol	1892
Plumb, George, 17, Havelock-road, Norwich	Regent's Park	1880
Plumbridge, James Henry, Southwell, Notts.	Metropolitan	1876
Pollard, Frank Ward, Sutton, Cross Hills, Keighley	Regent's Park	1886
Pollard, Thomas George, Brentford	Metropolitan	1895
Pontifex, William, Old Way, Fownhope, Herefordshire	..	1870
Pope, George W., 1, Roseford-gardens, Shepherd's Bush, London, W. (*Shepherd's-bush-road*)	Metropolitan	1878
Porteous, James, Eversleigh, Branstone-road, Burton-on-Trent	Ed. Un. & Raw.	1880
Porteous, James Ferguson, 22, Oxford-place, Doncaster	E. London Inst.	1889
Porter, James, Necton, Swaffham, Norfolk	Metropolitan	1870
Potter, Frank, Harston, Cambridge	Metropolitan	1882
Poulton, James Sylvester, 3, Avenue Villas, Child's Hill, London, N.W. (*Child's Hill*)	Metropolitan	1885
Povey, William James, M.A. (CANTAB.), Tintern House, Great Malvern	Cam. Univ. and Regent's Park	1889
Powell, David, 28, Osborne-road, Anfield, Liverpool	Haverfordwest	1882
Powell, R. Hill, Oakville, Eden-Bridge, Kent	Bristol	1874
Powell, Rees, Briton Ferry, Glam.	Pontypool	1889
Powell, Thomas Charles, 2, North Parade-terrace, Monmouth (*Penalt*)	..	1867
Powell, William, 35, Drysiog-st., Ebbw Vale R.S.O., Mon.	Pontypool	1880
Preece, Harry John, Ænon, Maidenhead	Metropolitan	1888

Name and Postal Address.	College.	Ministry commenced
Preston, Alfred Benjamin, North-street, Halstead	Metropolitan	1884
Price, David, Merthyr Tydvil	Llangollen	1890
Price, Paul, Northgate-street, Chester	.. ..	1857
Price, Rees, Cilfowyr, Boncath R.S.O., Pemb.	Pontypool	1851
Price, William, 82, Newtown-road, Hereford (*Whitestone*)	.. ..	1884
Price, William, Hafod, Holyhead	.. ..	1882
Price, William, Westbury, Wilts	.. ..	1884
Price, William Frederic, Paignton, Devon	Metropolitan	1885
Prichard, John, Tonyrefail, Porth R.S.O., Glam.	Pontypool	1863
Prichard, Owen Mathew, Newcastle Emlyn, Llandyssil	Haverfordwest	1886
Priestnall, William, 367, Humberstone-road, Leicester	E. London Inst.	1886
Pring, Gad, 6, Havelock-road, Norwich	Metropolitan	1875
Pringle, James, Chipperfield, King's Langley R.S.O., Herts	Bristol	1879
Priter, Albert, Preston	Metropolitan	1889
Probert, Enoch Evan, Siluria Villa, Pontypridd	Pontypool	1877
Probert, Evan, Whitebrook, Monmouth	Haverfordwest	1871
Prosser, William Henry, 45, Charles-street, Milford Haven	Pont. & Met.	1885
Pryse, Daniel Michael, 15, Redcar-road East, South Bank R.S.O., Yorks.	Haverfordwest	1883
Pugh, Frederick, 97, Clifton-street, New Swindon, Wilts	.. ..	1866
Pugh, Frederick William Walker, 37, Well Close-terrace, Leeds	Regent's Park	1893
Pugh, James, 158 Haverstock-road, Wells-road, Bristol	.. ..	1867
Pughe, John Myllon, Llansadwrn, Llanwrda R.S.O., Carm. (*Cwmdu*)	Llangollen	1874
Pulford, William, Lower Largo R.S.O., Fife	Bristol	1890
Pullen, Edgar R., 1, Richmond-road, Freemantle, Southampton (*Shirley*)	Metropolitan	1889
Purchase, Walter Henry, Cotswold, Poplar-avenue, Edgbaston, Birmingham	.. ..	1883
Purser, Thomas S., Holme Side House, Biggleswade	Regent's Park	1868
Pursey, Richard, Chilwell, Nottingham (*Beeston*)	Metropolitan	1884
Pywell, Joseph, 49, Greek-street, Stockport	Bradford	1844
RADBURN, William, Henley-in-Arden, near Birmingham	Stepney	1857
Rankine, John, 50, Stoke-road, Guildford	Metropolitan	1879
Ranson, Walter H., Somersham, Ipswich	.. ..	1888
Rawlings, Thomas Ebenezer, 2, Spring-grove, Idle, Bradford	Metropolitan	1867
Raymond, John, 17, Gloddaeth-crescent, Llandudno	Metropolitan	1873
Read, John, Prospect House, Priory-square, Studley R.S.O., Warwickshire	Regent's Park	1893
Readman, James Henry, Wootton, Bedford	.. ..	1870
Realff, A. E., 4, Hatherley-villas, Dollis-road, Church End, Finchley, London, N.	Culham	1878
Reed, Thomas Morgan, Loughor R.S.O., Glam.	Bangor	1892
Reed, Walter W., Wedmore, Weston-super-Mare	.. ..	1890
Rees, Charles, Tongwynlais, Cardiff	Llangollen	1883
Rees, David, 46, Park-avenue, Oswestry	Haverfordwest	1882
Rees, Frederick Abijah, Apsley House, Bury, Lancs	Pontypool	1892
Rees, George, John-street, Thornbury R.S.O., Gloucestershire	Haverfordwest	1863
Rees, Henry, 2, Arfryn, Llangollen	E. London Inst.	1888
Rees, John, 12, City-road, Haverfordwest	.. ..	1873
Rees, John C., Pensarn, Amlwch, Anglesey	Llangollen	1883
Rees, John D., Pontrhydyryn, near Pontypool, Mon.	Pont. & Reg. Pk.	1880
Rees, Morgan Thomas, Green Hall, Kidwelly, Carm.	Llangollen	1884
Rees, Thomas, Glyn Elan, Rhayader	Haverfordwest	1887
Rees, Thomas Leyshon, North-road, Milford Haven	Haverfordwest	1871
Rees, Thomas Morgan, Bethel Villa, Holyhead	Haverfordwest	1873
Rees, William, Harmony, St. Nicholas, Fishguard, Pemb. (*Pencaer*)	Llangollen	1879
Rees, William, Llandewi Rhydderch, Abergavenny	Pontypool	1887
Rees, William, Thompson-street, Hopkinstown, Pontypridd	Llangollen	1876

Name and Postal Address.	College.	Ministry commenced
Rees, William, Ton Mawr House, Blaenavon S.O., Mon. ..	Llangollen	.. 1867
Reid, Andrew John, Croydon (*Croham-road, South Croydon*)	Metropolitan	.. 1889
Reid, Henry, 39, Mill-bank, Wellington, Salop..	.. ..	.. 1884
Rendell, Alfred C. G., Long Buckby, Rugby	Bristol ..	.. 1883
Reynolds, Frederick William, 7, Penventon-terrace, Redruth	Metropolitan	.. 1892
Reynolds, John, Kidwelly, Carmarthenshire	.. ..	.. 1861
Reynolds, Philip, Albury, Ardilaun-road, Highbury-park, London, N. (*Highbury-place, Islington*)	.. ..	.. 1880
Reynolds, William, Hendre House, Penycwm R.S.O., Pembs.	.. ..	.. 1840
Reynolds, William, Martletwy, Narberth	Haverfordwest	.. 1890
Reynolds, W. L., Trecynon, Aberdare	Manchester	.. 1883
Rhys, William Casnodyn, 6, Beauchamp-road, Forest Gate, London, E.	Pontypool	.. 1876
Rice, George Miller, Lineholme, Todmorden	Bristol ..	.. 1888
Rice, W. E., Tuffley, near Gloucester (*Gloucester*)	Metropolitan	.. 1879
Richard, Richard, 33, Redland-grove, Bristol	Llangollen	.. 1879
Richards, David T., St. Ishmael's, Milford Haven (*Marloes*)	Haverfordwest & Aberystwyth U.	1891
Richards, David Bowen, 42, Robert-street, Manselton, Swansea	Pontypool	.. 1877
Richards, David, Cwmduad, Conwill Elfet, via Carmarthen..	Haverfordwest	.. 1865
Richards, John, Heol-las Farm, Verwig, Cardigan	Haverfordwest	.. 1879
Richards, Richard, 9, Worcester-buildings, Brynmawr R.S.O., Breconshire	Haverfordwest	.. 1876
Richards, Thomas, Cross Inn, Llantwit Vardre, Pontypridd	Llangollen	.. 1887
Richards, Thomas, Aberavon Academy, Aberavon, Port Talbot	Bristol ..	.. 1869
Richards, Thomas Myrddin, White Gate-terrace, Nelson, Treharris R.S.O., Glam.	Pontypool	.. 1885
Richards, Walter, 8, Oakville-terrace, Lochend-road, Leith	Metropolitan	.. 1882
Richards, William Williams, Greenfield-villas, Aberkenfig, Bridgend, Glam. (*Tondu*)	Pontypool and Bangor U.C..	.. 1885
Richardson, George Brooks, 5, White Rock-gardens, Hastings (*Battle*)	Metropolitan	.. 1876
Rickard, William, Homelea, Child's-hill, London, N.W. ..	.. ..	.. 1862
Riddell, Alexander M., Tottlebank, Ulverston	Glas. U. & B.U.S.	1885
Rigby, Joseph, 7, Brooklyn Terrace, Halifax-road, Dewsbury (*Staincliffe*)	Manchester	.. 1869
Rigby, Richard Henry, 44, Alfred-street, Harpurhey, Manchester	Rawdon ..	.. 1893
Rignal, Charles, Melbourne-terrace, Bradford	Manchester	.. 1881
Riley, Albert Fitzgibbon, 47, Whitehall Park, London, N. (*Archway-road, Highgate*)	Rawdon ..	.. 1873
Riseborough, Charles, 2, Ashley-avenue, Horehills-road, Leeds	Manchester	.. 1894
Robarts, Frederick H., 24, Belmont-gardens, Glasgow ..	Edinburgh Univ.	1859
Robert, George William, Clarence-avenue, Queen's-park, Northampton (*Kingsthorpe*)	Metropolitan	.. 1887
Roberts, David, Talog-road, Carmarthen	Haverfordwest	.. 1879
Roberts, David Evan, 21, Fitzhamon Embankment, Cardiff..	.. ..	.. 1879
Roberts, Ebenezer, 34, Camden-grove, Peckam, London, S.E. (*South London Tabernacle, Peckham*)	Metropolitan	.. 1874
Roberts, Hugh Ellis, Thrapston	Bangor ..	.. 1894
Roberts, Jesse, Cresswell Quay, Pembroke	Aberystwyth	.. 1895
Roberts, John, Ynys Farm, Clynnog, Carnarvonshire ..	.. ..	.. 1853
Roberts, John, Desert-terrace, Newtown, Mont. (*New Wells*)	Pontypool	.. 1881
Roberts, John Edward, M.A. (LON.), B.D. (ST. ANDREW'S), 378, Upper Brook-street, Manchester	Reg.Pk. & Lon.U.	1890
Roberts, Josiah, Gwern-y-Gerion, Treforest, Pontypridd (*Rhydfelen*)	.. ..	..
Roberts, Leyshon Mathaiarn, M.A. (U.S.), 15, Spencer-street, Ebbw Vale R.S.O., Mon.	Lewisburg Univ. (U.S.A.)	.. 1875
Roberts, Moses, Blaenau Festiniog (*Festiniog*)	Bangor ..	.. 1893
Roberts, Robert, Morriston, near Swansea	.. ..	.. 1865

Name and Postal Address.	College.	Ministry commenced
Roberts, Robert Henry, B.A. (Lon.), *President*, The College, Regent's-park, London, N.W.	Bristol ..	.. 1861
Roberts, Robert Younger, Oakdale House, Melton-road, Leicester..	Midland ..	.. 1868
Roberts, Rowland Charles, 22, Laws-street South, Pembroke Dock	Llangollen	.. 1876
Roberts, Samuel Foster, Pontllyw, Glam.	.. ..	.. 1882
Roberts, Thomas, 3, Park Villas, Abergele R.S.O., Denbigh	Llangollen	.. 1889
Roberts, Tobias John, Barmouth	Aberystwyth	.. 1891
Roberts, William, Felinganol, Solva R.S.O., Pemb. (*Middle-mill*)	Llangollen	.. 1882
Robertson, Frederic, Eastdowne, Coombe-park, Bath ..	Regent's Park	.. 1865
Robertson, John Donald, Alloa	Glas. U. & Bap. Th.	1895
Robinson, Frank Edward, B.A. (Lon.), B.D. (St. Andrew's), 28, Albany-road, Leighton Buzzard	Bristol ..	.. 1887
Robinson, Greenwood, The Knoll, Westham, Weymouth ..	Midland ..	.. 1883
Robinson, John Alexander Grant, M.A. (Glas.), Auchnafairn, Moncrieff-terrace, Craigie, Perth	Edin. U. & B.U.S.	1890
Robinson, John Henry, 7, Lilac-street, Lee Mount-road, Halifax	Metropolitan	.. 1885
Robinson, Josiah, Little Kingshill, Gt. Missenden R.S.O., Bucks	.. ..	.. 1867
Robinson, W. E., Victoria-place, Llantarnam, near Newport, Mon.	.. ..	.. 1890
Robinson, William Venis, B.A. (Lon.), Serampore, Boscombe, Bournemouth	Regent's Park	.. 1877
Robinson, William Wright, Hemel Hempstead	Metropolitan	.. 1873
Rock, George, Derryneil, Castlewellan, co. Down	.. ..	.. 1891
Roderick, William, 11, River-street, Rhyl	Llangollen	.. 1875
Rodway, Eusebius Joseph, 6, St. John's-terrace, Weston-super-Mare	.. ..	.. 1849
Rodway, John Daniel, Floraine Villa, Dartmouth-road, Paignton..	.. ..	.. 1872
Rogers, Robert, Ruthin R.S.O., Denbighshire	Regent's Park	.. 1876
Rollason, Alfred, Audley-road, Saffron Walden	Rawdon ..	.. 1872
Rollo, P. J., 645, Alexandra-place, Dennistoun, Glasgow ..	Glas. U. & B.U.S.	1869
Rootham, John Norris, Pier-street, Ventnor, I.W.	Metropolitan	.. 1874
Rose, James, Sandhurst, Wokingham	.. ..	.. 1865
Rose, William Henry, 23, Carey-street, Reading	.. ..	.. 1880
Rosevear, William Trenouth, 43, Percy-park, Tynemouth, North Shields	Bristol ..	.. 1850
Ross, David, 16, Shaftesbury-street, Stockton-on-Tees ..	Glasgow Univ.	.. 1884
Ross, Donald, Bowmore, Islay, Argyllshire	.. ..	.. 1878
Ross, William, Belle Vue, Coleford, Glos.	Bristol ..	.. 1883
Rosser, Henry, Treherbert, Pontypridd..	.. ..	.. 1855
Rosser, William, 10, Walters'-road, Melincrythan, Neath ..	.. ..	.. 1880
Roughton, George W., 47, East-street, Warminster	Bristol ..	.. 1866
Rowe, Philip Popplestone, M.A. (Lon.), The Limes, Tettenhall, Wolverhampton	Regent's Park	.. 1861
Rowland, Morris, Llanfair, near Harlech, Merioneth ..	.. ..	.. 1850
Rowland, W. S., M.A. (Cantab), Bluntisham, St. Ives, Hunts	Camb. Univ.	.. 1893
Rowlands, John, D.D. (U.S.), Llanelly, Carmarthenshire ..	Pontypool	.. 1851
Rowling, William Henry, Hamsterley, near Bishop Auckland	Manchester	.. 1890
Rowson, Henry, 336, Dudley-road, Birmingham	Bradford	.. 1856
Rowson, Thomas, 3, New-street, Welshpool	.. ..	.. 1873
Rowton-Parker, William, Crowle, Doncaster	.. ..	.. 1869
Rudge, C., Lynwood, Sevenoaks, Kent	Metropolitan	.. 1885
Rumsey, George Hunt, 1, Havelock-villas, Park-road, Merton, Surrey (*Longley-road, Lower Tooting*)	Metropolitan	.. 1888
Rumsey, William, Brockley, Bury St. Edmunds	.. ..	.. 1877
Rush, Thomas, Tipson-green, near Hounslow	.. ..	.. 1863
Rushby, Charles, Stock's-lane, Stalybridge	Midland ..	.. 1881

Name and Postal Address.	College.	Ministry commenced
Russell, David, 8, Queen's-road, Lower Edmonton (*Lower Edmonton*)	Metropolitan	1863
Russell, Frank, 11, Lothair-road, Anfield, Liverpool	Metropolitan	1885
Russell, John R., Astwood Bank, Redditch	Rawdon	1874
Russell, William Thomas, 11, Manor-place, Paddington-green, London, W. (*John-street, Marylebone*)	.. .. ..	1871
Ruthven, William, 16, Osborne-villas, Hellesdon-road, Norwich	Metropolitan	1886
Ryall, Charles Henry, 18, Glebe-road, Bromley, Kent	.. .. ..	1888
SAGE, John, West-road, Saffron Walden	Bradford	1855
Sage, William Carey, M.A., B.D. (EDIN.), Greenhill-lane, near Alfreton (*Riddings and Swanwick*)	Rawdon & Ed. U.	1888
Salathiel, Thomas, 96, High-street, Cefncoedycymmer, Merthyr Tydvil	Llangollen	1873
Salisbury, James, M.A. (U.S.), 32, Otter-street, Strutt's Park, Derby	Brdfd. & St. And.	1851
Salt, Henry Richard, St. Peter-street, Wallingford	.. .. ..	1869
Sampford, John, Ware, Herts	.. .. ..	1860
Samuel, David, Vicarage-road, Morriston, Swansea	Haverfordwest	1875
Samuel, Walter, 16, Borrowdale-road, Sefton Park, Liverpool	Haverfordwest	1860
Samuels, E., Sleaford, Lincolnshire	.. .. ..	1862
Samuels, Frederick, 14, Richmond-street, Stoke-on-Trent	.. .. ..	1879
Sanders, Harry, Belmont Villa, Trowbridge	E. London Inst.	1886
Satchwell, Walter, Lutterworth-road, Attleborough, Nuneaton	.. .. ..	1874
Saunders, James, Dinton, Aylesbury	Hackney	1847
Saunders, William Roberts, 16, Penrallt-road, Upper Bangor	Pontypool	1875
Savage, A. A., 18, Lower Cliff-road, Gorleston T.S.O., Great Yarmouth	.. .. ..	1893
Saville, Alfred Alexander, West Parade, Lincoln	Metropolitan	1880
Saville, Charles, Middleton Cheney, near Banbury	.. .. ..	1883
Sawday, Charles Burt, 9, Clarendon-place, Leeds	Metropolitan	1863
Sawday, Charles Pike, 36, Kitto-road, Nunhead, London, S.E. (*Edith-road, Nunhead*)	Metropolitan	1893
Scamell, Tom Webb, Meadowlands, Lyndhurst S.O., Hants	Metropolitan	1879
Schaffer, Edwin, 8, Harold-street, Roath, Cardiff	.. .. ..	1883
Schofield, James Thomas, Milthorpe, Towcester (*Weston-by-Weedon*)	Regent's Park	1893
Scilley, John, Victoria-road, Bridlington Quay, Yorks.	Metropolitan	1880
Scoones, John Richard, 37, Philip-road, Peckham, London, S.E. (*Uxbridge*)	.. .. ..	1882
Scorey, Philip George, Ellesmere, Venner-road, Sydenham, London, S.E.	Stepney	1856
Scott, Edward, Prospect-place, Bampton R.S.O., Devon	.. .. ..	1870
Scott, James, Scarfskerry, Thurso	Bap.Th.In.,Edin.	1849
Scott, John George, 4, Sea View, Dartmouth	.. .. ..	1879
Scott, Robert, Guiseley, Leeds	Met. & Ed. Un.	1883
Scriven, W., 228, Walworth-road, London, S.E.	Bristol	1867
Scudamore, George, 47, Boundary-road, St. John's Wood, London, N.W.	.. .. ..	1880
Seager, James, Cobourg-road, Montpelier, Bristol	Rawdon	1873
Seaman, William, 3, Waverley-cottages, Hawick	Metropolitan	1878
Sears, Robert Edward, 49, Battersea Rise, New Wandsworth, London, S.W. (*Meyrick-road, Clapham Junction*)	.. .. ..	1859
Selby, Robert Albert, Park View, Far Cotton, Northampton	.. .. ..	1887
Sexton, Walter, 13, Vauxhall-terrace, Boston	Metropolitan	1880
Shackleford, Lewis John, Ripley, Derby	Rawdon	1879
Shakespeare, John Howard, M.A. (LON.), The Wilderness, Bracondale, Norwich	Regent's Park & U. Coll., Lond.	1883
Shankland Thomas, Wheatville, Rhyl	Llangollen and Bangor U.C.	1888
Sharman, William, Station-road, Fleet (Hants.), Winchfield	Midland	1857

Name and Postal Address.	College.	Ministry commenced
Sharp, Daniel, Frankfort Villa, Easton-road, Bristol.. ..	Metropolitan ..	1877
Sharpe, William, 10, Arklow-square, Ramsgate	.. .. ..	1845
Shaw, Albert Oliver, Frithelstock, Great Torrington ..	Midland	1886
Shaw, Frederick, Brighton..	.. .. ..	1862
Shearer, John Fleming, 18, High Lever-road, St. Quintin's-park, N. Kensington, London, W. (*Ladbroke-grove Chapel, Cornwall-road, Notting Hill*)	Glas. U. & Metro.	1886
Shelley, Joseph, Croxton, Eccleshall, Staffs.	.. .. ..	1860
Shephard, John Edward, 26, Albany-street, Hull	.. .. ..	1875
Shepherd, Edwin Burfield, 2, Belmont-terrace, Newark ..	Regent's Park ..	1872
Shepherd, William Thomas, Upton-on-Severn, Worcester ..	Metropolitan ..	1894
Shindler, Robert, Maxwell House, Kelvin-grove, Sydenham, London, S.E.	.. .. ..	1850
Shinn, Arthur, Broseley R.S.O., Salop	.. .. ..	1887
Shipley, Cecil Edgar, Highfields, Bryn-road, Swansea ..	Bristol	1892
Short, Alfred George, Beaulieu House, Sandown R.S.O., I.W.	Metropolitan ..	1871
Short, George, B.A. (LON.), 4, The Cedars, Manor-road, Salisbury	Stepney	1851
Sidey, William Wilson, 54, Lansdowne-road, Tottenham (*High-road, Tottenham*)	Regent's Park ..	1880
Silby, Robert, 91, Burford-road, Nottingham	Midland ..	1870
Silvey, Robert, 34, Glebe-road, Bromley, Kent (*Park-road, Bromley*)..	Regent's Park ..	1893
Simmonds, Henry Walter, Cavendish-road, Aylestone Park, Leicester	Metropolitan ..	1876
Simmons, George, Granville-road, Sidcup R.S.O., Kent (*Sidcup*)	Metropolitan ..	1875
Simpson, Matthew, 5, Caulfield-terrace, Dungannon (*Knockconny*)	.. .. ..	1864
Simpson, William Robertson, Caledonia Cottage, Crieff ..	Edin. U.& B.U.S.	1889
Singleton, Hugh, Edgbaston-road, Smethwick, Birmingham	Rawdon	1882
Sirett, Caleb, Cutsdean, Broadway, Worcestershire	.. .. ..	1884
Skelly, John G., Brimpton, Reading	Madison, U.S.A.	1868
Skemp, Charles Widlake, 21, Marlborough-road, Bradford ..	Rawdon	1869
Skemp, John G., M.A. (EDIN.), 110, Langworthy-road, Pendleton T.S.O., Manchester	Rawdon & Edin. Univ... ..	1884
Skerry, William Richard, 177, The Grove, Camberwell, London, S.E. (*Denmark-place, Camberwell*)	Rawdon	1868
Skingle, Samuel, West Retford, Notts	Metropolitan ..	1872
Slack, Charles Augustus, Market Harborough..	Metropolitan ..	1878
Slater, Peter Forrester, 40 Jane-street, Blythswood-square, Glasgow	Glas. U. & B.U.S.	1881
Slater, William, 212, Highbury-road, Bulwell, Nottingham..	Metropolitan ..	1883
Small, George, M.A. (EDIN.), 4, Hartley-road, Leytonstone, London, N.E.	Bris. & Edin. Un.	1840
Smalley, James, 40, Burlington-street, Blackburn	Bristol	1873
Smart, Edwin, 29, St. John's-villas, Upper Holloway, London, N. (*Hornsey-road, Holloway*)..	.. .. ..	1893
Smart, Percy John, White House, High-street, Hadley T.S.O., Barnet (*Barnet*)	Metropolitan ..	1893
Smathers, Robert, Market-place, Whitchurch S.O., Hants ..	Metropolitan ..	1880
Smith, Amos, 61, Oliver-street, Kingsley-park, Northampton	Midland	1842
Smith, E. Ashford, Great Northern-road, Dunstable	Bristol	1890
Smith, Ernest Edwin, Trowbridge-road, Bradford-on-Avon	Bristol	1890
Smith, Frank, 5, Hurst-street, Oxford	Western Congl.	1882
Smith, Frank M., 9, East Dulwich-rd., London, S.E.	Metropolitan ..	1870
Smith, George K., Tintern Lodge, Bexley Heath S.O., Kent (*Bexley Heath*)	Metropolitan ..	1877
Smith, Henry, Faringdon	Metropolitan ..	1889
Smith, Henry Samuel, Aylesbury-street, Fenny Stratford, Bucks	Metropolitan ..	1875
Smith, James, 5, Hanover-road, Tunbridge Wells	Metropolitan ..	1863

Name and Postal Address.	College.	Ministry commenced
Smith, James, 6, Cowell-terrace, Soham..	Theol. Educ. Soc.	1847
Smith, James, Westbourne Villa, Corsham R.S.O., Wilts. ..	Metropolitan ..	1873
Smith, James Henry Pope, 99, Prospect-road, Scarborough	.. .. ..	1887
Smith, John Laxon, Sainthill, Kentisbere, Cullompton, Devon	Bristol (Ind.) ..	1870
Smith, John Nathan, Blaengavenny, Llanfihangel Crucorney, Abergavenny (*Capel-y-Ffin, Breconshire*)	Pontypool ..	1890
Smith, Joseph Manton, 75, Bedford-road, Clapham, London, S.W. (*Evangelist*)	Metropolitan ..	1877
Smith, Philip Henry, Kingsley-road, Northampton	Rawdon	1894
Smith, Robert, Histon, Cambridge	Manchester ..	1890
Smith, Thomas Henry, Walsworth-road, Hitchin	Metropolitan ..	1877
Smith, Thomas Napoleon, Tetbury	Metropolitan ..	1889
Smith, W. Harvey, 178, Stamford-hill, London, N. (*Bethnal Green-road*)	Midland.. ..	1875
Smith, William, Kirton Lindsey R.S.O., Lincs.	Metropolitan ..	1870
Smith, William, Avon Manse, Melksham	.. .. ..	1891
Smith, William Henry, Cotton End, Bedford	Metropolitan ..	1870
Smythe, Frank Tompson, 192, Kettering-road, Northampton	Bristol	1887
Smythe, James Francis, Boxwell-road, Berkhamsted.. ..	Bristol	1858
Somers, Samuel James, 28, Christchurch-street, Frome ..	E. London Inst.	1889
Soper, Walter Tucker, 56, Lansdown, Stroud	Metropolitan ..	1882
Sowerby, Robert Cochrane, 27, Queen-street, Stirling ..	.. .. ..	1837
Spanswick, John, Longford, Coventry	Metropolitan ..	1868
Spanton, Emery, Modbury, Devon	Metropolitan ..	1876
Sparham, T. H., Gt. Ellingham, Attleborough, Norfolk ..	.. .. ..	1854
Sparks, George, Victoria Villa, Mill Hill, West Cowes, I.W.	.. .. ..	1866
Spence, Daniel Andrew, 12, Osborne-terrace, South Shields	Glasgow Univ. ..	1890
Spence, John, 49, Oakley-crescent, Chelsea, London, S.W. (*Lower Sloane Street, Chelsea*)	.. .. ..	1891
Sprague, Alfred, Boroughbridge, near Bridgwater	.. .. ..	1873
Springthorpe, William, Cramer-street, Stafford	Midland.. ..	1894
Spufford, Hy. Thomas, Beechcroft-road, Bushey-grove, Watford	Metropolitan ..	1872
Spurgeon, Charles, Haddon, Dartmouth-row, Blackheath, London, S.E. (*South-street, Greenwich*)	Metropolitan ..	1879
Spurgeon, James Archer, D.D., LL.D. (U.S.), Campbelton, White Horse-road, Croydon (*West Croydon*)	Regent's Park ..	1859
Spurgeon, Thomas, 87, Knatchbull-road, Camberwell, London, S.E. (*Metropolitan Tabernacle*)	Metropolitan ..	1879
Spurr, Frederick Chambers, 35, Ladywell-park, Lewisham, London, S.E. (*Baptist Union Missioner*)	.. .. ..	1881
Spurrier, Edward, 33, Wellesley-road, Colchester	Metropolitan ..	1866
Stalberg, Isaac Octavius, 83, Windsor-road, Penarth.. ..	Metropolitan ..	1885
Stanley, Charles, 37, Washington-terrace, North Shields ..	Metropolitan ..	1889
Stanley, George, Eythorne, Dover	Metropolitan ..	1869
Stanley, James L., 1, Idmiston-road, West Norwood, London, S.E. (*Chatsworth-road, West Norwood*)	.. .. ..	1892
Stanley, John, Aston House, Bampton, Faringdon (*Coate*)..	Metropolitan ..	1885
Steedman, Leven Stuart, Tullymet, Ballinluig R.S.O., Perthshire	Metropolitan ..	1889
Steele, G., Cam, near Dursley, Gloucestershire	.. .. ..	1864
Stembridge, Hy. George, Biggleswade	Regent's Park ..	1884
Stenlake, Edwin W., 58, Trinder-road, Crouch-hill, London, N.	.. .. ..	1873
Stephens, James. M.A. (GLAS.), 46, Dartmouth Park-road, London, N.W. (*Highgate-road*)	Glas. & Ed. Uns.	1871
Stephens, W. E., Blaenavon R.S.O., Mon.	Haverfordwest ..	1893
Steven, J. M., London-road, Romford	Glasgow Univ. ..	1877
Stevens, George, Blackmore, Ingatestone, Essex	.. .. ..	1864
Stevenson, Edward, Southfield-road, Loughborough	Midland.. ..	1834
Stevenson, William, 33, Sotheby-road, Highbury-park, London, N. (*Highbury-hill*)	Glasgow Univ. & B.U.S. ..	1886
Stevenson, William Lewis, Lydgate, near Todmorden ..	Midland.. ..	1877

Name and Postal Address.	College.	Ministry commenced
Stock, Alfred, B.A. (Lon.), B.D. (St. And.), St. Michael's Mount, Honiton	Regent's Park	1884
Stone, Charles Ernest, 18, Park-road North, Middlesborough	Metropolitan	1883
Stone, H. E., 14, Abbey-road, St. John's Wood, London, N.W. (*Abbey-road, St. John's Wood*)	Metropolitan	1871
Stone, Hy., Farnham Common, Slough, Bucks	.. ..	1867
Stone, William, Birthright-view, Cornholme, Todmorden	Midland	1881
Storey, John, Letterkenny, Donegal	.. ..	1859
Stott, William, 11, Chatsworth-road, West Norwood, London, S.E. (*Battersea-park Tabernacle*)	.. ..	1862
Stovell, Charles, Chudleigh, Newton Abbot	Bristol	1865
Streuli, Arnold W. H., 138, Withington-road, Whalley Range, Manchester	Regent s Park	1891
Stuart, James, Beechen-grove Manse, Watford	Rawdon & Glas. University	1864
Sturge, Alfred, Highfield-road, Dartford	.. ..	1850
Styles, William Jeyes, 1, College-street, Islington, London, N.	Metropolitan	1863
Sullivan, William, Budleigh Salterton S.O., Devon	Metropolitan	1872
Sumner, William, 30, Edinburgh-grove, Armley, Leeds	Metropolitan	1876
Suter, Henry John Allison, Oakham	Metropolitan	1892
Swift, John T., 50, Wiltshire-road, Brixton, London, S.W.	Metropolitan	1872
Tait, David, Union street, South Leith	Metropolitan	1889
Tanswell, George Robert, Milford-on-Sea, Lymington	.. ..	1861
Tarbox, Edward William, Epsom-road, Guildford (*Horsell*)	Regent's Park	1876
Tarn, T. Graham, 56, St. Andrew's-street, Cambridge	Metropolitan	1872
Taylor, David, 41, Gore-road, South Hackney, London, N.E.	.. ..	[illegible]
Taylor, George, 164, Dereham-road, Norwich	M[illegible]	[illegible]
Taylor, Henry William, Florence Villa, St. Albans	M[illegible]tan	[illegible]
Taylor, John, Tandragee, co. Armagh	.. ..	18[illegible]
Taylor, John, 19, South-street, Isleworth	M[illegible]politan	[illegible]
Taylor, John Cameron, Gordon-street, Burslem	Manchester	1892
Taylor, Thomas, Tottlebank, Greenodd, near Ulverston	Bradford	1841
Taylor, W. Bampton, Chesham R.S.O., Bucks	Regent's Park	1883
Taylor, William John, 200, Euston-road, London, N.W.	.. ..	1878
Tessier, Alexander, Madras Cottage, Bromley, Kent	Metropolitan	1862
Tetley, John P., Glenthorne, Taunton	Midland	1865
Tettmar, Alfred B., Clare R.S.O., Suffolk	Metropolitan	1894
Thew, James, 28, De Montfort-street, Leicester	Rawdon	1872
Thirsk, William, Market-place, Beverley	.. ..	1853
Thomas, Benjamin, Letterston R.S.O., Pemb.	Haverfordwest	1865
Thomas, Benjamin, 15, St. Albans-road, Harlesden, London, N.W. (*Harlesden*)	Haverfordwest	1882
Thomas, C. H., Waterlooville, Cosham R.S.O., Hants	Metropolitan	1873
Thomas, Charles, 3, Mount Pleasant, Chepstow	Pontypool	1892
Thomas, Daniel, Mount Zion, Swansea	Llangollen	1871
Thomas, David, 5, Sawel-terrace, Llandilo R.S.O., Carm.	.. ..	1864
Thomas, David, 22, Waenfelin-road, Pontypool	Pontypool	1868
Thomas, David, Cwmbach, Aberdare	Pontypool	1888
Thomas, David, Rock, Penybont R.S.O., Radnor	Aberystwyth	1895
Thomas, Edw[illegible]ry-street, Merthyr Tydvil	.. ..	1889
Thom[illegible] Garmon, Morriston, Swansea	Llangollen	1881
Thomas, Evan, Pant-teg, Mount-avenue, Ealing, London, W. (*Haven-green, Ealing*)	Haverfordwest & Regent's Park	1865
Thomas, Evan, Elm-terrace, Pembroke	Haverfordwest	1875
Thomas, Evan Ungoed, Tabernacle Villa, Carmarthen	Pontypool	1881
Thomas, George William, Grosvenor-road, Watford	.. ..	1882
Thomas, Hector Vortigern, The Poplars, Atherton, Manchester	Pontypool	1881
Thomas, Hopkin B., Deri, Cardiff	Pontypool	1892
Thomas, Ioan, Goginan R.S.O., Cardiganshire	Cardiff Univ.	1887
Thomas, Isaac, Llangyfelach-road, Landore, Swansea	Pontypool	1861

Name and Postal Address.	College.	Ministry commenced
Thomas, J. B., Talgarth R.S.O., Breconshire	Aberystwyth	.. 1895
Thomas, J. D., Clarbeston R.S.O., Pembs.	Aberystwyth	.. 1895
Thomas, J. E., Cwmgors, Gwauncaegurwen R.S.O., Glam.	Pontypool	.. 1894
Thomas, James Evan, Maesucha, Farmers, Llanwrda R.S.O., Carm. (*Caio*)	Pontypool	.. 1879
Thomas, John, Colwyn Bay R.S.O. Denbighshire	Pontypool	.. 1863
Thomas, John, Bay View, Penclawdd, near Swansea.. ..	Pontypool	.. 1874
Thomas, John, 10, Ruskin-road. Crewe..	Manchester	.. 1893
Thomas, John, 15, Morton-crescent, Exmouth	.. .. ..	.. 1872
Thomas, John, M.A. (LON.), 22, Devonshire-road, Liverpool	Pont. & Bangor	1887
Thomas, John Albert, Mayfield, Narberth	Haverfordwest	.. 1890
Thomas, John Hobson, 1, Erddig-terrace, Wrexham.. ..	Pontypool	.. 1892
Thomas, John Pardoe, Home-cottage, Cardiff-road, Newport, Mon.	.. .. ..	.. 1866
Thomas, Joseph William, Gainsborough Villa, Cambridge-road, New Malden S.O., Surrey (*Mill End, Herts.*) ..	Metropolitan	.. 1874
Thomas, Joshua, Coedpenmaen, Pontypridd	Pontypool	.. 1868
Thomas, Lewis Morgan, 907, Belmont Villas, Fairfield, Manchester	Manchester	.. 1894
Thomas, Robert Pritchard, Llangendeirn, Kidwelly	Llangollen	.. 1892
Thomas, Seth, Glyn Elan, Rhayader, Radnor	.. .. ..	.. 1859
Thomas, Stephen, Garth R.S.O., Breconshire (*Pantycelyn*)..	Haverfordwest	.. 1863
Thomas, Thomas, 18, Stanley - buildings, Crawshawbooth, Manchester (*Goodshaw*)	Bristol ..	.. 1879
Thomas, Thomas, Risca, Newport, Mon.	Pontypool	.. 1872
Thomas, Thomas, Cwm, Waunllwyd R.S.O., Mon. (*Victoria, Ebbw Vale*)	Pontypool	.. 1865
Thomas, Thomas A., Abercarn, Newport, Mon.	.. .. ..	.. 1882
Thomas, Thomas Lewis, 19, Osborne-road, Pontypool, Mon.	Haverfordwest	.. 1879
Thomas, W., Cloth Hall, Mountain Ash (*Aberdare*)	Haverfordwest	.. 1882
Thomas, William, Queen-street, Chester	.. .. ..	.. 1877
Thomas, William, 5, Cawley-road, South Hackney, London, N.E. (*Grove-road, Victoria-park*)	.. .. ..	.. 1877
Thomas, William Ceinfryn, Pant-road, Dowlais	Llangollen	.. 1880
Thomason, Thomas William, 11, Park-view, Queen's Park, Manchester	Metropolitan	.. 1865
Thompson, Douglas, 25, Grange-road, Kingston-on-Thames (*Norbiton*)	Metropolitan	.. 1892
Thompson, Frank, 18, Stockwood-crescent, Luton	Metropolitan	.. 1886
Thompson, John Charles, Heathfield S.O., Sussex	Metropolitan	.. 1875
Thompson, Oliver, Aldwinckle, Thrapston	.. .. ..	.. 1880
Thomsett, William Ellis, 161, Oxford-road, Reading	.. .. ..	.. 1852
Thomson, Alexander, 35a, Queen-street, Galashiels	.. .. ..	.. 1852
Thomson, Malcolm Macmillan, Guilsborough, Northampton	.. .. ..	.. 1892
Thomson, Peter Taylor, M.A. (GLAS.), Leeds	Glas. U. & B.U.S.	1893
Thomson, Robert, 18, Harbutt-road, New Wandsworth, London, S.W.	Glasgow Univ.	.. 1882
Thorpe, Samuel John, Hermon-road, Teignmouth	Metropolitan	.. 1894
Throssell, John Nottes, High-street, Ramsey, Huntingdon	.. .. ..	.. 1892
Tidman, Owen, Ebenezer Cottage, Magor, Newport, Mon...	.. .. ..	.. 1872
Tildsley, Alfred, 3, Westwood-terrace, Rawtenstall, Manchester (*Sunnyside*)	Manchester	.. 1894
Tilly, Alfred, Cardiff	Stepney	.. 1846
Tipple, Samuel A., Howden-rd., Upper Norwood, London, S.E. (*Upper Norwood*)	.. .. ..	.. 1850
Titmuss, Thomas Edgar, 313, Rotton Park-road, Birmingham	Metropolitan	.. 1892
Todd, John Wood, D.D., Lynwood, Forest Hill, London, S.E.	Pontypool	.. 1845
Tolhurst, Adolphus Henry, Oakleigh, Melton-road, Leicester	Rawdon ..	.. 1894
Toll, James, Great Ellingham, Attleborough, Norfolk ..	.. .. ..	.. 1850
Tomkins, William John, Rushden R.S.O., Northants ..	Metropolitan	.. 1874
Toogood, John, 31, Croft-terrace, Jarrow	Metropolitan	.. 1893

Name and Postal Address.	College.	Ministry commenced
Tooke, William, 37, Queen's-road, Bury St. Edmunds ..	.. ..	.. 1887
Tooley, George Walter, Beverley, Fairmile-avenue, Streatham, London, S.W.	Metropolitan	.. 1876
Toone, Joseph Frank, B.A. (LON.), Sydney House, Tiverton	Regent's Park	.. 1888
Tovey, Aaron, Beaufort R.S.O., Breconshire	.. ..	.. 1861
Towler, Edward, Littleborough, Manchester	.. ..	.. 1887
Towler, George, Atch Lench, Evesham	Midland	.. 1860
Towler, Robert Edward, 7, Eltham-terrace, Levenshulme, Manchester (*Financial Secretary, Manchester College*) ..	Manchester	.. 1881
Townsend, William, 38, St. George's-place, Canterbury ..	Metropolitan	.. 1874
Tranter, John Ernest, Marshfield-road, Chippenham ..	Regent's Park	.. 1892
Tree, Henry Arthur, Broughton, Stockbridge S.O., Hants ..	Metropolitan	.. 1891
Trotman, Herbert, 133, Spring Vale-road, Sheffield	Metropolitan	.. 1882
Trotman, William, 5, St. George's-terrace, Stonehouse, Plymouth	.. ..	.. 1847
Trueman, Hugh, 96, Berkhampstead-road, Chesham R.S.O., Bucks.	Metropolitan	.. 1890
Tucker, William, Cornwallis-avenue, Clifton Vale, Bristol ..	.. ..	.. 1871
Tuckwell, John, 15, Craven-park-road, Harlesden, London, N.W. (*Westbourne grove*)	Regent's Park	.. 1868
Tulloch, William, Mount Pleasant, Bridge of Allan.. ..	Edinburgh Univ.	1843
Turner, Fred. Willey, 9, New-street, Pudsey, Leeds	Rawdon ..	.. 1893
Turner, George, Kilmeedy, Ringstead-road, Sutton, Surrey (*Sutton*)	Metropolitan	.. 1870
Turner, John, Southdown College, Chatsworth-gardens, Eastbourne	Metropolitan	.. 1862
Turner, Joseph, Blaby, near Leicester	Midland ..	.. 1877
Turner, Thomas, 40, Windmill-lane, Stratford, London, E...	.. ..	.. 1867
Turner, William, Naseby, Foster Hill-road, Bedford	Rawdon ..	.. 1869
Tweedie, William Lawrence, Woodbine Cottage, Montenotte, Cork	Metropolitan	.. 1894
Tydeman, Ebenezer Alfred, 11, May's-villas, Foots Cray S.O., Kent	Metropolitan	.. 1872
Tymms, T. Vincent, *Principal*, The College, Rawdon, Leeds	Regent's Park	.. 1865
Tyrrell, John, Woodford, Thrapston	.. ..	.. 1860
UNDERWOOD, Alfred, M.A. (GLAS.), 29, Charnwood-street, Derby	Mid. & Glas. U.	1875
Underwood, William, D.D. (U.S.), 29, Charnwood-street, Derby	Midland	.. 1836
Urquhart, John, 10, Paternoster-row, London, E.C.	Glas. U. & B. U.S.	1865
Usher, William, M.D. (ROY. U. I.), (*Tutor, Pastors' College*), Falkland Lodge, Orpington R.S.O., Kent..	Metropolitan	.. 1872
VANSTONE, William John Newton, 12, Vancouver-road, Catford, London, S.E. (*Catford Hill*)	Metropolitan	.. 1883
Varley, John William, St. Andrew's road South, St. Anne's-on-the-Sea, Preston	Manchester	.. 1885
Varley, Thomas, Keysoe, St. Neots	.. ..	.. 1887
Vasey, William Brown, Fern Bank, John-street, Sale, Manchester	Bury ..	.. 1872
Vaughan, Cornelius Wallace, 13, Rowell-street, Hartlepool ..	Metropolitan	.. 1890
Vick, Charles William, 2, Dyne-road, Brondesbury, London, N.W. (*Brondesbury*)	Midland..	.. 1880
Vince, Henry, Foulsham, Dereham, Norfolk	.. ..	.. 1882
Vincent, Samuel, 9, Woodside, Plymouth	Bristol ..	.. 1867
Virgo, George, 31, Upper Rock-gardens, Brighton	.. ..	.. 1856
WADDELL, Thomas Frederick, Derwick, South-street, Dorking	Metropolitan	.. 1885
Wainwright, George, Nelson-road, Bournemouth	Metropolitan	.. 1876
Walker, Albert, 62, Cromwell-road, Belfast	Manchester	.. 1893
Walker, Alfred, 28, Lady Margaret-road, London, N.W. ..	Metropolitan	.. 1867

Name and Postal Address.	College.	Ministry commenced
Walker, Arthur Turpin, Allerton, Bradford	Rawdon	1892
Walker, George, 27, Brewer-street, Maidstone	Metropolitan	1864
Walker, George, Shrigley View, Poynton, Stockport	.. .. ..	1862
Walker, James, South Parade, Frome	Rawdon	1877
Walker, Joseph, 18, Hazelwood-road, Northampton	.. .. ..	1881
Walker, Richard, Clyde Villa, Poole	Regent's Park	1879
Walker, William, Prospect-villas, Warley-road, Brentwood	Metropolitan	1886
Walker, William, Portland-road, Bishops Stortford	Metropolitan	1887
Wall, George Frederick, Bardwell, near Ixworth, Suffolk	.. .. ..	1882
Wall, Walter, Eglos, Ellington, Ramsgate	Regent's Park	1890
Wallace, Robert, Chapel House, Tottenham	Glasgow & Edin.	1834
Wallace, Robert Bruce, Little Tew, Enstone, Oxon	.. .. ..	1868
Walsh, Walter, 4, Malvern-street, Newcastle-on-Tyne	Glas. U. & B. U. S.	1882
Walter, Eli Elijah, 111, Botanic-road, Edge-hill, Liverpool	Metropolitan	1869
Walter, Frederick W., Bildeston S.O., Suffolk	Metropolitan	1893
Ward, Alfred, Beech Hill, near Reading	.. .. ..	1880
Ward, Ebenezer, 10, St. Helen's-street, Ipswich (*Framsden*)	.. .. ..	1881
Ward, Isaac Arthur, 9, Talbot-place, The Park, Sheffield	Metropolitan	1881
Warren, Charles Barrett, Little Staughton, St. Neots	Metropolitan	1867
Waters, D. W., Plasbach, Cwmsarnddu, Llandovery R.S.O., Carm.	.. .. ..	1893
Waterton, Clement, 1, Haven-villas, Haven Bank, Boston	Midland	1886
Watkins, Benjamin, 2, Sunny-cottages, Loughor R.S.O., Glam.	Haverfordwest	1849
Watkins, Charles Henry, 46, Claude-road, Cardiff	Pontypool	1881
Watkins, Edwin, Llangunog, near Carmarthen	Haverfordwest	1889
Watkins, Evan, Ryeford, near Ross, Herefordshire	Pontypool	1876
Watkins, Samuel, The Lock, Withington, Hereford	.. .. ..	1868
Watkins, William Evans, Frondeg Villa, Pemberton-avenue, Burry Port R.S.O., Carmarthenshire (*Pembrey*)	Haverfordwest	1863
Watmough, Joseph, Headcorn, Ashford, Kent	Midland	1875
Watson, Isaac, Egerton House, Radcliffe, Manchester	Metropolitan	1890
Watts, Frederick Charles, Moulton, Northampton	Metropolitan	1891
Watts, Henry, 9, Sidney-street, Grantham	.. .. ..	1858
Watts, Isaac, 4, Calthorpe-road, Banbury	Regent's Park	1869
Watts, James Gomer, Hanbury-terrace, Pontnewynydd, Pontypool	.. .. ..	1879
Watts, John, Mapledene, Whitecross-rd., Weston-super-Mare	Bristol	1872
Watts, Thomas, 6, Alexandra-road, Bedford	Stepney	1856
Way, Thomas Wreford, 136, Gilmore-place, Edinburgh	Regent's Park	1888
Webb, Evan, 6, Lawson-avenue, Long Eaton R.S.O., Derbyshire	Haverfordwest	1893
Webb, G. A., Ivy Bank, Staple Hill, Bristol (*Downend*)	Metropolitan	1880
Welch, Archibald William, Enfield Villa, Putney Road, Enfield Wash, Ponder's End (*Totteridge-road, Enfield Highway*)	Metropolitan	1888
Wells, J. G., Woodside, Wealdstone R.S.O., Middlesex	.. .. ..	1894
Welton, Charles, 34, Church-street, Morley, Leeds	Metropolitan	1867
West, Frederick George, 21, Washington-street, Liverpool	Metropolitan	1889
West, George, Jaffray-road, Erdington, Birmingham	Metropolitan	1875
Westlake, Francis Thomas Bartlett, Sea Level House, Queen's Promenade, Douglas	Metropolitan	1886
Westwood, Andrew, 2, South View, Bishop Auckland	Rawdon	1886
Whatford, John, Crowborough, near Tunbridge Wells	.. .. ..	1868
Wheatley, Thomas, 7, Vernon-road, Hornsey, London, N.	Metropolitan	1870
Wheeler, Frederick G., 46, Arodene-road, Brixton, S.W. (*Barrington-road, Brixton*)	Metropolitan	1894
Wheeler, Thomas A., Hoveton St. John, Norwich	Stepney	1843
Whetnall, Matthew Henry, 28, Burlington-street, Blackburn	Metropolitan	1877
Whitaker, John, 25, Norley-villas, Hardinge-road, Ashford, Kent	Regent's Park	1870
Whitaker, John Thompson, Witton, Birmingham	Rawdon	1889
Whitaker, Joshua Cecil, Prince's End, Tipton	Regent's Park	1864
White, Edwin, 16, Delafield-road, Charlton S.O., Kent	Metropolitan	1874

Name and Postal Address.	College.	Ministry commenced
White, F. Thos., Stogumber, Taunton	Metropolitan ..	1893
White, George W., Arlesdene, London road, Enfield (*Enfield Tabernacle*)	Metropolitan ..	1870
White, William, Watchet R.S.O., Somerset	Metropolitan ..	1894
Whiteside, Thomas, Mount-street, Ballymena, co. Antrim ..	Metropolitan ..	1880
Whiting, George James, Dolton R.S.O., North Devon ..	.. .. ..	1892
Whittet, George, Belhaven-terrace, Wishaw, Lanark.. ..	Metropolitan ..	1873
Whittle, Thomas, 30, Nebo-street, Daubhill, Bolton	Metropolitan ..	1882
Wicks, Henry James, Minchinhampton, Stroud	Bristol	1889
Wicks, William Ager, 3, Westminster-road, Handsworth, Birmingham	Metropolitan ..	1882
Wigner, John Thomas, Breakspears-road, St. John's, London, S.E.	Stepney	1839
Wilkin, Martin Hood, Sydney House, Hampstead, London, N.W. (*Bassett-street, Kentish Town*)	.. .. ..	1869
Wilkins, Joseph, Wendover, Tring	Metropolitan ..	1873
Wilkinson, George William, 2, Waterloo-bank, Wadsworth, via Manchester	Manchester ..	1875
Wilkinson, James, 10, Melbourne-grove, Bramley, Leeds ..	Bury	1869
Wilkinson, John, 149, Upton-lane, Forest Gate, London, E. (*Upton Cross*)	Metropolitan ..	1868
Wilkinson, Samuel Hamill, St. Peter's, Oak Hill-road, Putney, London, S.W. (*Werter-road, Putney*)	Metropolitan ..	1892
Wilkinson, Thomas, High-street, Tewkesbury	Bradford ..	1847
Wilks, W. Willis, Beaconsfield-terrace, Alnwick	Metropolitan ..	1892
Williams, Anthony, Ystrad Rhondda, Pontypridd	Llangollen ..	1872
Williams, Charles, Accrington	Newport Pagnell	[illegible]
Williams, Charles Baines, Truro	[illegible] ..	[illegible]
Williams, David, Commerce House, St. Clears, Carmarthenshire	Haverfordwest ..	[illegible]
Williams, David, 31, Regent-street, Llangollen	Llangollen ..	[illegible]
Williams, David Sinclair, 32, Athol-road, Bradford	Pontypool ..	1883
Williams, Edward Richard, Talybont, Glendovey R.S.O., Card.	Bangor	1895
Williams, Evan, Rhosllanerchrugog, Ruabon	Llangollen and Bangor U.C.	1887
Williams, George, Amlwch Port, Amlwch R.S.O., Anglesey (*Amlwch*)	Llangollen ..	1888
Williams, George, 40, Seymour-road, Astley Bridge, Bolton ..	.. .. ..	1857
Williams, George Charles, 325, Kellinghall-road, Bradford ..	Metropolitan ..	1878
Williams, George Nathaniel, Cromwell Villa, Stretford, Manchester	.. .. ..	1881
Williams, Griffith Llechidon, Cadoxton, Cardiff	Llangollen ..	1872
Williams, Hugh, Hermon House, Nantyglo R.S.O., Mon. ..	Llangollen ..	1874
Williams, Hugh Cernyw, Corwen, North Wales	Llangollen ..	1865
Williams, J. Gwyddno, Briensiencyn, Llanfairpwll, R.S.O., Anglesey..	.. .. ..	1890
Williams, J. Prue, Rochelle, St. Ursula Grove, Southsea ..	Bristol	1869
Williams, James, Camrose R.S.O., Pemb.	Haverfordwest ..	1880
Williams, James, 11, Cross Francis-street, Dowlais	Haverfordwest ..	1866
Williams, James Gyles, 214, Jenkin-road, Brightside, Sheffield	Metropolitan ..	1881
Williams, John, Pembroke House, Park-terrace, Pontypool..	Haverfordwest ..	1863
Williams, John, Bryn Gogarth, Cardigan	Llangollen ..	1874
Williams, John, Ynysddu, Pontllanfraith, Newport, Mon.		
Williams, John, 73, Bailey-street, Brynmawr, Brecon ..	Haverfordwest ..	1876
Williams, John, 74, Clive-street, Grangetown, Cardiff ..	Haverfordwest ..	1882
Williams, John, Porth R.S.O., Glam.	Haverfordwest ..	1868
Williams, John, Maesteg, Bridgend, Glam.	Pontypool and Cardiff U.C. ..	1893
Williams, John Ceulanydd, Maesteg R.S.O., Glam.	Llangollen ..	1891
Williams, John Glyn, Nantyglo R.S.O., Mon.	Pontypool and Cardiff U.C...	1890

Name and Postal Address.	College.	Ministry commenced
Williams, John Lloyd, Woodville, Glasbury R.S.O., Breconshire	Pontypool	1892
Williams, John William, D.D. (U.S.), 102, Walters-road, Swansea	Haverfordwest	1866
Williams, Joseph, 5, Greville-street, Hanley, Staffs.		1881
Williams, Joseph Frederick, Navigation R.S.O., Glam. (*Glancynon*)	Pontypool	1889
Williams, Joseph John, Brynmor, Penygroes R.S.O., Carn.	Haverfordwest	1861
Williams, Lewis Rowe, Hill Park, Trimsaran, Kidwelly	Haverfordwest	1894
Williams, Peter, Tredegar, Mon.		1881
Williams, Price, Bosworth House, Hinckley	Llangollen	1882
Williams, Richard Edward, Cefnmawr, Ruabon	Pontypool and Cardiff U.C.	1888
Williams, Richard Ellis, 103, Park-street, Grosvenor-square, London, W. (*Castle-street, Marylebone*)	Llangollen and Bangor U.C.	1885
Williams, Robert Ellis, 2, Bute-terrace, Aberdare (*Ynyslwyd*)		1868
Williams, Samuel, Stevington, Bedford	Pontypool	1862
Williams, Samuel Turner, 9, Chester-road, Whitchurch, Salop	Metropolitan	1867
Williams, T. E., Brynllys, Newtown, Mont.	Pontypool	1867
Williams, T. Ferwig, Ammanford R.S.O., Carmarthenshire	Pontypool	1861
Williams, Thomas, Ewias Harold, Pontrilas R.S.O., Herefordshire	Pontypool	1860
Williams, Thomas, B.A. (LOND)., 9, Queen's-terrace, Aberystwyth	Regent's Park	1869
Williams, Thomas E., Chapel-terrace, Gaerwen R.S.O., Anglesey	E. London Inst.	1891
Williams, Thomas Henry, Govilon, near Abergavenny (*Llanwenarth*)	Haverfordwest	1884
Williams, Thomas Robert, Bryn Emlyn, Clifton Wood, Clifton, Bristol	Bangor	1893
Williams, W. A., Ferryside R.S.O., Carmarthenshire	Haverfordwest	1887
Williams, William, Fernleigh, Lansdown-road, South Lambeth, London, S.W. (*Upton, Lambeth*)	Metropolitan	1874
Williams, William, Wednesbury	Pontypool	1892
Williams, William, 38, Ynyscynon-street, Cwmbach, Aberdare		1884
Williams, William, 63, Cardiff-road, Mountain Ash		1845
Williams, William, Knighton, Radnor	Haverfordwest	1878
Williams, William, 2, School-street, Elliot Town, New Tredegar, Cardiff	Haverfordwest	1865
Williams, William Henry, 58, Cottles Oak, Frome, Somerset		1877
Williams, William Llewellyn, Laburnum House, Pool-street, Bolton	Rawdon	1890
Williams, William Prichard, Landore, Swansea	Llangollen	1865
Williamson, Robert John, Beulah-villas, Queen's-road, Teddington S.O., Middlesex	Metropolitan	1886
Willis, George Alfred, Oakwood, Northumberland-road, Leamington	Regent's Park	1884
Willis, Richard Elgar, Stoke Manse, Ipswich	Metropolitan	1886
Willis, Samuel, Chelmsford		1866
Wilson, George, 11, Joannah-street, Newcastle-road, Sunderland		1873
Wilson, George Armitstead, East King-street, Helensburgh	Glas.Un.&B.U.S.	1883
Wilson, John, Montague House, Lower-road, Charlton S.O., Kent (*Parson's-hill, Woolwich*)	Metropolitan	1877
Wilson, John Alexander, Isleham, Soham	Metropolitan	1867
Wilson, John Lacy, Oak Cottage, Ulverston	Raw. & Edin. U.	1886
Wilson, Reuben, Dorman's Land, East Grinstead, Surrey	E. London Inst.	1872
Winks, William Edward, 58, Richmond-road, Cardiff	Midland	1865
Winslow, W., Wadhurst S.O., Sussex		1862
Winsor, Henry W. H., 34, Swathmore-terrace, Thornaby-on-Tees	Metropolitan	187

Name and Postal Address	College.	Ministry commenced
Wintle, William James, 3, St. Agnes-place, Kennington Park, London, S.E	Metropolitan ..	1890
Wood, Arthur William, 43, Portland-terrace, Winchester ..	Metropolitan ..	1882
Wood, Henry, 26, High-street, Long Eaton R.S.O., Derbyshire	Midland	1870
Wood, John Roskruge, 56, St. John's-park, London, N. (*Upper Holloway*)	Regent's Park ..	1863
Wood, Robert, 10, Albemarle-crescent, Scarborough	Metropolitan ..	1882
Wood, William, 58, High-street, Berkhamsted (*Bedmond*) ..	.. .. ..	1872
Woodgate, Philip Baker, 2, Fairy Croft-terrace, Saffron Walden	.. .. ..	1842
Woodhouse, Thomas, 59, Worcester-street, Stourbridge ..	Bristol	1892
Woodrow, Samuel George, 50, St. Swithin-street, Aberdeen	Regent's Park ..	1864
Woods, Edward Burchell, B.A. (LON.), 35, Plymouth-avenue, Longsight, Manchester	Regent's Park ..	1886
Woods, William, 11, Winslade-road, Brixton, London, S.W.	.. .. ..	1852
Woodward, Albert, 134, New-lane, Oswaldtwistle, Accrington	Bristol	1892
Wren, John William, 16, Ashburnham-road, Bedford ..	.. .. ..	1877
Wright, Henry, 2, Seyton-avenue, Langside, Glasgow ..	Regent's Park ..	1877
Wright, George, 18, Gibbon-road, Kingston-on-Thames ..	Metropolitan ..	1862
Wyard, George Luther, Hasland House, Penarth, Cardiff ..	Regent's Park ..	1883
Wyard, John S., 13, Dagmar-terrace, Gosport	.. .. ..	1859
Wyatt, Henry, Blisworth R.S.O., Northants	Bristol	1893
Wyatt, Mark, Chittering, Cambridge	.. .. ..	1856
Wyle, William Samuel, Burton, Stogursey, near Bridgwater	.. .. ..	1882
Wylie, Alexander, M.A. (GLAS.), 51, Mardale-crescent, Merchiston, Edinburgh	Glas.Un.& B.U.S.	1869
Wynn, Frederick, Batley	E. London I[illegible]	[illegible]
Wynn, Walter, Earby-in-Craven, Leeds	Midland	[illegible]
Wynne, Maurice Foulks, 1, Sibell-street, Chester	[illegible]	[illegible]
YAULDREN, Thomas, Semley, Shaftesbury, Wilts .. .		
Yemm, Edmund, Countesthorpe, via Leicester	Regent's Park ..	1866
Youlden, Harry, 85, Unthanks-road, Norwich	Rawdon	1895
Young, James, 17b, North-street, Rugby	Metropolitan ..	1880
Young, John, 1, Grange-vale, New Chester-road, Rockferry, Birkenhead	.. .. ..	1846
Young, John, 242, Sheffield-road, Barnsley	Rawdon	1881
Young, Jonathan, Kirton Lindsey R.S.O., Lincs.	.. .. ..	1859
Young, Joseph, 28, Wardlaw-avenue, Rutherglen, Glasgow ..	Metropolitan ..	1889
Young, Sidney Rogers, The Hawthorns, Abergavenny ..	Pontypool ..	1854
Young, Thomas, Semblester, Sandsting, Shetland	Glasgow Univ. ..	1859
Young, William Davies, Llanbister-road R.S.O., Radnorshire (*Dolau*)	Haverfordwest ..	1885
Young, William James, Sulgrave, Banbury	.. .. ..	1889
Yuille, George, 15, Victoria-place, Stirling	Glas. U. & B.U.S.	1870

MISSIONARIES

IN CONNECTION WITH THE BAPTIST MISSIONARY SOCIETY NOVEMBER, 1895.

ABBREVIATIONS, NOTES, &c.

B.M.=The words "Baptist Missionary" should follow the name in all addresses so indicated.

N.W.P.=North-Western Provinces, India.

All Congo Missionaries should be addressed:—Rev. ——, c/o the Missionary in charge, Baptist Mission Station, Underhill, Matadi, Congo Free State, West Central Africa; and letters marked "*via* Antwerp."

All Shansi Missionaries should be addressed:—c/o Agent, China Inland Mission, Tientsin, North China.

All Shantung Missionaries should be addressed:—c/o Messrs. Fergusson & Co., Chefoo, North China.

Name and Postal Address.	College.	Appointed
*ALLEN, I., M.A. (U.S.), B.M., Cortes Island, British Columbia	Oberlin & Bristol	1863
Anderson, Herbert, B.M., 37, Elliot-road, Calcutta, India ..	Rawdon	1886
*Anderson, J, H., Belmont, Loughton, S.O., Essex ..	Stepney	1853
BAILEY, Thomas, B.M., Cuttack, Orissa, India	Midland	1861
Balfour, J., M.A. (EDIN.), Calabar College, Kingston, Jamaica	Glasgow Univ. & B. U. S. ..	1883
Banerjea, B.N., B.M., Maldah, Northern Bengal, India ..	.. .. ..	1872
Barnett, T. H., B.M., 67, King's-road, Howrah, Calcutta, India	Rawdon	1880
Bate, J. D., M.R.A.S., B.M., Allahabad, Northern India ..	Regent's Park ..	1865
Beedham, Richard, Congo	Rawdon	1895
Bell, John, Congo	Regent's Park ..	1895
Bentley, W. Holman, Congo	.. .. ..	1879
Bevan, G. W., B.M., Calcutta, India	Haverfordwest ..	1889
*Bion, R., B.M., Monghyr, Bengal, India	Basle	1850
Biswas, Kristanga, 41, Lower Circular-road, Calcutta ..		
Bruce, J. P., B.A. (LON.), B.M., Shantung, China	Regent's Park ..	1886
Burt, E. W., M.A. (OXON.), B.M., Shantung, China	Bristol & Oxford Univ.	1892
CAMERON, G., Congo	.. .. ..	1884
Carey, W. B.M., Barisal, Eastern Bengal, India	Rawdon	1884
Chand, Prem, Gya, Northern India		
Chowdhery, Romanath R., 41, Lower Circular-rd. Calcutta		
Clarke, J. A., Congo..	Metropolitan ..	1888
Collier, A. E., B.M., Sultangunge, Mahendru, Patna, N. India	Bristol	1893
Couling, S., B.M., Shantung, China	Bristol	1884
Crudgington, H. E., B.M., Delhi, India	Rawdon	1879
DANN, G. J., B.M., Delhi, India	Metropolitan ..	1884
Davies, P., B.A. (LON.), Congo	Regent's Park ..	1885
Davies, W., B.M., Maldah, Northern Bengal, India	Haverfordwest ..	1889
Davy, E. P., B.M., Patna, Northern India	.. .. ..	1892
D'Cruz, J. A., B.M., Serampore College, Bengal, India ..	Serampore ..	1881
Dixon, ,H., B.M., Shansi, China	Regent's Park ..	1879
Dodds, Charles John, Congo	Rawdon	1895
Donald, David L., B.M., Chittagong, Eastern Bengal, India..	Metropolitan ..	1893
Drake, S. B., B.M., Shantung, China	Metropolitan ..	1886
Duncan, Moir B., M.A. (GLAS.), c/o Agent, China Inland Mission, Hankow, Hu-pe, North China	Glas. & Oxfd Uns.	1886
Dutt, G. C, B.M., Khoolna, Bengal, India	.. .. ..	1867

* Retired from active service.

Name and Postal Address.	College.	Appointed
*EAST, D. J., Watford	Stepney ..	.. 1851
Edwards, T. R., B.M., Sorry, Beerbhoom, Bengal, India ..	Pontypool	.. 1879
El Karey, Youhannah, B.M., Nablous, via Jaffa, Palestine ..	Pont. & Reg. Pk.	1886
Ellison, J. R., B.M., Rungpore, Bengal, India	Manchester	.. 1881
Evans, B., B.M., Monghyr, Northern India	Bristol ..	.. 1880
*Evans, T., B.M., Mussoorie, N.W.P., India	Pontypool	.. 1854
FARTHING, G. B., B.M., Shansi, China	Rawdon ..	.. 1886
Field, S. M., Congo	.. ..	.. 1894
Forfeitt, J. Lawson, F.R.G.S., Congo	.. ..	.. 1889
Forfeitt, W. L., Congo	Regent's Park	.. 1889
Forsyth, R. C., B.M., Shantung, China	.. ..	.. 1884
Fuller, J. A. A., Congo	.. ..	.. 1889
*Fuller, J. J., 2, Salisbury-villas, Cleveland-road, Barnes, London, S.W.		
GAMMON, R. E., B.M., Port of Spain, Trinidad, West Indies	Metropolitan	.. 1875
Ghose, Bhagaboti Churn, B.M., Serampore College, Bengal, India		
Glennie, Robert, Congo	Bristol ..	.. 1889
Gordon, S. C., Congo	Metropolitan	.. 1890
Graham, R. H. Carson, Congo	Metropolitan	.. 1886
Grenfell, G., F.R.G.S., Congo	Bristol ..	.. 1874
HALE, F. W., B.M., Agra, N.W.P., India	Bristol ..	.. 1893
Hankinson, W. D., B.M., Matale, Colombo, Ceylon ..	Rawdon ..	.. 1893
Harmon, Frank, B.M., Shantung, China	.. ..	.. 1887
Harvey, C. H., Cuttack, Orissa, India .. [illegible]	[illegible] Univ. [illegible]	[illegible]
Hasler, J. I., B.A. (LON.) B.M., Delhi, India [illegible]	[illegible]	[illegible]
Hay, R. Wright, B.M., Dacca, Eastern Bengal, [illegible]	[illegible]	[illegible]
Heberlet, P. E., B.M., Sumbulpore, Central [illegible]	[illegible]	.. [illegible]
Howells, George, B.A. (LON.) B.D. (ST. AND [illegible], Orissa, India	Reg. Pk. & Ox. U.	1895
JAMES, Arthur, B.A., President, Calabar College, Kingston, Jamaica	Regent's Park	.. 1893
James, W. Bowen, B.M., Julpaigori, Bengal, India	Haverfordwest	.. 1878
James, W. R., B.M., Madaripore, Furreedpore, Eastern Bengal, India	Pontypool	.. 1877
Jarry, F. W., Berhampore, Ganjam, India	Metropolitan	.. 1895
Jenkins, A. L., B.M., Morlaix, Finisterre, France	Regent's Park	.. 1872
Jewson, A., B.M., 48, Ripon-street, Calcutta, India	Regent's Park	.. 1881
Jones, A. G., B.M., Shantung, China	Lancs. Indep.	.. 1876
Jones, D., B.M., Patna, Northern India	Pontypool	.. 1878
Jordan, C., 3, Middle-road, Intally, Calcutta, India	Regent's Park	.. 1869
KERRY, G., 84, South-road, Intally, Calcutta, India	Bristol ..	.. 1856
Kerry, J. G., B.M., Barisal, Eastern Bengal, India	Rawdon ..	.. 1881
Kirkland, R. H., Congo	.. ...	.. 1893
LACEY, R. L., B.M., Berhampore, Ganjam, India	Midland ..	.. 1887
Landels, W. K., B.M., 51, Corso Siccardi, Turin, Italy ..	Regent's Park	.. 1875
Lapham, H. A., B.M., Matale, Ceylon	Regent's Park	.. 1880
Lewis, Thomas, Congo	Haverfordwest	.. 1882
Long, Arthur, Russool Khonda, Ganjam, Orissa, India ..	.. ..	.. 1893
MCCALLUM, J., M.A., B.D., c/o Rev. F. D. Waldock, Maradana, Colombo, Ceylon	Regent's Park and Glasgow Univ.	1894
McIntosh, R. M., B.M., Muttra, N.W.P., India	Pontypool	.. 1884
MacLean, A. J., B.M., Chittagong, Eastern Bengal, India ..	Serampore	.. 1887
*Martin, Thomas, 14, St. Michael's-avenue, Northampton ..	Bristol ..	.. 1854

* Retired from active service.

Name and Postal Address.	College.	Appointed
Massih, Imam, B.M., 41, Lower Circular Road, Calcutta, India		
Mitchell, W. S., B.M., Patna, Northern India	Metropolitan ..	1885
Mookerjee, Sat Soron, B.M., Dacca, Eastern Bengal, India		
Morgan, Evan, B.M., c/o Agent, China Inland Mission, Hankow, Hu-pe, North China	Bristol	1884
Morris, J. D., B.M., Dacca, Eastern Bengal, India	Serampore ..	1887
NICKALLS, E. C., B.M., Shantung, China	Bristol	1886
Norledge, T. W., B.M., Jessore, Eastern Bengal, India ..	Regent's Park ..	1889
PATERSON, H., B.M., Patna, Northern India	E. Lond. Inst. ..	1884
Paterson, T. C., M.B. (EDIN.), C.M., B.M., Shantung, China	Edinburgh Univ.	1892
Phillips, H. R., Congo	Metropolitan ..	1886
Pike, J. G., B.M., Cuttack, Orissa, India	Regent's Park ..	1874
Pinnock, John, Congo	.. .. ..	1887
Pople, George R., Congo	Bristol	1892
Potter, J. G., B.M., Agra, N.W.P., India	Metropolitan ..	1881
Price, W. J., B.M., Bankipore, Northern India	Pontypool ..	1877
Pusey, J. H., B.M., Grand Turk, Turk's Island, West Indies	Calabar, Kingston, Jamaica..	1880
RICHARD, T., B.M., 1, Quinsan-road, Shanghai, China ..	Haverfordwest ..	1869
Robinson, Denham, B.M., Serampore College, Bengal, India	Regent's Park ..	1884
Roger, Joseph L., Congo	Metropolitan ..	1888
Rouse, G. H., M.A., LL.B. (LON.), D.D. (U.S.), 41, Lower Circular-road, Calcutta, India	Regent's Park ..	1860
SAHU, Shem, B.M., Cuttack, Orissa, India	.. .. ..	1861
Scrivener, A. E., Congo	.. .. ..	1885
Shaw, N. H., B.M., 1, Piazza Cavour, Florence, Italy ..	Midland	1878
Shorrock, A. G., B.A. (LON.), B.M., c/o Agent, China Inland Mission, Hankow, Hu-pe, North China	Regent's Park ..	1886
Sircar, John, B.M., Barisal, Eastern Bengal, India		
Smith, George Anstie, B.M., Simla, N.W.P., India	.. .. ..	1891
Smith, James, B.M., Simla, N.W.P., India	.. .. ..	1852
Smith, Kenrid, Congo	Bristol	1895
Smyth, E. C., B.M., Shantung, China	Rawdon	1884
Sowerby, A., B.M., Shansi, China	Regent's Park ..	1881
Spurgeon, R., B.M., Barisal, Eastern Bengal, India	Metropolitan ..	1873
Stapleton, W. H., Congo	.. .. ..	1889
Stephens, J. R. M., Congo	.. .. ..	1894
Stonelake, Henry T., Congo	Bristol	1894
Stubbs, J., B.M., Patna, Northern India	Metropolitan ..	1884
Summers, E. S., B.A. (CANTAB.), B.M., Serampore College, Bengal, India	Camb. Univ. ..	1876
TEICHMANN, A., B.M., Pirijpore, Backergunge, Eastern Bengal, India	Regent's Park ..	1883
Thomas, F. V., B.A., M.B., B.M., Kharar, Simla, N.W.P., India	Edinburgh Univ.	1894
Thomas, H. J., B.M., Delhi, India	Bristol	1888
Thomas, J. W., 41, Lower Circular-road, Calcutta	Bristol	1867
Thomas, S. S., B.M., 27, Civil Lines, Delhi, India	Bristol	1885
Tregillus, R. H., B.M., Madaripore, Furreedpore, Eastern Bengal, India	Regent's Park ..	1885
Tucker, Leonard, M.A. (LON.), Calabar Coll., Kingston, Jamaica	Regent's Park ..	1891
Turner, J. J., B.M., Shansi, China	Metropolitan ..	1883
VAUGHAN, J., B.M., Cuttack, Orissa, India	Midland	1878

Name and Postal Address.	College.	Appointed
WALDOCK, F. D., B.M., Maradana, Colombo, Ceylon	Regent's Park	1862
Walker, R., B.M., 175, Via Foria, Naples, Italy	..	1880
Wall, J., B.M., 35, Piazza di San Lorenzo, near Lucina, Rome, Italy	Bristol	1871
Wall, J. C., B.M., 154a, Via Urbana, Est, Rome, Italy	Regent's Park	1889
Watson, J. R., M.D.(DURH.), M.R.C.S.(ENG.), B.M., Shantung, China	Durham Univ.	1884
Watson, Thomas, B.M., Barisal, Eastern Bengal, India	Bristol	1893
Weeks, J. H., Congo	Metropolitan	1881
White, H., Congo	Regent's Park	1889
Whitehead, John, Congo	Rawdon	1890
Whitewright, J. S., B.M., Shantung, China	Bristol	1881
Wilkins, Gordon S., B.M., Sambalpur, Central Provinces, India	Midland	1892
Willkinson, A. B., Udayagiri, Ganjam, Orissa, India	..	1893
Wills, W. A., B.M., Shantung, China	..	1885
Wilson, C. E., B.A., B.M., Serampore College, Bengal, India	Regent's Park	1894
YOUNG, A. H., M.A. (EDIN.), B.M., Cuttack, Orissa, India	..	1885

PASTORS OF ENGLISH CHURCHES IN INDIA, CEYLON, AND THE WEST INDIES.

NOT SUPPORTED BY THE BAPTIST MISSIONARY SOCIETY.

Name and Postal Address.	College.	Date.
Barrell, H. E., English Baptist Church, Bellasis-road, Byculla, Bombay, India	Metropolitan	1892
Dann, Chas. A., Zion Church, Nassau, N.P., Bahamas, West Indies	Metropolitan	1892
Hook, G. H., Lal Bazar, Calcutta, India	Metropolitan	1880
Jones, S. J., Dinapore Baptist Church, Northern India	Manchester	1892
Julian, Robert Martin, Circular-road Baptist Church, Calcutta, India	Midland	1892
Pratt, Wm., M.A. (Oxon.), East Queen-street Church, Kingston, Jamaica	Oxford Univ.	1890
Stockley, Thomas Ings, Cinnamon Gardens Baptist Church, Colombo, Ceylon	Metropolitan	1894

MINISTERIAL SETTLEMENTS.

Name.	Settled at	College.
Bennett, J.	Banbridge	
Black, J. W.	Millport	Glasgow U. & B. U. S.
Bowen, J. L.	Brynmawr	Cardiff.
Brown, A. D.	Herne Bay	
Brown, H...	Sible Hedingham	
Butler, J. ..	Shipston-on-Stour	
Chandler, A. V. G.	Bermondsey	Metropolitan.
Chilvers, H. T.	Bloomsbury	
Chisnall, W.	Colchester	
Collins, T.	Glasgow	Glasgow Univ.
Dawson, M. V. F., M.A.	Carrickfergus	Trinity Coll., Dublin.
Dickerson, A.	Brixton Hill	
Durbin, E. M.	Church ..	Rawdon.
Earney, L.	Damerham	
Evans, D. C.	Bryncethin	
Fidge, T. S.	Fleet	Metropolitan.
Flook, J. S.	Athlone	
Garrow, A. D.	Waterfoot	
Gibbon, O. R.	Wellington	Metropolitan.
Good, R. A.	Exmouth	Metropolitan.
Gray, A. ..	Briercliffe	Rawdon.
Griffiths, A.	Netherton	Metropolitan.
Harris, C...	Franksbridge	
Harris, H. J.	Abercanaid	Cardiff.
Harvey, J. L.	Berwick	Glasgow U. & B.U.S.
Heap, J. ..	Paddington	Midland.
Holdsworth, W. H., M.A.	Huddersfield	Rawdon.
Hunter, R. M.	Reading	Metropolitan.
Jackman, J. H.	Peterborough	Metropolitan.
James, R. A.	Tongwynlais	Cardiff.
Jenkins, D. H.	Groes ..	Aberystwyth.
Jones, A. E. O.	Leeds ..	Rawdon.
Jones, E. T.	Meinciau	
Jones, J. M.	Pengam	Cardiff.
Jones, O. ..	Llanddoget	
Jones, R. ..	Ceinewydd	
Joynes, J. E.	Marlow..	
Kirby, F. J.	Accrington	Bristol.
Knight, H. J.	Peckham Rye	
Lee, W. T.	Cardiff ..	
Livingston, W. A.	Manchester	Manchester.
Llewellyn, W.	Llangynidr	Cardiff.
Lloyd, J. ..	Waterford	
Love, J. ..	King's Cross	
Matthews, M. H...	Tredegar	
Minchin, T. T.	Faversham	Metropolitan.
Mitchell, W.	Stoke Newington	
Monk, E. C.	Okehampton	Shebbear.
Morris, A...	Festiniog	Aberystwyth U.C.
Morris, R. L.	Henllys..	Haverfordwest.
Padfield, J. W.	Cheddar	

Name.	Settled at	College.
Pay, A. W.	Swansea	
Payn, G. F.	Liskeard	Rawdon.
Phillips, T.	Blaenavon	Cardiff.
Pollard, T. G.	Silvertown	Metropolitan.
Povey, W...	Chester..	
Read, G. S.	Peckham	
Roberts, J.	Cresswell Quay	Aberystwyth.
Robertson, J. D... ..	Alloa	Glasgow U. a B. U. S.
Rumsby, F. W.	Stradbroke	
Rush, T.	Claygate	
Russell, G.	South Moreton	
Saunders, W.	Rhymney	Aberystwyth.
Shearman, C. E... ..	Hook Norton	Metropolitan.
Slater, F.	Halifax	Rawdon.
Sneesby, G.	Somersham	
Thomas, D.	Rock	Aberystwyth.
Thomas, J. B.	Talgarth	Aberystwyth.
Thomas, J. D.	Clarbeston	Aberystwyth.
Williams, D.	Llanstephan	
Williams, E. R.	Talybont	Bangor.
Williams, J.	Ynysybwl	
Williams, W. C.	Cilfowyr	Aberystwyth.
Winch, H. M.	Chatteris	
Yeomans, J.	Westray	Manchester.
Youlden, H. H.	Norwich	Rawdon.

MINISTERIAL RESIGNATIONS AND REMOVALS.

Name.	Place from	Place to
Aldis, J., Junr.	Batley	Little Leigh.
Alford, J. D.	Stony Stratford	Barrow-on-Soar.
Allsop, S. S.	Burton-on-Trent	Ripley.
Andrew, C.	*U.S. America*	Latchford.
Andrews, J.	Waldringfield	
Antram, C. E. P.	Broomhaugh and Broomley	Ipswich.
Archer, J. K.	Peterborough	Hepstonstall Slack.
Aubrey, E.	Abercarn	Glasgow.
Bailey, J., B.A.	Sheffield	
Baily, R.	Brentford	
Baker, S. J.	Bacup	Bury St. Edmunds.
Barker, A. W. L.	Evesham	Worthing.
Bergin, J. M.	Sutton	York Town.
Birch, C. B.	Willenhall	
Blaikie, P. H.	Wick	Coleraine.
Blomfield, W. E., B.A., B.D.	Ipswich	Coventry.
Bonner, C.	Sale	Southampton.
Bosher, A.	Northchurch	
Breewood, T.	*Australia*	Brayford.
Briggs, J.	Longton	Paddington
Briscoe, J. T.	Peckham	Bristol.
Broome, C.	Fressingfield	
Buchanan, W. J.	Portsmouth	
Campbell, O. D., M.A.	Newport	Haverfordwest.
Chambers, C.	Southgate	
Chambers, W.	Newcastle-under-Lyme	
Chesterton, W. R.	Christchurch	
Cliff, G. J.	Ripley	Wigan.
Cobb, G.	Stradbroke	
Colls, L. H.	Beccles	
Cook, G. S.	Chenies	
Coombs, W.	Princes Risborough	
Cotton, A. F.	Ponder's End	Brabourne.
Croome, C. G.	Shipley	Nottingham.
Crouch, C. D.	Worthing	
Curtis, G.	Sheerness	King's Cross.
Dakin, E.	Kingstanley	*Established Church.*
Darby, R. D.	*Congo (B.M.S.)*	Hornsey Rise.
Davies, D.	Harlech	Harlech.
Davies, D. R. S.	Resolven	
Davies, J.	Llandyssil	Aberayron.
Davies, T. C.	Shrewton	
Davies, T. J.	Briton Ferry	Waunarlwydd.
Davies, W.	Briton Ferry	Neath.
Davies, W. P.	Blakeney	Weston-super-Mare.
Davis, C. A.	Reading	Stroud.
Davis, E. T.	Wandsworth	Walworth.
Day, J.	Horwich	Devizes.
Denmee, W. J.	Maidstone	Hoxne.

Name.	Place from	Place to.
Dickins, B.	Swadlincote	Husbands Bosworth.
Dickins, W.	Herne Bay	
Dunkley, H.	Eynsford	
Dunnett, G.	Coseley	Halesowen.
Dye, J.	Saxlingham	
Earney, H.	Damerham	
Edgerton, W. F.	Woolwich	Harlington.
Edwards, G. P.	Fleet	Evenjobb.
Edwards, H. C.	Dolau	Newbridge-on-Wye.
Edwards, J.	Ffynnon	
Eland, F. G.	Athlone	
Elder, J.	Glasgow	
English, A.	Shefford	
Ennals, G. T.	Leytonstone	
Etheridge, B. C.	Balham	
Evans, D.	Machen	Newport, Mon.
Evans, E. H.	Glais	Merthyr Vale.
Evans, G.	Blackwood	Newport, Mon.
Evans, L. T.	*Hayti*	Pontyclun.
Ewing, J. W., M.A.	Wandsworth	Peckham.
Fellowes, C. A.	Jersey	Eastleigh.
Foote, W. E.	Bridport	
Forbes, F.	Alloa	
Forbes, J. T., M.A.	Newcastle	Edinburgh.
Foster, W. R.	Earls Colne	
Gardiner, T.	Penzance	
Gill, G. H.	Brabourne	
Godfrey, W. S.	Croydon	
Golding, W. R.	Leeds	
Goodman, W. E.	Naunton	
Graham, A.	Pembury	
Grant, J. H.	Goldhill	Coalville.
Gray, A. C.	Greenwich	
Green, M. E.	Swavesey	
Greenwood, T.	Catford-hill	Balham.
Grey, J.	Holbeach	
Griffith, T. G.	*Jamaica*	Cheam.
Griffiths, J.	Aberdare	
Griggs, D. B.	Eastleigh	Portsmouth.
Haddock, E.	Blakenham	
Hadler, E. S.	Thorpe-le-Soken	Fivehead.
Hadler, J. R.	Sheerness	Sheerness.
Hanson, J.	North Bradley	
Harris, I.	Blaenavon	*South Africa.*
Harris, G. H.	Chipping Campden	
Hasler, J.	Andover	
Hatton, G. E.	Holborn	
Herring, G.	Notting-hill Gate	
Hewson, J. C.	Stratford	*Western Australia.*
Hobbs, C.	Bourton-on-the-Water	High Wycombe.
Hopkins, D. W.	Blaenycwm	Neath.
Howells, W.	Sirhowy	*U.S. America.*
Howes, J.	Battle	
Hudgell, P. A.	Waterford	Derby.
Hughes, E.	*Congo (B.M.S.)*	Fraserburgh.
Humby, L.	Ford	Shefford.
Ingram, C.A.	Leafield	New Romney.
Jackson, F., M.A.	Worcester	Reading.
Jardine, A.	Fivemile Hill	Poyntz Pass.
Javan, R. P.	Nottingham	

Name.	Place from.	Place to.
Jenkins, D. W.	Glasgow	Salendine Nook.
Jennings, A. E.	Cheam	
Jermine, T.	Tredegar	
John, J.	Staylittle	
John, W. J.	Swansea	Swansea.
Johns, R. O.	Cardiff	Dalston.
Johnson, A. E.	Westbury	Ibstock.
Johnson, F.	Usk	
Johnston, R.	Peckham	
Jones, A. G., Ph.D.	*Nova Scotia*	Sarn.
Jones, J. L.	Pentre	Glynceiriog.
Jones, M. H.	Llanrwst	
Jones, R. B.	Berthlwyd	Llanelly.
Jones, S. J.	Kensington	Liverpool.
Jones, T.	Bagillt	
Jones, W. B.	Ynysybwl	Penycae.
Jones, W. S.	Chester	
Judd, T. A.	Grimsby	
Juniper, W. J.	Rotherhithe New-road	*Burmah.*
Latimer, R. S.	Colne	Weston-super-Mare.
Lawrence, E.	Sarn	Neyland.
Lewis, D.	Saundersfoot	Honeyborough.
Lewis, D.	Abersychan	
Lewis, E. D.	Llancarvan	Treorky.
Lewis, J. M.	Cemaes	Cymmer.
Lewis, P.	Romsey	Chipping Campden.
Lewis, W.	Cilfynydd	
Lindsay, S.	Lochfyneside	Burray.
Longhurst, T. J.	Cheltenham	Weston-super-Mare.
McKeracher, J. H.	Forres	Leeds.
Mackey, H. O.	Hendon	
McKittrick, A.	Sheffield	
M'Mechan, W. H.	Old Kent-road	Barnes.
Martin, H. J.	Plumstead	Tring.
Mathews, J.	Stantonbury	
Maynard, W.	Kirkby Stephen	Syston.
Miller, P.	Millport	Fenton.
Morgan, C.	Brayford	Hay.
Morgan, M.	Tondu	Birmingham.
Morgan, T.	Dowlais	Cardiff.
Morgan, W.	St. Brides	
Morris, D. G.	Talgarth	Pentre.
Morris, W. M.	Cresswell Quay	*Established Church.*
Morrison, P.	Norwich	Coventry.
Mursell, W. A.	Coventry	Blackburn.
Muxworthy, D.	Padiham	
Neighbour, G.	Longhope	Ruardean Hil
Neighbour, J.	Cirencester	
Newman, J. P.	Ibstock	Burnley.
Oakley, H.	Devizes	Upper Tooting.
Oldring, G. W.	Long Sutton	
Owen, D. R.	Clipston	
Owen, J. M. G.	Southampton	Birmingham
Owen, O. M.	Gefailyrhyd	
Ovendon, G. W.	Dalston	
Packer, W. J.	Rochdale	
Page, E. J.	Bideford	Woking.
Parkinson, L. C., B.A.	*Bahamas* (*B.M.S.*)	Nottingham.
Parnell, J.	Pimlico	Stepney.
Parrish, J.	Bargoed	

Name.	Place from.	Place to.
Pates, C.	Bilston	York.
Payne, W. H.	Arnsby	Bovey Tracey.
Perry, C. F.	Liskeard	Liverpool.
Phillips, H. A. B.	Southport	Cheltenham.
Pollard, T. G.	Silvertown	Brentford.
Priter, A.	Shipley	Preston.
Probert, E.	Whitebrook	
Prout, A. T.	Coventry	*Established Church.*
Pugh, J.	Stratford-on-Avon	
Pywell, J.	Stockport	
Realff, A. E.	Guildford	
Rees, F. A.	Berwick	
Rees, M. T.	Meinciau	
Rees, W.	Blaenavon	
Reid, A. J.	Shoreham	Croydon.
Richards, H. N.	Cymmer	Aberdare.
Richards, T.	Ogmore Vale	
Richards, W.	Fraserburgh	Leith.
Richardson, G. B.	Eynsford	Battle.
Rigby, R. H.	Aylsham	
Roberts, C.	Liverpool	*Canada.*
Roberts, D. W.	Warrington	
Roberts, S. F.	Llanfyrnach	Pontllyw.
Robins, S. J.	Cadoxton	Blakeney.
Rodger, H.	Bromley Common	St. Leonards.
Russell, J. R.	High Wycombe	Astwood Bank.
Sage, J.	Ashdon	
Sampson, R.	Bloomsbury	Richmond.
Saunders, J.	Kenninghall	
Sawday, C. B.	Leeds	
Scott, R.	Wolsingham	Guiseley.
Sears, R. E.	Whitechapel	Clapham Junction.
Shaw, F.	Gravesend	Brighton.
Shephard, J. E.	Holborn	Hull.
Silvey, R.	Swaffham	Bromley, Kent.
Smathers, R.	Whitchurch	
Smith, E. A.	Bovey Tracey	Dunstable.
Smith, F. G.	Truro	
Smith, F. M.	Peckham Rye	
Smith, R.	Horsforth	Histon.
Smith, T. N.	*U. S. America*	Tetbury.
Smith, W.	King's Cross	Kirton Lindsay.
Somers, S. J.	Beckington	
Soper, E. H.	Birmingham	
Stanley, J.	Semley	Coate.
Stansfield, T.	Bacup	Blackburn.
Stephens, W. E.	Crickhowell	Blaenavon.
Stevens, W. H.	Whitechapel	Stratford.
Stone W.	Vale	
Sullivan, W.	Budleigh Salterton	
Thomas, E.	Bryncethin	
Thomas, J. W.	Willesden Junction	Mill End.
Thomas, T.	Cefnmawr	Ebbw Vale.
Thomson, M.M.	Guilsborough	
Thomson, P. T., M.A.	Lochee	Leeds.
Thorn, W.	Loose	
Toogood, J.	Burton-on-Trent	Jarrow.
Tooke, W.	Lee	Bury St. Edmunds.
Towler, G.	Sawley	Atch Lench.
Townsend, J. W.	Wickwar	

Name.	Place from.	Place to.
Turner, J.	Trowbridge	
Vanstone, W. J. N. ..	Bow	Catford Hill.
Wagnall, H. C.	Manchester	Morecambe.
Walker, A.	Chalk Farm	
Westby, F. W.	Chadwell Heath	
Whetnall, M. H... ..	Blackburn	
Whitaker, J. T.	Coseley..	
White, F. T.	Faversham	Stogumber.
Williams, C. B.	Beverley	
Williams, J.	Rock	Sutton, Pembs.
Williams, J. G.	Ffynongroew	Brynsiencyn.
Willis, S...	Whittlesea	
Woodward, A.	Carrickfergus	Oswaldtwistle.
Wynn, F.	Barrow-in-Furness	Batley.
Yauldren, T.	Ashwater	Semley.

PART IX.

COLONIAL AND FOREIGN.

EUROPE.

FRANCE.

(*Population*, 38,218,903.)

Churches.	Formed.	Pastors.	Members.
Brittany—			
Morlaix, 5 stations † ..	1834	A. L. Jenkins	41
Tremel, 14 stations § ..	..	G. Le Coat	66
Brest §	1880		35
Paris—			
48, Rue de Lille* .. .. New Places of Worship:— Versailles, 21, Rue Montreuil*, Mesnil St. Denis* (Seine and Oise), and others.	1850	Ph. Vincent, 46, Rue de la Santé. Second Pasteur; S. Vincent, 20, Rue Hallé. M. Dez, Ancien Pasteur, 22, Avenue Bellevue à Sèvres .. .. .. J. Vignal, Evangéliste, 43, Rue Vanneau M. Maneval, Evangéliste, 50, Avenue d'Orléans .. .. M. Meyer, 3, Cité Thure .. .. Mme. Lambert, Bible Woman, 76, Rue de Moulin Vert, à Montrouge, Paris	310
123, Rue St. Denis	1889	R. Saillens, 2, Rue Antoine Roucher, Auteuil .. .. M. Sagnol, Evangéliste à Rueil (Seine) Miss Douglas, Bible Woman, Bougival (Seine)	295
Niort et Chatelleraut (Deux Sevres)	..	J. Sainton	27
Neuilly (Seine)	..	Anciens: Bentz-Audéoud and Paul Passy	22

FRANCE—*continued.*

Churches.	Formed.	Pastors	Members.
Marseilles	1892	M. Colin	47
Toulon et La Seyne	1892	De Robert	35
Nice	1892	— Long	28
Chauny* (Aisne)	1832	A. Cadot .. .. M. Béguelin, Lay Preacher	132
La Fère* (Aisne)	1848	M. Cadot	83
St. Sauveur* (Oise)	1838	F. Lemaire (invalid), H. Andru, Pasteur M. Ferret, Colporteur-Evangéliste ..	113
Denain* (Nord)	1851	M. Vincent, père, Lay Preacher .. M. Capon, Colporteur-Evangéliste .. Miss Dinoir, Bible Woman, Tourcoing	258
Lens*	1875	S. Farelly and C. Vautrin	67
Sallan	..		
L'Epinette (près Lens) ..	..		
Haisnes (sous station) ..	..		
Loos (environs de Lens) ..	..		
Bruay	1885	C. Vautrin	47
Béthune	1894	S. Farelly, 76, Rue de la Gare, Béthune	..
Marles			
Auchel	..	P. Hugon, Rue de la Colonne, Grand Rue à Auchel	32
Rembert			
Isbergues			
St. Pierre			
Lyons* (Rhone)	1868	M. Laügt, 62, Rue Molière, Lyon ..	68
Montélimar (Drôme) ..	..		
St. Didier*	..		
Villefranche	..		
St. Etienne* (Loire)	1855	S. Ralinesque, Evangéliste, 13, Place Chavanelle	64
Montbéliard* (Doubs) ..	1872	M. Biéler, Evangéliste	94
Chaux de Fonds (Switzerland)	..	.. ..	..
Valentigney (Doubs)	1891	M. Lucien Louys	32
Rouen (Seine-Inferieure) ..	1891	M. Guignard; 10, Rue Aux Anglais, Evangéliste, Jaccard	32
Tramelan (Switzerland) ..	1892	P. Juillerat, Evangéliste, Sancey	174
Neuchatel	1894	M. Revel	46
Ougrée (Belgium)	1892	A. Brogniez, Pasteur; M. Debaker, Evangéliste: Monseur, Colporteur	60

The Churches marked (†) are aided by the Baptist Missionary Society; those marked (*) are connected with the American Baptist Missionary Union; and those marked (§) are aided by the Brittany Mission.

The French Baptists have a paper called *L'Echo de la Vérité*, published twice a month, at Paris. Editor, Pasteur Ruben Saillens.

695 Sunday-school scholars. Number of baptisms, 265.

ITALY.

(*Population*, 30,158,408.)

BAPTIST UNION OF ITALY.

(Unione Cristiana Apostolica Battista.)

Founded 1883.

President—N. H. SHAW. ***Vice-President***—Dr. J. H. EAGER.

Treasurer—W. K. LANDELS. ***Secretary***—N. NARDI-GRECO.

Churches.	Date.	Address of Halls.	Members.	S. S. Scholars.	Pastors.
		BAPTIST MISSIONARY SOCIETY.			
Avellino	1885	Corso V. Emanuele, Pal. Curcios	7	13	F. Libonati.
Calitri	1892	88, Vico Zorrilli	38	15	A. Barone.
Florence ..	1880	6, Vià Borgognissanti ..	47	30	N. H. Shaw. G. Allegri
Prato	1890	.. ..	4		
Genova	1879	36, Piazza De Ferrari ..	133	24	N. Nardi-Greco.
Leghorn	1876	2, Vià dei Fulgidi	23	26	G. Baratti.
Naples	1877	175, Vià Foria	47	*35	R. Walker and V. Tummolo.
Rome	1870	35, Piazza in Lucina ..	*375	*366	James Wall. J. C. Wall. A. Dal Canto. A. Giordani. A. Petocchi. E. Nesi.
	1875	154, Vià Urbana			
		102, Vià Consolazione ..			
		125, Vià Lungaretta ..			
		140, Piazza V. Emanuele ..			
Civitavecchia	1871	4, Vià dei Campani ..			
S. Benedetto	1892	3, Vià Ariana			
Tivoli	..	.. ..			
Susa	1894	S. Lazaro Lungo Dora ..	10	10	P. E. Jahier.
Meana ..	1894	Campo del Carro, Casa Bolei	12	16	" "
Gravere ..	1895	.. ..	..	..	" "
Turin	1878	27, Vià M. Vittoria .. 102, Vià Frejus	62	40	W. Kemme Landels.
Viterbos	..	.. ..	..	..	A. Ageno.

ITALY—*continued.*

Churches.	Date.	Address of Halls.	Members.	S. S. Scholars.	Pastors.
	SOUTHERN BAPTIST CONVENTION OF AMERICA.				
Bari	1877	91, Viâ Dante Alighieri ..	18	18	E. Volpi.
Barletta ..	..	16, Piazza Ferrovia.. ..	6	..	,,
Boscoreale ..	1886	20, Viâ Garibaldi	18	..	F. Martinelli.
Cagliari	1877	6, Piazza Yenne	31	34	P. Arbanasich.
Cannes (France)	1892	19, Rue Chateaudun ..	20	10	O. Ferraris.
Carpi, &c. ..	..	54, Corso Alberto Pio ..	34	7	C. Boglione.
Cuglieri	1894	.. ..	..	..	A. Cossû.
Florence ..	1890	Lungarno Guicuardini ..	37	70	J. H. Eager and
Sesto & Rifredi	..	.. ..	..	..	L. M. Galassi.
Genoa	1895	4, Piazza Paolo da Novi ..	4	..	G. Colombo.
Sampierdavena	1894	4, Corso dei Colli	..	..	,,
Gravina	1894	7, Viâ Giosia Gentile ..	25	10	A. Fiore.
Iglesias, &c. ..	1893	Viâ Circonvallazione ..	27	20	G. Tortonese.
Miglionico ..	1891	Piazza Purgatorio	27	45	C. Piccinni.
Milano	1874	39, Viâ del Pesce	41	18	N. Papengouth.
Novara ..	1894	16, Corso Roma	6	..	,,
Naples	1890	6, Viâ San Giacomo ..	26	12	G. Fasulo.
Palermo	1894	57, Viâ Bandiera	7	10	S De Gaetano.
Portici	1892	9, Viâ Cannito	11	..	A. Basile.
Rome	1874	26, Viâ Teatro Valle ..	26	11	G. B. Taylor, D.D. & E. Paschetto.
San Remo, &c. ..	1890	Viâ Francia, Rondo ..	14	25	D. Stanganini.
Torre Pellice, &c.	1871	Viâ Angrogna	26	20	D. B. Malan.
Venice	1876				
		INDEPENDENT MISSIONS.			
Naples, &c. ..	1873	13, Largo S. Domenico M...	50	14	O. Papengouth.
Sestri	1892	17, Viâ Travi	*25	*18	Sig. Baci.

* Last year's Statistics.

Summary of Statistics, including estimate for non-reporting Churches: 40 Churches; 1,279 members; 917 Sunday-school scholars. About 150 baptized.

SPEZIA MISSION FOR ITALY.

Founded 1866.

Director—Rev. E. CLARKE. *Co-Director*—Rev. H. H. Pullen.

Station.	Formed.	Locality.
Casa Alberto..	1866	Spezia
Casa Massa	1870	Spezia
Piazza M. Adelaida	..	Spezia
Via Volturno	1888	Spezia
Arcola	1865	Spur of the Apennines
Baccano	1880	Spur of the Apennines
Belluno	1880	Province of Venezia
Campiglia	1882	Gulf of La Spezia
Conegliano	1882	Province of Venezia
Feltre	..	Province of Venezia
Lerici	1879	Gulf of La Spezia
Levanto	..	Province of Liguria
Marola*	1887	Gulf of La Spezia
Montebelluna	..	Province of Venezia
Oderza	..	Province of Venezia
Pistoja	1875	Province of Tuscany
Pordenone	1870	Province of Venezia
Porto Venere	1883	Gulf of La Spezia
Rebocco	1883	Gulf of La Spezia
Sarzana	1883	Borders of Tuscany
Sereno	..	Province of Venezia
St. Terenzo	..	Gulf of La Spezia
Treviso	1887	Province of Venezia

* In Marola, in connection with the Mission, there is a Girls' Orphanage, with 23 orphans.

23 Stations, besides numerous sub-stations, 164 communicants, 8 Bible day-schools, with over 800 scholars, 15 Sunday-schools, with 280 scholars. The whole superintended by British missionaries, aided by over 33 native missionaries, assistants and school-teachers, and 91 catechumens.

GERMAN BAPTIST UNION.

INCLUDING CHURCHES IN

GERMANY, AUSTRIA, HUNGARY, SWITZERLAND, HOLLAND, ROUMANIA, BULGARIA, AND SOUTH AFRICA.

COMMITTEE

For the distribution of the Funds sent from Great Britain in aid of Mission-work in Germany.

Rev. F. B. MEYER, B.A., London.

Pastor WIEHLER, Bremen.
„ K. MASCHER, Dresden.
Rev. E. MILLARD, Wiesbaden.
Mr. W. S. ONCKEN, Lincoln.
Mr. HARTUNG, Hamburg.
Mr. PIELSTICK, Hamburg.

Rev. PHILIPP BICKEL, D.D., Hamburg, *Treasurer.*
Mr. MARTIN HOOD WILKIN, Hampstead, N.W., *Treasurer for Great Britain.*

The Baptist Churches in *Germany* form one Union, including seven Associations. The Associations have their Conferences every year. The Union's Conference is a triennial one. The next Conference of the Union will be held in 1897 (probably in Konigsberg, East Prussia). The work of the Union is done by the following three Commissions of seven :—

1. *Publications Commission*, in charge of the publishing and printing office in *Hamburg*—Borgfelde, 98, Mittelweg, Rev. P. Bickel, D.D., director and chief editor

J. G. Lehmann, editor; and Karl Bickel, manager. Here the *Wahrheitszeuge* (the organ of the Baptist denomination in Germany) and five other periodicals for Sunday-school teachers and children, for young men and women, sermons from English and American pulpits, and illustrated tracts and books are issued. The Conference authorised Rev. P. Bickel to collect funds for the building of a Publication House.

2. *School Commission*, in charge of the Theological College in Hamburg, which has now its own building in Horn, Rennbahnstr. The Professors are Rev. Joseph Lehmann and Rev. J. G. Fetzer. There are at present 47 students preparing for the ministry, 42 in two classes, the course of studies lasting four years, and 5 of more advanced years, taking a course of one year's study.

3. *Finance Commission*, in charge of the funds of the Union:—
   a. Chapel-Building Fund, £3,650;
   b. Invalid Ministers' Fund, £2,426;
   c. Ministers' Widows' and Orphans' Fund, £1,946.

For representing the Union before public authorities, the following three brethren were elected:—Rev. Philipp Bickel, J. Braun, Rev. Chr. Rode. The three Commissions together form the "United Bundes Verwaltung," the secretary of which is Rev. J. G. Fetzer.

The Dutch Baptist Union is now part of the larger circle of the German Baptist Union.

DUTCH COMMITTEE.

G. DE VRIES, *President*. | J. DE HART, *Vice-President*.
B. ROELES, *Secretary*. | J. KATUIN, *Vice-Secretary*.

F. J. VAN MEERLOO, *Treasurer*.

MR. R. KLICKMANN, 82, Ondine Road, East Dulwich, Lambeth, S.E., *Treasurer for Great Britain*.

GERMANY.

(*Population*, 49,421,064.)

Town and Address.	Date.	Members.	S. S. Tchrs.	S. S. Schlrs.	Local Prchrs.	Pastors.
Albrechtsdorf (East Prussia)	1876	517	15	250	10	F. Schirrmann.
Alexen (East Prussia) ..	1873	251	..	..	..	Ch. Kickstat.
Altenburg (Saxony)—						
Johannisgraben, 3A.. ..	1881	160	24	260	5	P. Betzou.
Altona (near Hamburg)—						
Gr. Gärtnerstrasse, 98 ..	1871	554	65	660	..	C. Rode. W. Haupt.
Backnang (Würtemberg)—						
Aspacherstrasse, 19.. ..	1874	54	5	41	2	
Barmen—						
Gasstrasse, 44	1852	213	24	500	7	C. Schröder.
Bartenstein (East Prussia)—						
Angerstrasse, 21	..	..	..	..	..	F. Schirrmann.
Bayreuth—						
Friedrichstrasse	..	..	..	..	..	F. Hermann.
Belgard, a. d. P. (Pomerania)—						
Burgstrasse, 7	1892	176	5	75	1	F. W. Nickel.
Berlin—						
Schmidstrasse, 17. S.O. ..	1837	1108	64	800	17	G. Mattes, C. Meyer.
Gubenerstrasse, 11. O. ..	..	1002	93	1150	14	C. Peters, F. Sturm.
Berlinchen (Brandenburg) ..	1869	128	3	40	..	R. Schwan.
Bladiau (East Prussia) ..	1869	153	3	40		

GERMANY—*continued.*

Town and Address.	Date.	Members.	S. S. Tchrs.	S. S. Schlrs.	Local Prchrs.	Pastors.
Bochum— Wittenerstrasse, 44 ..	1874	285	26	550	4	G. Kickstat.
Bremen— Langenstrasse, 115	1845	145	8	50	..	J. Wiehler.
Bremerhafen— Am Hafen 73 and Kirchenstrasse, 1						
Lehe (near Bremerhaven)— Geeststrasse, 11	1863	94	17	375		
Breslau— Löschstrasse, 11A	1846	347	18	210	2	R. Kromm.
Briesen (West Prussia) ..	1891	91	1	20	3	H. Flüggo.
Bromberg (Prov. Posen)— Jakobstrasse, 2	1874	197	12	105	4	F. Curant.
Brome (Hanover)	1849	173	9	90	5	H. Riemenschneider.
Bruiszen (East Prussia) ..	1881	168	..	..	2	A. Nelaimiszkis.
Brunswick— Am alten Petrithor, 9 ..	1869	137	15	157	5	H. Fiehler.
Büdingen (Ober Hessen) ..	1856	..	..	..	..	E. Schirrmann.
Bütow (Pomerania)	1886	79	..	..	..	F. W. Nickel.
Cassel— Mönchebergerstrasse, 10	1847	213	12	125	3	W. Ratter.
Cologne— Severinstrasse, 33	1868	215	21	350	2	H. W. Grage.
Danzig— Schiesstange, 13, 14 ..	1875	254	18	250	2	J. Hermann.
Derschlag (Rhein Provinz) ..	1882	197	11	130	2	Fr. Herrmann.
Dirschau— Podlitzstrasse, 13	1859	203	8	70	3	L. Helmetag.
Dortmund, Godenstrasse ..	1894	87	4	50	..	J. B. Wilkens.
Dresden— Altstadt, Mathildenstr., 111	1892	85	10	90	2	K. Mascher.
Düsseldorf— Charlottenstrasse, 32 ..	1889	91	12	110	..	A. Hoefs.
Eberswalde (Brandenburg)— Eichwerderstrasse, 61 ..	1879	97	5	34	2	O. Schmidt.
Einbeck (Hanover)— Baustrasse	1843	160	13	80	5	S. Knappe.
Elberfeld Teichstrasse, Vereinshaus	1894	107	12	200	..	G. Fehr.
Elbing— Heiligengeiststrasse, 13 ..	1844	480	49	471	11	J. L. Hinrichs. L. Horn.
Elmshorn (Holstein)— Osterfeld, 1	1866	168	19	180	3	K. Mahr.
Elsfleth (Gr. Duchy, Oldenburg)— Mühlenstrasse	1854	53	3	65	2	
Emden— Beuljenstrasse, 3						
Essen an der Ruhr— Frohnhäuserstrasse, 4 ..	1879	244	12	96	2	M. Palm.
Eydtkuhnen (Russian frontier)	1878	259	6	80	4	— Schilling.
Felde (Oldenburg)	1849	111	11	80	2	H. Cording
Fischausen (E. Pr.)	1865	400	20	250	4	A. Pipereit.

GERMANY—*continued.*

Town and Address.	Date.	Members.	S. S. Tchrs.	S. S. Schlrs.	Local Prchrs.	Pastors.
Forst (Brandenburg)	1892	32	2	30		
Frankfort-on-Maine—						
Am Tiergarten, 100 ..	1868	150	16	170	3	B. Weerts.
Freiburg (Silesia)—						
Neuebahnhofstrasse ..	1858	235	12	176	5	M. Knappe.
Fulda, Karlstrasse						
Gerstungen Ober-Ellen (Saxony-Weimar-Eisenach) ..	1878	140	11	124	3	Fr. Ehmer.
Göttingen, Gronerstrasse, 451	1894	21	4	25	2	B. Naumdorf.
Goyden (E. Pr.)	1855	279	5	70	2	
Graudenz (W. Pr.)—						
Marienwerderstrasse, 22 ..	1881	201	8	70	..	C. G. Schultz.
Grodszisko (E. Pr.)	1868	137	2	40	2	J. Lübeck.
Grundschöttel (Westphalia) ..	1854	283	40	400	8	G. Maier.
Gundelfingen (nr. Freiburg in Baden) Konvicstrasse, 13 ...	1877	96	8	73	3	J. Winhold.
Halle a. d. Saale—						
Forsterstrasse, 12						
Giebichenstein, Triftstr., 19A	1864	157	28	261	5	D. Janssen
Hamburg—						
Böhmkenstrasse, 21 ..	1834	601	60	650	..	Th. Duprée.
Eilbeck, Kiebitzstrasse 40	1884	227	45	350	2	L. Schunke.
Hanover—						
Semmernstrasse, 1C ..	1854	294	18	225	6	A. Mundhenk.
Harburg—						
Maretstrasse, 11						
Hassenhausen, Hesse ..	1840	162	9	111	7	H. Brucker.
Heilbronn (Würtemburg)—						
Aüssere Rosenbergstr., 35 ..	1847	106	3	55	10	Chr. Friz.
Heiligenbeil	1893	145	6	50	1	O. H. Licht.
Herford (Westphalia)—						
Am Gange, 849	1865	82	6	110	4	C. Haydt.
Hersfeld (Hessen)—						
Am Neumarkt	1845	244	29	300	5	M. Gute.
Hildesheim						
Friesenstrasse						
Hohenkirch (W. Pr.)	1863	274	7	92	1	
Ihren (Ostfriesland)	1846	440	33	480	12	H. Mechels.
Ickschen (E. Pr.)	1862	306	8	80	3	P. Weist. E. Liedtke.
Inowrazlaw (Prov. Posen)—						
Bahnhofstrasse, 11	1885	323	12	115	11	Helm. Liebig.
Insterburg (E. Pr.)—						
Ziegelstrasse, 14	1883	572	20	350	3	F. Hinzke and Cl. Lorenz.
Jennelt (Ostfriesland)	1865	195	11	110	5	S. U. Janssen.
Jever (Oldenburg)—						
Am Pferdegraben, 650 ..	1840	23	3	40		
Kiel—						
Wilhelminenstrasse, 12 ..	1872	182	13	124	..	W. Clasen.
Königsberg i/P.—						
Hinter Tragheim, 12 Unterhaberberg, 12	1857	1500	86	1250	12	J. Kradolfer. F. Wargenau.
Küstrin-Tschernow ..	1890	210	10	90	7	F. Pahlke.

GERMANY—*continued.*

Town and Address.	Date.	Members.	S. S. Tchrs.	S. S. Schlrs.	Local Prchrs.	Pastors.
Landsberg, a. d. W.—Heinersdorferstrasse, 22 ..	1862	196	7	120	6	P. Grögor.
Leipzig—Johannisgasse, 15	1880	50	8	85	1	
Liegnitz (Silesia)—Carthaus, 6	1849	67	4	35	1	
Lübeck—Meynstrasse, 42						
Lyck (East Prussia)	1888	205	4	50	3	G. Kuczewski.
Magdeburg—Prälatenstrasse, 30	1888	79	5	130	2	G. Späth
Mainz—Lotharstrasse, 14	1866	29	4	50		
Mannheim—Neckar Vorstadt, Dammstrasse, 29						
Marburg—Hofstadt						
Marienburg (W. Pr.)—Ziegelgasse, 27						
Marköbel, near Hanau ..						
Massenbach (Würtemberg) ..	1882	45	2	20	3	C. Fritz.
Memel (E. Pr.)—Neuer Park, ...	1841	334	35	500	4	F. W. Herrmann.
Metz—Friedhofstrasse, 33-35	..	..	..	..	..	C. Breidenbach.
Möckmühl (Würtemberg)—An d langen Staffel, 81 ..	1863	37	1	25	1	
Mülhausen (Elsass)—Langegasse, 23	1856	130	20	200	6	G. F. Weidkuhn.
Mülheim a. Rh.—Salzstrasse, 4						
Neudorf (Ostfriesland) ..	1865	66	1	27	1	J. Jelten.
Neuenflügel	1893	51	3	76	..	H. Braun.
Neuwied a. Rh.—Schloss strasse, 57						
Norgau, near Königsberg i/P.	1876	55	..	..	2	
Oberkaufungen (Hessen)—Jägerhof, 63	1855	68	6	50	1	C. Fuchs.
Oldenburg—Wilhelmstrasse, 6	1837	80	6	30	1	A. Thesmacher.
Ottensen, near Altona—Bahrenfelderstrasse, 131 ..	..	..	..	..	..	W. Haupt.
Parsau	1889	109	6	40	2	B. Knoch.
Piassutten (E. Pr.)	1884	445	2	23	12	
Planitz (Saxony)—Schlossbergstrasse, 337 ..	1891	157	41	360	4	N. Capek.
Pobethen (E. Pr.)	1869	127	4	50	3	E. Ziehl.
Potsdam—Junkerstrasse, 50						
Prenzlau (Brandenburg)—Am Berliner Thor, 69 ..	1880	104	2	20	3	
Przesdzenk (E. Pr.)	1882	302	..	..	3	
Reetz, near Arnswalde (Brandenburg	1856	276	8	52	..	C. Krüger.

GERMANY—*continued.*

Town and Address.	Date.	Members.	S. S. Tchrs.	S. S. Schlrs.	Local Prchrs.	Pastors.
Rogahlen (E. Pr.)	1887	118	3	35	2	
Romanowen (E. Pr.)	1872	204	1	45	6	C. Frassa.
Rositten, near Pr. Eylau (E.Pr.)	1855	173	6	80	6	A. Baumgärtner.
Rummy, near Mensguth (E.Pr.)	1861	269	6	49	9	F. W. Kottke.
Russ Prökuls (E. Pr.)	1864	128	1	30	..	F. Stein.
Salzgitter—						
Sackstrasse, 43	1840	54	4	40	2	J. Bobrowski.
Schalke-Gelsenkirchen—						
Blumenstrasse, 4	1891	308	13	108	..	A. Broda.
Schleswig—						
Stadtweg, 80 A.	1856	403	24	350	8	H. Schröder.
Schmalkalden—						
Pfaffengasse	1893	102	9	80	4	J. Dietzel
Schmölln—						
Wilhelmstrasse, 454 ..						
Seefeld (G. D. Ol'burg)—						
Seefelder Aussendeich ..	1856	17				
Seehausen (Brandenburg)—						
Grabenstrasse, 50	1856	109	11	120	3	R. Nehring.
Selters-Marköbel (Hessen) ..	1856	57	8	25	1	E. Schirrmann.
Solingen—						
Kronenbergerstrasse ..						
Spangenberg (Hesse-Nassau)—						
Vor der Judenschule ..	1847	135	7	110	10	R. Hoppe.
Stettin—						
Johannisstrasse, 4	1846	463	23	185	4	Herm. Liebig, and C. Böhme.
Stolzenberg (East Prussia) ..	1849	161	4	45	..	C. F. Lardon.
Stralsund	1877	10	..	..	1	
Strasburg—						
Metzgergiessen, 19	1893	80	12	74	5	L. Grüber.
Stuttgart—						
Kasernenstr., 16 Hinterhaus	1863	227	12	120	8	F. W. Liebig.
Süd-Georgsfehn (Ostfriesland)	1865	61	4	55		
Tangstedt (Holstein)	1854	57	3	32	1	
Templin (Brandenburg) ..	1845	261	9	80	5	
Tilsit (East Prussia)—						
Teichstrasse, 7	1885	250	6	85	2	G. Klempel.
Tübingen—						
Neustadt, 4						
Uslar	1891	76	3	20	1	
Varel (Grand Duchy of Oldenburg)—						
Mühlenstrasse, 19	1856	43	7	50	..	A. F. W. Haese.
Velten (near Berlin)	1891	83	7	88	..	O. Weinhold.
Wermelskirchen	1893	46	6	50	1	H. Braun.
Wiesbaden—						
Kirchgasse, 32, Hinterhaus	1880	114	5	60	2	E. Millard.
Wilhelmshaven—						
Ostfriesenstrasse, 70 ..	1886	87	12	90	1	P. Winderlich.
Wittenberge—						
Zimmerstrasse, 5	..	..	..	..	..	W. Märtens.
Worms (a. Rhein)—						
Schmidstrasse, 10	1864	91	16	130	1	J. Harnisch.
Zeinicke, near Freienwalde, (Pomerania) ..	1883	299	6	80	..	A. Kühn.

AUSTRIA-HUNGARY.

(*Population*, 42,749,329.)

Town and Address.	Date.	Members.	S. S. Tchrs.	S. S. Schl's.	Local Prchrs.	Pastors.
Buda-Pesth— Wesselenyigasse, Ecke Lindengasse	1874	2088	120	1200	87	H. Meyer.
Feketehegy	1894	83	8	50	..	J. Peter.
Graz— Haydngasse, 10	1882	31	..	..	1	
Kesmark, Alter Markt, 276 ..	1888	180	5	50	7	A. Meereis.
Prague (Bohemia)— Königl. Weinberge Halekstrasse, 52	1885	159	7	44	9	H. Nowotny.
Sniatyn (Gallicia)	1885	176	14	120	11	F. Massier.
Temesvar	1894	66	8	20	..	M. Kuss.
Vienna— VII Bezirk, Breitegasse, 7 ..	1869	170	9	50	5	H. Koch.

SWITZERLAND.

(*Population*, 2,933,334.)

Town and Address.	Date.	Members.	S. S. Tchrs.	S. S. Schl's.	Local Prchrs.	Pastors.
Basel	1893	46	3	28	1	J. Gamper.
Bischofzell— Z. Chorherrenhof	1867	132	18	280	3	J. Gossweiler.
Bruggen— J. Kürsteiner's						
St. Gallen— Speiserthor, Linsebühlstr...	1881	83	4	35	2	T. Fisch.
Herisau— Oberdorfstrasse	1867	81	14	300	1	A. Waldvogel.
Zürich— Neumarkt, 13	1849	161	10	100	7	Aug. Meyer.

HOLLAND.

(*Population*, 4,450,870.)

Churches in the German Union.

Town and Address.	Date.	Members.	S. S. Tchrs.	S. S. Schlrs.	Local Prchrs.	Pastors.
Amsterdam— Rozengracht, 166	1848	62	4	70	2	F. J. van Meerloo.
Deventer, Aan het Singel ..	1884	36	3	50	1	B. Roeles.
Franeker	1864	211	11	200	..	A. Karssiens.
Foxhol	1876	60	4	110	1	J. Deuzeman (Deacon).
'sGravenhage	1892	45	7	120	2	F. J. van Meerloo.
Groningen— Warmoerstraat	1876	281	13	130	2	J. Horn.
Haarlem	1876	25	1	25	..	E. van der Steur (Deacon).
Haulerwyk	1878	30	4	90	2	G. de Vries.
Heeg	1883	13	2	30	1	J. de Vries (Deacon).
Hengeloo (O)	1879	98	2	51	2	J. Katuin.
Nieuw-Pekela	1885	56	2	40	..	E. H. de Groot (Deacon).
Sneek	1879	87	12	300	2	J. de Hart.
Valthermond	1882	48	2	80	..	K. Hesseling.
'tZandt	1882	18	2	30	1	S. Engelsman. (Deacon).
Zutphen— Rykenhage, 16	1888	41	5	135	1	B. Roeles.

1,111 members; 74 teachers; 1,461 scholars in the Union.

CHURCHES NOT IN THE UNION.

Churches	Formed.	Members.	S. S. Teachrs	S. S. Scholars	Pastors.
Hoorn	1883	19	2	30	D. Velde (Deacon).
Rotterdam	1888				
Stadskanaal	1845	143	3	175	N. van Beek.
Weerdingermond ..	1875				

ROUMANIA.

(*Population, about* 5,376,000.)

Town and Address.	Date.	Members.	S. S. Tchrs.	S. S. Schlrs.	Local Prchrs.	Pastors.
Bukarest—						
Strada Arcului, 3	1883	30	4	50	3	D. Schwegler.
Catalui	1869	245	25	250	16	L. Liebig, M. Issler.

BULGARIA.

(*Population*, 3,154,375.)

Town and Address.	Date.	Members.	S. S. Tchrs.	S. S. Schlrs.	Local Prchrs.	Pastors.
Rustschuk—						
Kara Ali Machala	1884	72	4	90	5	Chr. Stvikoff.
Tultscha	1891	37	3	45	2	Kensseff.

SUMMARY.

Up to 1890 the Russian and Danish Unions sent the statistics of their churches to Hamburg; now they publish their own statistical reports. This fact must be remembered in comparing the following summary with that of former years.

CLOSE OF 1894.

Country.	Churches.	Chapels.	Members.	Baptisms in 1894.	Clear increase in 1894.	S. S. Teachers.	S. S. Scholars.
Germany	144	116	24,571	1,928	813	1,565	18,364
Austria-Hungary	8	17	2,953	1,020	874	171	1,534
Switzerland	6	2	503	24	12	49	743
Holland	19	13	1,273	77	27	79	1,666
Roumania and Bulgaria	4	11	384	32	17	36	435
South Africa (See page 430) ..	5	14	1,018	104	90	59	472
Totals	186	173	30,702	3,185	1,843	1,959	23,214

RUSSIA.

(Including POLAND.)

Population, including Poland and excluding Finland and Asiatic Russia, 89,685,489.

RUSSIAN BAPTIST UNION.

The Baptist Churches in Russia now form a separate Union, but continue to take part in the use and support of the German Union funds. They are divided into four Associations:—The Baltic (Kurland), Polish, West Russian, and South Russian.

Town and Address.	Date.	Members.	S. S. Tchrs.	S. S. Schlrs.	Local Prchrs.	Pastors.
St. Petersburg, Offizierstr., 49	1880	201	..	..	5	Schiewe, Tetermann.
Hapsal (Esthland)	1894	163	1	22	2	A. Johannsohn.
Kertel (Livland)	1894	168	1	30	10	Kaups.
Riga (Kurland)..	1881	251	15	150	8	S. Lehmann.
Kowno (Gub. Kowno) ..	1888	81	..	..	..	A. Stoltenhoff.
Agenskalno (Kurland) ..	1884					J. Eichmann.
Aisup (Kurland)	..					J. A. Frey.
Bachte (Kurland) ..	1886					J. Eidemann, M. Ries.
Galitscha (Kurland)	..					T. Tuke.
Grobin (Kurland)	..					K. Ruschewitz.
Gr. Irben (Kurland)	1885					P. Weidemann.
Kandawa (Kurland)	..					S. Aisupis.
Leepaja (Kurland)	1881					M. Matthische.
Mitau (Kurland)	1879					F. Kruming.
Nikolai-Datscha (Kurland) ..	..					T. Ubberts.
Pilten (Kurland)	..					M. Ehwert.
Prekuln (Kurland)	1876					M. Wihtinsch.
Renges (Kurland)	..	5902	152	1747	53	P. Samet.
Sakas (Kurland)	1883					P. Klawintsch.
Saldus, Sohkehde, Sirgen, Skatre..	..					Freimann.
Tadaiki, Turlau, Uschawa, Windau	..					Erdmannsohn Andermann.
Dundanga, Dinamunde (Livland)	1876					F. Puschkewitz.
Jaunjelgawa (Livland) ..	1878					Klabbis.
Paltmale (Livland)	1881					Puschis.
Kurino (Gub. Warsaw) ..	1886					Alps.
Schimirscha (Gub. Simbirsk)	..					Kesser.
Trubatschina (Gub. Simbirsk)	..					T. Kulberg.
Kicin (Gub. Plock. Poland) ..	1861	601	18	230	4	Alf, Hinz, Rossoll, Assmann.
Kuruwek (Gub. Petrikan, Poland)	1870	154	..	..	10	
Lodz (Gub. Petrikan, Poland)	1878	1019	69	755	6	Gutsche, Eichhorst.
Ploutschewize (Gub. Lublin)	1889	181	8	90	8	Aschendorf.
Radawtschik (Gub. Lublin) ..	1884	338	12	120	7	Mantei.
Warsaw (Gub. Warsaw) ..	1888	138	4	45	8	Pufahl, Hass.
Zdonskawola (Gub. Kalisch)..	1885	346	14	120	8	Hohense.
Zelow (Gub. Petrikan) ..	1886	112	4	50	4	Pospisil.
Zezulin (Gub. Petrikan) ..	1873	318	8	101	9	Lasch.
Zyrardow (Gub. Warsaw) ..	1875	207	17	122	1	Brauer, Schweiger.

RUSSIA—*continued.*

Town and Address.	Date.	Members.	S. S. Tchrs.	S. S. Schlrs.	Local Prchrs.	Pastors.
Cholossna (Gub. Wolhynien)	1875	289	..	..	..	Rosenau.
Friedenberg (Gub. Samara) ..	..	102	2	40	..	Hammer, Lorenz.
Hortschik (Gub. Wolhynien)	1864	297	3	40	..	R. Wardetzke.
Iwanowitsch (Gub. Wolhynien)	1885	649	..	..	3	Tiedtke.
Luzinow (Gub. Wolhynien) ..	1881	802	3	50	3	Klenysel. Jesske.
Moor (Gub. Saratow).. ..	1885	169	2	41	..	Hammer. Kirsch.
Moisejewka (Gub. Wolhynien)	1888	323	..	..	14	Wenslaw.
Neudorf (Gub. Wolhynien) ..	1866	1072	..	..	..	Baier. Spingath.
Nowo-Rudnia (Gub. Wolhynien)	1884	270	..	..	..	Koschinsky.
Roschitsche (Gub. Wolhynien)	1884	324	3	25	1	Breier.
Sorotschin (Gub. Wolhynien)	1864	367	8	111	6	Schulz. Freizang.
Toporischst (Gub. Wolhynien)	1878	425				
Ust-Kulalinka (Gub. Saratow)	1890	214	6	200	1	Husmann. Schleunig.
Alt-Danzig (Gub. Cherson) ..	1869	101	5	80	5	F. Pritzkaw.
Bellagwesch (Gub. Mariupul)	1888	167	3	58	4	H. Liedtke. W. Dell.
Eupatoria (Crimea)	1887	19	..	..	..	
Friedrichsfeld (Kuban District)	..	196	..	..	..	
Johannisthal (Gub. Cherson)..	1885	521	14	210	..	Hornbather, Busse.
Klein-Liebenthal (Gub. Ekaterinoslaw)	1888	358	6	111	5	W. Bechthold.
Michaelowka (Gub. Ekaterinoslaw)	1885	171	5	80	6	Golbeck. Müller.
Neuburg (Gub. Ekaterinoslaw)	1887	190	5	120	..	C. Füllbrandt.
Neu-Danzig (Gub. Cherson)..	1875	180	6	80	6	Kessler, Matthiess.
Neuheim (Gub. Charkow) ..	1889	120	3	40	3	H. Schimpke.
Odessa (South Russia) ..	1870	100	3	62	3	Triesen. Kessler.

SUMMARY.

No. of Chapels and places where Meetings are held.	Churches.	Chapels.	Members.	S. S. Teachers	S. S. Scholars.	Sittings.	Baptisms.
513	102	94	17,606	400	4,930	..	1,079

FINLAND.

(*Population in* 1891, 2,412,134.)

AMERICAN BAPTIST MISSIONARY UNION AND FINNISH BAPTIST MISSION.

Churches.	Date.	Chapels.	Members.	S. S. Tchrs.	S. S. Schlrs.	Local Prchrs.	B'ptisms	Pastors.
Abo (City) ..	1887	..	29	1	6	1	5	J. G. Johansson.
Aland	1887	..	21	..	..	1	8	A. Hallsten.
Amossa, Petalax	1881	1	302	9	100	5	32	E. Jansson.
Djupsund.. ..	1885	..	46	..	..	..	8	K. Strom.
Esse	1874	1	76	1	25	1	1	J. Radmans.
Forsby	1873	1	78	4	35	3	2	A. Niss.
Fogle	..	..	13	..	..	..	..	K. W. Sjoblom.
Helsingfors (City)	1886	..	25	4	50	1	..	P. Malmquist.
Jakobstad (City)..	1891	1	38	3	20	1	2	J. E. Soderman.
Jungsund.. ..	1887	1	16	2	75	1	1	A. Wahlstedt.
Jurva	1879	1	67	..	..	1	2	J. Nostaja.
Karis	..	..	33	1	30	..	1	G. Hagstrom.
Kuopio (City) ..	1886	1	27	..	..	..	..	G. W. Nygren.
Laihela	1879	..	13	..	..	..	..	Johan Fast.
Larsmo	1874	1	54	2	20	1	3	E. Kackur.
Mono	1873	1	95	9	75	1	4	E. Nygard.
Nempnes.. ..	1884	1	64	3	35	2	..	M. Eriksson.
Nerpes	1887	1	47	3	30	2	..	G. Soderman.
Ofverpurmo ..	1873	..	104	..	..	1	3	J. Sundquist.
Osterhankmo ..	1889	..	43	..	..	2	6	J. Akerholm.
Osterpurmo ..	1873	..	29	1	15	1	9	J. Kasen.
Pensala	1873	1	48	2	30	3	7	J. Rausk.
Sibbo	..	..	23	..	..	..	3	K. Wikstrom.
Tammerfors (City)	1890	..	58	1	20	1	9	J. Andersson.
Tolby	1885	1	28	..	..	2	4	J. Liljestrand.
Wasa (City) ..	1881	..	92	3	25	3	25	J. S. Osterman.
Woro	1873	..	25	..	..	..	..	M. Bertils.
Ylistaro	1894	..	15	..	..	..	13	J. Kokki.
Totals ..	..	13	1,509	49	591	34	148	

DENMARK.

(*Population*, 2,172,205.)

BAPTIST UNION OF DENMARK.

Churches.	Date.	Chapel Seats.	Members.	S. S. Tchrs.	S. S Schlrs.	Local Prchrs.	Pastors.
Aalborg	1879	300	92	22	230	4	B. Andreasen.
Amager	1891	250	110	9	90	..	A. Broholm.
Bornholm	1848	850	442	19	240	2	Ipsen, Holm.
Eskildstrup	1861	350	128	7	105	1	L. Andersen.
Falster and Ostlolland	1877	..	24	1	54	..	B. Jensen.
Frederikshavn	1860	400	230	21	453	5	R. E. Holm.
Hals	1856	..	81	7	125	2	
Hjörring	1886	450	223	20	350	6	A. Jensen.
Jetsmark	1856	500	232	9	250	4	E. Jensen.
Kjöbenhavn	1839	650	536	35	500	4	M. Larsen.
Langeland	1840	300	75	10	116	1	
Lolland	1857	150	54	2	30	1	N. Larsen.
Lögstör	1863	..	45	2	40	..	B. Sönder.
Nyrup	1891	150	36	..	..	..	
Oure	1855	250	116	9	182	..	J. A. Petersen.
Saaby	1881	150	51	5	108	1	
Samsö	1890	100	18	2	14	1	
Slagelse	1842	250	49	2	20	2	H. Larsen.
Snede	1863	150	103	7	120	3	
Snevre	1865	550	78	9	187	3	N. Hansen.
Syd-Aalborg	1840	500	164	10	250	4	C. Nörgaard.
Thyland	1891	..	66	4	115	..	A. Jörgensen.
Vandlöse	1857	400	247	12	400	9	B. Lensen.
Vantinge	1875	100	40	1	30	3	J. Larsen.
Vejle	1866	250	70	8	80	2	
Totals ..	..	7,050	3,310	233	4,089	58	

Baptisms, 251.

SPAIN.

(*Population*, 17,550,216.)

AMERICAN BAPTIST MISSIONARY UNION AND SWEDISH BAPTIST MISSION.

Churches.	Formed.	Pastors.	Members.
Barcelona	..	E. Lund .. .. / M. C. Marin	30 (Barcelona and La Escala)
La Escala	..	.. ..	
Sabadell	..	J. Uhr	23
Valencia	..	.. ..	44 (Valencia, Alcacer and Alginet)
Alcacer	..	.. ..	
Alginet	..	.. ..	

Baptisms, 5.

SWEDEN.

(*Population*, 4,784,675.)

Place.	Pastors.
Norrbotten Association—	
(MEMBERS 226.)	
Kalix	H. Lindgren.
Börjeslandet	A. Olson.
Broby	L. J. Larson.
Ersnas	L. O. Larson.
Pitea	A. A. Hortlander
Ranea	W. E. Winberg.
Lulea	C. J. Bergström.
Bensby	N. P. Petterson.
Jemtland Association—	
(MEMBERS 902.)	
Föllinge	J. Edström.
Hammerdal	J. Edström.
O. Offerdal	E. Janson.
Bracke	J. Åkeson.
Gransjolandet	
Hackas	J. Gerdin.
Hasjo	J. Johanson.
Mardsjo	P. Magnusson.
Sveg	
Ytteran	O. Anderson.
Hjerpen	S. Johanson.
Aspas	
Ostersund	J. Johanson.
Hallen	A. Norberg.
Sunne	J. Gårdlund.
Welje	
Oviken	A. Svelander.
Näs	
Myssjö	
Berg	P. A. Alm.
Stugun	A. Petterson.
Ragunda	J. Amcoff.
Palgard	
Langa	
Storsjön	G. Palson.
Angermanland Association—	
(MEMBERS 1,240.)	
Bjertra	
Bjurholm	O. Agren.
Bjorna	J. Edlund.
Anundsjö	J. W. Bergström.
Backe	
Gudmundra	
Nätra	J. O. Nyberg.
Umea	J. Nyqvist.
Asele	J. P. Olzén.
Nordmaling	E. Oldberg.
Gidea	E. J. Lundström.
Grundsunda	J. Jonson.
Arnäs	
Ornsköldsvik	M. Ohman.
Mo	Kr. Andersson
Skorped	J. Forssén.
Ramsele	L. Molander.
Helgum	E. Engman.
Graninge	E. Källman.
Solleftea	J. G. Roos.
Styrnäs	
Högsjö	N. P. Lund.
Botea	
Husum	E. Anderson.
Sidensjö	J. O. Nyberg.
Hernösand	M. Olson.
Sjalevad	M. Forsén.
Kramfors	P. Söderlof.
Medelpad Association—	
(MEMBERS 3,317.)	
Liden	L. Byqvist.
Holm	J. F. Sundman.
Ljustorp	F. M. Näss.
" Upper Church	C. Wigg.
Lögdö	M. W. Hammarberg.
Indal	
" North Church	L. O. Billström.
Hässjö	E. G. Akerlind.
Tynderö	P. Dahlin.
Selånger	
Sättna	A. O. Wallin.
" Lower Church	N. E. Karlmark.
Timra	P. Sundin.
Alnö	K. V. Lindblom.
" North Church	G. T. Johanson.
Sundsvall	
Skonsberg	
Tunadal	A. Osterman.
Tuna, Upper Church	L. S. Franson.
" Lower Church	E. Westerlund.
Svartvik	A. E. Backman.
Njurunda	P. O. Romberg.
Galtström	J. W. Wagberg.
Sörbygden	A. Backlund.
Bredby	E. M. Jonson.
Karläng	J. O. Larson.
Norr-Hassela	P. C. Jacobson.
Gransjö	J. P. Wiklander.

SWEDEN—*continued.*

Place.	Pastors.
Stöde	S. Eklund.
Knutnäs	O. Nilson.
Munkby	P. Hammarström
Torp	E. O. Nordberg.
Hjeltanstorp	J. O. Anderson.
Borgsjö	E. M. Karlson.
" Lower Church	L. A. Borg.
Havero, First Church	
" Second Church	
Skönvik	
Stigsjö	J. A. Westberg.
Orsvik	P. O. Tjernberg.
Johannedal	K. Ostling.
Mjösund	E. Hegner.
Wike	
Ostrand	
Helsingland Association—	
(MEMBERS 1,986.)	
Lindsjön	L. Olsson.
Berge	P. Jonson.
Furuberg	E. Jonson.
Alfta	K. Roos.
Ansjön	L. A. Thunberg.
Bollnäs	O. Dreiwitz.
Bjuraker	O. Andersson.
Gränsfors	P. Lindh.
Gnarp	L. Norlin.
Grängsjö	H. Norin.
Jättendal	N. Nilson.
Bergsjö	P. Selander.
Harmanger	L. J. Oquist.
Iggesund	G. Pihlström.
Ingesarfve	J. Enlund.
Ilsbo	D. Danielsson.
Hudiksvall	N. Engström.
Ljusdal, First Church	C. Englund.
" Second Church	P. O. Ström.
Lervik	B. Person.
Idenor	N. Hedlund.
Ljusne	O. Henrikson.
Forssa	E. Jonsson.
Enanger	
Mo	O. Jonson.
Wallsta	
Soderhamn	J. Nygren.
Wagbro	A. Jonsson.
Farila	A. Rask.
Helsing Tuna	E. Wiberg.
Haddangsnäs	J. Hallberg.
Woxna	J. Kihlström.
Nybo	J. A. Strömstedt.
Wattlang	A. Thomason.

Place.	Pastors.
North Dala Association—	
(MEMBERS 828.)	
Asen	
Elfdalen	A. W. Westling.
Stenberg	C. S. Nord.
Bonäs	H. Petterson.
Skattungbyn	P. Holdst.
Vamhus	
Wikarbyn	O. Erson.
Mora	G. Nilson.
Rättvik	P. Anderson.
Westmanland Association—	
(MEMBERS 1,590.)	
Bagga	G. Erikson.
Sala	H. Anderson.
Björksta	J. A. Lindevall.
Norberg	E. G. Ekebom.
Vestanfors	A. F. Huzén.
Westeras	G. A. Engdahl.
Kolbäck	
Munktorp N.	A. G. Olson.
Munktorp S.	
Köping	K. S. Akerlund.
Kungsör	K. Fröling.
Arboga	J. G. Obrström.
Fellingsbro	C. J. Frisk.
Broby	A. W. Carlson.
Gunnilbo	A. G. Anderson.
Bjorskog	J. V. Widberg.
Westermo	E. Widlund.
Hed	G. D. Sjörberg.
Odensvi	J. Jonson.
Tärna, West	A. F. Torgren.
" East	J. Englöf.
Skinnskatteberg	G. Erikson.
Ramsberg	C. J. Anderson.
Gestrikland Association—	
(MEMBERS 1,339.)	
Ockelbo	J. A. Selén.
Elfkarleby	
Forsbacka	A. Nyström.
Gefle	J. A. Jäder.
Torsaker	J. Agren.
Tierp	L. Peterson.

SWEDEN—*continued.*

Place.	Pastors.
Tierp, South	C. Wiklund.
Orbyhus	A. Forsman.
Hofors	
Hollnäs	
O. Fernebo	E. Olson.
Hamrange	E. Erikson.
Nora	A. G. Sedvall.
Skutskär	C. O. Trybom.
Söderfors	A. Aberg.
Wessland	E. Wesslander.
Sandviken	L. Torell.
Oster Löfsta	K. Johanson.
Oster Wahla	E. Wahlström.
South Dala Association—	
(MEMBERS 2,197.)	
Wika	J. Person.
Husby	A. Hed.
Folkärna	J. Roslund.
Hedemora	
Great Tuna	G. Agren.
Borlänge	J. G. Johanson.
Svärdsjö	P. M. A. Erikson.
Falun	C. A. Berner.
Aspeboda	E. G. Sundgren.
Bjursas	H. Hammar.
Sundborn	L. Larson.
Skedevi	A. G. Hanson.
Torsang	J. E. Zetterlund.
By	J. G. Sålgström.
Ludvika	A. Lindblom.
Smedjebacken	K. A. Moden.
Söderbärke	A. G. Friedfelt.
Leksand	J. A. Wahlborg.
Grangarde:	
North Church	J. A. Johnson.
South Church	V. P. Anderson.
Garpenberg	E. V. Norberg.
Grytnäs	D. Larson.
Gagnef	M. A. Persson.
Gonäs	P. Janson.
Al	O. Lindgren.
Korsnas	J. Dahlström.
Langshyttan	A. G. Sjöberg.
Grängesberg	N. J. Lindgren.
Stockholm Association—	
(MEMBERS 6,247.)	
Skederid	K. P. Gustafson.
Sundbyberg	O. Lindblom.
Sanga	S. P. Johanson.

Place.	Pastors.
Söderö	
Trosa	J. Filippiss.
Walö Forsmark	A. Forsman.
Orsundsbro	J. W Fredrikson.
Osterunda	K. W Anderson.
Edebo	S. A. Bergtson.
Grillby	E. A. Erikson.
Gráso	J. A. Hallerström
Munsö	G. J. Carlson.
Aker	A. Alard.
Almunge	O. Lundgren.
Heby	A. V. Petterson.
Husby Langhundra	
Hatuna	G. Lindberg.
Widbo	F. Eklund.
Jerna	P. A. Sandholm.
Lena	J. E. Wahlen.
Loharad	F. Nilson.
Mariefred	J. Lundgren.
Riala	
Sigtuna	
Sicklaö	
Balsta	E. A. Alsén.
Morkarla	
Dannemora	P. Film.
Alunda	
Ramhäll	A. P. Blom.
Wendel	J. Ytterberg.
Upsala	A. Ullmark.
Rasbo	P. G. Peterson
Skogs Tibble	K. F. Lödstrom.
Biskopskulla	E. Oman.
Kulla	
Enköping	O. Lantz.
Osthamar	
Wäddö	A. G. Olson.
Norrtelje	
Karsta	J. H. Djupström.
Ossbygarn	C. A. Ostervall.
Ostuna	
Haga	P. G. Wallbom.
Adelsö	A. G. Rydberg.
Täby	L. J. Renaldo.
Gustafsberg	
Södertelje	
Grödinge	C. Tobiasson.
Stockholm:	
First Church	W. Lindblom.
Salem Church	S. A. Moreln.
Ebenezer	J. Hedberg.
Fourth Church	R. Söderberg.
Fifth Church	J.O.Hammarberg
Kungsholm Church	E. Bergström.
Enaker	A. G. Sandell.
Gnesta	K. S. Bergqvist.
Strengnäs	M. Palm.

SWEDEN—*continued.*

Place.	Pastors.	Place.	Pastors.
Härad..	A. Eriksson.	Degerfors	G. Lindberg.
Toresund	S. Dahlberg.	Bofors..	A. Linderberg.
Söderbykarls ..		Brattfors	A. Bihl.
Bred		Forshaga	
Westerhanninge ..	J. F. Gussander.	Boda	
		Gasborn	
Sodermanland Association—		Skare..	C. W. Wetterstrand.
(MEMBERS 1,882.)		Säfsnäs	A. Asker.
		Wäse	A. Kolmodin.
Flen	E. Osterholm.	Blomskog	A. Lindé.
Wadsbro	J. A. Anderson.	Karlanda	L. D. Löfgren.
Nyköping	F. Lindberg.	Torskog	G. Nordquist.
Tuna	J. A. Anderson.		
Blacksta	Daniel Janson.		
Eskilstuna	O. Larson.	*Nerike Association—*	
Floda	L. Larson.		
Hellby	A. Jonson.	(MEMBERS 4,153.)	
Kantorp	E. Osterholm.		
Katrineholm.. ..	A. Palmborg.	Brefven	A. F. Erikson.
Little Mellösa ..	L. A. Theorin.	Aspa	A. Larson.
Johanneberg ..	O. Friberg.	Tysslinge	L. E. Eriksson.
Näshulta		Vintrosa	E. Larsson.
Rekarne		Orebro	J. Ongman.
Torshälla	E. A. Ekström.	Glanshammar ..	K. J. Berglund.
Wrena	K. Hägg.	Norrbyas	K. E. Bergman.
Arila	N. Hutt.	Gt. Mellösa	C. Halgren.
Osteraker	A. Palmborg.	Lennäs	E. G. Cederborg.
Kila	J. A. Lindberg.	Asker	J. P. Dubois.
		Ekeby..	G. Jonsson.
Wermland Association—		Sköllersta	J. Person.
		Palsboda	A. G. Anderson.
(MEMBERS 2,189.)		Svennevad	F. A. Anderson.
		Kumla	A. F. Schager.
Mangskog		Haddebo	J. Olson.
Längstad	A. Olson.	Jernboas	A. Larson.
V. Emtervik ..	F. Petterson.	Halsberg	N. Lyberg.
O. Emtervik	L. E. Dahlstrand.	Hardemo	P. A. Hallqvist
Frykerud	S. Lundborg.	Hackvad	G. Ohrn.
Frykerud, South ..		Hafla	P. Anderson.
Ullerud, Upper Ch...	J. Arvidson.	Wiby	K. J. Lundholm.
Ullerud, Lower Ch...	E. A. Axell.	Asbro	G. Danielson.
Filipstad	A. J. Ekholm.	Lerbäck	
Nyed	E. M. Nilsson.	Boo	
Kihl		Askersund	C. G. Högberg.
Grafva		Zinkgrufvan	C. G. Wikman.
Karlstad	G. Erikson.	Ammeberg	J. L. Dahl.
Fogelvik		Vingaker	J. G. Bjurström.
Kristinehamn ..	J. Mattheus.	Skedevi	R. Blomqvist.
Langbanshyttan ..		Nora	A. Larson.
Ransäter	N. Olsonn.	Kopparberget ..	E. Fridman.
Arvika	J. H. Björk.	Lillkyrka	L. E. Erikson.
Rämen		Fyrby	L. Larson.
Nykroppa	N. Berglund.	Finnerödja	E. Erikson.
Loka		Guldsmedshyttan ..	P. E. Petterson.
Nor	A. Mellqvist.	Axberg	F. W. Olson.

SWEDEN—*continued.*

Place.	Pastors.
West of Sweden Association—	
(MEMBERS 1,866.)	
Falköping	N. A. Nilson.
Sköfde	K. Olson.
Hornborga	L. Jonson.
Amal	S. P. Gerdin.
Or	L. Peterson.
Venersborg	C. Erikson.
Storegarden	O. J. Nilson.
Tisselskog	A. Larsson.
Trollhättan	M. Hedlund.
Blidsberg	A. Frisell.
Brismened	
Göteborg	T. Truvé.
Veddige	J. Bengtson.
Boras	K. V. Schedvin.
Drared	A. Bergquist.
Hudened	B. A. Anderson.
Mariestad	J. A. Ahlin.
Dimbo	J. Sten.
Ulricehamn	C. Ekström.
Wing	A. Huttgren.
Lysekil	J. Lundell.
Sörby	J. Anderson.
Uddevalla	O. Länsberg.
Vilska Klefva	A. Broms.
Animskog	L. M. Petterson.
Lidköping	Chr. Lowseth.
Wanga	A. G. Lind.
Smaland Association—	
(MEMBERS 787.)	
Svinhult	S. J. Tyhr.
W. Ed.	S. Svenson.
O. Ed.	G. Nilson.
Hallingberg	N. M. Peterson
Locknevi	A. M. Lindqvist
Wimmerby	J. P. Sundberg.
Westervik	A. Jonason.
Westerum	N. J. Petterson.
Misterhult, North	C. G. Nilsson.
,, South	S. A. Svenson.
Oskarshamn	M. Lignell.
Hjorthed	Z. Erikson.
Ukna	S. A. Halldén.
Gunnebo	K. Wiking.
Borgholm	A. J. Anderson.
Böda	N. P. Olson.
Ankarsrum	O. Stämberg.
Kalmar	S. U. Högendal.

Place.	Pastors.
Skane Association—	
(MEMBERS 1,913.)	
Rösvid	
Isjöa	
Grytasa	J. P. Johanson.
Ekeryd	
Magnarp	S. Jönson.
Ausas	
Röshult	
Barkhult	J. Akeson.
Halmstad	C.G. Salmonson.
Hessleholm	C. E. Sundbom.
Oppmanna	
Svenstorp	
Kristianstad	W. Hammar.
Ullstorp	P. L. Lundberg.
Nockarp	P. Dalberg.
Wenestad	A. Persson.
Ugerup	
Yngsjö	
Wallby	
Helsingborg	E. Berg.
Malmö	H. Waxberg.
Trelleborg	
Vesterstad	A. Olson.
Kivik	H. Akeson.
Börringe	M. Person.
Böste	Kr. Olson.
Perstorp	
Ramlösa	
Cimbrishamn	B. Löfgren.
Skärhus	
Skurup	
Sparrarp	
Lund	J. Jönson.
Rataryd	
Ronkarp	A. Salmonson.
Ahus	N. Hakanson.
Oraholma	
Hör	
Karsholm	L. Nilson.
Löfvesta	A. Olson.
Bleking Association—	
(MEMBERS 962.)	
Karlshamn	F. A. Magnuson.
Karlskrona	K. G. Hellstrom.
Kristianopel	G. Andersson.
Torsas	
Jemjö	P. Pettersson.
Tving	
Mariefröjd	J. Johnson.
Skärgöl	E. Anderson.

SWEDEN—*continued.*

Place.	Pastors.
Ronneby	C. P. Anderson.
Senoren	S. J. Manson.
Lyckeby	A. Svenson.
Sibbamåla	
Wexiö	A. L. Rignell.
Sjösas	C. F. Berggvist.
Ramquilla	P. J. Röst.
Gotland Association— (MEMBERS 1,088.)	
Slite	A. F. Höglund.
Wisby	J. N. Gustafson.
Lärbro	J. Hällström.
Vestergarn	
Tofta	
Eksta	P. Olofsson.
Hafdhem	L. Qviberg.
Fröjel	K. A. Lingström.
Grötlingbo	J. Rosendahl.
Fide	C. Jonson.
Näs	O. Närström.
Hamra	H. Olsson.
Wamlingbo	H. L. Hansson.
Vall	C. J. Lidqvist.
Garda	J. Ockander.
Stenkumla	A. Ahlstedt.
Eskilhem	P. Engström.
Fardhem	L. P. Hagström.
Gothem	O. P. Larson.
Halla	C. F. Lavergren.
Rone	N. Fridin.
Ardre	J. Gahnström.
Ostergarn	A. Fält.
Wäte	J. Jakobson.
Ostgöta Association— (MEMBERS 2,889.)	
Aneby	G. A. Anderson.
Boxholm	O. Strutz.
Fifvelstad	F. William.
Frinnaryd	
Godegard	
Hellestad	
Kristberg	K. Hällman.
Krokek	C. J. Fredmark.
Kullerstad	C. L. Arvidson.
Linköping	
Marbäck	
Mjolby	A. G. Strutz.
Motala	A. Wiberg.
Normlösa	
Norrkoping	Fred. Anderson.
Regna	
Ringarum	F. Carlson.
Ringstorp	A. G. Flärd.
Rinna	
Söderköping	P. E. Sorbom.
Tjällmo	
Tranas	K. J. Eriksson.
Torpa	K. L. Johanson.
Trehörna	K. G. Anderson.
Vestrany	P. A. Agren.
Askeryd	K. Peterson.
Fridsby	J. M. Gustafson.
Lotorp	K. Nilson.
Linderas	
Mogata	
O. Rinna	J. G. Sköld.
Rök	K. L. Karlson.
Skeninge	F. O. Johanson.
Gt. Aby	K. O. Hagman.
Stralsnäs	G. A. Hammarlund.
Sunneränga	
Sommen	
Westerlösa	
Wäderstad	C. A. Wall.
Wadstena	P. J. Ternström.
W. Ryd	
Wordsberg	
O. Husby	
Adelöf	
Asby	
Bälaryd	S. A. Carlson.
Hvarf	C. J. Hjort.
Mantorp	
Rogslösa	C. Petterson.
Skeda	
Sund	
Ulrika	A. J. Kullberg.
W. Harg	K. J. Anderson.
W. Tollstad	
Fornas	C. A. Tapper.
Kisa	C. A. Eiksell.
Tjärstad	
Flisby	

In the whole of Sweden there were, at the beginning of 1895, 553 Churches united in 19 Associations, with a total membership of 37,601. During the year 1894, 2,595 were added by baptism. The Churches have 301 Places of Worship of their own, and 644 preachers. In Sunday-schools connected with the Baptist Churches, 40,353 children were instructed by 3,175 teachers. During the year, 419,833 crowns (£23,324) were contributed for benevolent objects.

THE STOCKHOLM MISSIONARY UNION aided, during the year 1894, 19 evangelists and preachers, at a cost of 6,894 crowns (£383).

THE BETHEL SEMINARY is a theological school, instituted 1866, for the instruction of young Baptist preachers in the truths of the Bible, and other subjects connected with the work of the ministry. In this school the students are instructed from one year to four years, according to their capabilities. During the years 1894-5, there were thirty-three students. *Principal*—Rev. K. O. BROADY, D.D., Stockholm.

THE BAPTIST BUILDING FUND, consisting of 12,000 crowns (£666), furnishes loans free of interest to Baptist churches, for the purpose of erecting places of worship—the loans to be repaid in instalments of a twentieth part every half-year.

THE SWEDISH BAPTIST MISSION, organized in 1889, supports one missionary to Spain, with two native helpers. It has sent three missionaries to China, and one to the Congo. It aids three evangelists in Finland and Russia. Expenditure, 21,291 crowns (£1,183).

BAPTIST HOME MISSION, organized in 1889, 33 evangelists. Expenditure, 8,377 crowns (£465).

PROGRESS OF THE BAPTISTS IN SWEDEN

From the year 1855 to the year 1895.

Year.	Churches.	Members.	Year.	Churches.	Members.	Year.	Churches.	Members.
1855	9	476	1865	176	6,606	1885	398	27,135
			1875	234	10,490	1895	553	37,601

NORWAY.

(*Population*, 2,000,000.)

Churches.	Date.	Chapel Seats.	Members.	Pastors.
Vardö	1876	150	30	S. Gunderson.
Tromsö	1871	800	201	O. B. Hansson.
Andenœs	1884	350	107	C. Pederson.
Bjarkö	1884	300	52	J. Jenson.
Aune	1887	150	51	J. Olson.
Kvœdfjord	1887	200	28	P. Fredrikson.
Sommerö	1892	250	51	K. O. Tonnœs.
Hadsel	1892	..	51	B. Dahl.
Vigten	1888	..	51	A. Olsen.
Vœrdalen	1880	200	107	Fr. Nilson.
Trondhjem	1876	600	164	P. Helbostad.
Kristiansund	1876	..	72	C. Stabell.
Opdal	1892	200	51	O. Ingebrigtson.
Sell	1890	..	111	S. Olson.
Bergen	1870	400	152	M. A. Ohrn.
Arendal	1868	350	110	B. Bakke.
Tvedestrand	1862	..	9	K. Knudson.
Risör	1872	400	51	E. P. Andréson.
Kragerö	1863	250	42	E. P. Andréson.
Langesund	1872	260	35	E. P. Andréson.
Skien	1860	300	93	A. Milde.
Melum	1872	250	38	J. A. Dola.
Svelvig	1885	150	13	N. Nilson.
Laurvig	1892	..	13	S. Sörenson.
Kristiania	1884	..	259	E. S. Sundt.
Sarpsborg	1890	150	12	F. Björk.
Fredrikshald	1884	900	220	C. Y. Hugo.
Eidsvold	1895	..	40	
Kongsberg	1895	..	30	A. Alfson.
			2,241	

ASIA.

INDIA.

Population, [*in* 1891] 286,114,210.)

BAPTIST MISSIONARY SOCIETY.

BENGAL.

Stations.	Missionaries.	Stations and Sub-Stations.	Members.	Sunday-School Teachers.	Sunday Scholars.	Baptisms.
Calcutta	G. Kerry and Mrs. Kerry, G. H. Rouse, M.A., D.D., and Mrs. Rouse, J. W. Thomas and Mrs. Thomas, Tara Choron Banerjea, Romonath Ray Chowdhery, C. Jordan and Mrs. Jordan, A. Jewson and Mrs. Jewson, Iman Masih *Zenana*—Mrs. Ellis, Mrs. Williamson, Miss Taylor, Miss Duval, Miss Ewing, Miss Pike, Miss Dyson, Miss Way	1				
" Circular Road	*R. M. Julian	..	126	11	59	5
" Lal Bazar ..	*G. H. Hook and Mrs. Hook	1	150	12	80	16
" South Colinga	*Gogon Chunder Dass ..	1				
" Intally (Bengali) Twenty-four Pergunnahs (South Villages and Mutlah District)	H. Anderson and Mrs. Anderson (in England), Khristanga Biswas	21	569	25	329	35
Alipore..						
Baraset..	.. ..	1	19	1	9	
Howrah	T. H. Barnett and Mrs. Barnett *Zenana*—Mrs. Langer	3	72	9	130	14
Serampore	E. S. Summers, B.A., and Mrs. Summers, D. Robinson and Mrs. Robinson, C. E. Wilson, B.A., J. A. D'Cruz (on sick leave), Bhagaboti Churn Ghose *Zenana*—Mrs. Manual, Miss Mackintosh	2	88	9	140	5
Jessore, Jhinida and Margoorah	T. W. Norledge and Mrs. Norledge	5	70	3	45	
.. ..	Gogon Chunder Dutt ..	17	300	7	210	16

BENGAL—*continued.*

Stations.	Missionaries.	Stations and Sub-Stations.	Members.	Sunday-School Teachers.	Sunday Scholars.	Baptisms
Dinagepore and Julpaigori	W. B. James and Mrs. James	11	236	5	60	10
Rungpore	J. R. Ellison and Mrs. Ellison	1	5	2	12	
Maldah..	W. Davies (in England), G. W. Bevan (in England), Brojo Nath Banerjea	1	5			
Dacca	R. Wright Hay and Mrs. Hay, J. D. Morris, Sat Saron Mookerjee *Zenana*—Miss K. Bonnaud, Miss M. Bergin	4	78	7	95	1
Cachar						
Backergunge District	R. Spurgeon and Mrs. Spurgeon, W. Carey and Mrs. Carey, J. Sircar, J. G. Kerry and Mrs. Kerry, T. Watson *Zenana*—Miss Finch, Miss Moore	30	1,133	34	503	44
Madaripore	W. R. James and Mrs. James (in England), R. H. Tregillus and Mrs. Tregillus	18	1,082	21	272	81
Pirojpore	A. T. Teichmann and Mrs. Teichmann	4	16	3	20	
Chittagong	A. J. McLean and Mrs. McLean (in England), D. L. Donald and Mrs. Donald	3	63	4	86	17
Soory, Beerbhoom ..	T. R. Edwards and Mrs. Edwards	1	55	4	63	

NORTHERN INDIA.

Stations.	Missionaries.	Stations and Sub-Stations.	Members.	Sunday-School Teachers.	Sunday Scholars.	Baptisms
Monghyr	B. Evans and Mrs. Evans, R. Bion and Mrs. Bion *Zenana*—Mrs. W. R. Bion, Miss Bion	2	83	9	201	1
Patna	H. Paterson and Mrs. Paterson, A. E. Collier, E. P. Davy and Mrs. Davy	1	14	3	104	

NORTHERN INDIA—*continued.*

Stations.	Missionaries.	Stations and Sub-Stations.	Members	Sunday-School Teachers.	Sunday Scholars.	aptisms
Bankipore	W. S. Mitchell and Mrs. Mitchell (in England), D. Jones and Mrs. Jones (in England), John Stubbs and Mrs. Stubbs, W. J. Price and Mrs. Price *Zenana*—Miss F. G. Smith, Miss Swinden, Miss Tresham	2	42	8	155	3
Dinapore	*S. J. Jones (in England)					
Gya	Prem Chand .. .. *Zenana*—Mrs. McLeod	1	37	2	60	
Tikari	*Zenana*—Mrs. Wince, Miss Wince					
Benares	*Zenana*—Miss Joseph, Miss de Souza, Miss Morris					
Allahabad	J. D. Bate and Mrs. Bate (in England),					
Agra	J. G. Potter and Mrs. Potter, F. W. Hale and Mrs. Hale *Zenana*—Miss Wrigley, Miss Eekhout, Miss Watson	3	93	10	250	9
„ Havelock Church (English) ..						
Muttra	R. M. McIntosh and Mrs. McIntosh	1				
Delhi	H. J. Thomas and Mrs. Thomas, S. S. Thomas and Mrs. Thomas, H. E. Crudgington and Mrs. Crudgington, G. J. Dann and Mrs. Dann, J. I. Hasler, B.A., and Mrs. Hasler *Zenana*—Miss Thorn, Miss Rooke (in Australia), Miss Gange, Miss Bate, Miss Williams, Miss Coombes, Miss Wells	14	295	32	1,484	16
Palwal	*Zenana*—Miss Fletcher, Miss Allen					
Bhiwani	*Zenana*—Miss I. M. Angus, Miss Theobald, Miss Farrer, M.B., B.S.					
Mussoorie						
Simla	J. Smith and Mrs. Smith, G. A. Smith, F. V. Thomas, B.A., M.D. *Zenana*—Mrs. Davies	15	371	..	..	1

WESTERN INDIA.

Stations.	Missionaries.	Stations and Sub-Stations.	Members.	Sunday-School Teachers.	Sunday Scholars.	Baptisms.
Bombay, English Church	*H. E. Barrell					

ORISSA.

Stations.	Missionaries.	Stations and Sub-Stations.	Members.	Sunday-School Teachers.	Sunday Scholars.	Baptisms.
Berhampore	R. L. Lacey and Mrs. Lacey (in England), G. H. Wilkins, F. W. Jarry	2	216	15	157	22
Padri Polli		2				
Russelkondah and Udayagiri	A. Long and Mrs. Long A. B. Wilkinson					
Cuttack, Macmillanpatna, Bhoirapore, and Houghpatna	T. Bailey, J. G. Pike (in England), J. Vaughan and Mrs. Vaughan, Miss Leigh, A. H. Young, M.A., G. Howells, B.A., B.D., C. H. Harvey, Miss Barrass, Miss Gleazer, Miss Thatcher, Shem Sahu	8	990	66	767	23
Chaga						
Khundittur						
Aquapadda						
Minchinpatna.. ..						
Mangalpore						
Kendrapara						
Khoordah						
Pipli and Puri, Bilepada, and Asrayapur ..	Visited by the Missionaries from Cuttack	5	272	14	132	11
Sylhet (Assam)						
Bonamalipore ..						
Bilepada						
Sambalpur	P. E. Heberlet ..	2	53	9	40	4

SOUTHERN INDIA.

Stations.	Missionaries.	Stations and Sub-Stations.	Members.	Sunday-School Teachers.	Sunday Scholars.	Baptisms.
Madras	*Zenana*—Mrs. Dawson, Miss Dawson, Mrs. W. S. Dawson, Miss Shepherd					
Totals	.. ..	183	6,534	325	5,463	350

There is also the American Free Baptist Mission in Orissa:—13 stations, 26 missionaries, 815 members, 1,429 Native Christian Community, 2,615 Sunday School Pupils, 3,619 in Schools. No Returns for 1894.

* Pastors supported by Churches that are independent of the Baptist Missionary Society.

LONDON STRICT BAPTIST MISSION.

Districts.	Missionaries.	Formed.	Stations.	Workers.	Church Members.	Day Scholars.	Sunday Scholars.
Madras :—							
St. Thomas' Mount ..	Jacob John	1866	1	8	13	179	50
Poonamallee..	Abel Michael	1869	3*	10	14	117	117
Madras City :—							
Pursawalkam .	M. Solomon	1888	1	3	13	35	10
Black Town ..	Dr. Narrayanaswamy ..	1888	1	3	13	..	5
North Tinnevelly	H. Noble and Miss Noble	1882	7†	38	706	312	312
Bangalore, St. John's Hill	Muttusawmy Pillay ..	1890	1	3	14	..	..
Totals ..	.. ..	..	14	65	773	643	494

* And 3 Sub-Stations. † And 50 Sub-Stations.

TELUGU MISSION.

AMERICAN BAPTIST MISSIONARY UNION.

Stations.	Missionaries.	Total Mission'y Workers.	Churches.	Members.	S.S. Scholars.	Baptisms.
Nellore	David Downie, D.D., and wife, Miss J. E. Wayte (in America), Miss Mary D. Faye, Miss K. Darmstadt, Miss O. W. Gould, M.D.	27	3	849	245	50
Ongole	J. E. Clough, D.D., and wife, L. E. Martin and wife, O. R. McKay and wife (in America), A. H. Curtis and wife, Mrs. Ellen M. Kelly, Miss Sarah Kelly, Miss Amelia G. Dessa, Miss L. B. Kuhlen, J. M. Baker.	106	16	18,000	700	273
Ramapatam ..	R. R. Williams, D.D., and wife, J. Dussman and wife.	20	1	610	130	11
Allur	W. S. Davis and wife ...	13	2	140	100	13
Secunderabad ..	W. B. Boggs, D.D., and wife, J. S. Timpany, M.D., and wife, C. R. Marsh and wife, R. Maplesden and wife (in America).	15	1	84	50	29

TELUGO MISSION—*continued.*

AMERICAN BAPTIST MISSIONARY UNION.

Stations.	Missionaries.	Total Mission'y Workers.	Churches.	Members.	S. S. Scholars.	Baptisms.
Kurnool	W. A. Stanton and wife, George N. Thomssen and wife (in America).	27	2	574	295	66
Madras	Charles Hadley and wife (in America), P. B. Guernsey and wife (in America), T. D. Dudley, jun., Miss M. M. Day, Miss S. I. Kurtz, Miss Johanna Schuff (in America).	42	2	167	507	13
Hanamakonda ..	W. H. Beeby and wife ..	12	4	263	69	72
Cumbum	John Newcomb and wife, Miss Erika A. Bergman, Miss Ida A. Skinner, Miss R. E. Pinney.	40	6	8,000	1,176	11
Vinukonda ..	J. Heinrichs and wife, F. Kurtz and wife.	34	1	5,960	328	29
Nursaravapetta ..	William Powell and wife, Miss Helen D. Newcomb.	53	20	6,009	893	41
Bapatla	William C. Owen and wife, Edwin Bullard and wife (in America), Miss L. H. Booker.	41	17	2,527	450	68
Udayagiri ..	William R. Manley and wife.	17	1	341	175	45
Palmur	Elbert Chute and wife ..	18	2	515	124	20
Nalgonda ..	A. Friesen and wife	30	1	606	56	83
Kanigiri ..	George H. Brock and wife ..	39	2	6,000	100	28
Bangalore ..	John McLaurin, D.D., and wife.	3				
Bolarum	W. E. Hopkins and wife ..	6				
Kavali	D. S. Bagshaw and wife ..	13	1	28	..	25
Kundakur ..	W. Boggess and wife.. ..	2	..	..	..	6
Atmakur	T. S. Hankins and wife ..	2				
Podili	A. C. Fuller	28	..	3,000	..	54
Darsi	F. H. Levering and wife ..	34	..	3,000		
Sattanapalli ..	W. E. Boggs and wife ..	2				
Ootacamund ..	Mrs. Lavinia P. Pearce ..	1				
Totals ..	.. ..	625	82	56,683	5,398	938

TELUGU MISSION OF REGULAR BAPTIST CONVENTION OF ONTARIO AND QUEBEC.

Stations.	Missionaries.	Churches.	Members.	S. S. Teachers.	S. S. Scholars.	Baptisms.
Akidu	J. Craig, B.A., and wife, Miss F. M. Stovel.	10	1,612	35	1,000	145
Cocanada ..	J. E. Chute, B.Th., Miss A. E. Baskerville, Miss E. A. Folsom, Miss C. McLeod, Miss S. A. Simpson.	2	188	28	475	33
Narsapatram ..	.. ..	1	35	4	25	11
Peddapuram ..	J. A. K. Walker and wife ..	3	175	7	65	64
Ramachandrapuram	A. A. McLeod and wife, Miss S. I. Hatch.	3	353	14	160	15
Samulcotta ..	J. E. Davies, B.A., and wife, J. R. Stillwell, B.A., and wife (in Canada).	2	121	27	320	5
Tuni	Miss Martha Rogers (in Canada), Miss Ellen Priest, Miss K. S. McLaurin.	1	87	10	142	15
Vuyyuru	J. G. Brown, B.A., and wife, Miss Anna Murray.	4	638	14	165	120
Yellamanchili ..	H. F. Laflamme and wife (in Canada), E. G. Smith, M.D., and wife.	1	6	4	25	
Totals ..	.. ..	27	3,215	143	2,377	408

TELUGU MISSION OF BAPTIST CONVENTION OF THE MARITIME PROVINCES OF CANADA.

Stations.	Missionaries.	Churches.	Members.	Baptisms.
Bimlipitam	L. D. Morse and wife, Miss A. C. Gray.	1	22	
Chicacole	I. C. Archibald and wife, Miss H. H. Wright.	2	59	3
Bobbili	G. Churchill (and wife in Canada)	1	25	1
Vizianagram	M. B. Shaw and wife, Miss K. McNeil.	1	28	3
Parla-Kimedy ..	W. V. Higgins and wife	2	42	2
Palcondah				
Totals	.. ..	7	176	9

EASTERN BENGAL.

AUSTRALASIAN BAPTIST MISSIONS.

*** BELOW THE DISTRICTS ARE PRINTED THE NAMES OF THE COLONIES UNDERTAKING THE WORK.

District.	Stations.	Missionaries.	Churches.	Members.	S.S. Teachers.	S.S. Scholars.	Baptisms.
Furreedpore (*South Australia and Tasmania*)	Furreedpore	Miss Alice G. Pappin, Miss Bertha S. Tuck, Miss Amy Parsons, Miss Ada J. Archer, Punchanon Biswas, Babu Horish C. Sanyal.					
Maimensing (*Victoria*)	Biri-Siri, Nasirabad, Tangail.	A. Neville and Mrs. Neville, A. E. Blackwell, Miss Bethel, Miss Chambers, Miss Ehrenberg, Miss Lamb, Miss Seymour, Miss Fuller, Babu JoyNathChowdry, Babu Chandra Kuma Shaha.	8	138	..	..	56
Noakhali .. (*Queensland*)	Sudharam	Miss Martha Plested, Miss E. Saker, Kisher Chandra Sircar, Shuran Chandra Sircar.	1	9	..	..	1
Pubna .. (*South Australia and Tasmania*)	Pubna ..	A. E. Summers and Mrs. Summers, Dr. C. S. Mead, B.A., Miss Ellen Arnold, Miss Lucy Kealley, Babu Upendra Das, Babu Nanda Lall.					
N. Tipperah (*New Zealand*)	Bramanbaria, Chandpore	W. La Barte and Mrs. La Barte, George Hughes, Miss Annie Bacon, Miss Lillian B. Peters, Miss Emma Beckingsale, Babu S. K. Chatterjee, Babu S. C. Battarcharjee.					
S. Tipperah (*New South Wales*)	Commillah, Madhya	Miss Lynne, Miss Middleton, Ram Chandra.	2	16	..	..	4
		Totals ..	11	163	..	..	61

BURMAH.

AMERICAN BAPTIST MISSIONARY UNION.

Stations	Missionaries.	Total Mission'y Workers.	Churches.	Members.	S. S. Scholars.	Baptisms.
Rangoon	*Burman Department.*—E. W. Kelly and wife, Mrs. E. L. Stevens, Miss Ella F. McAllister, Miss Ruth W. Ranney, Miss Hattie Phinney, Miss Marie M. Coté, M.D., A. T. Rose, D.D., and wife, Miss A. E. Fredrickson. *Sgaw-Karen Department.*—Albert E. Seagrave and wife, Mrs. Julia H. Vinton. *Pwo-Karen Department.*—Durlin L. Brayton. *Karen Theological Seminary.* —D. A. W. Smith, D.D., and wife, W. F. Thomas and wife, Mrs. C. B. Thomas. *Rangoon Baptist College.*—Josiah N. Cushing, D.D. (Mrs. Cushing in America), David C. Gilmore and wife, L. E. Hicks and wife, W. O. Valentine. *Eurasian School.*—W. A. Sharp and wife. *Baptist Mission Press.* —E. B. Roach and wife, Frank D. Phinney.	109	112	5,824	970	530
Moulmein ..	*Burman Department.* — Edward O. Stevens and wife, Miss Susie E. Haswell, Miss Sarah B. Barrows, Miss Martha Sheldon, Miss Lydia M. Dwyer, Miss Agnes Whitehead (in America). *Karen Department.* — William C. Calder, Mrs. C. H. R. Elwell, Miss Ellen J. Taylor, J. L. Bulkley and wife (in America). *Telugus and Tamils and English Church.*—William F. Armstrong and wife. *Eurasian Home.*—Miss Sarah R. Slater, Miss Alice L. Ford. *Medical Work.*—Miss Ellen E. Mitchell, M.D., Miss Elizabeth Carr.	51	22	2,042	76	15
Tavoy	*Karen Department.*—H. Morrow and wife. *Burman Department.*—H. W. Hale and wife.	26		1,074		

BURMAH—*continued.*

Stations.	Missionaries.	Total Mission'y Workers.	Churches.	Members.	S. S. Scholars.	Baptisms.
Bassein	*Burman Department.* — E. Tribolet and wife, *Sgaw-Karen Department.*--Charles A. Nichols and wife, Miss Isabel Watson, Miss Amy B. Harris, Miss Harriet E. Hawkes, Miss May C. Fowler, M.D. *Pwo-Karen Department.*—L. D. Cronkhite and wife, Miss Louise E. Tschirch; in America, B. P. Cross and wife, Miss Lillian R. Black.	179	128	11,249	3,327	626
Henzada	*Burman Department.* — John E. Cummings (in America), Neil D. Reid, Mrs. L. A. Crawley, Miss Annie Hopkins, Miss. J. V. Smith (in America). *Karen Department.* — Washington I. Price and wife, Miss Annie M. Modisett (in America), Miss M. M. Larsh.	57	56	2,684	1,524	188
Toungoo	*Burman Department.*—Henry P. Cochrane and wife. *Paku-Karen Department.* — Edmund B. Cross, D.D., and wife, A. V. B. Crumb and wife (in America), Miss Frances E. Palmer, Miss Elma R. Simons. *Bghai-Karen Department.*—Alonzo Bunker, D.D. (Mrs. Bunker in America), Truman Johnson, M.D., and wife (in America), C. H. Heptonstall, Miss Naomi Garton, M.D., Miss Joanna Anderson, Miss H. W. Eastman (in America).	198	149	5,576	1,794	330
Shwegyin ..	*Karen Department.*—E. N. Harris and wife.	32	45	1,825	153	135
Prome	L. H. Mosier and wife; Henry H. Tilbe and wife (in America).	15	4	244	300	10
Thongze	Mrs. Murilla B. Ingalls, Miss Kate F. Evans.	14	2	332	40	42
Zigon	Miss Zillah A. Bunn	4	2	146	126	20
Tharrawaddy ..	Miss S. J. Higby	30	25	718	261	52
Bhamo	*Kachin Department.*—W. H. Roberts and wife, Ola Hanson and wife, Miss Eva C. Stark. *Burman-Shan Department.*—W. C. Griggs, M.D., and wife.	12	1	112	72	27

BURMAH—*continued.*

Stations.	Missionaries.	Total Mission'y Workers.	Churches.	Members.	S.S. Scholars.	Baptisms.
Maubin	Walter Bushell and wife (in America), M. E. Fletcher and wife, Miss Carrie E. Putnam, Miss Kate Knight.	21	17	761	240	36
Thaton*						
Mandalay ..	John McGuire (Mrs. McGuire in America), Mrs. H. W. Hancock (in America), T. H. Burhoe and wife, Miss Ellen E. Fay, Miss Flora E. Ayres.	17	2	122	150	23
Thayetmyo ..	Arthur E. Carson and wife ..	10	4	177	92	31
Myingyan ..	John E. Case and wife ..	3	1	11	30	
Pegu	Miss Emily H. Payne ..	10	2	222	106	23
Sagaing	Frederick P. Sutherland and wife (in America).	3	1	23		
Sandoway ..	*Burman Department.*—Frederick H. Eveleth (Mrs. Eveleth in America). *Chin Department.*—Ernest Grigg and wife, Miss Melissa Carr, Miss A. M. Lemon.	39	15	437	305	21
Meiktila	John Packer, D.D., and wife	3	..	..	16	
Thibaw	M. B. Kirkpatrick, M.D., and wife.	5	1	21	30	3
Moné	W. M. Young and wife, A. H. Henderson, M.D., and wife, Mrs. H. W. Mix.	14	1	9	20	1
Myitkyina ..	George J. Geis and wife ..	5	..	4	6	
Namkham ..	W. W. Cochrane and wife ..	6	..	3	25	3
Totals	.. ..	863	613	33,616	10,391	2,318

* Statistics under Moulmein.

ASSAM.

AMERICAN BAPTIST MISSIONARY UNION.

Stations.	Missionaries.	Total Mission'y Workers.	Churches.	Members.	S.S. Scholars.	Baptisms in 1893.
Sibsagor	C. E. Petrick and wife, O. L. Swanson and wife, Miss I. Wilson, Miss H. Morgan.	15	8	451	92	91
Nowgong.. ..	Pitt H. Moore and wife, Penn E. Moore and wife, Miss Laura A. Amy, A. K. Gurney (Mrs. Gurney in America), J. M. Carvell, Miss N. M. Yates (in America).	19	2	144	50	38
Gauhati	C. D. King and wife, Charles E. Burdette and wife.	8	5	614	400	109

ASSAM—*continued.*

Stations.	Missionaries.	Total Mission'y Workers.	Churches.	Members.	S. S. Scholars.	Baptisms.
Goalpara.. ..	A. E. Stephen and wife, James Craighead and wife (in America).	6				
Tura	E. G. Phillips and wife, William Dring and wife, S. A. D. Boggs and wife, Miss Stella H. Mason, Miss A. J. Rood. In America, M. C. Mason and wife, Miss Ella C. Bond.	85	13	2,378	1,626	242
Molung	Edward W. Clark (Mrs. Clark in America), F. P. Haggard and wife, S. A. Perrine and wife.	3	5	76	60	
Kohima	Sidney W. Rivenburg, M.D., and wife.	2				
North Lakimpur	John Firth and wife, J. Paul and wife.	5	1	54	..	43
Impur	.. ..	4	1	4	100	
Totals	.. ..	147	35	3,721	2,328	523

CEYLON.

(*Population*, 3,008,239.)

BAPTIST MISSIONARY SOCIETY.

Stations.	Missionaries.	Stations and Sub-Stations.	Members.	S. S. Teachers.	S. S. [Scho]lars.	Baptisms.
Colombo District	F. D. Waldock and Mrs. Waldock, J. McCullum, M.A., B.D.	72	715	70	892	13
English Church	T. I. Stockley*	2	177	14	160	2
Sabaragamuwa District	W. D. Hankinson	14	21	9	84	
Kandy District..	H. A. Lapham and Mrs. Lapham	11	126	26	323	13
Totals ..	.. ..	99	1,039	119	1,459	28

* Pastor of English Church maintained entirely by local funds.

LONDON STRICT BAPTIST MISSION.

Districts.	Missionaries.	Formed.	Stations.	Workers.	Church Members.	Day Scholars.	Sunday Scholars.
Jaffna :—							
Nallur ..	Mrs. Noble	1888	1	1	..	25	25
Nunâville ..	.. ..	1888	1	1	..	45	35
Tinnevelly ..	.. ..	1889	1	1	..	25	30
Pettah.. ..	.. ..	1889	1	2	20	40	40
Totals ..	.. ..	..	4	5	20	135	130

CHINA.

(*Population*, [*about*] 300,000,000.)

BAPTIST MISSIONARY SOCIETY.

Stations.	Missionaries.	Stations and Sub-Stations.	Members.	S. S. Teachers.	S. S. Scholars.	Baptisms
Shansi ..	A. Sowerby and Mrs. Sowerby, G. B. Farthing and Mrs. Farthing (in England), J. J. Turner and Mrs. Turner (in England), H. Dixon (Mrs. Dixon in England).	10	100	..	..	30
Shantung ..	J. S. Whitewright and Mrs. Whitewright, S. Couling (Mrs. Couling in England), R. C. Forsyth and Mrs. Forsyth, J. R. Watson, M.B., and Mrs. Watson (in England), J. P. Bruce, B.A., and Mrs. Bruce, T. C. Paterson, M.B., C.M., A. G. Jones and Mrs. Jones, W. A. Wills (in England), S. B. Drake and Mrs. Drake (in England), F. Harmon and Mrs. Harmon, E. C. Nickalls and Mrs. Nickalls (in England), E. C. Smyth and Mrs. Smyth, E. W. Burt, M.A., and Mrs. Burt. *Zenana.*—Miss Shalders, Miss Kirkland, Miss Aldridge, Miss Simpson.	187	2,535	47	518	319
Shens ..	M. B. Duncan, M.A., and Mrs. Duncan, A. G. Shorrock, B.A., E. Morgan and Mrs. Morgan.	16	61	..	172	10
Shanghai ..	T. Richard (Mrs. Richard in England)					
Totals..	.. ..	213	2,696	47	690	359

AMERICAN BAPTIST MISSIONARY UNION.

Stations.	Missionaries.	Total Mission'y Workers.	Churches.	Members.	S. S. Scholars.	Baptisms.
Bangkok (Siam)..	Lewis A. Eaton and wife (in America).	4	1	13	..	6
Ningpo	W. H. Cossum and wife, J. S. Grant, M.D., and wife, J. R. Goddard and wife, Miss H. L. Corbin, Miss M. E. Barchet, Miss Elizabeth Stewart, Miss E. M. Boynton, Miss Emily A. Parker (in America).	32	6	287	150	16

CHINA—*continued.*

AMERICAN BAPTIST MISSIONARY UNION.

Stations.	Missionaries.	Total Mission'y Workers.	Churches.	Members.	S. S. Scholars.	Baptisms.
Swatow ..	William Ashmore, D.D., and wife (in America), Sylvester B. Partridge, D.D., and wife, William Ashmore, Jr., and wife, John M. Foster and wife (in America), H. A. Kemp and wife, Mrs. Anna K. Scott, M.D., W. K. McKibben (Mrs. McKibben in America), Miss Mary K. Scott, Miss M. E. Magee, Miss J. M. Bixby, M.D.	59	1	902	150	51
Shaohing..	Horace Jenkins and wife, W. S. Sweet and wife, A. Copp and wife, Miss M. A. Dowling, Miss L. A. Snowden.	13	1	24	100	5
Munkeuliang	.. ..	1	2	43	10	5
Kinhwa ..	S. P. Barchet, M.D. and wife, T. D. Holmes and wife, Miss Annie S. Young, Miss Clara E. Righter	15	6	118	..	1
Huchau ..	George L. Mason and wife, E. N. Fletcher and wife, Miss L. J. Wyckoff, M.D.	8	2	43	20	3
Suichaufu	George Warner and wife, C. H. Finch, M.D., and wife, Robert Wellwood and wife, F. B. Malcolm M.D., Miss Bessie G. Forbes, Miss M. A. Gardelin.	14	1	12	35	
Kayin ..	George Campbell and wife (in America), G. E. Whitman and wife, Edward Bailey, M.D., and wife, Miss Ella Campbell, Miss M. L. Ostrom.	9	..	..	18	
Ung-Kung	J. W. Carlin, D.D., and wife	13	1	32	..	18
Hanyang..	.. ..	7	1	9		
Kiating ..	C. F. Viking and wife, W. F. Beaman, Miss F C. Bliss, Miss E. Inveen (in America).	4	1	8	40	
Yachau ..	W. Upcraft, G. W. Hill and wife, H. J. Openshaw, F. J. Bradshaw.	6				
Chungking	C. A. Salquist, W. G. Silke and wife (in England).					
Hankow ..	J. S. Adams and wife, W. F. Gray and wife.					
Totals ..	.. ..	185	23	1,491	523	105

CHINA—*continued.*

SOUTHERN BAPTIST CONVENTION OF AMERICA.

NORTH CHINA.—P.O. CHEFOO. *Founded* 1860.

Stations.	Missionaries.	Churches.	Out Stations.	Members.	S. S. Scholars.	Bap sms.
Tung Chow ..	Miss Laura G. Barton, J. B. Hartwell and wife.	1	3	64	50	12
Hwanghien..	C. W. Pruitt and wife, Peyton Stephens and wife.	1	2	30	40	5
Pingtu ..	Miss Lottie Moon, W. H. Sears and wife. H. A. Randle and wife.	1	1	44	..	17
	CENTRAL CHINA. *Founded* 1847.					
Shanghai ..	E. F. Tatum and wife, R. T. Bryan and wife, Miss Willie Kelly, Miss Lottie W. Price.	1	5	86	49	1
Soochow (*P. O., Shanghai*) ..	T. C. Britton and wife, W. W. Lawton	1	1	12	21	1
Quinsau	.. ..	1	1	12		
Chinkiang .. (*Formed* 1880)	W. J. Hunnex and wife, L. N. Chappell and wife, Miss Julia K. Mackenzie.	1	23	11	35	
Yangchow .. (*Formed* 1880)	L. W. Pierce and wife ..	1	8	6	36	
	SOUTH CHINA. *Founded* 1845.					
Canton and Vicinity	R. H. Graves and wife, Miss Lula Whilden, E. Z. Simmons and wife, Thomas McCloy and wife, G. W. Greene and wife, Miss H. F. North, Miss Mollie McMinn, Miss C. J. White, Miss Anna B. Hartwell, and twenty-two native assistants and Bible-women	8	6	866	..	82
Totals ..	.. ..	16	50	1,131	231	118

JAPAN.

(*Population*, 40,072,684.)

SOUTHERN BAPTIST CONVENTION OF AMERICA.

Church.	Missionaries.	Churches.	Out Stations.	Members.	S. S. Scholars.	Baptisms.
Moji .. .. Fukuoka ..	J. W. McCollum and wife .. E. N. Walne and wife, N. Maynard and wife	1	8	40	166	9

JAPAN—*continued.*

AMERICAN BAPTIST MISSIONARY UNION.

Stations.	Missionaries.	Total Mission'y Workers.	Churches.	Members.	S. S. Scholars.	Baptisms.
Yokohama ..	Albert A. Bennett and wife, Charles K. Harrington and wife (in America), John L. Dearing and wife, Frederick G. Harrington and wife (in America), W. B. Parshley and wife, Miss Clara A. Converse, Miss E. L. Rolman, Miss Nanna J. Wilson Miss M. A. Hawley.	24	6	491	416	64
Tokyo	C. H. D. Fisher and wife, George W. Taft and wife, J. C. Brand and wife, E. W. Clement and wife, Miss Anna H. Kidder, Miss M. Antoinette Whitman, Miss Anna M. Clagett,	33	5	403	356	30
Kobe	Henry H. Rhees, D.D., and wife, Robert A. Thompson and wife, Miss Ella R. Church (in America), Miss D. B. Barlow, Miss H. M. Witherbee.	18	1	190	232	28
Sendai	Samuel W. Hamblen and wife, Ephraim H. Jones and wife (in America), Miss Lavinia Mead, Miss A. S. Buzzell, Miss Nellie E. Fife (in America).	11	1	204	369	6
Shimonoseki ..	Richard L. Halsey and wife, (in America), W. E. Story and wife, Miss Harriet M. Browne, Miss Olive M. Blunt, Mrs. Ellen Sharland	23	2	163	167	23
Morioka	.. ..	2	2	79	25	5
Nemuro	Mrs. H. E. Carpenter, Miss L. Cummings.	6	1	55	205	14
Osaka	William Wynd and wife, J. H. Scott and wife, Miss M. Walton, Miss F. A. Duffield.	11	1	48	100	9
Totals ..	.. ..	128	19	1,633	1,870	179

PALESTINE.

BAPTIST MISSIONARY SOCIETY.

Stations.	Missionaries.	Stations and Sub-Stations.	Members.	S.S. Teachers.	S.S. Scholars.	Baptisms.
Nablous, Samaria, Bate Mreen, Coorcood, Boorkeen, Rafidia, Burka, Nus Jebeen	Youhannah El Karey and Mrs. El Karey	7	112	6	51	

AFRICA.

SOUTH AFRICA.

(*Population*, [*estimated*] 2,200,000.)

BAPTIST UNION OF SOUTH AFRICA.

President—Rev. JOHN GIFFORD. *Vice-President*—Rev. H. J. BATTS.
Secretary—Rev. G. W. CROSS. *Treasurer*—Mr. J. W. VARDER.
Financial Secretary—Rev. H. J. BATTS.

Church.	Date.	Chapel Seats.	Members.	S. S. Teachers.	S. S. Scholars.	Local Preachers.	Pastor.	When Settled.
Alice and stations ..	1874	600	84	6	40	..	F. W. King ..	1893
Cape Town	1878	520	191	16	160	4	E. Baker ..	1893
Wynberg	1892	110	64	10	140	..	J. Russell ..	1893
Cradock	1881	250	53	9	90	..	J. Maginnes ..	1893
Durban— Natal	1864	200	95	12	85	..	J. B. Rose ..	1891
East London	1884	300	103	12	100	4	D. H. Hay ..	1890
Graham's Town	1820	400	208	16	180	..	G. W. Cross ..	1886
Kariega	..	80	58	..	..	..	E. G. Evans ..	1893
Kimberley..	1890	500	170	11	128	..	J. Hughes ..	1889
King William's Town .. *Kei Road*	1882	400	204	16	160	4	J. E. Ennals, B.A., B.D.	1895
Port Alfred	1878	120	16	3	17	..	R. H. Brotherton	1893
Port Elizabeth .. .. *Corrney & Alicedale.*	1860	450	221	21	213	6	John Gifford .. G. P. Burbidge.	1889
Port Elizabeth— South End .. .. *Walmer*	1888	250	45	7	90	..	C. H. Homer ..	1892
Pietermaritzburg ..	1885	300	65	19	107	..	J. B. Heard ..	1885
Pretoria	1890	400					W. E. Kelly ..	1889
Johannesburg	1888	350	94	..	60	..	F. Davis.	
Krugersdorp							C. Pittman ..	1895
Bloemfontein	1892	250	43	5	30	..	A. J. Edwards..	1893
Mowbray	1894	..	22	6	63	..	Geo. Eales ..	1894
Totals ..	..	5480	1736	169	1663	18		

Revs. L. Nuttall, H. J. Batts, W. J. Staynes, J. Whitford. I. Harris and F. Ochse are without pastoral charge.

CHURCHES IN GERMAN BAPTIST UNION. (*See Page* 402.)

Town and Address.	Date.	Chapel Seats.	Members.	S. S. Tchrs.	S. S. Scholrs.	Local Prchrs.	Pastors.	Settled.
Berlin	1893	800	143	14	100	4	H. G. F. Meier ..	1895
East London ..	1894	315	120	5	40	..	H. Gutsche, jun.	1894
King William's Town	1867	880	309	11	123	4	H. Gutsche, sen. L. Preuss ..	1867 1895
Stutterheim ..	1867	1,000	286	25	150	3	M. Schmidt ..	1889
Sugarloaf ..	1886	150	160	4	59	4	J. D. Odendaal ..	1886
Totals ..	..	3,145	1,018	59	472	15		

Rev. E. P. Reimer without pastoral charge.

SOUTH AFRICA—*continued.*

NATIVE MISSION.

urch.	Date	Chapel Seats.	Members.	S. S Teachers.	S.S. Scholars.	Local Preachers.	Missionaries.
King William's Town ..	1894	300	..	..	..	..	Miss Joyce L. Pearse.
Tehabo	1889		26	5	34	2	Miss Bellin. Miss Box.

CENTRAL AFRICA.

CONGO.

BAPTIST MISSIONARY SOCIETY.

Stations.	Missionaries.	Stations and sub-Stations.	Members.	S.S. Teachers.	S.S. Scholars.	Baptisms.
Lower River— San Salvador .. .. *Mbanza Mputu* .. *Mawuinse* .. .. *Kimpesi* .. .. Tunduwa, or Underhill Lukunga (for Transport work only) .. .. Ngombe, or Wathen .. Upper River— Stanley Pool, or Arthington .. .. Lukolela, or Liverpool *Bolobo* .. .. *Munsembe* .. .. *Bopoto* .. .. *Mojembo*	W. H. Bentley and Mrs. Bentley, G. Grenfell and Mrs. Grenfell, J. H. Weeks and Mrs. Weeks, G. Cameron, P. Davies, B.A., A. E. Scrivener and Mrs. Scrivener, R. H. C. Graham (Mrs. Graham in England), H. R. Phillips (Mrs. Phillips in England), Thomas Lewis and Mrs. Lewis (in England), J. Pinnock and Mrs. Pinnock, J. A. Clark, J. L. Roger and Mrs. Roger, W. L. Forfeitt and Mrs. Forfeitt, H. White and Mrs. White, J. L. Forfeitt and Mrs. Forfeitt, R. Glennie and Mrs. Glennie, W. H. Stapleton and Mrs. Stapleton, J. A. A. Fuller, S. C. Gordon (on furlough), J. Whitehead and Mrs. Whitehead, G. R. Pople (in England), R. H. Kirkland, S. M. Field, H. T. Stonelake, J. R. M. Stephens, John Bell, R. Beedham, C. J. Dodds, K. Smith, Miss Lily M. deHailes.	15	114	15	336	41

AFRICA—*continued.*

AMERICAN BAPTIST MISSIONARY UNION.

Stations.	Missionaries.	Total Missionary Workers.	Churches	Members.	S. S. Scholars.	Baptisms.
Palabala	C. H. Harvey, Miss Lulu C. Fleming (in America).	6	1	25	24	11
Banza Manteke..	Henry Richards and wife, W. H. Leslie, M.D., A. L. Bain and wife, Miss F. A. Cole (in England), J. S. Burns, Miss J. S. Edmunds, Miss Clara R. Hill.	23	3	635	200	162
Matadi	T. Hill	1				
Lukunga ..	Theodore H. Hoste, C. B. Antisdel, Lyman H. Morse (Mrs. Morse in America), Miss Clara A. Howard (in America), Miss Bessie E. Gardner (in America), Miss Nora A. Gordon (in America).	55	8	541	70	63
Mukimvika ..	F. P. Lynch, M.D., and wife, Wesley M. Biggs and wife.	4				
Leopoldville ..	A. Sims, M.D., Thomas Adams.	8	1	26	..	20
Bolengi	Charles B. Banks and wife, J. B. Murphy (Mrs. Murphy in England), E. V. Sjoblom.	5	1	16	50	1
Bwemba	A. Billington and wife, Charles B. Glenesk and wife, *The steamer "Henry Reed."*	7	..	1	10	1
Kinjila	P. Frederickson and wife, Christian Nelson and wife.	10	1	35	57	13
Irebu	Thomas Moody and wife (in America), Joseph Clark and wife, J. A. Finch (Mrs. Finch in America), W. A. Hall and wife, R. Milne, Miss G. Milne.	7	..	4	10	
Ikoko	.. ..	7	..	4		
	Totals ..	133	15	1,287	421	271

WEST AFRICA.

CAMEROONS AND VICTORIA.

35 stations, 19 sub-stations 1,446 members, 100 Sunday-school teachers, and 2,500 Sunday-school scholars.

AMERICAN SOUTHERN BAPTIST CONVENTION.

Churches.	Missionaries.	Churches.	Members.	S.S. Scholars.	Baptisms.
Lagos	M. L. Stone, and three native assistants and teachers.	1	106	50	24
Abbeokuta	W. T. Lumbley and wife, L. O. Fadipe.	1	20	30	1
Awyaw	S. G. Pinnock and wife, and Miss Alberta Newton.				
Ogbomoshaw	C. E. Smith and wife, and native teacher.	1	81	60	25
Hausser Farm	A. Eli	1	29	..	14
Debari	.. ..	..	3	..	3
	Totals ..	4	239	140	67

ST. HELENA.

(*Population*, 4,116.)

Church.	Date.	Seats.	Members.	Teachers.	Scholars.	Local Pchrs.	Pastor.	Settled.
Jamestown	1865	200	102	14	100	4	J. R. Way ..	1893
Knollcombe ..	..	150						
Sandy Bay ..	..	130						
High Peak ..	..	100						

CAPE VERDE ISLANDS.

Population, 107,026.)

St. Vincent	1884	50	9	1	7	..	G. S. C. Eveleigh.

AMERICA.

DOMINION OF CANADA.

(*Population*, 4,829,411.)

BAPTIST CONVENTION OF ONTARIO AND QUEBEC.

OFFICERS OF CONVENTION FOR 1895-96.

President.—Rev. JOHN DEMPSEY, D.D., Ingersoll.

Vice-Presidents.—Rev. T. S. JOHNSON, Brantford; Mr. A. A. AYER, Montreal.

Secretary and Treasurer.—Rev. D. M. MIHELL, M.A., B.Th., St. George.

BAPTIST CONVENTION OF MANITOBA AND THE NORTH-WEST TERRITORIES—*President*—Mr. S. J. MCKEE, B.A., Brandon, Man. *Secretary*—Rev. H. G. MELLICK, B.D., Winnipeg.

SUMMARY OF STATISTICS IN ONTARIO, QUEBEC, MANITOBA, AND NORTH-WEST TERRITORIES.

Associations.	Churches.	Members.	S. S. Teachers.	S. S. Scholars.	Pastors.	Baptisms
Amherstburg	13	583	..	..	3	26
Brant	17	2,574	227	2,296	12	157
Canada Central	24	1,948	159	1,332	17	187
Eastern	20	2,039	220	2,065	11	174
Elgin	22	2,370	176	1,417	10	173
Grand Ligne (French)	20	379	..	..	11	43
Guelph	21	2,215	228	1,822	17	87
Hamilton	11	1,183	164	1,291	7	79
Middlesex and Lambton ..	31	2,948	325	2,628	18	130
Niagara	22	1,832	236	1,569	12	134
Norfolk	30	3,153	268	2,453	18	227
Northern	23	1,309	142	1,204	13	..
North Western	34	2,568	..	..	19	224
Ottawa	33	2,789	199	1,631	17	..
Owen Sound	22	1,287	153	1,161	13	148
Peterborough	19	1,491	189	1,477	11	111
Toronto	29	5,135	700	6,152	20	356
Walkerton	19	959	103	817	9	59
Western	28	2,350	234	2,172	17	361
Whitby and Lindsay	22	1,288	121	1,133	8	174
Woodstock	19	2,271	242	1,903	12	167
Manitoba and North-West ..	48	2,841	..	..	33	253
Totals	527	45,512	4,086	34,523	308	3,270

Details of Churches and Pastors are to be found in the "Baptist Year-Book for Ontario, Quebec, Manitoba, and N.-W. Territories."

AMERICA—*continued*

McMASTER UNIVERSITY

OFFICERS:

Chancellor—Rev. O. C. S. WALLACE, M.A.

Chairman—Hon. JOHN DRYDEN, M.P.P., Brooklin.

Treasurer—Mr. J. S. MCMASTER, Toronto *Secretary*—Mr. T. F. WEBB, Toronto.

UNIVERSITY FACULTY.—*Principal*—O. C. S. WALLACE, M.A., Homiletics and Pastoral Theology; ALBERT H. NEWMAN, D.D., LL.D., Prof. of History and Civil Polity; DANIEL M. WELTON, D.D., Ph.D., Prof. of Hebrew and Cognate Languages and Old Testament Exegesis; THEODORE H. RAND, M.A., D.C.L., Prof. (Emeritus) of Education and English; PETER S. CAMPBELL, B.A., Prof. of Latin and Greek Languages and Literatures; JONES H. FARMER, B.A., Prof. of New Testament and Patristic Greek; A. C. MCKAY, B.A., Prof. of Mathematics and Physics; CALVIN GOODSPEED, D.D., Prof. of Systematic Theology and Christian Evidences; M. S. CLARK, B.A., Prof. of Modern Languages and Literatures; A. B. WILLMOTT, M.A., B.Sc., Prof. of Natural Sciences, Philosophy, Ethics and Logic; WALTER S. W. MCLAY, B.A., Lecturer in the English Language and Literature; W. H. PIERSOL, B.A., Demonstrator in the Natural Sciences; J. W. RUSSELL, B.A., Fellow in Physics; H. N. SHAW, B.A., Lecturer in Elocution.

WOODSTOCK COLLEGE.—*Principal*—J. I. BATES, B.A., Ph.M., The Bible, Latin and Greek; NEIL MCKECHNIE, B.A., English Language and Literature; DONALD K. CLARKE, B.A., Modern Languages and Manual Training; WILSON R. SMITH, Science and Mathematics; ABRAHAM L. MCCRIMMON, M.A., Latin and Greek; H. L. MCNEILL, B.A., Preparatory Department.

MOULTON COLLEGE.—*Principal*—ADELAIDE L. DICKLOW, Ph.M., The Bible and Science; ANNIE M. MCKAY, B.A., Mathematics; ELIZA P. WELLS, B.A., English Language and Literature; MARY H. SMART, Music; H. GERTRUDE HART, Elocution and Physical Culture; LOTTIE V. PORTER, Preparatory Department; Mrs. MARY E. DIGNAM, Drawing and Painting.

SOCIETIES IN ONTARIO, QUEBEC, MANITOBA, AND NORTH-WEST TERRITORIES.

LA GRANDE LIGNE MISSION.—OBJECT:—"The diffusion of the benefits of education and the propagation of the Gospel of Jesus Christ among the people of Quebec." *President*—Mr. A. A. AYER, Montreal. *Secretary*—Rev. T. LAFLEUR, Montreal. *Treasurer*—Mr. JOSEPH RICHARDS, Montreal. 20 churches, 11 pastors, 379 members.

FELLER INSTITUTE.—OBJECT:—"To give an evangelical education to any who may desire it, and to train Preachers and Teachers for the Churches and Schools." *Principal*—Rev. G. N. MASSÉ. *Assistant*—Mr. A. MASSÉ. *Instructors*—Madame MASSÉ, E. RAINVILLE, M.D., Miss S. PICHE, Miss B. SCOFIELD, and Rev. M. B. PARENT, B.A.

HOME MISSIONARY BOARD OF THE BAPTIST CONVENTION OF ONTARIO AND QUEBEC.—OBJECT:—"To promote the preaching of the Gospel, and the dissemination of the principles held by the denomination known as Regular Baptists." *Chairman*—Mr. JOHN STARK, Toronto. *Secretary*—Rev. J. B. KENNEDY, B.A., Toronto. *Superintendent*—Rev. J. P. MCEWEN, Toronto. *Treasurer*—Mr. E. T. FOX, Toronto.

AMERICA—*continued.*

FOREIGN MISSIONARY BOARD OF THE BAPTIST CONVENTION OF ONTARIO AND QUEBEC.—Mission among the Telugus, South India (*see* page 420). *Established* 1874. *Chairman*—Rev. S. S. BATES, B.A., Toronto. *Treasurer*—Mr. W. E. WATSON, Toronto. *Secretary*—Rev. A. P. MCDIARMID, M.A., Toronto.

BOARD FOR THE RELIEF OF SUPERANNUATED MINISTERS, &c. (1864).—*Chairman*—Rev. W. H. PORTER, Brantford. *Secretary*—Rev. W. H. CLINE, Paris. *Treasurer*—Mr. CHAS. RAYMOND, Guelph.

WOMEN'S BAPTIST FOREIGN MISSIONARY SOCIETIES OF ONTARIO AND QUEBEC.—Western Board: *Secretary*—Miss JANE BUCHAN, Toronto. Eastern Board: *Secretary*—Miss N. E. Green, Montreal.

WOMEN'S BAPTIST HOME MISSIONARY SOCIETY OF ONTARIO.—*Secretary*—Mrs. JOHN LILLIE, Toronto. *Treasurer*—Miss EMMA J. DRYDEN.

BROOKLYN WOMEN'S BAPTIST HOME MISSIONARY SOCIETY (EAST)—*Secretary*—Mrs. C. E. PARSON.

CHURCH EDIFICE BOARD.—*President*—JOHN STARK, Toronto. *Secretary and Treasurer*—Mr. P. C. PARKER, Toronto.

BOARD OF PUBLICATION.—*Chairman*—Rev. O. C. S. WALLACE, M.A., Toronto. *Secretary*—Mr. G. R. ROBERTS, Toronto.

BAPTIST PERIODICALS.—*Canadian Baptist:* the weekly newspaper of the denomination, published at 9, Richmond Street, Toronto: *Editor*—Prof. J. E. WELLS, M.A.; *Manager*—Mr. G. R. ROBERTS; price 1 dol. 50c. a year, when paid in advance. *The Canadian Missionary Link:* Monthly, devoted to the interests of the Women's Foreign Missionary Societies of Ontario, Quebec, and Maritime Provinces; 25c. a year; *Editor and Manager*—Mrs. NEWMAN, 116, Yorkville Avenue, Toronto. *Baptist Visitor:* Monthly, devoted to the interests of the Women's Home Missionary Societies of Ontario and Quebec; *Editor*—Mrs. A. R. MCMASTER, Toronto. *The Baptist Year-Book*, for Ontario, Quebec, Manitoba and North-West Territories: Under the direction of the Denominational Societies; *Editor*—Rev. D. M. MIHELL, M.A., B.Th., St. George, Ont. *McMaster University:* a Monthly magazine, published by the McMaster University.

BAPTIST CONVENTION OF THE MARITIME PROVINCES OF CANADA, EMBRACING—

NOVA SCOTIA, NEW BRUNSWICK AND PRINCE EDWARD ISLAND.

Organised 1846.

The Canadian Census of 1891 gives the number of Baptist adherents, 169,000; Church of England, 114,000; Methodists, 104,000; Presbyterians, 183,000; Roman Catholics, 286,000. The total *population* was 880,737.

The objects of the Convention are to maintain the educational and missionary operations of the Body, and to advance the general interests of the denomination. It is composed of representatives of the associations, delegates from contributing Churches, ordained ministers of the denomination, and life members constituted by the payment of fixed amounts.

AMERICA—*continued.*

OFFICERS OF CONVENTION FOR 1895-96.

President—Mr. JONATHAN PARSONS, B.A., Halifax, N.S.

Vice-Presidents—Mr. J. S. SIMMS, St. John, N.B.; Mr. GEORGE W. WARREN, Summerside, P.E.I.

Secretary—Rev. E. M. KEIRSTEAD, M.A., D.D., Acadia University, Wolfville, N.S.

Assistant Secretaries—Rev. W. C. GOUCHER, B.A., St. Stephen, N.B.; Rev. H. G. ESTABROOKE, B.A., Amherst, N.S.

Treasurer—Mr. DONALDSON HUNT, St. John, N.B.

Associations.	Date of Organisation.	Churches.	Members.	Baptisms.	S. Schools.	S.S. Teachers.	S.S. Scholars.
NOVA SCOTIA—							
Western	1851	72	5,861	580	127	846	7,370
Central	1851	54	9,757	575	95	652	6,368
Eastern	1851	67	11,558	277	73	436	4,172
African	1884	16	570	14	13	50	460
NEW BRUNSWICK—							
Western	1848	75	4,905	600	59	484	3,101
Southern	1879	46	5,114	472	54	400	3,707
Eastern	1848	47	5,967	436	24	94	1,245
PRINCE EDWARD ISLAND ..	1868	25	2,006	112	28	132	1,390
TOTALS		402	45,738	3,066	473	3,094	27,813

INSTITUTIONS IN THE CONVENTION.

ACADIA UNIVERSITY, Wolfville, N.S.—*Founded* 1838. *Faculty of Instruction*—*President*—A. W. SAWYER, D.D., LL.D., Metaphysics; F. HIGGINS, M.A., Ph.D., Professor of Mathematics; R. V. JONES, M.A., Ph.D., Professor of Greek and Latin; E. M. KEIRSTEAD, M.A., D.D., Professor of English Literature and Moral Philosophy; A. E. COLDWELL, M.A., Professor of Chemistry and Geology; L. E. WORTMAN, M.A., Professor of German and French; J. F. TUFTS, M.A., Mark Curry Professor of History and Political Economy; F. R. HALEY, M.A., Alumni Professor of Physics and Astronomy.

The university has 125 students. The regular course in arts extends over four years. Supported by endowment fund and contributions from the churches.

HORTON ACADEMY, Wolfville, N.S.—*Established* 1828. *Principal*—INGRAM B. OAKES, M.A. Five teachers, 90 pupils.

ACADIA SEMINARY, Wolfville, N.S.—A school for girls. *Principal*—Miss ADELAIDE F. TRUE, B.A. Nine teachers, 90 pupils.

Horton Academy and Acadia Seminary are under the control of the Board of Governors of Acadia University. *Secretary*—Rev. S. B. KEMPTON, D.D., Dartmouth, N.S.

THE BAPTIST SEMINARY AT ST. MARTIN'S, N.B., is managed by the Baptists and Free Baptists of New Brunswick. *Principal*—Rev. W. E. MCINTYRE, B.A.

BOARD OF FOREIGN MISSIONS.—Located at St. John, N.B. *Secretary*—Rev. J. W. MANNING, B.A., St. John, N.B. Has 13 missionaries at work among the Telugus of India. (*See* page).

BOARD OF HOME MISSIONS.—*Secretary*—Rev. A. COHOON, M.A., Wolfville, N.S.

AMERICA—*continued.*

BAPTIST BOOK AND TRACT SOCIETY.—120 Granville Street, Halifax, N.S. *Secretary*—GEORGE A. MACDONALD. Publishes "The Canadian Baptist Hymnal."

THE BAPTIST INSTITUTE.—*Secretary*—Rev. B. N. NOBLES, Hillsburg, N.S. Meets annually for discussion of topics of current interest.

PERIODICALS.—*The Messenger and Visitor:* Published weekly at St. John, N.B *Editor*—Rev. S. McC. BLACK, M.A. *The Acadia Athenæum:* Published monthly by the Students of Acadia University. *The Rema:* Published monthly by the Students of St. Martin's Seminary. *The Baptist Year Book of the Maritime Provinces:* Published by the Publication Society, Halifax.

The Free Baptists publish the *Religious Intelligencer* at Fredericton, N.B. *Editor*—Rev. J. McLEOD, D.D.

UNITED STATES.

(*Population*, 62,622,250.)

SUMMARY OF STATISTICS.

States and Territories	Associations.	Ordained Ministers.	Churches.	Membership.	Baptisms.	Sunday Schools.	Officers and Teachers.	Scholars.
Alabama	135	2,729	3,058	256,223	15,402	1,231	4,157	47,547
Arizona	1	6	7	262	19	6	..	265
Arkansas	79	1,241	810	118,454	6,757	553	1,585	24,256
California	12	249	195	14,043	894	175	1,598	12,161
Colorado	3	55	62	5,558	500	62	636	6,017
Connecticut ..	6	162	137	24,135	1,327	134	1,807	19,170
Delaware	1	14	13	2,455	165	22	365	2,513
District of Columbia	3	74	58	16,444	788	61	956	10,273
Florida	31	364	800	44,032	1,404	282	1,054	9,610
Georgia	136	2,602	3,709	367,498	15,460	1,645	6,689	76,974
Idaho	2	12	13	515	69	11	94	753
Illinois	43	942	1,110	109,335	8,087	845	7,348	72,498
Indiana	33	322	564	58,096	4,004	485	3,760	33,762
Indian Territory ..	15	250	309	14,440	798	53	291	2,395
Iowa	29	406	436	33,431	3,167	362	3,305	25,143
Kansas	30	407	609	37,697	2,921	344	3,101	22,903
Kentucky	69	1,309	1,933	225,970	9,033	1,038	4,874	63,854
Louisiana	41	845	1,444	100,750	2,749	726	2,354	35,073
Maine	12	145	244	18,789	824	198	..	17,047
Maryland	1	62	77	13,350	1,021	84	1,302	12,654
Massachusetts ..	16	460	318	65,315	3,429	373	5,009	65,323
Michigan	23	340	423	39,488	4,594	409	5,562	40,335
Minnesota ..	10	170	224	17,042	1,502	186	1,864	15,006
Mississippi ..	98	1,476	2,595	201,025	7,287	1,085	3,331	34,102
Missouri	88	1,588	2,078	155,706	11,464	1,115	7,199	67,847
Montana	1	16	18	938	81	18	163	1,458
Nebraska	17	171	280	15,722	1,568	254	2,239	17,622
Nevada	..	..	1	105	36	1	12	106
New Hampshire ..	6	91	86	9,757	518	83	1,178	8,653
New Jersey ..	6	266	239	43,762	3,276	287	5,326	41,042
New Mexico ..	2	12	13	260	22	9	48	425
New York	43	964	923	142,779	9,389	942	14,587	121,352
North Carolina ..	90	1,368	2,642	259,775	8,700	1,619	8,477	93,947
North Dakota ..	5	24	46	1,776	66	32	172	1,499
Ohio	33	520	646	66,039	5,228	564	6,148	55,020
Oklahoma	4	70	69	1,882	250	17	40	600

SUMMARY OF STATISTICS—*continued.*

States and Territories.	Associa-tions.	Ordained Ministers.	Churches.	Member-ship.	Baptisms.	Sunday Schools.	Officers and Teachers.	Scholars.
Oregon	8	67	116	6,568	305	77	648	5,222
Pennsylvania ..	25	629	682	96,175	7,543	683	10,044	81,687
Rhode Island ..	3	90	76	13,898	982	77	1,649	13,036
South Carolina ..	70	1,004	1,795	218,414	8,236	1,365	7,266	75,992
South Dakota ..	8	64	105	5,009	602	99	726	5,046
Tennessee.. ..	67	1,171	1,954	163,782	8,402	1,023	4,037	54,367
Texas	127	2,578	3,881	260,868	24,500	1,289	5,017	58,075
Utah	1	5	8	550	55	11	106	1,062
Vermont	7	79	100	8,463	461	92	1,048	8,274
Virginia	50	1,158	2,102	318,355	16,007	1,402	10,939	100,187
Washington ..	5	47	113	6,758	673	94	634	6,476
West Virginia ..	19	289	566	39,358	3,100	298	1,919	15,628
Wisconsin.. ..	15	164	214	16,000	1,492	195	2,103	16,575
Wyoming	1	6	9	375	..	..	..	..
TOTALS ..	1,530	27,083	37,910	3,637,421	205,157	22,016	152,767	1,500,832

Whole amount reported Contributions, 11,672,691 dols.
Full information to be found in the American Baptist Year-Book.

PROGRESS OF THE REGULAR BAPTISTS (U. S. A.) SINCE A.D. 1770.
(See also below.)

Year.	Churches.	Ministers.	Members	Sunday Scholars.
1770	77	..	..	..
1784	471	424	35,101	..
1792	891	1,156	65,345	..
1812	2,164	1,605	172,972	..
1832	5,320	3,618	384,926	..
1840	7,771	5,208	571,291	..
1851	9,552	7,393	770,839	..
1860	12,279	7,773	1 016,134	..
1871	18,397	12,013	1,489,191	..
1879	24,794	15,401	2,133,044	..
1889	32,900	21,420	2,997,794	1 158,665
1890	34,767	22,850	3,174,885	1,280,663
1891	36,165	23,792	3,276,359	1,307,628
1892	37,501	24 799	3,399,028	1,390,601
1893	38,238	24,279	3,510,187	1,430,933
1894	37,910	27,091	3,637,421	1,500,834

SOCIETIES.

AMERICAN BAPTIST MISSIONARY UNION.—*Established* 1814. Executive Board located at Boston, Massachusetts. *Hon. Secretary*—Rev. J. N. MURDOCK, D.D., LL.D. *Corresponding Secretaries*—Rev. S. W. DUNCAN, D.D., and Rev. H. C. MABIE, D.D. Supports missions to the Burmese, the Karens, the Chins, the Assamese, the Telugus, the Chinese, and the Japanese (in Asia), to the French, the Germans, the Swedes, the Danes, the Finns, the Norwegians, and the Spaniards (in Europe); and to various tribes in Central Africa. *Income,* including 94,984.45 dols. from the Woman's Baptist Foreign Missionary Society, and 38,103.27 dols. from the Woman's Baptist Foreign Missionary Society of the West, 485,000.12 dols.; *expenditure,* 713,714.37 dols.

AMERICAN BAPTIST HOME MISSION SOCIETY.—*Organised* 1832. Executive Board at New York. *Secretary*—Rev. THOS. J. MORGAN, D.D., New York. *Receipts*, 405,213.45 dols.

AMERICAN BAPTIST PUBLICATION SOCIETY (1824).—Head-quarters at Philadelphia. *Secretary*—Col. C. H. BANES. *Receipts* in business department, 556,847.76 dols.; in missionary department, 159,225.55 dols.; in Bible department, 29,297.23 dols.

SOUTHERN BAPTIST CONVENTION (1845).—*Secretaries*—Rev. LANSING BURROWS, D.D., Augusta, Georgia, and Rev. O. F. GREGORY, D.D., Baltimore.—*Receipts of Home Missions*—138,263.49 dols.; *Ditto of Foreign Mission*—219,645.30 dols. Has missions in China, Italy, Africa, Mexico, Brazil, Japan. *Receipts of Sunday School Board*—56,502 dols.

AMERICAN BAPTIST HISTORICAL SOCIETY (1853).—The works belonging to this Society are numerous and valuable. *Secretary*—Rev. B. MACMACKIN, Philadelphia.

WOMAN'S BAPTIST FOREIGN MISSIONARY SOCIETY (1871).—*Receipts*—94,692.72 dols. Has female missionaries labouring for the Burmese, the Shans, the Karens, the Telugus, Chinese, Japanese, the Chins, the Kachins, Eurasians, Assamese, and in Africa, France and Sweden. *Secretary*—Mrs. H. G. SAFFORD.

WOMAN'S BAPTIST FOREIGN MISSIONARY SOCIETY OF THE WEST (1871).—*Receipts*—50,485.63 dols. Has female missionaries at work for Karens, Burmese, Assamese, Telugus, Chinese, Japanese, and in Africa. *Secretary*—Mrs. A. M. BACON, Chicago, Illinois.

WOMAN'S MISSIONARY UNION (SOUTHERN) co-operates with the Southern Baptist Convention in support of its missionaries, home and foreign. *Receipts*—45,128.59 dols. *Secretary*—Miss ANNIE W. ARMSTRONG, Baltimore.

WOMEN'S BAPTIST HOME MISSION SOCIETY (1877).—Chicago, Ill. *Secretary*—Miss M. G. BURDETTE, Chicago. *Receipts*—61,884.48 dols.

WOMEN'S AMERICAN BAPTIST HOME MISSION SOCIETY (1877).—Boston, Mass. *Secretary*—Miss M. C. REYNOLDS, Cambridgeport, Mass. *Receipts*—36,241.68 dols.

There are in the United States seven Baptist Theological Institutions, having 67 instructors, 937 students. There are also 35 Universities and Colleges, having 722 instructors, and 9,385 students. 27 Institutions for Female Education exclusively, with 401 instructors, and 3,433 pupils; 56 Seminaries and Academies, Male and Co-educating, with 397 instructors, and 12,774 pupils; and 34 Institutions for Negroes and Indians, with 259 instructors, and 4,808 pupils.

FREE BAPTISTS IN AMERICA.

States.	Associations.	Churches.	Ministers.	Members.
Maine	1	250	172	13,795
New Hampshire	1	100	97	8,212
Vermont	1	42	38	2,134
Massachusetts	1	17	22	3,124
Rhode Island	2	35	40	4,369
New York	6	136	109	8,523
Pennsylvania	3	40	39	2,108
Ohio	4	130	136	8,341
West Virginia	4	31	38	1,096
Indiana	1	27	23	1,651
Michigan	1	130	117	5,623
Illinois	3	135	107	6,179
Wisconsin	1	39	39	1,580
Minnesota	5	35	41	2,150
Iowa	7	44	30	1,609
Nebraska	4	19	22	930
Kansas	6	18	18	925
California	1	3	5	200

FREE BAPTISTS IN AMERICA—*continued.*

States.	Associations.	Churches.	Ministers.	Members.
Virginia	2	22	21	1,950
Kentucky	1	34	34	1,218
Louisiana	1	30	34	714
Mississippi	5	90	44	8,516
North Carolina	4	100	92	13,250
South Carolina	2	19	15	2,120
Missouri	4	70	64	2,415
Tennessee	6	98	89	6,130
Georgia	3	41	37	3,640
Alabama	1	10	8	1,220
Florida	1	4	4	525
Texas	1	8	8	410
Arkansas	1	5	6	512
Ontario	1	7	2	320
Totals	85	1,769	1,551	115,489

FREE BAPTIST BENEVOLENT SOCIETIES.*

FOREIGN MISSION.—*Secretary*—Rev. T. H. STACY, Auburn, Maine. *Income*—35,000 dols.

HOME MISSION.—*Secretary*—Rev. A. L. GERRISH, Obneyville, R.I. *Income*—20,000 dols.

WOMAN'S MISSION SOCIETY.—*Secretary*—Mrs. J. A. LOWELL, Danville, N.H. *Income*—18,000 dols.

BATES COLLEGE, Lewistown, Maine.—*President*—Rev. G. C. CHASE, M.A., *Invested Capital*—500,000 dols.

HILLSDALE COLLEGE, Hillsdale, Michigan.—*President*—Hon. G. F. MOSHER, M.A. *Invested Capital*—560,000 dols.

STORER COLLEGE, West Virginia.—*President*—Rev. N. C. BRACKETT. *Invested Capital*—130,000 dols.

RIO GRAND COLLEGE, Ohio.—*President*—Rev. JOHN M. DAVIS, M.A. *Invested Capital*—90,000 dols.

PARKER COLLEGE, Minnesota.—*President*—Rev. G. A. BURGESS, M.A. *Invested Capital*—120,000 dols.

KEUKA COLLEGE, New York.—*President*—Rev. GEO. H. BALL, D.D. *Invested Capital*—160,000 dols.

Eight classical schools. *Invested Capital*—80,000 dols.

PUBLICATIONS.—*Morning Star*, Boston, Mass., weekly. *Free Baptist*, Minneapolis, Minnesota, weekly. *Missionary Helper*, Boston, Mass.

THE GENERAL BAPTISTS.

Essentially Free Baptists, found mostly in Indiana, Kentucky, Missouri, and Tennessee, have a Foreign Mission, a Home Mission, and an Education Society. Membership, about 20,000.

The American Baptist Year-Book for 1895 publishes the following estimates of OTHER BAPTIST BODIES, *not included* in the foregoing statements :—

Denomination.	Churches.	Ministers.	Members.
Baptist, German or Tunkers	989	..	73,795
Baptist, Primitive	3,222	..	121,347
Baptist, Separate	24	40	1,599
Baptist, Seventh Day	105	130	9,500
Baptist, Six Principle	18	16	937
Totals	4,358	186	207,178

MEXICO.

(*Population*, [*estimated*] 10,447,974.)

SOUTHERN BAPTIST CONVENTION OF AMERICA.

States.	Stations.	Missionaries.	Churches.	Members.	S. S. Scholars.	Baptisms.
Mexico ..	Toluca ..	W. D. Powell and wife	6	114	75	20
Coahuila .. (Mission commenced 1880)	Musquiz	A. C. Watkins and wife, Pablo Rodriquez	12	295	172	74
	Saltillo ..	A. B. Rudd and wife, Miss L. A. McDavid, Miss Addie Barton, Miss Ida Hayes, José M. Cardenas	4	494	173	29
	Patos ..	A. Trevino				
	San Rafael	M. T. Flores				
	San Pedro	E. Barocio				
Nuevo Leon	Doctor Arroyo	J. G. Chastain and wife, Porfirio Rodriguez, Eliseo Recio	2	25	35	11
Zacatecas .. (Mission commenced 1887)	Zacatecas	M. Gassaway	3	67	55	23
	Colotlan	Benjamin Müller				
Michoacan..	Morelia..	H. P. McCormick and wife	1	48	65	40
Jalisco .. (Mission commenced 1887)	Gwadalajara	D. A. Wilson and wife, Samuel Dominquez, Miss Sallie Hale, F. de P. Stephenson	3	63	40	18
Vera Cruz ..	Orizaba..	I. N. Steelman and wife, Miss L. C. Cabaniss, native assistant	1	14	14	11
		Totals	32	1,120	629	226

WEST INDIES.

JAMAICA.

(*Population*, 650,000; Area, 4,193 square miles.)

JAMAICA BAPTIST UNION.

Chairman, 1895—Rev. CHARLES CHAPMAN; *Vice-Chairman*—Rev. T. S. JOHNSON; *Secretary and Treasurer*—Rev. P. WILLIAMS, Bethel Town P.O. Churches (in Jamaica), 187; ministers, 64 (4 retired); members, 36,227; inquirers, 4,832; baptised in 1894, 2,413; Sunday-school teachers, 2,282; scholars, 25,596; day-schools, 240; scholars, 26,100. Churches connected with the Union (in neighbouring countries), 7; members, 391; inquirers, 98.

Jamaica Baptist Missionary Society—OBJECTS:—Home evangelization; maintenance of Calabar College; extension of the Gospel in the surrounding Islands, Central America, and Africa; assistance of Day and Sunday-schools; and the aiding of Churches in their building operations. *Secretary*—Rev. E. J. HEWETT, Anchovy P.O. *Treasurer*—Rev. J. KINGDON, Falmouth P.O. *Income* from all sources in 1894—£2,569 13s. 3d.

Jamaica Baptist College.—Founded at Calabar in 1843; removed to Kingston, 1869. *President*—Rev. ARTHUR JAMES, B.A. *Normal School Tutor*—Rev. L. TUCKER. M.A. *Classical Tutor*—Rev. JAMES BALFOUR, M.A. *Secretary*—Rev. P. WILLIAMS. *Students* Theological, 6; Normal School, 25; Total 31.

Denominational Paper.—Jamaica Baptist Reporter—Published Monthly. *Editor*—Rev. W. M. WEBB, Stewart Town P.O.

The prefixed asterisk indicates that the name of the Pastor appears in more than one place.

Parishes and Churche	Date.	Chapel Seats.	Members.	S. S. Teachers.	S. S. Scholars.	Local Preachers.	Pastors.	When Settled.
Kingston—								
East Queen-street	1816	1000	550	28	340	5	*W. Pratt, M.A. ..	1890
Hanover-street ..	1827	500	130	..	..	..	W. D. Brown ..	1895
St. Andrew—								
Ebenezer	1867	300	96	..	..	1	J. C. Duhaney ..	1866
Bethlehem ..	1868	300	60	..	..	1	" ..	1866
Temple Hall ..	1877	350	48	..	..	1	" ..	1877
Providence ..	1875	200	58	..	..	..	" ..	1875
Bethany	1877	200	20	..	..	..	*C. E. Henderson..	1892
Hope Hill	1886	150	126	12	113	2	*W. Pratt, M.A. ..	1891
Dallas Castle ..	1886	200	32	..	..	..	*E. H. Cunning ..	1891
Mount Privilege ..	1887	200	160	4	36	2	" ..	1887
Hopeful Ville ..	1887	200	34	..	..	1	" ..	1887
St. Thomas—								
Morant Bay ..	1867	650	310	12	165	4	A. P. Watson ..	1871
Prospect Pen ..	1868	600	235	7	95	3	" ..	1871
Arcadia	1868	500	280	10	210	3	" ..	1873
Hebron	1884	250	95	11	65	3	" ..	1884
Shiloh	1884	200	42	5	70	2	" ..	1884
Monklands ..	1867	400	460	7	111	4	E. Mowl	1895
Richmond	1872	250	319	5	66	7	" ..	1895
Minto Gap ..	1889	150	84	..	..	2	" ..	1895
River Head ..	1888	200	83	..	..	1	" ..	1895
Yallahs	1827	500	284	9	106	6	T. G. Somers ..	1893
Stokes Hall ..	1846	500	165	11	204	3	*W. P. Sibley ..	1890
Leith Hall	1864	400	180	6	107	3	" ..	1890
Sunning Hill ..	1887	300	142	3	43	2	*E. H. Cunning ..	1887

JAMAICA—*continued.*

Parishes and Churches.	Date.	Chapel Seats.	Members.	S. S. Teachers.	S. S. Scholars.	Local Preachers.	Pastors.	When Settled
Portland—								
Port Antonio ..	1856	400	102	8	115	..	S. C. Morris ..	1886
Tabernacle ..	1864	500	61	..	..	..	„ ..	1886
Hephzibah.. ..	1864	300	29	7	90	..	„ ..	1886
Belle Castle ..	1831	500	91	21	253	5	*W. P. Sibley ..	1890
St. Margaret's Bay	1871	400	83	..	..	1	R. R. James ..	1889
Mount Carmel ..	..	200	47	..	..	2	„ ..	1879
Beulah	1890	150	21	..	..	..	„ ..	1890
Fellowship ..	1871	400	297	..	..	..	„ ..	1891
Buff Bay	1824	500	158	9	98	4	W. J. Thompson	1895
Tranquillity ..	1873	300	106	..	..	2	„ ..	1895
Bethbara	1871	200	62	7	76	1	„ ..	1895
Mill Bank	1886	140	36	4	35	1	*E. H. Cunning ..	1886
Hope Bay	..	..	54					
St. Mary—								
Port Maria ..	1828	800	395	33	426	4	W. D. Henderson	1883
Oracabessa ..	1829	700	359	27	363	3	„ ..	1883
Mount Lebanon ..	1862	160	74	14	97	1	„ ..	1883
Zion Hill	1889	150	83	18	134	1	„ ..	1889
Annotto Bay ..	1824	1000	419	30	214	3	C. Barron ..	1890
Robin's Bay ..	..	100	29	..	..	..	„	
Clonmel	1862	350	132	16	131	2	*C.S.Brown ..	1892
Barronville ..	1888	150	92	8	84	1	„ ..	1891
Mount Angus ..	1842	600	406	30	308	2	„ ..	1890
Wallingford ..	1871	400	86	11	67	4	„ ..	1890
Wheeler's Mount ..	..	200	50	..	..	2	*J. Duthie ..	1890
Three Hills ..	1890	300	98	..	..	1	*F. Edmonds ..	1894
St. Catherine—								
Spanish Town (1)	1819	1000	484	..	..	..	*C. E. Henderson	1889
Sligoville	1836	300	160	..	..	..	„ ..	1889
Ebenezer, Spanish Town	1852	700	446	10	50	1	W. A. Tucker ..	1876
Hartlands	1872	200	75	7	103	..	„ ..	1876
Bower Wood ..	1890	300	80	..	..	..	„ ..	1890
Mount Nebo ..	1825	550	335	22	121	4	*J. Duthie	1889
Jericho	1834	1200	510	52	565	12	J. J. Kendon ..	1880
Mount Hermon ..	1834	1000	374	52	459	4	„ ..	1880
Ewarton	1884	700	223	36	261	6	„ ..	1884
Redwood	1887	250	124	15	235	6	„ ..	1887
Bybrook	1884	400	207	..	..	1	E. Arnett	1892
Zion Hill	1833	350	214	..	..	1	„ ..	1892
Linstead	1885	500	63	..	..	2	„ ..	1892
Buxton Town ..	1885	200	150	..	..	2	„ ..	1892
Mount Industry ..	1890	200	65	..	..	2	„ ..	1892
Old Harbour ..	1825	400	97	..	..	2	*J. T. Dillon ..	1892
Shiloh	1886	250	103	..	..	3	„ ..	1892
Brown's Hall ..	1847	200	61	..	..	1	„ ..	1892
Ebenezer	1860	..	46	..	..	..	*E. V. Donaldson..	1895
Point Hill	1835	600	315	28	213	3	*T. S. Johnson ..	1861
Mount Merrick ..	1843	400	201	18	240	3	„ ..	1868
Ashley Ville ..	1867	200	72	6	39	..	„ ..	1889
Lucky Valley ..	1879	..	102	4	50	2	Edward Jones ..	1878
Mount Olivet ..	1881	..	100	10	77	2	„ ..	1886
Shady Grove ..	1846	300	43	..	..	..	*G. Turner ..	1895

JAMAICA—*continued.*

Parishes and Churches.	Date	Chapel Seats.	Members	S. S. Teachers.	S. S. Scholars.	Local Preachers.	Pastors.	When settled.
Clarendon—								
Ebenezer, Four Paths	1834	400	263	12	109	3	*R. H. Hobson ..	1895
Jubilee	1844	300	236	..	..	3	*S. J. Washington	1895
Elim	1861	350	76	..	..	3	*R. H. Hobson ..	1895
Mount Zion ..	1848	300	186	14	204	3	*T. S. Johnson ..	1868
Bethlehem ..	1867	400	195	6	82	1	*E. V. Donaldson..	1895
Spring Mount ..	1870	250	60	..	..	..	" ..	1895
Croft's Hill ..	1888	400	72	..	..	..	*G. Turner ..	1895
Hayes	1829	600	108	..	..	..	*J. T. Dillon ..	1895
Enon	1859	300	91	9	57	5	*R. H. Hobson ..	1886
The Cross	1859	250	47	5	39	2	" ...	1888
Free Town ..	1886	200	90	..	..	2	*J. T. Dillon ..	1892
Rosewell	1888	250	87	..	..	2	" ..	1892
Mount Zion ..	1843	400	268	13	215	7	J. Yair and J. McCauly.	1894
Kilsythe	1860	300	237	7	75	..	" ..	1894
Leicesterfield ..	1878	250	203	13	161	6	" ..	1894
Smithville	1860	300	289	25	184	8	" ..	1894
Prospect	1878	400	149	10	143	3	" ..	1892
John Austins ..	1881	200	119	7	90	3	" ..	1892
Top Hill	1887	200	104	10	97	2	" ..	1892
Frankfield	..	..	62	..	..	2		
Douce	..	..	62	..	..	3		
John's Hall ..	1863	300	133	13	125	4	*W. Head	1888
Tweedside	1886	150	103	7	100	3	" ..	1886
Thompson Town..	1841	800	410	21	315	10	*G. Turner ..	1889
Staceyville	1839	600	210	22	144	5	" ..	1885
Paradise	1839	600	214	16	214	5	" ..	1885
Brandon Hill ..	1886	550	138	14	166	4	" ..	1886
Milk River.. ..	1869	450	90	13	142	3	*A. M. Gooden ..	1889
Whitefield	1844	250	84	6	116	2	" ..	1889
Manchester—								
Porus	1840	800	367	30	420	5	*S. J. Washington	1886
Mandeville ..	1840	300	178	11	131	3	" ..	1886
Zion Hill	1872	400	152	5	78	4	" ..	1886
Mount Lebanon ..	1872	400	52	5	50	3	*A. M. Gooden ..	1895
Harmon	1885	250	105	6	100	2	" ..	1886
Resource	1892	250	36	4	70	2	" ..	1886
St. Ann's—								
St. Ann's Bay ..	1830	1500	344	34	420	3	*G. House ..	1894
Liberty	1889	300	87	15	179	1	" ..	1889
Clark Town ..	1892	..	107	14	171	..	" ..	1892
Brown's Town ..	1829	1250	916	48	558	..	*G. E. Henderson	1879
Bethany	1836	800	467	2	53	..	" ..	1890
Stepney	1889	400	274	18	252	..	" ..	1889
Sturge Town ..	1857	400	164	21	169	..	" ..	1879
Moneague	1835	250	85	9	58	3	*J. Duthie .	1891
Harmony Vale ..	1835	300	60	6	65	2	J. Balfour, M.A (*acting*).	1895
Coultart Grove ..	1891	200	14	2	26	2	" ..	1895
Waltham	1877	350	209	20	154	6	*G. Turner ..	1885
Salem	1846	500	216	14	109	..	J. G. Bennett ..	1854
Grateful Hill ..	1843	400	201	5	75	..	*G. E. Henderson	1894

JAMAICA—*continued.*

Parishes and Churches.	Date.	Chapel Seats.	Members.	S. S. Teachers.	S. S. Scholars.	Local Preachers.	Pastors.	When Settled.
St. Ann's (*contd.*)—								
Ocho Rios	1830	1000	250	30	224	3	*F. Edmonds ..	1894
Orange Park ..	1891	200	62	4	73	..	" ..	1894
Clarksonville ..	1841	400	367	23	207	5	*W. Head ..	1881
Mount Moriah ..	1870	250	94	5	64	2	" ..	1881
Gibraltar	1858	700	444	24	270	3	*W. M. Webb ..	1862
Jarretton	1891	450	135	17	175	3	" ..	1891
Keith	1894	200	70	9	103	2	" ..	1894
Trelawny—								
Falmouth	1827	2000	623	22	326	2	J. Kingdon ..	1868
Unity	1835	500	408	35	326	1	" ..	1861
Refuge	1839	900	448	..	..	2	E. Fray ..	1891
Kettering	1844	500	321	18	222	5	" ..	1891
Clarkstown ..	1883	700	198	14	523	4	" ..	1891
Stewart Town ..	1829	700	372	23	271	3	*W. M. Webb ..	1862
The Alps	1840	250	83	12	66	3	" ..	1888
Waldensia	1838	700	374	32	352	6	A. G. Eccleston ..	1894
Trittonville ..	..	..	98	10	85			
Rio Bueno	1829	700	356	43	405	3	J. J. Steele ..	1869
Ulster Spring ..	1871	400	297	19	183	4	P. O'Meally ..	1860
Ebenezer	1852	400	168	16	130	2	" ..	1860
Hastings	1842	700	557	37	370	6	*P. F. Schoburgh ..	1888
Worsup	1863	250	78	11	85	..	W. J. Mornan ..	1894
Litchfield Mountain	1885	300	79	..	..	..	" ..	1894
Freeman Hall ..	1889	250	35	..	..	..	" ..	1894
St. James—								
Montego Bay (1) ..	1824	2000	457	..	..	4	H. L. Webster ..	1895
Montego Bay (2) ..	1849	900	647	33	283	..	*C. Chapman ..	1888
Salter's Hill ..	1825	1700	581	37	310	6	W. N. Brown ..	1884
Sudbury	1879	800	201	34	245	2	" ..	1884
Lottery	1893	200	96	17	174	1	" ..	
Bethtephil	1835	700	593	31	486	1	*P. F. Schoburgh	1888
Mount Carey ..	1838	1800	863	61	877	4	*E. J. Hewett ..	1883
Shortwood ..	1835	800	548	41	676	..	*P. Williams ..	1883
Maldon	1865	700	384	38	394	..	*T. C. Hutchins E. J. Touzalin ..	1874 1894
Springfield ..	1881	400	302	38	390	..	*T. C. Hutchins ..	1874
Bass Grove ..	1875	200	77	9	123	..	" ..	1874
Buckingham ..	1894	200	87	..	..	..	" ..	1894
Hanover—								
Lucea	1827	1500	202	12	145	2	W. Burke ..	1872
Mount Moriah ..	1878	300	127	13	108	2	" ..	1878
Claremont	..	..	69	..	..	1		
Fletcher's Grove ..	1841	400	131	6	70	..	*C. Chapman ..	1889
Watford Hill ..	1838	800	405	27	221	1	W. M. Christie ..	1894
Friendship	1881	300	164	23	218	1	" ..	1894
Gurney's Mount ..	1830	700	440	27	310	4	" ..	1894
Mount Peto ..	1851	300	411	27	371	4	*E. J. Hewett ..	1893
Green Island ..	1831	600	74	8	96	2	*R. E. Bennett ..	1888
Kendal	1894	180	62	..	..	3	" ..	1894

JAMAICA—*continued.*

Parishes and Churches.	Date.	Chapel Seats.	Members.	S. S. Teachers.	S. S. Scholars.	Local Preachers.	Pastors.	When Settled.
Westmoreland—								
Savannah-la-Mar ..	1829	1000	241	13	144	2	A. G. Kirkham ..	1885
Sutcliffe Mount ..	1868	500	332	28	279	3	" ..	1885
Grace Hill	1888	250	138	14	139	4	" ..	1888
Bethel Town ..	1838	800	627	54	896	3	*P. Williams ..	1867
St. Leonards ..	1893	400	78	11	229	..	" ..	
Fullersfield ..	1828	600	167	15	116	1	*R. E. Bennett ..	1886
Townhead	1890	280	106	8	95	3	Isaac S. Tate ..	1889
Williamsfield ..	1890	200	111	9	93	2	" ..	1887
St. Elizabeth—								
Sharon	1873	500	133	11	158	1	S. I. Marson ..	1888
Burn's Savannah ..	1880	250	98	8	114	1	" ..	1888
Hewett's View ..	1848	300	146	11	110	2	T. E. Marston ..	1891
Nightingale Grove	1879	250	79	6	98	3	" ..	1891
Arlington	1886	150	54	4	56	2	" ..	1891
Wallingford ..	1852	700	258	23	272	5	C. Sibley ..	1886
Vauxhall	1840	300	133	12	89	3	" ..	1889
Elderslie	1879	200	95	10	74	2	" ..	1887
Cayman Islands—								
Ebenezer	1887	200	63	8	75	2		
Sobeyville	1887	180	45	..	..	1		
Union Tabernacle	1892	200	31	4	44	1		
Little Cayman ..	1887	150	21	2	12	1		

HAYTI.

(*Population*, 550,000.)

Churches.	Date.	Chapel Seats.	Members.	S. S. Teachers.	S. S. Scholars.	Local Preachers.	Pastor or Missionary.	When Settled.
Port-au-Prince ..	1890	200	26	3	20	1	†L. Hippolyte, M.A.	1890
Jacmel	1845	300	54	5	42			
Cape Hayti	1855	150	24	4	20	2	†R. H. Rowe ..	1894
Fort Liberté	1887	60	9	2	9	2	" ..	1894
Le Trou	1887	50	19	3	17	..	" ..	1894
Port de Paix	..	50	24	1	4	2	" ..	1894
St. Marc	1871	..	30	..	50	..	Geo. Angus ..	1874

† Missionaries of Jamaica Baptist Missionary Society.

THE BAHAMAS.

BAPTIST MISSIONARY SOCIETY.

(*Population*, 48,000.)

Principal Stations.	Formed.	Missionaries.	Stations and Sub-Stations.	Membr's	S. S. Teach'rs	S. S. Scholars	Bap-tisms.
Nassau	1833	C. A. Dann,	67	3,412	303	2,510	178
Inagua	1853	Miss Dann					

SAN DOMINGO, TURK'S ISLAND, AND CAICOS.

BAPTIST MISSIONARY SOCIETY.

Principal Stations.	Formed.	Missionaries.	Stations and Sub-Stations.	Membr's	S. S. Teach'rs	S. S. Scholars	Bap-tisms.
St. Domingo, Puerto Plata	1843	J. H. Pusey	13	888	96	969	48
Monte Christi	1880						
Grand Turk	..						
Salt Cay	..						
Kingston..	..						

TRINIDAD.

BAPTIST MISSIONARY SOCIETY.

Principal Stations.	Formed.	Missionaries.	Stations and Sub-Stations.	Membr's	S. S. Teach'rs	S. S. Scholars	Bap-tisms.
Port of Spain	1843	R. E. Gammon and Mrs. Gammon	23	1,104	41	509	64
San Fernando	1861						

CUBA.

(*Population*, 2,000,000.)

SOUTHERN BAPTIST CONVENTION OF AMERICA.

(HOME MISSION BOARD.)

5 stations; 24 missionaries; 2,698 members; 7 Sunday schools having 900 scholars; 118 baptisms.

CENTRAL AMERICA AND VARIOUS ISLANDS.

(*Population*, 3,053,000.)

Churches.	Date.	Chapel Seats.	Members.	S. S. Teachers.	S. S. Scholars.	Local Preachers.	Pastor or Missionary.	When Settled.
COSTA RICA—								
Port Limon ..	1889	450	100	9	110	4	†J. H. Sobey ..	1888
							†J. Hayter ..	1893
B. HONDURAS—								
Belize	..	400	312	25	300	8	†C. Brown ..	1889
Crooked Tree ..	..	150	..	12	150	4		
S. HONDURAS, RUATAN—								
Flowers Bay ..	..	200	90	10	100	6	C. C. Tharpe ..	1894
West End	..	..						
Coxen's Hole ..	..	..						
Oak Ridge.. ..	..	..	85	..	..	..	R. Cleghorn ..	1891
Bocas del Toro ..	..	..	71	7	108	1	†A. W. Meredith..	1894

† Missionaries of Jamaica Baptist Missionary Society.

SOUTH AMERICA.

ARGENTINE REPUBLIC.*

(*Population*, 4,200,000.)

Churches.	Date.	Chapel Seats.	Members.	S. S. Teachers.	S. S. Scholars.	Local Preachers.	Baptisms.	Pastor.	When Settled.
Buenos Ayres ..	1882	..	42	6	60	..	5	Paul Besson ..	1882
Santa Fé ..	..	..	45						
Quilmes ..	..	..	3						
Las Flores ..	..	..	5						

* No returns for 1894.

BRAZIL.

(*Population*, 14,000,000.)

SOUTHERN BAPTIST CONVENTION OF AMERICA.

Stations.	Date formed.	Missionaries.	Churches.	Out Stations.	Members.	S. S. Scholars.	Baptisms.
Rio de Janeiro ..	1884	W. B. Bagby and wife, J. J. Alves..	2	3	63	..	5
Juis de Fora..	..	J. J. Taylor and wife ..	2	2	26	..	9
Barbacena ..	..	Rodrigues da Silva					
Bahia—	1882	Z. C. Taylor, R. E. Neighbour, José Dominquez	1	4	139	..	6
Maceio ..	..	Jos. Aden, Joao Baptista	1	5	66	..	9
Valenca ..	..	Antonio Morgues	1	3	71	..	11
Alogoinhas ..	..	.. ..	1	..	3	..	..
Campos	1890	S. L. Ginsburg and wife, A. Campos	1	2	122	50	48
San Fidelas ..	..	Jcas Manhaes..	2	..	11	..	7
Pernambuco ..	1889	W. E. Entzminger and wife ..	1	..	61	..	28
V. Grande	..	.. ..	1	4	18	..	10
Santa Barbara ..	..	.. ..	1	..	30	..	..
		Totals	14	23	610	50	133

PATAGONIA.

Church	Formed.	Sittings.	Members.	Teachers	Scholars.	Pastor.	Settl d.
Brondeg, Chupat ..	1877	200	24	4	46		

AUSTRALASIA.

NEW SOUTH WALES.

(*Population*, 1,268,150.)

BAPTIST UNION OF NEW SOUTH WALES.

Formed 1868.

Chairman for 1895-96—Mr. HUGH DIXSON. *Vice-Chairman*—Rev. SETH JONES.
Hon. Treasurer—Mr. JOHN WELLS.
Hon. Secretary—Rev. F. E. HARRY, Darlinghurst, Sydney.
Hon. Treasurer Foreign Missionary Society—Mr. W. H. BURTON.
Hon. Secretary Foreign Missionary Society—Rev. F. HIBBERD.
Denominational Paper—*New South Wales Baptist*. *Editor*—Rev. E. PRICE.

Churches.	Formed.	Chapel Seats.	Members.	S. S. Teachers	S. S Scholars.	Local Preachers.	Baptisms.	Pastor.	Settled.
Ashfield	1884	200	112	21	178	..	19		
Auburn	1889	150	43	12	168	..	5	J. Straughen ..	1889
Balmain	1882	150	74	14	140	..	6	W. Taylor ..	1891
Bathurst	1863	300	117	..	..	..	16	J. Worboys ..	1893
Bournewood ..	1892	..	..	..	..	..	..	J. Mayo	1893
Burwood	1895	..	25	7	36	..	2		
Garra	1889	150	66	8	62	10	4	J. Mayo	1893
Goulburn	1893	..	58	9	120	1	23	D. J. Graham ..	1893
Grafton	1876	500	50	13	134	2	11	C. Stark	1893
Granville	1888	150	23	6	83	..	..	J. Straughen ..	1888
Hinton	1857	250	29	5	90	2	4		
Islington	1888	150	56	13	125	..	8	S. Sharp	1893
Kal Kal	1895	..	8	..	..	..	..	J. K. McIntyre ..	1895
Kingsgrove and Rockdale	1881	100	22	3	48	3	..	C. Palmer ..	1895
Leichardt	..	130	41						
Lower Southgate ..	1881	100	20	..	..	..	..	T. H. Jaggers ..	1881
Marrickville	1887	150	50	..	..	..	4		
New England ..	1883	100	61	11	126	8	6	S. Hotston ..	1891
Newcastle	1860	500	136	21	284	..	7	S. Jones	1885
Newtown	1860	650	163	23	210	5	17	W. Coller ..	1889
Orange	1869	200	22	5	33	2	4	W. A. Southwell	1893
Parramatta	1851	300	66	9	79	2	3	J. Straughen ..	1882
Petersham	1882	500	307	30	496	2	18	T. Porter ..	1894
Plattsburg	1860	300	83	17	125	..	11	H. Halmarick ..	1892
Rooty Hill	1887	150	11	3	29	..	..	J. D. Brown ..	1887
Smithfield	1857	100	8						
Springhill	1869	..	23	..	..	..	..	W. A. Southwell	1893
Sydney:—									
Bathurst-street ..	1836	700	167	14	112	..	21	F. E. Harry ..	1892
Harris-street ..	1862	400	127	16	135	2	2.	H. Clark ..	1892
Burton-street ..	1871	700	216	31	360	..	15	W. R. Hiddlestone	1891
Tamworth	1890	300	29	..	..	..	..	M. H. Morris ..	1890
Thalaba	1881	150	69	6	40	7	10	R. J. Middleton	1890
Woollahra	1885	250	31	7	64	2			
Totals ..	..	7780	2313	304	3277	48	235		

Honorary Members of Union:—Revs. F. Hibberd, J. Voller, and E. Price, Personal Members:—Revs. J. Moss, W. V. Young, W. G. Wilson, H. R. Pigott. and Mr. J. A. Packer.

Affiliated Home Missions: In Blackheath, Rev. W. Page; Burwood and Carlton, Rev. C. Palmer; Wyalong, Rev. Keith McIntyre. Preaching stations, 49.

Baptist Foreign Missionary Society, Ladies' Zenana Missionary Society, and Girls' Zenana Aid Society. Field of operations, Tipperah, E. Bengal (*see* page 421).
Missionaries—Misses Lynne and Middleton.

VICTORIA.

(*Population in* 1895, 1,174,000.)

BAPTIST UNION OF VICTORIA.

President—Rev. F. J. WILKIN, B.A., Kerang.
Vice-President—Mr. W. G. STEPHENS, Malvern Road, Toorak.
Hon. Treasurer—Mr. R. STONE, Royal Arcade, Melbourne.
Hon. Secretary—Mr. C. W. WALROND, Cotham Road, Kew.

HOME MISSIONARY SOCIETY.

For establishing Churches and carrying on Mission Work. Expenditure, £2,340.
Hon. Secretary—Mr. C. W. WALROND, Cotham Road, Kew.
Hon. Treasurer—Mr. J. HIGGINS, 62, Elizabeth Street, Melbourne.
General Superintendent—Rev. F. J. WILKIN, B.A., Kerang.
Sixteen agents are employed, who conduct services at seventy-eight stations.

FOREIGN MISSIONS.

Hon. Secretary—Rev. A. W. WEBB, Aberdeen Street, Geelong.
Hon. Treasurer—Mr. D. C. REES, 209, Punt Road, Prahran.
Mission Field—Maimensing, Eastern Bengal (*see* page 421). Expenditure £1,068.

BAPTIST COLLEGE, MELBOURNE.

President—Rev. S. CHAPMAN, Baptist Church, Collins Street.
Principal—Rev. W. T. WHITLEY, M.A., LL.M. (Cantab.), 32, Jolimont Terrace East Melbourne.
Hon. Secretary—Mr. H. S. MARTIN, B.A., LL.B., Wattletree Road, Malvern.
Training five students for work in Victoria and one for New South Wales.

VICTORIAN BAPTIST FUND.

Chairman—Rev. S. CHAPMAN, Baptist Church, Collins Street.
Hon. Treasurer—Mr. W. G. STEPHENS, Malvern Road, Toorak.
The Fund amounts to £64,659.
Denominational Paper—*The Southern Baptist* (Bi-monthly).

Church.	Date.	Chapel Seats.	Members.	S. S. Teachers.	S. S. Scholars.	Local Preachers.	Pastor.	Settled.
(Metropolitan.)								
Albert Park	1890	350	110	22	232	2		
Port Melbourne	..	..	..	12	150			
Bacchus Marsh ..	1867	100	26	8	70	2	J. C. Martin ..	1894
Balwyn	1891	250	40	8	52			
Brighton	1852	200	139	14	148	2	J. E. Harrison ..	1895
Brunswick	1861	675	261	26	478	6	J. Carson.. ..	1894
Camberwell	1891	..	68	19	200			
Carlton	1883	350	91	20	225	1	W. Clark	1892
Clifton Hill	1890	..	67	15	250			
Coburg	1890	220	49	9				
Collingwood	1874	1,500	81	45	535			
Elsternwick	1894	..	21	8	73			
Essendon	1894	..	21	8	56	1		

VICTORIA—*continued.*

Church.	Date.	Chapel Seats.	Members.	S. S. Teachers.	S. S. Scholars.	Local Preachers.	Pastor.	Settled.
Fitzroy	1863	575	320	39	377	1	E. Isaac	1894
Footscray	1883	300	67	13	138	1		
Hawthorn	1888	500	204	29	293	4		
Kew	1856	300	113	19	163	..	S. Howard ..	1894
Lilydale	1880	120	68	9	74			
Wandin	..	..	..	4	30			
Melbourne:—								
Albert-street ..	1850	675	238	14	83	..	T. J. Malyon ..	1894
Collins-street ..	1843	1,000	637	9	62	8	S. Chapman ..	1877
Bouverie-st. ..	..	400	..	15	111			
Hoddle-st. ..	..	250	..	18	141			
Little Bourke-st.	..	250						
South, Dorcas-st...	1865	600	248	28	243	..	H. G. Blackie ..	1894
West, Victoria-st.	1870	..	251	35	334	8		
Friendly Soc. Hall	..	..	..	12	129			
Moonee Ponds ..	1892	225	73	18	137	1	A. Steele	1895
Murrumbeena ..	1890	250	35	8	77	3		
Newmarket	1886	200	106	16	147	..	A. Steele	1895
Prahran	1879	..	60	8	52	..	J. J. Mackenzie ..	1879
Richmond	1870	260	54	21	217	..	J. H. Carter ..	1894
South Yarra	1854	450	245	27	316	15		
Malvern	..	..	..	3	28			
St. Kilda, Crimea-st.	1864	400	84	11	90	..	R. Williamson ..	1893
Blanch-st.	1880	..	35	7	57	..	J. T. Evans ..	1887
Williamstown, Cecil-st.	1868	350	123	26	179	6		
(Country Districts)								
Ballarat	1860	600	341	20	400	4	J. A. Soper ..	1894
Bendigo	1859	400	148	33	261	3	G. Weller ..	1892
Castlemaine	1861	400	96	15	116	3	W. A. Whitney ..	1880
Wesley Hill ..	..	150						
Daylesford	1886	180	39	10	70	..	D. Corbet.. ..	1894
Eaglehawk	1868	150	27	7	45	..	W. C. Tayler ..	1891
Echuca	1887	170	43	16	122	..	A. A. Medley ..	1894
Geelong Aberdeen-st.	1852	550	271	32	290	12	A. W. Webb ..	1890
Belmont	..	200	..	5	79			
Breakwater ..	..	150	..	3	18			
Fenwick-st. ..	1857	300	145	13	110	..	W. J. Eddy ..	1888
Hamilton	1867	200	110	14	99	1	C. Pickering ..	1893
North Hamilton	..	50	..	3	33			
South Hamilton	..	50	..	3	30			
Kyneton	1860	250	60	10	60	2	J. H. Pryce ..	1892
East Tylden ..	..	60						
Laang	..	..	14	..	..	1		
Maldon	1860	290	107	10	94	..	T. Beeson ..	1887
Parkins Reef ..	..	50						
Portland	1859	300	71	13	75	4	J. R. Cooper ..	1887
Sebastopol	1864	150	5	3	19			
Stawell	1892	400	42	5	73	..	F. Clemens ..	1894
Warrnambool ..	1864	350	131	21	173	8	F. Boyling ..	1895
White Hills	1858	150	28	6	65	2		

VICTORIA—*continued.*

Church.	Date.	Chapel Seats.	Members.	S. S. Teachers.	S. S. Scholars.	Local Preachers.	Pastor.	Settled.
(Home Mission.)								
Beechworth	1888	150	35	3	16	1	*F. Harris	1893
Cohuna	1892	120	21	4	30	5		
Crymelon and District	1890	90	34	5	49	6		
Beulah	..	60	..	3	28	..	*W. Robertson ..	1893
Brentwood ..	..	60						
Brim								
Goyura								
Hopetoun ..	..	80	..	..	..	..	*W. Kennedy ..	1895
Pepper's Plains	..	60						
Warracknabeal	1895	130	..	..	..	..	*E. Dybing ..	1892
Goulburn Valley ..	1885	..	63	..	30	4		
Shepparton ..	..	100	..	..	..	..	*S. Pitman ..	1893
Tatura	..	200	..	..	..	..	*G. B. W. Filmer ..	1893
Kerang and District..	1883	120	43	7	74	11	F. J. Wilkin, B.A.	1881
Barrapoort ..	..	100	..	2	29	..	*H. Stewart ..	1894
Benjeroop ..	..	110	..	3	27	..	*H. H. Jeffs ..	1895
Macorna ..	..	90	..	2	29	..	*M. L. Murphy ..	1895
Minmindie ..	..	100	..	2	26			
Tragowel ..	..	100	..	3	29			
Koondrook	1892	100	21	3	27	5	*W. O. Ward ..	1893
Koroit..	1864	200	8	2	17	3	*H. D. Archer ..	1895
Korumburra	1895	150	..	..	..	2	*J. Pollock ..	1895
Newport	..	150						
Oxley and District ..	1888	150	59	3	20	1	*J. Ottaway ..	1895
Wangaratta East	..	120	..	2	20			
Port Campbell ..	1884	80	14	..	..	2	*A. Robertson ..	1893
Sea Lake	..	..	..	..	..	..	*J. J. Proctor ..	1895
Totals.. ..	..	18,920	5,911	889	8,630	141		

* Home Mission Agents.

Baptisms in 1894, 466; cost of buildings, £122,319; debts on buildings, £14,536; members, Y.P.S.C.E. 1,268.

There is a Particular Baptist Association of Australasia, to which belong six churches in Victoria; secretary, Pastor F. Fullard, Ebenezer Church, Victoria Parade, Melbourne.

SOUTH AUSTRALIA.

(*Population*, [*estimated*] 347,120.)

SOUTH AUSTRALIAN BAPTIST UNION.

President—Mr. W. GILBERT, M.P. *Vice-President*—Rev. W. GILMOUR.

Hon. Secretaries: General—Rev. G. HOGBEN. *Finance*—Mr. N. J. HONE.

Minute—Rev. A. HYDE.

Treasurer—Mr. J. R. FOWLER.

Committee Room—Flinders Street Baptist Church, Adelaide.

Denominational Paper—*Southern Baptist*.

* An asterisk against a Pastor's name indicates that he has the oversight of more than one church

Church.	Date.	Sittings.	Members.	S.S. Teachers.	S.S. Scholars.	Local Preachers.	Pastor.	When Settled.
Adelaide, North ..	1848	570	444	50	640	..	E. H. Ellis ..	1894
Adelaide, South ..	1861	940	413	37	420	7	Silas Mead, M.A., LL.D. J. G. Raws ..	1861 1895
Alberton	1862	400	223	20	300	5		
Aldinga	1867	120	32	7	70	..	*J. H. Sexton ..	1893
Angaston	1849	300	55	10	75	..	J. Barker	1889
Appila	1879	90	46	5	60	..	* C. F. Smith ..	1892
Barootа	1885	90	13	5	24	3	*T. Dowding ..	1890
Black Rock	1889	140	60	10	95	..	*E. Bungay ..	1893
Broken Hill, N.S.W.	1888	275	68	12	130	4	T. E. Jones ..	1895
Broken Hill, South ..	1890	300	71	12	180	..	*E. J. Tuck ..	1890
Broken Hill, West ..	1890	120	24	11	129	..	*E. J. Tuck ..	1891
Clare	1889	120	63	7	63	2	E. B. Turner ..	1893
Clover Hill	1873	100	25	5	37	4	*J. Nancarrow ..	1894
Coromandel	1858	100	39	7	77	3	*R. Woolcock ..	1888
Coobowie	1885	60	..	..	..	..	*J. R. Wallbank ..	1894
Curramulka	1881	80	8	2	25	1	*J. R. Wallbank ..	1894
Diamond Lake ..	1876	50	..	..	..	..	*J. R. Wallbank ..	1894
Gawler	1866	280	151	25	206	5	D. Davis	1893
George-town	1874	120	16	6	40	..	*J. Nancarrow ..	1894
Glen Osmond ..	1883	200	54	14	165	3	*S. Fairey	1893
Goodwood	1877	400	91	23	320	5	*A. Hyde	1893
Grange	1884	70	8	5	43	..	*G. J. Clarke ..	1893
Gumeracha	1843	250	86	9	82	3	*E. J. Henderson	1893
Hilton..	1871	200	28	8	91	1	*G. J. Clarke ..	1884
Hindmarsh	1876	450	91	15	210	1		
Jamestown	1875	180	41	6	60	..	R. Taylor ..	1895
Kapunda	1865	500	68	19	123	5	A. Metters ..	1893
Kenton Valley ..	1849	250	24	4	30	2	*E. J. Henderson	1893
Knightsbridge ..	1884	120	22	7	50	..	*S. Fairey	1894
Laura	1876	150	112	17	166	3	*C. F. Smith.. ..	1892
Lyndoch	1859	150	33	4	35	..	J. Renney ..	1890
Magill	1858	200	86	10	121	2	*G. Hogben ..	1881

SOUTH AUSTRALIA—*continued.*

Church.	Date.	Sittings.	Members.	S. S. Teachers.	S. S. Scholars.	Local Preachers.	Pastor.	When Settled.
Mannum	1888	140	46	9	90	3	H. E. Hughes ..	1895
Minlacowie	1875	84	18	..	..	..	*J. R. Wallbank ..	1894
Minlaton	1877	150	54	6	46	6	*J. R. Wallbank ..	1894
Mitcham	1858	250	77	11	130	3	*R. Woolcock ..	1888
Morphett Vale ..	1865	266	44	5	50	..	*J. H. Sexton ..	1893
Mount Barker ..	1873	180	81	9	97	..	John Price ..	1881
Mount Gambier ..	1864	250	57	8	66	..	J. Paynter ..	1893
Norton's Summit ..	1876	150	50	5	70	3	*G. Hogben ..	1881
Norwood	1867	562	256	34	436	5	C. Bright	1892
Orroroo	1880	150	52	10	96	2	*E. Bungay ..	1893
Parkside	1880	350	144	16	267	..	R. McCullough ..	1893
Petersburg	1882	208	102	14	130	3	W. Gilmour ..	1893
Port Pirie	1884	350	64	9	80	3	*T. Dowding ..	1890
Richmond	1894	150	17	8	96	..	*A. Hyde	1894
Saddleworth	1869	130	37	3	13	5	*F. J. Steward ..	1890
Salt Creek	1862	150	16	..	..	..	*W. O. Ashton ..	1890
Sanderston	1884	130	29	3	12	5	*W. O. Ashton ..	1890
Semaphore	1878	330	181	19	260	..	W. Bell, M.A. ..	1893
Stockport	1868	200	22	4	22	3	*F. J. Steward ..	1890
South Rhine	1867	150	24	..	..	..	*W. O. Ashton ..	1890
Southwark	1884	300	94	26	221	2	J. Murray	1891
Tarlee	1868	120	39	6	42	3	*F. J. Steward ..	1890
Tea Tree Gully ..	1860	150	47	9	72			
Telowie	1878	80	28	3	33	..	*T. Dowding ..	1890
Terowie	1877	140	81	12	99	2	*R. Grant	1892
Wayville	1894	100	19	10	80	..	T. Adcock ..	1894
Yorketown	1883	60	36	3	33	..	*J. R. Wallbank ..	1894
PREACHING STATIONS—								
Beetaloo	..	..	..	2	25	..	*C. F. Smith ..	
Blumberg	..	..	..	6	87	..	*E. J. Henderson	
Brown Hill Creek ..	..	50	..	..	..	..	*R. Woolcock ..	
Finsbury Park ..	..	100	..	3	29			
Forreston	..	..	..	4	50	..	*E. J. Henderson	
Parnaroo	..	60	..	..	..	..	*R. Grant	
Prairie	..	50	..	4	30	..	*E. J. Henderson	
Totals	..	12,915	4,210	633	6,829	107		

Value of property, churches, schools, manses, £83,312. Amount raised for all purposes during the year from 1st September, 1893, to 31st August, 1894, £11,170. Debt on churches, schools, and manses, £11,640. Baptisms for the year, 152.

FURREEDPORE MISSION.—*Secretary*—Rev. R. MCCULLOUGH, Parkside. *Mission Field*—Furreedpore and Pubna, Eastern Bengal (*see* page 421).

SOUTH AUSTRALIAN BAPTIST BUILDING AND JUBILEE FUND.—*Capital*—£6,875. *Secretary*—Mr. J. T. MELLOR.

AGED MINISTERS' RELIEF FUND.—*Secretary*—Mr. WILLIAM NEILL. *Capital*—£4,798.

"JAMES WHITE" FUND (for relief of aged or poor Baptists).—*Secretary*—Mr. A. S. NEILL. *Capital*—£750.

FURREEDPORE BIBLE SOCIETY.—*Secretary*—Rev. G. HOGBEN.

QUEENSLAND.

(*Population*, 393,718. *Census* 1891.)

BAPTIST ASSOCIATION OF QUEENSLAND.

OFFICERS FOR 1895-6:—

President—Rev. J. B. SNEYD. *Vice-President*—Rev. J. GLOVER.

Treasurer—Mr. W. C. POOLE. *Secretary*—Rev. W. HIGLETT.

Denominational Paper—*The Queensland Baptist* (monthly).

Church.	When Formed.	Sittings.	Members.	S. S. Teachers.	S. S. Scholars.	Local Preachers.	Pastor	When Settled.
BRISBANE DISTRICT:								
City Tabernacle ..	1855	800	371	25	205	5	William Whale ..	1885
Samford Road ..	..	250	..	5	60			
Taringa	..	200	..	14	114			
Jireh	1861	250	97	17	190	3	John Kingsford ..	1862
Petrie Terrace ..	1870	300	64	14	172	2	John Alexander ..	1891
Oxford Estate ..	..	130						
South Brisbane ..	1872	300	151	18	200	..	William Poole ..	1880
Fairfield ..	..	100	..	8	100			
Thompson Estate	..	120	..	8	116			
Windsor Road ..	1877	400	170	30	231	..	Thomas Leitch ..	1878
Toowong	1881	200	39	11	90	2	A. G. Weller ..	1895
Albion	1892	150	58	13	181	1	William Higlett ..	1890
Bulimba	..	100	..	5	50			
Ipswich	1859	350	83	11	103	7		
Dinmore	..	180	..	6	60	2		
Rockhampton ..	1862	215	92	14	120	..	Edwin R. Makin	1895
Toowoomba	1875	180	68	6	65	1	John Glover ..	1894
Murphy's Creek ..								
Koojarewon	1894	100	19	3	25	..	Ezekiel Barnett ..	1894
Engelsburg (German)	1875	300	152	3	45	3	Carl Krueger ..	1886
Boonah	..	100						
Fassifern Scrub ..	..	..	..	3	30			
Maryborough ..	1883	150	108	10	85	1	C. Boyall	1885
Minden (German) ..	1884	120	61	2	22	1	August Schmidt	
Hatton Vale ..								
Laidley								
Redland Bay ..								
Lower Freestone Creek (Danish) ..	1886	..	19	2	16	..	J. P. Hansen ..	1892
Swan Creek ..								

QUEENSLAND—*continued.*

Church.	When Formed.	Sittings.	Members.	S. S. Teachers.	S. S. Scholars.	Local Preachers.	Pastor.	When Settled.
Sandgate	1887	400	53	6	100	..	J. B. Sneyd	1894
Rosewood	1887	200	74	6	70	6	Thos. U. Symonds	1893
Marburg	..	..	..	2	15			
Rosevale	..	..	..	3	20			
Grandchester ..								
Townsville	1888	..	54	9	120	5	F. G. Buckingham	1892
Black River ..								
Charters Towers ..	1888	220	63	11	156	..	Thomas Vigis ..	1889
Sellheim								
Hendra	1888	300	45	19	185	..	H. Cairns, M.A...	1895
Coolabunia	1890	50	11	4	15			
Beandesert	..	..	..	3	30			
Nundah	..	..	..	..	..	..	A. D. Shaw ..	1893
Totals	..	6,165	1,852	291	2,991	39		

Baptisms 91.

QUEENSLAND BAPTIST MISSIONARY SOCIETY.—*President*, Rev. J. B. SNEYD. *Treasurer*, Mr. W. R. SMITH. *Secretary*, Rev. A. G. WELLER. *Mission Station*, Noakhali, Eastern Bengal (*see* page 421). *Expenditure*, £300 per annum.

GERMAN BAPTIST CHURCHES, NOT IN THE ASSOCIATION.

Church.	When Formed.	Sittings.	Members.	S. S. Teachers.	S. S. Scholars.	Local Preachers.	Pastor.	When Settled.
Fernvale, Brisbane River	1870	100	81	3	25	2	Wilhelm Litzow..	1870
Lowood								
Esk								
Sandy Creek ..								
Marburg	1887	200	35	..	..	..	Gottfried Nitz ..	1890
Sandy Creek ..								
Ma. Ma. Creek ..								
Marburg (Bethel) ..	1880	150	55					
Mount Walker ..	1872							
McGrath's Water-course								

NEW ZEALAND.

(*Population*, 668,181.)

BAPTIST UNION OF NEW ZEALAND.

President—Rev. W. R. WOOLLEY, Thames.

Vice-President—Mr. H. OLNEY, Christchurch.

Treasurer—Mr. J. T. GARLICK, Auckland.

Secretary—Rev. A. H. COLLINS, Ponsonby, Auckland.

Committee—Revs. A. NORTH, A. DEWDNEY, J. BLAIKIE, J. J. DOKE, and Mr. G. CARSON.

Students' Committee—Revs. A. DEWDNEY, A. NORTH, Messrs. H. B. KIRK, M.A., and H. H. DRIVER.

Evangelistic Committee—Revs. J. BLAIKIE and A. NORTH, C. DALLASTON, and Mr. W. INGS.

Union Solicitor—Mr. HERBERT WEBB, Dunedin.

NEW ZEALAND BAPTIST MISSIONARY SOCIETY.

Established 1885.

Officers for the year 1894-5.

President—Rev. W. R. WOOLLEY, Thames.

Vice-President—Mr. H. OLNEY, Christchurch

Treasurer—Mr. S. G. MARTIN, " National Mutual," Wellington.

Secretary—Rev. H. H. DRIVER, George-street, Dunedin.

Committee—The above and the Executive of the Union.

Mission Field.—Bramanbaria, N. Tipperah, E. Bengal (see page 421).

Income—£700.

Denominational Organ—*The New Zealand Baptist*.

Churches.	Date.	Sittings	Members	Teachers	Scholars	Local Preacher	Pastor.	Settled
NORTH ISLAND—								
Auckland	1852	1300	565	59	440	0	J. Blaikie.. ..	1892
Otahuhu	..	100						
Mount Eden	1886	230	96	24	132			
Ponsonby	1880	400	18	25	173		A. H. Collins ..	1893
Minnisdale	1866	..	10	2	30		E. S. Brookes ..	1867
Napier	1887	200	65		72	3	G. D. Cox ..	1894
New Plymouth	1893	150	41	8	50		W. Drew	1893
Palmerston, North ..	..	..	15				J. Muirhead ..	1896
Thames	1869	300	28	19	16		W. R. Woolley ..	1883

NEW ZEALAND—*continued.*

Churches.	Date.	Sittings.	Members.	Teachers.	Scholars.	Local Preachers.	Pastor.	Settled.
Wanganui	1882	150	57	11	92	3	H. Peters.. ..	1893
Wellington	1878	300	213	20	208	10	C. Dallaston ..	1891
Kilbirnie	..	..	..	5	42			
Ohiro	..	..	..	9	109			
SOUTH ISLAND—								
Ashburton	1882	100	46	8	41			
Caversham	1872	400	55	16	129	5		
Mornington	..	..	24	..	..	1		
Portobello								
Hooper's Inlet ..								
Caversham (John-st.) ..	1884	300	93	21	159			
Christchurch	1871	700	274	27	225	4	J. J. Doke.. ..	1894
Dunedin..	1863	560	501	45	402	15	A. North	1882
N. E. Valley	..	250	..	23	187	..	E. Richards ..	1893
Kaikorai	..	..	..	20	174			
Maori Hill	..	100	..	8	60			
South Dunedin.. ..	..	250	60	30	324	6		
Greendale	1873	100	54	8	86	9		
Invercargill	1878	200	45	10	60	..	J. F. Jones	1894
Appleby	..	..	..	4	55			
Kirwee	1878	100	18	6	36	..	D. Dolamore ..	1884
Lincoln	1876	160	43	10	55			
Ladbrooks	..	..	..	5	42			
Mosgiel	..	210	93	14	127	4		
Riccarton	..	..	..	3	40			
Nelson	1851	200	73	15	104	4		
Oamaru	1883	300	98	21	223	4	A. Dewdney ..	1892
Owake District.. ..	..	120	53	2	34	9		
Oxford	1873	100	14	8	75	3	T. W. Wagstaff ..	1888
Richmond (Nelson) ..	1851	100	26	6	45			
South Malvern	1873	100	8	5	45			
Spreydon (Christchurch)	1864	300	66	24	190	4		
Sydenham	1880	300	35	14	153	..	T. A. Williams ..	1896
Timaru	1880	320	79	15	152	..	C. C. Brown ..	1885
Totals	..	8,400	3,066	561	4,732	98		

Total number of baptisms, 148.

The Revs. P. H. Cornford, Charles Carter and J. T. Hinton are without pastoral charge.

TASMANIA.

(*Population*, [*estimated*] 151,480.

President—Rev. E. VAUGHAN. *Vice-President*—Rev. J. E. WALTON.

Treasurer—Mr. J. T. SOUNDY. *Secretary*—Rev. E. HARRIS

TASMANIAN BAPTIST MISSIONARY SOCIETY

Secretary—Miss L. A. DOWLING, "Ellerslie," Perth.

Treasurer—Mr. D. SMART, Perth.

Missionary—Miss KEALLEY.

Mission Field—Pubna, E. Bengal (*see page* 421).

Name of Church.	Date.	Sittings.	Members.	S.S. Teachers.	S.S. Scholars.	Local Preachers.	Pastor.	Settled.
Deloraine	1880	300	30	7	70	..	S. A. Harris ..	1895
Dunorlan	..	60						
Devonport	1888	200						
Spreyton	..	50						
Hobart	1884	700	122	22	230	1		
Latrobe	1887	300	38	6	40	1	H. Wood	1895
Sassafras	..	80						
Launceston—								
The Tabernacle ..	1884	900	131	23	360	2	E. Harris	1894
York-street ..	1841	200	34	4	25	1	W. White	1877
Longford	1881	300	43	5	54	..	J. F. Macallister	1894
Perth	..	350	125	13	146	3	J. E. Walton ..	1888
The Nile								
Snake Banks ..								
Cleveland								
Sheffield	1890	300	43	4	32	1	E. Vaughan	1893
Promised Land ..								
Paradise								
Constitution Hill ..	..	100	..	2	20	1		
Bracknell	1885	70	} ..	6	100	1	W. Kenner ..	1890
Blackwood	1885	70						
Totals..		3,980	566	92	1,077	11		

Baptisms in 1894, 15.

Rev. J. Chamberlain is without pastoral change.

SUMMARY OF STATISTICS OF BAPTIST CHURCHES THROUGHOUT THE WORLD.

Countries.	Churches.	Pastors and Missionaries.	Members.	Scholars in Sunday Schools.	Baptisms.
EUROPE.					
England, Wales, Scotland, Ireland, and Channel Islands... ...	2,917	1,935	353,967	513,638	15,795
Austria-Hungary	8	7	2,953	1,534	1,020
Belgium	1	1	60	—	—
Denmark	25	18	3,310	4,089	251
Finland...	28	28	1,509	591	148
France	55	25	1,994	705	265
Germany	144	106	24,571	18,364	1,928
Holland...	19	10	1,273	1,666	77
Italy	62	39	1,423	1,187	150
Norway...	29	26	2,244	—	—
Roumania and Bulgaria...	4	5	384	435	32
Russia, including Poland	102	75	17,606	4,930	1,079
Spain	6	3	97	—	5
Sweden	553	430	37,601	40,353	2,595
Switzerland...	8	5	677	743	24
	3,961	2,713	449,669	588,235	23,369
ASIA.					
Ceylon	103	8	1,059	1,589	28
China	252	164	5,318	1,444	582
India, including Burmah & Assam	985	557	105,696	29,066	4,607
Japan	20	60	1,673	2,036	188
Palestine	7	2	112	51	—
	1,367	791	113,858	34,186	5,405
AFRICA.					
South	25	29	2,780	2,169	104
Central	30	88	1,401	757	312
West	39	10	1,685	2,640	67
St. Helena and Cape Verdes ...	2	2	111	107	—
	96	129	5,977	5,673	483
AMERICA.					
Dominion of Canada—					
Canada	527	308	45,512	54,523	3,270
Nova Scotia, New Brunswick & Prince Edward Island	402	177	45,738	27,813	3,066
United States	44,037	28,820	3,980,088	1,500,832	205,157
Mexico	32	30	1,120	629	226
West Indies and Central America	310	96	45,173	31,414	2,821
South America	16	19	729	156	133
	45,321	29,450	4,118,360	1,595,367	214,673
AUSTRALASIA.					
New South Wales	36	24	2,313	3,277	235
New Zealand	30	18	3,066	4,732	148
Queensland	28	21	2,023	3,016	91
South Australia	59	35	4,210	6,829	152
Tasmania	12	8	566	1,077	15
Victoria	65	46	5,911	8,630	466
	230	153	18,089	27,561	1,107

TOTALS.

	Churches.	Pastors and Mission-aries.	Members.	Scholars in Sunday Schools.	Baptisms.
Europe	3,961	2,713	449,669	588,235	23,369
Asia	1,367	791	113,858	34,186	5,405
Africa	96	129	5,977	5,673	483
America	45,324	29,450	4,118,360	1,595,367	214,673
Australasia	230	153	18,089	27,561	1,107
Grand Totals, 1895	50,978	33,236	4,705,953	2,251,022	245,037
" " 1892	46,502	30,548	4,136,152	2,002,877	216,349
" " 1889	42,650	27,858	3,786,603	—	—
British Empire.					
Great Britain, Ireland, and Channel Islands	2,917	1,935	353,967	513,638	15,795
Dominion of Canada	929	485	91,250	62,336	6,336
India and Ceylon	1,088	565	106,755	30,655	4,635
Australasia	230	153	18,089	27,561	1,107
Other Colonies	312	90	44,712	32,045	2,826
Foreign Countries	45,502	30,008	4,091,180	1,584,787	214,338
Grand Totals, 1895	50,978	33,236	4,705,953	2,251,022	245,037
" " 1892	46,502	30,548	4,136,152	2,002,877	216,349
" " 1889	42,650	27,858	3,786,603	—	—

Note.—This summary is corrected to the year 1895. The sources from which it has been compiled are the returns from the English Churches, collected principally through the Associations; the statistics supplied by the Colonial and Foreign Unions and Associations, and information contained in the reports of various missionary societies. The figures given above include the approximate number of accredited members in recognised Baptist Churches, but do not include those who, holding the principle that baptism is a profession of faith in the Lord Jesus Christ, are to be found in other denominations. On the other hand, deductions should be made of those who, not being Baptists, are to be found among Baptist Churches having Open Fellowship.—S. H. Booth, D.D., *Secretary*, Baptist Union of Great Britain and Ireland, 19, Furnival Street, London, E.C., *December*, 1895.

APPENDIX.

CONGREGATIONAL UNION OF ENGLAND AND WALES.

Founded 1831.—*Chairman* 1895—Rev. J. Morlais Jones. *Treasurer*—Mr. W. Holborn. *Secretary*—Rev. W. J. Woods, B.A., Memorial Hall, Farringdon-street, E.C.

LONDON CONGREGATIONAL UNION.

Chairman, 1896—Mr. A. Pye Smith; *Treasurers*—Mr. W. Holborn and Mr. Edward Spicer, J.P.; *Secretary*—Rev. A. Mearns; *Superintendent of Philanthropic Work*—Mr. E. W. Gates. *Office*—Memorial Hall, Farringdon-street, E.C.

District Secretaries—Central (City of London), Rev. T. Grear; East, Rev. J. R. Fisher; Metropolitan Essex, Rev. E. T. Egg; North-East, Rev. T. C. Udall; North, Rev. E. Griffith-Jones, B.A.; North-West, Mr. W. Chapple; West, Rev. Dr. Davies; South-West (Metropolitan Surrey), Rev. T. Jarratt and Mr. T. E. Tydeman; South-East (Metropolitan Kent), Rev. A. J. Viner; Extra Metropolitan Surrey, Rev. W. Baxendale.

LIST OF MINISTERS.

After the name of each Pastor the name of his Church is given in italics.
Members of the Congregational Board are indicated by an asterisk.

*Adams, Joseph, 19, Boscombe-road, Shepherd's Bush, W. (*Shepherd's Bush, Oaklands.*)
*Adeney, W. F., M.A., West House, North-end, Hampstead, N.W.
*Alden, P., M.A., Mansfield House, University Settlement, Barking-road, Canning Town, E.
*Allen, Bevill, The Manse, Tooting, S.W. (*Tooting.*)
Allen, G. J., B.A., 299, Oxford-street, W.
*Allen, W. Herwood, 49, St. Augustine-road, N.W. (*Kentish Town, Hawley-road.*)
Allpress, G. T., 613, Barking-road, Plaistow, E. (*Plaistow, Greengate.*)
*Anderton, W. E., M.A., Ambleside, Woodford-green, Essex. (*Woodford Green.*)
*Arkell, H. E., 46, Carholme-road, Forest-hill, S.E. (*Catford, Trinity.*)
*Arnold, Herbert, 24, Sisters'-avenue, Clapham Common, S.W. (*Clapham, Lavender Hill.*)
*Ashbery, H., 23, Lebanon-gardens, West-hill, Wandsworth, S.W.
Atchison, G., Snakes-lane, Woodford-green, Essex. (*Woodford U.*)
*Atkinson, J., Claremont, Cawley-road, South Hackney, N.E.
*Atkinson, J. W., Claremont, Cawley-road, South Hackney, N.E. (*Stepney, Latimer.*)
Attenborough, A. B., Woodstock, Marlborough-road, Ealing, W.
Aveling, F. W., M.A., B.Sc., Christ's College, Blackheath, S.E.

*Bagley, Thomas, 9, Hydeside-terrace, Edmonton. (*Edmonton and Tottenham.*)
Baker, Bagnall, Maybury-road, Tooting, S.W.
*Balgarnie, Robert, 51, Crouch Hall-road, Hornsey, N.
Barlow, W. Crosbie, M.A., 12, Dumbleton-road, Loughborough Junction, S.W.
*Barnes, John, Lilian House, Hornsey-lane, N.
Barnes, Philip, 160, Claremont-road, Forest-gate, E.
*Barron, Henry, 12, Crockerton-road, Upper Tooting, S.W.

*Bartlet, G. D., M.A., Solsgirth House, South-grove, Highgate, N.
Bartlett, John, Cedar Cottage, London-road, Forest Hill, S.E.
Batcock, W., 4, Thornhill-square, Barnsbury, N. (*Caledonian-road.*)
*Baxendale, W., 5, Auckland-hill, West Norwood, S.E. (*Norwood, West.*)
Beazley, Joseph, 13, The Paragon, Blackheath, S.E.
Bedolfe, J. Chisman, 9, Berkeley-road, Regent's Park, N.W.
Begg, A. P., B.A., 25, High-road, South Tottenham.
Bennett, H. E., B.A., Uxbridge, Middlesex. (*Uxbridge, Providence.*)
*Bennett, W. H., M.A., 18, Denning-road, Hampstead, N.W.
*Berry, Robert, 43, Highbury-crescent West, N. (*Islington Chapel.*)
Billing, F. A., LL.D., 7, St. Donatt's-road, New Cross, S.E. (*Southwark-park.*)
Blenkin, A. G., 6, Earlham-grove, Wood Green, N. (*Wood Green*).
Blomfield, J. B., Clifton House, George-lane, Lewisham, S.E.
Blore, J. W., 92, High-street, New Barnet.
*Bolton, Francis, B.A., 16, Haycroft-road, Brixton-hill, S.W.
*Bolton, William, M.A., 4, Cumberland-park, Acton, W. (*Acton.*)
*Boseley, Ira, 16, Cambridge-gardens, Kilburn, N.W.
*Bourne, Alfred, B.A., 45, Park-road, Bromley, Kent.
*Bowman, J. W., M.A., B.D., 7, Waveney-avenue, Peckham-rye, S.E. (*Peckham Hanover.*)
*Boyle, Joseph, 44, Aberdeen-road, Highbury, N.
Bradford, W. H., 52, Hayter-road, Brixton, S.W. (*Brixton, Trinity.*)
*Bridge, A. G., 119, Selhurst-road, South Norwood, S.E. (*Norwood, Selhurst-road.*)
Brierley, Jonathan, B.A., Helensleigh, Dean-road, Willesden-green, N.W.
*Brooks, J. L., 8, Castlenau-gardens, Barnes, S.W. (*Hammersmith Broadway.*)
*Brown, Frederick, Brooklyn, Thistlewaite-road, Lower Clapton, N.E.
*Bull, H. Davis, 122, Claremont-road, Forest Gate, E. (*Manor-park.*)
Burn, J. W., Carleton, The Avenue, Surbiton Hill, Kingston-on-Thames. (*Surbiton.*)
Byles, John, The Manse, Ealing, W.

Calvert, A., M.A., 2, Walpole-road, Twickenham.
*Cave, Alfred, B.A., D.D., Hackney College, Finchley-road, Hampstead, N.W.
Cecil, E. D., 59, Selhurst-road, South Norwood, S.E.
*Chamberlain, J. A., 1, Mallinson-road, Wandsworth-common, S.W.
Chambers, Charles, (*Stepney Meeting.*)
Charke, Thos., 49, Wharton-road, West Kensington, W. (*Notting Hill, Horbury.*)
Chisholm, Samuel, Gladsmuir, Malmsbury-road, South Woodford, Essex.
*Christie, George A., M.A., 21, Denning-road, Hampstead, N.W.
Clark, Henry W., 41, Conduit-street, W.
Clarke, John, 42, Springfield-road, South Tottenham.
Clarke, W. E., 31, Blyth-hill, Catford, S.E.
*Colborne, Philip, 41, Brailsford-road, Tulse Hill, S.W.
Colborne, George, M.A., Ph.D., 41 Brailsford-road, Tulse Hill, S.W.
*Coley, Henry, 1, Lady Margaret-road, Kentish Town, N.W. (*Camden Town, Park Chapel.*)
Collins, Robert, 109, Belvedere-road, Upper Norwood, S.E.
Comer, Sidney T., Ingleside, Oakfield-road, Long-lane, Church End, Finchley, N. (*North Finchley.*)
*Cooper, R. Denness, South View, The Drive, Walthamstow. (*Walthamstow, Trinity.*)
Cottingham, J. C., 194, Devonshire-road, Honor Oak-park, Forest-hill, S.E. (*Forest Hill, Queen's-road.*)
*Cousins, George, 59, Finsbury Park-road, N.
Cowper, Benjamin Harris, 230, Evering-road, Upper Clapton, N.E.
Crickmer, W. St. John, Moultan Hill, Swanley Junction S.O., Kent.
*Critchley, George, B.A., 18, Handen-road, Lee, S.E. (*Lee, Burnt Ash.*)
Cropper, John, The Manse, Enfield Highway, N. (*Enfield Highway.*)
Cullen, G. F., Woodville, Cleveland-road, South Woodford, Essex. (*Wanstead.*)

Daniel, W., 151, Jamaica-road, Bermondsey, S.E. (*Bermondsey, Rouel-road.*)
*Darby, W. Evans, LL.D., 67, Oakley-road, Essex-road, N.
*Darlow, T. H., M.A., 155, Fellows-road, South Hampstead, N.W. (*South Hampstead, New College Chapel.*)
Davies, Herbert, 35, Buxton-road, Chingford, Essex. (*Chingford.*)

Davies, Isaac, 38, Wheathill-road, Anerley, S.E.
*Davies, J. Alford, B.A., B.D., Woodview, Clifford-road, New Barnet. (*New Barnet.*)
Davies, James T., 11, Shore-road, South Hackney, N.E. (*Bethnal Green-road.*)
Davies, Lewis John, 6, South Hill Park-gardens, Hampstead, N.W.
*Davies, Thomas, 23, Linton-road, Barking, E. (*Barking, Broadway.*)
Davies, Thomas, M.A., Ph.D., 1, Peterborough-villas, Fulham, S.W. (*Edith-grove.*)
Davis, Henry R., 19, Lancefield-street, Harrow-road, W. (*North Kensington.*)
Davis, J. Teesdale, 43 Beaconsfield-road, St. Margaret's, Twickenham.
*Dawson, Robert, B.A., Lynton Grange, Fortis-green, N.
*Dawson, W. J., 17, Highbury-terrace, N. (*Highbury Quadrant.*)
*Devine, W. P., 32, Chesterton-road, Notting-hill, W. (*Notting-hill, Lancaster-road.*)
Dickenson, W. H., 216, Ashmore-road, Paddington, W. (*Notting Dale.*)
Dixon, Geo., Templeton Mansion, Fopstone-road, Earl's Court, W.
Docker, F., 83, Montpelier-road, Peckham, S.E. (*Southwark Pilgrim Church.*)
*Dorling, William, Buckhurst Hill, Essex. (*Buckhurst Hill, King's-place.*)
*Dothie, Elvery, B.A., 47, Longton-grove, Sydenham, S.E.
Duffill, M., 31, Springdale-road, Green Lanes, N.

*Edmondson, W., 3, Stanley-villas, Pembury-road, Tottenham.
*Edwards, W., 1, Trimmer-villas, Brentford. (*Brentford.*)
Edwards, W. Henry, 2, Capel-road, Harlesden, N.W.
*Egg, E. T., Sydney Villa, Woodford-green, Essex. (*East Ham.*)
*Ellis, James, 63, Kelvin-road, Highbury Park, N. (*Barnsbury.*)
England, Alfred John, 62, Annandale-road, Vanbrugh-hill, S.E.
*Essery, W. A., 147, Peckham-rye, S.E.
Evans, J. Benson, Nevern, Morland-road, Croydon. (*Croydon. Addiscombe.*)
*Evans, Owen, D.D., 28, Freegrove-road, West Holloway, N. (*King's Cross Tabernacle, Welsh.*)
*Evans, Thos., 64, Victoria Park-road, N.E. (*Victoria Park.*)
Evershed, Samuel, 329, Liverpool-road, N.

*Farren, John, Iona, Waveney-avenue, Peckham Rye, S.E.
*Farrer, William, LL.B., Oakleigh, Arkwright-road, N.W.
*Fisher, John, Lyndhurst, Harlesden-road, N.W. (*Willesden.*)
*Fisher, J. Rolfe, 26, Cottage-grove, Bow-road, E. (*Stepney, Burdett-road.*)
*Flower, James Edward, M.A., Highfield, Allfarthing-lane, Wandsworth, S.W.
Forrester, Alexander, 145, Malpas-road, Brockley, S.E.
*Forster, J. Lawson, LL.B., D.D., 21, Highbury New Park, N. (*Hare-court.*)
*Foster, Josiah, Linton House, Plaistow, E. (*Victoria Docks.*)
Fotheringham, R., M.A., Fernwood, Blackheath-park, S.E. (*Blackheath.*)
*French, J. Bryant, 75, Grosvenor-park, Camberwell, S.E.

Gates, William J., 143, Lower Addiscombe-road, Croydon.
*Geddes, J., Thanet Villa, Bexley Heath, Kent. (*Bexley Heath.*)
*Gibbon, J. Morgan, 116, Clapton Common, N.E. (*Stamford Hill.*)
*Giddins, Geo. H., Clyde House, Fairlop-road, Leytonstone, N.E.
*Gilfillan, Thomas, 57, Burrard-road, West Hampstead, N.W.
*Gladstone, J. P., 63, Upper Tulse Hill, S.W. (*Streatham Hill.*)
Gookey, H. de Vere, The Manse, Gresham-road, Staines. (*Staines.*)
*Grainger, Henry, 8, Durand-gardens, Stockwell, S.W.
Grant, Duncan, East Finchley, N. (*East Finchley.*)
Gray, B., B.A., Langley Villa, Sunny-gardens, Hendon, N.W.
*Grear, Thomas, 252, Dalston-lane, N.E. (*City, Bishopsgate.*)
Green, J. L., 103, Elm-park, Brixton-hill, S.W.
Gregory, B. D. W., 9, Cavendish-road, Clapham Common, S.W.
*Gregory, John, 38, Groombridge-road, South Hackney, N.E. (*Hackney-road, Adelphi.*)
Greig, Walter, 7, Victoria-avenue, Surbiton, S.W. (*Thames Ditton.*)
*Grenville, Palmer, B.A., LL.B., 22, Ellerker-gardens, Richmond, Surrey.
*Griffith, Arthur, LL.B., B.Sc., 9, Philip-terrace, S. Tottenham.
*Griffith, W., 61, Wellesley-road, Croydon.

Griffith-Jones, E., B.A., 61, Cecile Park, Crouch End, N. (*Stroud Green.*)

*Haffer, H. J., 143, Dulwich-grove, S.E. (*Dulwich-grove.*)
*Hall, Frederick, Rockdale, 182, Worple-road, Wimbledon. (*Wimbledon.*)
*Hall, Newman, LL.B., D.D., Vine House, Hampstead-heath, N.W.
Halsey, Joseph, The Hawthorns, 10, Crescent-road, S. Norwood Park, S.E. (*Anerley.*)
Hamilton, Andrew, M.A., 23, Nassington-road, Hampstead, N.W. (*Hampstead, Lyndhurst-road.*)
*Hammond, T., Studley, Grove-road, Woodford, Essex. (*South Woodford, George-lane.*)
*Hampden-Cook, Ernest, M.A., Mill Hill School, N.W.
Hanson, G. A. (*Twickenham.*)
Hardiman, Henry C., 49, Clarendon-road, Walthamstow.
* Harley, Robert, M.A., F.R.S.. Rosslyn, Westbourne-road, Forest-hill, S.E.
*Harries, H., M.A., Anlaby House, High-road, Upper Clapton, N.E. (*Clapton Park.*)
Hartill, Isaac, 19, Acacia-road, St. John's-wood, N.W. (*St. John's Wood-terrace.*)
*Harwood, William Hardy, 25, Aberdeen-park, N. (*Islington Union.*)
Hastings, Frederick, 40 Royal-avenue, Chelsea, S.W. (*Chelsea, Markham-square, S.W.*)
Hawker, John G., 79, Cecile-park, Crouch End, N.
Heathcote, H. J., Memorial Hall, Farringdon-street, E.C.
Herschell, D. A., 4, Overton-road, Brixton, S.W.
*Hewett, Henry, 18, Lansdowne-gardens, Clapham-road, S.W. (*Clapham-road, Claylands.*)
*Higgins, E. Hinchcliffe, Mycenæ-road, Westcombe-park, S.E. (*Greenwich, Maze-hill.*)
*Hill, Thomas, Parsonage, North Finchley, N. (*North Finchley.*)
*Hinds, George, 178, Merton-road, Wimbledon.
*Hitchens, E. Theodore, 90 Gloucester-street, Belgravia, S.W. (*Eccleston-square.*)
*Hitchens, J. Hiles, D.D., 90 Gloucester-street, Belgravia, S.W. (*Eccleston-square.*)
Holborn, Alfred, M.A., 50, Windsor-road, Ealing, W.
Holmes, James, 33, Arlington-park-gardens North, Chiswick, (*Gunnersbury.*)
*Hooke, D. Burford, Bonchurch Lodge, Manor-road, High Barnet.
*Hooper, Thomas, 29, De Crespigny-park, Denmark Hill, S.E. (*Camberwell-green.*)
*Horne, C. Silvester, A.M., 9, Campden Hill-gardens, Kensington, W. (*Kensington, Allen-street.*)
*Horton, Robert F., M.A., D.D., The Chesils, Christchurch-road, Hampstead, N.W. (*Hampstead.*)
*Hurndall, W. Evans, M.A., 90, St. Ermin's Mansions, Westminster, S.W. (*Westminster Chapel.*)
*Hurry, Nicholas, Ferncliff, Orleans-road, Hornsey Rise. N.
Hurst, G. L., 86, Englefield-road, Canonbury, N. (*Barbican.*)

Ingram, J. W., Lyntonia, Cranbrook-road, Ilford. (*Ilford, Christ Church.*)
*Irving, James, 116, King Edward-road, South Hackney, N.E. (*Hackney Old Gravel Pit.*)

*Jackson, J. Southwood, 15, Barrington-road, Brixton, S.W. (*Stockwell-road.*)
*Jameson, John, Melgund House, Melgund-road, Highbury, N. (*Arundel-square.*)
*Jarratt, T., Era House, Surrey-lane, Battersea, S.W. (*Battersea, Bridge-road.*)
Jeffrey, A. D., 73, Pepys-road, New Cross, S.E. (*Peckham, Clifton.*)
*Jenkins, D. M., 202, Portsdown-road, Maida Vale, W. (*Craven Hill.*)
Jermyn, Jno., 6, Stonard-road, Palmer's Green, N. (*Winchmore Hill.*)
Johnson, Arthur Newton, M.A., 75, South Hill-park, Hampstead, N.W.
*Johnson, Richard Alexander, B.A., 28, Springdale-road, Green Lanes, N.
*Johnston, John, 15, Burma-road, Green Lanes, N. (*Stoke Newington, Raleigh Memorial.*)
Jones, D. C., 8, Hilda-road, Brixton, S.W. (*Southwark Bridge-road, W.*)
*Jones, Daniel Lloyd, Glenthorne, Southwood-road, New Eltham, Kent. (*New Eltham.*)
*Jones, Edward Henry, 3, Upper Cheyne-row, Chelsea, S.W.
Jones, Hampden B., 3, Church-road, Leyton.

*Jones, Joseph, M.A., The Limes, Grange-crescent, Sutton, Surrey. (*Sutton.*)
*Jones, J. Morlais, Hafod, College-park, Lewisham, S.E. (*Lewisham.*)
*Jones, William, 9, Surbiton Hill-park, Surbiton, Kingston-on-Thames.
*Joscelyne, A. F., B.A., 37, Peak Hill-gardens, Sydenham, S.E. (*Sydenham.*)
Jude, R. Chatfield, 17 Mill-road, Northumberland Heath, Kent. (*Erith-avenue.*)

Keen, C. C., 3, Fern Villas, Feltham, Middlesex. (*Feltham and Sunbury.*)
*Keesey, G. W., 47, Grosvenor-park, Camberwell, S.E. (*Walworth, Sutherland.*)
*Kennedy, James, M.A., 16, Christchurch-road, Hampstead, N.W.
*Kennedy, John, M.A., D.D., Cluny Cottage, Rudall-crescent, Hampstead, N.W.
Kick, William, 17, John's Avenue, Hendon, N.W.
King, Alexander, 11, Sutton Court-road, Chiswick, Middlesex.
Kirkby, Charles, 8, Salisbury-square, Fleet-street, E.C.
*Knaggs, James, Claremont, 247, Romford-road, Stratford, E. (*Stratford.*)

Lansdown, M., 65, Oakley-square, N.W. (*Tolmer's-square.*)
Lansdowne, Thomas P., 137, Whitechapel-road, E. (*Whitechapel, Brunswick.*)
Laver, Robert, The Retreat, Belvedere, Kent. (*Belvedere.*)
*Leach, Charles, D.D., Homestead, Brondesbury-road, West Kilburn, N.W. (*Queen's Park, Harrow-road.*)
*Le Blond, S. J., 225, Evering-road, Upper Clapton, N.E.
Le Marchant, Alexander, The Manse, Hendon, N.W. (*Hendon.*)
Le Pla, Henry, Chapel House, South-hill-park, Hampstead, N.W. (*Gospel Oak.*)
Le Pla, James, 53, Lausanne-road, Hornsey, N. (*Harringay.*)
*Le Pla, Matthew Henry, 176, Amhurst-road, N.E. (*Kingsland.*)
Legg, W. A. H., B.A., Ellangowan, Kempshott-road, Streatham Common, S.W. (*Streatham.*)
*Legge, J. R., M.A., 2, St. John's-terrace, Buckhurst-hill, Essex. (*Buckhurst-hill, Palmerston-road.*)
*Lennox, William Marshall, 70, Ivydale-road, Nunhead, S.E.
Leonard, T. A., 1, Carlingford-road, Green Lanes, N.
Lewin, William, 65, Park-road, Portway, West Ham, E. (*West Ham-park.*)
Lewis, Dolfan, Trinity Chapel, Hanhury-street, E. (*Mile End, New Town.*)
*Lewis, William, The Parsonage, St. Mary Cray, Kent. (*St. Mary Cray.*)
*Linington, W. A., 62, Nightingale-lane, Balham, S.W. (*Horselydown, Parish-street.*)
Lister, J. B., 18, St. Mary Abbott-terrace, Kensington, W.
Lloyd, E., 67, Abberville-road, Clapham-common, S.W.
Long, Sidney J., 28, Albert-road, Stroud-green, N.
*Lovett, Richard, M.A., 42, Sisters'-avenue, Clapham Common, S.W.
Lucas, Mark, Granville Lodge, Wellesley-road, Gunnersbury, W.
Lummis, John Henry, 12, Water-lane, Brixton-rise, S.W.

*Mabbs, Goodeve, Silverleigh, Constantine-road, Hampstead, N.W.
*Macbeth, Robert, 36, Waterloo-street, Hammersmith, W.
*Macgregor, George Douglas, Blenheim Lodge, Marlborough-hill, Harrow.
*Mackay, Robert, 23, Durand-gardens, Clapham-road, S.W.
*MacNeill, Nigel, 131, Camden-road, N.W. (*Charrington-street.*)
Macwilliam, W. B., 2, Ridge-road, Hornsey, N.
*Manington, George, The Manse, New Malden, Surrey. (*New Malden.*)
*Marsden, John, B.A., 9, Cromartie-road, Hornsey Rise, N.
*Marshall, William, Home Lyn, Woodberry Down, Stamford-hill, N.
*Martin, George, St. Aubyn's, Harold-road, Upper Norwood, S.E. (*Upper Norwood.*)
Martin, Henry, Oakhurst, Anerley-road, S.E.
Martin, Percy, B.A., 10, The Barons, St. Margaret's-on-Thames, Twickenham. (*Richmond, Vineyard.*)
*Matthews, Edward W., 61, Cawley-road, Victoria-Park, N.E.
*Matthews, John, Holmlea, High Barnet. (*Barnet.*)
*Mearns, Andrew, 277, Coldharbour-lane, Brixton, S.W.
Meaton, W. A., 2, Newton-avenue, Acton, W.
Merchant, Herbert, B.A., Glady's-road, West Hampstead, N.W. (*Greville-place, Kilburn.*)
*Milnes, John, M.A., Park Side, Oakleigh-park, N. (*Whetstone.*)
Moffett, Joseph, 42, St. Julian's-road, Kilburn, N.W.

*Mottram, W., The Mount, Friern-road, East Dulwich, S.E.
*Moulson, H., 7, Manor-road, Leyton, Essex. (*Leyton, Grange Park-road.*)
Muirhead, W., D.D., 149, Highbury New Park, N.
Muncaster, W., 53, Abingdon-villas, Kensington, W. (*Brompton, Trevor.*)

*Nachim, M., 72, Mildmay-park, N.
New, Alfred H., Fernleigh, Canning-road, Croydon.
Newell, H. C. W., 269, Victoria-park-road, N.E. (*Hackney, South.*)
*Newth, Samuel, M.A., D.D., 3, Perrhyn-road, Acton, W.
Nichols, John B., 30, Maitland-park-villas, Haverstock-hill, N.W. (*Haverstock-hill.*)
*Nicholson, T., Cartref, Elmfield-road, Bromley, Kent. (*Bromley, Kent.*)
*Nimmo, David, 51, Ladbroke-grove, Notting-hill, W.
*Nobbs, Robert, 77, Windsor-road, Forest-gate, E. (*Upton, Forest-gate.*)
*Noble, R. H., Wilmington House, New Southgate, N.
*Norton, George, 14, Cliff-terrace, St. John's, S.E. (*Greenwich-road.*)
*Nunn, John, 6, Maitland-park-villas, Haverstock-hill, N.W.

Onley, John, 11, Springfield-road, Kingston-on-Thames. (*Kingston-on-Thames.*)

*Park, John, Laurieknowe, Earlsfield-road, Wandsworth, S.W. (*Wandsworth, East-hill.*)
*Park, William, 3, South-park-hill-road, Croydon. (*Croydon, George-street.*)
*Parker, Joseph, D.D., Tynehome, Lyndhurst-gdns., South Hampstead, N.W. (*City Temple.*)
*Parsons, Llewellyn H., Rutland House, Portland-road, Finsbury-park, N. (*Finsbury-park.*)
*Partner, R., The Manse, Howard-road, Plaistow, E. (*Plaistow.*)
Pattenden, Thomas James, Albert House, Miranda-road, Upper Holloway, N.
Peace, J. T., Ponder's End, N. (*Ponder's End.*)
*Pedley, C. S., B.A., New Southgate, N. (*New Southgate.*)
*Penford, E. J., Eltham, Kent. (*Eltham.*)
*Pierce, William, 30, Ashley-road, Crouch-hill, N. (*Tollington-park.*)
*Poole, Thomas, 46, Leander-road, Josephine-avenue, Brixton-hill, S.W.
*Postans, J. Chetwode, 71, Oakhurst-grove, East Dulwich, S.E. (*Peckham, Linden-grove.*)
*Poulter, James Ford, B.A., The Ferns, 26, King's-road, South Wimbledon.
Preston, William C., 39, Stile Hall-gardens, Chiswick, Middlesex.
*Pryce, Robert Vaughan, M.A., LL.B., New College, Hampstead, N.W.
Pulsford, John, D.D., 20, Belsize-crescent, Hampstead, N.W.

*Ramsey, A. Averell, Cardell, Overhill-road, Dulwich, S.E. (*Dulwich, Emmanuel, Barry-road.*)
Randall, Uriah Brodribb, M.A., Westridge, Sunningfields-road, Hendon, N.W.
Ray, Thomas, LL.D., Forest-hill-road, Peckham, S.E.
*Read, S. Sabine, Burton Lodge, Lewisham, S.E. (*Deptford.*)
Reason, Will, M.A., University Settlement, Mansfield House, Barking-road, Canning Town, E.
*Redford, Robert Ainslie, M.A., LL.B., Crest House, Putney-bridge-road, S.W. (*Putney Union.*)
*Reed, Andrew, B.A., Ellenslea, Parsifal-road,South Hampstead, N.W.
*Rees, J. Machreth, 42, Kersley-street, Battersea-park, S W. (*Chelsea, Radnor-street, W.*)
*Reynolds, Henry Robert, B.A., D.D., Sandholme, Broxburne, Herts.
Rice, E. P., B.A., 123, Milton-road, Stoke Newington, N.
Richards, J. R., 63, Victoria-park-road, N.E. (*Hackney, Cambridge Heath.*)
Ridgway, G., Melford House, High-road, Chingford, Essex.
*Roberts, William, B.A., 26, Sanfoin-road, Balham, S.W.
*Rogers, James Guinness, B.A., D.D. 81, North Side, Clapham Common, S.W. (*Clapham, Grafton-square.*)
*Rogers, James William, B.A., 81, North Side, Clapham Common, S.W.
*Rook, J. Colwell, 77, Sunderland-road, Forest-hill, S.E.
Rosier, Heber, 121, Portland-terrace, Lower-road, Rotherhithe, S.E. (*Bermondsey, Jamaica-row.*)
*Rowland, Alfred, LL.B., B.A., Selwood, Crescent-road, Crouch End, N. (*Crouch End.*)

*Rudd, Thomas, B.A., 10, Oliver-grove, South Norwood, S.E.
*Rutherford, T. Dixon, M.A., 38, Filey-avenue, Filey-road, Stoke Newington, N. (*Stoke Newington, Abney.*)
*Ryley, G. Buchanan, 34, Bow-road, E. (*Bow, Harley-street.*)

*Sackett, Benjamin, 14, Albert-square, Commercial-road, E. (*St.George's-in-the-East, Ebenezer.*)
*Sandison, Alex., The Parsonage, Thomas-street, Grosvenor-square, W. (*Weigh House, Duke-street, Grosvenor-square.*)
Sandison, Robert C., St. Peter's, Thurlow-hill, West Dulwich, S.E. (*West Dulwich.*)
*Sargent, Richard J., Norfolk House, London-road, Enfield. N.
Saville, W. G., 32, Bartholomew-road, Kentish Town, N.W.
Schnadhorst, E., 34, St. Stephen's-road, North Bow, E. (*North Bow.*)
Scott, Alex., Chase Side, Southgate, N.
Scott, D. Wardlaw, Woodland Villa, Clarence-road, Wood Green, N.
Scott, Harry, Lennox Villa, Friern Barnet-road, New Southgate, N.
Scott, William, 37, Ravensdale-road, Craven-park, Stamford-hill, N.
*Selbie, W. B., M.A., 11, North-road, Highgate, N. (*Highgate.*)
Selfe, Francis C., 19, Royal-hill, Greenwich, S.E.
Shadforth, W., 91, Listria-park, Stoke Newington, N. (*Stoke Newington, Abney.*)
Shalders, Edward William, B.A., 73, Digby-road, Green Lanes, N.
Shaw, G. A., Ambahy, Handworth-avenue, Higham-park, Chingford, Essex.
*Shrewsbury, A. R., 28, Bridge-avenue, Hammersmith, W. (*Hammersmith, Dalling-rd.*)
Sime, A. H. Moncur, 9. Dalmeny-avenue, Tufnell-park, N. (*Holloway, Camden-road.*)
*Simon, Thomas, The Parsonage, Rowfant-road, Upper Tooting, S.W. (*Balham.*)
Simpson, Robert, 10, Bellevue-villas, Southgate-road, Wood Green, N.
*Sissons, Thomas, Elm Lodge, Albemarle-road, Beckenham, Kent.
*Skinner, W., 86, Hampton-road, Forest Gate, E. (*Forest Gate.*)
Skipper, J. H., 129, High-road, Willesden-green, N.W.
Smith, F. Seth, 3, Belsize-road, South Hampstead, N.W.
*Smith, James S. Tamatoa W., 2, Alexandra-road, South Hampstead, N.W.
*Smith, Matthew, 51, Marquess-road, Canonbury, N. (*Islington, Britannia-row.*)
*Smith, Samuel Joseph, B.A., Forty-hill, Enfield, N. (*Enfield, Baker-street.*)
*Snashall, George, B.A., 25, The Crescent, Gore-road, Victoria Park, N.E. (*Victoria-park Tabernacle.*)
*Snell, Bernard J., M.A., B.Sc., 94, New-park-road, Brixton Hill, S.W. (*Brixton.*)
*Snowdown, R., 26, Grove-green-road, Leyton, Essex. (*Leyton, Frith-road.*)
Spears, A. G., A.T.S., Georgina House, Clement's-road, Ilford. (*Ilford.*)
*Stead, F. Herbert, M.A., Robert Browning Hall, York-street, Walworth, S.E. (*Browning Hall, York-street, Walworth.*)
Stephens, F., 65, St. Augustine's-road, Camden-square, N.W.
*Storrow, Arthur H., 31, Tyrwhitt-road, St. John's, S.E. (*City, Falcon-square.*)
Stoughton, John, D.D., Athenæum Club, Pall Mall, S.W.
Stuchbery, Joseph, B.A., 5, Charlotte-villas, Brockley, S.E.
Sturges, Thomas Richard Henry, 65, Victoria-avenue, Upton-park, E. (*Plashet-park.*)
Suttle, G. A., 57, Agate-road, Hammersmith, W. (*Tottenham Court-road.*)
*Sweet, Frederick, The Manse, Romford. (*Romford.*)
*Symes, Colmer Boaz, B.A., Runswick, Cambridge Park, Leytonstone, N.E. (*Leytonstone High-road.*)

Temple, W. J., 32, Stafford-street, West Ferry-road, Millwall, E. (*Millwall.*)
Terry, F. G., 12, Elm-road, Camden-square, N.W.
Thacker, Leonard J., Kingtyre, Spratt Hall-road, Wanstead. (*Leytonstone, High-road.*)
Thomas, David, 1, The Terrace, Cheshunt, Waltham Cross, N. (*Cheshunt, Crossbrook-street.*)
*Thomas, F. Fox, Ottery, Uplands-park, Enfield, N.
Thomas, F. W. Danetree, Chaucer-road, Ashford, Middlesex. (*Ashford*).
*Thomas, James, 33, Leyland-road, Lee, S.E.
*Thomas, Owen, M.A., 95, Greenwood-road, Dalston, N.E. (*Dalston, Middleton-road.*)
*Thompson, R. Wardlaw, Bellary, Frognal, Hampstead, N.W

*Thomson, J. Radford, M.A., Spelthorne, Upper Teddington, Middlesex.
*Thorn, G. Ernest, 8, Latymer-road, Lower Edmonton, N. (*Lower Edmonton.*)
Thorpe, James, 261, London-road, Thornton Heath, Surrey.
*Tinling, J. F. B., B.A., 4, Dalmeny-road, Tufnell-park, N. (*City-road*).
Todd, Stephen, 52, Disraeli-road, Putney, S.W.
*Toms, H. Storer, The Manse, Enfield. (*Enfield.*)
*Touzeau, T. F., 81, Loughborough-park, S.W. (*Loughborough-park.*)
Townley, James, 12, Osbaldeston-road, Stoke Newington, N.
*Tuck, Robert, B.A., 40, Carholme-road, Forest-hill, S.E.
*Turner, G. Lyon, M.A., 8, Carlton-road, St. John's, S.E. (*Lewisham, Algernon road.*)
*Turquand, Paul James, 3, Lynette-avenue, Clapham Common, S.W.
*Twentyman, George, M.A., B.D., Green-hill-park, New Barnet.

*Udall, Thomas Charles, 69, Greenwood-road, Dalston, N.E. (*Dalston, Shrubland-road.*)

*Valentine, J. M. Hannay, 12, Douglas-road, Canonbury, N.
Vaughan, D. W., M.A., 21, Bartholomew-road, N.W. (*Kentish Town.*)
Veevers, John W., 34, Sibley-grove, East Ham, E.
*Verrall, R. T., B.A., 1, Homefield-road, Bromley, Kent.
*Viner, Albert James, 118, Herbert-road, Plumstead, Kent. (*Woolwich.*)
*Viney, Josiah, Alleyne House, Caterham Valley, Surrey.

*Waite, Edward, M.A., Blackheath, S.E.
*Walker, George, B.A., 85, Marquess-road, Canonbury, N.
Walker, Geo. S., Orchard Leigh, Granville-road, Sidcup, Kent. (*Sidcup.*)
Wallace, J. Bruce, M.A., 1, Downham-road, Kingsland, N. (*Southgate-road.*)
*Waterhouse, Samuel N., Moorlands, Hampton-road, Teddington, Middlesex. (*Hampton-hill.*)
*Waterman, T. T., B.A., Eskdale, 11, Fairfield-road, Croydon.
*Watt, D. G., M.A., 6, Deerbrook-road, Herne-hill, S.E.
Watt, James Gordon, M.A., 10, Winchester-place, Cromwell-avenue, Highgate, N.
Weatherhead, H. J., 23, Tomlin's-grove, Bow, E.
Welch, Hy., 83, Chesterton-road, Plaistow, E. (*Canning Town.*)
White, Edward, Hildas Mount, Mill-hill, N.W.
Whitehouse, J. O., 10, Marriott-road, High Barnet.
*Whitehouse, Owen Charles, M.A., Holly Lodge, Cheshunt, Waltham Cross.
Whitmee, S. J., 20, Lordship-park, N.
*Whittley, W., 5, Carlton-villas, Chichele-road, Cricklewood, N.W. (*Cricklewood.*)
*Whyte, Peter, Woodside, Rydal-road, Streatham, S.W.
*Wickson, Arthur, LL.D., 20, Portsdown-road, Maida-vale, W.
*Wilkins, John, 135, Avondale-square, Old Kent-road, S.E. (*Old Kent-road, Marlborough.*)
Wilkinson, George, Claremont-villa, Woodford-green, Essex.
*Williams, C. Fleming, 56, Kenninghall-road, Clapton, N.E. (*Stoke Newington, Rectory-road.*)
*Williams, S. Tamatoa, Kelvin Lodge, Blythe-hill, Catford, S.E.
Williams, William, Beauparc, Hounslow-road, Hampton-hill, Middlesex.
*Williams, W. Pedr, 102, Brooke-road, Stoke Newington, N. (*Lower Clapton.*)
Willifer, R. Merridew, 8, Denton-road, Hornsey, N.
*Wills, John Bynglass, 28, Brigstock-road, Thornton Heath. (*West Croydon.*)
*Wilson, James Hall, D.D., Dacre Lodge, Lee-terrace, Blackheath, S.E.
*Wilson, Charles, M.A., 16, St. Germain's-place, Blackheath, S.E.
Wilson, J. W., 92, Herbert-road, Manor Park, E.
Wilson, R. D., Trinity Parsonage, Poplar, E. (*Poplar, Trinity.*)
*Wood, Charles Frederick William, M.A., 148, Norwood-road, West Norwood, S.E.
Woodhouse, Joseph, 18, Hinckley-road, East Dulwich, S.E.
*Woodhouse, J. T., Oakdene, Hurst-road, Bexley, Kent. (*Bexley.*)
*Woods, William James, B.A., Memorial Hall, Farringdon-street, E.C.
Wright, Chas., Malverns, Epping, Essex. (*Epping.*)
*Wright, I. Morley, 105, Sutherland-avenue, W. (*Paddington*).

*Young, H. P., 57, Fairholme-road, West Kensington, W. (*West Kensington.*)

Zucker, Leon, 1, Werndee-road, South Norwood, S.E.

s.
, N.

GENERAL BODY OF PROTESTANT DISSENTING MINISTERS OF THE THREE DENOMINATIONS

RESIDING IN AND ABOUT THE CITIES OF LONDON AND WESTMINSTER.

Place of Meeting—Congregational Memorial Hall, Farringdon-street, E.C.

Secretary—Rev. J. HUNT COOKE, Ramleh, Coolhurst-road, Crouch End, N.

Clerk—Mr. J. Minshull, Memorial Hall, Farringdon-street, E.C.

The three Boards of Presbyterian, Independent, and Baptist Ministers, resident in and about the cities of London and Westminster, were formed in the early part of the eighteenth century. These bodies were accustomed to unite in presenting addresses to the Throne on suitable occasions, from the date of the Revolution, but were not organized into one "General Body" till July 11th, 1727. At that time it was agreed, and the rule continues still in force, "That no person be allowed to join with the body of Protestant Dissenting Ministers in any public act but such as are approved by one or other of the three."

The business of the General Body is conducted by a committee chosen from the three denominations, and which meets as occasion requires.

The meetings of the General Body are always special and by summons, excepting the annual meeting which is held at one o'clock on the Tuesday following the second Lord's Day in April of every year.

The secretary is chosen triennially from each of the three Boards in rotation.

The chairman is chosen only for the meeting over which he presides, and from each Board in succession.

PRESBYTERIAN BOARD.

This Board holds its annual meeting at the College, Queen's-square, on the Tuesday after the third Sunday of March; and at other times as business demands.

Secretary.—Rev. Alex. Jeffrey, Forest-gate, E.

Committee for 1895-6.—Rev. Dr. Morison, Rev. D. Fotheringham, Rev. Wm. Dale, Rev. J. Mackintosh, M.A.. and Secretary.

In the following complete list of Presbyterian Ministers in London, those are members of the Presbyterian Board against whose names the dates of admission to the Board are placed :—

1884	Alexander, A. Crighton	135, Bethune-road, Stoke Newington, N.
1888	Ballantyne, Wm.	31, Clissold-road, Stoke Newington, N.
1886	Carlyle, Gavin, M.A.	174, Kensington-park-road, W.
	Carmichael, Peter, B.D.	20, Alwyne-square, N.
	Connan, D. M., M.A.	84, Bartholomew-road, Kentish Town, N.W.
	Crombie, Henry	7, Thyra-grove, Finchley, N.
	Connell, Alex., M.A., B.D. ..	39, Upper Bedford-place, W.C.
1889	Cunningham, J., M.A.	1, Keswick-road, Putney, S.W.
1884	Dale, William	New Barnet.
	Davidson, J. Thain, D.D.	23, Park-hill, Ealing, W.
1888	Davison, Matthew	98, Downs-park-road, Clapton, N.E.
	Duff, Robert, M.A.	13, Walpole-street, Sloane-square, W.
	Dykes, J. Oswald, D.D.	38, Coolhurst-road, Crouch End, N.
1889	Elder, George, M.A.	4, The Grove, Blackheath, S.E.
	Fergusson, J. Moore, M.A. ..	134, Herbert-road, Plumstead, S.E.
	Fotheringham, D.	Northumberland-park, Tottenham.

	Gibb, John, D.D.	The College, Guilford-street, W.C.
1888	Gibson, J. Monro, D.D.	15, Cleve-road, West Hampstead, N.W.
	Gillie, R. C., M.A., A.Sc.	65, Craven-park-road, N.W.
1892	Gillies, Jas. R., M.A.	8, Thurlow-road, Hampstead, N.W.
1895	Grierson, J. G., M.A.	22, Harley-street, Bow, E.
1884	Harris, William	85, Balaam-street, Plaistow, E.
1889	Hester, Samuel	129, Victoria-park-road, N.E.
	Howatt, J. Reid	92, Grove-lane, Denmark-hill, S.E.
1889	Jeffrey, Alexander	70, Earlham-grove, Forest-gate, E.
	Johnston, Wm., B.A.	36, Mildenhall-road, Clapton, N.E.
	Johnstone, J. Jeffrey	Uplands, Honor-oak-road, Forest-hill, S.E.
	Kidd, William	56, Forest Drive West, Leytonstone, N.E.
1875	MacEwan, David, D.D.	Kelvindale, Clapham-common, S.W.
	McGaw, J. T., D.D.	7, East India-avenue, E.C.
1882	McIntosh, Hugh, M.A.	The Manse, Brockley, S.E.
1893	McKee, W. Aikman	The Manse, Silvertown, E.
1894	McQueen, David	297, Burdett-road, E.
	Macgregor, Geo. H. C., M.A. ..	11, Hanover-terrace, Notting-hill, W.
	Macgregor, D. C., M.A.	Wimbledon, S.W.
	Mackenzie, Hugh M.	32, Sisters'-avenue, New Wandsworth, S.W.
1889	Mackintosh, James, M.A... ..	115, Stepney-green, E.
	Mackray, A. N., M.A.	7, Park-hill-road, Croydon.
1887	Macphail, W. M., M.A.	2, Wavertree-road, Streatham-hill, S.W.
1888	Macrae, Duncan	Gloucester House, Bowes-pk., Wood-gn., N.
1891	Matheson, D., M.A.	13, Dealtry-road, Putney, S.W.
	Mathews, G. D., D.D.	25, Christ Church-road, Brondesbury, N.W.
1879	Mauchlen, John	Aden House, Kew Gardens, S.W.
	Meharry, John B., B.A.	2, Hillside Lawn, Hornsey-lane, N.
	Miller, Henry	214, Goldhawk-road, W.
	Milne, P.A.	169, Fentiman-road, Clapham, S.W.
	Milne, Robert	3, Alma-terrace, Kensington, W.
	Moinet, Chas., D.D.	16, Cromwell-crescent, S.W.
	More, John	144, Herbert-road, Plumstead, S.E.
1871	Morison, Walter, D.D.	27, Powis-square, Talbot-road, W.
1895	Murray, T. G.	134, Avondale-square, Old Kent-road, S.E.
	Norwell, Henry, M.A.	15, Clephane-road, Canonbury, N.
1888	Patterson, J. R.	6, Dulwich-rise, S.E.
1894	Pentecost, George F., D.D. ..	3, Cambridge-square, W.
	Raitt, Wm., M.A., Ph.D.	St. George's Church, Southwark, S.E.
1889	Ramsay, A., B.D.	15, Cromwell-place, Highgate, N.
1892	Scott, Charles Anderson, B.A. ..	Woodbury, Acton-lane, Harlesden, N.W.
	Simpson, P. Carnegie, M.A. ..	Helmsley, Wallington.
	Skinner, John, D.D.	3, Wolseley-road, Crouch End, N.
1886	Stuart, James, M.A.	Wallington, Carshalton.
1888	Taylor, Robert	14, Evelyn Mansions, Carlisle-place, S.W.
1886	Thomson, J. H., B.D.	37, St. John's-park, Blackheath, S.E.
	Thornton, R. M., D.D.	72, Carleton-road, N.
	Train, John G.	18, Harold-road, Norwood, S.E.
	Welsh, R. E., M.A...	6, Walm-lane, Willesden-green, N.W.
	Wilson, David, M.A.	67, Maitland-park-road, N.W.
1888	Wilson, G., M.A., F.L.S.	Bible Soc. House, Queen Victoria-st, E.C.
	Woffendale, Z. B.	White House, Dartmouth-park-avenue, N.
1895	Wright, W. D., M.A.	6, Surbiton-road, Kingston-on-Thames.
1890	Wylie, Robert	The Manse, Church-road, Canonbury, N.

CONGREGATIONAL BOARD.

(*See pages 464 to 471.*)

Formed 1772.

THE FOLLOWING ARE THE PRINCIPAL RULES OF THE BOARD:—

The Congregational Board is a union of ministers of the Congregational Denomination residing in and about the cities of London and Westminster, and is formed to promote fraternal intercourse and to take cognizance of all public questions affecting the interest of that denomination and of religion in general.

Any Congregational minister wishing to be admitted to the Board shall be recommended, in writing, by at least five of its members, who shall attest that his moral character is unimpeachable, and that he holds, or has held, the pastoral office, and has been in some form publicly recognized by the representatives of neighbouring churches; or that, with the consent of the church, he is an assistant to a pastor in or about the Metropolis; or that, having had ministerial training, he is or has been officially connected with some of the religious or collegiate institutions of, or recognised by, the Congregational Body.

Such recommendation shall also be sustained by the personal testimony of a majority of those by whom he is nominated, and by an official testimonial from the County Association, College, or Denomination whence the candidate comes.

Candidates for membership shall be nominated only twice in the session—viz., in the months of October and February.

The names of candidates for nomination, with the names of their nominators, shall be transmitted to the Minute-Secretary fourteen days at least before the meeting at which the nomination shall take place; and in the agenda for that meeting the names of all such candidates, with those of the nominators, shall be forwarded to each member of the Board; the personal and official testimony required by Rule II. shall be given at the time of nomination, and the election shall take place by ballot at the meeting next ensuing.

No candidate shall be admitted to membership except by the votes of three-fourths at least of the members actually voting by ballot.

No member shall be excluded, but by three-fourths at least of the members actually voting by ballot, at a meeting, of which due notice of such proposed exclusion shall be given.

Every member shall pay the sum of twenty shillings on admission, and also contribute his proportion of the yearly expenditure of the Board.

Former members seeking re-admission shall be nominated in the same way as new members, and with similar testimonials. The election shall be taken immediately after nomination, and by open voting. If re-admitted, no entrance fee will be required.

The ordinary business of the Board shall be transacted at meetings to be held on the Tuesday after the second Lord's Day in the months commencing with September and ending with April, at four for five o'clock precisely.

Nomination Forms may be obtained on application to the Clerk.

OFFICERS.

Chairman—Rev. GEORGE MARTIN.

Deputy-Chairman—Rev. I. MORLEY WRIGHT.

Committee.

Rev. W. F. ADENEY, M.A.
„ J. L. BROOKS.
„ JAMES ELLIS.
„ OWEN EVANS, D.D.
Rev. J. M. GIBBON.
„ J. JOHNSTON.
„ J. MATTHEWS.
„ J. PARKER, D.D.
Rev. A. J. VINER.

Secretaries.

Minutes and Correspondence—Rev. THOMAS SISSONS, Elm Lodge, Beckenham.

Finance—Rev. P. J. TURQUAND, 3, Lynette-avenue, Clapham Common, S.W.

Clerk—Mr. J. MINSHULL.

Office of the Board:—

CONGREGATIONAL MEMORIAL HALL, FARRINGDON-STREET, E.C.

BAPTIST BOARD.

(*For Officers, Committee and Rules, see page* 105.)

List of Members.

(*For addresses, see pages* 334 *to* 378.)

Angus, J., D.D.
Baillie, J.
Baster, W.
Bergin, J. M.
Blake, J. H.
Blake, W. A.
Booth, S. H., D.D.
Boud, J. W.
Box, J.
Brock, W.
Brown, C.
Brown, J. A.
Bruce, J. S.
Burns, D., M.A., D.D.
Carlile, J. C.
Cattell, J.
Chadwick, J.
Charlesworth, V. J.
Clark, J. P., M.A.
Clifford, J., M.A., LL.B., B.Sc., F.G.S., D.D.
Cole, J. W.
Cole, T. J.
Cooke, J. H.
Cowdy, S., LL.D.
Cox, J. M.
Cox, J. R.
Cuff, W.
Davies, G.
Davis, E. T.
Dowen, Z. T., F.G.S.
Dunington, H.
Dunlop, J.
Dyson, W.
Edgerton, A. G.
Edgerton, W. F.
Elvey, R. A.
Ennals, G. T.
Etheridge, B. C.
Ewing, J. W., M.A.
Field, J.
Fleming, R. S., M.A.
Fletcher, J.
Foster, J. C.
French, J. H.
Gange, E. G.
Gould, G. P., M.A.
Gray, A. C.
Green, S. W., M.A.
Griffiths, P.
Haines, W. W.
Hamilton, W.
Hanger, T.
Hawker, G.
Hazzard, T. J.
Henderson, W. T.
Hewson, J. M.
Hill, W.
Hillman, J.
Honour, D.
Hughes, F. C.
James, F.
Jones, A. E.
Jones, F. A.
King, W. H.
Lardner, T.
Le Riche, E. M.
Levinsohn, I.
Lynn, J. H.
Mackey, H. O.
Martin, J. E.
Meyer, F. B., B.A.
Miall, W.
Middleditch, A. B.
Mills, W. J.
Mitchell, E.
Monti, F. B.
Morgan, G. H., B.Sc.
Myers, J. B.
Page, W., B.A.
Parker, J., M.A.
Pettman, W.
Pope, G. W.
Reynolds, P.
Riley, A. F.
Roberts, R. H., B.A.
Scorey, P. G.
Scriven, W.
Scudamore, G.
Sears, R. E.
Shindler, R.
Simmance, J.
Simmons, G.
Skerry, W. R.
Smith, G. K.
Spendelow, H.
Spurgeon, J. A., D.D., LL.D.
Spurr, F. C.
Stone, H. E.
Stott, W.
Stuart, J.
Sturge, A.
Styles, W. J.
Taylor, D.
Tessier, A.
Thomas, E.
Thomas, J. W.
Thomas, W.
Thomson, R.
Todd, J. W., D.D.
Tydeman, E. A.
Vick, C. W.
Walker, A.
Wallace, R.
Wilkinson, S. H.
Williams, W.
Wood, J. R.
Woods, W.

Printed in the United States
128804LV00002B/2/A

9 781437 151459